DEPARTMENT OF THE ARMY
U.S. Army Corps of Engineers
Washington, D.C. 20314-1000

EM 385-1-1

CESO-ZA

Manual
No. 385-1-1

28 November 2014

Safety

SAFETY AND HEALTH REQUIREMENTS

1. Purpose. This manual prescribes the safety and health requirements for all Corps of Engineers activities and operations.

2. Applicability. This manual applies to Headquarters, US Army Corps of Engineers (HQUSACE) elements, major subordinate commands, districts, centers, laboratories, and field operating activities (FOA), as well as USACE contracts and those administered on behalf of USACE. Applicability extends to occupational exposure for missions under the command of the Chief of Engineers, whether accomplished by military, civilian, or contractor personnel.

3. References.

   a. 29 Code of Federal Regulation (CFR) 1910, Occupational Safety and Health Standards   for General Industry

   b. 29 CFR 1926, Occupational Safety and Health Standards for Construction

   c. 29 CFR 1960, Basic Program Elements for Federal Employees, OSHA

   d. Executive Order (EO) 12196, Occupational Safety and Health Programs for Federal Employees, 26 Feb, 1980

   e. Federal Acquisition Regulation (FAR) Clause 52.236-13, Accident Prevention, Nov 1991

   f. Department of Defense Instruction (DODI) 6055.1, DOD Sfety and Occupational Health Program, 14 Oct 2014

   g. Army Regulation (AR) 40-5, Preventive Medicine

   h. AR 385-10, Army Safety Program

This manual supersedes EM 385-1-1, 15 September 2008

4. <u>General</u>.

a. The provisions of this manual implement and supplement the safety and health standards and requirements referenced above. Where more stringent safety and occupational health standards are set forth in these requirements and regulations, the more stringent standards shall apply.

b. Mission applicability introduced in paragraph 2 above shall include the following:

(1) Construction contract work under the provisions of FAR Clause 52.236-13. Contractors shall comply with the latest version of EM 385-1-1 (including interim changes) that is in effect on the date of solicitation. Prior to making an offer, bidders should check the HQUSACE Safety and Occupational Health web site (see paragraph c) for the latest changes. No separate payment will be made for compliance with this paragraph or for compliance with other safety and health requirements of this contract. Note: Existing contracts will continue to apply the provisions of the previous edition of this manual until contract completion.

(2) Service, supply, and research and development contracting actions. Compliance with this manual shall be a contract requirement for such activities unless technical representatives (in coordination with safety and health professionals) advise that special precautions are not appropriate due to extremely limited scope of services or similar. However, it is understood that this manual in its entirety may be too complex for the type of work being performed under these contracts. These contractors may reference Appendix A, for abbreviated Accident Prevention Plan (APP).

(3) Contracting actions for hazardous, toxic, and radioactive waste site investigation, design, or remediation activities. Compliance with this manual shall be a contract requirement.

c. Changes. All interim changes (changes made between publication of new editions) to this manual, and the effective date of change, will be posted on the Safety and Occupational Health Office web site: http://www.usace.army.mil/CESO/Pages/Home.aspx and in USACE Electronic bid Sets. Hard copies of this manual are available from the local contracting official.

d. Interpretations. Within the Corps of Engineers, interpretations to the requirements contained within this manual shall be executed in accordance with the process contained in Appendix <u>C</u>. Interpretations will apply only to the specific situation in question and may not be used as a precedent to determine the meaning of a requirement as it may apply to another circumstance.

     e. Variances and Waivers. Within the Corps of Engineers, variances and waivers to provisions of this manual require the approval of the Chief of Safety and Occupational Health, HQUSACE. Variances or waivers shall provide an equal or greater level of protection, shall be substantiated with a hazard analysis of the activity and shall be documented and forwarded through channels to Chief of Safety and Occupational Health, HQUSACE. The process for requesting variances or waivers is contained in Appendix D.

     f. Activities performed OCONUS. Some of the technical requirements of this manual may not be applicable to overseas activities due to conflicting circumstances, practices, and laws or regulations of the locality or the unavailability of equipment. In such instances, means other than the ones specified in this manual may be used to achieve the required protection. In such instances, a hazard analysis must be developed to document that the required protection will be achieved by the alternate means.

     g. Unless otherwise indicated, when publications are referenced in this manual, the most recent edition is to be used.

     h. The use of underlining in this manual indicates new or changed text from the 2008 version.

     i. Supplementation of this manual is not authorized except as published by the Safety and Occupational Health Office, HQUSACE.

     (1) Local USACE organizations may develop Standard Operating Procedures (SOPs) to implement the provisions contained within this manual, but may not implement new requirements (e.g., more stringent, differing intent, etc.) without the specific approval of HQUSACE.

(2) Locally developed Safety and Health Requirements will not be included in contract requirements without the approval of HQUSACE.

FOR THE COMMANDER:

WILLIAM H. GRAHAM
COL, EN
Chief of Staff

DEPARTMENT OF THE ARMY
U.S. Army Corps of Engineers
Washington, DC 20314-1000

CESO

Manual
No. 385-1-1

Safety
Safety and Health Requirements Manual
TABLE OF CONTENTS

10. Welding and Cutting

11. Electrical

12. Control of Hazardous Energy

13. Hand and Power Tools

Appendices

Index

Figures

THIS PAGE INTENTIONALLY LEFT BLANK

SECTION 1 Program Management

Table of Contents

01.A General. This Section provides the overall programmatic guidance for developing, managing and implementing a safety and occupational health (SOH) program.

01.A.01 No person shall be required, instructed or allowed to work in surroundings or under conditions that are unsafe or dangerous to his or her health.

01.A.02 The employer is responsible for initiating and maintaining a SOH program that complies with the US Army Corps of Engineers (USACE) SOH requirements.

➢*Note 1: Supplementation of this manual is not authorized except as published by the HQUSACE SOH Office.*

➢*Note 2: Local USACE Commands may develop Standard Operating Procedures (SOPs) to implement the provisions contained within this manual, but may not implement new requirements (e.g., more stringent, differing in intent, etc.), without the specific approval of HQUSACE-SO.*

01.A.03 Each employee is responsible for complying with applicable SOH requirements, wearing prescribed SOH equipment, reporting unsafe conditions or activities, preventing avoidable mishaps, and working in a safe manner.

01.A.04 Supervisors shall remove employees from exposure to work hazards, or the work site when they are observed acting in an unsafe manner, or otherwise pose a potential SOH threat to themselves or others. Employees may return to the work environment after appropriate supervisory action has occurred (i.e., re-training on proper safe procedures, etc.).

01.A.05 SOH programs, documents, signs, and tags shall be communicated to employees in a language that they understand.

01.A.06 Worksites with non-English speaking workers shall have a person(s), fluent in the language(s) spoken as well as English, on-site when work or training is being performed, to interpret and translate as needed.

01.A.07 SOH Bulletin Board. The Contractor or USACE Project shall erect and maintain a SOH bulletin board in a commonly accessed area in clear view of the on-site workers. The bulletin board shall be continually maintained and updated and placed in a location that is protected against the elements and unauthorized removal. It shall contain, at minimum, the following SOH information:

a. A map denoting the route to the nearest emergency care facility;

b. Emergency phone numbers;

c. A copy of the most current Accident Prevention Plan (APP) or Project Safety and Occupational Health (SOH) Plan, mounted on/adjacent to the bulletin board, or a notice on the bulletin board stating the location of the Plan. The location of the Plan shall be accessible on the site by all workers;

d. The Occupational Safety and Health Administration (OSHA) Form 300A, *Summary of Work Related Injuries and Illnesses*, posted in accordance with OSHA requirements (from February 1 to April 30 of the year following the issuance of this form). It shall be mounted on/adjacent to the bulletin board, accessible on the site by all workers;

e. A copy of the SOH deficiency tracking log mounted on/adjacent to the bulletin board or a notice on the bulletin board shall state the location where it may be accessed by all workers upon request; > *See 01.A.1 13.d.*

f. SOH promotional posters;

g. Date of last lost workday injury and date of last OSHA recordable injury;

h. OSHA Safety and Health Poster;

i. A copy of the hazardous material inventory, identification of use, approximate quantities and site map detailing location as required by Section 06.B.01.a.

01.A.08 USACE Business Process. USACE Project Managers (PMs), in accordance with the SOH Reference Document (Ref Doc 8016G) contained in the USACE Business Manual, shall ensure that a SOH plan is developed for funded projects and incorporated into each Project Management Plan (PMP)/Program Management Plan (PrgMP).

a. The PM shall collaborate with the customer and the local SOH office (SOHO) on project safety goals and objectives and communicate these through the PMP/PrgMP SOH plan and Project Delivery Team (PDT) meetings.

b. Coordination between local SOHOs of the design district and the construction district shall occur during the development of the PMP.

01.A.09 USACE Project Management Plan. USACE PMs and the PDT shall develop the SOH program requirements to be incorporated in the PMP and are responsible for assuring that SOH requirements are properly addressed and executed throughout the life cycle of each project.

a. The PM shall ensure that identified hazards, control mechanisms, and risk acceptance are formally communicated to all project stakeholders.

b. The current Unified Facilities Guide Specification (UFGS) for Safety and Health in effect on the date of solicitation shall be used in all USACE contract work administered on behalf of the USACE under the provisions of FAR Clause 52.236-13 and on other contracts as deemed appropriate based on the risk assessment.

c. Military Construction (MILCON) Transformation contracts will include the Federal Acquisition Regulation (FAR) Clause 52.236-13 as well as the Model Request for Proposal (RFP).

d. Locally developed SOH requirements will not be included in contract requirements without the concurrence of the Contracting Officer (KO) and local SOHO.

e. When an employee is deemed to be in imminent danger, the COR or a designated representative shall immediately stop the unsafe work being performed. > See Federal Acquisition Regulation (FAR) Clause 52.236-13(d).

01.A.10 USACE Project SOH Plan. For USACE activities where USACE employees are engaged in functions other than routine office or administrative duties, a Project SOH Plan shall be developed, implemented, and updated as necessary.

a. Such activities include operations and maintenance; recreational resource management; in-house conducted environmental restoration (investigation, design, and remediation); surveying, inspection, and testing; construction management; warehousing; transportation; research and development; and other

activities when the Government Designated Authority (GDA) and the command's local SOHO agree on the benefit of such a program for accident prevention.

b. The Project SOH Plan shall address applicable items listed in Appendix A, and in addition, any local SOPs or requirements identified in the USACE Command's SOH Program. > See Section 01.A.02, Notes 1 and 2.

c. For Hazardous Waste Operations and Emergency Response (HAZWOPER) sites, refer to Section 33 for Site Safety and Health Plan (SSHP) guidance.

01.A.11 Position Hazard Analyses (PHA) for USACE Employees. A PHA shall be prepared, updated as necessary, documented by the supervisor, and reviewed by the command's SOHO for each USACE position according to the hazards associated with the position's tasks. A generic PHA may be used for groups of employees performing repetitive office/administrative tasks where the primary hazards result from ergonomic challenges, lighting conditions, light lifting and carrying tasks, and indoor air quality. > See Figure 1-1 for an outline of a PHA. An electronic, fillable version of a PHA may be found on the HQUSACE Safety Office Website.

a. The USACE Supervisor, in coordination with the SOHO, shall determine the need for analysis of each position within his or her area of responsibility.

b. In developing the analysis for a particular position, supervisors shall draw upon the knowledge and experience of employees in that position in addition to that of the SOHO.

c. A complete PHA document shall indicate that the hazards, medical surveillance requirements, control mechanisms, personal protective equipment (PPE) and training required for the position were discussed with the employee. The PHA shall be signed by the supervisor and employee. A PHA shall contain a copy of the employee's training certificate of completion for all required training.

d. Supervisors shall review the PHAs with employees upon initial assignment to a position, whenever there is a significant change in hazards and during their annual performance review or at least annually.

FIGURE 1-1

Position Hazard Analysis (PHA)

Position Hazard Analysis (PHA) for USACE Employees		
Name: (Print - Last, First, Mi): _____	Prepared By: (Print – Last, First, MI): _____	
Job Series: _____ Job Title: _____ Job Number (SF52): _____	Reviewed By (SSHO):_____ Date (Mo) _ _ (Day) _ _ (Year) _ _ _ _	
Command Name & Organization Code: _____ Primary Duty Location: _____		
Clearances Required EM OPS Team First Aid/CPR Respirator CDL Crane Operator Diver HTRW Other ☐ ☐ ☐ ☐ ☐ ☐ ☐ ☐		
Position Tasks	Safety and/or Occupational Health Hazards*	Recommended Controls
1. 2. 3. 4. 5.	1. 2. 3. 4. 5.	1. 2. 3. 4. 5.

*Note - Examples of potential hazards are as follows:

Safety:	Excavating; electrical; slips, trips, falls; falls from heights, motor Vehicle/equipment operation; compressed air; fire; etc.
Physical Agent:	Exposure to heat/cold; noise; stress; vibration; radiation, hot substances; radio frequency; EMF, etc.
Chemical Agent:	Exposure to solvents; cadmium; paints; welding fumes; lead; asbestos; pesticides; etc.
Biological Agent:	Exposure to bloodborne pathogens; poison ivy; insects; fungi; etc.

Equipment, Materials & Chemicals To Used	Inspection Requirements	Training Requirements
List for each task [include Material Safety Data Sheets(MSDSs)]	List inspection requirements for each work task	List safety/health training requirements
1.	1.	1.
2.	2.	2.
3.	3.	3.
4.	4.	4.
5.	5.	5.
6.	6.	6.

Note: This PHA serves as the hazard assessment required by Sections 01, 05, and 06 of this Manual. The employee covered by this PHA has been instructed in the tasks to be performed, the hazards that may be encountered, potential adverse effects of the hazards and controls to be used. He/she has received adequate, specific training related to safe work practices, administrative and engineering controls and PPE to be used to ensure assigned work tasks are conducted in a safe/healthful manner. He/she has demonstrated an understanding of the safety/health equipment/PPE to be used, including its limitations, useful shelf-life, how to properly don, doff, adjust, and wear required PPE, how to properly care for, inspect, maintain, store, and dispose of same. Attached is documentation of the training received, dates of such training, and the subject matter taught.

Supervisor Signature: _____ Employee Signature: _____

Date __ _/_ _/__ _ _ _ _   Date __ _/_ _/__ _ _ _ _

01.A.12 Accident Prevention Plans (APP) for Contract Work. Before initiation of work at the job site, an APP shall be reviewed and found acceptable by the GDA. > See Appendix A.

a. APPs shall be developed and submitted by the Contractor. The Contractor shall address each of the elements/sub-elements in the outline contained in Appendix A in the order that they are provided in the manual. If an item is not applicable because of the nature of the work to be performed, the Contractor shall state this exception and provide a justification.

(1) The Contractor shall identify each major phase of work that will be performed on this contract. Within each major phase, all activities, tasks or Definable Features of Work (DFOWs) shall be identified that will require an Activity Hazard Analysis (AHA). > See Section 01.A.14 and Appendix A, paragraph 3.j.

(2) The APP shall also address any unusual or unique aspects of the project or activity.

b. The APP shall be written in English by the Prime Contractor and shall articulate the specific work, work processes, equipment to be used, and hazards pertaining to the contract. The APP shall also implement in detail the pertinent requirements of this manual.

c. The APP shall contain appropriate hazard-specific plans as needed for the work being performed (e.g., appendices that include a SSHP for hazardous waste site cleanup operations; a Lead Compliance Plan when working with lead, or an Asbestos Hazard Abatement Plan when working with asbestos).

d. All highly complex or high-hazard projects shall be coordinated with the local SOH office.

e. For limited-scope supply, service and R&D contracts, the KO and local SOHO may authorize an abbreviated APP. > See Appendix A, Paragraph 2 for details.

f. The APP shall be developed and signed by Qualified Person (QP) and then signed. The Contractor shall be responsible for documenting the QPs' credentials.

g. The Contractor's APP shall be job-specific and must include work to be performed by subcontractors.

(1) If at the time of submission of the APP, portions of the work have yet to be known or sub-contracted, that portion will be added to the APP, submitted and accepted by the GDA prior to initiation of the sub-contracted work.

(2) In addition, the APP shall include measures to be taken by the Contractor to control hazards associated with materials, services, or equipment provided by suppliers.

(3) Each sub-contractor shall be provided a copy of the APP by the prime contractor and be required to comply with it.

h. The contractor shall provide on-going evaluations of the APP throughout the life of the project. Changes, revisions and updates to the APP shall be reviewed and accepted by the GDA.

➢ Note: When USACE or other government employees are on a site that is controlled by a contractor and are affected by the contractor-managed APP (e.g., QA's on construction sites, etc.), they shall comply with the contractor's APP and associated programs (i.e., Fall Protection, Hazardous Energy Control, Diving, Blasting, etc.).

01.A.13 Inspections - Contractor and USACE Projects.

a. The APP or the USACE Project SOH Plan shall provide for frequent safety inspections/audits, conducted by a Competent Person (CP), of the work sites, material, and equipment to ensure compliance with the plan and this manual. These inspections/audits shall be documented in writing and available upon request to the GDA. They shall include the name of the inspector, date, and all findings.

b. In addition, Contractor Quality Control (QC) and USACE Quality Assurance (QA) personnel as part of their QC and QA responsibilities, shall conduct and document daily SOH inspections in their daily logs.

c. Inspection reports shall document any identified SOH issues and deficiencies, and the actions, timetable, and responsibility for correcting the deficiencies. Follow-up inspections to ensure correction of any identified deficiencies must also be conducted and documented in inspection reports.

d. The Contractor or USACE Project shall establish a SOH deficiency tracking system that lists and monitors the status of SOH deficiencies in chronological order. The tracking system provides useful information that must be used to evaluate the effectiveness of the APP. A monthly evaluation of the data should be discussed in the QC or SOH meeting with everyone on the project. The list shall be posted on the project bulletin board, be updated daily, and should provide the following information:

(1) Date deficiency identified;

(2) Description of deficiency;

(3) Name of person responsible for correcting deficiency;

(4) Projected resolution date;

(5) Date actually resolved.

e. The Contractor shall immediately notify the GDA of any OSHA or other regulatory agency inspection and provide GDA an opportunity to accompany the Contractor on the inspection. The inspection will not be delayed due to non-availability of the GDA. The Contractor shall provide the GDA with a copy of any citations or reports issued by the inspector and any corrective action responses to the citation(s) or report(s).

f. The GDA shall notify the local SOHO of any regulatory visits.

g. The USACE Project personnel shall immediately notify the local SOHO of any OSHA or other regulatory agency inspection. The Project shall provide the local SOHO with a copy of any citations or reports issued by the inspector and any corrective action responses to the citation(s) or report(s). Local SOHO shall immediately provide this documentation to HQUSACE-SO.

01.A.14 Contractor Risk Management Process. Risk management is a business process that includes the identification, assessment, and prioritization of risks, followed by coordinated and economical application of resources to minimize, monitor, and control the probability and/or impact of unfortunate events to an acceptable level. The USACE uses the Activity Hazard Analysis (AHA) as part of a total risk management process. > See Figure 1-2 for a *NON-MANDATORY formatted outline* of an AHA. An electronic version AHA may be found on the HQUSACE Safety Office Website.

➤ *Note: Contractors and other individual employer's typically use Job Safety Analyses (JSAs), Job Hazard Analyses (JHAs), or similar Risk Management assessment tools. These documents are considered equivalent to, and acceptable substitutes for, the* USACE's AHA provided the data collected is the same as that required by the AHA.

a. AHAs shall define the steps being performed within the activity, task or Defined Feature of Work (DFOW), and identify the work sequences, specific anticipated hazards, site conditions, equipment, materials, personnel and the control measures to be implemented.

b. Before beginning each work activity, task or DFOW, the *Contractor performing that work activity* shall prepare the initial AHA. A Risk Assessment Code (RAC) is assigned to each step, to the risk that remains after controls have been applied (residual risk).

(1) Once this process has occurred, a RAC will be assigned to the activity as a whole (cannot be lower than the highest step RAC).

(2) Acceptance of risk. This residual risk must then be communicated to the proper authority for acceptance in order to proceed with the activity.

(3) The names of the Competent Person(s) (CP) and Qualified Person(s) (QP) required for a particular activity (e.g., excavation, scaffolding, fall protection, or other activities as specified by OSHA and this manual) shall be identified and included in the AHA, as well as proof of their competency/qualification.

(4) If more than one CP/QP is used on the AHA activity, a list of names and appropriate qualifications shall be submitted as an attachment to the AHA. Those listed must be CPs/QPs for the type of work involved in the AHA and familiar with current site safety issues.

c. Work shall not begin until the AHA with RAC for the work activity has been accepted by the GDA and discussed with all engaged in the activity, including the Contractor, subcontractor(s), and Government on-site representatives at preparatory and initial control phase meetings.

d. AHA's are intended to be developed and used by the field crews/workers performing the work, with the assistance of others (SSHO, QC, Superintendent, etc) as needed. The initial, accepted AHA shall be provided to and used by the field crews/workers that are performing that activity. AHAs are to be considered living documents and are intended to be created in the field and updated by the workers as needed.

e. The AHA shall be reviewed and modified as necessary to address changing site conditions, operations, or change of CP(s)/QP(s).

(1) If a new CP/QP (not on the original list) is added, the list shall be updated (an administrative action not requiring an updated AHA). The new CP/QP shall acknowledge in writing that they have reviewed the AHA and is familiar with current site safety issues.

(2) If the initial RAC increases due to a change made to the AHA by the workers, the AHA shall be resubmitted to GDA for acceptance prior to work proceeding.

(3) Changes to or updates to an AHA that do not increase the RAC are not required to be resubmitted for acceptance by the GDA.

(4) Workers/crews shall have in their possession the current AHA that reflects current site conditions, personnel, equipment, control measures, etc while the work is being performed.

f. The AHA shall be used by the contractor and USACE personnel to assure work is being performed consistent with the AHA. In the event that the work is not being conducted in a safe manner, the contractor and/or the USACE (COR or designated representative) shall immediately stop the unsafe work being conducted until it is in compliance with this manual, APP and the AHA or the APP/ AHA is revised and accepted by the GDA, if necessary.

g. AHAs for completed work for the same contract or project work shall be readily available on site (e.g., office, trailer, etc.) and accessible on site by all workers, for a period of 12 months or, for contract work, the length of the contract;

01.A.15 USACE Risk Management Process. Risk management is a business process that includes the identification, assessment, and prioritization of risks, followed by coordinated and economical application of resources to minimize, monitor, and control the probability and/or impact of unfortunate events to an acceptable level. The USACE uses the Activity Hazard Analysis (AHA) as part of a total risk management process. > *See Figure 1-2 for a NON-MANDATORY formatted outline of an AHA and an electronic version of this AHA may be found on the HQUSACE Safety Office Website. Work crews may use other forms/formats as long as the information contained within is the same.*

a. An AHA shall be prepared and documented for each USACE activity as warranted by the hazards associated with the activity. Typically, an AHA shall be prepared for all field, laboratory, industrial and maintenance activities.

b. The supervisor, utilizing the recommendations of the SOHO, should determine the need for an AHA for each activity within his/her area of responsibility. AHAs shall define the steps being performed within the activity or task, identify the work sequences, specific anticipated hazards, site conditions, equipment, materials, personnel and the control measures to be implemented.

c. Before beginning each work activity, the *workers performing that work activity* shall prepare the initial AHA. A Risk Assessment Code (RAC) is assigned to each step, to the risk that remains after controls have been applied (residual risk). In developing the AHA for

a particular activity, the involved workers should draw upon the expertise (knowledge, skill and experience) of the USACE supervisor for that activity as well as the SOH Office.

(1) Once this process has occurred, a RAC will be assigned to the activity as a whole (cannot be lower than the highest step RAC).

(2) Acceptance of risk. This residual risk must then be communicated to the proper authority for acceptance in order to proceed with the activity.

(3) The names of the Competent Person(s) (CP) and Qualified Person(s) (QP) required for a particular activity (e.g., confined space entry, scaffolding, fall protection or other activities as specified by OSHA/this manual) shall be identified and included in the AHA, as well as proof of their competency/qualification.

(4) If more than one CP/QP is used on the AHA activity, a list of names and appropriate qualifications shall be noted on the AHA. Those listed must be CPs/QPs for the type of work involved in the AHA and familiar with current site safety issues.

d. Work shall not begin until the AHA with RAC for the work activity has been discussed with all engaged in the activity in a job pre-brief (to include Supervisor and/or local SOHO if applicable).

e. AHA's are intended to be developed and used by the field crews/workers performing the work, with the assistance of others (CDSO, Superintendent, etc.) as needed. The initial AHA shall be provided to and used by the field crews/workers that are performing that activity. AHAs are to be considered living documents and are intended to be created in the field and updated by the workers as needed.

f. The AHA shall be reviewed and modified as necessary to address changing site conditions, operations, or change of CP(s)/QP(s).

(1) If a new CP/QP (not on the original list) is added, the list shall be updated (an administrative action not requiring an updated AHA). The new CP/QP shall acknowledge in writing that he/she has reviewed the AHA and is familiar with current site safety issues.

(2) If the initial RAC increases due to a change made to the AHA by the workers, the AHA shall be re-reviewed by the supervisor and local SOHO for acceptance prior to work proceeding.

(3) Changes to or updates to an AHA that do not increase the RAC are not required to be re-reviewed.

FIGURE 1-2

Activity Hazard Analysis (AHA)

Activity/Work Task:	Overall Risk Assessment Code (RAC) (Use highest code)				
Project Location:	Risk Assessment Code (RAC) Matrix				
Contract Number:	Severity	Probability			
Date Prepared: / /		Frequent	Likely	Occasional	Seldom	Unlikely
Prepared by (Name/Title):	Catastrophic	E	E	H	H	M
	Critical	E	H	H	M	L
Reviewed by (Name/Title):	Marginal	H	M	M	L	L
	Negligible	M	L	L	L	L
Notes: (Field Notes, Review Comments, etc.)	Step 1: Review each "Hazard" with identified safety "Controls". Determine RAC (See above)				
	Probability: likelihood the activity will cause a Mishap (near miss, incident or accident). Identify as Frequent, Likely, Occasional, Seldom or Unlikely.	RAC Chart			
	Severity: the outcome if a mishap occurred. Identify as Catastrophic, Critical, Marginal, or Negligible	E = Extremely High Ri			
		H = High Risk			
	Step 2: Identify the RAC (probability vs. severity) as E, H, M, or L for each "Hazard" on AHA. Annotate the overall highest RAC at the top of AHA.	M = Moderate Risk			
		L = Low Risk			
Job Steps	Hazards	Controls			RAC
1.	1.	1.			1.
2.	2.	2.			2.
Equipment to be Used	Training Requirements & Competent or Qualified Personnel name(s)	Inspection Requirements			

(4) Workers/crews shall have in their possession the current AHA that reflects current site conditions, personnel, equipment, control measures, etc while the work is being performed.

g. The AHA shall be used to assure work is being performed consistent with the AHA. In the event that the work is not being performed/conducted in a safe manner, work shall stop until it is in compliance with this manual, and the AHA.

h. Once the activity has been completed, the AHA shall be available and kept on file on site for 6 months minimum.

01.A.16 To ensure compliance with this manual, the Contractor may be required to prepare for review specific SOH submittal items. These submittal items may be specifically required by this manual or may be identified in the contract or by the Contracting Officer's Representative (COR). All SOH submittal items shall be written in English and provided by the Contractor to the GDA.

01.A.17 Contractor Site Safety and Health Officer (SSHO). The Contractor shall employ a minimum of one CP at each project site to function as the SSHO (primary), depending on job complexity, size and any other pertinent factors.

a. The SSHO shall:

(1) Be a full-time responsibility. The SSHO shall be present at the project site, located so they have full mobility and reasonable access to all major work operations during the shift.

(2) Be an employee other than the supervisor, unless specified differently in the contract and coordinated with the local SOH Office, and

(3) Report to a senior project (or corporate) official.

b. The SSHO, as a minimum, must produce a copy of their instructor-signed OSHA 30- hour training card (or course completion if within 90 days of having completed the training and card has not yet been issued). They will have completed:

(1) The 30-hour OSHA General Industry safety class (may be web-based training if the student is able to directly ask questions of the instructor by chat or phone) or

(2) The 30-hour OSHA Construction Industry safety class (may be web-based training if the student is able to directly ask questions of the instructor by chat/phone), or

(3) As an equivalent, formal construction or industry safety and health training covering the subjects of the OSHA 30-hour course and the EM 385-1-1 [see Appendix A, Paragraph 3.d.(3)] applicable to the work to be performed and given by qualified instructors - may be web-base training if the student is able to directly ask questions of the instructor by chat/phone).

➤Note: The local SOHO having jurisdiction over the work shall evaluate the proposed equivalent training for applicability to the contract work to be performed.

c. In addition, the SSHO is also required to have proof of employment for:

(1) Five (5) years of continuous construction industry safety experience in supervising/ managing general construction (managing safety programs or processes or conducting hazard analyses and developing controls), or

(2) Five (5) years of continuous general industry safety experience in supervising/ managing general industry (managing safety programs or processes or conducting hazard analyses and developing controls), or

(3) If the SSHO has a Third-Party, Nationally Accredited (ANSI or National Commission for Certifying Agencies - NCCA) SOH-related certification, only 4 years of experience is needed. > See Appendix Q for list of certifications.

d. SSHOs shall maintain competency through having taken 8 hours of documented formal, on-line, or self-study safety and health related coursework every year. Examples of continuing education activities that meet this requirement are: writing an article, teaching a class, reading/writing professional articles, attendance/participation in professional societies/ meetings, etc.

e. For projects with multiple shifts, an Alternate SSHO as identified in the AHA will be assigned to insure SSHO coverage for the project at all times work activities are conducted.

➤Note: The Alternate SSHO must meet the same requirements and assume the responsibilities of the project SSHO. > See Appendix Q for "Alternate SSHO" and "SSHO" definitions.

f. If the SSHO is off-site for a period longer than 24 hours, an Alternate SSHO shall be provided and shall fulfill the same roles and responsibilities as the primary SSHO.

g. When the SSHO is temporarily (up to 24 hours) off-site, a Designated Representative (DR), as identified in the AHA may be used in lieu of an Alternate SSHO, and shall be on the project site at all times when work is being performed.

➤Note: DRs are collateral duty safety personnel, with safety duties in addition to their full-time occupation.

h. If an activity, task or DFOW contains multiple sites and has been assessed and given an activity RAC of low or medium, a DR shall be appointed for each site where remote work locations are more than 45 minutes travel time from the SSHO's duty location.

(1) DRs shall perform safety program tasks as designated by the SSHO and report safety findings to the SSHO.

(2) A DR may NOT be assigned to projects that have a RAC level of high or extremely high.

i. The Contractor's project management team, with the assistance of the SSHO, is responsible for managing, communicating, implementing and enforcing compliance with the Contractor's APP and other accepted safety and health submittals.

➤Exception 1: For dredging contracts, the SSHO requirements established in the standardized contract clause for dredging project site safety personnel shall be used as it is included in the current UFGS for Governmental Safety Requirements.

➤Exception 2: For limited service contracts, for example, mowing only, park attendants, rest room cleaning, etc., the KO and SOH Office may modify SSHO requirements and waive the more stringent elements of this Section. > See Appendix A, Paragraphs 2 and 3.i.

➤Exception 3: For field walk-over, surface soil sampling, or long term water sampling, in which there *is no exposure to mechanical or explosive hazards, the SSHO may be collateral duty and shall have a minimum of 8 hours of training annually and specific knowledge of the potential hazards of the tasks being completed.*

01.A.18 USACE SOH Professional and Collateral Duty Safety Officer (CDSO). > *See Appendix Q.* Organizations shall assign a safety point of contact (POC) for all construction and/or maintenance activities, dredging, field sampling, drilling and any other potentially hazardous tasks. A safety POC is a worker that has knowledge of the work being performed and the associated hazards and controls associated with it.

a. For all activities with a high potential for injury or illness and/or a RAC on the AHA of high or extremely high, a SOH Professional shall be on site full time. The SOH Professional shall have reviewed the hazards and appropriate controls with the local SOHO.

b. If a project or task has been assessed with a RAC of low:

(1) A Safety POC or CDSO as identified in the AHA, shall be on the project site at all times when work is being performed.

(2) And it contains multiple sites, a Safety POC shall be appointed for each site where remote work locations are more than 45-minutes travel time from the CDSO's main duty location. POCs shall perform safety program tasks as designated by the SOH Professional, Project Safety Officer or CDSO and report safety findings to the appropriate level.

➢ *Note: CDSOs are formerly identified personnel with safety duties in addition to their full-time occupation.*

c. If a project or task has been assessed with a RAC for the project of medium:

(1) A CDSO, as identified in the AHA, shall be on the project site at all times when work is being performed.

(2) And it contains multiple sites, a Safety POC shall be appointed for each site where remote work locations are more than 45-minutes travel time from the CDSO's main duty location. POCs shall perform safety program tasks as designated by the SOH Professional, Project Safety Officer or CDSO and report safety findings to the appropriate level.

d. A CDSO may NOT be assigned to projects that have a RAC level of high or extremely high.

e. The responsibilities of the government Safety POC/CDSO are:

(1) To ensure the hazards identified in the AHA are appropriately addressed;

(2) Provide training on the hazards of the activity and PPE or controls to be utilized;

(3) Provide feedback on the work activities as to how to improve the safety of the activity, and

(4) Document the safety and health controls being used and implemented.

f. Project SO, CDSO and Safety POC shall seek support and information from the local SOHO if there is a verbalized concern or someone becomes injured or ill.

01.A.19 USACE Collateral Duty Safety Officers (CDSOs). USACE organizations shall designate CDSOs as recommended by the SOH Office. CDSOs shall:

a. Be selected, then trained per Section 01.A.19.b, then appointed through written orders;

b. On appointment of an employee to CDSO, SOH training commensurate with the scope of their assigned responsibilities shall be provided. > *See 29 CFR 1960.58.* Training shall include:

(1) USACE EM 385-1-1;

(2) Section 19 of the OSH Act, Executive Order 12196 and 29 CFR 1960.58;

(3) USACE procedures for the reporting, evaluation and abatement of hazards;

(4) Hazard recognition and Risk Management Processes;

(5) USACE procedures for mishap reporting and investigation and use of lessons learned;

(6) Any local SOH SOPs, to include other appropriate rules and regulations; or

(7) A USACE-instructed or provided (e.g., Prospect classes) 30-hour OSHA General Industry safety class or 30-hour Construction Industry safety class can be taken and will successfully satisfy all training material above except for local SOPs and information.

c. Maintain their competency through taking a minimum of 24-hours of documented formal or online safety and health related coursework, training and webinars over a period of 4-years. The training must be applicable to the work being performed. Teaching is not considered the equivalent of attending training.

d. Give their safety duties proper priority;

e. Report directly to their unit manager concerning safety–related matters;

f. Coordinate activities with their supporting SOHO.

01.A.20 Fatigue Management Plan (FMP).

a. A FMP shall be completed as part of the APP/Project SOH Plan whenever work hours:

(1) Exceed 10-hours a day for more than 4 consecutive days;

(2) Exceed 50-hours in a 7-day work week;

(3) Exceed 12-hours a day for more than 3 consecutive days, or

(4) Exceed 58-hours a week for sedentary (to include office) work.

b. The FMP shall address the following conditions for operator work hour limitations:

(1) Equipment Operators. Operators of equipment, such as hoisting equipment and draglines, mobile construction equipment, electrical power systems, hydropower plants, industrial manufacturing systems, hydraulically operated equipment, powered vessels, and boats, shall not be permitted to exceed 12-hours of duty time in any 24- hour period, including time worked at another occupation. A minimum of 8 consecutive hours of rest between shifts in a 24-hour period is required.

➤ Note: See "Rest", in Appendix Q.

(2) Motor Vehicle Operators. Operators of motor vehicles, while on duty, shall not operate vehicles for a continuous period of more than ten 10-hours in any 24-hour period; moreover, no employee, while on duty, may operate a motor vehicle after being in a duty status for more than 12-hours during any 24-hour period. A minimum of 8 consecutive hours shall be provided for rest in each 24-hour period.

(3) Floating Plant. All floating plant personnel shall be scheduled to receive a minimum of 8-hours rest in any 24-hour period, except:

(a) When quarters are provided immediately adjacent to, or aboard the work site, these hours of rest may be divided into no more than 2 periods,

one of which must be at least 6 continuous hours in length.

(b) Rest periods may be interrupted in case of emergency, drill, or other overriding operational necessity.

c. FMP shall identify affected workers, management responsibility, training, and the controls established at the worksite.

(1) Training shall include symptoms of fatigue, habits and actions the worker may take to avoid fatigue, actions workers should take if they observe fatigue in a co-worker, and controls in place to prevent fatigue.

(2) Controls for fatigue shall include a discussion of driving to and from work and any possible mitigation of driving as a factor of fatigue. > See Appendix Q, "Rest".

(3) Controls for fatigue may include work scheduling (limit number of consecutive night shifts), rotating jobs to prevent repetitive work, breaks at critical times in the work cycle, control of environmental factors (heat, cold, use of personal protective equipment), buddy check-in for individuals working alone, and alternate transportation for long commutes.

01.B Indoctrination and Training.

01.B.01 A Competent Person (CP), qualified in the material presented, shall conduct all training required by this manual. All training shall correspond to American National Standards Institute (ANSI) regulation Z490.1.

01.B.02 Employees shall be provided an SOH indoctrination prior to the start of work as well as continuous SOH training to enable them to perform their work in a safe manner. All training, meetings and indoctrinations shall be documented in writing by date, name, content and trainer.

01.B.03 Indoctrination and training should be based upon the existing SOH program of the Contractor or Government agency, as applicable, and shall include but not be limited to:

a. Requirements and responsibilities for accident prevention and the maintenance of safe and healthful work environments;

b. General SOH policies and procedures and pertinent provisions of this manual;

c. Employee and supervisor responsibilities for reporting all mishaps;

d. Provisions for medical facilities and emergency response and procedures for obtaining medical treatment or emergency assistance;

e. Procedures for reporting and correcting unsafe conditions or practices;

f. Job hazards and the means to control/eliminate those hazards, including applicable PHAs and/or AHAs;

g. Specific training as required by this manual.

01.B.04 Visitors and Authorized Entrants.

a. A visitor is anyone coming to the site for short-term action (e.g., inspection, meetings, deliveries, etc.). An authorized entrant is anyone entering the site that is assigned to the site but is not a site worker (e.g., security forces, other military forces, etc.). Signs shall be posted at all site entrances requiring anyone entering the site to report to the project office for a safety briefing.

b. All visitors and authorized entrants to USACE Government- or Contractor-controlled sites presenting hazardous conditions shall be briefed by a CP on the hazards to be expected on the site and the safety and health controls required (e.g., hard hat, foot protection).

c. All personnel who escort visitors are responsible for their visitors and shall ensure that all visitors entering the site are properly protected and are wearing or provided the appropriate PPE.

➤ Note: If visitors can be escorted along a designated safe path through the site where they are not exposed to the hazards, the use of PPE is not necessary.

d. Contractor and/or Project site personnel shall maintain a stock of common PPE, such as hard hats, eye protection, ear plugs, and reflective vests, for use by visitors

e. All visitors shall be escorted by appropriate site personnel.

f. A visitor sign-in/out log shall be maintained on site. The site manager shall maintain a roster of all authorized entrants that enter the site.

01.B.05 Safety meetings shall be conducted to review past activities, plan for new or changed operations, review pertinent aspects of appropriate AHA (by trade), establish safe working procedures for anticipated hazards, and provide pertinent SOH training and motivation.

a. Meetings shall be conducted at least once a month for all supervisors on the project location and at least once a week for all workers by SSHO, supervisors, foremen or CDSO's.

b. Meetings shall be documented, including the date, persons in attendance, subjects discussed, and names of individual(s) who conducted the meeting. Documentation shall be maintained and copies furnished to the GDA on request.

c. The GDA shall be informed of all scheduled meetings in advance and be invited to attend.

01.B.06 Emergency situations.

a. The employer shall provide training in handling emergency situations that may arise from project activities or equipment operation.

b. All persons who may have occasion to use emergency and rescue or lifesaving equipment shall be familiarized with the equipment location, trained in its proper use, be instructed in its capabilities and limitations, and medically qualified for its use.

01.C Physical Qualifications of Employees.

01.C.01 All persons shall be physically and medically qualified for performing the duties to which they are assigned. Some factors to be considered in making work assignments are strength, endurance, agility, coordination, and visual and hearing acuity.

a. At a minimum, employees shall meet the physical requirements for specific job tasks and hazards as required by this document, the position, the job description, OSHA guidelines, applicable Department of Transportation (DOT) regulations or applicable U.S. Coast Guard (USCG) requirements.

b. Medical documentation shall be recorded using applicable medical screening and/or medical history and examination forms and shall be maintained in accordance with 5 CFR 293 and Privacy Act requirements.

01.C.02 While on duty, employees shall not use or be under the influence of alcohol, narcotics, intoxicants, or similar performance or mind-altering substances.

a. Contractors shall enforce the drug-free workplace requirements. Employees found to be under the influence of or consuming such substances will be immediately removed from the job site.

b. Any employee under a physician's treatment and taking prescribed narcotics or any medication that may prevent one being ready, willing and able to safely perform position duties shall provide a medical clearance statement to his supervisor.

01.C.03 Operators of any equipment or vehicle shall be able to read and understand the signs, signals, and operating instructions in use.

01.D Mishap Reporting and Investigation.

01.D.01 A mishap is any unplanned, undesired event that occurs during the course of work being performed. The term "mishap" includes accidents, incidents and near misses. > See Appendix Q and reporting thresholds and criteria in Section 01.D.03.

01.D.02 All mishaps occurring incidentally to an operation, project, or facility for which this manual is applicable shall be reported, investigated and analyzed as prescribed below and in accordance with ER 385-1-99.

a. Employees are responsible for reporting ALL mishaps immediately to their employer or supervisor.

b. Employers and supervisors are responsible for reporting all recordable mishaps to the GDA within 24-hours after notification from the affected employee. > See also immediate notification requirements in Sections 01.D.04 and 01.D.05.

c. No supervisor may decline to accept a report of a mishap from a subordinate.

01.D.03 In addition to the reporting requirements identified above, the employer is required to report:

a. Property damage (exceeding $5,000 is recordable);

b. Days Away Injuries;

c. Days Away Illnesses;

d. Restricted/Transfer Injuries.

01.D.04 Boards of Investigation. Any accident that has, or appears to have, any of the consequences listed below shall be immediately reported to the GDA. These accidents shall be investigated in depth to identify all causes and to recommend hazard control measures. The GDA shall immediately notify the SOHO when any of these occurs and subsequently follow-up with official accident reports as prescribed by regulation.

a. Fatal injury/illness;

b. Permanent totally disabling injury/illness;

c. Permanent partial disabling injury/illness;

d. One (1) or more persons hospitalized as inpatients as a result of a single occurrence;

e. $500,000 or greater accidental property damage;

f. Three (3) or more individuals become ill or have a medical condition which is suspected to be related to a site condition, or a hazardous or toxic agent on the site;

g. USACE aircraft destroyed or missing;

h. Contractors are responsible for notifying OSHA in accordance with 29 CFR 1904.39 within 8-hours when their employee(s) is fatally injured or 1 or more persons are hospitalized as inpatients as a result of a single occurrence.

01.D.05 In addition to the above, any mishap occurring in any of the following high hazard areas shall be immediately reported to the GDA. These mishaps shall be investigated in depth to identify all causes and to recommend hazard control measures. The GDA shall immediately notify the local SOHO when any one of these occurs and subsequently followup with official reports as prescribed by regulation. HQUSACE-SO must also be notified immediately (within 24-hours) and provided follow-up investigative findings within 10-days of occurrence.

a. Electrical – to include Arc Flash, electrical shock, etc.;

b. Uncontrolled Release of Hazardous Energy (includes electrical and non-electrical);

c. Load Handling Equipment (LHE) or Rigging;

d. Fall-from-Height (any level other than same surface), and

e. Underwater Diving.

➤ Note: The reporting and associated investigation of these mishaps is considered a leading indicator. As such, this information is to be used for data collection, data trending and correction of hazards or program deficiencies before they result in an accident. To encourage reporting of these mishaps, for the betterment of all, this data is NOT to be used for any other reason. > See Appendix Q for "Mishap" definitions.

01.D.06 Except for rescue and emergency measures, the mishap scene shall not be disturbed until it has been released by the investigating official.

01.D.07 The Contractor is responsible for obtaining appropriate medical and emergency assistance and for notifying fire, law enforcement, and regulatory agencies. The Contractor shall assist and cooperate fully with the GDA conducting the Government investigation(s) of any mishap.

01.D.08 Records of all first aid treatments shall be maintained and submitted to the GDA upon request.

a. Records shall include, at a minimum, employee's name, job title, date and type of mishap , causes and corrective actions taken (i.e., AHA review, process changes, establishment of controls, personnel qualifications and training, etc.).

b. This data shall be reviewed and analyzed by the SSHO and/or SOHO for corrective action as appropriate.

01.E Emergency Planning.

01.E.01 Emergency Plans to ensure employee safety in case of fire, inclement weather or other emergency shall be prepared, in writing, and reviewed with all affected employees. Emergency plans shall be tested to ensure their effectiveness.

a. Plans shall include escape procedures and routes, critical plant operations, employee accounting following an emergency evacuation, rescue and medical duties, means of reporting emergencies, and persons to be contacted for information or clarification.

b. On-site emergency planning shall be integrated with off-site emergency support. Documentation of specific on-site emergency services shall be made and may include written agreements, memoranda for record, telephone conversation logs, etc. The emergency services provider should be offered an on-site orientation of the project and associated hazards.

c. The SSHO or designated on-site personnel, shall be responsible for checking the weather conditions at a minimum of twice a day.

d. The employer's APP or Project SOH Plan shall include a discussion of:

(1) Severe weather triggers to alert the SSHO to monitor weather conditions continuously;

(2) Training on severe weather precautions and actions;

(3) Identified area of retreat, or other actions to be taken such as evacuation, work delay, etc.

(4) If lightning is observed, all Load Handling Equipment (LHE), drill rigs, work on elevated platforms or scaffolding, roofing activities, tree trimming activities, pole climbing activities, or work in open areas shall stop. A determination shall be made as to the proximity to the operation being performed. Once lightning is seen, count the number of seconds until you hear the thunder. Divide number of seconds by 5 to get the distance the lightning is away from you. If lightning is 10-miles away or less, work should stop until 30minutes after the last audible thunder or visible flash of lightning.

(5) For floating plant, boats, and marine activities, the APP shall address securing the vessel and evacuation of personnel during severe weather. > See Sections 19.A.03 and 19.A.04.

01.E.02 Planning for any operation shall include the total system response capabilities to minimize the consequences of accidents or natural disaster and shall consider communications, rescue, first aid, medical, emergency response, emergency equipment, and training requirements.

01.E.03 The number of persons permitted in any location shall correspond to rescue and escape capabilities and limitations.

01.E.04 Emergency alert systems shall be developed, tested, and used to alert all persons likely to be affected by existing or imminent disaster conditions and to alert and summon emergency responders.

01.E.05 Emergency telephone numbers and reporting instructions for ambulance, physician, hospital, fire, and police shall be clearly communicated to all employees, conspicuously and clearly posted at the work site.

01.E.06 Employees working alone in a remote location or away from other workers shall be provided an effective means of emergency communications (i.e., cellular phone, twoway radios, land-line telephones or other acceptable means).

a. The selected communication shall be readily available (easily within the immediate reach) of the employee and shall be tested prior to the start of work to verify that it effectively operates in the area/environment.

b. An employee check-in/check-out communication procedure shall be developed to ensure employee safety.

01.F Emergency Operations. In addition to the other pertinent parts of this manual, Civil Disaster Emergency Operations for floods, earthquakes, hurricanes and other natural disasters shall be conducted in accordance with this manual, generally and with Appendix B specifically, for both USACE and Contractor activities.

01.G Explosives Activities and Operations.

a. The requirements for the safe use, storage and transportation of commercial explosives on non-military lands/installations are found in Section 29 of this manual.

b. The requirements for the safe use, storage and transportation of commercial explosives on military lands/installations, are found in EM 385-1-97, *Explosives Safety and Health Requirements Manual.*

c. For all work performed under USACE activities and operations dealing with ammunition and explosives (military munitions), refer to EM 385-1-97.

THIS PAGE INTENTIONALLY LEFT BLANK

SECTION 2 Sanitation

Table of Contents

02.A General. Employers shall establish and maintain hygienic sanitation provisions for all employees in all places of employment as specified in the following paragraphs.

02.B Housekeeping.

02.B.01 Places of employment shall be kept as clean as possible, taking into consideration the nature of the work. Regular cleaning shall be conducted in order to maintain safe and sanitary conditions in the workplace.

a. Periodic sanitation inspections of food preparation areas (kitchens and dining facilities) shall be conducted at least weekly and documented.

b. In workplaces where toxic dusts, fumes, or mists are generated, all surfaces in the work area and adjacent common use areas shall be cleaned in accordance with a written Housekeeping Plan based on the frequency and quantity of toxic material generation.

02.B.02 The floor of every workroom shall be kept as dry as possible. Drainage shall be maintained where wet processes are used, and false floors, platforms, mats, or other dry standing places shall be provided, when possible. Appropriate footwear shall also be provided.

02.B.03 To facilitate cleaning, every floor, working place, and passageway shall be kept free from protruding nails, splinters, loose boards, clutter and unnecessary holes and openings.

02.C Drinking Water.

02.C.01 An adequate supply of potable water shall be provided in all places of employment, for both drinking and personal cleansing.

a. Drinking water shall be provided, whenever possible, from a local municipal water supply that is in compliance with federal, state, and local drinking water standards.

b. When drinking water is obtained from an on-site well, the water shall be tested and the system supplied in accordance with the Safety Drinking Water Act, 40 CFR 141-143, and any state or local drinking water regulations.

c. If water is not available from a local municipal water supply or on-site well, a temporary potable water system shall be provided from a licensed drinking water source.

d. Outside the Continental Unites States (OCONUS), drinking water at military fixed facilities shall be provided in compliance with country-specific Final Governing Standards (FGS). In the absence of FGS, the National Primary Drinking Water Regulations (NPDWR) as outlined in the Overseas Environmental Baseline Guidance Document (OEBGD), Department of Defense Instruction (DODI) 4715.5-G shall be followed. In addition, sanitary control and surveillance of water supplies and chlorination and fluoridation shall be conducted according to applicable Department of Defense (DoD) Component guidelines, or if more stringent, the host nation requirements.

e. Drinking water on all Army floating vessels shall be provided according to 40 CFR 141 and Chapter 6 of Navy Medical (NAVMED) P-5010. Drinking water and water for washing on all Army floating vessels shall be provided from a potable water source which meets the federal and state requirements or, if generated on the vessel, shall be tested and shall meet the federal and state drinking water requirements.

(1) All hoses, pumps, and valves, shall be dedicated to potable drinking water only and shall be rinsed before each use.

(2) Before connecting at shore side, the supply water should be flushed for 30 seconds.

(3) After transfer is complete, the vessel hose shall be removed first, then the shore side hose removed, and the supply source shall be flushed again and capped.

(4) Drain all hoses, pumps, and valves after each use.

(5) Storage tanks on vessels shall be either chemically or mechanically disinfected when the water fails to meet two consecutive drinking water tests.

02.C.02 Cool drinking water shall be provided during hot weather.

02.C.03 Only approved potable water systems may be used for the distribution of drinking water. Construction trailers and other temporary or semi-permanent facilities shall be properly connected to the local municipal water supply unless the remoteness of the location makes this prohibitive. When unable to connect to the municipal supply, temporary potable water systems shall be utilized and the services provided by a licensed potable water contractor. "Reclaimed water" (treated wastewater) use in potable systems is strictly prohibited.

02.C.04 Drinking water shall be dispensed by means that prevent contamination between the consumer and the source.

02.C.05 Portable drinking water dispensers shall be designed, constructed, and serviced to ensure sanitary conditions, shall be capable of being closed and shall have a tap. Any container used to distribute drinking water shall be clearly marked "DRINKING WATER" and may not be used for other purposes.

02.C.06 Open containers (i.e., barrels, pails, or tanks) or any container (with or without a fitted cover) from which the water is dipped or poured are prohibited for drinking water. Lid shall remain on a container except when being sanitized, washed or filled.

02.C.07 Fountain dispensers shall have a guarded orifice.

02.C.08 Use of a common cup (a cup shared by more than one worker) and other common utensils is prohibited. Employees shall use cups when drinking from portable water coolers/containers. Unused disposable cups shall be kept in sanitary containers and a waste receptacle shall be provided for used cups.

02.C.09 Potable drinking water dispensers shall only contain drinking water and shall not be used to store or cool drinks or food or other items.

02.C.10 All potable wells intended for drinking water or human contact shall include appropriate wellhead protection to ensure sanitary quality. Wellhead protection shall include methods or accessories to prevent fecal contamination, insect infestation, and deliberate human actions that might jeopardize the quantity and quality of the water supply.

02.D Non-Potable Water.

02.D.01 Outlets dispensing non-potable water shall be conspicuously posted "CAUTION-WATER UNSAFE FOR DRINKING, WASHING, OR COOKING". Outlets dispensing non-potable water at Corps Dumping Stations within campgrounds may, in lieu of this requirement, be posted in accordance with USACE's Engineering Pamphlet (EP) 310-1-6A and EP 310-1-6B.

02.D.02 There shall not be any cross-connection, open or potential, between a system furnishing potable water and a system furnishing non-potable water.

02.D.03 Non-potable water may be used for cleaning work areas, except food processing and preparation areas and personal service rooms, provided this non-potable water does not contain concentrations of chemicals, fecal coliform or other substances which could create unsanitary conditions or be harmful to employees.

02.E Toilets.

02.E.01 General. Toilets shall be present in all places of employment and shall contain the following:

➢ *Exception: The requirements below do not apply to mobile crews or to normally unattended work locations if employees working at these locations have transportation readily available to nearby toilet and/or washing facilities which meet the other requirements of this paragraph.*

a. Separate toilet facilities, in toilet rooms provided for each sex shall be provided in all places of employment according to Table 2-1. Separate toilet rooms for each sex need not be provided if toilet rooms can only be occupied by one person at a time, can be locked from the inside and contain at least one toilet seat (where such single- occupancy rooms have more than one commode, only one commode in each toilet room may be counted);

b. Hot and cold running water, or tepid running water [tepid water is 60° F - 100° F (15.5° C - 37.8° C)];

c. Hand soap or similar cleansing agents shall be provided;

d. Individual disposable paper towels or warm air blowers designed for hand-drying, convenient to the lavatories;

e. An adequate supply of toilet paper and a holder for each seat;

f. Contained within an individual compartment and equipped with a door and separated from other toilet fixtures by walls or partitions sufficiently high to ensure privacy;

g. Adequate interior lighting;

h. Washing and toilet facilities shall be cleaned regularly and maintained in good order;

i. Each commode shall be equipped with a toilet seat and toilet seat cover. Each toilet facility - except those specifically designed and designated for females shall be equipped with a metal, plastic or porcelain urinal trough; and

j. Adequate ventilation. All windows and vents shall be screened; seat boxes shall be vented to the outside [minimum vent size 4 in (10.1 cm)] with vent intake located 1 in (2.5 cm) below the seat.

02.E.02 Construction Sites. Toilet facilities on construction sites shall be provided as follows (the requirements of this subsection do not apply to mobile crews or to normally unattended work locations if employees working at these locations have transportation immediately available to nearby toilet facilities):

a. Where sanitary sewers are not available, job sites shall be provided with chemical toilets, re-circulating toilets, or combustion toilets unless prohibited by state/local codes;

b. Each toilet facility shall be equipped with a toilet seat and toilet seat cover. Each toilet facility - except those specifically designed and designated for females - shall be equipped with a metal, plastic, or porcelain urinal trough. All shall be provided with an adequate supply of toilet paper and a holder for each seat;

TABLE 2-1

Minimum Toilet Facilities

(Other than Construction Sites)

Number of Employees	Minimum Number of Toilets[1]
1 to 15	One (1)
16 to 35	Two (2)
36 to 55	Three (3)
56 to 80	Four (4)
81 to 110	Five (5)
111 to 150	Six (6)
Over 150	Refer to Note[2]

Note:

[1] Where toilet facilities will not be used by women, urinals may be provided instead of commodes, except that the number of commodes in such cases shall not be reduced to fewer than 2/3 of the minimum number specified.

[2] One additional toilet fixture for each additional 40 employees.

c. Toilets shall be provided for each sex according to Table 2-2. Separate toilet rooms for each sex need not be provided if toilet rooms can only be occupied by one person at a time, can be locked from the inside and contain at least one toilet seat;

d. Where it is not practical to provide running water, hand sanitizers may be used as a substitute for running water. Hand sanitizers must contain at least 60% ethyl alcohol as its active ingredient and workers shall be trained to properly use the sanitizer.

e. Toilet facilities shall be constructed so that the occupants are protected against weather and falling objects; all cracks shall be sealed; the door shall be tight-fitting, selfclosing, and capable of being latched from the inside;

f. Adequate ventilation shall be provided; all windows and vents shall be screened; seat boxes shall be vented to the outside [minimum vent size 4 in (10.1 cm)] with vent intake located 1 in (2.5 cm) below the seat;

g. Toilet facilities shall be constructed so that the interior is lighted; and

h. Provisions for routinely servicing and cleaning all toilets and disposing of the sewage shall be established before placing toilet facilities into operation. The method of sewage disposal and the placement location selected shall be in accordance with Federal, state, and local health regulations.

TABLE 2-2

Minimum Toilet Facilities

(Construction Sites)

Number of Employees	Minimum Number of Toilets[1]
20 or fewer	One (1)
20 or greater	One (1) toilet seat and One (1) urinal per 40 workers.
200 or greater	One (1) toilet seat and One (1) urinal per 50 workers.

Note: [1] Where toilet facilities will not be used by women, urinals may be provided instead of commodes, except that the number of commodes in such cases shall not be reduced to fewer than 2/3 of the minimum number specified.

02.E.03 Employees working in temporary field conditions, in mobile crews or in normally unattended work locations shall be provided at least one toilet facility unless transportation to nearby toilet facilities is readily available.

02.F Washing Facilities.

02.F.01 Washing facilities shall be provided at toilet facilities and as needed to maintain healthful and sanitary conditions.

02.F.02 Each washing facility shall be maintained in a sanitary condition and provided with water from an approved potable water supply. Water shall be either hot and cold or tepid running water. Soap and either individual disposable paper towels or warm air blowers designed for hand-drying shall be provided. If impractical to provide running water, hand sanitizer <u>and individual disposable paper towels</u> may be used.

02.F.03 Washing facilities shall be in close proximity to the worksite.

02.G Showers.

02.G.01 Washing facilities for persons engaged in application of paints, coatings, herbicides, insecticides, or other operations where contaminants may be harmful shall be at or near the work site and shall be equipped to enable employees to remove such substances.

02.G.02 Whenever showers are required by a particular standard, the showers shall be provided in accordance with the following:

a. One shower shall be provided for every ten employees (or fraction thereof) of each sex, who are required to shower during the same shift;

b. Body soap or other appropriate cleansing agents for the showers shall be provided;

c. Showers shall be equipped with hot and cold water <u>from an approved potable water supply</u> feeding a common discharge line; and

d. Employees who use showers shall be provided with individual clean towels.

02.H Changing Rooms. Whenever employees are required by a particular standard to wear protective clothing, changing rooms shall be equipped with separate storage facilities for both street clothes and protective clothing.

02.I <u>Laundry of Work Clothing.</u> <u>If non-disposable work clothing provided by the employer becomes contaminated, provisions shall be made to ensure clothing is laundered and decontaminated by the employee prior to reuse. Employees shall not wear contaminated clothing when leaving the worksite. If contaminated work clothing is taken to a commercial laundry, the laundry representative must be advised of the potential contaminants on the clothing.</u>

02.J Food Service.

02.J.01 <u>All USACE food service facilities and facilities operated under USACE contracts, including galleys aboard vessels, shall be compliant with the US Public Health Service (USPHS) Food and Drug Administration (FDA) Food Code.</u>

02.J.02 All employee food service facilities and operations shall be conducted in accordance with sound hygienic principles.

02.J.03 In places of employment where all or part of the food service is provided, the food dispensed shall be wholesome, free from spoilage, and shall be processed, prepared, handled, and stored in such a manner as to be protected against contamination.

02.J.04 No employee may be allowed to consume food or beverages in a toilet room or in any area exposed to a toxic material.

02.J.05 No food or beverages may be stored in toilet rooms or in an area exposed to a toxic material.

02.J.06 <u>Food handlers are not required to have a general medical exam, but must obtain a statement from a licensed physician, physician's assistant, or nurse practitioner attesting that they are free of communicable diseases. Food handlers shall complete at least 8 hours of food service sanitation training annually.</u>

02.J.07 <u>All USACE food service facilities and facilities operated under USACE contracts, including galleys aboard vessels, shall be inspected for compliance with the USPHS FDA Food Code at least semi-annually.</u>

02.K Waste Disposal.

02.K.01 An adequate number of waste receptacles shall be provided in a food service area and used for the disposal of waste food. Receptacles shall be constructed of smooth, corrosion-resistant, easily cleanable, or disposable materials, provided with solid tight-fitting covers, emptied at least daily and maintained in a sanitary condition.

02.K.02 Receptacles used for putrescible solid or liquid waste or refuse shall be constructed in order to prevent leakage and to allow thorough cleaning and sanitary maintenance. Such receptacles shall be equipped with solid tight-fitting covers, unless they can be maintained in sanitary conditions without covers.

02.K.03 All sweepings, solid or liquid wastes, refuse, and garbage shall be removed in a manner which avoids creating a menace to health and should be discarded as often as necessary or appropriate to maintain sanitary conditions in the place of employment.

02.L Vermin Control.

02.L.01 Every enclosed workplace shall be constructed, equipped, and maintained, as practicable as possible, in order to prevent the entrance or harborage of rodents, insects, or other vermin.

02.L.02 A continuing and effective extermination program shall be instituted when the presence of vermin is detected. The use of licensed exterminators/pest control personnel is required.

THIS PAGE INTENTIONALLY LEFT BLANK

SECTION 3 Medical and First Aid

Table of Contents

03.A General.

03.A.01 Prior to the start of work by a contractor and for all USACE locations, arrangements shall be made for medical facilities and personnel to provide prompt attention to injured employees. For work or tasks with a high or extremely high risk assessment code (RAC) on the Activity Hazard Analysis (AHA), the arrangements with the medical facility shall be confirmed in writing. > See Sections 01.A.14 and 01.A.15.

a. An effective means of communication (i.e., hardwired or cellular telephone, two-way radio, etc.) with #911 access or other emergency response source, and transportation to effectively care for injured workers shall be provided. Communication devices shall be tested in the area of use to assure functionality.

b. The telephone numbers of physicians, hospitals, or ambulances shall be conspicuously posted, at a minimum, on the safety bulletin board and near the on-site project office telephones. Medical facilities and personnel expected to treat injured employees shall be informed of the nature of the work to be performed and the injuries/illnesses prevalent on such jobsites. Depending on the scope and size of the job, the GDA may require a formal written agreement.

c. A highly visible map delineating the best route to the nearest medical facility shall be prepared and posted on the safety bulletin board. For mobile field crews, it shall be readily available.

03.A.02 First aid and cardiopulmonary resuscitation (CPR) availability.

a. When emergency medical services are not accessible within 5 minutes of work location and there are 2 or more workers at the location, at least 2 employees on each shift shall be qualified to administer first aid and CPR. > Minimum qualifications are listed in Section 03.D.

b. For job sites with more than 100 employees on one shift, a list of qualified individuals shall be maintained by the site security personnel and in the site trailer. > Minimum qualifications are listed in Section 03.D.

c. Training and Retraining. First aid attendants shall hold current certification in first aid and CPR from the American Red Cross (ARC), the American Heart Association (AHA), or from an organization whose training adheres to the standards of the International Liaison Committee on Resuscitation (as stated in writing), or from a Licensed Physician.

(1) All classes shall contain a hands-on component that cannot be taken online.

(2) The certificate(s) shall state the date of issue and length of validity.

(3) All first aid and CPR attendants shall be retrained every 2 years.

d. Individuals who are required to work alone in remote areas shall be trained in first aid and shall be provided with an effective means of communication to call for assistance in the event of an emergency.

03.A.03 First aid and medical facility requirements.

a. All projects, activities, or contracts (USACE or contractor operated), for which fewer than 100 persons are employed (greatest total number of employees on a shift) at the site of the work, and where neither a first aid station nor a health clinic is available or the site is more than 5 minutes from a hospital, medical clinic, or doctors' office which has agreed to provide emergency medical support, shall be provided with a first aid kit complying with the criteria contained in ANSI Z308.1.

(1) There shall be one first aid kit for every 25 (or fewer) employees.

(2) In addition to the basic fill requirements of the first aid kit, the contractor or local USACE Safety and Occupational Health Office (SOHO), in consultation with a health care professional, shall evaluate the hazards found in the work environment to determine the necessity of optional fill contents.

b. All projects, activities, or contracts (USACE or contractor operated) for which more than 99 and fewer than 300 persons are employed (greatest total number of employees on a shift) at the site of the work, shall establish and equip a first aid station (per Section 03.C). In non-rural locations, the use of a medical clinic, hospital, or doctor's office, that has agreed to provide emergency medical support and is accessible within 5 minutes of the work location, may be approved instead of a first aid station, provided at least two employees per shift are CPR qualified as defined in 03.A.02.c and a first aid kit complying with the criteria contained in ANSI Z308.1 is available.

c. Where tunnels are being excavated, a first aid station and transportation facilities shall be provided so that treatment is available within 5 minutes of the occurrence of an injury.

d. All <u>medium, high, or extremely high risk operations,</u> projects, activities, or contracts (<u>USACE or contractor operated)</u> for which 300 or more persons are employed (greatest total number of employees on a shift) at the site of the work shall establish and equip, as directed by a licensed physician, a <u>health clinic.</u> <u>Requirements for health clinics are in Section 03.C.</u>

e. All locations where the work efforts are primarily administrative, such as a district or regulatory office, shall have either: an accessible, staffed infirmary in the building or a medical clinic, hospital, or doctors' office that has agreed to provide emergency medical support and is accessible within 5 minutes. If an outside emergency medical clinic, hospital, or doctor's office is used, the location shall also have a minimum of 2 employees on each shift qualified to administer first aid and CPR and are trained according to Section 03.A.02.c. The work location shall also have several first aid kits meeting the requirements of this document.

03.A.04 Should work activities present any potential exposure (of any part of the body) to toxic or corrosive materials, drenching and/or flushing facilities shall be provided in the work area for immediate emergency use. > *See Section 06.B.*

03.A.<u>05</u> Blood-Borne Pathogen (BBP) Program. Employees designated as responsible for rendering first aid or medical assistance shall be included in their employer's BBP program in accordance with 29 CFR 1910.1030 and shall:

a. Be instructed in the sources, hazards, and avoidance of BBPs and be provided the training specified in 29 CFR 1910.1030;

b. Be provided with, and shall use and maintain, PPE (i.e., breathing barrier, latex-free gloves, gowns, masks, eye protectors, and/or resuscitation equipment) when appropriate for rendering first aid or other medical assistance to prevent contact with blood or other potentially infectious materials;

c. Institute a site-specific BBP program to include a site-specific Exposure Control Plan with provisions for engineering and administrative controls, Hepatitis B vaccination, PPE, training, recordkeeping, and a Post-Exposure Control Plan in the event of a blood-borne exposure. Post-exposure protocol shall include a plan to ensure immediate medical evaluation of exposed individual(s) per current recommendations of the Center for Disease Control (CDC) for human immunodeficiency virus (HIV), Hepatitis B virus (HBV), <u>and</u> Hepatitis C virus (HCV).

03.A.<u>06</u> Prior to the start of work outside the employee's normal geographical area, the employer shall inform

employees of parasitic, <u>bacterial,</u> viral and environmental diseases endemic to the geographical work location (i.e., Lyme Disease, West Nile Virus, Hantavirus, Histoplasmosis, Rocky-Mountain Spotted Fever, Dengue Fever, Malaria, etc.)

a. For guidance on the potential biological and environmental diseases in the work location, the employer shall consult the CDC Travel webpage, U.S. Army <u>Public Health Command – Institute of Public Health</u> web site, and the health department in the local area.

b. Information to be provided to the employee traveling in areas where such diseases are endemic shall include:

(1)   Modes of disease transmission;

(2)   Specific health risks associated with the disease;

(3)   Preventive measures such as available vaccines and PPE (gloves, eye and skin protection, respirator);

(4)   Appropriate work practices to prevent contact with infected agents (bird/rodent droppings, etc.), such as watering areas prior to dust-generating activities;

(5)   Vaccine information, to include information on the effectiveness, risk, and availability;

(6)   Safe removal of source where applicable;

(7)   Symptom recognition and medical referral.

03.B First Aid Kits.

03.B.01 The performance requirements of the first aid kits shall be based on the storage area location of the first aid kit and shall conform to ANSI/ISEA Z308.1. <u>Content of all first aid kits shall be to the level of training attained by the responders</u> using the first aid kit.

a. Type I <u>kits</u> are intended for use in stationary, indoor settings <u>where the potential for damage of kit supplies due to environmental factors and rough handling is minimal.</u> Type I first aid kits are required to <u>contain the minimum fill in Table 3-1.</u>

b. Type II , Type III, and <u>Type IV</u> first aid kits shall, at a minimum, meet the requirements <u>of the minimum fill in Table 3-1:</u>

(1) Type II kits are for portable indoor settings where the potential for damage of kit supplies due to environmental factors and rough handling is minimal;

(2) Type III kits are for portable use in mobile, indoor and/or outdoor settings where the potential for damage of kit supplies due to environmental factors is not probable (includes general indoor, sheltered outdoor use).

(3) Type IV kits are intended for portable use in mobile industries (i.e., utilities, construction, transportation, armed forces) and/or outdoor settings where the potential for damage of kit supplies due to environmental factors and rough handling is significant.

c. The contents of the first aid kit shall, at a minimum, contain the items detailed in Table 3-1.

d. First aid kits shall be easily accessible to all workers and protected from the weather. The individual contents of the first aid kits shall be kept sterile. First aid kit locations shall be clearly marked and distributed throughout the site(s).

03.B.02 The contents of first aid kits shall be checked by the employer prior to their use on site and at least every 3 months when work is in progress to ensure that they are complete, in good condition, and have not expired.

TABLE 3-1
Requirements for Basic First Aid Unit Package

Unit first aid item	Minimum Size or Volume (metric)	Minimum Size or Volume (US)	Item quantity per unit package	Unit package size
Absorbent Compress	206 cm^2	32 in^2	1	1
Adhesive Bandage	2.5 x 7.5 cm	1 x 3 in	16	1
Adhesive Tape	2.3 m	2.5 yd (total)	1 or 2	1 or 2
Antiseptic Wipe	2.5 x 2.5 cm	1 x 1 in.	10	1
Aspirin, Individually Wrapped	325 mg		2	2
Bandage Compress (2 in-4 in)	5 x 91 cm	2 x 36 in.	4	1
Burn Dressing	10 x 10 cm	4 x 4 in	1	1-2
Burn Treatment	0.9	1/32 fl. Oz.	6	1
Cold Pack	10 x 12.5 cm	4 x 5 in	1	1
*Combat style Tourniquet with Windlass	95.3 x 3.8	37.5 x 1.5 in. width	1	1
CPR Breathing Barrier			1	1
Eye Covering, with means of attachment	19 cm^2	2.9 in^2	2	1
Eye/Skin Wash	118 ml (total)	4 fl. oz total	1	2
First Aid Guide			1	1
Gloves, latex free	XL	XL	2 pair	1
Hand Sanitizer	0.9 g	1/32 oz.	6	
Occlusive Dressing	10.2 x 10.2	4 x 4	1	2
Roller Bandage (2 in.)	5 x 366 cm	2 in. x 4 yd.	2	1
Roller Bandage (4 in.)	10 x 366 cm	4 in. x 4 yd.	1	1
Sterile pad	7.5 x 7.5 cm	3 x 3 in.	4	1
Triangular Bandage	101 x 101 x 14 cm	2 40 x 40 x 56 in.	1	1

*Required when power tools in use.

03.B.03 All employees who work where there is a first aid kit shall receive a tool box training on the content and use of the kit supplies

03.B.04 Automatic External Defibrillator (AED). The placement of AEDs is optional (except for health clinics, see 03.C.03.d) but highly recommended. The placement of AEDs on the worksite shall be preceded by an assessment of the time and distance to emergency medical services (EMS) and a justification for such equipment. For the ease of use and program maintenance, all AEDs in a location and/or Command should be the same manufacturer and model. For guidance, USACE facilities should refer to Guidelines for Public Access Defibrillation Programs in Federal Facilities (www.foh.dhhs.gov/whatwedo/aed/hhsaed.asp). An AED program shall include, at minimum:

a. Training and Retraining: Workers required to use an AED shall be trained per Section 03.A.02.c. All classes shall contain a hands-on component and cannot be taken online. Training shall be on the same model and manufacturer of AED available in the work area. The certificate(s) shall state the date of issue and length of validity;

b. Licensed Physician direction and oversight;

c. Documented weekly battery and functionality checks;

d. Standard Operating Procedures (SOPs) for placement, maintenance, inspections, and EMS activation;

e. Equipment Maintenance Program based on the manufacturer's recommendations that, at a minimum, shall include pad replacement (regular and after use) and battery replacement.

03.C First Aid Stations and Health Clinics.

03.C.01 General.

a. For activities requiring a first aid station or a health clinic, the type of facilities and equipment provided shall be determined after consideration is given to the proximity and quality of available medical services. The facilities and equipment shall also be in accordance with the recommendation of a Licensed Physician, Board-Certified and Licensed, Physician's Assistant (PA-C), or Licensed Nurse Practitioner (LNP). Alternative facilities that provide the quantity and quality of services outlined in this section may be used if recommended by the consulting Licensed Physician, PA-C or LNP.

b. Identification and directional markers shall be used to readily denote the location of all first aid stations and health clinics.

c. Emergency lighting shall be provided for all first aid stations and health clinics.

03.C.02 A certified first aid provider shall be on duty in first aid stations at all hours when work is in progress (except when on emergency calls).

03.C.03 Health Clinics.

a. Health Clinics shall provide privacy, adequate lighting, climate control, adequate toilet facilities, hot and cold water, drainage, and electrical outlets. Walls and ceilings shall be finished with the equivalent of two coats of white paint; windows and doors shall be screened; floors shall be constructed with impervious materials.

b. In remote locations where medical care is not available within 5 minutes, a properly equipped emergency vehicle, helicopter, or mobile first aid unit shall be provided during work hours at sites requiring a health clinic. The emergency vehicle shall not be used for any other purpose, except in the case of a helicopter, which may be used for shift crew changes.

c. A Registered Nurse (RN), a certified Emergency Medical Technician (EMT), Intermediate/Paramedic, or a Licensed Practical Nurse (LPN), with physician oversight, shall be assigned on a full-time basis to each installation requiring a health clinic.

d. Health clinics shall be equipped with an AED.

03.D Personnel Requirements and Qualifications.

03.D.01 All projects, activities, or contracts (USACE or contractor) where work or tasks with a high or extremely high risk assessment code (RAC) exists and which 1,000 persons or more are employed (greatest total number of employees on a shift) shall have the fulltime services of a Licensed Physician.

➢ Note: A certified Nationally Registered Emergency Medical Technician (NREMT) Intermediate/Paramedic, RN, LPN, LNP, or a PA-C having direct communication with a Licensed Physician, may be used when a full-time Licensed Physician is not available.

03.D.02 First aid attendants shall hold certification in first aid and CPR training as defined in Section 03.A.02. The certificate(s) shall state the date of issue and length of validity.

03.D.03 First aid attendants, RNs, LPNs, NREMT-Intermediates/Paramedics, LNP and PA-C shall be under the direction of a Licensed Physician.

03.D.04 Military personnel with equivalent qualifications and certifications may be used in lieu of the above personnel.

THIS PAGE INTENTIONALLY LEFT BLANK

SECTION 4 Temporary Facilities

Table of Contents

4

04.A General.

04.A.01 Plans for the layout of temporary construction buildings, facilities, fencing, access routes and anchoring systems for temporary structures shall be submitted to and approved by the GDA. > *See Section 09.A.18 for temporary building spacing requirements; Section 11 for temporary power distribution approval requirements; Section 24 for temporary ramp, trestle, scaffold, and platform approval requirements.*

04.A.02 The design and construction of temporary structures shall consider the following loadings. > *See American Society of Civil Engineers (ASCE) 7-10, Minimum Design Loads for Buildings and Other Structures:*

    a. Dead and live loads;

    b. Soil and hydrostatic pressures;

    c. Wind loads;

    d. Rain and snow loads;

    e. Flood and ice loads, and

    f. Seismic forces.

04.A.03 Trailers and other temporary structures used as field offices, as personnel housing, or for storage shall be anchored with rods and cables or by steel straps to ground anchors. The anchor system shall be designed to withstand winds and must meet applicable state or local standards for anchoring mobile trailer homes.

04.A.04 Fencing and warning signs.

    a. Temporary project fencing (or a substitute acceptable to the GDA and delineated in the APP) shall be provided on all projects located in areas of active use by members of the public, including those areas in close proximity to family housing areas and/or school facilities.

    b. Fencing shall extend from grade to a minimum of 4 ft (1.2 m) above grade and shall have a maximum mesh size of 2 in (5 cm). Fencing shall remain rigid/taut with a minimum of 200 lbs (.9 kN) of force exerted on it from any direction with less than 4 in (10 cm) of deflection.

    c. Signs warning of the presence of construction hazards and requiring unauthorized persons to keep out of the construction area shall be posted on the fencing. At minimum, signs shall be posted every 150 ft (45.7 m). Fenced sides of projects that are less than 150 ft shall, at minimum, have at least one warning sign. > *See also Section 8.*

    d. Depending upon the nature and location of the project site, the GDA may determine that fencing is not required. This will be based on a risk analysis of public exposure and other project specific considerations, and will be included in the applicable AHA. In those locations where the GDA has determined fencing is not required, signs, warning of construction hazards, shall be conspicuously posted.

04.A.05 Temporary Work Camps (Floating plant excluded). The design and construction of work/labor camps shall be IAW 29 CFR 1910.142.

    a. All sites used for temporary work camps shall be adequately drained. They shall not be subject to periodic flooding nor located within 200 ft (61 m) of swamps, pools, sink holes, or other surface collections of water unless adequate mosquito control methods have been implemented. The sites shall be graded, ditched, and rendered free from depressions in which water may become a nuisance.

    b. Sites shall be sized to prevent overcrowding of necessary structures.

    c. The grounds and open areas surrounding the shelters shall be maintained free of rubbish, debris, waste paper, garbage, or other refuse.

    d. Shelters will provide protection from the elements, and each room used for sleeping purposes shall contain at least 55 ft^2 (5.06 m^2) of floor space for each occupant and at least 7 ft-6 in (2.3 m) ceilings. The floor space does not include areas occupied by closets or wall lockers.

    e. Beds, cots, or bunks, and suitable storage facilities (such as wall lockers for clothing and personal articles) shall be provided in every room used for sleeping purposes. Beds shall be spaced not closer than 3 ft (1 m) both laterally and end-to-end and shall be elevated at least 1 ft (.3 m) from the floor. Double-decked bunk beds shall be spaced not fewer than 4 ft (1.2 m) both laterally and end-to-end with a minimum space of not fewer than 27 in (68.5 cm) between the upper and lower bunk. Triple deck bunks are prohibited.

    f. Floors shall be constructed of wood, asphalt, or concrete. Wooden floors shall be of smooth and tight construction. Floors shall be kept in good repair.

    g. All wooden floors shall be elevated not less than 1.5 ft (0.5 m) above the ground level at all points to prevent dampness and permit free circulation of air beneath, and for easier and safer maintenance.

    h. Living quarters shall be provided with windows that may be opened for purposes of ventilation.

    i. All exterior openings shall be effectively screened with 16-mesh material and screen doors shall be equipped with self-closing devices.

j. Temporary sleeping quarters shall be heated, cooled, ventilated, lighted, and maintained in a clean and safe condition.

k. Sleeping quarters must comply with applicable provisions of the National Fire Protection Agency (NFPA) 101, Life Safety Code.

04.A.06 Unless otherwise indicated, throughout this manual, lumber dimensions are given in nominal sizes.

04.A.07 Temporary Explosives Storage Areas. Temporary Explosives Storage Areas shall be IAW the EM 385-1-97, Explosives Safety and Health Requirements.

04.B Access and Haul Roads.

04.B.01 Prior to construction, the Contractor shall provide the GDA with a copy of an Access/Haul Road plan for review and acceptance. Access/haul roads shall be designed in accordance with current engineering criteria. Work on the haul road shall not commence until the GDA has accepted the plan. The plan shall address the following items:

a. Equipment usage, traffic density and patterns, right-of-way rules, and hours of operation;

b. Road layout and widths, horizontal and vertical curve data, and sight distances;

c. Sign and signalperson requirements, road markings, and traffic control devices;

d. Drainage controls;

e. Points of contact between vehicles and the public, vehicles and pedestrians, and safety controls at these points;

f. Maintenance requirements, including roadway hardness and smoothness and dust control, and

g. Hazards adjacent to the road (e.g., bodies of water, steep embankments).

04.B.02 No employer shall move, or cause to be moved, any equipment or vehicle upon an access or haul road unless the roadway is constructed and maintained to safely accommodate the movement of the equipment or vehicle involved.

04.B.03 When road levels are above working levels, berms, barricades, or curbs shall be constructed to prevent vehicles overrunning the edge or end of embankment. Berms/curbs shall be constructed to one-half the diameter of the tires of the largest piece of equipment using the roadway.

04.B.04 Roadways shall have a crown and ditches for drainage. Water shall be intercepted before reaching a switch back or large fill and be led off.

04.B.05 Haul roads shall be constructed to widths suitable for safe operation of the equipment at the travel speeds proposed by the Contractor and accepted by the GDA.

04.B.06 All roads, including haul roads, shall be posted with maximum speed limits.

04.B.07 An adequate number of turn-outs shall be provided on single lane roads with two-way traffic. When turn-outs are not practical, the Contractor shall provide a traffic control system to prevent accidents.

04.B.08 Whenever possible, use a right-hand traffic pattern on two-way haul roads.

04.B.09 Curves.

a. All curves shall have open sight lines and as great a radius as practical.

b. Vehicle speed shall be limited on curves so that vehicles can be stopped within one-half the visible distance of the roadway.

c. The design of horizontal curves shall consider vehicle speed, roadway width and surfacing, and super elevation.

04.B.10 Grades.

a. When necessary, based on grade and machine and load weight, machines shall be equipped with retarders to assist in controlling downgrade descent.

b. Access/haul roads should be kept to less than a 10% grade. There should be no more than 400 ft (121.9 m) of grade exceeding 10%.

c. The maximum allowable grade shall not exceed 12% ppp.

04.B.11 Adequate lighting shall be provided. > See Section 7.

04.B.12 Traffic control lights, barricades, road markings, signs, and signalpersons for the safe movement of traffic shall be provided in accordance with the DOT Federal Highway Administration's "Manual on Uniform Traffic Control Devices" and this Section.

04.B.13 Roadway hardness, smoothness, and dust control shall be used to maintain the safety of the roadway.

04.B.14 All roads shall be maintained in a safe condition and eliminate or control dust, ice, and similar hazards.

04.B.15 The deposition of mud and or other debris on public roads shall be minimized to the extent possible and in accordance with local requirements.

THIS PAGE INTENTIONALLY LEFT BLANK

SECTION 5 Personal Protective and Safety Equipment

Table of Contents

5

05.A General.

05.A.01 Responsibilities.

a. The use of personal protective and safety equipment (PPE) is a control measure that is to be used only after a hazard evaluation identifies hazards associated with a particular job or activity, and it is determined that the hazards cannot be eliminated and/or controlled to an acceptable level through engineering design or administrative actions. Utilize process and engineering controls before PPE to protect employees.

b. Based on hazard evaluations conducted by supervisors, employers shall identify and select, and each affected employee shall use PPE that will provide appropriate protection. > *See 29 CFR 1910.132.*

c. Employers shall communicate PPE decisions to each affected employee. Employees shall use all PPE that may be required to maintain their exposure within acceptable limits.

d. The employer will make all reasonable efforts to accommodate employees with religious beliefs that may conflict with determined PPE requirements. However, when reasonable efforts to accommodate employee's religious beliefs do not provide the necessary safe working environment (without PPE), then the employee must use the appropriate PPE or the employee will not be allowed to work in the area where the hazard requiring protection exists.

05.A.02 Employees shall be appropriately trained in the use, care, and limitations of all required PPE.

a. Employees must be trained in and shall demonstrate an understanding of the following aspects of PPE prior to use: selection (for specific hazard); donning, doffing and adjusting; limitations and useful life; inspection and testing; and proper care including maintenance, storage and disposal.

b. When the employer has reason to believe that any affected employee who has been trained does not have the understanding and skill required for the use of the PPE, the employer shall make certain that the employee receives the necessary re-training to acquire the appropriate skills.

c. The employer shall verify through written certification that each affected employee has received and understood the required training. The written certification shall identify the name of each employee trained, the date(s) of the training, and the subjects taught.

05.A.03 A copy of the manufacturer's use, inspection, testing, and maintenance instructions shall be maintained at the job site and be readily available to personnel using the PPE and safety equipment.

05.A.04 PPE shall be tested, inspected, and maintained in a serviceable and sanitary condition as recommended by the manufacturer.

a. Defective or damaged equipment, or equipment that has exceeded its useful life, shall not be used. It shall be tagged as out of service and/or immediately removed from the work site to prevent use.

b. Previously used PPE must be cleaned, inspected, and repaired as necessary before issuing to another employee.

05.A.05 When employees provide their own PPE, the employer is responsible for assuring its adequacy in protecting against the hazard and its state of repair.

05.A.06 Minimum requirements.

a. Employees shall wear clothing suitable for the weather and work conditions. For fieldwork (e.g., construction sites, industrial operations and maintenance activities, emergency operations, regulatory inspections, etc.), at a minimum, this shall be:

(1) Short sleeve shirt;

(2) Long pants (excessively long or baggy pants are prohibited); and

(3) Leather or other protective work shoes or boots. Open-toed shoes are prohibited. > *See Section 5.E.*

b. Protective equipment shall be of heat, fire, chemical, and/or electrical-resistive material when conditions require protection against such hazards.

05.A.07 Persons involved in activities that subject the hands to injury (for example, cuts, abrasions, punctures, burns, chemical irritants, toxins, vibration, and forces that can restrict blood flow) shall select and use hand protection appropriate for the hazard in accordance with ANSI/International Safety Equipment Association (ISEA) 105. > *See Section 5.H.*

05.A.08 Protective leg chaps shall be worn by workers who operate chainsaws. Protective leg chaps must meet the specifications in American Society for Testing and Materials (ASTM) Standard F1897.

05.A.09 <u>For personal fall arrest equipment, including lineman's equipment (electrically rated harnesses), see Section 21.I.05.</u>

05.B Eye And Face Protection.

05.B.01 Persons shall be provided with eye and face protection <u>for the specific jobsite hazards</u>, as <u>listed</u> in Table 5-1, when machines or operations present potential eye or face injury.

a. Eye and face protection shall meet the requirements of ANSI/American Society of Safety Engineers (ASSE) Z87.1, and bear a legible and permanent "Z87" logo to indicate compliance with the standard.

b. Eye and face protection shall be distinctly marked to identify manufacturer.

05.B.02 When eye protection is required by this regulation, persons whose vision requires the use of corrective lenses, <u>whether via the use of contact lenses or eyeglasses</u>, shall be protected by one of the following:

a. Prescription safety glasses providing optical correction and equivalent protection;

b. Protective glasses with sideshields designed to fit over corrective lenses without disturbing the adjustment of the glasses;

c. Goggles that can be worn over corrective lenses without disturbing the adjustment of the glasses, or

d. Goggles that incorporate corrective lenses mounted behind the protective lenses.

05.B.03 Personnel who are considered blind in one eye and are working in other than administrative functions shall wear safety glasses with sideshields at all times.

05.B.04 Operations that require the use of, or exposure to, hot or molten substances (e.g., babbitting, soldering, pouring or casting of hot metals, handling of hot tar, oils, liquids, and molten substances) shall require eye protection, such as goggles with safety lenses and screens for side protection, or face masks, shields, and helmets giving equal protection. Lens mountings shall be able to retain in position all parts of a cracked lens.

05.B.05 Operations that require handling of harmful materials (e.g., acids, caustics, hot liquids, or creosoted materials) and operations where protection from gases, fumes, and liquids is necessary, shall require the wearing of goggles with cups of soft pliable rubber and suitable faceshields, masks, or hoods that cover the head and neck, and other protective clothing appropriate to the hazards involved.

05.B.06 Operations where protection from radiant energy with moderate reduction of visible light is necessary, including welding, cutting, brazing, and soldering, shall require eye and face protection suitable to the type of work, providing protection from all angles of direct exposure, and with lenses of the appropriate shade. > *See Table 5.2.*

05.B.07 Glare-resistant glasses that comply with ANSI Z80.3 with an ultraviolet A- region (UVA) and ultraviolet B-region (UVB) 99% filtration shall be worn when conditions require protection against glare. When conditions so warrant, polarized lenses shall also be considered.

05.B.08 Tinted or automatically darkening lenses should not be worn when work tasks require the employee to pass often from brightly to dimly lighted areas.

5

Eye and Face Protector Selection Guide

A. Spectacle,
   No sideshield

E. Spectacle,
   Non-Removable
   Lens

I. Cover Goggle,
   Direct Ventilatior

B. Spectacle, Half
   Sideshield

F. Spectacle,
   Lift Front

J. Cup Goggle,
   Direct Ventilatior

C. Spectacle, Full
   Sideshield

G. Cover Goggle,
   No Ventilation

K. Cup Goggle,
   Indirect Ventilatior

D. Spectacle,
   Detachable
   Sideshield

H. Cover Goggle,
   Indirect Ventilation

L. Spectacle,
   Headband
   Temple

TABLE 5-1 (Continued)

Eye and Face Protector Selection Guide

M. Cover Welding
Goggle, Indirect
Ventilation

Q. Welding Helmet,
Lift Front

S. Respirator

5

N. Faceshield

R. Respirator

T1. Respirator

T2. Respirator

U. Respirator

O. Welding
Helmet,
hand Hold

P. Welding Helmet,
Stationary Window

Table 5-1 (Continued)

Eye and Face Protector Selection Guide

IMPACT: Chipping, grinding, machining, masonry work, riveting and sanding				
Assessment See Note (1)	Protector Type	Protectors	Limitations	Not Recommended
Flying fragments, objects, large chips, particles, sand, dirt, etc.	B, C, D, E, F, G, H, I, J, K, L, N	Spectacles, goggles, faceshields See Notes (1)(3)(5)(6)(10) For severe exposures: add N	Protective devices do not provided unlimited protection. See Note (7)	Protectors that do not provide protection from side exposure See Note (10) Filter or tinted lenses that restrict light transmittance, unless it is determined that a glare hazard exists. Refer to Optical Radiation.
HEAT: Furnace operations, pouring, casting, hot dipping, gas cutting, and welding				
Assessment See Note (1)	Protector Type	Protectors	Limitations	Not Recommended
Hot sparks	B, C, D, E, F, G, H, I, J, K, L, N	Faceshields, goggles, spectacles For severe Exposure, add N See Notes (2)(3)	Spectacles, cup and cover- type goggles do not provide unlimited facial protection See Note (2)	Protectors that do not provide protection from side exposure
Splash from Molten Metals	N	Faceshields worn over goggles H,K See Notes (2)(3)		
High Temperature Exposure	N	Screen faceshields, reflective faceshields	See Note (3)	

Table 5-1 (Continued)

Eye and Face Protector Selection Guide

CHEMICAL:
Acid and chemical handling, degreasing, plating

Assessment See Note (1)	Protector Type	Protectors	Limitations	Not Recommended
Splash	G, H, K N	For severe exposure add N	Ventilation should be adequate but protected from splash entry	Spectacles, welding helmets, hand shields
Irritating mists	G	Special purpose goggles	See Note (3)	

DUST: Woodworking, buffing, general industry conditions

Assessment See Note (1)	Protector Type	Protectors	Limitations	Not Recommended
Nuisance dust	G, H, K	Goggles, eyecup and cover types	Atmospheric conditions and the restricted ventilation of the protector can cause lenses to fog. Frequent cleaning may be required.	

OPTICAL RADIATION: Welding: electric arc

Assessment See Note (1)	Protector Type	Protectors	Limitations	Not Recommended
O, P, Q	Typical filter lens shade		Protection from optical radiation is directly related to filter lens density. See Note (4). Select the darkest shade that allows adequate task performance.	Protectors that do not provide protection from optical radiation.

NOTES:

(1) Care should be taken to recognize the possibility of multiple and simultaneous exposure to a variety of hazards. Adequate protection against the highest level of each of the hazards must be provided.

(2) Operations involving heat may also involve optical radiation. Protection from both hazards shall be provided.

(3) Faceshields shall only be worn over primary eye protection.

(4) Filter lenses shall meet the requirements for shade designations in Table 5-2.

(5) Persons whose vision requires the use of prescription (Rx) lenses shall wear either protective devices fitted with prescription (Rx) lenses with sideshields or protective devices designed to be worn over regular prescription (Rx) eyewear.

(6) Wearers of contact lenses shall also be required to wear appropriate covering eye and face protection devices in a hazardous environment. It should be recognized that dusty and/or chemical environments may represent an additional hazard to contact lens wearers.

(7) Caution should be exercised in the use of metal frame protective devices in electrical hazard areas.

(8) Refer to ANSI/ASSE Z87-1, Section 6.5, Special Purpose Lenses.

(9) Welding helmets or hand shields shall be used only over primary eye protection.

(10) Non-sideshield spectacles are available for frontal protection only

.

TABLE 5-2

Required Shades for Filter Lenses/Glasses in Welding, Cutting, Brazing and Soldering

OPERATION	SHADE NUMBER
Soldering	2
Torch Brazing	3 or 4
Cutting (light) up to 1 in (2.5 cm)	3 or 4
Cutting (medium) 1 to 6 in (2.5 to 15.2 cm)	4 or 5
Cutting (heavy) 6 in (15.2 cm) or more	5 or 6
Gas welding (light) up to 1/8 in (0.3 cm)	4 or 5
Gas welding (medium) 1/8 to 1/2 in (0.3 to 1.2 cm)	5 or 6
Gas welding (heavy) 1/2 in (1.2 cm) or more	6 or 8
Atomic hydrogen welding	10 – 14
Inert-gas metal-arc welding (nonferrous): 1/16 in to 5/32 in (0.1 to 0.4 cm) electrodes	11
Inert-gas metal-arc welding (ferrous) - 1/16 to 5/32 in (0.1 to 0.4 cm) electrodes	12
Shielded metal-arc welding - 1/16 to 5/32 in (0.1 to 0.4 cm) electrodes	10
Shielded metal-arc welding - 3/16 to 1/4 in (0.4 to 0.6 cm) electrodes	12
Shielded metal-arc welding - 5/16 to 3/8 in (0.7 to 0.9 cm) electrodes	14
Carbon arc welding	14
Plasma arc cutting up to 100 amps	8
Plasma arc cutting 100 to 200 amps	10
Plasma arc cutting 200 to 400 amps	12
Plasma arc cutting greater than 400 amps	14

05.C Hearing Protection and Noise Control.

05.C.01 The employer shall evaluate the workplace for noise hazards initially and regularly during the course of work. When noise hazards are known or expected, the employer shall develop a Hearing Conservation Program that includes identification and assessment of noise hazards and the measures to taken to protect personnel against them.

a. USACE workplace hearing conservation programs shall comply with the requirements of ER 385-1-89.

b. Contractors programs shall comply with American Conference of Governmental Industrial Hygienists (ACGIH) Threshold Limit Values (TLVs) and this manual at a minimum.

05.C.02 Identification of noise hazards.

a. Noise measurements shall be made whenever there is difficulty in communicating at distances greater than 2 ft (0.6 m), upon worker complaint of excessive noise, or whenever hazardous noise levels are suspected.

b . Noise assessments and/ or measurements shall be performed and documented when any new facility or new equipment is placed in service and when areas that in the past were not noise hazardous become noise hazardous for any reason.

05.C.03 Assessment of noise hazards.

a. Instruments used to measure noise shall meet or exceed the requirements listed below.

b. For continuous (steady-state) noise and impact (impulse) noise, the instrument settings shall be in accordance with Table 5-3.

c. Dosimeters shall measure the entire employee's work shift to be considered full- shift sampling.

d. Calibration of noise measuring equipment shall be in accordance with manufacturer's instructions (USACE refer to ER 385-1-89).

e. Workplaces known or suspected to include hazardous noise will be surveyed initially, annually and whenever site conditions change impacting noise generation.

f. Exposure standards.

(1) For impact (impulse) noise, personnel exposures may not exceed 140 dBA (unweighted) without effective hearing protection devices.

(2) For continuous (steady-state) noise, personnel exposures may not exceed 85 dBA without effective hearing protection devices.

(3) Contractor personnel shall comply with the ACGIH, TLV continuous noise exposure standards, outlined in Table 5-4.

(4) USACE personnel shall refer to ER 385-1-89.

(5) When the daily noise exposure is composed of two or more periods of noise exposure of different levels, the combined effects must be considered. Exposure to different levels for various periods of time shall be computed according to the following formula:

$$C_n = T_1 / L_1 + T_2 / L_2 + \ldots + T_x / L_x$$

Where:

C_n = combined noise exposure factor;

T = the total time of exposure at a specified sound-pressure level (in hours), and

L = the total time of exposure permitted at that level (in hours), from Tables 5-2 or 5-3, as appropriate

If the sum exceeds 1, the mixture of exposure periods exceeds the TLV.

05.C.04 Noise controls. Practical engineering or administrative controls shall be considered and implemented when personnel exposed to continuous (steady-state) soundpressure levels exceeding the limits specified stated above.

a. Engineering controls are the primary means of controlling exposures to excessive noise in the workplace. These controls may include lubrication, isolation, damping, baffles, or other methods.

b. Administrative controls.

(1) Noise-hazardous areas include all areas where the noise values exceed the standards above and shall be posted to indicate the presence of hazardous noise levels and the requirement for hearing protection. Equipment identified as noise hazardous shall be labeled as a noise hazard requiring the use of hearing protection. If noise hazards impact personnel working in adjacent areas, the individuals in the adjacent areas shall be notified of the noise values and offered hearing protection.

(2) If noise exposure to employees cannot be reduced to below the required standard, operating time limits may be imposed.

TABLE 5-3

Settings for Noise Measuring Equipment

Feature	Dosimeter (ACGIH)	Dosimeter (DoD and USACE)*	Type 2 (or better) Sound Level Meter for Continuous Noise (USACE)*	Type 1 Sound Level Meter for Impulse Noise (USACE)*
Criterion Time	8 hours	8 hours	8 hours	8 hours
Criterion Level	85 dB	85 Db	85 dB	85 dB
Weighting	A	A	A	Unweighted, linear, or Z
Peak Weighting	Unweighted	Unweighted, linear, or Z	Unweighted, linear, or Z	Unweighted, linear, or Z
Threshold Level	80 dB	80 dB	80 dB	140 dB
Upper bound on integration	130 dB	None	None	None
Time Weighting	Slow	Slow	Slow	Impulse
Exchange Rate	5 dB	3 dB	3 dB	3 dB

TABLE 5-4

Non-DoD Continuous Noise Exposures (OSHA Standard)

Duration per day (hours)	Permissible sound-pressure level (dBA)
8	85
4	88
2	91
1	94
0.5 = 30 min	97
0.25 = 15 min	100

c. Personal Protective Equipment (PPE).

(1) Hearing protection devices shall provide for the attenuation of noise to acceptable levels (i.e., 85 dBA for continuous (steady-state) noise). If necessary to hear audible warnings, hearing protection devices should not attenuate hearing levels below an individual's hearing threshold.

(2) Dual hearing protection (earplugs and a second method such as ear muffs worn concurrently), shall be based on the attenuation of the specific hearing protection. Generally, double hearing protection should be used whenever employees are exposed to continuous noise greater than 115 dBA.

(3) The attenuation of the specific hearing protection, except custom ear mold hearing protection, shall be determined using the NIOSH de-rating scheme.

(4) Ear insert devices, to include disposable, pre-formed, or custom-molded earplugs, shall be fitted to the exposed individual by an individual trained in such fitting and able to recognize the difference between a good and poor fit. Plain cotton is not an acceptable hearing protection device.

05.C.05 Hearing Conservation Program (HCP) Requirements.

a. A HCP shall include all personnel who are exposed to hazardous noise or ototoxic chemicals (including arsenic, carbon disulfide, carbon monoxide, cyanide, lead and derivatives, manganese, mercury and derivatives, n-hexane, Stoddard solvent, styrene, trichloroethylene, toluene, and xylenes). The usage of these chemicals shall be considered in development of the HCP.

b. All contractors who expose employees to noise greater than the values listed above shall have a written HCP as part of their APP which includes:

(1) The identification, documentation, engineering controls, PPE and hearing testing for all employees;

(2) Employee training on the hazards of noise and the methods of protection provided;

(3) Labeling of all noise hazardous equipment and areas as required above, and

(4) Pre-employment and end-of-employment hearing testing of individuals who will be working in noise hazardous environments greater than 30 days a year for the contractor.

05.D Head Protection.

05.D.01 All persons working in or visiting hard hat areas shall be provided with and required to wear Type I or Type II, Class G (General – not to exceed 2,200 volts) or Class E (Electrical-not to exceed 20,000 volts) headgear as appropriate. The selection of the type of hardhat shall be based on the activity and identified in the AHA. For emergency response operations and other activities with greater need for side impact protection, Type II head protection is required. > *See Appendix B.*

a. Hard hat areas or activities are those areas with potential hazard of head injury; in general, all construction areas are considered hard hat areas. However, specific areas may be designated as non-hard hat areas, or activities may be considered non-hard hat activities, if identified and properly documented in the associated AHA. The identification and analysis of head hazards will be documented in an AHA or project safety and health plan, as appropriate.

b. Points of entry to a hard hat area shall have a sign warning of the requirement to wear hard hats.

05.D.02 All protective headgear shall meet the requirements of ANSI Z89.1.

a. No modification (i.e., paint) to the shell or suspension is allowed except when such changes are applied or approved by the manufacturer. Stickers are allowed on the hard hat provided they do not interfere with the ability to properly inspect it. > *See 05.D.03.*

b. Hard hats shall be worn with the bill facing forward unless the GDA has determined exceptions for certain trades in order to accommodate appropriate mission accomplishments. Headgear must be designed to accommodate these needs.

c. Protective headgear worn near electric lines and equipment shall be Class E.

d. No ball caps, knit caps, or other headdress shall be worn under the hard hat that could interfere with the fit or stability of the hard hat.

05.D.03 Protective headgear and components shall be visually inspected daily for signs of damage (dents, cracks, etc.) that might reduce the degree of safety integrity originally provided. Headgear will be periodically inspected for ultraviolet degradation as evidenced by cracking or flaking of the helmet.

05.D.04 Drilling holes or in any way changing the integrity of the hard hat is prohibited. Alterations that will reduce the dielectric or impact strength will not be made.

05.D.05 Protective headgear worn by USACE employees shall (in addition to complying with the preceding specifications) be:

a. White in color and marked with a 1 in (2.5 cm) band of red reflective material placed along the base of the crown with a 5 in (12.7 cm) break in front. A red Corps of Engineers castle insignia will be centered at the front of the hat with the base of the insignia approximately ¾ in (1.9 cm) above the base of the crown. Personnel may place their name above the insignia and their organization title below the insignia: the rank of military personnel should precede their name. An American Flag insignia may be worn on the back of the hard hat.

b. Requests for variations in color and marking to accommodate occupational specialties shall be submitted for consideration to HQUSACE Safety and Health Office.

c. Chin straps will be worn when wearers are subject to high wind conditions and/or working on elevated structures.

05.E Protective Footwear.

05.E.01 Protective footwear that is rated to protect against the hazard(s) identified in the PHA/AHA shall be provided and worn.

05.E.02 All protective footwear shall meet ASTM F2413 standards.

05.E.03 Add-on type devices, such as strap-on foot, toe or metatarsal guards, shall not be used as a substitute for protective footwear and must be demonstrated by the employer to be equally effective via independent testing data for these devices.

05.E.04 For activities in which USACE or contractor personnel or official visitors are potentially exposed to foot hazards, the applicable PHA/AHA, APP, or project safety and health plan shall include an analysis of, and prescribe specific protective measures to be taken for, reducing foot hazards.

05.E.05 Personnel shall, as a minimum, wear safety-toed boots meeting ASTM Standard F2413 while working on construction sites unless it can be demonstrated by a PHA/AHA to the GDA's satisfaction that a different type of foot protection is required.

05.E.06 Footwear providing protection against impact and compressive forces, conduction hazards, electrical hazards, and sole puncture shall comply with the applicable requirements of ASTM F2413. Footwear providing protection against impact and compression hazards shall be rated as I/75 and C/75.

a. Unexploded ordnance (UXO) personnel whose job tasks required protective footwear but require no metal parts in or on their footwear shall wear Conductive footwear (Cd) with protective toe cap/composite toe footwear.

b. Personnel participating in wild land fire management activities shall wear leather lace-up boots with slip-resistant soles, such as a hard rubber lug-type or tractor tread, a top height of 8 in (20.3 cm) or more with composite toes. Soles shall not be made of composition rubber or plastic, which have low melting points.

05.F High-Visibility Apparel.

05.F.01 High-visibility apparel meeting, at minimum, ANSI/ISEA 107, Performance Class 2 requirements, shall be worn by workers (i.e., signal persons, spotters, survey crews, inspectors, etc.) whenever:

a. There is limited visibility of workers exposed to mobile/heavy equipment operations, vehicles, load handling, or other hazardous activities;

b. Reduced visibility conditions exist due to weather conditions, illumination, or visually complex backgrounds where ambient visibility is at least 50 ft (15.2 m); OR

c. Workers are exposed to vehicular or equipment traffic at speeds up to 35 mph (56.3 kph).

05.F.02 If any or all of the following conditions exist, Class 3 high-visibility apparel meeting ANSI/ISEA 107 shall be worn for higher visibility (i.e., signal persons, spotters, survey crews, inspectors, etc.) whenever:

a. Reduced visibility conditions exist due to weather conditions, illumination, or visually complex backgrounds where ambient visibility is less than 50 ft (15.2 m);

b. Workers are exposed to vehicular or equipment traffic in excess of 35 mph (56.3 kph);

c. Workers are performing tasks which divert attention from approaching vehicular traffic, traveling in excess of 35 mph (56.3 kph), as posted; OR

d. Workers are involved in activities in close proximity to vehicular traffic with no protective barriers.

05.F.03 When working at night, on or near sites where vehicles are present, workers (i.e., signal persons, spotters, survey crews, inspectors, etc.) shall wear, at a minimum, a Class 3 high-visibility safety coverall/jumpsuit or a Class 3 high-visibility safety jacket and Class E high-visibility pants, or bib overalls.

05.F.04 If the use of high-visibility apparel proves to create a greater hazard due to moving machinery, pinch points, heat stress or other reasons, an AHA detailing rationale for infeasibility of use and alternate safety measures to be used to ensure same level of worker safety, shall be developed, signed and submitted by the responsible person and accepted by the GDA, supervisor or the command's local Safety and Occupational Health Office (SOHO). Work shall not commence until such acceptance has been obtained.

05.F.05 The apparel background material color shall be either fluorescent yellow-green, fluorescent orange-red, or fluorescent red (see ANSI/ISEA 107). When choosing color, optimization of color conspicuity between the wearer and work environment shall be considered.

05.F.06 The apparel shall be:

a. Free of roughness, sharp edges and projections that could cause irritation or injury;

b. Should fit correctly to ensure that the vest remains in place for the expected period of use, environmental conditions, and wearer movements;

c. Cleaned, laundered and/or dry-cleaned in accordance with the label located on the apparel; and

d. In useable condition with limited rips, tears or fading; and

e. Replaced if it fails to comply with and of the above or ANSI/ISEA 107.

05.G Respiratory Protection.

05.G.01 General. The use of respirators is required when occupational exposure levels exceed OSHA Permissible Exposure Limits (PELs) or ACGIH TLVs, and engineering or administrative exposure controls are not feasible to implement.

05.G.02 The employer may allow the voluntary use of respirators, such as a filtering face pieces (nuisance dust masks) in atmospheres that are not hazardous. Prior to use of the voluntary respirators, the respirator must be evaluated and approved by the respiratory program administrator to ensure that its use will in itself not create a hazard. The employee shall be instructed in the limitations of the respirator and the correct method of wearing and using the respirator.

05.G.03 Written respiratory protection program. A written respiratory protection program shall be developed and implemented when respirators are used.

a. All employees using respirators, with the exception of employees voluntarily using only filtering face pieces (NIOSH-approved dust masks), shall be included in the respiratory protection program.

b. A respiratory protection program administrator with the technical qualifications (training and experience) and administrative authority to develop, implement and update (as necessary) the respiratory protection program shall be identified and so designated in the program.

(1) The program administrator shall ensure that all respirator users comply with the requirements of the program.

(2) Program Administrator Qualifications. The program administrator shall have the documented knowledge and experience to understand OSHA's respiratory protection standard (29 CFR 1910.134), evaluate respiratory hazards at the facility/project or similar facility/project, select appropriate respirators based on similar hazards as the facility/project hazards or potential hazard, and train employees on the use of similar respirators.

c. Respiratory protection programs shall address each of the following topics:

(1) Methods used to identify and evaluate workplace respiratory hazards;

(2) Procedures for selecting respirators for use in the workplace;

(3) Medical evaluations of employees required to use respirators;

(4) Fit testing procedures for tight-fitting respirators;

(5) Procedures for proper use of respirators in routine and reasonably foreseeable emergency situations;

(6) Procedures and schedules for cleaning, disinfecting, storing, inspecting, cartridge and canister change-out, repairing, discarding, and otherwise maintaining respirators;

(7) Procedures to ensure adequate air quality, quantity, and flow of breathing air for atmosphere-supplying respirators;

(8) Training of employees in the respiratory hazards to which they are potentially exposed during routine and emergency situations;

(9) Training of employees in the proper use of respirators, including putting on and removing (donning and doffing) the respirator, any limitations

on their use of the respirator, pre-use testing procedures, and respirator maintenance;

(10) Procedures for regularly evaluating the effectiveness of the program; and

(11) Project/facility-specific voluntary use guidelines and a requirement for voluntary users to learn and understand the contents of 29 CFR 1910.134 Appendix D, *Information for Employees Using Respirators When Not Required Under the Standard*.

05.G.04 Medical evaluation. All employees, with the exception of employees voluntarily using filtering face pieces, shall be medically evaluated to ensure they are fit enough to wear the selected respirators before being fit tested. Evaluation options for respirator use are as follows:

a. Completion of the respirator questionnaire from 29 CFR 1910.134, Appendix C which is reviewed by a medical professional and a follow-up of the recommended medical exam and testing if required by the reviewing medical professional. Medical clearances to wear respirators shall include the following:

(1) Telephone, e-mail, and physical address of the medical facility/provider;

(2) Printed name of the licensed, certified health care provider along with his/her signature;

(3) The statement of clearances or respiratory limitations only (no personal medical information shall be included. Employee identification shall not include the full social security number);

(4) Date of examination and date that clearance expires.

b. Respirator Medical Evaluation Service. An on-line, mail-in or in-person evaluation service for the purpose of clearing an employee to wear selected respirators may be used provided it is supervised by a Board-Certified or Board-Eligible Occupational Medicine Physician and based upon Appendix C to 29 CFR 1910.134, OSHA Respirator Medical Evaluation Questionnaire. Medical clearances to wear respirators shall include the information in (1) – (4) above.

c. Additional medical evaluations shall be provided when:

(1) An employee reports medical signs or symptoms that are related to the ability to use a respirator;

(2) A change occurs in workplace conditions (e.g., physical work effort, protective clothing, temperature, etc.,) that may result in a substantial increase in the physiological burden placed on an employee.

d. All USACE respirator users shall have a pre-placement history and targeted physical. The exam shall include a pulmonary function test, evaluation of the cardiovascular and respiratory systems, and any tests required by the Occupational Health Provider.

05.G.05 Respirator Selection. Respirator selection shall be completed by the Respirator Program Administrator (RPA).

a. The selection shall be based on objective industrial hygiene data for this or similar operations.

b. Before industrial hygiene data is obtained, the RPA shall use knowledge of the hazard and work methods to determine the highest potential exposure, which shall be used to select the respiratory protection.

c. To determine the change out schedule of the respirator cartridge or respirator canister, the respirator program administrator shall use manufacturer recommended change-out based on the operations or the objective industrial hygiene data or data from similar operations.

d. An air purifying respirator shall not be used in an atmosphere with less than 19% oxygen or an atmosphere that is immediately dangerous to life and health (IDLH).

05.G.06 Fit testing. Employees wearing respirators with tight-fitting face pieces [Supplied Air Respirators (SARs) and Self-Contained Breathing Apparatus (SCBAs) included] shall be fit tested to ensure that selected respirators achieve a proper face-to- facepiece seal. Fit testing shall be performed before initial use of the selected respirator, whenever respirator size, make or model is changed, and at least annually. Fit testing requirements shall comply with respiratory protection program requirements.

05.G.07 Airline Respirators (SARs and SCBAs). If airline respirators are used, the following apply (excludes underwater diving SCBAs, see Section 30):

a. All SARs or SCBA respirators shall meet the Grade D Breathing Air requirements from ANSI/Compressed Gas Association Commodity Specification for Air;

b. If an airline respirator is used in an environment that has the potential to become IDLH, the respirator shall have an alternate source of breathing air for escape from the environment;

c. If an airline respirator is used in an environment that has the potential to become IDLH, there shall be a respirator air attendant to prevent the lines from becoming tangled or tied, to change the air supply tanks, and/or to confirm the air source (compressor or air supply tank manifold) is adequately working. If the air supply is interrupted, the attendant shall notify the respirator users to leave the area where the respirators are required.

05.G.08 Training and information. The RPA or his designee shall provide respirator training annually (or earlier if the requirements change significantly due to process changes or changes in site specific operations) to personnel using respirators at the facility or project. Annual training shall ensure that each employee using a respirator can demonstrate knowledge of the following topics:

a. Why the respirator is necessary and how improper fit, usage, or maintenance can compromise the protective effect of the respirator;

b. Limitations and capabilities of the respirator;

c. How to use the respirator effectively in emergency situations, including situations in which the respirator malfunctions;

d. How to inspect, put on and remove, use, and check the seals of the respirator;

e. Procedures for maintenance and storage of the respirator;

f. How to recognize medical signs and symptoms that may limit or prevent the effective use of respirators; and

g. The general requirements of the OSHA respirator standard at 29 CFR 1910.134.

05.G.09 Recordkeeping. Establish and retain written information regarding medical evaluations, fit testing, and the respirator program. The following shall be made available upon request:

a. Records of medical approval must be retained and made available, as needed;

b. Fit test records must be maintained for respirator users until the next fit test is administered. Establish a record of the Qualitative Fit Test (QLFT) and Quantitative Fit Test (QNFT) administered to an employee including:

(1) The name or identification of the employee tested;

(2) Type of fit test performed and name of the test administrator;

(3) Specific make, model, style, and size of respirator tested;

(4) Date of test; and

(5) The pass/fail results for QLFTs or the fit factor and strip chart recording or other recording of the test results for QNFTs.

c. Retain a written copy of the current respirator program.

05.H Hand Protection.

05.H.01 Employers shall select, and require employees to use, appropriate hand protection when employees' hands are exposed to hazards such as skin absorption of harmful substances, severe cuts or lacerations, severe abrasions, punctures, chemical burns, thermal burns, harmful temperature extremes, high hand vibration and sharp objects. > See Table 5-5.

05.H.02 Employers shall base the selection of the appropriate hand protection on an evaluation of the performance characteristics of the hand protection relative to the task(s) to be performed, conditions present, duration of use, and the hazards and potential hazards identified.

05.H.03 Employees shall be trained to recognize hand hazards, select appropriate gloves for all anticipated hazards and to inspect and properly store gloves.

05.H.04 Gloves should fit snugly. Workers shall wear the correct gloves for the hazard (e.g., heavy-duty rubber gloves for concrete work, welding gloves for welding, insulated gloves and sleeves when exposed to electrical hazards, etc.).

05.H.05 Gloves will be inspected thoroughly prior to use to assure they are in good condition and will provide the protection required.

05.I Electrical Protective Equipment.

05.I.01 Persons working on electrical distribution systems shall be provided with the appropriate electrical protective equipment. This equipment shall be inspected, tested, and maintained in safe conditions in accordance with Table 5-6.

05.I.02 Employees shall use rubber gloves, sleeves, blankets, covers and line hoses as required by special conditions for work on energized facilities. Rubber goods provided to protect employees who work on energized facilities must meet ASTM F18 standards. Electrical workers' rubber insulating protective equipment shall be visually inspected for damage and defects prior to each use.

05.I.03 Rubber protective equipment must be subjected to periodic electrical tests. Rubber insulating gloves shall be inspected before first issue and every 6 months thereafter; rubber insulating blankets and sleeves shall be inspected before their first issue and every 12 months thereafter. Rubber insulating covers shall be inspected upon indication that insulating value is suspect (per 29 CFR1910.137).

TABLE 5-5

Hand and Arm Protection

Metal Mesh, Leather, or Canvas Gloves	- Sturdy gloves made from metal mesh, leather, or canvas provide protection from cuts, burns, and sustained heat.
Leather Gloves	- Protection against sparks, moderate heat, blows, chips, and rough objects. - Welders in particular need the durability of higher-quality leather gloves.
Aluminized Gloves	- Provide reflective and insulating protection against heat. Usually used for welding, furnace, and foundry work. - Normally require an insert made of synthetic material that protect against heat and cold.
Aramid Fiber Gloves	- Aramid is a synthetic material that protects against heat and cold and is also used to make gloves that are cut- and abrasive-resistant and wear well.
Fabric and Coated Fabric Gloves	- Gloves made of cotton or other fabric protect against dirt, slivers, chafing, and abrasion but do not provide sufficient protection to be used with rough, sharp or heavy materials. - Cotton flannel gloves coated with plastic transform fabric gloves into general-purpose hand protection offering slip- resistant qualities. - Coated fabric gloves are used for tasks ranging from handling bricks and wire rope to handling chemical containers in laboratory operations. - For protection against chemical exposure hazards, always check with manufacturer to determine the gloves' effectiveness against the specific chemicals/conditions in the workplace.
Chemical and Liquid-Resistan Gloves	- Gloves made of rubber (latex, nitrile, or butyl), plastic, or synthetic rubber-like material such as neoprene protect workers from burns, irritation, and dermatitis caused by contact with oils, greases, solvents, and other chemicals. - Use of rubber gloves also reduces the risk of exposure to blood and other potentially infectious substances.
Butyl Rubber Gloves	- Protect against nitric acid, sulfuric acid, hydrofluoric acid, red fuming nitric acid, and peroxide. Resist oxidation, ozone corrosion, abrasion and remain flexible at low temperatures.
Natural Latex or Rubber Gloves	- Comfortable wear and pliability along with their protective qualities make them popular general purpose glove. - Resist abrasions caused by sandblasting, grinding, and polishing and protect workers' hands from most water solutions of acids, alkalis, salts and ketones. - Hypoallergenic gloves, glove liners, and powderless gloves possible alternatives for those allergic to latex.

Neoprene Gloves	- Good pliability, dexterity, high density, and tear resistance. - Provide protection from hydraulic fluids, gasoline, alcohols, organic acids, and alkalis.
Nitrile Rubber Gloves	- Provide protection from chlorinated solvents such as trichloroethylene and perchloroethylene. - Intended for jobs requiring dexterity and sensitivity, yet stand up to heavy use even after prolonged exposure that cause other gloves to deteriorate. - Resist abrasion, puncturing, snagging, and tearing.
Anti-vibration Gloves	-Gloves with gel insert and padding to absorb the tool vibration. For best effectiveness, gloves should meet the requirements of ANSI S2.73

05.I.04 Electric arc flash protection shall be provided for any person entering the flash protection boundary. > See Section 11.B.

a. Arc-rated clothing and PPE must be worn as determined by the incident exposure associated with the specific task. Refer to NFPA 70E for specific Hazard Risk Classifications and NFPA PPE Category Level Chart for Clothing/Equipment Requirements). > See Table 5-7.

b. Synthetic clothing such as acetate, nylon, polyester, rayon, either alone or in blends with cotton, may not be worn while in the flash protection boundary.

c. Employees must wear protective eye equipment whenever there is a danger from electric arcs, flashes, flying objects, or electrical explosion.

d. Employees must wear arc-rated clothing whenever they may be exposed to potentially energized electrical equipment.

(1) Arc-rated suits and their closure design must permit easy and rapid removal.

(2) The entire arc-rated suit, including the window, must have energy-absorbing characteristics suitable for arc flash exposure.

(3) Clothing and equipment required by the degree of electrical hazard exposure can be worn alone or be integrated with normal apparel.

(4) Protective clothing and equipment must cover associated parts of the body and all normal apparel that is not flame-resistant, while allowing movement and visibility.

e. Employees must wear rubber-insulating gloves where there is a danger of hand or arm injury from electric shock or arc flash burns due to contact with energized parts. Gloves made from layers of flame-resistant material provide the highest level of protection. Leather glove protectors should be worn over voltage-rated rubber gloves.

f. Dielectric overshoes are required where electrically insulated footwear is used for protection against step and touch potential.

05.I.05 An air test shall be performed on electrical workers' rubber insulating gloves before each use.

05.I.06 Protective equipment of material other than rubber shall provide equal or better electrical and mechanical protection.

05.I.07 Tools must be insulated and manufactured to meet ASTM F18. The insulating tool portion shall be made of fiberglass-reinforced plastic (FRP).

05.I.08 Only live-line tool poles having a manufacturer's certification to withstand at least the following test shall be used: 100 (kilovolts) kV AC per ft (305 mm) of length for 5 minutes or 75 kV AC per ft (305 mm) for FRP tools. Records shall be maintained for all live-line tools to demonstrate satisfactory accomplishment of laboratory and shop test.

05.I.09 Wooden tools are not authorized for use.

05.I.10 When using live-line tools, workers shall use voltage rated gloves and not place their hands closer than necessary to energized conductors or to the metal parts of the tool

05.I.11 Only tools and equipment intended for live-line bare hand work should be used on transmission lines. The tools shall be kept dry and clean and shall be visually inspected before use each day.

05.I.12 See Section 05.A.09 for requirements on lineman's personal fall protection equipment.

TABLE 5-6

Standards for Electrical Protective Equipment

SUBJECT	NUMBER AND TITLE
Head Protection	ISEA/ANSI Z89.1, Requirements for Protective Headwear for Industrial Workers
Eye and face Protection	ANSI Z87.1, Practice for Occupational and Educational Eye and Face Protection
Gloves	ASTM D120-02a, Standard Specification for Rubber Insulating Gloves
Sleeves	ASTM D1051, Standard Specification for Rubber Insulating Sleeves
Gloves and sleeves	ASTM F496, Standard Specification for In-Service Care of Insulating Gloves and Sleeves
Leather protectors	ASTM F696, Standard Specification for Leather Protectors for Rubber Insulating Gloves and Mittens
Footwear	ASTM F1117, Standard Specification for Dielectric Overshoe Footwear
	ASTM 2412, Standard Test Methods for Foot Protection ASTM 2413, Standard Specification for Performance Requirements for Foot Protection
Visual inspection	ASTM F1236, Standard Guide for Visual Inspection of Electrical Protective Rubber Products
Apparel	ASTM F1506, Standard Performance Specification for Flame Resistant Textile Materials for Wearing Apparel for Use by Electrical Workers When Exposed to Momentary Electric Arc and Related Thermal Hazards

5

TABLE 5-7

Arc Flash Protective Clothing and PPE

Hazard/Risk Category	Protective Clothing and PPE
0	Protective Clothing, Non-melting or Untreated Natural Fiber (i.e., untreated cotton, wool, rayon, or silk, or blends of these materials) with a fabric weight of at least 4.5 oz/yd² Shirt (long sleeve) Pants (long Protective Equipment: Hard hat; Safety glasses/ goggles (SR); Hearing Protection (ear canal inserts); Heavy-duty leather gloves (AN) (See Note 1); Leather work boots
1	Arc-Rated Clothing, Minimum Arc Rating of 4 cal/cm² (See Note 3) Arc-rated long-sleeve shirt and pants or arc-rated coverall Arc-rated faceshield (See Note 2) or arc flash suit hood Arc-rated jacket, parka, rainwear, or hard hat liner (AN) Protective Equipment: Hard hat; Safety glasses/goggles (SR); Hearing protection (ear canal inserts); Heavy-duty leather gloves (See Note 1); Leather work boots
2	Arc-Rated Clothing, Minimum Arc Rating of 8 cal/cm² (See Note 3) Arc-rated long-sleeve shirt and pants or arc-rated coverall Arc-rated flash suit hood or arc-rated faceshield (See Note 2) and arc-rated balaclava Arc-rated jacket, parka, rainwear, or hard hat liner (AN) Protective Equipment: Hard hat; Safety glasses/goggles (SR); Hearing protection (ear canal inserts); Heavy-duty leather gloves (See Note 1); Leather work boots
3	Arc-Rated Clothing selected so the System Arc Rating meets the required minimum arc rating of 25 cal/cm² (See Note 3) Arc-rated long-sleeve shirt (AR) Arc-rated pants (AR) Arc-rated coverall (AR) Arc-rated arc flash suit jacket (AR) Arc-rated arc flash suit pants (AR) Arc-rated arc flash suit hood Arc-rated gloves (See Note 1) Arc-rated jacket, parka, rainwear, or hard hat liner (AN) Protective Equipment: Hard hat; Safety glasses/goggles (SR); Hearing protection (ear canal inserts); Leather work boots

4	Arc-Rated Clothing selected so the System Arc Rating meets the required minimum Arc Rating of 40 cal/cm² (See Note 3)
	Arc-rated long-sleeve shirt (AR) Arc-rated pants (AR)
	Arc-rated coverall (AR)
	Arc-rated arc flash suit jacket (AR)
	Arc-rated arc flash suit pants (AR)
	Arc-rated arc flash suit hood
	Arc-rated gloves (See Note 1)
	Arc-rated jacket, parka, rainwear, or hard hat liner (AN) Protective Equipment: Hard hat; Safety glasses/goggles (SR);
	Hearing protection (ear canal inserts); Leather work boots

AN: as needed (optional). AR: as required. SR: selection required.

Notes:

(1) If rubber insulating gloves with leather protectors are required by NFPA 70E. Table 130.7(C)(9), additional leather or arc-rated gloves are not required. The combination of rubber insulating gloves with leather protectors satisfies the arc flash protection requirement.

(2) Face shields are to have wrap-around guarding to protect not only the face but also the forehead, ears, and neck, or, alternatively, an arc-rated arc flash suit hood is required to be worn.

(3) *Arc rating* is defined in Article 100 and can be either the arc thermal performance value (ATPV) or energy of break open threshold (EBT). ATPV is defined in ASTM F 1959, *Standard Test Method for Determining the Arc Thermal Performance Value of Materials for Clothing*, as the incident energy on a material, or a multilayer system of materials, that results in a 50 percent probability that sufficient heat transfer through the tested specimen is predicted to cause the onset of a second-degree skin burn injury based on the Stoll curve, in cal/cm2. EBT is defined in ASTM F 1959 as the incident energy on a material or material system that results in a 50 percent probability of breakopen. Arc rating is reported as either ATPV or EBT, whichever is the lower value.

05.J Personal Flotation Devices.

05.J.01 Inherently buoyant Type III, Type V work vests, or better USCG-approved personal flotation devices (PFDs) shall be provided and properly worn in closed fashion (zipped, tied, latched, etc.) by all persons in the following circumstances: > See 05.J.02 and Figure 5-1.

a. On floating pipelines, pontoons, rafts, or stages;

b. On structures or equipment extending over or next to water except where guardrails, personal fall protection system, or safety nets are provided for employees;

c. Working alone at night where there are drowning hazards, regardless of other safeguards provided;

d. In skiffs, small boats, or launches, unless in an enclosed cabin or cockpit; or

e. Whenever there is a drowning hazard.

05.J.02 Automatic-Inflatable PFDs Type V or better, USCG-approved for Commercial Use, may be worn by workers in lieu of inherently buoyant PFDs (see conditions 05.J.01.a-e above), provided the following criteria is met:

a. PFDs are worn only by workers over 16 years of age and those who weigh 90 lb (40.8 kg) or more;

b. An AHA shall be developed for the intended activity and shall be used to select the most appropriate PFD for the activity;

c. PFDs must be inspected, maintained, stowed and used in accordance with the manufacturer's instructions. PFDs used in heavy construction or maintenance activities or where hot work (welding, brazing, cutting, soldering, etc.) is to be performed must be designed, tested and certified by the manufacturers for this type of work;

➤*Note: The standard commercial auto-inflatable PFD does not meet these requirements.*

d. PFDs shall provide a 30-pound minimum buoyancy, post-deployment, and shall have a status indicator window;

e. Personnel shall be trained in the use, maintenance, restrictions, care, storage, inspection and post-deployment procedures per manufacturer's instructions;

f. The USCG-approval for auto-inflatable PFD's is contingent upon the PFD being worn, not stowed. All auto-inflatable PFDs must be worn at all times a drowning hazard exists.

g. In-water testing is required for all first time users so that wearers become familiar with the <u>feel and performance</u> of the PFD.

05.J.03 All wearable PFDs shall be of an international orange (or orange/red) or ANSI 107 yellow-green color.

a. Each inherently buoyant PFD shall have at least 31 in^2 (200 cm^2) of retroreflective material attached to its front side and at least 31 in^2 (200 cm^2) on its back side, per USCG requirements (46 CFR Part 25.25-15).

b. Each auto-inflatable PFD shall have at least 31 in^2 (200 cm^2) of retroreflective material attached to its front side **and** at least 31 in^2 on its bladder, to be visible when deployed (with the exception of Work Vests, which are allowed to have a total of 31 in^2 front and back, combined).

05.J.04 Each PFD shall be equipped with a USCG-approved automatically activated light. Lights are not required for PFDs on projects performed exclusively during daylight hours.

05.J.05 Before and after each use, the PFD shall be inspected for defects that would alter its strength or buoyancy.

05.J.06 Throwable devices (Type IV PFD).

a. On USCG-inspected vessels, ring buoys are required to have automatic floating electric water lights (46 CFR 160).

b. On all other floating plant and shore installations, lights on life rings are required only in locations where adequate general lighting (e.g., floodlights, light stanchions) is not provided. For these plant and installations, at least one life ring, and every third one thereafter, shall have an automatic floating electric water light attached.

c. All PFDs shall be equipped with retroreflective tape in accordance with USCG requirements.

d. Life rings (rope attachment not required) and ring buoys (rope attachment required) shall be USCG-approved; shall have at least <u>9</u>0 ft (<u>27.4</u> m) of 3/8 in (0.9 cm) of attached solid braid polypropylene, or equivalent. Throw bags may be used in addition to life rings or ring buoys. These throwable devices and lifelines shall be inspected at a minimum, every 6 months and shall be stored in such a manner as to allow immediate deployment and will be protected from degradation from weather and sunlight. Life rings or ring buoys shall be readily available and shall be provided at the following places:

(1) At least one not less than 20 in (51 cm) on each safety skiff up to 26 ft (7.9 m) in length (46 CFR 117.70);

(2) At least one (1) 24 in (61 cm) in diameter on all motor boats longer than 26 ft (7.9 m) in length up to 65 ft (19.8 m) in length and for motor boats 65 ft (19.8 m) in length or longer, a minimum 3 life buoys of not less than 24 in (61 cm) and one additional for each increase in length of 100 ft (30.4 m) or fraction thereof; and

(3) At least one (1) at intervals of not more than 200 ft (60.9 m) on pipelines, walkways, wharves, piers, bulkheads, lock walls, scaffolds, platforms, and similar structures extending over or immediately next to water, unless the fall distance to the water is more than 45 ft (13.7 m), in which case a life ring shall be used. (The length of line for life rings at these locations shall be evaluated, but the length may not be less than <u>9</u>0 ft (<u>27.4</u> m).

FIGURE 5-1

Personal Flotation Devices

Off-Shore Life Jacket (Type I PFD)

Best for open, rough or remote water, where rescue may be slow coming.

Near-Shore Buoyant Vest (Type II PFD)

Good for calm, inland water, or where there is a good chance of fast rescue

Flotation Aid (Type III PFD)

Good for calm, inland water, or where there is a good chance of fast rescue

Throwable Device (Type IV PFD)

For calm, inland water with heavy boat traffic, where help is always nearby

Special Use Devices (Type V PFD)

Only for special use or conditions

Inflatable Device (Type V Hybrid)

Only for special use or conditions

05.J.07 At navigation locks, an analysis of the benefits versus the hazards of using floating safety blocks (blocks that may be quickly pushed into the water to protect individuals who have fallen in the water from being crushed by vessels) shall be made.

a. This analysis shall be documented as an AHA.

b. If the use of blocks is found acceptable, consideration shall be given to the size and placement of the blocks, the appropriate means of securing and signing the blocks, etc. When the use of blocks is found unacceptable, alternative safety measures shall be developed.

05.K Lifesaving and Safety Skiffs.

05.K.01 During construction activities, at least one skiff shall be immediately available at locations where employees work over or immediately next to water.

➢Note: This requirement is applicable to any Operations and Maintenance activities that cause an employee to work outside the designed, permanently installed safety controls (i.e., guardrails).

05.K.02 Personnel trained in launching and operating the skiff shall be readily available during working hours. Lifesaving personnel shall perform a lifesaving drill, including the launching and recovery of the skiff, before the initiation of work at the site and periodically thereafter as specified by the GDA (but at least monthly or whenever new personnel are involved).

05.K.03 Skiffs shall be kept afloat or ready for instant launching.

05.K.04 Required equipment must be onboard and meet or exceed USCG requirements and the requirements of Section 19 of this manual. Skiffs shall be equipped as follows:

a. Four (4) oars (two (2) if the skiff is motor powered);

b. Oarlocks attached to gunwales or the oars;

c. One (1) ball-pointed boat hook;

d. One (1) ring buoy with 90 ft (21.3 m) of 3/8 in (0.9 cm) solid braid polypropylene, or equivalent, line attached; and

e. PFDs in number equaling the skiff rating for the maximum number of personnel allowed on board.

f. Fire Extinguisher.

05.K.05 In locations where waters are rough or swift, or where manually operated boats are not practical, a power boat suitable for the waters shall be provided and equipped for lifesaving.

05.K.06 Skiffs and power boats shall have buoyant material capable of floating the boat, its equipment, and the crew.

05.K.07 On vessels (such as skiffs) without permanently mounted navigation lights, portable battery-operated navigation lights will be available and used for night operations.

SECTION 6 Hazardous or Toxic Agents and Environments

Table of Contents

6

06.A General.

06.A.01 Exposure standards.

a. Exposure, through inhalation, ingestion, skin absorption, or physical contact, to any chemical or biological agent in excess of the acceptable limits specified in the current American Conference of Governmental Industrial Hygienist (ACGIH) guideline, "*Threshold Limit Values and Biological Exposure Indices*," published Department of the Army (DA) or Department of Defense (DoD) Exposure Limits, or by OSHA shall be prohibited. For the purpose of this document, the applicable standard is the Occupational Exposure Limit (OEL). Physical agents are addressed individually in this section.

> *Note: For Beryllium, the Department of Energy's exposure value of 0.2 ug/m3 may be allowed with written permission from the HQUSACE-SO.*

b. In case of conflicts between ACGIH, OSHA, DoD or DA standards or regulations referenced in this manual, the more stringent shall be used as the OEL.

c. The employer shall comply with all applicable standards and regulations to reduce contaminant concentration levels As Low As is Reasonably Achievable (ALARA).

d. Activities where occupational exposure to a chemical or biological warfare agent is possible, shall comply with current DA safety and occupational health requirements for chemical and biological agents.

e. Activities involving ammunition and explosives or their constituents or chemical warfare agents may have additional requirements as specified in EM 385-1-97, *Explosives Safety and Health Requirements Manual.*

06.A.02 Hazard evaluation.

a. Jobsite operations, materials, and equipment involving potential exposure to hazardous or toxic agents or environments shall be evaluated by a qualified Industrial Hygienist, or equivalent competent person in Industrial Hygiene operations, to formulate a hazard control program. A description of the methods to be used must be accepted by the GDA or local Safety and Occupational Health Office (SOHO) before the start of the specific operation. > *This evaluation shall be performed at least annually for USACE operations.*

b. Activity Hazard Analysis (AHA) and/or Position Hazard Analysis (PHA) shall be used to document the evaluation of the hazards and the controls present. The hazard evaluation shall identify all substances, agents, and environments that present a health, explosive or fire hazard to workers or visitors, the risk of the hazard, and recommend hazard control measures. Engineering and administrative controls shall be used to control hazards; in cases where engineering or administrative controls are not feasible, personal protective equipment (PPE) may be used.

c. The hazard evaluation shall document: the nature of the evaluation (air, biological or radiological samples, etc.); that it serves as certification of hazard evaluation; the workplace and activity evaluated; the name, position and credentials of the person certifying that the evaluation has been performed; any controls and training being utilized; and the date of the evaluation. This evaluation shall be documented in a written report and available for review by the GDA or SOHO for USACE operations.

06.A.03 Testing and monitoring.

a. Approved and calibrated testing devices shall be provided to measure hazardous or toxic agents and environments. Devices shall be labeled with calibration information (name of individual performing the calibration and date of the most current calibration). Calibration results shall be maintained in a calibration log.

b. Individuals performing testing and monitoring shall be trained in hazards and testing and monitoring procedures. Testing devices shall be used, inspected, and maintained in accordance with the manufacturer's instructions, a copy of which shall be maintained with the devices.

c. NIOSH, OSHA, Environmental Protection Agency (EPA) or DA sampling and analytical methods or other independently verified sampling and analytical methods shall be used. Laboratories used for analysis shall be accredited by nationally recognized bodies, such as the American Industrial Hygiene Association (AIHA), for the type of analysis performed.

d. Determination of the concentration of, and hazards from, hazardous or toxic agents and environments shall be made by a qualified industrial hygienist or other competent person during initial startup and as frequently as necessary to ensure the safety and health of the workers or other potentially exposed individuals.

e. Records of testing/monitoring shall be maintained on site and shall be available to the GDA or SOHO for USACE operations upon request.

06.A.04 The following methods shall be utilized for the control of exposure to hazardous or toxic agents and environments and shall be followed in the order below, unless infeasible:

a. Substitution: if the substitute process or product is determined to provide the same outcome and to be less of a hazard;

b. Engineering controls: (i.e., local/general ventilation), to limit exposure to hazardous or toxic agents and environments within acceptable limits;

c. Work practice controls: when engineering controls are not feasible or are not sufficient to limit exposure to hazardous or toxic agents and environments within acceptable limits;

d. Appropriate PPE (i.e., respirators, gloves, etc.) and associated programs: shall be instituted when engineering, work practice controls, or material substitution are not feasible or are not sufficient to limit exposure to hazardous or toxic agents;

e. Regular housecleaning (work and break area surface cleaning) and personal decontamination procedures: shall be instituted in areas where the operations generate toxic dust and fume hazards. The frequency of surface cleaning and of decontamination procedures is dependent on the nature of the hazard, and frequency and risk from the exposure and shall be documented in the Project Safety and Occupational Health (SOH) Plan or Accident Prevention Plan (APP).

06.B Hazardous or Toxic Agents Handling.

06.B.01 Chemical Hazard Communication (HazCom). A written HazCom program shall be developed when hazardous or toxic agents (any chemical which is a physical/health hazard) are present or procured, stored or used at a project site (per 29 CFR 1910.1200). The written HazCom program shall address the following in project- specific detail:

a. Hazardous or Toxic Agent Inventory. A list of the hazardous or toxic agents with the following information:

(1) Explanation of how the agents are to be used at the project.

(2) For emergency response purposes, approximate quantities (e.g., liters, kilograms, gallons, pounds) that are onsite or will be on site at any given time shall be provided for each material. If the chemical name and/or quantity and/or location are classified information, it shall be maintained in a location so that it can be provided to emergency responders during an emergency. This could be in a secure area outside of the area the chemical is used or stored, or just outside the entrance to the location in a secure box.

(3) A site map will be attached to the inventory showing where inventoried substances are stored.

(4) The inventory and site map will be updated annually at a minimum, but as frequently as necessary to ensure it is current and accurately reflects those materials on site.

b. Hazardous or Toxic Agent Labeling. Procedures for assuring that containers used to store and transport hazardous or toxic agents around the project site are appropriately labeled to communicate the physical and health hazards associated with the agents in the containers. The pictorial labels required by the OSHA HazCom standard are acceptable labels.

c. Material Safety Data Sheet (MSDS) or Safety Data Sheet (SDS) Management. Procedures to ensure MSDSs (SDSs) are maintained at project site for each chemical, combustible dust, or product. During the period of 2013 through 2016, the MSDS will be phased out and replaced with the SDS. The new SDSs content is mandated and allows for the toxicological hazard to be based on similar chemicals. For the purpose of this manual, either a MSDS or SDS meeting the criteria of the OSHA globally harmonized system standard is acceptable.

(1) Employees shall have access to the MSDSs (SDSs) and the safety and health protection procedures.

(2) Applicable information contained in the MSDS (SDS) shall be incorporated in the AHA/PHAs. If the chemical or toxic agent is used extensively in the operation, the applicable information shall be incorporated into the AHA and MSDS (SDS) shall be attached to the AHA.

(3) The information will be followed in the use, storage, and disposal of material and selection of hazard control and emergency response measures.

d. Employee Information and Training. Procedures to ensure employees are trained initially and periodically when use of hazardous or toxic agents is altered or modified to accommodate changing on-site work procedures. Training shall be provided to employees working with or in the area of use of any potentially hazardous chemical. Training shall cover the following topics:

(1) Requirements of the HazCom program on the project;

(2) The location of all hazardous or toxic agents at the project;

(3) Identification and recognition of hazardous or toxic agents on the project;

(4) Physical and health hazards of the hazardous or toxic agents pertinent to project activities;

(5) Protective measures employees can implement when working with project- specific hazardous or toxic agents.

(6) The location and content of the MSDS (SDS) for the chemicals. The content and meaning of the information provided on the MSDS.

(7) All workers in locations covered by the HazCom standard shall be briefed on the recent changes to the standard. These changes include MSDS to SDS, label content, the new pictographs on the labels, and an explanation of chemical banding.

06.B.02 When engineering and work practice controls or substitution are either infeasible or insufficient, appropriate PPE and chemical hygiene facilities shall be provided and used for the transportation, use, and storage of hazardous or toxic agents.

a. When irritants or hazardous substances may contact skin or clothing, chemical hygiene facilities and PPE shall be provided. PPE may include suitable gloves, face/eye protection and chemical protective suits.

(1) The qualified IH or other competent person shall determine the scope and type of PPE required.

(2) Special attention shall be given to selecting proper chemical protection when working with materials designated with a "skin" notation by OEL. Such materials may produce systemic toxic effects through absorption through unbroken skin. > *See Section 5.*

(3) Before commencing use of epoxy resins, concrete, or other dermatitis- producing substances, employees shall be made aware of the manufacturer's skin protection recommendations. Barrier cream ointment or other skin protection measures recommended by the manufacturer for the specific exposure shall be available for use.

b. When eyes or body of any person may be exposed to hazardous or toxic agents, suitable facilities that comply with ANSI Z358.1, *Emergency Eyewash and Shower Equipment,* for quick drenching or flushing of the eyes and body shall be provided in the work area for immediate emergency use and shall be no more

than 10 seconds from the hazardous material. > *See ANSI Z358.1.*

(1) Emergency eyewash equipment must be provided where there is the potential for an employee's eyes to be exposed to corrosives, strong irritants, or toxic chemicals.

(2) The emergency eyewash equipment must irrigate and flush both eyes simultaneously while the operator holds the eyes open.

(3) The emergency eyewash equipment must deliver at least 0.4 gal (1.5 L) of water per minute for 15 minutes or more, providing a minimum of 6 gal (22.7 L) of water).

(4) Water used in emergency eyewashes and showers shall meet drinking water standards. When these items are exposed to the elements, steps will be taken to ensure the water does not freeze or become stagnate.

(5) Personal eyewash equipment may be used to supplement emergency washing facilities. They must not be used as a substitute. Personal eyewash fluids shall be visually inspected monthly to ensure they remain sanitary with no visible sediments.

(6) All plumbed emergency eyewash facilities and hand-held drench hoses shall be connected to an approved potable water supply and activated weekly and inspected annually to ensure that they function correctly and that the quality and quantity of water is satisfactory for emergency washing purposes.

c. When personal protective clothing is required:

(1) An area shall be established for the removal of the personal protective clothing which limits the spread of any chemical waste, dust, or fume;

(2) Workers shall be trained in the removal of personal protective clothing and equipment to prevent further spread or contamination.

06.B.03 Storage prior to transportation of hazardous chemicals, materials, substances and wastes shall be under the supervision of a qualified person.

a. Transportation, use, and storage of hazardous or toxic agents shall be planned and controlled to prevent contamination of people, animals, food, water, equipment, materials, and environment.

b. All storage of hazardous or toxic agents shall be in accordance with the recommendations of the manufacturer, OSHA and NFPA requirements and accessible only to authorized personnel.

c. Disposal of surplus or excess hazardous or toxic agents shall occur in a manner that will not contaminate or pollute any water supply, ground water, or streams; and will comply with Federal, State, and local regulations and guidelines.

d. Containers used to hold hazardous or toxic agents should not be used to hold other materials unless they have been managed or cleaned under hazardous waste and DOT regulatory requirements.

e. Every hazardous or toxic agent being transported for disposal shall be transported with a copy of the substance's MSDS (SDS) whenever applicable.

f. Persons who prepare shipments of hazardous chemicals, materials, substances and/or wastes that are defined as hazardous material under DOT regulations are required to be DOT trained, certified and issued an appointment letter in accordance with Defense Transportation Regulation 4500.9-R, Chapter 204.

06.B.04 A Process Safety Management (PSM) Program of highly hazardous chemicals shall be employed in accordance with 29 CFR 1910.119 or 29 CFR 1926.64 whenever a work activity involves:

a. A process that involves a chemical at or above the threshold quantities listed in Appendix A of the above-cited CFRs; or

b. A process that involves a flammable liquid or gas on site in one location in a quantity of 10,000 lb (4,535.9 kg) or more as defined in 29 CFR 1926.59(c), except:

(1) Hydrocarbon fuels used solely for workplace consumption as a fuel if such fuels are not part of a process containing another highly hazardous chemical covered by the standards cited above; or

(2) Flammable liquids stored in atmospheric tanks or transferred that are kept below their normal boiling point without benefit of chilling or refrigeration.

06.C Lead and Asbestos Hazard Control.

06.C.01 General.

a. No asbestos-containing materials (ACMs) shall be used or brought onto any USACE projects. Lead-based paints (LBP) shall only be used with written approval of the GDA or USACE SOHO and shall never be used inside a residence, child care facility, or medical treatment facility.

b. All construction or maintenance projects will be evaluated for the potential to contact ACM and LBP.

(1) Lead and asbestos sources are to be labeled as a lead or asbestos hazard that should not be disturbed without proper protection. If infeasible to label each source, a site map may be posted which points out the location of the lead and asbestos hazards.

(2) If the evaluation shows the potential for activities to generate unacceptable occupational exposure to LBP, a written lead compliance plan shall be written. The lead compliance plan shall be in accordance with 29 CFR 1910.1025 and 29 CFR 1926.62.

(3) If the evaluation shows the potential for activities to disturb ACM, an asbestos abatement plan shall be developed. The plan shall be in accordance with 29 CFR 1910.1001; 29 CFR 1926.1101; and 40 CFR 61, Subpart M.

(4) These plan(s) shall be developed as an appendix to the APP or, for USACE operations, the Project SOH Plan. The written plan(s) shall be submitted for acceptance by the GDA or local SOHO before beginning work.

06.C.02 Lead Compliance Plan. A lead compliance plan shall describe the procedures to be followed to protect employees from lead hazards while performing lead hazard control activities. The Plan shall address the following:

a. A description of each work activity in which lead is emitted, to include equipment and materials used, controls in place, crew size, job responsibilities, operating procedures, and maintenance practices, work activity locations and lead- containing components keyed to the project drawings;

b. Description of means to be used to achieve exposure compliance, including any engineering controls;

c. Employee exposure assessment procedures to monitor and document employee lead exposure. Exposure monitoring shall include two types:

(1) Initial determination (may be omitted if there is sufficient objective/historical data showing action level compliance according to the requirements); and

(2) Continued exposure monitoring required as a result of initial exposure determinations.

d. Protective clothing, housekeeping procedures to prevent spread of lead contamination both in and beyond the lead hazard control area, and hygiene facilities and practices to prevent employees from inadvertent ingestion of lead;

e. Administrative controls to limit employee exposure to lead, including employee rotation schedule to be employed, if engineering controls or PPE fail to eliminate exposures exceeding the PEL;

f. Medical surveillance procedures to monitor employee exposures and ensure fitness for wearing respiratory protection;

g. Competent person (CP) and employee training required;

h. Detailed sketches identifying lead hazard control areas, including decontamination areas and facilities, critical barriers, and physical and air distribution boundaries;

i. Perimeter or other area air monitoring outside or adjacent to the regulated area;

j. Security required for each lead hazard control area; and

k. Waste generation, characterization, transportation, and disposal (including recordkeeping).

06.C.03 Asbestos Abatement Plan. An asbestos abatement plan shall describe procedures to be followed to protect employees from asbestos hazards while performing work that will disturb ACM. It shall address the following:

a. A description of each activity where asbestos will be disturbed, including OSHA class of work, equipment required, controls to be used, crew size, job responsibilities, maintenance practices, and locations keyed to the project drawings;

b. The method of notification of other employers at the worksite;

c. A Description of regulated areas, types of containment, decontamination unit plan, and engineering controls;

d. Air monitoring plan - personal, environmental and clearance. Employee exposure assessment procedures shall address monitoring and documenting employee exposures.

(1) An initial determination (may be omitted if there is sufficient objective/historical data showing compliance with the requirements);

(2) Continued exposure monitoring may be required as a result of initial exposure determinations;

(3) Environmental monitoring shall demonstrate the absence of asbestos fiber migration outside the regulated area; and

(4) Clearance monitoring to document that the area has met specified clearance criteria.

e. PPE, including respirators and clothing;

f. Housekeeping procedures that address prevention of spread of contamination both in and beyond the regulated area;

g. Hygiene facilities and practices;

h. CP and employee training required;

i. Medical surveillance, as required, to assess exposure and to monitor employee fitness to perform work tasks while wearing PPE to include respiratory protection devices;

j. Waste generation, containerization, transportation, and disposal (including recordkeeping); and

k. Security, fire, and medical emergency response procedures.

06.D Hot Substances.

➤Note: For *heating devices and melting kettles*, see *Section 09.E.*

06.D.01 Protection from Hot Substances. Hazards from hot substances include increased inhalation and skin hazards and burns from the heat. When working with hot substances the following shall be considered:

a. PPE (respirators, gloves, etc.) shall be evaluated for efficiency in hot atmospheres and protectiveness from heat as well as the chemical hazard;

b. Heat stress precautions and measurements shall be taken as required by Section 06.I;

c. Location where hot substances are heated shall be located away from any ventilation intake air vents. If hot substances are being applied to a roof, the ventilation intake air vents shall be temporarily relocated so as to prevent the uptake of the fumes into the building or the work shall be completed at a time when the building is not occupied.

06.D.02 Transporting and handling hot substances.

a. Runways or passageways, clear of obstructions, shall be provided for all persons carrying hot substances.

b. Hot substances shall not be carried up or down ladders.

c. When hoists are used to raise or lower hot substances, attention shall be given to assuring that the hoisting mechanism is adequate for the loads imposed and is securely braced and anchored.

d. All persons handling hot substances shall be provided protection against contact with, or exposure to radiant heat, glare, fumes, and vapors of the substances. At a minimum, roofers handling roofing materials shall be fully clothed including long sleeved shirts, shoes secured and at least 6 in (15 cm) in height, and gloves up to the wrist. > See Section 5.

e. Containers for handling and transporting hot substances shall be of substantial construction (minimum 24-gauge sheet steel), free from any soldered joints or attachments, and shall not be filled higher than 4 in (10.1 cm) from the top.

f. Piping used to transport hot substances shall have an entry and exit shut off valve and shall be made of flexible metallic hoses fitted with insulated handles. In cold climates, piping shall be insulated to prevent material from solidifying on the inside of the pipe.

06.E Harmful Plants, Animals and Insects.

06.E.01 Protection against hazards from insects and/or animals harboring fleas or disease-carrying insects shall include, as applicable, the following:

a. PPE such as netted hoods, leather work gloves, and high-top work boots worn in conjunction with trousers and long-sleeved shirts;

b. Clothing treated at the factory with DEET or Permethrin are recommended in areas of high insect population;

c. Drainage or spraying of breeding areas;

d. Destroying or flagging (marking as hazard) of nests;

e. Smudge pots and aerosols for protecting workers and small areas;

f. Elimination of actions or conditions that propagate insects or vermin;

g. Extermination measures by a certified pesticide applicator or, for over the counter items, following the instructions on the label;

h. Approved first aid procedures for employees; employees allergic to bee stings shall be encouraged to self identify to the supervisor and to carry an EpiPen;

i. Inoculation against diseases known to be a local hazard; and

j. Instruction in recognition of the animals and insects and their common nesting habits, aggressiveness, etc.

06.E.02 In areas where there is exposure to poisonous snakes or lizards, employees shall be required to:

a. Wear snake chaps or knee-high snake boots worn in conjunction with trousers and long-sleeved shirts;

b. Be trained in recognition of the snakes and their common nesting habits, aggressiveness, etc.; and

c. Be trained in the proper first aid procedures for bites.

06.E.03 In areas where employees are exposed to poisonous plants, the following protective measures, as applicable, shall be provided:

a. Removal or destruction of plants, where practical;

b. Appropriate protective clothing such as gloves;

c. Protective ointments;

d. Soap and water for washing exposed parts; and

e. Instruction in recognition and identification of the plants.

06.E.04 When burning poisonous plants, controls shall be instituted to prevent contact with or inhalation of toxic elements contained in the smoke.

06.F Ionizing Radiation.

06.F.01 Anyone who procures, uses, possesses, transports, transfers, or disposes of radioactive materials or radiation generating devices shall:

a. Notify, in writing, the GDA or USACE Command Radiation Safety Officer (RSO) of the nature of the material or device, a description of intended use, the location of use and storage, and all transportation and disposal requirements;

b. Secure appropriate authorization or permit if <u>any radioactive material or a radiation generating</u> device is to be used on a DoD installation (a lead time of at least 45 days should be allowed for obtaining a DoD authorization or permit);

c. Provide to the GDA <u>or USACE Command RSO</u> a copy of all US Nuclear Regulatory Commission (NRC) or Agreement State licenses, the Army Radiation Authorization (ARA), Army Radiation Permit, and reciprocity forms (to include NRC Form 241), as applicable.

d. When a USACE Radiation Safety Program exists at a location/facility that has potential Radon-222 emissions from radioactive material use, the more restrictive of the specific limits, the specific license condition or the NRC requirements in 10 CFR 20 for Radon-222 shall apply. If USACE employees work in a building, structure, or tunnel that has naturally occurring Radon-222, then OSHA requirements in 29 CFR 1910.1096 are applicable as specified in Section 06.F.14, Radon.

➤*Note: See OSHA Directive CPL 02–00–086, Memorandum of Understanding between OSHA and the U.S. Nuclear Regulatory Commission, 22 December 1989, for a delineation of radiation sources regulated by each agency.*

06.F.02 Qualified Personnel.

a. Operations involving radiation hazards or use of radioactive material or radiation generating devices shall be performed under the direct supervision of a RSO, who is qualified and responsible for radiological safety.

b. The RSO will be technically qualified and will meet the experience, training, and education requirements listed below:

(1) Formally trained in radiation protection topics including the following: physics of radiation; radiation's interaction with matter; mathematics necessary for the subject matter; biological effects of radiation; type and use of instruments for detection, monitoring and surveying radiation; radiation safety techniques and procedures; and use of time, distance, shielding, engineering controls, and PPE to reduce radiation exposure;

(2) Hands-on training in the uses of equipment, instrumentation, procedures, and theory used in their unit;

(3) Knowledge of applicable regulations including those of the NRC, EPA, DOE, <u>OSHA</u>, DOT and DoD,

to include all applicable DoD Components, pertaining to radioactive materials, radiation generating devices, and radioactive and mixed waste; and

(4) Knowledge of the USACE Radiation Safety Program, and recordkeeping requirements for work with radioactive materials and radiation generating devices.

06.F.03 Radiation Safety Program.

a. Operations involving radiation hazards, and users of radioactive material or radiation generating devices, shall develop and implement a Radiation Safety Program.

(1) The program shall be managed by the RSO and based on sound radiation safety principles that shall keep occupational doses and doses to the public ALARA.

(2) The RSO is responsible for performing or ensuring the performance of an annual review of the program. Documentation of the review shall be retained for two (2) years.

(3) A Radiation Safety Committee (RSC) shall be established in accordance with 10 CFR 20 and DA PAM 385-24 as part of the Radiation Safety Program.

b. All personnel entering an area where radioactive material or radiation generating devices are used, and where there is a potential for an individual to receive a Total Effective Dose Equivalent (TEDE) of 100 mrem or more in one (1) year, shall receive instruction in:

(1) The presence of the material or device;

(2) Health and safety problems associated with exposure to radiation, including the potential effects of radiation on a pregnant female, the fetus, or embryo;

(3) Precautions and controls used to control exposure;

(4) Proper use of instrumentation and dosimetry in the area;

(5) The Radiation Safety Program required in 06.F.03.a; and

(6) Their rights and responsibilities.

c. Users of radioactive material or radiation generating devices without a potential to receive a TEDE of 100 mrem or more in one (1) year and visitors to a site shall coordinate with the RSO for appropriate training.

d. The Radiation Safety Program will include plans and procedures for handling credible emergencies involving radiation and radioactive materials. This will include coordination with civilian and/or military emergency response organizations as necessary.

06.F.04 Dose Limits.

a. Occupational dose limits shall be based on the TEDE. > *See Table 6-1.*

(1) An annual (calendar year) limit that is the more limiting of: 5 rem [0.05 sieverts (Sv)] TEDE, or the sum of the deep dose equivalent and the committed dose equivalent to any individual organ or tissue of 50 rem (0.5 Sv), or 15 rem (0.15 Sv) to the lens of the eye, or 50 rem (0.05 Sv) shallow dose equivalent to the skin or any extremity.

TABLE 6-1

Occupational Dose Limits

Body part	Annual limits with RSSO approval	Annual limits without RSSO approval	Suggested ALARA limit
Whole body	5 rem (0.05 Sv)	0.5 rem (0.005 Sv)	0.1 rem (0.001 Sv)
Individual organ	50 rem (0.5 Sv)	5 rem (0.05 Sv)	0.5 rem (0.005 Sv)
Lens of eye	15 rem (0.15 Sv)	1.5 rem (0.015 Sv)	0.15 rem (0.0015 Sv)
Skin or extremity	50 rem (0.5 Sv)	5 rem (0.05 Sv)	0.5 rem (0.005 Sv)

(2) Without the written approval of the USACE Radiation Safety Staff Officer (RSSO), the annual occupational dose shall not exceed the more limiting of: 0.5 rem (0.005 Sv) TEDE, or the sum of the deep dose equivalent and the committed dose equivalent to any individual organ or tissue of 5 rem (0.05 Sv), or 1.5 rem (0.015 Sv) to the lens of the eye, or 5 rem (0.05 Sv) shallow dose equivalent to the skin, or any extremity.

(3) To keep doses ALARA, the user shall set administrative action levels below the annual dose limits. These action levels shall be realistic and attainable. Suggested action levels are the more limiting of: 0.1 rem (0.001 Sv) TEDE, or the sum of the deep dose equivalent and the committed dose equivalent to any individual organ or tissue of 0.5 rem (0.005 Sv), or 0.15 rem (0.0015 Sv) to the lens of the eye, or 0.5 rem (0.005 Sv) shallow dose equivalent to the skin or any extremity.

(4) Any exposure in excess of an ALARA limit requires investigation by the RSO.

b. In accordance with DA PAM 385-24, planned special exposures shall not be performed.

c. No employee under 18 years of age shall receive occupational exposure to ionizing radiation (excluding exposure to Radon-222).

d. The dose to a declared pregnant employee shall not exceed 0.5 rem (0.005 Sv) during the entire gestation period and efforts shall be made to avoid variations in a uniform monthly exposure rate. If the dose to the embryo/fetus is between 0.05 rem and 0.5 rem at the time of declaration, then dose to the embryo/fetus is limited to 0.05 rem for the remainder of gestation.

06.F.05 Radiation Monitoring, Surveys, and Dosimetry.

a. Users of radioactive material or radiation generating devices shall conduct surveys and monitoring to ensure occupational dose limits are not exceeded.

b. Instruments used for radiation monitoring and surveying shall be:

(1) Available and used whenever radioactive material or radiation generating devices are used;

(2) Properly calibrated at least annually to a National Institute of Standards and Technology (NIST) traceable source;

(3) Appropriate for the type and intensity of the radiation surveyed;

(4) Operationally checked against a dedicated check source before each use; and

(5) The RSO must maintain at least two survey instruments to accommodate maintenance and calibration downtime.

c. Users of radioactive material or radiation generating devices and visitors or personnel performing work tasks in the area shall coordinate with the RSO for appropriate dosimetry use whenever any of the following situations exist:

(1) An individual enters a Radiation Area (> 5 mrem [50 microsieverts (µSv)] in any one (1) hour at 1 ft (30 cm) from the radiation source), or a High Radiation Area (> 100 mrem [1 mSv] in any one (1) hour at 1 ft (30 cm) from the radiation source), or a Very High Radiation Area (>500 rad [5 Gray (Gy)] in 1 hour at 3.3 ft (1 m) from the radiation source);

(2) An individual has the potential to receive greater than the ALARA limits established pursuant to Section 06.F.04.a.(3) in 1 year.

d. All external dosimetry shall be processed by a National Voluntary Laboratory Accreditation Program (NVLAP) certified laboratory. USACE personnel shall use dosimetry provided by the Army Dosimetry Center.

e. Users of unsealed radioactive material sources shall institute an internal dosimetry program:

(1) When there is a potential for an employee to receive an internal dose of greater than 0.5 rem (5 mSv) per year;

(2) That is reviewed and approved by a qualified health physicist, and

(3) That contains provisions for a pre-exposure bioassay, a bioassay method capable of detecting internal radioactive materials, at a level below 10% of the annual limits of intake (ALI) listed in Appendix B of 10 CFR 20 for each radionuclide used, appropriate action levels for requiring additional bioassay, actions for individuals found to have

internally deposited radioactive materials, and provisions for post-exposure bioassay.

06.F.06 Access, Storage, and Control.

a. All radiological devices and radioactive materials shall be designed, constructed, installed, used, stored, transported, and disposed of in such a manner to ensure personnel exposures are kept ALARA.

b. Users of radioactive materials or radiation generating devices shall post signs and control access to radiation areas in accordance with Section 06.F.08.

c. Where radiation levels exceed 2 mrem (20 µSv) in any 1 hour period, users shall use engineering controls, shielding, access time limitation, and/or physical separation to keep doses to the public ALARA.

d. Users shall secure radioactive material and radiation generating devices against theft or unauthorized use.

e. Storage shall be in accordance with any license or permit requirements.

f. Radioactive material and radiation generating devices, not in storage, shall be under constant control and surveillance.

g. Operations involving regulated radiation hazards or users of regulated radioactive material or radiation generating devices shall conduct surveys to ensure that the public dose limit of 0.01 rem (0.0001 Sv) is not exceeded.

06.F.07 Respiratory Protection and other Controls.

a. Users of radioactive material shall, to the extent practicable, institute process or engineering controls to limit concentrations of radioactive materials in air.

b. Where process or engineering controls are unable to control airborne radioactive material concentrations, users shall increase monitoring and limit intakes of radioactive materials through control of access, limitation of exposure times, use of respiratory protection equipment, or other controls.

c. The use of respiratory protection equipment shall be in compliance with Section 05.G of this manual, and shall be limited by the protection factors listed in Appendix A of 10 CFR 20.

06.F.08 Signs, Labels, and Posting Requirements.

a. The RSO shall post in a conspicuous location a sign or signs bearing the standard radiation symbol shown in Figure 8-7 and the following words:

(1) "Caution, Radiation Area" - areas where radiation field is equal to or greater than 5 mrem (0.05 mSv) in any 1 hour and less than 100 mrem (1 mSv) in any 1 hour at 30 cm from the radiation source;

(2) "Caution, High Radiation Area" - areas where radiation field is equal to or greater than 100 mrem (1 mSv) in any 1 hour at 12 in (30 cm) from the radiation source and less than 500 rads (5 Gy) in any 1 hour at 3.3 ft (1 m) from the radiation source;

(3) "Grave Danger, Very High Radiation Area" - areas where the radiation field is equal to or greater than 500 rads (5 Gy) in any 1 hour;

(4) "Caution, Airborne Radioactivity Area" – rooms, enclosures, or areas where airborne radioactive material concentrations are greater than the derived air concentration (DAC) limits listed in 10 CFR 20, Appendix B or where concentrations (excluding Radon222) exist to such a degree that an individual present in the area without respiratory protective equipment could exceed, during the hours an individual is present in a week, an intake of 0.6% of the annual limit on intake (ALI) or 12 DAC- hours; or

(5) "Caution, Radioactive Material" – areas or rooms where quantities of radioactive materials in excess of ten times the 10 CFR 20, Appendix C quantities are used or stored.

b. Users who receive or expect to receive a package containing radioactive material shall follow the package receipt procedures listed in 10 CFR 20.1906.

c. When a site has an NRC license, the RSO shall post an NRC Form 3 in a location visible to all employees who work with or around radioactive materials

06.F.09 Radioactive Waste Disposal

a. Radioactive sealed sources (and gauges) when no longer needed may be returned (transferred) to the manufacturer. The local USACE RSO must be notified and any applicable licenses or permits amended or terminated.

b. Radioactive waste disposal shall be coordinated with the GDA. For disposal actions specific to USACE operations and activities the GDA or Project Manager shall coordinate with the USACE Command RSO and the USACE Environmental and Munitions Center of Expertise.

c. Tritium (H-3) and Carbon-14 used in liquid scintillation counting, at concentrations below 0.05 microcuries per gram (μCi/g), may be disposed without regard to its radioactivity. (Note: Many liquid scintillation fluids are hazardous wastes and must be disposed of as such.)

06.F.10 Records.

a. All users of radioactive material or radiation generating devices shall prepare and maintain records of the Radiation Safety Program for three (3) years after termination of the license or permit.

b. For any individual for whom monitoring was required by Section 06.F.05, the RSO shall prepare and maintain documentation of that person's occupational dose during the current year. The RSO shall also attempt to obtain records of cumulative occupational radiation dose.

c. All users of radioactive material or radiation generating devices shall prepare and maintain records of all calculated or monitored radiation dose to individual members of the public so as to document compliance with Section 06.F.05.

06.F.11 Reports.

a. Any loss, theft, damage, or overexposure shall immediately upon discovery be reported to the RSO who will then file a report (if required) with NRC in accordance with the requirements of 10 CFR 20.

b. Mishaps involving radioactive material or radiation generating devices shall be reported immediately to the RSO and the USACE RSSO.

c. Annual reports shall be issued by the RSO for each individual USACE radiation employee with the recorded or calculated dose assigned to the USACE individual for the year or specific work project. These shall be maintained in such a manner that accumulated exposure can be determined at a future date.

06.F.12 Transportation.

a. Users of radioactive material shall comply with the requirements of the DOT for inter- and intra-state transport contained in 49 CFR.

b. Persons who prepare shipments of radioactive materials that are defined as hazardous material under DOT regulations are required to be trained (49 CFR 173.1(b)), certified, and issued an appointment letter in accordance with DoD 4500.9-R, Chapter 204.

06.F.13 Medical surveillance. > *See Section 33 for requirements specific to work conducted under the provisions of 29 CFR 1910.120 and 29 CFR 1926.65.*

6

a. Medical examinations are not routinely required before occupational exposure to ionizing radiation. For USACE personnel, a medical examination shall be conducted in accordance with DA PAM 40-501, when deemed necessary, by a physician, the RSO, or other regulations. The RSO will coordinate with supporting medical personnel to help ensure that personnel receive appropriate occupational health surveillance.

b. All cases of overexposure and suspected ingestion or inhalation of radioactive materials shall be referred to a physician for examination.

06.F.14 Radon-222.

a. If a work area is occupied for 40-hours per week or more by an individual 18 years of age or older, and average natural occurring radon-222 concentration is greater than 100 pCi/L, then number of hours worked in the area by the individual shall be reduced or engineering controls introduced to reduce the radon-222 concentration. If the exposure is due to a regulated radiation source, the requirements of the NRC license shall apply. > See 29 CFR 1910.1096(c)(1) which references 10 CFR 20 Appendix B Table 1 and Table 2.

b. Any work area in a structure, building, or tunnel, wherein workers may be reasonably expected to be exposed to naturally occurring radon-222 exceeding 25 pCi/L averaged over a 40-hour work week, is an Airborne Radioactivity Area and shall be posted in accordance with 29 CFR 1910.1096(e)(4)(ii).

c. All individuals working in or frequenting any portion of an area posted per Section 06.F.14.b shall receive instruction regarding exposure to radiation as per 29 CFR 1910.1096(i).

06.G Non-ionizing Radiation, Magnetic and Electric Fields.

06.G.01 Lasers.

a. Only qualified and trained employees may be assigned to install, adjust, and operate laser equipment. Proof of qualification of the laser equipment operator shall be in the operator's possession during operation. A qualified employee shall design or review for adequacy all radiation safety Standard Operating Procedure (SOP).

b. Laser equipment shall bear a label to indicate make, maximum output, and beam spread.

c. Areas in which lasers are used shall be posted with standard laser warning signs.
> See Figures 8-5 and 8-6

d. Employees whose work requires exposure to laser beams shall be provided with appropriate laser safety goggles that will protect for the specific wavelength of the laser and be of optical density adequate for the energy involved, as specified in Table 6-2. Protective goggles shall bear a label identifying the following data: the laser wavelengths for which use is intended, the optical density of those wavelengths, and the visible light transmission.

TABLE 6-2

Laser Safety Goggle Optical Density Requirements

Intensity, continuous wave maximum power density (watts/cm^2)	Attenuation	
	Optical density	Attenuation factor
0.01	5	10,000
0.1	6	100,000
1.0	7	1,000,000
10.0	8	10,000,000

e. Beam shutters or caps shall be used, or the laser turned off, when laser transmission is not required. When the laser is left unattended for a period of time (e.g., during lunch hour, overnight, or at change of shifts) the laser shall be turned off.

f. Only mechanical or electronic means shall be used as a detector for guiding the internal alignment of the laser.

g. The laser beam shall not be directed at employees: whenever possible, laser units in operation shall be set above the heads of employees.

h. When it is raining or snowing or when there is dust or fog in the air, the operation of laser systems shall be prohibited (as practical); during such weather conditions employees shall be kept out of range of the areas of source and target.

i. Employee exposure to laser power densities shall be within the TLVs as specified by the ACGIH in "Threshold Limit Values and Biological Exposure Indices."

j. Only Class 1, 2, or 3a lasers may be used as hand-held pointing devices. Lasers used as pointing devices (e.g., during briefings) shall not be directed toward employees and shall be handled and stored in accordance with the manufacturer's recommendations.

k. Suspected LASER eye injuries: Immediately evacuate personnel suspected of experiencing potentially damaging eye exposure from LASER radiation to the nearest medical facility for an eye examination. LASER eye injuries require immediate specialized ophthalmologic care to minimize long-term visual acuity loss. Medical personnel should obtain medical guidance for LASER injuries from the Tri-Service LASER Incident Hotline, (800) 473-3549 (24-hour phone line).

06.G.02 Radio frequency and electromagnetic radiation.

a. Ensure that no employee is exposed to electric or magnetic fields, radio frequency (RF) including infrared, ultraviolet, and microwave radiation levels exceeding the values listed in the ACGIH Threshold Limit Values and Biological Exposure Indices.

b. Routine use of RF protective clothing to protect personnel is prohibited.

(1) Protective equipment, such as electrically insulated gloves and shoes for protection against RF shock and burn, or for insulation from the ground plane, is permissible when engineering controls or procedures cannot eliminate exposure hazards.

(2) Users will identify, attenuate, or control potentially hazardous RF electromagnetic fields and other radiation hazards associated with electronic equipment by engineering design, administrative actions, or protective equipment, (in that order), or a combination thereof. Use process and engineering controls before PPE to protect employees.

c. All personnel routinely working with RF emitting equipment where exposures may exceed TLVs will receive training in RF hazards, procedures for minimizing these hazards, and their responsibility to limit potential overexposures. Operator's manuals, Training Orders, Equipment SOPs, etc. will be available for all RF generating equipment and safety guidance will be followed.

d. Whenever personnel are potentially exposed to RF fields exceeding PELs, the fields will be measured and evaluated using Institute of Electrical and Electronics Engineers (IEEE) guidance. District and/or project safety personnel will use this information and document RF environments. Where multiple RF electromagnetic radiation emitters are located in fixed arrangements, RF evaluation data will include a determination of weighted contributions from expected simultaneously operated emitters.

06.H Ventilation and Exhaust Systems.

06.H.01 Portable and Temporary Ventilation Systems.

a. All portable or temporary ventilation systems shall remove dusts, fumes, mists, vapors and gases away from the worker and the work environment or provide air to prevent an oxygen deficient atmosphere.

b. Portable or temporary ventilation systems shall be used as designed by the manufacturer. All hoses shall be only as long as the maximum allowed by the manufacturer to provide the required air flow at the supply or exhaust point. If adding or changing hoses, only hoses and/or connectors shall be used that are comparable and compatible with the hoses and connectors provided by the manufacturer.

c. Make-up air for air supply ventilation systems shall draw air free of contaminants and away from any potential contaminant source.

d. Any portable or temporary ventilation system and the locations where the systems are to be used shall be approved by the GDA or SOHO before use. Manufacturer information or design criteria shall be provided with the request for approval.

e. Airborne contaminants created by portable or temporary ventilation systems (such as drills, saws, and grinding machines) in concentrations exceeding acceptable safe limits shall be effectively controlled at the source. > *See Section 06.A.03.*

f. The use of high efficiency, filtered, recirculated ventilation units shall be allowed when:

(1) The filtration system lowers the levels of any of the toxic fumes or dust from the operation to less than half of the OEL. This shall be documented by an IH or CP through sampling for the contaminants.

➤*Note: Welding, carbon monoxide, ozone, and carbon dioxide are common contaminants that are not filtered out by most filtration devices.*

(2) The unit and filtration are regularly maintained and the maintenance procedure and schedule is written and documented when maintenance is completed.

(3) The air is not recirculated into a confined space.

(4) The contaminant is not beryllium or chromium. Fumes or particulate from beryllium or chromium are not to be filtered and recirculated.

06.H.02 Ventilation systems shall be operated and maintained in such a manner to ensure the maintenance of a volume and velocity of exhaust air sufficient to gather contaminants and safely transport them to suitable points for removal.

06.H.03 Duration of operation.

a. Ventilation systems shall be operated continuously during operations when persons are exposed to airborne contaminants or explosive gases at or above acceptable safe limits as defined in Section 06.A.01 or as otherwise specified by this manual, referenced standards, or regulations.

b. Ventilation systems shall remain in operation for a period of time after the work process or equipment has ceased to ensure the removal of any contaminants in suspension or vaporizing into the air.

06.H.04 Local exhaust ventilation systems shall be periodically evaluated to ensure that proper contaminant capture, movement through the system and filtration or exhaust to the outside.

06.H.05 Dusts and refuse materials removed by exhaust systems or other methods shall be disposed of in a manner that will not create a hazard to employees or the public and in accordance with Federal, State, and local requirements.

06.H.06 Ventilation systems used to remove hazardous dusts, fumes, gases, or substances shall be evaluated annually to determine if the system requires cleaning. The cleaning of the ventilation system shall be part of the written housekeeping program section of the Project SOH Plan or APP.

06.I Abrasive Blasting.

06.I.01 General. Silica sand shall NOT be used as an abrasive blasting media. Alternative abrasive blasting materials are available and listed in Table 6-3. Depending on the application, one of these alternative materials is suggested for use as an abrasive blasting media.

a. Abrasive blasting operations shall be evaluated to determine composition and toxicity of the abrasive and the dust or fume generated by the blasted material, including surface coatings. This determination shall be documented on the AHA (Activity Hazard Analysis) developed for the abrasive blasting activity.

b. Written operating procedures shall be developed and implemented for abrasive blasting operations, including pressurized pot procedures (filling, pressurizing, depressurizing, and maintenance and inspection). The procedures should be added as an appendix to the APP.

c. The concentration of respirable dust and fume in the breathing zone of individuals exposed to the blasting operation shall be maintained below any OEL for the material being blasted and the blasting agents or its byproducts.

d. No employee will be allowed to work in abrasive blasting operations unless he has met the medical surveillance and training and experience requirements, and has been provided the appropriate PPE.

TABLE 6-3

Abrasive Blasting Media: Silica Substitutes

Applications	Media	Advantages
Cleaning Hard Metals (Titanium); Removing Metal Etch Glass; Carve Granite	Aluminum Oxide	Recyclable
General Paint Removal Stripping Aircraft Skins Cleaning Surfaces in Food Processing Plants Removing Paint from Glass	Baking Soda (Sodium Bicarbonate)	Less Material Used/Less Cleanup Low Nozzle Pressures (35-90 PSI) Non-Sparking Water Soluble
General Paint, Rust, & Scale Removal from Steel Paint Removal from Wood Exposure of Aggregates	Coal Slag	Less than 1% Free Silica Inert, Fast Cutting Creates Anchor Profile
General Paint, Rust & Scale Removal from Steel Paint Removal from Wood	Copper Slag	Rapid Cutting
Deburring Paint & Rust Removal from Wood & Metal	Corn Cob Granules	Low Consumption Low Dust Levels Biodegradable
Cleaning Aircraft Parts Cleaning Exotic Metals	Dry Ice (Carbon Dioxide)	No Residue Remains Minimal Cleanup
General Paint, Rust & Scale Removal from Steel	Garnet	Lower Nozzle Pressure (60-70 PSI) Low Dust Levels Fast Cleaning Rates Can be Recycled 6-7 Times Low Free Silica
Cleaning & Polishing Deburring	Glass Beads	Uniform Size and Shape Recyclable Provide High Luster Polished Surface
General Paint, Rust & Scale Removal from Steel	Nickel Slag	Rapid Cutting
Cleaning Soft Materials (e.g. Aluminum, Plastic, Wood Cleaning Surfaces in the Petroleum Industry	Nut Shells	High Removal Speed Non-Sparking Low Consumption
Clean Light Mill Scale/Rust from Steel 2.5 MIL Profile & Finer	Olivine	Low Chloride Ion Level Low Conductivity

e. All production and control systems used in a stationary abrasive-blasting process shall be designed or maintained to prevent escape of airborne dust or aerosols in the work environment and to ensure control of the abrasive agents.

f. Pressurized systems and components shall be inspected, tested, certified and maintained in accordance with the requirements of Section 20.

g. Engineering controls for noise and dust shall be used even if they cannot reduce the exposures to below OEL (significantly reduces noise and dust exposure to the employees).

06.I.02 Blast Cleaning Enclosures and Rooms.

a. The ventilation in all blast enclosures shall be measured annually to confirm the flow is adequate and the system does not require cleaning or maintenance. Exhaust systems shall be part of a regular cleaning and maintenance program.

b. All air inlets and access openings shall be baffled to prevent the escape of abrasive agent and contaminant and the recommended continuous airflow into the air inlets is a minimum of 250 fpm (4.6 kph).

c. Negative pressure shall be maintained inside during blasting.

d. The rate of exhaust shall be sufficient to provide prompt clearance of the dust- laden air within the enclosure after cessation of the blasting.

e. If abrasive blasting is automated, the blast shall be turned off before the enclosure is opened. The exhaust system shall be run for a sufficient period of time to remove the dusty air within the enclosure to minimize the escape of dust into the workroom and prevent any health hazard.

f. In the room, a cleanup method other than broom sweeping or compressed air blowing shall be used to collect the abrasive agent after blasting (e.g., vacuum cleaning). If the blasting agent is removed manually, appropriate personal protective equipment, including respiratory protection shall be worn and not removed until outside the blasting room.

06.I.03 Blasting without Enclosures.

a. If abrasive blasting must be performed inside a building without enclosures, respiratory protection shall be provided for all employees in the area. Portable engineering control devices shall be used at the location to collect the entire used abrasive agent as it is applied.

b. When airborne abrasive-blasting dust becomes sufficiently heavy in an area to cause a temporary safety hazard by reduced visibility, or discomfort to the unprotected employees not engaged in abrasive blasting, such operations in the affected area shall be discontinued until the airborne dust is removed by exhaust ventilation and the settled dust has been removed from the horizontal surfaces in the area. If such operations have to continue, appropriate respiratory protection shall be provided to those employees remaining in the area.

c. Abrasive materials shall not be allowed to accumulate on aisles and walkways to create a slipping hazard.

d. If wet abrasive blasting is employed to reduce dust exposures, the aerosols produced and the dried residues that become airborne might be potential hazards and shall be considered.

06.I.04 Confined spaces. Abrasive blasting work conducted in a confined space shall be performed in accordance with Section 34. If the space is mechanically ventilated, means shall be provided to collect dust before release to the open atmosphere.

06.I.05 Blasting Outdoors.

a. Work completed outside has been shown to create exposures to health hazards for the worker and other trades in the area. Air and noise samples shall be taken to document the level of exposure to the worker and the workers in the area, unless similar operations documented no exposure. Blasters shall be protected in a manner equivalent to Section 05 and/or 29 CFR 1910.94(a)(5), whichever is more stringent.

b. Engineering controls and work practices, such as wet blasting methods, shall be used to prevent the dust cloud from spreading to other work areas. Check with Local and State requirements which may add restrictions to outdoor abrasive blasting. If the surface to be blasted is painted or contains high levels of silica and/or heavy metals, such as lead, chromium, or cadmium, an enclosure may be required to prevent disbursement of the hazard.

c. Hearing protection and respiratory protection shall be available to all employees in the area unless noise and air sampling documents the workers are not exposed to the blasting agent or contaminants from the blasted surface.

06.I.06 Personal Protective Equipment (PPE).

a. Selection and use of PPE shall be in accordance with Section 05. If reusable coveralls are used, they shall be vacuumed before all breaks and removed at the end of the shift. Clothes shall not be taken home to be cleaned by the worker or family, but shall be laundered by the employer.

b. Air-supplied helmets, blast helmets/hoods, dust respirators, ear muffs, safety boots or toe guards, durable coveralls, closeable at wrists, ankles, and other openings, and safety glasses should be an individual issue item, identified with and used by only one employee. Such equipment may be reissued to another employee only after complete cleaning, repair, and decontamination.

c. Means shall be provided to clean and store air-supplied respiratory equipment after each shift of use. Storage shall be in a clean enclosure such as locker, footlocker, plastic container or zip-lock type bag. Employees shall be trained to maintain issued equipment in clean and good working condition.

d. Replacement of prescription or plano safety glasses shall be made if multiple pitting or etching is visible in the center of the lenses.

e. Replacement of faceplates in air-supplied helmets and blast helmets/hoods shall take place when a side-on light source produces obscuring visible reflections and glare from the etched spots and pit holes in the faceplate. Mylar coating, or similar transparent plastic material, is recommended to protect the glass or plastic faceplate.

f. Length of air hose may not be altered from the manufacturer's specifications.

g. Daily checks shall be performed by the wearer of PPE to maintain it in good working condition. Rips, tears, and openings of PPE that expose skin to abrasive agents shall be mended or replaced. Functional tests for leaks, proper respiration, and good connections shall be performed on the complete air-supply system.

h. Air supply - portable.

(1) The breathable air supplied to the blast helmet or hood shall be drawn from an oil and carbon monoxide free air compressor. The compressor used for blasting cannot be used for breathing air. Breathable air-supply system should be equipped, if possible, with audible alarm at the helmet or hood to warn the user of low air pressure.

(2) Hearing protection. Suitable hearing protection, capable of attenuating employee noise exposure as discussed in Section 05.C, shall be worn inside the blast helmet or hood unless hearing protection is an integral part of such helmet or hood.

(3) Heat stress. Cooling of breathable air, supplied to the blast helmets/hoods, should be considered depending on season and employee exposure to heat sources.

06.J Heat/Cold Stress Management.

06.J. General. Employer's APP or Project SOH plans shall include control of heat and/or cold stress hazards, as appropriate for the season and work location. Heat/Cold Stress sections in the APP or Project SOH plans, shall take into consideration the influence of environmental conditions, workload, and personal factors.

06.J.01 Heat Stress: The APP or Project SOH Plan and individual AHAs shall address heat stress under the following working conditions:

a. CONUS and OCONUS locations when hot/dry or hot/humid environments are forecasted;

b. Work in conducted in semi-permeable or impermeable clothing and/or heavy clothing such as arc-rated suits;

c. Work in confined work environment with minimal air movement;

d. Work when heat index is greater than 75° F (24° C) or dry temperature is 75° F with 55% humidity or Wet-Bulb-Glove Temperature (WBGT) exceeds the action level for various exertion levels in Table 2 of the TLV and Action Limit for Heat Stress Exposure in the current ACGIH TLV/ BEI booklet;

e. Work around heat-producing equipment, furnaces, boilers, asphalt pots, engines, compressors, etc.

06.J.02 Heat Stress Monitoring Plan (HSMP). The written HSMP shall be incorporated into the APP or Project SOH Plan and shall cover the following topics relative to the on- site conditions expected:

a. Training on heat-related illnesses and how it can be prevented and the control measures to be taken;

b. Method used to monitor for heat stress, including standards being utilized and the responsible party for monitoring heat stress;

c. Signs and symptoms of heat-related illnesses and first aid procedures for each condition;

d. Exacerbation of heat related injury and illness based on various types of clothing, including general work clothing, semi-permeable and non-permeable clothing, arc flash clothing, and other protective clothing which reduces the evaporation rate;

e. The dangers of using drugs and alcohol in hot work environments.

06.J.03 In hot environments as defined above, the following shall be required:

a. Potable drinking water shall be available to employees and employees are encouraged to frequently drink small amounts, (e.g., 1/2 cup every 15-20 minutes). The water shall be kept reasonably cool $50-60^{\circ}$ F ($10-15^{\circ}$ C) to encourage consumption. > See Section 02.C.

6

b. Tool box training which addresses the requirements in the HSMP, anticipated weather conditions for the day, any heat-related incidents, etc.

c. When possible, work should be scheduled for cooler periods during the day.

d. Implement a buddy system. Workers should not only monitor themselves, but also be alert to changes and the symptoms of their co-workers.

e. Workers who have not previously worked in a hot environment or have had a previous heat-related injury, or are known to be on medication, shall acclimatize with a regimen of increasing exposure each day of work.

f. Provide recovery areas where possible, such as air-conditioned enclosures, or shaded areas, with intermittent breaks and water breaks.

g. If a worker is required to wear semi-impermeable or impermeable clothing, then physiological monitoring shall include:

(1) Heart rate monitoring with a standard of a sustained heart rate in excess of 180 beats per minute (bpm) minus the age of the worker in years, recovery heart rate at one minute after a peak work effort is greater than 120 bpm, or

(2) Monitoring of the core body temperature with a standard of greater than 100.4°F (38.0°C) for unacclimatized workers, and 101.3°F (38.5°C) for acclimated workers.

(3) Workers exceeding the above standards are required to have work/rest regimens and fluid replacement schedules.

h. If a worker is wearing permeable clothing:

(1) Environmental monitoring or physiological monitoring shall be conducted and work/rest regimens established.

(2) Monitoring shall be conducted when temperature exceeds 75°F (24°C) and 55% humidity.

(3) Use of a WBGT instrument is preferred, however, if a WBGT instrument is not available, and the WBGT cannot be obtained from local weather stations, then Figure 6-1. the Approximate WBGT Temperature Chart, should be used to approximate the WBGT.

(4) If Figure 6-1 is used, direct radiant sun exposure, air velocity, temperature, and humidity and adjustment factors for various work clothing should be taken into consideration.

i. Employees exposed to solar radiation with the potential for sunburn, should be encouraged to use sun screen with a sun protection factor (SPF) of 30 or greater, and should wear hats, long sleeve shirts, sunglasses, and other protective attire.

j. Workers who experience heat stress shall seek medical attention. Workers who have more than one heat-related episode within a month shall have a doctor's written release prior to returning to exposures in a potential heat stress environment.

06.J.04 Cold Stress Management Plan (CSMP). A CSMP shall be incorporated into the APP or Project SOH Plan for the following work activities:

a. Extended work duration in refrigerated rooms;

b. Work in cold environments taking into consideration heat loss from wind speeds (e.g., when air temperature or wind chill could drop below 40°F (4.4°C);

c. Extended bare-hand work in cold weather;

d. Working with hands or parts of the body in cold water for periods greater than 10-12 minutes or potential cold water emersion;

e. Working in snow or ice.

06.J.05 The CSMP shall address:

a. Training on the signs, symptoms, and first aid for hypothermia, frostbite, and trench foot;

b. Control and prevention measures to include PPE, engineering and administrative controls, eating, drinking, and safe work practices;

c. Conditions and limitations in which bare hand work can be performed;

d. Frequency. Air temperature and wind speed shall be taken should be taken at least every 4 hours when the temperature drops below 20°F (-6°C) and wind speed exceeds 5 mph (8 kmph) or broadcasted wind chill factors may be used if the reading is within 10 miles of the location.

Figure 6-1

Approximate Wet-Bulb Globe Temperature (WBGT) Chart

Degrees F

Relative Humidity (%)	68	70	72	73	75	77	79	81	82	84	86	88	90	91	93	95	97	99	100	102	104	106	108
0	59	61	61	63	64	64	66	66	68	68	70	72	72	73	73	75	75	77	77	79	81	81	82
5	61	61	63	64	63	66	66	68	70	70	72	72	73	75	75	77	79	79	81	81	82	84	84
10	61	63	63	64	66	66	68	70	70	72	73	73	75	77	77	79	81	81	82	84	86	86	88
15	63	63	64	66	66	68	70	70	72	73	73	75	77	79	79	81	82	84	84	86	88	90	91
20	63	64	64	66	68	70	70	72	73	75	75	77	79	81	81	82	84	86	88	90	90	91	95
25	64	64	66	68	68	70	72	73	75	75	77	79	81	82	82	84	86	88	90	91	93	95	97
30	64	66	68	68	70	72	73	73	75	77	79	81	82	84	84	86	88	90	91	93	95	97	99
35	64	66	68	70	72	72	73	75	77	79	81	82	84	86	88	90	91	93	95	97	99	100	102
40	66	68	70	70	72	73	75	77	79	81	82	84	86	88	90	91	93	95	97	99	100	102	
45	66	68	70	72	73	75	77	79	81	81	82	84	86	90	91	93	95	97	99	100			
50	68	70	72	73	73	75	77	79	81	82	84	86	88	91	93	95	97	99	102				
55	68	70	72	73	75	77	79	81	82	84	86	88	90	93	95	97	99	100					
60	70	72	73	75	77	79	81	82	84	86	88	90	91	95	97	99	100						
65	70	72	73	75	77	79	81	82	84	88	90	91	93	97	99	100							
70	72	73	75	77	79	81	82	84	86	88	91	93	95	97	100	102							
75	72	73	75	77	79	81	84	86	88	90	91	95	97	99	102								
80	73	75	77	79	81	82	84	86	90	91	93	97	99	100									
85	73	75	77	79	82	84	86	88	90	93	95	99	100	102									
90	75	77	79	81	82	84	88	90	91	95	97	99	102										
95	75	77	79	81	84	86	88	91	93	95	99	100											
100	75	79	81	82	84	88	90	91	95	100	100	102											

Chart assumes full sunshine and light wind. Using this chart on a cloudy or windy day will result in an overestimation of heat stress

06.J.06 In cold environments the following guidelines shall be followed to prevent cold-related injury.

a. Warming shelters should be made available nearby when the wind chill drops below 10°F (-12°C).

b. A change of clothing shall be available if there is an opportunity for a worker to become wet.

c. When the wind chill drops below 0°F (-17°C), the following work practices shall apply.

(1) Workers shall use the buddy system to watch for signs and symptoms of cold related injuries or illnesses.

(2) The work rate shall be moderated to prevent sweating.

(3) Heat shelters shall be provided.

(4) New workers shall be given time to acclimate.

d. Workers exposed to -15°F (-26°C) shall use the work/warm-up schedule specified in the ACGIH TLVs/BEIs booklet.

e. If any extremity or body part is immersed in water where the air temperature is below 40°F (4°C), the employee shall be required to change any clothing that became wet and to dry off in a warm area.

f. Environmental monitoring. As the wind chill drops below 20°F (-7°C), the air temperature and wind speed (wind chill index) shall be monitored a minimum of every 4 hours or as warranted.

g. When the wind chill falls below 0°F (-17°C), the air temperature and wind speed shall be monitored every 2 hours or more frequently if it drops below this level.

06.K Cumulative Trauma Disorder Prevention.

06.K.01 Work activities that require employees to conduct lifting, handling, or carrying; rapid and frequent application of high grasping forces; repetitive hand/arm manipulations; tasks that include continuous, intermittent, impulsive, or impact hand-arm vibration or whole body vibration; and other physical activities that stress the body's capabilities shall be evaluated by a competent person to ensure the activities are designed to match the capabilities of the employees.

06.K.02 When work activities that stress the body's capabilities are identified, the employer shall identify it as a hazard in the APP or Project SOH Plan. The plan shall incorporate processes that recognize cumulative trauma hazards, isolate causative factors, inform and train employees, provide and implement PPE and engineering controls, if appropriate.

06.K.03 Control measures to minimize hand-arm vibration (HAV) shall include: use of anti-vibration tools and/or gloves; implementation of work practices that keep the employee's hands and body warm/minimize vibration coupling between employee and the vibration tool; application of specialized medical surveillance to identify personnel susceptible to vibration, and adherence to TLV guidelines as specified by ACGIH in "*Threshold Limit* Values and Biological Exposure Indices". For USACE only, the evaluation shall include:

a. Acceleration measurements made according to ANSI S2.70 or acceleration data from the manufacturer (ISO 8662) or an online HAV database that has collected tool specific data via ISO 5349. If using manufacturer's data, a safety factor of 2.0 should be incorporated and if using an online database, a safety factor of 1.25 is warranted.

b. Using an estimate or measurement for each individual piece of equipment used by an operator, a time weighted average of the vibration exposure shall be determined. Detailed description of the proper method of completing the vibration evaluations is found in ANSI S2.70.

c. If the estimate or monitored HAV exposure is greater than 2.5 m/s^2, then controls shall be implemented in the following order: changing the process to use lower vibrating equipment; using anti-vibration handles, mounts, tension chains; limited tool usage; providing training or techniques such as tool speed and proper shut off times; and the use of anti-vibration gloves that meet ANSI S2.73.

06.L Indoor Air Quality (IAQ) Management.

06.L.01 Investigations. Supervisors shall report employee concerns or complaints of IAQ problems to the facility manager/owner or other designated representative. That individual will be responsible for investigating and resolving the IAQ complaint in a timely manner and reporting back to the supervisor. For leased facilities, procedures for resolving IAQ issues should ultimately be investigated and resolved by the lessor. An IH or other qualified and competent person shall initiate an IAQ investigation using appropriate guidelines published by ACGIH; AIHA; ANSI; American Society of Heating, Refrigeration, and Air Conditioning Engineers (ASHRAE); EPA; OSHA; NIOSH; or other Federal, DOD, State, local, and host nation requirements. At a minimum the following shall be investigated:

a. Ensure building activities, such as painting, roof repairs, carpet installation and repair and other activities likely to involve usage of chemicals or solvents, are conducted after normal working hours where possible or in a manner that will prevent exposure to occupants.

b. Evaluate condition of the air-handling system for proper operation, make-up air supply, blocked dampers or diffusers, cleanliness of ducts and filters, and standing water or wet areas.

c. Educate employees and supervisors concerning measures they can take to help maintain acceptable IAQ in their work areas. Employees shall be instructed not to make unauthorized modifications to the heating, ventilation, and air conditioning (HVAC) systems (i.e., blocking off vents, removing ceiling tiles).

06.L.02 Environmental tobacco smoke (ETS). Employees shall be protected from involuntary exposure to ETS in working and public living environments.

a. Smoking, to include the use of smokeless cigarettes or cigars, shall be prohibited inside all DoD vehicles, aircraft, vessels, and work buildings.

b. Designated smoking areas only in outdoor locations that are not commonly used or accessed by nonsmokers shall be provided. In accordance with Executive Order 13058, all outside smoking areas shall be a minimum of 25 ft (7.6 m) from building entrances. Before establishing outside smoking area, local ordinances shall be reviewed and most stringent shall apply. Receptacles shall be provided in designated smoking areas for the containment of cigarette butts and other smoking by-products.

c. Designated smoking areas shall be located away from supplied-air intakes and building entryways/egresses to prevent ETS from entering occupied buildings and structures.

06.L.03 Mold Evaluation. Because mold can contribute to health problems ranging from minor irritation to serious debilitation if found in high quantities or improper locations, a mold assessment shall be performed when need is indicated.

a. Assessments/remediation shall be overseen by a competent mold inspector with a minimum of 5 years experience in evaluation of indoor air problems and an understanding both the properties of mold behaviors and building design or construction. This person shall be an IH, microbiologist, or a qualified indoor air specialist or mold inspector who has been certified by an independent IAQ certifying agency and/or who can demonstrate training and experience in the IAQ investigative field. Some states, local authorities and host nations also require this person to be licensed.

b. A visual assessment of potential mold hazards shall be performed, based on criteria in the, U.S. Army Public Health Command TG 278, *Industrial Hygiene Preventive Medicine Mold Assessment Guide*, the EPA *Indoor Air Quality Checklists*, and guidance from AIHA. Bulk and/or air samples are generally not necessary to evaluate mold hazardous environments.

c. A mold assessment shall be written and shall contain the following:

(1) Description of the area assessed including size (footprint), ventilation, and occupancy;

(2) Name and qualifications of the individual completing the assessment;

(3) Any sample results taken, including location of the sample result, date and time of the sample, temperature and humidity at the time of the sample; and laboratory procedure used to analyze the sample;

(4) Drawing of the area showing location of samples, location of visible mold or mildew and the type of substrate it is growing on, ventilation sources in the room, and other information thought to be important;

(5) Potential sources of the moisture which has caused the mold growth;

(6) Recommendations for controlling the problem and remediating the mold.

d. Causes of mold (i.e., water leakages, seepages, drainage, HVAC/ insulation repaired, etc.) shall be addressed before completing mold remediation.

06.L.04 Mold Remediation. If the assessment reveals mold remediation is required, then USAPHC TG 277, *Army Facilities Management Information Document on Mold Remediation Issues,* and any local, state, or host nation guidelines or regulations shall be used.

a. A Mold Remediation Plan shall be written by a competent mold expert and shall include: location and extent of the mold, description of conditions found (i.e. wet or dry), type of materials or 'substrate' that the mold is growing on, whether the substrate will be cleaned or removed, source or problem which created the mold, repair of building structure or component that is the source, and whether the mold contaminated area will be isolated from the remainder of the building and or its occupants. The plan shall also include the steps involved in remediation, identified hazards, recommended controls, equipment and materials (i.e., fungicide used for removal), inspection requirements and worker and occupant training requirements.

b. Mold remediation should not be performed by the same entity that performed the mold assessment.

c. Employees in the immediate area of the mold contamination shall be informed of the remediation, results of any testing, and symptoms of the hazard. The employees shall not be in the area during the remediation.

d. Post-remediation air sampling shall be done in the immediate area and in any areas in the mold spore or vegetative air-pathway and compared to outside air

samples. Mold in areas above drop ceilings with combined air plenums shall have air samples taken within the plenum as well as in air-serviced areas. Air samples should be taken in the immediate area of remediation and analyzed by a laboratory in the AIHA Environmental Microbiology Laboratory Accreditation Program

06.M Control of Chromium (VI) Exposure.

06.M.01 General. All activities which could generate chromium (VI) fumes, mists, or dusts shall be evaluated by an IH to determine potential personnel exposure over the OSHA Chromium (VI) standards. Typical operations where chromium exposures are high include: cutting or breaking up of cement surfaces made from Portland cement with a high chromium content, painting or paint removal operations, welding using rods or wire with a chromium coating, heating or welding on stainless steel, and handling or applying anti-corrosive substances or coatings.

a. The evaluation shall include a risk assessment of the type and frequency of exposure and breathing zone air samples and swipe sampling on surfaces in the work and surrounding area as described in 29 CFR 1910.1026.

b. The evaluation shall be added as an appendix to the APP or the Project SOH Plan. Individual sample results shall be provided to the employee and add to their official occupational health record and a summary of the sample results should be posted in the work area.

06.M.02 To prevent exposure to chromium (VI), the use of paints with chromium pigments, Portland cement with greater than 20 ppm chromium, or chromium/arsenic treated lumber shall be avoided when possible. Should chromium (VI) containing products be required, a justification and similar non-chromium (VI) product evaluation shall be conducted and submitted for review by the GDA or the USACE SOHO.

06.M.03 If chromium containing compounds are used and the objective determination is inconclusive, before air sampling confirms the level of exposure, the employer shall comply with the requirements of 1910.1026, 1915.1026, or 1926.1126, whichever is applicable. At a minimum, employers shall provide appropriate PPE, respirators, decontamination facilities, and a lunch room/area clean from chromium dust and/or fume.

06.M.04 If air sampling confirms chromium (VI) exposure over the OEL, and there is no adequate substitute or work practice change (i.e., use of argon instead of carbon dioxide when arc welding), then the employer shall provide appropriate engineering controls, i.e., local HEPA filtered ventilation systems, medical surveillance, housekeeping, and air sampling

6

as required by the applicable chromium (VI) standard. If adequate engineering controls are not feasible or appropriate due to the length of the task, then PPE shall be provided.

06.M.05 In areas where chromium (VI) is generated or used, there shall be a housekeeping and decontamination program instituted.

a. Employees shall clean all surfaces a minimum of once a day or at the end of the shift that the chromium (VI) dust or fume was generated.

b. At a minimum all exhaust and ventilation systems shall be cleaned and filters changed annually.

c. At a minimum, workers shall remove outer work clothing before eating, drinking, or smoking.

06.N Crystalline Silica.

06.N.01 Occupational Standards.

a. Employee airborne exposure to crystalline silica shall not exceed the 8-hour time weighted average (TWA) OEL.

b. Mandatory requirements.

(1) Employee exposure shall be eliminated through the implementation of feasible engineering controls.

(2) After all such controls are implemented and they do not control to the OEL, each employer must rotate its employees to the extent possible in order to reduce exposure.

(3) When all engineering or administrative controls have been implemented, and the level of respirable silica still exceeds OEL, respirators may be used in accordance with mandatory requirements of Section 5 E. and 29 CFR 1910.134.

(4) Employees shall be trained on the hazards of silica, the controls required to control the potential exposure, any sampling results and work practices to lower their exposure.

06.N.02 Monitoring.

a. Each employer who has workplaces where silica is occupationally produced, reacted, released, transported, stored, handled, or used shall inspect each workplace and work operation to determine if any employee may be exposed to silica at or above the OEL. This evaluation shall be documented in the AHA for the job/task to be completed or PHA for government worker.

b. Air monitoring and analysis. Sampling and analytical methods shall be in accordance with those specified in Section 06.A.

06.N.03 Medical Surveillance. Each employer shall institute a medical surveillance program for all employees who are exposed to airborne concentrations of silica above the OEL for more than 30 days a year. The employer shall provide each employee a medical examination performed by or under the supervision of a licensed physician and shall provide the examination during the employee's normal working hours without cost to the employee. The content of the medical exam shall be determined by the physician based on the exposure records of the employee and guidance provided by NIOSH Standard DHS pub. No 92-102 Aug 1992 or OSHA Instruction CPL 2-2.7 Oct 30, 1972.

a. Medical examinations shall also be made available:

(1) At least annually for each employee exposed to airborne concentrations of silica above the OEL for more than 30 days during the last year; and

(2) Upon notification by the employee that he/she has developed signs or symptoms commonly associated with chronic exposure to silica.

b. Where medical examinations are performed, the employer shall provide the examining physician with the following information:

(1) The reason for the medical examination requested;

(2) A description of the affected employee's duties as they relate to the employee's exposure;

(3) A description of any PPE used or to be used;

(4) The results of the employee's exposure measurements, if available; and

(5) Upon request of the physician, information concerning previous medical examination of the affected employee.

c. Physician's written opinion. The employer shall obtain and furnish the employee with a written opinion from the examining physician containing the following:

(1) The signs or symptoms of silica exposure manifested by the employee, if any;

(2) A report on the findings of any medical tests completed.

(3) The physician's opinion as to whether the employee has any detected medical condition that would place the employee at increased risk of material impairment to the employee's health from exposure to silica or would directly or indirectly aggravate any detected medical condition;

(4) Any recommended limitation upon the employee's exposure to silica or the use of PPE; and

(5) A statement that the employee has been informed by the physician of any medical condition that requires further examination or treatment.

06.N.04 Training. Each employee who may be potentially exposed to silica shall be instructed at the beginning of his/her employment or assignment of potential silica exposure in the following:

a. Relevant symptoms; appropriate emergency procedures; and proper conditions and precautions for safe use or exposure;

b. To advise the employer of the development of the signs and symptoms of prolonged exposure to silica;

c. Specific nature of operations that could result in exposure to silica above the OEL, as well as safe work practices for the release of the silica and the types and function of engineering controls;

d. Proper housekeeping practices;

e. The purpose, proper use, and limitations of respirators;

f. A description of, and explain the purposes for, the medical surveillance program; and

g. The increased risk of impaired health due to the combination of smoking and silica dust exposure.

06.N.05 Respiratory Protection.

a. When the exposure to silica cannot be lowered below the OEL by engineering and administrative controls, an employer shall use respiratory protection.

b. Properly fitted particulate-filter respirators may be used for short, intermittent, or occasional dust exposures such as cleanup, dumping of dust collectors, or unloading shipments of sand at a receiving point when it is not feasible to control the dust by enclosure, exhaust ventilation, wetting, or other means.

06.N.06 Protective Clothing. Where exposure to airborne silica or other substances is above the OEL, work clothing shall be HEPA vacuumed before removal unless it is wet. Clothes shall not be cleaned by blowing or shaking.

06.N.07 Housekeeping.

a. To prevent the dispersal of silica dust, all exposed surfaces shall be maintained free of accumulation of silica dust.

b. Dry sweeping and the use of compressed air for the cleaning of floors and other surfaces shall be prohibited. If vacuuming is used the exhaust air shall be HEPA filtered to prevent generation of airborne respirable silica concentrations. Gentle wash down of surfaces is preferred.

c. Emphasis shall be placed upon preventive maintenance and repair of equipment, proper storage of dust producing materials, and collection of dusts containing silica. Sanitation shall meet the requirements of 29 CFR 1910.141.

06.N.08 Personal Hygiene Facilities and Practices. All food, beverages, tobacco products, nonfood chewing products, and unapplied cosmetics shall be discouraged in work areas.

06.N.09 Engineering Controls.

a. Dust suppression. Moisture, mists, fogs, etc., shall be added where such addition can substantially reduce the exposure to airborne respirable silica dust.

b. Ventilation. Where a local exhaust ventilation and collection system is used in a building, it shall be designed and maintained to prevent the accumulation or recirculation of airborne silica dust into the workplace. The system shall be inspected periodically. Adequate measures shall be taken to ensure that any discharge will not produce health hazards to the outside environment.

c. Additional control measures. When mobile equipment is operated in areas of potential silica exposure, engineering controls shall be provided to protect the operator from such exposure.

06.N.10 Itinerant Work. When employees are exposed to airborne silica at temporary work sites away from the primary worksite, emphasis shall be placed on respiratory protection, protective clothing, portable engineering controls, and provisions for personal hygiene and sanitation. Training of employees shall be provided to protect them as well as others from airborne silica dust exposure.

THIS PAGE INTENTIONALLY LEFT BLANK

SECTION 7 Lighting

Table of Contents

7

07.A General. Proper illumination of work spaces, project sites, roadways and vessels is imperative to a safe working environment. It is of significant importance in safe vehicular operation and the prevention of slips and falls. The lighting standards provided in this section are minimal standards. This section is applicable to both contractor and government operations.

07.A.01 A review of the lighting requirements for specific tasks or operations shall be evaluated as part of the activity hazard analysis (AHA).

07.A.02 Lamps and fixtures will be guarded and secured to preclude injury to personnel. Open fluorescent fixtures will be provided with wire guards, lenses, tube guards and locks, or safety sockets that require force in the horizontal axis to remove the lamp.

07.A.03 Lamps for general illumination shall be protected from accidental contact or breakage.

a. Protection shall be provided by elevation of at least 7 ft (2.1 m) from normal working surface, suitable fixture or lamp holder with a guard.

b. Fixtures may be no closer than 18 in (0.5 m) to overhead sprinkler systems, if the building is so equipped, per NFPA Standards.

c. Open fluorescent fixtures will be provided with wire guards, lenses, tube guards or other means to prevent damage to the bulb.

07.A.04 Generator-powered portable lighting units shall be grounded in accordance with manufacturer's instructions. In addition, a survey of the area to be lighted will be conducted and documented to ensure overhead power lines do not pose a hazard.

07.A.05 For temporary lighting, see Section 11.E.06.

07.B Lighting Levels.

07.B.01 While work is in progress, offices, facilities, accessways, working areas, construction roads, etc., shall be lighted by at least the minimum light intensities specified in Table 7-1. Illumination readings shall be taken and recorded whenever proper lighting of an area is in question. A calibrated light meter shall be provided, maintained and used as necessary to provide illumination readings.

07.B.02 Office lighting shall be a minimum of 50 foot -candles (lm/ft2) or 540 luminance (lx) at the working surface, in accordance with the Illuminating Engineering Society of North America (IESNA) Handbook, RP-1. In office areas, attention shall be paid to the control of glare.

07.B.03 Roadway lighting shall be in accordance with IESNA RP-8.

07.B.04 Marine lighting shall be in accordance with American Bureau of Shipping, *Guide for Crew Habitability on Ships.*

07.B.05 Means of egress.

a. Means of egress shall be illuminated, with emergency and non-emergency lighting, to provide a minimum of 5 lm/ft^2, (55 lx), measured at the floor. > *Reference IESNA Handbook.*

b. The illumination shall be arranged so that the failure of any single lighting unit, including the burning out of an electric bulb, will not leave any area darkened to the point of impeding the means of egress.

07.B.06 If work is to be performed at night, a night operations lighting plan shall be developed to ensure that all activities, areas and operations are adequately illuminated to perform work safely. On-task lighting shall be in conformance with Table 7-1. Lighting near roadways and other public transportation areas shall be positioned as to avoid creating a glare hazard.

TABLE 7-1

Minimum Lighting Requirements

Facility or Function	Lux	Foot Candles (lm/ft2)
Accessways		
- general indoor	55	5
- general outdoor	33	3
- exitways, walkways, ladders, stairs	110	10
Administrative areas (offices, drafting and meeting rooms, etc.)	540	50
Chemical laboratories	540	50
Construction areas		
- general indoor	55	5
- general outdoor	33	3
- tunnels and general underground work areas (min 110 lux required at tunnel/shaft heading during drilling, mucking, and scaling)	55	5
Conveyor routes	110	10
Dam Operating Areas (Interior)		
-Tunnels and underground work areas	55	5
-Control Stations	150	15
Docks and loading platforms	33	3
Elevators, freight and passenger	50	5
Temporary Electrical Panels (Interior)	300	30
Temporary Electrical Panels (Exterior)	50	10
First-aid stations and infirmaries	300	30
Maintenance/operating areas/shops		
- vehicle maintenance shop	300	30
- carpentry shop	110	10
- refueling area, outdoors	55	5
- shops, fine - medium detail work	540-325	50-30
- welding shop	300	30
Mechanical/electrical equipment rooms	110	10
Outdoor parking areas	33	3
Toilets, wash, and dressing rooms	110	10
Visitor areas	215	20
Warehouses and storage rooms/areas		
- indoor rack storage	270	25
- outdoor storage	33	3
Work areas – general (not listed above)	325	30

7

THIS PAGE INTENTIONALLY LEFT BLANK

SECTION 8 Accident Prevention Signs, Tags, Labels, Signals, Piping System Identification and Traffic Control

Table of Contents

8

08.A Signs, Tags, Labels and Piping Systems.

08.A.01 Signs, tags, and labels shall be provided to give adequate warning and caution of hazards. They are provided to instruct and direct workers and the public.

08.A.02 All warning systems such as signs, tags, and labels shall be visible at all times when the hazard or problem exists, and shall be removed or covered when the hazard or problem no longer exists.

08.A.03 All employees shall be informed as to the meaning of the various signs, tags, and labels used throughout the workplace and any special precautions that may be required.

08.A.04 The safety and occupational health (SOH) related signs in the USACE Sign Standards Manual (EP 310-1-6a) have been determined to meet or exceed ANSI and/or OSHA requirements. USACE facilities shall use signs based upon the specifications in the USACE Sign Manual at permanent USACE-owned and USACE-operated sites. USACE employees and contractors may opt to use signs meeting either the OSHA or ANSI standards for temporary use during the life of a project.

08.A.05 Signs, Tags, Placards, Labels, and Piping Systems shall meet or exceed the following standards:

a. USACE *Graphic Standards Manual*, EP 310-1-6;

b. USACE Sign Standards Manual, Volume 1, EP 310-1-6a;

c. 29 CFR 1910.145; Specifications for Accident Prevention Signs and Tags;

d. 29 CFR 1926.200; Accident Prevention Signs and Tags;

e. ANSI/IEEE C95.2;

f. ANSI Z136.1;

g. ANSI Z535.1;

h. ANSI Z535.2;

i. ANSI Z535.5;

j. ANSI/ASME A13.1; and

k. DOT Federal Highway Administration, Manual on Uniform Traffic Control Devices for Streets and Highways (MUTCD).

08.A .06 The type of sign or tag used in a particular situation shall be appropriate for the degree of hazard or intent of message. The workplace safety signs with *Danger* and *Caution* headings have standard legends that must be used exactly as shown in the USACE Sign Standards Manual. If a sign with a unique legend not appearing on pages 114 to 11-7 or in the UNICOR catalog is needed, the procedures detailed on page 1-13 should be followed. The sign legend shall be concise, easy to read and should contain enough information to be easily understood. > *See Figure 8-1 for Sign and Tag Signal Word Headings, Figure 8-2 for Example Tag Layout, Figure 8-3 for Example Sign Layout, Table 8-1 for Accident Prevention Sign Requirements.*

a. Danger Signs. Danger signs must conform to the following requirements:

(1) Danger signs will be used only when the circumstances indicate an imminently hazardous situation that, if not avoided, will result in death or serious injury.

(2) Signal word.

(a) USACE Standard: The signal word "Danger" is white on a red background at the top of the sign.

(b) ANSI Alternate Standard: Danger signs must have the signal word "DANGER" in white letters placed at the top of a rectangular safety red background placed at the top of the sign. The safety alert symbol shall precede the signal word. The base of symbol shall be on the same horizontal level as the base of the letters of the signal word - the height equaling or exceeding the signal word height. > *See Figure 8-1.*

(c) OSHA Alternate Standard: As an alternative, Danger Signs may have "DANGER" in white letters on a safety red oval background with a white border on a black rectangular field. This distinctive panel shall appear in the uppermost portion of the sign. No other signal word or symbol shall be used within this distinctive shape and color arrangement.

(3) The message panel.

(a) USACE Standard: For workplace safety signs the lettering describing the specific danger is black letters on a white background. On other approved Danger Signs, the message is white lettering on a red background.

(b) OSHA or ANSI Alternate Standard: The lettering shall be black letters on a white background or white letters on a black background and the symbol/pictorial panel, if used, shall be square with a black safety red, or black and safety red symbol on a white background.

b. Warning Signs. Warning signs must conform to the following requirements:

(1) Signs may be used only when the circumstances indicate a potentially hazardous situation that, if not avoided, **could** result in death or serious injury. The hazards may be the same as those associated with Danger signs but are of significantly less magnitude.

(2) Signal Word

(a) USACE Standard: On approved Warning Safety signs the signal word "Warning" appears in black lettering on an orange background under a black top border. There are no Warning workplace safety signs in the Corps system.

(b) ANSI Standard: Warning signs must have the signal word "WARNING" in black letters on a rectangular orange background placed at the top of the sign. The safety alert symbol shall precede the signal word. The base of symbol shall be on the same horizontal level as the base of the letters of the signal word – the height equaling or exceeding the signal word height. > See Figure 8-1.

(c) OSHA Standard Alternative: As an alternative, Warning Signs may have the signal word "WARNING" in black lettering within a safety orange truncated diamond on a black rectangular background. The distinctive panel shall be located at the uppermost portion of the sign. No other word or symbol shall be used within this distinctive shape or color arrangement.

(3) The message panel.

(a) USACE Standard: On approved Warning signs the message panel shall be in black lettering on an orange background.

(b) OSHA or ANSI Alternate Standard: The message panel shall be in black lettering on a white background or white lettering on a black background. The message may, as an alternative, be in black letters on a safety orange background. The symbol/pictorial panel, if used, shall be square with a black symbol on a white background. The symbol panel used as an alternative may be square with a black symbol on an orange background.

c. Caution Signs. Caution signs must conform to the following requirements:

(1) Caution signs may be used only when circumstances indicate a potentially hazardous

situation that, if not avoided, may result in a minor or moderate injury. It may also be used to alert against unsafe practices that may result in property damage. The hazards may be the same as those associated with Danger signs but are of significantly less magnitude.

(2) Signal Word

(a) USACE Standard: On Workplace Safety Signs the word "Caution" appears in yellow lettering on black bar at the top of the yellow message panel. On other approved Caution Safety Signs the signal word "Caution" appears in black lettering on a yellow background under a black top border.

(b) Alternate ANSI Standard: Caution signs must have the signal word "CAUTION" in black lettering on a rectangular yellow background placed at the top of the sign. The safety alert symbol shall precede the signal word if the hazard is a potential personal injury hazard. (The alert symbol is not used when the situation is used to indicate property damage hazards.) The base of the symbol shall be on the same horizontal level as the base of the letters of the signal word – the height shall equal or exceed the signal word height. > See Figure 8-1.

(c) Alternate OSHA Standard: As an alternative, caution signs may have the signal word "CAUTION" in safety yellow letters within a black rectangular background, and this distinctive panel shall be located in the uppermost portion of the sign. No other signal word or symbol shall be used with this distinctive color or signal shape arrangement.

(3) Message Panel.

(a) USACE Standard: The descriptive legend appears in black lettering on a yellow panel.

(b) OSHA or ANSI Alternate Standard: The message panel shall be in black lettering on a white background or white lettering on a black background. The message may, as an alternative, be in black lettering on a safety yellow background. The symbol/pictorial panel, if used, shall be square with a black symbol on a white background. As an alternative, it may be square with a black symbol on a safety yellow background.

d. Notice Signs. Notice signs should conform to the following requirements:

(1) Notice signs may be used to indicate a statement of company policy directly or indirectly related to the safety of personnel or protection of property. The signal word should not be associated directly with a hazard or hazardous situation, and shall not be used

in place of "DANGER", "WARNING", or "CAUTION." These signs are used to control or define access and circulation. They are used primarily for information and are not placed to identify a hazard.

(2) Notice signs shall have the signal word "NOTICE" in white lettering on a safety blue background on a rectangular field, and this distinctive panel shall be located in the uppermost portion of the visual alerting device. No other signal word or symbol shall be used within this distinctive shape and color arrangement.

(3) Message panel.

(a) General Standards for Workplace: The message shall be in safety blue or black letters on a white background. The symbol/pictorial panel, if used, shall be square with a safety blue or black symbol on a white background.

(b) USACE Alternative for Outdoor Use: Notice signs posted on USACE managed property for public viewing in areas accessible to the public, including recreation areas, may have white letters on blue background. Text for these custom signs shall be approved by the District Sign Manager. Other signs used to define access and use may include prohibition symbol signs or Restricted Area signs.

e. General Safety Signs: General safety signs should conform to the following requirements:

(1) General safety signs may be used to indicate general instructions relative to safe work practices, remind of proper safety procedures or indicate the location of safety equipment. These signs identify rules and facilities relating to health, first aid, medical equipment, sanitation, housekeeping practice and general safety information.

(2) Legend Panel: White signal word "SAFETY" on safety green header with black text on white panel.

f. Fire Safety Signs. Fire safety signs shall conform to the following requirements:

(1) Fire safety signs may be used to indicate the location of emergency firefighting equipment. Fire extinguisher signs shall be placed where fire extinguishers are not visible from designated exit pathways. > See NFPA 10 D2.2.2.

(2) These signs do not have a signal word.

(3) The message panel shall be in safety red letters on a white background in either a square or rectangular field. The symbol/pictorial panel, if used, shall be safety red on white or white on safety red.

g. Directional Arrow Signs: Directional arrow flow signs should conform to the following requirements:

(1) Directional arrow signs may be used to indicate the direction to emergency equipment, safety equipment, and other locations important to safety.

(2) Directional signs that relate to accident prevention use a format similar to all other Workplace Safety signs. The header shall have white lettering on a black rectangular background. The arrow symbol shall be in black lettering on a white background.

h. Colors. Color coding shall be in accordance with Table 8-2 of this manual. Color specifications for Corps safety signs are found in the USACE Sign Standards Manual.

i. Piping systems shall be identified. The identification of piping systems (including pipes, fittings, valves, and pipe coverings) shall be in accordance with Table 8-3 of this manual and comply with ANSI/ASME A13.1 color scheme and directional flow requirements.

j. The RF radiation hazard-warning symbol specified in Figure 8-4 of this manual shall be used in the identification of RF radiation hazards.

k. Laser caution and warning signs shall be in accordance with ANSI Z136.1. > See Figures 8-5 and 8-6.

l. Ionizing radiation warning signs, labels, and signals shall contain the symbol shown in Figure 8-7 of this manual. > See Section 06.F for posting requirements.

m. Vehicles or equipment that, by design, move at 25 mph (40 km/h) or less on public roads shall display the slow-moving vehicle emblem. > See Figure 8-8.

08.A.07 Safety sign finishes shall be of durable materials with colors in accordance with the USACE Signs Standards Manual, or ANSI Z535.1.

08.A.08 Safety signs shall be placed to alert and inform the viewer in sufficient time to take appropriate evasive actions to avoid potential harm from the hazard. They shall be legible, non- distracting, and not hazardous in themselves. They shall be fabricated with retro-reflective sheeting as appropriate for adequate visibility under normal and emergency operating conditions.

08.A.09 Each container of hazardous material shall be labeled, tagged or marked with the identity of the material(s), appropriate hazard warnings, potential health effects and the name and address of the manufacturer, importer or other responsible party. > *See 06.B.01.*

a. Signs, placards, process sheets, batch tickets, operating procedures, or other written means may be used in lieu of affixing labels to stationary process containers if the alternative method identifies the containers to which it is applicable and conveys the information required above. The written information shall be readily available to employees in their work area throughout each work shift.

b. Portable containers into which hazardous material(s) are transferred from labeled containers and which are intended only for the immediate use by the employee who performs the transfer are not required to be labeled. However, there shall be a means of indicating that the hazardous material has been used in the container.

08.A.10 Signs, tags and labels shall be located as close as safely possible to their respective hazards. Tags will be affixed by a positive means (such as wire, string, or adhesive) that prevents their loss or unintentional removal.

08.A.11 Signs, tags, and labels shall be legible and in English.

a. In areas where a significant percentage of the workforce or the visiting population speaks primarily in a foreign language, the use of symbol signs is strongly encouraged. > *See USACE Sign Standards Manual, Section 8.*

b. When no symbols exist or where words are essential, two signs - one in English and one in the foreign language - should be placed side by side.

c. These signs will follow the same format: same overall size, letter size and style, color, and mounting.

d. Because of variations in dialect, the legends on non-English signs shall be developed at the local level.

e. Two languages should never appear on the same sign. > *See 01.A.05.*

08.A.12 Signs shall be furnished with rounded or blunt corners and shall be free from sharp edges, burrs, splinters, or other sharp projections. The ends or heads of bolts or other fastening devices shall be located so that they are not a hazard.

08.A.13 Construction areas shall be posted with legible traffic signs at points of hazard in accordance with the MUTCD.

08.A.14 Signs required to be seen at night shall be reflectorized.

08.A.15 Accident prevention tags shall be used only as a temporary means of warning employees of an existing hazard (i.e., defective tools, equipment, caution orders and tags for hazardous energy control). > *See Figure 8-9; See Section 12 for lockout/tagout requirements.*

08.A.16 Tags shall contain a signal word (either "DANGER" or "CAUTION") and a major message (presented in either pictographs, written text, or both) to indicate the specific hazardous condition or the instruction to be communicated to the employee. The signal word shall be readable at a minimum distance of 5 ft (1.5 m) or such greater distance as warranted by the hazard. The signal word and major message shall be understandable to all employees who may be exposed to the hazard. > *See 08.A.06 for basic design criteria.*

08.A.17 Accident prevention tags shall be rectangular in shape and shall be no smaller than 3 in x 5 in (8 cm x 13 cm). The corners may be square cut, chamfered, or rounded.

08.A.18 Kerosene lamps and open flame pots shall not be used for, or with, warning signs or devices.

08.A.19 Warning signs shall be placed on unattended government-owned floating plant and land-based heavy equipment accessible to the public and shall read "No Trespassing – U.S. Government Property".

08.B Signal Systems, Personnel and Procedures.

08.B.01 A standard signal system shall be used on all operations.

a. Hand signals for crane operations shall conform to ANSI/ASME B30 series. > *See Figure 16-1.*

b. Traffic flagging procedures shall be in accordance with the DOT Federal Highway Administration's MUTCD.

c. For Marine signals, see Section 19 of this manual.

d. For helicopter hand signals, see Section 16.P of this manual.

08.B.02 Standard hand signals shall be posted at the operator's position, signal control points and other points as necessary to inform those concerned.

08.B.03 Manual (hand) signals may be used when the distance between the operator and signal person is not more than 100 ft (30.5 m). Radio, telephone, or a visual and audible electrically-operated system shall be used

8

when the distance between operator and signal person is more than 100 ft or when they cannot see each other.

08.B.04 A signal person shall be provided when the point of operation (includes area of load travel and area immediately surrounding the load placement) is not in full view of the vehicle, machine, or equipment operator; when vehicles are backed more than 100 ft (30.5 m); when terrain is hazardous; or when two or more vehicles are backing up in the same area.

> ➢Note: This applies to all equipment operations covered in Section 18.

08.B.05 A flag person or other controls shall be provided when operations or equipment on or next to a highway create a traffic hazard. An exception shall be made only when an adequate mechanical signaling or control device is provided for safe direction of the operation.

08.B.06 Where manual (hand) signals are used, only one person shall be designated to give signals to the operator. This signal person shall be located to see the load and be clearly visible to the operator at all times.

08.B.07 Flag signaling shall be accomplished by use of red flags at least 18 in (45.7 cm) square or sign paddles. In periods of darkness, red lights shall be used.

08.B.08 High visibility apparel shall be worn by flag and signal persons. > *See Section 05.F.*

08.B.09 Signal systems shall be protected against unauthorized use, breakage, weather, or interference; any malfunction shall be cause to stop all work.

08.B.10 Only persons who are competent and qualified by experience and/or training with the operations being directed shall be used as signal persons.

08.B.11 Signal persons shall back one vehicle at a time. While under control of a signal person, the driver shall not back or maneuver until directed and the driver shall stop when visual contact with the signal person is lost.

> ➢Note: This applies to operations covered in Section 18.

08.B.12 The signal person shall have a warning device of clear range and penetrating sound to warn persons when the load is coming in so they have time to get in the clear.

> ➢Note: This applies to operations covered in Section 18.

08.C Traffic Control.

08.C.01 Traffic control shall be accomplished in accordance with DOT Federal Highway Administration's MUTCD.

08.C.02 The Contractor shall conduct his operations in such a manner as to offer the least possible obstruction to the safe and satisfactory movement of traffic over the existing roads during the life of the contract.

08.C.03 The Contractor shall be responsible for providing, erecting, maintaining, and removing all traffic signs, barricades, and other traffic control devices necessary for maintenance of traffic.

08.C.04 All barricades, warning signs, lights, temporary signals, other devices, flagmen, and signaling devices shall meet or exceed the minimum requirements of the local DOT requirements.

08.C.05 Prior to the commencement of contract operations, the Contractor shall submit for acceptance the complete details of the proposed traffic control plan for the maintenance of traffic and access through the contract work area.

08.C.06 The Contractor shall coordinate with the GDA and obtain approval and any required permits from local authorities prior to closing or restricting any roads.

08.C.07 Barricades, danger, warning and detour signs, as required, shall be erected before any roads are closed.

a. When roads are temporarily closed to public access, barricades or gates shall be used that are highly visible in day or night conditions. At a minimum, barriers shall be coated with reflective paint or be applied with highly reflective tape on both sides, and be signed as "ROAD CLOSED".

b. Affected roads shall also be posted with appropriate warning signs a minimum of 100 ft (30.5 m) before the barrier per W 20-3, DNG-11, W RN-24, or other appropriate signs from the MUTCD or USACE Sign Standards Manual. Size and placement of signs depends on viewing distance and speed limit of roadway.

FIGURE 8-1
Sign and Tag Signal Word Headings

USACE	ANSI	OSHA
WARNING Warning	⚠ **WARNING** Warning	**WARNING** Warning
DANGER Danger	⚠ **DANGER** Danger	**DANGER** Danger
CAUTION Caution - Workplace Safety	⚠ **CAUTION** Caution	**CAUTION** Caution
CAUTION Caution - Undesignated Safety		
SAFETY Safety		
NOTICE Notice		

8

FIGURE 8-2
Example Tag Layout

TABLE 8-1
Accident Prevention Sign Requirements

TYPE	PURPOSE	DESIGN
DANGER	Indicates a specific immediate and grave danger, a hazard capable of producing irreversible damage or injury, and prohibition against harmful activity.	Layout as shown in Fig 8-1. Shall have "DANGER" in white letters at top of rectangular safety red background placed at top of sign. Safety alert symbol shall precede signal word. Base of symbol shall be on same horizontal level as base of letters of signal word- height equaling or exceeding signal word height. Alternate OSHA or ANSI requirement calls for lettering to be black letters on white background or white letters on black background and symbol/pictorial panel, if used, shall be square with black safety red, or black and safety red symbol on a white background. The USACE standard requires that the specific danger be described in black letters on a white background. On other approved Danger signs, the message is white lettering on a red background.
CAUTION	Call attention to a specific potential hazard capable of resulting in severe, but not irreversible, injury or damage.	Layout as shown in Fig 8-1. Shall have "CAUTION" in yellow on black background and lower panel for additional sign wording in black on a yellow background.
GENERAL SAFETY	Includes notices of general practice and rules relating to health, first aid, medical equipment, sanitation, housekeeping, and general safety.	Layout as shown in Fig 8-1 or consisting of single panel. Shall have appropriate keyword as signal word in white on a green background in the upper panel and a lower panel for additional sign wording or symbols in black or green on a white background. Alternatively, the entire sign may be white letters on a green background.
FIRE AND EMERGENCY	Used only to label or points the way to fire extinguishing equipment, fires escapes and exits, gas shutoff valves, sprinkler drains, and emergency procedures.	Layout as shown in Fig 8-1 or consisting of a single red panel. Shall have the appropriate keyword as the signal word in white on a red background in the upper panel and a lower panel for additional sign wording or symbols in red on a white background. Alternatively, the entire sign may be white letters on a red background.
INFORMATION	Provide information of a general nature, such as designation of facilities or services, in order to avoid confusion or misunderstanding.	Layout as shown in Fig 8-1 or consisting of a single panel. Should have signal word "NOTICE" in white on blue background in upper panel and lower panel for additional wording or symbols in blue or black on a white background OR entire sign may be white letters on blue background.
EXIT	Used to indicate exits.	Lettered in legible letters, not less than 6 in (15.2 cm) high, on white field. The principal stroke of letters shall be at least 3/4 in (5.1 cm) in width.

TABLE 8-2
Accident Prevention Color Coding

COLOR	PURPOSE
Red	Red shall be the color used for identifying dangerous conditions, emergency controls, fire detection equipment and fire suppression systems, and containers of flammable liquids.
Orange	Orange shall be the color used for designating dangerous parts of machines and energized equipment. Orange shall also be used for temporary traffic control signs in construction zones.
Yellow	Yellow shall be the color for designating conditions requiring caution, marking dangerous chemicals, marking physical hazards, and markings for ionizing radiation.
Green	Green shall be the color for designating safety equipment and operator devices and the location of first-aid and safety equipment (other than firefighting equipment).
Blue	Blue shall be the color used for designating information of a non-safety nature.
Purple	Purple shall be the color used to designate ionizing radiation hazards.

8

FIGURE 8-3
Example Sign Layout

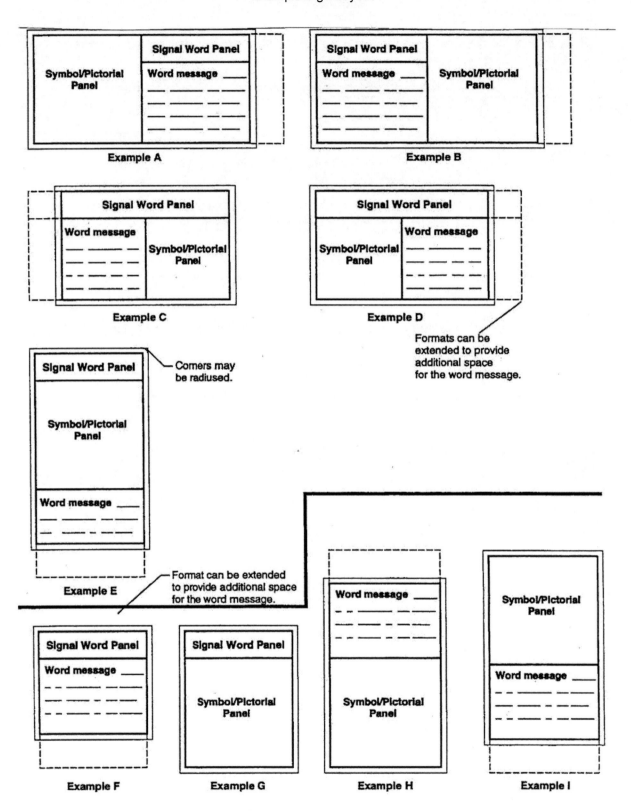

TABLE 8-3

Identification of Piping Systems

Outside diameter of pipe or covering	Length of color field "A"	Size of letters "B"
3/4 to 1 1/4 inches	8 inches	1/2 inch
1 1/2 to 2 inches	8 inches	3/4 inch
2 1/2 to 6 inches	12 inches	1 1/4 inch
8 to 10 inches	24 inches	2 1/2 inch
over 10 inches	32 inches	2 1/2 inch

8

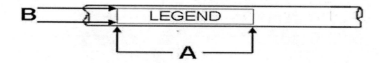

FIGURE 8-4

Radio Frequency Warning Symbol

D = scaling unit

Lettering: ratio of letter height to thickness of letter lines

Upper triangle: 5 to 1 = large
                       6 to 1 = medium

Lower triangle: 4 to 1 = small
                       6 to 1 = medium

Symbol is square; triangles are right-angle isosceles.

FIGURE 8-5

Laser Caution Sign

FIGURE 8-6
Laser Warning Sign

FIGURE 8-7

Radiological Warning Symbol

1. Cross-hatched area is to be magenta or purple.
2. Background is to be yellow.

FIGURE 8-8

Slow-Moving Vehicle Emblem

NOTE: All dimensions are in inches

FIGURE 8-9

Accident Prevention Tags

Keyword/Phrase	Keyword/Phrase Print Color	Background Color	Tag Color
"DANGER"	White in red oval	Black	White
"CAUTION"	Yellow	Black	Yellow
"DO NOT OPERATE	White	Red	White
"OUT OF ORDER"	White	Black	White
"DO NOT USE"			
Informational message or inspection	Black or green	N/A	Green & white OR White & black

8

THIS PAGE INTENTIONALLY LEFT BLANK

SECTION 9 Fire Prevention and Protection

Table of Contents

9

09.A General.

09.A.01 A fire prevention plan shall be developed for all USACE facilities and project sites. > *For Construction operations see NFPA 241; for Marine operations see Section 19.A.04.*

a. It shall include, as a minimum: A list of the major workplace fire hazards; potential ignition sources; the types of fire suppression equipment or systems appropriate to the control of fire; assignments of responsibilities for maintaining the equipment and systems; personnel responsible for controlling the fuel source hazards; and housekeeping procedures, including the removal of waste materials.

b. It shall be used to brief employees and emergency first responders on the fire hazards, the materials and processes to which they are exposed, and the emergency evacuation procedures.

09.A.02 An annual survey of the suitability and effectiveness of fire prevention and protection measures and facilities at each project or installation shall be made by a qualified person. Records of the survey findings and recommendations shall be retained on file at the project or installation.

09.A.03 When unusual fire hazards exist or fire emergencies develop, additional protection shall be provided as required by the GDA.

09.A.04 The GDA shall survey all activities and determine which require a hot work permit. All hot work and hot work permits shall conform to local policy, when present.

a. Hot work permits shall be required when performing activities which generate or have the potential to generate, heat, sparks, or open flames, such as abrasive blasting, burning, brazing, cutting, grinding, powder-actuated tools, hot riveting, soldering, thawing activities, welding, or any similar operation capable of initiating fires or explosions.

b. Areas shall be surveyed prior to performing any hot work to ensure they are free of fire hazards and to determine if a fire watch is required.

c. Fire watches shall be conducted in accordance with Sections 09.K.01 and 09.K.03.

d. A fully charged fire extinguisher, minimum 10 lbs, shall be readily available in the immediate area of the hot work.

e. Hot work permits shall include date(s) authorized for hot work and identify the objects on which the hot work is to be performed. The permit shall be kept on file until the completion of the hot work.

f. Hot work is prohibited in the following areas:

(1) In areas not authorized by GDA;

(2) In sprinklered buildings while such protection is impaired, unless equivalent protection is provided for the hot work and approved by the GDA;

(3) In the presence of explosive atmospheres, areas where an explosive atmosphere may develop, or where there is an accumulation of combustible dust;

(4) In area near the storage of large quantities of exposed, readily ignitable materials such as bulk sulfur, baled paper, or cotton.

g. See NFPA 51B, *Fire Prevention During Welding, Cutting, and Other Hot Work* for a sample hot work permit and further information. *See also Sections 09.E and 10.D.*

09.A.05 Fires and open flame devices shall not be left unattended.

09.A.06 All sources of ignition shall be prohibited within 50 ft (15.2 m) of operations with a potential fire hazard. The area shall be conspicuously and legibly posted "NO SMOKING, MATCHES, or OPEN FLAME."

09.A.07 Smoking shall be prohibited in all areas where flammable, combustible, or oxidizing materials are stored. "NO SMOKING, MATCHES, or OPEN FLAME" signs will be posted in all prohibited areas.

09.A.08 Areas where there is danger of underground fire shall not be used for the storage of flammable or combustible materials.

09.A.09 A barrier having a fire resistance rating equivalent to a listing of at least 1 hour shall segregate DOT-identified non-compatible materials that may create a fire hazard. > *See Section 20.D for compressed gas cylinders.*

09.A.10 A good housekeeping program that provides for prompt removal and disposal of accumulations of combustible scrap and debris shall be implemented on the site. Self-closing containers shall be used to collect waste saturated with flammable liquids. Only non-combustible or UL labeled nonmetallic containers may be used to dispose of waste and rubbish.

09.A.11 Measures must be taken to control the growth of tall grass, brush, and weeds adjacent to facilities. A break of at least 3 ft (0.9 m) shall be maintained around all facilities.

09.A.12 Paint-soiled clothing and drop cloths, when not in use, shall be stored in well ventilated steel cabinets or containers.

09.A.13 Disposal of combustible waste materials shall be in compliance with applicable fire and environmental laws and regulations.

09.A.14 Burning operations.

a. Burning areas shall be established in coordination with the GDA and with the agency responsible for monitoring fire potential at the location of the proposed burning area.

b. Burning operations shall be in compliance with Federal, State, and local regulations and guidelines.

c. A sufficient force to control and patrol the burning operations shall be maintained until the last embers have been extinguished.

d. Bump blocks shall be provided where trucks back to a fire or burning pit.

e. Prescribed burning activities for natural resource management shall be conducted in accordance with guidelines set forth in Section 09.K.

09.A.15 Low-density fiberboard, combustible insulation, or vapor barriers with a flame spread rating greater than 25 shall not be installed in permanent buildings.

09.A.16 Temporary enclosures shall be covered with flame- resistant tarpaulins or material of equivalent fire-resistant characteristics.

09.A.17 When outside help is relied upon for fire protection, a written agreement shall be made, or a memorandum of record, stating the terms of the arrangement and the details for fire protection services, and shall be provided to the GDA.

09.A.18 Temporary building spacing shall be in accordance with the International Building Code (IBC).

09.A.19 Fire lanes providing access to all areas shall be established and maintained free of obstruction.

09.A.20 Vehicles, equipment, materials, and supplies shall not be placed so that access to fire hydrants and other firefighting equipment is obstructed.

09.A.21 Hazardous locations.

a. Electrical lighting shall be the only means of artificial illumination in areas where flammable liquids, vapors, fumes, dust, or gases are present.

b. All electrical equipment and installations in hazardous locations shall be in accordance with the National Electrical Code (NEC) for hazardous locations.

c. Globes or lamps shall not be removed or replaced nor shall repairs be made on the electrical circuit until it has been de-energized.

d. Miners' lights and flashlights used around explosives, and in atmospheres likely to contain explosive vapors, dusts, or gases shall be approved by a private sector organization recognized by OSHA under the Nationally Recognized Testing Laboratory Program.

09.A.22 Sufficient clearance shall be maintained around lights and heating units to prevent ignition of combustible materials.

09.A.23 All combustibles shall be shielded from the flames of torches used to cut or sweat pipe.

09.A.24 Precautions shall be taken to protect formwork and scaffolding from exposure to, and spread of, fire.

09.A.25 Fire protection in the construction process.

a. Fire cut-offs shall be retained in buildings undergoing alterations or demolition until operations require their removal.

b. Where a water distribution system is required for the protection of buildings or other structures, water mains and hydrants shall be installed before or concurrent with the construction of facilities. Until the permanent system is in operation, an equivalent temporary system shall be provided.

c. Permanent (fixed) extinguishing equipment and water supply for fire protection shall be installed and in operable condition as soon as possible. The scheduling of sprinkler installation shall closely follow the building construction and, following completion of each story, shall be placed in service as soon as possible.

d. During demolition or alterations, existing automatic sprinkler systems shall be retained in service as long as reasonable. Modification of sprinkler systems to permit alterations or additional demolition should be expedited so that the system may be returned to service as quickly as possible. Sprinkler control valves shall be checked daily at close of work to ascertain that the protection is in service. The operation of sprinkler

9

control valves is permitted only when approved by the GDA.

e. During the construction process, the construction of fire walls and exit stairways required for completed buildings shall have priority; fire doors, with automatic closing devices, shall be hung on openings as soon as practical.

09.A.26 Water supply and distribution facilities for fire fighting shall be provided and maintained in accordance with NFPA recommendations.

09.A.27 Recommendations of the NFPA shall be complied with in situations not covered in this section. Where local building codes are established, the more stringent requirements shall apply.

09.B Flammable Liquids.

09.B.01 All storage, handling, and use of flammable liquids shall be in accordance with NFPA 30, NFPA 30A, or other applicable standards under the supervision of a qualified person.

09.B.02 All sources of ignition shall be prohibited in areas where flammable liquids are stored, handled, and processed. Suitable "NO SMOKING, MATCHES, or OPEN FLAME" signs shall be posted in all such areas.

09.B.03 Fire protection requirements.

a. At least one portable fire extinguisher rated 20-B:C shall be provided on all tank trucks or other vehicles used for transporting and/or dispensing flammable liquids.

b. Each service or refueling area shall be provided with at least one fire extinguisher rated not less than 40-B:C and located so that an extinguisher shall be within 100 ft (30.4 m) of each pump, dispenser, underground fill pipe opening, and lubrication or service area.

09.B.04 Category 1 or 2 flammable liquids or Category 3 flammable liquids with a flashpoint below 100°F (37.8°C) shall be kept in closed containers or tanks when not in use.

09.B.05 Workers shall guard carefully against any part of their clothing becoming contaminated with flammable fluids. They shall not be allowed to continue work if their clothing becomes contaminated, and they must remove or wet down the clothing as soon as possible.

09.B.06 No flammable liquid with a flash point (closed cup test) below 100°F (37.8°C) shall be used for cleaning purposes or to start or rekindle fires.

09.B.07 Ventilation adequate to prevent the accumulation of flammable vapors to hazardous levels shall be provided in all areas where flammable liquids are handled or used.

09.B.08 Only labeled/listed (by a nationally-recognized testing laboratory) containers and portable tanks shall be used for the storage of flammable liquids.

a. Metal containers and portable tanks less than 660 gal (2.5 m3) individual capacity meeting the requirements of, and containing products authorized by, Chapter I, 49 CFR (U.S. DOT Hazardous Materials Regulations), Chapter 9 of the United Nations' *"Recommendations on the Transport of Dangerous Goods,"* or NFPA 386 shall be acceptable.

b. Plastic containers meeting the requirements of, and used for petroleum products within the scope of, one or more of the following specifications shall be acceptable: ASTM F852, ASTM F976, and ANSI/UL 1313.

c. Plastic drums meeting the requirements of and containing products authorized by 49 CFR or by Chapter 9 of the United Nations' *"Recommendations on the Transport of Dangerous Goods"* shall be acceptable.

d. Fiber drums that meet the requirements of Item 296 of the National Motor Freight Classification (NMFC) or Rule 51 of the Uniform Freight Classification (UFC) for Types 2A, 3A, 3B-H, 3B-L, or 4A and meet the requirements of and contain liquid products authorized either by Chapter I, 49 CFR (U.S. DOT Hazardous Materials Regulations) or by DOT exemption shall be acceptable.

09.B.09 Portable tanks less than 660 gal (2.4 m^3) individual capacity shall be provided with one or more devices installed in the top with sufficient emergency venting capacity to limit internal pressure under fire exposure conditions to 10 pounds per square inch (psi) [68.9 kilopascal (kPa)] gauge or 30% of the bursting pressure of the portable tank, whichever is greater.

a. At least one pressure-actuated vent having a minimum capacity of 6000 ft^3 (170 m^3) of free air per hour shall be used. It shall be set to open at not more than 5 psi (35 kPa) gauge.

b. If fusible vents are used, they shall be actuated by elements that operate at a temperature not exceeding 300°F (148.8°C).

c. Where plugging of a pressure-actuated vent can occur, fusible plugs or venting devices that soften to failure at a maximum of 300°F (148.8°C) under fire exposure shall be permitted to be used for the entire emergency venting requirement.

09.B.10 The design, construction, and use of storage tanks containing flammable liquids shall be as specified in NFPA 30. Tanks greater than 660 gal (2.5 m^3) capacity shall be in accordance with NFPA 30, Chapter 22 and NFPA 30A.

09.B.11 The maximum allowable size for a container or metal portable tank less than 660 gal (2.5 m^3) individual capacities shall not exceed those shown in Table 9-1.

09.B.12 The design, construction, and use of storage cabinets, indoor storage areas, outdoor storage areas, hazardous materials storage lockers, and other occupancies shall be in accordance with NFPA 30 or, for marine applications, 46 CFR 147 covers use of cabinets and 46 CFR 92.05-10 specifies design and construction.

09.B.13 Flammable liquids in quantities greater than that required for 1 day's use shall not be stored in buildings under construction and not more than a 2 day supply shall be stored on paint barges.

09.B.14 Flammable liquids shall not be stored in areas used for exits, stairways, or safe passage of people.

09.B.15 Safety cans and other portable containers for flammable liquids having a flash point at or below 73°F (23°C) shall be labeled/listed and painted red with a yellow band around the can and the name of the contents legibly indicated on the container.

09.B.16 Unopened containers of flammable liquids, such as paints, varnishes, lacquers, thinners, and solvents, shall be kept in a well ventilated location, free of excessive heat, smoke, sparks, flame, or direct rays of the sun.

09.B.17 In areas where flammable liquids are handled or stored, a self-closing metal refuse can, listed by a nationally recognized testing laboratory, shall be provided and maintained in good condition.

TABLE 9-1

Maximum Allowable Size of Portable Containers and Tanks for Flammable Liquids

| Container type | Flammable Liquids Categories | | | |
	1	2	3	4
Glass	16 oz (473 mL)	32 oz (946 mL)	1gal (3.8 L)	1 gal (3.8 L)
Metal (other than DOT drums) or approved plastic)	1 gal (3.8 L)	5 gal (19 L)	5 gal (19 L)	5 gal (19 L)
Safety cans	2 gal (7.6 L)	5 gal (19 L)	5 gal (19 L)	5 gal (19 L)
Metal drum (DOT) specification	60 gal (8.1 ft^3) (0.23 m^3)	60 gal (8.1 ft^3) (0.23 m^3)	60 gal (8.1 ft^3) (0.23 m^3)	60 gal (8.1 ft^3) (0.23 m^3)
Approved metal portable tanks	660 gal (88.3 ft^3) (2.5 m^3)	660 gal (88.3 ft^3) (2.5 m^3)	660 gal (88.3 ft^3) (2.5 m^3)	660 gal (88.3 ft^3) (2.5 m^3)

NOTE: Flammable liquid means any liquid having a flashpoint at or below 199.4°F (93°C).
Flammable liquids are divided into four categories as follows:
-Category 1 shall include liquids having flashpoints below 73.4°F (23°C) and having a boiling point at or below 95°F (35°C).
-Category 2 shall include liquids having flashpoints below 73.4°F (23°C) and having a boiling point above 95°F (35°C).
-Category 3 shall include liquids having flashpoints at or above 73.4°F (23°C) and at or below 140°F (60°C). When a Category 3 liquid with a flashpoint at or above 100°F (37.8°C) is heated for use to within 30°F (16.7°C) of its flashpoint, it shall be handled in accordance with the requirements for a Category 3 liquid with a flashpoint below 100°F (37.8°C).
-Category 4 shall include liquids having flashpoints above 140°F (60°C) and at or below 199.4°F (93°C).When a Category 4 flammable liquid is heated for use to within 30°F (16.7°C) of its flashpoint, it shall be handled in accordance with the requirements for a Category 3 liquid with a flashpoint at or above 100°F (37.8°C).

9

09.B.18 Storage areas/tanks shall be surrounded by a curb, earthen dike or other equivalent means of containment of at least 6 in (15 cm) in height and higher as needed to contain the contents in the event of a leak.

a. Other secondary containment methods that are approved by the EPA or USCG can be used in lieu of curbs or dikes (double-walled tanks, etc.).

b. When dikes or curbs are used, provisions shall be made for draining off accumulations of ground or rain water or spills of flammable liquids.

c. Drains shall terminate at a safe location and shall be accessible to operation under fire conditions. If fuel and oil storage areas are subject to the provisions of 40 CFR 112 (Spill Prevention Control and Countermeasures), those provisions shall apply as well.

09.B.19 Where liquids are used or handled, provisions shall be made to promptly and safely dispose of leakage or spills.

09.B.20 Flashlights and electric lanterns used while handling flammable liquids shall be listed by a nationally recognized testing laboratory for the intended use.

09.B.21 Dispensing flammable liquids - general.

a. All pumping equipment used for the transfer of Category 1 or 2 flammable liquids or Category 3 flammable liquids with a flashpoint below 100°F (37.8°C) shall be listed by a nationally recognized testing laboratory or approved by, and labeled or tagged in accordance with, the Federal agency having jurisdiction, such as the DOT.

b. Dispensing systems for Category 1 or 2 flammable liquids or Category 3 flammable liquids with a flashpoint below 100°F (37.8°C) shall be electrically bonded and grounded. All fuel tanks, hoses, and containers of 5 gal (18.9 L) or less shall be kept in metallic contact while flammable liquids are being transferred; transfer of flammable liquids to containers in excess of 5 gal shall be done only when the containers are electrically bonded.

c. Flammable liquids shall be drawn from, or transferred into, vessels, containers, or tanks within a building or outside only through a closed piping system, from safety cans, by means of a device drawing through the top, or from a container, or portable tanks, by gravity or pump, through an approved self-closing valve. Transferring by means of air pressure on the container or portable tanks is prohibited.

d. Areas in which flammable liquids are transferred in quantities greater than 5 gal (18.9 L) from one tank or container to another, shall be separated from other operations by at least 25 ft (7.6 m) or a barrier having a fire resistance of at least 1 hour. Drainage or other means shall be provided to control spills. Natural or mechanical ventilation shall be provided to maintain the concentration of flammable vapor at or below 10% of the lower flammable limit.

e. Dispensing units shall be protected against collision damage by suitable means and permanent dispensing units shall be securely bolted in place.

f. Dispensing nozzles and devices for Category 1 or 2 flammable liquids or Category 3 flammable liquids with a flashpoint below 100°F shall be listed.

g. Lamps, lanterns, heating devices, small engines, and similar equipment shall not be filled while hot: these devices shall be filled only in well ventilated rooms free of open flames or in open air and shall not be filled in storage buildings.

h. Dispensing devices shall be in all cases at least 20 ft (6 m) from any activity involving fixed sources of ignition.

09.B.22 Service and refueling areas.

a. Dispensing hoses shall be listed. Dispensing nozzles shall be an approved automatic-closing type without a latch-open device.

b. Equipment using flammable liquids as fuel shall be shut down during refueling, servicing, or maintenance, except for emergency generators. Waiver requests may be reviewed and granted by the local SOHO for operations in remote sites or regions where cold weather conditions pose a significant risk when equipment fails to restart (copy provided to CESO).

c. Dispensing of Category 1 or 2 flammable liquids or Category 3 flammable liquids with a flashpoint below 100°F (37.8°C) from tanks of 55 gal (0.20 m^3) capacity or more shall be by listed pumping arrangement. Transferring by air pressure on the container or portable tank is prohibited.

d. Clearly identified and easily accessible switch(es) shall be provided at a location remote from dispensing devices to shut off the power to all dispensing devices in an emergency.

e. A listed emergency breakaway device designed to retain liquid on both sides of the breakaway point shall be installed on each hose dispensing Category 1 or 2 flammable liquids or Category 3 flammable liquids with a flashpoint below 100°F (37.8°C) liquids.

09.B.23 Tank cars/trucks.

a. Tank cars/trucks shall be spotted and not loaded or unloaded until brakes have been set and wheels chocked.

b. Tank cars/trucks shall be attended for the entire time they are being loaded or unloaded. Precautions shall be taken against fire or other hazards.

c. Tank cars/trucks shall be properly bonded and grounded while being loaded or unloaded. Bonding and grounding connections shall be made before dome covers are removed on tank cars/trucks and shall not be disconnected until such covers have been replaced. Internal vapor pressure shall be relieved before dome covers are opened.

09.C Liquefied Petroleum Gas (LP-Gas).

09.C.01 Storage, handling, installation, and use of LP-Gas and systems shall be in accordance with NFPA Standard 58 and USCG regulations, as applicable.

09.C.02 LP-Gas containers, valves, connectors, manifold valve assemblies, regulators, and appliances shall be of an approved type.

09.C.03 Any appliance that was originally manufactured for operation with a gaseous fuel other than LP-Gas and is in good condition may be used with LP-Gas only after it is properly converted, adapted, and tested for performance with LP-Gas.

09.C.04 Polyvinyl chloride and aluminum tubing shall not be used in LP-Gas systems.

09.C.05 Safety devices.

a. Every container and vaporizer shall be provided with one or more safety relief valves or devices. These valves and devices shall be arranged to afford free vent to the outside air and discharge at a point not less than 5 ft (1.5 m) horizontally from any building opening that is below the discharge point.

b. Container safety relief devices and regulator relief vents shall be located not less than 5 ft (1.5 m) in any direction from air openings into sealed combustion system appliances or mechanical ventilation air intakes.

c. Shut-off valves shall not be installed between the safety relief device and the container, or the equipment or piping to which the safety relief device is connected, except that a shut-off valve may be used where the arrangement of the valve is such that full required capacity-flow through the safety relief device is always afforded.

09.C.06 Container valves and accessories.

a. Valves, fittings, and accessories connected directly to the container, including primary shut off valves, shall have a rated working pressure of at least 250 psi (1723.6 kPa) gauge and shall be of material and design suitable for LP-Gas service.

b. Connections to containers (except safety relief connections, liquid level gauging devices, and plugged openings) shall have shutoff valves located as close to the container as practical.

09.C.07 Multiple container systems.

a. Valves in the assembly of multiple container systems shall be arranged so that replacement of containers can be made without shutting off the flow of gas in the system (this is not to be construed as requiring an automatic changeover device).

b. Regulators and low-pressure relief devices shall be rigidly attached to the cylinder valves, cylinders, supporting standards, building walls, or otherwise rigidly secured and shall be installed or protected from the elements.

09.C.08 LP-Gas containers and equipment shall not be used in unventilated spaces below grade in pits, below-decks, or other spaces where dangerous accumulations of heavier than-air gas may accumulate due to leaks or equipment failure.

09.C.09 Welding is prohibited on LP-Gas containers.

09.C.10 Dispensing.

a. Equipment using LP-Gas shall be shut down during refueling operations.

b. Filling of fuel containers for motor vehicles from bulk storage containers shall be performed not less than 10 ft (3 m) from the nearest masonry-walled building, not less than 25 ft (7.6 m) from the nearest building of other construction, and, in any event, not less than 25 ft from any building opening.

c. Filling, from storage containers, of portable containers or containers mounted on skids shall be performed no less than 50 ft (15.2 m) from the nearest building.

9

09.C.11 Installation, use, and storage outside buildings.

a. Containers shall be upright upon firm foundations or otherwise firmly positioned. Flexible connections (or other special fixtures) shall be provided to protect against the possibility of the effect of settlement on the outlet piping.

b. Containers shall be in a suitable ventilated enclosure or otherwise protected against tampering.

c. Storage outside buildings, of containers awaiting use, shall be located from the nearest building or group of buildings in accordance with Table 9-2.

d. Storage areas shall be provided with at least one approved portable fire extinguisher rated no less than 20-B:C.

TABLE 9-2

Outside Storage of LP-Gas Containers and Cylinders - Minimum Distances

Quantity of LP-Gas stored	Distance
Less than 500 lb (227 kg)	0 ft
500 lb (227 kg) 6,000 lb (2730 kg)	10 ft (3 m)
6,000 lb (2730 kg) 10,000 lb (4545 kg)	20 ft (6 m)
More than 10,000 lb (4545 kg)	25 ft (7.6 m)

09.C.12 Installation, use, and storage inside of buildings.

a. Storage of LP-gas containers (empty or full) in industrial buildings (not normally frequented by the public) shall not exceed 300 lbs (2,598 ft^3 in vapor form). When stored inside, empty containers which have been in LP-Gas service shall be considered as full containers for the purpose of determining the maximum quantity of LP-Gas permitted.

➤Exemption: A total of 5 one-pound propane cylinders may be stored indoors as long as they are stored away from exits and stairways, or in areas normally used for the safe exit of people.

b. Containers stored inside shall not be located near exits, stairways, or in areas normally used for the safe exit of people.

c. Container valves shall be protected while in storage as follows: by setting into recess of container to prevent the possibility of it being struck if the container is dropped upon a flat surface, or by ventilated cap or collar fastened to the container capable of

withstanding blow from any direction equivalent to that of a 30 lb (13.6 kg) weight dropped 4 ft (1.2 m).

d. Outlet valves of containers in storage shall be closed.

e. Storage locations shall be provided with at least one approved portable fire extinguisher having a minimum rating of 8-B:C.

f. Containers, regulating equipment, manifolds, pipe, tubing, and hose shall be located to minimize exposure to high temperatures or physical damage.

g. The maximum water capacity of individual containers shall be 245 lb (111.1 kg), nominal 100 lb (45.3 kg), LP-Gas capacity.

h. Containers having a water capacity greater than 2.5 lb LP-Gas capacity (1.1 kg), (nominal 1 lb (0.4 kg), that are connected for use shall stand on a firm and substantially level surface and, when necessary, shall be secured in an upright position. Systems using containers having a water capacity greater than 2.5 lb shall be equipped with excess flow valves internal either with the container valves or in the connections to the container valve outlets.

i. Regulators shall be directly connected to either the container valves or to manifolds connected to the container valves. The regulator shall be suitable for use with LP-Gas. Manifolds and fittings connecting containers to pressure regulator inlets shall be designed for at least 250 psi (1723.6 kPa) gauge service pressure.

j. Valves on containers having water capacity greater than 50 lb (22.6 kg) (nominal 20 lb (9 kg) LP-Gas capacity) shall be protected from damage while in use or storage.

k. Hoses shall be designed for working pressure of at least 250 psi (1723.6 kPa) gauge. Design, construction, and performance of hoses and connections shall have been suitability determined by listing by a nationally recognized testing agency. Hose length shall be as short as possible but long enough to permit compliance with spacing requirements without kinking, straining, or causing the hose to be so close to a burner as to be damaged by heat.

09.D Temporary Heating Devices.

09.D.01 Only temporary heating devices approved by the GDA shall be used. Each heater should have a safety data plate permanently affixed by the manufacturer. The plate shall provide requirements or recommendations for:

a. Clearances from combustible materials;

b. Ventilation (minimum air requirements for fuel combustion);

c. Fuel type and input pressure;

d. Lighting, extinguishing, and relighting;

e. Electrical power supply characteristics;

f. Location, moving, and handling; and

g. Name and address of the manufacturer.

➤Note: If this information is not available on a data plate, it shall be in writing at the job site.

09.D.02 A positive operating procedure shall be established to assure the following:

a. Proper placement and servicing;

b. Safe clearance from combustible material;

c. Close surveillance;

d. Safe fuel storage and refueling;

e. Proper maintenance; and

f. Ventilation and determination of gaseous contamination or oxygen deficiency.

09.D.03 Heater installation and maintenance shall be in accordance with the manufacturer's instructions.

09.D.04 Open-flame heating devices having exposed fuel below the flame are prohibited.

09.D.05 Heaters, when in use, shall be set horizontally level, unless otherwise permitted by the manufacturer's specifications.

09.D.06 Heaters unsuitable for use on wood floors shall be so marked. When such heaters are used, they shall rest on suitable heat insulating material, such as concrete of at least 1 in (2.5 cm) thickness or equivalent; the insulating material shall extend 2 ft (0.6 m) or more in all directions from the edges of the heater.

09.D.07 Heaters used near combustible tarpaulins, canvas, or similar coverings shall be located at least 10 ft (3 m) from such coverings; coverings shall be securely fastened to prevent them from igniting or upsetting the heater due to wind action.

09.D.08 Heaters shall be protected against damage.

09.D.09 Installation of temporary heating devices shall provide minimum clearances to combustible materials as specified in Table 9-3.

TABLE 9-3

Temporary Heating Device Clearances

Heater type	Sides	Rear	Chimney Connector
Room heater – circulating	12 in (30.5 cm)	12 in (30.5 cm)	18 in (45.8 cm)
Room heater – radiant	36 in (91.5 cm)	36 in (91.5 cm)	18 in (45.8 cm)

09.D.10 Fuel combustion space heating devices used in any enclosed building, room, or structure shall be vented by a flue pipe to the exterior of the structure.

a. Fresh air shall be supplied, by natural or mechanical means, in sufficient quantities to ensure the health and safety of workers. Particular attention shall be given to areas where heat and fumes may accumulate.

b. When heaters are used in confined spaces, precautions shall be taken to ensure proper combustion, maintenance of a safe and healthful atmosphere for workers, and limitation of temperature rise in the area. These precautions shall be addressed in the confined space entry permit. > *See Section 34.*

c. Vent pipes shall be located at least 18 in (0.5 m) from flammables and combustibles. Where vent pipes pass through combustible walls or roofs, they shall be properly insulated and securely fastened and supported to prevent accidental displacement or separation.

09.D.11 When a heater is placed in operation, initial and periodic checks shall be made to ensure it is functioning properly.

09.D.12 Fuel combustion heater CO hazards.

a. When heaters are used in enclosed or partially enclosed structures, CO shall be continuously monitored. If not feasible, this shall be so stated in the AHA and tests for the presence of CO shall be made within 1 hour of the start of each shift and at least every 4 hours thereafter.

b. CO concentrations greater than 25 ppm (TLV) of air volume at worker breathing levels shall require extinguishing of the heater unless additional ventilation is provided to reduce the CO content to acceptable limits.

09.D.13 Personnel involved in fueling heaters shall be trained in, and thoroughly familiar with, the manufacturer's recommended safe fueling procedures.

09.D.14 Heaters shall be equipped with an approved automatic device to shut off the flow of fuel if the flame is extinguished (on liquid fuel heaters, barometric or gravity oil feed shall not be considered a primary safety control).

09.D.15 Spark arresters shall be provided on all smoke stacks or burning devices having forced drafts or short stacks permitting live sparks or hot materials to escape.

09.D.16 Solid fuel heaters are prohibited in buildings and on scaffolds.

09.D.17 Gas Heaters - General.

a. All piping, tubing, and hose shall be leak tested using soap suds or other noncombustible detection means (tests shall not be made with a flame) after assembly and proven free of leaks at normal operating pressure.

b. Hose and fittings shall be protected from damage and deterioration.

c. All hoses and fittings shall be checked to ensure that the type, capacity, and pressure ratings are as specified by the heater manufacturer. Hose shall have a minimum working pressure of 250 psi (1723.6 kPa) gauge and a minimum bursting pressure of 1250 psi (8618.4 kPa) gauge.

d. All hose connectors shall be capable of withstanding, without leakage, a test pressure of 125 psi (861.8 kPa) gauge for natural gas, and 500 psi (3,447 kPa) gauge for LP-Gas and shall be capable of withstanding a pull test of 400 lb (181.4 kg).

e. Hose connectors shall be securely connected to the heater by mechanical means. Neither "slip-end" connectors (connections that allow the hose end to be held only by the friction of the hose material against the metal fitting of the unit) nor ring keepers (tightened over the hose to provide an increased force holding the hose to the metal fitting) are permitted.

09.D.18 Natural gas heaters. When flexible gas supply lines are used, the length shall be as short as practical and shall not exceed 25 ft (7.6 m).

09.D.19 Portable LP-Gas Heaters.
> *See also Section 09.C.*

a. If LP-Gas is supplied to a heater by hose, the hose shall not be less than 10 ft (3 m), or more than 25 ft (7.6 m), in length.

b. Heaters shall be equipped with an approved regulator in the supply line between the fuel cylinder and the heater unit. Cylinder connectors shall be provided with an excess flow valve to minimize the flow of gas in the event the fuel line ruptures.

c. LP-Gas heaters having inputs above 50,000 British Thermal Unit (BTU)/hour shall be equipped with either a pilot, which must be lighted and proved before the main burner can be turned on, or an electronic ignition. > *These provisions do not apply to portable heaters under 7,500 BTU/ hour when used with containers having a maximum water capacity of 2.5 lb (1.1 kg).*

d. Container valves, connectors, regulators, manifolds, piping, and tubing shall not be used as structural support for LP-Gas heaters.

e. Heaters, other than integral heater-container units, shall be located at least 6 ft (1.8 m) from any LP-Gas container (this shall not prohibit the use of heaters designed specifically for attachment to the LP-Gas container or to a supporting standard, provided they are designed and installed to prevent direct or radiant heat application from the heater into the containers). Blower and radiant type heaters shall not be directed toward any LP Gas container within 20 ft (6 m).

f. If two or more heater-container units (of either the integral or non-integral type) are located in an unpartitioned area of the same floor, the container or containers of each unit shall be separated from the container or containers of any other unit by at least 20 ft (6 m).

g. When heaters are connected to containers for use in an unpartitioned area on the same floor, the total water capacity of containers, manifolded together for connection to a heater(s), shall not be greater than 735 lb (333.3 kg), [nominal 300 lb (136 kg) LP-Gas capacity]. Such manifolds shall be separated by at least 20 ft (6 m).

09.D.20 Installation of heating equipment in service or lubrication areas.

a. Heating equipment installed in lubrication or service areas where there is no dispensing or transferring of flammable liquids shall be installed such that the bottom of the heating unit is at least 18 in (.5 m) above the floor and is protected from damage.

b. Heating equipment installed in lubrication or service areas where flammable liquids are dispensed shall be of a type approved for garages and shall be installed at least 8 ft (2.4 m) above the floor.

09.E Heating Devices and Melting Kettles.

09.E.01 Heating devices and melting kettles shall be placed on firm, level, noncombustible foundations and shall be protected against traffic, accidental tipping, or similar hazards and, whenever possible, shall be placed downwind from employees or occupied buildings.

09.E.02 A method to contain uncontrolled spills of the heated material, which might be on fire, shall be developed. The placement of a fire retardant tarp under the kettle (or other effective means) shall be used.

09.E.03 A minimum of 2 fire extinguishers, rated not less than 2A:20B:C shall be available within 25 ft (7.6 m) of the working kettles. > *Hot work permits shall be required on Government installations unless otherwise indicated by the GDA.*

09.E.04 The kettle operator must be trained in the proper operation of the kettle and have knowledge of the material being heated so as to not allow the material to be heated beyond the allowable temperature. A working thermometer shall be provided and used.

09.E.05 Heating devices and melting kettles shall not be left unattended when in use. When the kettle is heating material to the working temperature, the operator must be located on the same level as the kettle, be within eyesight and be within 25 ft (7.6 m) of the kettle. > *See 09.K.03.*

09.E.06 Bituminous-material melting kettles shall be provided with an effective tight fitting lid or hood, and a calibrated thermometer in operating condition.

a. The temperature shall be maintained 25° below the flash point of the bituminous material.

b. All melting kettles shall be sized for the job.

c. Asphalt and tar kettles shall not be located on roofs.

09.E.07 Bituminous-material melting kettles shall not be used or operated inside or within 25 ft (7.6 m) of combustible materials, including propane tanks stored or in use. The lid for the kettle should open away from the building.

09.E.08 The liquid propane container(s) used as the heat source shall be kept at least 10 ft (3 m) away from the kettle and shall be placed in an upright and secured position to insure it doesn't tip over.

09.E.09 Kettles shall be located so that means of egress is not restricted and shall be no closer than 10 ft (3 m) of egress path.

09.E.10 Enclosed areas in which hot substances are heated or applied shall be ventilated.

09.E.11 Ladles, equipment, and material shall be moisture-free before being used or placed in heated material.

09.E.12 Flammable liquids with a flash point below 100°F (37.8°C) shall not be used to thin the mixture or to clean equipment.

09.E.13 An effective fire prevention plan shall be included in the APP, AHA and maintained at the jobsite. All workers shall be trained in the specifics of the plan.

9

TABLE 9-4

Fire Extinguisher Distribution

	Occupancy					
	Low Hazard		Medium Hazard		High Hazard	
	Class A	Class B	Class A	Class B	Class A	Class B
Minimum rating for single extinguisher	2-A	5-B or 10-B[1]	2-A	10-B or 20-B	4-A	40-B or 80-B[2]
Maximum coverage (floor area) per unit of A-rating	3,000 ft²	n/a	1,500 ft²	n/a	1,000 ft²	n/a
Maximum floor area for extinguisher	11,250 ft²	n/a	11,250 ft²	n/a	11,250 ft²	n/a
Maximum travel distance to extinguisher	75 ft	30 ft for 5-B 50 ft for 10-B	75 ft	30 ft for 10-B 50 ft for 20-B	75 ft	30 ft for 40-B 50 ft for 80-B

1) Up to 3 foam extinguishers of at least 2 1/2 gal (9.5 L) capacities may be used to fulfill low hazard requirements

2) Up to 3 aqueous film foaming foam (AFFF) extinguishers of at least 2 1/2 gal (9.5 L) capacities may be used to fulfill high hazard requirements

Derived from NFPA 10: In multiple-story facilities, at least 1 extinguisher shall be adjacent to stairways.   On construction and demolition projects, a 1/2 in (1.2 cm) diameter garden hose, not to exceed 100 ft (30.4m) in length and equipped with a nozzle, may be substituted for a 2-A rated fire extinguisher provided it its capable of discharging a minimum of 5 gal (18.9 L) per minute with minimum hose stream range of 30 ft (9.1m) horizontally. The garden hose lines shall be mounted on conventional racks or reels. The number of location of hose racks or reels shall be such that at least 1 hose stream can be applied to all points in the area.

09.F First Response Fire Protection.

09.F.01 Portable fire extinguishers shall be provided where needed as specified in Table 9-4.

a. Fire extinguishers shall be inspected monthly and maintained as specified in NFPA 10.b. Records shall be kept on a tag or label attached to the extinguisher, on an inspection check list maintained on file, or by an electronic method that provides a permanent record. Record/tag shall include date inspection was performed and initials of the person performing the inspection..

09.F.02 Approved fire extinguishers.

a. Fire extinguishers shall be approved by a nationally recognized testing laboratory and labeled to identify the listing and labeling organization and the fire test and performance standard that the fire extinguisher meets or exceeds.

b. Fire extinguishers shall be marked with their letter (class of fire) and numeric (relative extinguishing effectiveness) classification.

c. Fire extinguishers using carbon tetrachloride or chlorobromomethane extinguishing agents are prohibited.

d. Soldered or riveted shell self-generating foam or gas cartridge water-type portable extinguishers that are operated by inverting the extinguisher to rupture or initiate an uncontrollable pressure generating chemical reaction to expel the agent are prohibited.

09.F.03 Fire extinguishers shall be in a fully charged and operable condition and shall be suitably placed, distinctly marked, and readily accessible.

09.F.04 When portable fire extinguishers are provided for employee use in the workplace, the employer shall provide training (upon initial employment and at least annually thereafter) in the following:

a. General principles of fire extinguisher use and the hazards involved with incipient stage fire fighting to all employees; and

b. Use of the appropriate firefighting equipment to those employees designated in an emergency action plan to use firefighting equipment.

09.F.05 Approved fire blankets shall be provided and kept in conspicuous and accessible locations as warranted by the operations involved.

09.F.06 No fire shall be fought where the fire is in imminent danger of contact with explosives. All persons shall be removed to a safe area and the fire area guarded against intruders.

09.F.07 Standpipe and hose system equipment.

a. Standpipes shall be located or otherwise protected against damage. Damaged standpipes shall be repaired promptly.

b. Reels and cabinets used to contain fire hose shall be designed and maintained to ensure the prompt use of the hose valve, hose, and other equipment. Reels and cabinets shall be conspicuously identified and used only for fire equipment.

c. Hose outlets and connections shall be located high enough above the floor to avoid their obstruction and to be accessible to employees. To ensure hose connections are compatible with support fire equipment, screw threads shall be standardized or adapters shall be provided throughout the system.

d. Standpipe systems shall be equipped with vinyl type or lined hoses of such length that friction loss resulting from water flowing through the hose will not decrease the pressure at the nozzle below 30 psi (206.8 kPa) gauge. The dynamic pressure at the nozzle shall be within 30 psi (206.8 kPa) gauge and 125 psi (861.8 kPa) gauge.

e. Standpipe hoses shall be equipped with basic spray nozzles with a straight stream to wide stream spray pattern. Nozzles shall have a water discharge control capable of functions ranging from full discharge to complete shutoff.

09.F.08 The following tests shall be performed on standpipe and hose systems before placing them in service:

a. Piping (including yard piping) shall be hydrostatically tested for at least 2 hours at not less than 200 psi (1378.9 kPa), or at least 50 psi (344.7 kPa) in excess of normal pressure when the normal pressure is greater than 150 psi (1034.2 kPa)); and

b. Hose shall be hydrostatically tested with couplings in place at a pressure of not less than 200 psi (1378.9 kPa). This pressure shall be maintained for at least 15 seconds, but not more than 1 minute, during which time the hose shall not leak nor shall the jacket thread break.

09.F.09 Standpipe and hose system inspection and maintenance.

a. Water supply tanks shall be kept filled to the proper level except during repairs. When pressure tanks are used, proper pressure shall be maintained at all times except during repairs.

b. Valves in the main piping connections to the automatic sources of water supply shall be kept fully open at all times, except during repairs.

c. Hose systems shall be inspected at least annually and after each use to assure that all equipment is in place, available for use, and in operable condition.

9

d. When the system or any portion of the system is found not to be serviceable, it shall be removed for repair and replaced with equivalent protection (such as fire watches and extinguisher) until the repairs are complete.

e. Hemp and linen hoses shall be unracked, physically inspected for deterioration, and reracked using a different fold pattern at least annually.

09.F.10 The minimum water supply for standpipe and hose systems provided for the use of employees shall be sufficient to provide 100 gal (0.37 m^3) per minute for at least 30 minutes.

09.F.11 For all structures in which standpipes are required, or where standpipes exist in structures being altered, the standpipes shall be brought up as soon as practical and maintained as construction progresses so that they are always ready for fire protection use. There shall be at least one standard hose outlet at each floor.

09.F.12 For employees that may encounter incipient stage wild land fires, local safety programs shall provide basic training (upon initial employment and at least annually thereafter) in techniques commonly used to extinguish incipient stage wild land fires and the hazards associated with such fire fighting activities.

09.G Fixed Fire Suppression Systems.

09.G.01 Fixed fire suppression systems shall be designed, installed, and acceptance tested in accordance with requirements of the NFPA.

09.G.02 Fixed fire suppression systems shall be inspected and maintained in accordance with UFC 3-600-02, *O&M: Inspection, Testing, and Maintenance of Fire Protection Systems*. Inspection and maintenance dates shall be recorded on the container, on a tag attached to the container, or in a central location.

09.G.03 Automatic sprinkler systems shall be protected from damage.

09.G.04 Vertical clearance of at least 18 in (45.7 cm) shall be maintained between the top of stored material and sprinkler deflectors.

09.G.05 If a fixed extinguishing system becomes inoperable, the employer shall notify the employees and take necessary precautions to assure their safety until the system is restored to operating order.

09.G.06 Effective safeguards shall be provided to warn employees against entry into fixed extinguishing system discharge areas where the atmosphere remains hazardous to employee safety and health. Manual operating devices shall be identified as to the hazard against which they will provide protection.

09.G.07 Warning or caution signs shall be posted at the entrance to, and inside, areas protected by fixed extinguishing systems that use agents in concentrations known to be hazardous to employee safety and health.

09.G.08 Dry chemical fixed extinguishing systems.

a. Dry chemical extinguishing agents shall be compatible with any foams or wetting agents with which they are used.

b. Dry chemical extinguishing agents of different compositions shall not be mixed together.

c. Dry chemical extinguishing systems shall be refilled with the chemical stated on the approval nameplate or an equivalent compatible material.

09.G.09 Gaseous agent fixed extinguishing systems.

a. Agents used for initial supply and replenishment shall be of a type approved for the system's application.

b. Employees shall not be exposed to toxic levels of the gaseous agent or its decomposition products.

09.G.10 When water and spray foam fixed extinguishing systems are used, the drainage of water shall be away from work areas and routes of emergency egress.

09.H Firefighting Equipment.

09.H.01 Firefighting equipment shall be provided and installed in accordance with applicable NFPA and OSHA regulations.

09.H.02 No fire protection equipment or device shall be made inoperative or used for other purposes, unless specifically approved by the GDA.

09.H.03 If fire hose connections are not compatible with local firefighting equipment, adapters shall be made available.

09.I Fire Detection and Employee Fire Alarm Systems.

09.I.01 Fire detection and employee fire alarm systems shall be designed and installed in accordance with requirements of NFPA and OSHA.

09.I.02 Fire detection systems and components shall be restored to normal operating condition as soon as possible after each test/alarm. Spare devices and components shall be maintained in sufficient quantities for the prompt restoration of the system.

09.I.03 Fire detection systems shall be maintained in operable condition except during maintenance or repairs.

a. Fire detectors and detector systems shall be tested and adjusted as often as necessary to maintain operability and reliability; factory calibrated detectors need not be adjusted after installation.

b. Pneumatic and hydraulic operated detection systems installed after January 1, 1981, shall be equipped with supervised systems.

c. The servicing, testing, and maintenance of fire detection systems shall be performed by a trained person knowledgeable in the operations and functions of the system.

d. Fire detectors that need to be cleaned of dirt, dust, or other particulate matter to be fully functional shall be cleaned at regular intervals.

09.I.04 Fire detection systems and devices shall be protected from weather, corrosion, and mechanical and physical damage.

09.I.05 Fire detectors shall be supported independently of their control wiring or tubing.

09.I.06 An alarm system shall be established by the employer so that employees on the site and the local fire department can be alerted of an emergency.

09.I.07 Manually operated alarm actuation devices shall be conspicuous and accessible and inspected and maintained in operable condition.

09.I.08 The alarm shall be distinctive and recognizable as a signal to evacuate the work area or to perform actions designated in the emergency action plan.

a. The alarm shall be capable of being perceived above ambient noise and light levels by all employees in the affected area.

b. Tactile devices may be used to alert those employees who would not otherwise be able to recognize the audible or visual alarm.

09.I.09 Employees shall be instructed in the preferred means of reporting emergencies, such as manual pull box alarms, public address systems, or telephones.

a. The alarm code and reporting instructions shall be conspicuously posted at phones and at employee entrances.

b. Reporting and evacuating instructions shall be conspicuously posted.

c. For work at installations that are equipped with radio wave fire alarm systems, a compatible fire alarm transmitter should be used at the construction site.

09.J Firefighting Organizations - Training and Drilling.

09.J.01 Firefighting organizations shall be provided to assure adequate protection to life and property. NFPA recommendations shall be used for determining type, size, and training of fire fighting organizations.

09.J.02 Fire brigade drills shall be held to assure a well-trained and efficient operating force. Records of such drills shall be maintained at the installation.

09.J.03 Demonstration and training in first-aid firefighting shall be conducted at intervals to ensure that project personnel are familiar with, and capable of operating, firefighting equipment.

09.K Fire Watch.

09.K.01 When fire watch personnel or guards are provided, they shall make frequent rounds through buildings and storage areas when work is suspended.

09.K.02 Smoke detectors shall be installed and maintained where personnel are quartered.

09.K.03 In any instance where combustible materials have been exposed to fire hazards (i.e., welding operations, hot metals, open flame, etc.), a fire watch shall be assigned to remain at the location for at least one (1) hour after the exposure has ended.

09.L USACE Wild Land Fire Control.

09.L.01 At all USACE facilities and areas with potential exposure to wild land fire, whether prescribed or planned, a wild land fire management plan shall be developed. The plan, which is further detailed in USACE Engineer Pamphlet (EP) 1130-2-540, shall address prescribed fire and wild fire prevention and suppression, shall include the following items, and shall be updated annually:

a. An individual prescribed fire burn plan procedure, as outlined in EP 1130-2-540, that requires individual burn plans to include an AHA and an on-site safety meeting to include discussion of predicted weather patterns, escape route(s), and safety zone(s);

b. An analysis of wild land fire causes and special wild fire hazards and risks;

c. Proposed measures to reduce wild fire occurrence and decrease fire damage;

d. Procedures for public education and wild fire prevention sign posting (including procedures for keeping the public informed of the current fire danger rating);

e. Provisions for cooperative efforts with all other neighboring wild land fire management protection agencies;

f. The in-house wild land fire management or control team organization and personnel roster, training and equipment requirements, and notification procedures;

g. A listing of cooperating agencies and notification procedures, (including any mutual aid agreements with adjacent fire departments and agencies);

h. A listing of additional available resources for work force, equipment, supplies, and facilities, and contracting or procurement information;

i. An up-to-date map(s) of the managed and/or protected area(s) that shows boundaries, roads, and other means of access, heliports, airports, water sources, special hazards, and special fire risks;

j. A listing of weather information sources;

k. Procedures for public notification; and

l. A pre-attack fire suppression plan as outlined in EP 1130-2-540.

09.L.02 Wild land fire management teams and operations should be organized and conducted in accordance with the requirements of NFPA 1143.

a. Wild land fire management team personnel shall, as a minimum, receive training that will include fire line safety, basic wild land fire behavior, basic wild land fire suppression tactics, communications procedures, first aid and use, limitations and care of protective and firefighting equipment.

b. Firefighting equipment shall be maintained in working and ready condition.

c. PPE, fire-resistant clothing, safety hard hats, safety toe (non steel-toe) leather boots, goggles, and fire resistant gloves, as required by NFPA 1143, part A.5.3.1.2 and NFPA 1977, shall be provided and maintained in working and ready condition. > See also Section 5.

d. Employees engaged in fire management activities shall be examined, as part of their medical surveillance, by a physician and certified to be physically able to perform assigned fire management duties.

e. Communication equipment shall be provided to personnel as necessary for coordination, control, and emergency needs.

09.L.03 Recommendations of NFPA 1143 shall be complied with in wild land fire situations not covered in this Section.

09.L.04 Wild land fire management teams shall consist of 2 or more qualified individuals.

SECTION 10 Welding and Cutting

Table of Contents

10

10.A General.

10.A.01 Welders, cutters, and their supervisor shall be trained in the safe operation of their equipment, safe welding/cutting practices, and welding/cutting respiratory and fire protection. > *AIHA publication "Welding Health and Safety: A Field Guide for OEHS Professionals" is recommended.*

10.A.02 All welding equipment shall be inspected before each use to ensure that all required safety devices and ancillary equipment are in place and properly functioning. Defective equipment shall be removed from service, replaced or repaired, and reinspected before again being placed in service.

10.A.03 Electrical and pressurized system requirements.

a. Welding cylinders and their use and maintenance shall meet the applicable requirements of Section 20.

b. Arc welding and cutting systems and their use shall meet the applicable requirements of this section.

10.A.04 Arc welding and cutting operations shall be shielded by noncombustible or flameproof screens that will protect employees and other persons working within 35 ft (10.7 m) from the direct rays of the arc, sparks, molten metal, spatter, and chipped slag.

a. Welding curtains shall be suitable for the welding process and amperage.

b. Welding curtains shall provide a high degree of safety against ultraviolet radiation and blue light.

c. Welding curtains shall be fade resistant and flame retardant.

d. The use of blue tinted welding curtains is prohibited if observers are in the work area as they provide very little blue light protection.

10.A.05 Cable, hoses, and other equipment shall be kept clear of passageways, ladders, and stairways.

10.A.06 Welding and cutting of hazardous materials.

a. When welding, cutting, or heating on steel pipelines containing natural gas, 49 CFR 192 shall apply.

b. Before welding, cutting, or heating is commenced on any surface covered by a preservative coating whose flammability is not known, a test shall be made to determine its flammability. Preservative coatings shall be considered highly flammable when scrapings burn with extreme rapidity.

c. Preservative coatings shall be removed a sufficient distance from the area to be heated to ensure any temperature increase of the un-stripped metal will not result in visually observable decomposition, or degradation of the coatings; artificial cooling of the metal surrounding the heating area may be used to limit the area to be stripped.

d. When welding, cutting, or heating toxic surface coatings (paints, preservatives, surface stripping chemicals, etc.) in enclosed spaces, all surfaces covered with the coatings shall be stripped of such for a distance of at least 4 in (10.1 cm) from the area of heat application or the employees shall be protected by airline respirators.

10.A.07 Critical Items. > *See Appendix Q.*

a. All structural welding performed on critical items, such as scaffolding, shoring, forms, ladders, piling, etc., as well as other critical items as determined by a Qualified Person (QP), shall only be performed by welders certified in accordance with American Welding Society (AWS) standards using qualified and approved welding practices and procedures (AWS certification or approved equivalent organization which trains to AWS standards).

b. Welds on critical items shall be inspected by either a current, AWS-certified Senior Certified Welding Inspector (CSWI) or Certified Welding Inspector (CWI) (or equivalent).

10.A.08 Before heat is applied to a drum, container, or hollow structure, a vent or opening shall be provided for the release of any built-up pressure generated during the application of heat. The use of the heat or spark producing tools to create or provide venting is not permitted.

10.A.09 Employees performing welding, cutting, and heating work shall be protected by PPE appropriate for the hazards that they may encounter and based upon the results of an AHA conducted specifically for the welding, cutting, or heating operation that they will be performing. All required respiratory, eye and face, noise, head, foot, and skin protection equipment shall be selected and used in accordance with Sections 10.B, 10.C. and Section 5.

10.A.10 All welding and cutting equipment and operations shall be in accordance with standards and recommended practices of ANSI/AWS Z49.1.

10.B Eye and Face Protection. The eyes and face of welders shall be protected against UV and infrared radiation and flying objects during welding, grinding and chipping operations.

10.B.01 Personnel performing and/ or exposed to these tasks shall have appropriate eye and face protection based on the hazards, in accordance with this section and Section 05.

10.B.02 Personnel performing and/ or exposed to work that produces UV, blue light, and Infrared light shall be protected from these hazards.

a. Shaded lenses shall be selected based on the type of equipment and work. > See Section 5, Table 5-2.

b. Protective helmets shall have non-reflective surfaces and shall be free of cracks or openings.

c. Lenses that are cracked or pitted shall not be used.

d. All filter lenses shall meet ANSI Z87.1.Ultraviolet, Luminous, and Infrared Transmittance requirements.

e. Welding Helmets shall always be used in conjunction with ANSI Z87.1 rated safety glasses with top and side protection.

f. Electronic-shading welding helmets shall not be used for welding processes requiring a higher shade than the helmet is capable of. Most auto-darkening helmets are not suited for welding processes requiring a Filter Shade of 14 or higher.

10.C Controls.

10.C.01 All welding, cutting, and heating operations shall be ventilated (natural or mechanical) such that personnel exposures to hazardous concentrations of airborne contaminants are within acceptable limits. > See Section 06.

10.C.02 Welding, cutting, and heating not involving conditions or materials described in this Section may normally be done without mechanical ventilation or respiratory protective equipment.

10.C.03 Either general mechanical or local exhaust ventilation shall be provided whenever welding, cutting, or heating is performed in a confined space. > See Sections 10.A.06.d and 10.C.05.

10.C.04 Materials of toxic significance. Welding, cutting, or heating operations that involve or generate any of the substances listed below shall be performed in accordance with the following subparagraphs: Antimony, Arsenic, Barium, Beryllium, Cadmium,

Chromium, Chromium (VI), Cobalt, Copper, Lead, Manganese, Mercury, Nickel, Ozone, Selenium, Silver, or Vanadium. > See also Section 10.A.06.d.

a. Whenever these materials are encountered in confined spaces, local mechanical exhaust ventilation and personal respiratory protective equipment shall be used. The use of local mechanical exhaust ventilation systems that permit the re-entry of exhaust air back into the work area, or local exhaust which incorporate a system for the filtration and recirculation of exhaust air back into the work area shall not be permitted.

b. Whenever these materials, except beryllium and chromium (VI), are encountered in indoor operations, local mechanical exhaust ventilation systems that are sufficient to reduce and maintain personal exposures to within acceptable limits shall be used and maintained in accordance with manufacturer's instruction. Care shall be taken to ensure replacement filters are from the same manufacturer and are the correct filter for the exhaust system. When either beryllium or chromium (VI) is encountered in indoor operations, approved local mechanical exhaust ventilation systems and personal respiratory protection shall be used.

(1) In areas where only welding is conducted, a general exhaust system ventilation rate of 2,000 CFM per welder is required in open welding areas.

(2) Local exhaust ventilation should have a capture velocity of 100 FPM as measured from the farthest distance from the work, and a duct transport velocity of 1,000 FPM minimum. Local exhaust ventilation systems which filter and return the air back into the work environment shall be allowed for welding, that is not in a confined space or does not include beryllium or chromium, if the provisions of Section 06.H.01.f. are followed.

c. Whenever these materials, except beryllium and chromium (VI), are encountered in outdoor operations, and local mechanical exhaust ventilation systems sufficient to reduce and maintain personal exposures to within acceptable limits are not provided, then appropriate respiratory protective equipment shall be used.

d. Whenever beryllium and chromium (VI) are encountered in outdoor operations, the need for and type of engineering and work practice controls to be implemented, as well as the need for and type of respiratory protection to be provided shall be based upon the results of an initial worker exposure assessment and exposure determination with regards to these substances.

e. Workers may be exposed to hazardous

10

concentrations of chromium (VI) while welding, cutting or performing hot work on stainless steel, high chrome alloys or chromecoated metal, or during the application and removal of chromate-containing paints and other surface coatings. > See Section 06.L.

f. Workers working with materials of toxic significance, shall remove outer clothing, vacuum off, and wash before taking a break, drinking, smoking, or leaving for the day.

g. A good housekeeping plan shall be developed and implemented for all work areas where welding, cutting, or heating operations involve materials of toxic significance. The plan shall require all surfaces to be regularly HEPA vacuumed and wet wiped. The frequency shall maintain the surfaces free of contamination and will be dependent on the frequency, type, and volume of welding, cutting, or heating completed in the area.

10.C.05 Welding, cutting, or heating operations that involve or generate fluorine or zinc compounds shall be performed in accordance with the following:

a. In confined spaces, local mechanical exhaust ventilation and personal respiratory protection sufficient to maintain exposures to within acceptable limits shall be used.

b. In open spaces, sampling shall be performed as required and following the procedures in Section 6.A.01 to determine concentrations of fluorides or zinc compounds and the need for local exhaust ventilation and personal respiratory protection sufficient to maintain exposures to within acceptable limits.

10.C.06 Arc and gas cutting. Oxygen cutting using either an iron powder or chemical flux, gas-shielded arc cutting, and plasma cutting shall employ local mechanical exhaust ventilation or other means adequate to remove the fumes generated.

10.C.07 Other persons exposed to the same atmosphere as welders or cutters shall be protected in the same manner as welders or cutters.

10.D Fire Protection.

10.D.01 Suitable fire extinguishing equipment of sufficient capacity shall be provided in the immediate vicinity of welding or cutting operations and maintained in a state of constant readiness for immediate use. Hot work permits shall be required on Government installations when welding, cutting, or heating operations are performed unless otherwise indicated by the GDA.

10.D.02 Before conducting welding or cutting operations, the area shall be surveyed to ensure it is free

of the following hazards:

a. Combustible materials located close to the operation;

b. The presence or possible generation of potentially explosive atmospheres (flammable gases, vapors, liquids, or dusts); and

c. The presence or nature of an oxygen-enriched atmosphere.

10.D.03 Hierarchy of fire control. Objects to be welded, cut, or heated shall be:

a. Moved to a location free of dangerous combustibles;

b. If the work cannot be moved, all moveable fire hazards in the vicinity shall be taken to a safe place (moved at least 35 ft (10.6 m) horizontally from the welding or cutting area) or the combustible material and construction shall be protected from the heat, sparks, and slag of welding;

c. When welding or cutting must be done in a location where combustible or flammable materials are located, inspection and authorization by the GDA shall be required before such operations are begun. During welding or cutting, a fire watch shall stand with a fire extinguisher equipment readily available and be trained in its use and in sounding an alarm in the event of a fire. A fire watch shall be maintained for at least an hour after completion of the welding or cutting operation to extinguish possible smoldering fires. > See also Section 09.J.03.

10.D.04 When a welding, cutting, or heating operation is such that normal fire prevention precautions are not sufficient, additional qualified fire watch personnel shall be assigned to guard against fire and shall be instructed in anticipated fire hazards and how firefighting equipment is to be used. > See Section 09.J.03.

10.D.05 When welding or cutting is to be done over combustible flooring, the flooring shall be protected by fire-resistant shielding, covered with damp sand, or kept wet. Where flooring is wet or damp, personnel operating arc welding or cutting equipment shall be protected from potential shock hazards.

10.D.06 Noncombustible barriers shall be installed below welding or burning operations in a shaft or raise,

10.D.07 Openings or cracks in walls, floors, or ducts within 35 ft (10.7 m) of the site of welding or cutting operations shall be tightly covered to prevent the passage of sparks to adjacent areas.

10.D.08 Where welding or cutting is to be done near walls, partitions, ceilings, or roofs of combustible construction, fire resistant guards shall be used to prevent ignition.

10.D.09 Where welding or cutting is to be done on a metal wall, partition, ceiling, or roof, precautions shall be taken to prevent ignition, due to heat conduction or radiation, of combustibles on the other side.

10.D.10 Welding or cutting shall not be done on a metal partition, wall, ceiling, or roof with a combustible covering nor on walls or partitions of combustible sandwich-type panel construction.

10.D.11 Before welding or cutting drums, tanks, or other containers and equipment that have contained hazardous materials, the containers shall be thoroughly cleaned in accordance with NFPA 326 and ANSI/AWS F4.1.

10.D.12 Hot tapping or other welding or cutting on a flammable gas or liquid transmission or distribution pipeline shall be performed only by personnel qualified to make hot taps and only with the permission of the GDA.

10.D.13 When welding or cutting is to be conducted near a sprinkler head, a wet cloth or equivalent protection shall be used to cover the sprinkler head and then removed at the completion of the welding or cutting operation.

10.D.14 When welding or cutting in areas protected by fire detection and suppression systems, precautions shall be taken to avoid accidental initiation of these systems.

10.E Oxyfuel Gas Welding and Cutting.

10.E.01 Oxyfuel gas welding and cutting equipment shall be listed by a nationally recognized testing laboratory.

10.E.02 Oxygen cylinders and apparatus.

a. Oxygen cylinders and apparatus shall be kept free from oil, grease, and other flammable or explosive substances and shall not be handled with oily hands or gloves.

b. Oxygen cylinders and apparatus shall not be used interchangeably with any other gas.

c. Oxyfuel cylinders shall not be placed in a confined space with the workers.

10.E.03 Hose and hose connections.

a. Fuel gas hose and oxygen hose shall be readily distinguishable from each other.

b. Oxygen and fuel gas hoses shall not be interchangeable. A single hose having more than one gas passage shall not be used.

c. Hose couplings of the type that can be unlocked or disconnected without a rotary motion are prohibited.

d. Hose that has been subject to flashback or that shows evidence of severe wear or damage shall be tested to twice the normal pressure to which it is subjected, and in no case less than 300 psi (2068.4-kPa) gauge. Damaged hose and hose connectors, or hose and hose connectors in questionable condition, shall not be used.

e. When parallel runs of oxygen and fuel gas hose are taped together, not more than 4 in out of every 12 in (10 cm out of every 30.4 cm) shall be covered by tape.

f. Boxes used for the storage of gas hoses and all enclosed spaces which hoses run through or are used shall be properly ventilated.

g. Hose connections shall be clamped or otherwise securely fastened in a manner that will withstand, without leakage, twice the pressure to which they are normally subjected in service, but not less than 300 psi (2,068 kPa) gauge.

10.E.04 Torches.

a. Torches shall be inspected before each use for leaking shutoff valves, hose couplings, tip connections and damaged torch tips. Defective torches shall not be used.

b. Hoses shall be purged individually before lighting the torch for the first time each day. Hoses shall not be purged into confined spaces or near ignition sources.

c. Clogged torch tip openings shall be cleaned with suitable cleaning wires, drills, or other devices designed for such purposes.

d. Torches shall be lighted by friction lighters or other approved devices, not by matches or from hot work.

10.E.05 Torch valves shall be closed and the gas supply shut off whenever work is suspended.

10.E.06 The torch and hose shall be removed from confined spaces whenever work is suspended.

10

10.E.07 Protective equipment.

a. Oxyfuel gas, and other oxygen-fuel gas welding and cutting systems using cylinder-regulator-hose-torch shall be equipped with both a reverse-flow check valve and a flash arrestor, in each hose, at the torch unless otherwise indicated by the manufacturer instructions.

b. When oxygen-fuel gas systems are manifolded together, the provisions of NFPA 51 shall apply.

10.E.08 Connection of multiple sets of oxyacetylene hoses to a single regulator on a single set of oxyacetylene tanks may only be accomplished by installing a commercially available fitting approved by Compressed Gas Association (CGA) standards and listed by a nationally-recognized testing laboratory. The fitting shall be installed on the output side of the regulator and shall have a built-in shut-off valve and reverse-flow check valve on each branch.

10.E.09 Acetylene regulators shall not be adjusted to permit a discharge greater than 15 psi (103.4 kPa) gauge.

10.F Arc Welding and Cutting.

10.F.01 Electric welding apparatus shall be installed, maintained, and operated in accordance with the NEC.

10.F.02 Manual electrode holders.

a. Only manual electrode holders specifically designed for arc welding and cutting of a capacity capable of safely handling the maximum rated current required by the electrodes shall be used.

b. All current carrying parts passing through the portion of the holder that is gripped by the welder or cutter, and the outer surfaces of the jaws of the holder, shall be fully insulated against the maximum voltage encountered to ground.

10.F.03 Welding cables and connectors.

a. Cables shall be completely insulated, flexible, capable of handling the maximum current requirements of the work in progress, and in good repair. Cables in need of repair shall not be used.

b. Welding cables shall be inspected for wear or damage before each use. Cables with damaged insulation or connectors shall be replaced or repaired to achieve the same mechanical strength, insulating quality, electrical conductivity, and water tightness of the original cable. Cables containing splices or repaired insulation within a minimum distance of 10 ft (3 m) from the end of the cable to which the electrode

holder is connected shall not be used.

c. Where it becomes necessary to connect or splice lengths of cable together, insulated connectors of a capacity at least equivalent to that of the cable shall be used. When connections are affected by cable lugs, they shall be securely fastened together to give good electrical contact and the exposed metal parts of the lugs shall be completely insulated. The joining of lengths of cable shall be accomplished by methods specifically intended for that purpose and connection methods shall provide insulation adequate for the service conditions.

10.F.04 The frames of arc welding and cutting machines shall be grounded either by a third wire in the cable connecting the circuit conductor or by a separate wire that is grounded at the source of the current.

10.F.05 Neither terminal of the welding generator shall be bonded to the frame of the welder.

10.F.06 Pipelines containing gases or flammable liquids or conduits carrying electrical conductors shall not be used for a ground return circuit.

10.F.07 Circuits from welding machines used for other than welding tools shall be grounded.

10.F.08 Welding supply cables shall not be placed near power supply cables or other hightension wires.

10.F.09 Welding leads shall not be permitted to contact metal parts supporting suspended scaffolds.

10.F.10 Switching equipment for shutting down the welding machine shall be provided on or near the welding machine.

10.F.11 Equipment shall be shut down when the leads are unattended.

10.F.12 Arc welding and cutting operations shall be shielded by noncombustible or flameproof screens to protect employees and other visitors from the direct rays of the arc as in Section 10.A.04.

10.F.13 Coiled welding cable shall be spread out before use.

10.G Gas Metal Arc Welding.

10.G.01 Chlorinated solvents shall be kept at least 200 ft (61 m) away from the exposed arc, unless shielded. Surfaces prepared with chlorinated solvents shall be dry before welding is permitted on such surfaces.

10.G.02 Persons less than 35 ft (10.7 m) from the arc

not protected from the arc by screening shall be protected by filter lenses. When two or more welders are exposed to each other's arc, filter lens goggles shall be worn under welding helmets. Hand shields shall be used to protect the welders against flashes and radiant energy when either the helmet is lifted or the shield is removed.

10.G.03 Welders and other persons who are exposed to radiation shall be protected so that the skin is covered to prevent burns and other damage by UV rays. Welding helmets and hand shields shall be free of leaks, cracks, openings, and highly reflective surfaces.

10.G.04 When gas metal arc welding is performed on stainless steel, chrome alloy steel, or chrome-coated metal, personnel shall be protected against dangerous concentrations of nitrogen dioxide and other air contaminants such as chromium (VI), by means of an approved local exhaust ventilation system. The system shall be capable of reducing and maintaining personal exposures to within permissible limits, or by means of other effective work practice and engineering controls such as the use of an argon- rich (> 75% argon) shielding gas for use in gas metal arc welding (GMAW) or flux cored arc welding (FCAW) operations. Wherever engineering and work practice controls are not sufficient to reduce employee exposures below permissible limits, the employer shall use them to reduce employee exposures to the lowest levels achievable, and shall supplement such methods by the use of respiratory protection that complies with the requirements of this Section and Section 05.

10.H Plasma Cutting.

10.H.01 Plasma arc cutting equipment shall be installed, maintained and operated in accordance with the NEC and manufacturer's instructions.

10.H.02 All cables and torch leads shall be inspected before each use. Any damaged cables and torch leads shall be replaced before use.

10.H.03 All consumables (nozzles, electrodes, etc.) shall be verified for proper installation before each use.

10.H.04 All torches used in plasma cutting shall contain a trigger safety device to prevent accidental contact.

10.I Thermite Welding. > *See Appendix Q.*

10.I.01 The mold for a thermite weld shall be dried thoroughly and provided cover before the charge is ignited to prevent spray back during the thermite welding reaction.

10.I.02 Storage of thermite welding supplies.

a. Bulk storage of thermite welding materials shall be maintained in a detached shed or building at least 50 ft (15 m) from the welding area.

b. Bulk storage areas for thermite welding materials shall be maintained dry and locked.

c. Storage containers for the starting material shall be closed tightly immediately after each use.

10.I.03 Thermite welding molds shall not be removed until sufficient cooling has taken place as stated in the manufacturer's literature.

10.I.04 Smoking shall not be allowed in areas where thermite welding material is being used or stored.

10

THIS PAGE INTENTIONALLY LEFT BLANK

SECTION 11 Electrical

Table of Contents

11

11.A General.

11.A.01 Approval and qualification. The term "Qualified Person (QP)", as used in this section, refers to "Qualified Person, Electrical". > *See Appendix Q.*

a. All electrical wiring and equipment shall be a type listed by a nationally recognized testing laboratory for the specific application for which it is to be used.

b. All electrical work shall comply with applicable National Electrical Safety Code (NESC), National Electric Code (NEC), National Fire Protection Association (NFPA), OSHA and USCG regulations. If the work being performed (as described within this chapter) conflicts with the above codes and regulations, the most stringent shall apply.

c. Electrical work shall be performed by QP with verifiable credentials who are familiar with applicable code requirements. Verifiable credentials consist of State, National and/or Local Certifications or Licenses that a Master or Journeyman Electrician may hold, depending on work being performed, and should be identified in the appropriate AHA. Journeyman/Apprentice ratio shall be in accordance with State, Local and Host Nation requirements applicable to where work is being performed.

d. USACE and/or other Government designated QPs must possess verifiable credentials and shall be familiar with applicable code requirements. Verifiable credentials consist of State, National and/or Local Certifications/Licenses that a Master or Journeyman Electrician may hold, or USACE -sponsored local training programs (e.g., hydropower training program, District navigation training program, etc.) but the following applies:

(1) Training shall be provided by an electrically qualified source to the level of work being performed;

(2) Training and qualifications shall be verifiable and documented;

(3) Qualification level shall be identified in the employee's PHA;

(4) QPs must demonstrate skills and knowledge related to the construction, operation and maintenance of the electrical equipment and installations and receive relevant safety training to recognize, avoid and control associated hazards.

e. Emergency Procedures and training. Employees exposed to shock hazard and those employees responsible for taking action in case of emergency shall be trained in methods of release of victims from contact with exposed energized electrical conductors or circuit parts. Employees shall be regularly instructed in methods of first aid and emergency procedures, such as approved methods of resuscitation, if their duties warrant such training. Training and re-training of employees in approved methods of resuscitation, including cardiopulmonary resuscitation and automatic external defibrillator (AED) use, shall be certified by the employer as required by *Section 03.A* and OSHA 29 CFR 1910.151 and NFPA 70E 110.2(c).

11.A.02 Isolation.

a. Before work begins, a Qualified Person in charge shall ascertain by inquiry, direct observation and by instruments, whether any part of an electric power circuit (exposed or concealed) is located such that the performance of work could bring any person, tool, or machine into physical or electrical contact with it. This verification procedure shall be documented prior to work beginning.

b. All equipment and circuits to be worked on shall be de-energized before work is started. Personnel shall be protected by a Hazardous Energy Control Program (HECP) and procedures (i.e. lockout/tagout, blanking, positive means of blocking, grounding, etc.). Positive means shall be provided for rendering controls or devices inoperable while repairs or adjustments are being made to the machines they control. > *See Section 12.*

➤ *Note: If work MUST be performed on an energized system, then the employer must first demonstrate that de-energizing introduces additional or increased hazards (i.e., interruption of life support equipment, removal of light for an area, etc.) or is infeasible due to equipment design or operational limitations (i.e., testing, troubleshooting, etc.).*

c. Energized work may never be performed without prior authorization. Once it has been determined that equipment must be worked on in an energized condition, an energized work permit shall be submitted to GDA for acceptance. > *See NFPA 70E.* Permits must be prepared in advance and include, as a minimum:

(1) Description of work and location;

(2) Justification for why the work must be performed in an energized condition;

(3) Description of work practices to be followed;

(4) An electrical shock analysis and boundaries (safe working distances);

(5) Arc flash hazard analysis and arc flash boundary determination;

(6) Identification of PPE necessary to safely perform the task;

(7) Means to restrict access of unqualified persons in work area;

(8) Evidence of completing the job briefing (includes safety, tools, PPE, any other hazards and controls).

d. Live parts of wiring or equipment shall be guarded to protect all persons or objects from harm.

e. High voltage equipment (i.e., switchyards, transformers, etc) shall be protected from unauthorized access. Entrances not under constant observation shall be kept locked; metallic enclosures shall be grounded and signs warning of high voltage and prohibiting unauthorized entrance shall be posted at entrances.

f. Enclosure gates or doors shall swing outward or provide clearance from installed equipment.

11.A.03 When it is necessary to work on energized lines or equipment, rubber gloves and other protective equipment and hotline tools meeting the provisions of ANSI and ASTM standards shall be used. For work on energized equipment, only tools insulated for the rated voltage shall be used.
> See Section 05.I and NFPA 70E.

11.A.04 Flexible cords.

a. Refer to NEC (NFPA 70) for minimum requirements on permanent use flexible cords for permanently installed equipment such as cranes and elevators.

b. For maintenance and construction activities, all portable flexible cords or cables (i.e., extension cords) shall be inspected by the user of the cord at least daily.

c. Portable flexible cords shall contain the number of adequately sized conductors required for the load plus an adequately sized equipment ground conductor. A QP shall determine appropriate hard or extra hard usage flexible cord length and size as specified in the NEC, Article 400. Portable flexible cords shall be minimum 14 AWG.

d. Portable flexible cords passing through work areas shall be protected from damage (including that caused by foot traffic, vehicles, sharp corners, protections, and pinching). Flexible cords and cables passing through holes shall be protected by bushings or fittings.

e. Portable flexible cords shall be used only in continuous lengths without splice or tap. The repair of hard-service cords/cord sets is permitted if conductors are spliced in accordance with NEC - the splices must be performed by a QP, the insulation is equal to the cable being spliced, and wire connections are soldered.

f. Patched, oil-soaked, worn, or frayed electric portable flexible cords shall not be used.

g. Portable flexible cords shall be supported in place at intervals that ensure that they will be protected from physical damage. Support shall be in the form of cable ties, straps or similar type fittings installed so as not to cause damage. They shall not be hung from nails, or suspended by bare wire.

11.A.05 The QP is responsible for determining the number of workers required to perform the job safely and shall identify work hazards and controls in the corresponding AHA. Work must be performed with a sufficient number of workers to provide a safe working environment.

11.A.06 Switchboxes, receptacle boxes, metal cabinets, enclosures around equipment, and temporary power lines shall be marked to indicate the maximum operating voltage.

11.A.07 Insulation mats or platforms of substantial construction and providing good footing shall be placed on floors and on the frames of equipment having exposed live parts so that the operator or persons in the vicinity cannot touch such parts unless standing on the mats, platforms, or insulated floors.

11.A.08 Suitable temporary barriers or other means shall be provided to designate arc flash and electrical shock boundaries. Boundaries shall ensure a workspace cannot be used as a passageway while electrical work is being performed.

11.A.09 When fuses are installed or removed with one or both terminals energized, use an insulated fuse pulling tool for the rated voltage.

11.A.10 Attachment plugs and receptacles.

a. Plugs and receptacles shall be kept out of water unless of an approved submersible type.

b. Attachment plugs for use in work areas shall be

11

constructed so that they will endure rough use and shall be equipped with a cord grip to prevent strain on the terminal screws.

c. Attachment plugs and other connectors supplying equipment at more than 240 volts shall be skirted or otherwise designed so that arcs will be confined.

d. Plugs and receptacles in power distribution networks of over 240 volts shall be inspected by a QP before each use.

e. Physical attachment of plugs into receptacles rated over 240 volts shall be made with the circuit de-energized.

f. Appropriate PPE shall be worn prior to energizing circuits feeding equipment plugged in to receptacles rated over 240 volts.

g. When a National Electrical Manufacturers Association (NEMA) standard configuration exists for a particular voltage, amperage, frequency, or type of current, the NEMA standard plug and receptacle shall be used.

11.A.11 Portable hand lamps.

a. Portable hand lamps shall be of molded composition or another type approved for the purpose.

b. Metal-shell, paper-lined lamp holders shall not be used.

c. Hand lamps shall be equipped with a handle and a substantial guard over the bulb. The guard shall be attached to the lamp holder or the handle.

11.A.12 Metal jewelry (i.e., wristbands, watch chains, rings, bracelets, necklaces, body jewelry, piercings, etc) shall not be worn when working on or near electrical equipment.

11.B Arc Flash.

11.B.01 Whenever work on or near energized parts greater than 50 volts is necessary, a hazard analysis/arc flash hazard analysis will be conducted in accordance with NFPA 70E. Either Appendices or Tables may be used to conduct the analysis. The flash protection boundary, approach distances, hazard/risk category and personal protective equipment (PPE) requirements shall all be identified.

11.B.02 PPE that provides appropriate arc flash protection is required for all personnel working on or near exposed energized electrical equipment operating at 50 volts or more. Identification of required PPE is based on equipment arc flash labels or NFPA 70E task tables. *> See Section 05.I.*

11.B.03 PPE garments shall meet and be labeled in accordance with ASTM F1506, *Standard Specification for Flame Resistant Textile Materials for Wearing Apparel for use by Electrical Workers Exposed to Momentary Electric Arc and Related Thermal Hazards.*

11.B.04 Arc rated clothing shall be properly worn. Long sleeves must be rolled down and buttoned, shorts are prohibited and trousers shall extend the full length of the leg. Garments with exposed metallic fasteners shall not be worn unless the garments are properly arc rated.

11.B.05 Garments, to include fall protection harnesses, worn over arc rated protective clothing, must also be arc rated.

11.B.06 Clothing that could increase the extent of injuries when exposed to electric arcs or open flames (i.e., acetate, nylon, polyester, rayon or any blend, celluloid or other flammable plastic), shall not be worn. No metal slides or zippers unless they are effectively covered.

11.B.07 Arc flash labels must be placed on energized equipment. Labels are required to warn of potential arc flash hazards and appropriate PPE. Labels, at minimum, shall include:

a. Limits of approach;

b. Nominal system voltage;

c. Hazard/Risk category (required PPE);

d. Incident energy at working distance.

11.B.08 All personnel entering the identified arc flash protection boundary must be QPs and properly trained in NFPA 70E requirements and procedures. Unless permitted by NFPA 70E, Article 130.4, no Unqualified Person shall be permitted to approach nearer than the Limited Approach Boundary of energized conductors and circuit parts. Training must be administered by an electrically qualified source and documented.

11.C Overcurrent Protection, Disconnects, and Switches.

11.C.01 All circuits shall be protected against overload.

a. Overcurrent protection shall be based on the current-carrying capacity of the conductors supplied and the power load being used.

b. No overcurrent device shall be placed in any

permanently grounded conductor except where the overcurrent device simultaneously opens all conductors of the circuit or where the device is required by NEC 430 for motor overload protection.

c. Overcurrent protection devices must be readily accessible, clearly labeled, not exposed to physical damage, not placed in the vicinity of easily ignitable materials, and located or shielded such that their operation will not expose employees to injury due to arcing or the sudden movement of parts.

d. Circuit breakers shall clearly indicate whether they are in the open (de- energized/off) or closed (energized/on) position.

e. Enclosures containing overcurrent protective devices shall be provided with lockable, close-fitting doors.

f. Access and working space shall be provided and maintained around all electrical equipment to permit ready and safe operation and maintenance in accordance with NFPA 70, Article 110.26, *Spaces About Electrical Equipment*. Where required clearance is not feasible (i.e., floating plant, vessels, etc.), procedures shall be in place to ensure sufficient clearance is maintained for fully opening the door and/or servicing the electrical enclosure.

11.C.02 Disconnects.

a. Disconnecting means shall be located or shielded so that persons will not be injured when the disconnect is operated.

b. Enclosures for disconnecting means shall be securely fastened to the surface and fitted with covers.

c. Disconnecting means shall be capable of accepting a lock and of being locked in the open (de-energized/off) position.

11.C.03 Switches.

a. A readily accessible, manually-operated switch shall be provided for each incoming service or supply circuit.

b. Switches shall be of the externally operable type mounted in an enclosure listed for the intended use and installed to minimize the danger of accidental operation.

11.C.04 Switches, fuses, and automatic circuit breakers shall be marked, labeled, or arranged for ready identification of the circuits or equipment that they supply.

11.C.05 Switches, circuit breakers, fuse panels, and motor controllers located outdoors or in wet locations shall be in a listed weatherproof enclosure or cabinet.

11.D Grounding.

11.D.01 All electrical circuits, equipment and enclosures shall be grounded in accordance with the NEC and the NESC to provide a permanent, continuous and effective path to ground unless otherwise noted in this manual.

a. A ground shall be provided for non-current carrying metallic parts of equipment such as generators (per NEC 250.34, portable and vehicle-mounted generators are exempt from grounding provided conditions if Section 11.D.01.b and c are met), non-engine driven electrically powered arc welders, light plants, switches, motor controller cases, fuse boxes, distribution cabinets, frames, non-current carrying rails used for travel and motors of electrically operated cranes, electric elevators, metal frames of non-electric elevators to which electric conductors are attached, other electric equipment, and metal enclosures around electric equipment.

b. Portable Generators. Portable describes equipment that is easily carried by personnel from one location to another. The frame of a portable generator is not required to be grounded and may serve as the grounding electrode for a system supplied by the generator under the following conditions:

(1) The generator supplies ONLY equipment mounted on the generator, cord-and-plug-connected equipment through receptacles mounted on the generator, or both; and

(2) The non-current-carrying metal parts of the equipment and the equipment grounding conductor terminals of the receptacles are bonded to the generator frame.

c. Vehicle-Mounted Generators. The frame of a vehicle need not be grounded and may serve as the grounding electrode for a system supplied by a generator located on the vehicle under the following conditions:

(1) The frame of the generator is bonded to the vehicle frame;

(2) The generator supplies only equipment located on the vehicle or cord-and-plug-connected equipment through receptacles mounted on the vehicle;

(3) The non-current-carrying metal parts of equipment and the equipment grounding conductor terminals of the receptacles are bonded to the generator frame; and

11

(4) The system complies with provisions of Section 11.D.01.

d. A system conductor that is required to be grounded (per NEC 250.34) shall be bonded to the generator frame where the generator is a component of a separately derived system.

e. Portable and semi-portable electrical tools and equipment shall be grounded by a multi-conductor cord having an identified grounding conductor and a multi-contact polarized plug and receptacle.

f. Floodlights, light plants and work lights shall be grounded.

g. Tools protected by an approved system of double insulation, or its equivalent, need not be grounded. Double-insulated tools shall be distinctly marked and listed by a nationally-recognized testing laboratory.

h. A grounding terminal or grounding type device on a receptacle, cord connector, or attachment plug may not be used for purposes other than grounding.

11.D.02 Grounding rod and pipe electrodes.

a. Electrodes of rod or pipe shall be free from non-conducting coatings and, if practicable, shall be embedded below permanent moisture levels.

b. Grounding rods and pipe electrodes shall be in unbroken 8 ft (2.4 m) lengths and driven to full depth. Where rock bottom is encountered, the electrode shall be driven at an angle not to exceed 45° from the vertical or shall be buried in a trench that is at least 2.5 ft (0.7 m) deep.

c. A single electrode that does not have a resistance to ground of 25 ohms or less, shall be augmented by one additional electrode spaced no closer than 6 ft (1.8 m) to the first electrode.

d. Electrodes or rods of iron or steel shall be at least 5/8 in (15 mm) diameter. Nonferrous rods, or their equivalent, shall be listed by a nationally-recognized testing laboratory and shall be at least ½ in (12 mm) diameter.

e. Electrodes or pipe or conduit shall be at least ¾ in (21 mm) trade size. Pipes and conduit of iron or steel shall have the outer surface galvanized or otherwise metal- coated for corrosion control.

f. Grounding electrode systems of permanent facilities shall be in accordance with NEC 250.

11.D.03 Conductors used for bonding or grounding stationary and movable equipment shall be of ample size to carry the anticipated current.

a. When attaching bonding and grounding clamps or clips, a secure and positive metal-to-metal contact shall be made.

b. The ground end shall be attached first. The equipment end shall be attached and removed by insulated tools or other suitable devices.

c. When removing grounds, the grounding device shall be removed from the line or equipment first, using insulated tools or other suitable devices.

d. Bonding and grounding attachments shall be made before systems are activated and shall not be broken until after systems are de-activated.

e. A designated grounding conductor shall not be used as a current carrying conductor.

11.D.04 Grounding circuits shall be checked to ensure that the circuit between the ground and a grounded power conductor has a resistance low enough to permit sufficient current flow to allow the fuse or circuit breaker to interrupt the current.

11.D.05 Ground-Fault Circuit-Interrupter (GFCI) Protection For Personnel. All receptacle outlets (125-volt, 15-, 20-, 30-amperage and greater) that provide temporary electrical power during construction, remodeling, maintenance, repair, or demolition shall have ground-fault circuit-interrupter (GFCI) protection for personnel. > See NEC, Article 590.6 and 29 CFR 1926.404(b); See also paragraph g below.

a. GFCI protection shall be provided on all circuits serving portable electric hand tools or semi-portable electric power tools (such as block/brick saws, table saws, air compressors, welding machines, and drill presses).

b. The GFCI device shall be calibrated to trip within the threshold values of 5 ma +/- 1 ma as specified in UL Standard 943. GFCI devices shall be tested before initial use and before use after modification.

c. Receptacle outlets that are not part of the permanent wiring of the building or structure shall be GFCI protected by one of the following means:

(1) A receptacle outlet with integral GFCI protection;

(2) A standard receptacle outlet connected downstream of a receptacle outlet with integral GFCI protection; or

(3) Receptacles protected by a GFCI-type circuit breaker.

d. Receptacle outlets that are part of the permanent wiring of the building or structure and are used for temporary electric power, (including portable generators) shall use a portable GFCI if the receptacle outlets are not already GFCI protected. The portable GFCI shall be as near as practicable to the receptacle outlet.

➤*Exception: In industrial facilities only, where conditions of maintenance and supervision ensure that only qualified personnel are involved, an Assured Equipment Grounding Conductor Program (AEGCP), see also Appendix E, shall be permitted for only those receptacle outlets used to supply equipment that would create a greater hazard if power was interrupted or having a design that is not compatible with GFCI protection.*

e. Electric tool circuits that are hard-wired directly to an electrical source of power shall be protected by a GFCI circuit-breaker type.

f. GFCIs shall be installed in accordance with the NEC. The permanent wiring shall consist of electrical circuits grounded in accordance with the NEC.

g. GFCIs may be sensitive to some equipment (such as concrete vibrators), or unavailable for the voltage and current rating. In these instances, an AEGCP in accordance with Appendix E is acceptable in lieu of GFCIs if the exception is documented on an AHA and contains the following:

(1) The conditions, or need, for the exception; and

(2) Implementation of the requirements of the AEGCP;

(3) The request for the exception, the AHA, and the AEGCP must be submitted and accepted by the GDA prior to implementing the program.

11.E Temporary Wiring and Lighting.

11.E.01   A sketch of proposed temporary power distribution systems shall be submitted to the GDA and accepted for use before temporary power is installed. The sketch shall indicate the location, voltages, and means of protection of all circuits, including receptacles, disconnecting means, grounding, GFCIs, and lighting circuits.

11.E.02 Testing.

a. Temporary electrical distribution systems and devices shall be checked and found acceptable for polarity, ground continuity, and ground resistance before initial use and before use after modification. GFCI shall be tested monthly.

b. Ground resistance and circuits shall be measured at the time of installation and shall comply with Sections 11.D.02 and 11.D.04. The measurement shall be recorded and a copy furnished to the GDA.

11.E.03 The vertical clearance of temporary wiring for circuits carrying 600 volts or less shall be:

a. 10 ft (3 m) above finished grade, sidewalks, or from any platform;

b. 12 ft (3.8 m) over areas other than public streets, alleys, roads and driveways, subject to vehicular traffic other than truck traffic;

c. 15 ft (4.5 m) over areas other than public streets, alleys, roads and driveways, subject to truck traffic;

d. 18 ft (5.5 m) over public streets, alleys, roads, and driveways.

11.E.04 Wet Locations. An Activity hazard Analysis (AHA) shall be developed by the work crew for these activities.

a. Submersible electric pumps may be used to support periodic maintenance and/or construction activities only when the pump is designed by the manufacturer to operate in wet locations.

(1) The pump shall be installed and tested by a QP and operated by personnel trained to the appropriate level.

(2) When personnel are, or could be, present in the water during pump operation, the pump shall be equipped with a Ground Fault Circuit Interrupter (GFCI), except as noted in (3) below.

➤*Note: If pump manufacturer does not allow personnel in the area when pumps are used in water, an appropriate Hazardous Energy Control Program, to include lockout/tagout, must be in place. > See Section 12.*

(3) Where conditions of maintenance and supervision ensure that only qualified personnel are involved, an Assured Equipment Grounding Conductor Program (AEGCP, see Appendix E) shall be permitted for those receptacle outlets used to

11

supply equipment that is not compatible with GFCI protection or that would create a greater hazard if power was interrupted. > *See Section 11.D.05.g, NEC Article 590.6 and 29 CFR 1926.404(b).*

> *Note: The AEGCP shall be continuously enforced at the site by one or more designated persons to ensure that equipment grounding conductors for all temporary power are installed and maintained in accordance with the AEGCP, NEC and OSHA.*

b. Where a receptacle is used in a wet location, it shall be contained in a weatherproof enclosure, the integrity of which is not affected when an attachment plug is inserted.

c. All temporary lighting strings in outdoor or wet locations (such as tunnels, culverts, valve pits, floating plant, etc.) shall consist of lamp sockets and connection plugs permanently molded to the hard service cord insulation.

11.E.05 Wires shall be insulated from their supports.

11.E.06 Temporary lighting.

a. Bulbs attached to temporary lighting strings and extension cords shall be protected by guards unless the bulbs are deeply recessed in a reflector.

b. Unless designed for suspension, temporary lights shall not be suspended by their electric wire.

c. Exposed empty light sockets and broken bulbs shall be replaced immediately.

d. Portable electric lighting used in wet and/or other conductive locations (e.g., drums, tanks, vessels, sumps, scroll cases, etc.) shall be rated and operated at 12 volts or less. > *See also Section 11.H.*

11.E.07 When temporary wiring is used in tanks or other confined spaces, an approved disconnect, properly identified, UL labeled, and rated for this application and environment, shall be provided at or near the entrance to such spaces for the purpose of readily disconnecting the electrical power in case of an emergency.

11.E.08 Non-metallic sheathed cable may be used as allowed by the NEC and as follows:

a. Along studs, joists, or similar supports closely following the building finish or running boards when 7 ft-8 in (2.3 m) or more above the floor;

b. When firmly attached to each cabinet, box fitting, or fixture by means of a cable clamp. > *Non-metallic sheathed cable may not be used when precluded by*

the NEC nor as portable extension cords, lying on the ground subject to any type of traffic, where subject to frequent flexing, or as service entrance cable.

11.E.09 Temporary lighting circuits shall be separate from electric tool circuits. Receptacle circuits shall be dedicated to either temporary lighting or electric tools and shall be labeled "LIGHTS ONLY" or "TOOLS ONLY," as applicable.

11.F Operations Adjacent to Overhead Lines.

11.F.01 Overhead transmission and distribution lines shall be carried on towers and poles that provide safe clearances over roadways and structures.

a. Clearances shall be adequate for the movement of vehicles and for the operation of construction equipment.

b. All electric power or distribution lines shall be placed underground in areas where there is extensive use of equipment having the capability to encroach on the clearance distances specified in Section 11.E.03. For voltages greater than 600, reference NESC for required clearance distance.

c. Protection of outdoor trolleys and portable cables rated above 600 volts for supplying power to moveable construction equipment such as gantry cranes, mobile cranes, shovels, etc., shall conform to NESC.

11.F.02 Work activity adjacent to overhead lines shall not be initiated until a survey has been made to ascertain the safe clearance from energized lines. > *See Section 11.A.02.*

11.F.03 Any overhead wire shall be considered energized unless the person owning such line or operating officials of the electrical utility supplying the line certifies that it is not energized and it has been visibly grounded and tested.

11.F.04 Operations adjacent to overhead lines are prohibited unless at least one of the following conditions is satisfied:

a. Power has been shut off and positive means taken to prevent the lines from being energized;

b. Equipment, or any part of the equipment, does not have the capability of coming within the minimum clearance from energized overhead lines as specified in Table 11-1, OR the equipment has been positioned and blocked to assure no part, including cables, wire rope, components and attachments, can come within those clearances; AND a notice of the minimum required clearance has been posted at the operator's position;

c. Electric line trucks and/or aerial lifts used for working on energized overhead lines must meet the requirements of OSHA 1910.269 and Table 11-I.

> NOTE: Cranes and other equipment (excavators, forklifts, etc) used to hoist loads with rigging: Equipment operations in which any part of the equipment, load line, or load (including rigging and lifting accessories) is closer than the minimum

approach distance in Table 11-1 to an energized power line is prohibited, except as allowed in Section 16.G.12.
> See 16.G.12 and Table 16-2.

TABLE 11-1

Minimum Clearance from Energized Overhead Electric Lines

NOTE: All dimensions are distances from live part to equipment and components at any potential reach

Voltage (nominal, kV, alternating current)	Minimum clearance distance
Up to 50	10 ft (3 m)
51 – 200	15 ft (4.6 m)
201 – 350	20 ft (6 m)
351 – 500	25 ft (7.6 m)
501 – 750	35 ft (10.7 m)
751 – 1000	45 ft (13.7 m)
Over 1,000	(As established by the utility owner/operator or registered professional engineer who is a qualified person with respect to electrical power transmission and distribution).

11

11.F.05 Work activity that could affect or be affected by overhead lines shall not be initiated until coordinated with the appropriate utility officials.

11.F.06 Standard emergency communication procedures shall be established and rehearsed to assure rapid emergency shutdown for all work being conducted on overhead power lines.

11.F.07 Floating plant and associated equipment shall not be sited or placed within 20 ft (6 m) of overhead transmission or distribution lines

11.F.08 Cage boom guards, insulating links, or proximity warning devices may be used on cranes, but such devices shall not alter the requirements of any other regulation of this part, even if such device is required by law or other regulation. Insulating links shall be capable of withstanding a 1 minute dry low frequency dielectric test of 50,000 volts AC.

11.F.09 Induced currents.

a. Before work near transmitter towers where there is potential for an electrical charge to be induced in equipment or materials, the transmitter shall be de-

energized or tests shall be conducted to determine if an electrical charge could be induced.

b. The following precautions shall be taken to dissipate induced voltages:

(1) The equipment shall be provided with an electrical ground to the upper rotating structure supporting the boom; and

(2) Ground jumper cables shall be attached to materials being handled by boom equipment when electrical charge could be induced while working near energized transmitters. Crews shall be provided with nonconductive poles having large alligator clips or other similar protection to attach the ground cable to the load and insulating gloves will be used.

11.G Batteries and Battery Charging.

11.G.01 Batteries shall be stored in enclosures with outside vents or in well-ventilated rooms and be so arranged as to prevent the escape of fumes, gasses, electrolyte spray, or liquid electrolyte into other areas.

11.G.02 Provisions shall be made for sufficient diffusion and ventilation of gases from storage batteries to prevent the accumulation of explosive mixtures.

11.G.03 Battery storage and handling.

a. Racks and trays shall be substantial and shall be treated to make them resistant to the electrolyte.

b. Floors shall be of acid resistant construction or protected from accumulation of acid.

c. Facilities for quick drenching of the eyes and body shall be provided for emergency use within 25 ft (7.6 m) of battery handling areas. > *See Section 06.B.02.b.*

d. Use only insulated tools in the battery area to prevent accidental shorting across battery connections.

e. PPE shall be used as prescribed in Section 11.G.06 and Section 5.

f. For lead acid batteries, bicarbonate of soda to neutralize any acid spillage [1 lb/gal (0.1 kg/L) of water] shall be provided for flushing and neutralizing spilled electrolyte and for fire protection.

11.G.04 Battery charging.

a. Battery charging installations shall be located in areas designated for that purpose.

b. Charging apparatus shall be protected against physical damage.

c. When charging batteries, the vent caps shall be kept in place to avoid spray of electrolyte. Care shall be taken to assure vent caps are functioning.

d. Prior to charging batteries, the electrolyte level shall be checked and adjusted to the proper level if necessary.

11.G.05 Exit route from battery area shall remain unobstructed.

11.G.06 PPE. The following shall be available and used for safe battery handling.

a. Goggles and faceshields appropriate to the chemical and electrical hazard;

b. Acid-resistant rubber gloves;

c. Protective rubber aprons and safety shoes;

d. Lifting devices of adequate capacity, when required.

11.H Hazardous (Classified) Locations.

11.H.01 Locations of electrical equipment and wiring shall be classified on the properties of the flammable vapors, liquids or gases, or combustible dusts or fibers that may be present and the likelihood that a flammable or combustible concentration or quantity is present. In classifying locations, each room, section, or area shall be classified on an individual basis in accordance with the definitions given in Table 11-2 and NEC Article 500. These hazardous locations within the facility, as designated, shall be documented by the employer.

11.H.02 All equipment, wiring methods, and installations of equipment in hazardous (classified) locations shall be either listed as intrinsically safe, listed for the hazardous location, or demonstrated to be safe for the location.

11.H.03 Only equipment wiring and installation of equipment in hazardous locations shall be permitted in those hazardous (classified) locations.

11.H.04 Equipment and wiring listed for the hazardous (classified) location shall be approved not only for the class of location but also for the ignitable or combustible properties of the specific gas, vapor, dust, or fiber that will be present.

a. This equipment shall be marked to show the class, group, and operating temperature or temperature range for which it is approved.

b. With the following exceptions, the temperature marking shall not exceed the ignition temperature of the specific gas or vapor to be encountered.

(1) Equipment of the non-heat producing type (e.g., junction boxes and conduit) and equipment of the heat producing type having a maximum temperature not more than 212°F (100°C) need not have a marked operating temperature or temperature range.

(2) Fixed lighting fixtures marked for use in Class I, Division 2 or Class II, Division 2 locations need not be marked to indicate the group.

(3) Fixed general-purpose equipment in Class I locations, other than lighting fixtures, that is acceptable for use in Class I, Division 2 locations need not be marked with the class, group, division, or operating temperature.

(4) Fixed dust-tight equipment, other than lighting fixtures, that is acceptable for use in Class II, Division 2, and Class III locations need not be marked with the class, group, division, or operating temperature.

TABLE 11-2

Hazardous (Classified) Locations

Class I — Gasses, Vapors or Liquids (A, B, C and D)	
Division 1	**Division 2**
Normally explosive and hazardous	Not normally present in an explosive concentration (but may accidentally exist).
Zone 0 (IEC Stds)	Zone 1 (IEC Stds)
Class II — Dusts (E, F and G)	
Division 1	**Division 2**
Ignitable quantity of dust that is normally or may be, in suspension or conduc dust may be present	Dust not normally suspended in an ignitable concentration (but may accidentally exist). Dust layers are present.
Class III — Fibers or Flyings (H)	
Division 1	**Division 2**
Handled or used in manufacturing	Stored or handled in storage (exclusive of manufacturing).

A - Acetylene

B – Hydrogen

C - Ethyl-ether vapors, ethylene, etc

D –Hydrocarbons, fuels, solvents, etc

E - Metal dust (conductive* and explosive);

F - Carbon dusts (some are conductive* and all are explosive)

G - Flour, starch, grain, Combustible Plastic or Chemical Dusts (explosive)

H – Textiles, woodworking, etc.,(easily ignitable, not likely to be explosive)

*Note: Electrically conductive dusts are dusts with a resistivity less than 10^5 OHM-centimeter

11.H.05 Equipment that is safe for the hazardous location shall be of a type and design that will provide protection from the hazards arising from the combustibility and flammability of vapors, liquids, gases, dusts, or fibers involved.

11.H.06 Equipment approved for a specific hazardous location shall not be installed or intermixed with equipment approved for another specific hazardous location.

11.H.07 All wiring components and utilization equipment shall be explosion proof (vapor, dust, or fiber tight) and shall be maintained in that condition.

a. There shall be no loose or missing screws, gaskets, threaded connections, or other impairments to this tight condition.

b. Conduits shall be threaded and made wrench-tight: where it is impractical to make a threaded joint tight, a bonding jumper shall be used.

11.I Power Transmission and Distribution.

11.I.01 The requirements in this subsection shall apply to the erection of new electric transmission and distribution lines and equipment, and the alteration, conversion, and improvement of existing electric transmission and distribution lines and equipment.

11.I.02 Before starting work, existing conditions shall be evaluated and determined. Such conditions shall include, but not be limited to, location and voltage of energized lines and equipment, conditions of poles, and location of circuits and equipment including power and communication lines and fire alarm circuits.

a. Electric equipment and lines shall be considered energized until determined to be de-energized by tests, or other means, and grounds applied.

b. New lines or equipment may be considered de-energized and worked as such where the lines or equipment are grounded or where the hazard of induced voltages is not present and adequate clearances or other means are implemented to prevent contact with energized lines or equipment.

c. The operating voltage of equipment and lines shall be determined before working on or near energized parts.

11.I.03 Clearance requirements of either subparagraph a or b below shall be observed.

a. No QP shall be permitted to approach or take any conductive object without an approved insulating handle closer to exposed energized parts than shown in Table 11-3 (phase to ground) unless:

(1) The QP is insulated or guarded from the energized part (gloves or gloves with sleeves rated for the voltage involved shall be considered insulation of the QP from the energized part);

(2) The energized part is insulated or guarded from the QP and any other conductive object at a different potential; or

(3) The QP is isolated, insulated, or guarded from any other conductive object(s), as during live-line, bare-hand work.

b. The minimum phase to ground working distance and minimum clear hot stick distances in Table 11-3 shall not be exceeded. The minimum clear hot stick distance refers to the distance from the hot end of live-line tools to the lineman when performing live-line work. Conductor support tools (such as link sticks, strain carriers, and insulator cradles) may be used provided the clear length of insulation is at least as long as the insulator string or as long as the minimum phase to ground distance in Table 11-3.

TABLE 11-3

AC Live Work Minimum Approach Distance
Reference 29 CFR 1910.269(L)(10), Table R-6

Voltage in kV (phase-to-phase)[1,2]	Distance to Employee			
	Phase-to-ground		Phase-to-phase	
	(m)	(ft-in)	(m)	(ft-in)
0 to 0.050	Not specified		Not specified	
0.051 to 0.300	Avoid contact		Avoid contact	
0.301 to 0.750	0.31	1-0	0.31	1-0
0.751 to 15	0.65	2-2	0.67	2-3
15.1 to 36.0	0.77	2-7	0.86	2-10
36.1 to 46	0.84	2-9	0.96	3-2
46.1 to 72.5	1.00[3]	3-3[3]	1.20	3-11
72.6 to 121	0.95[3]	3-2[3]	1.29	4-3
138 to 145	1.09	3-7	1.50	4-11
161 to 169	1.22	4-0	1.71	5-8
230 to 242	1.59	5-3	2.27	7-6
345 to 362	2.59	8-6	3.80	12-6
500 to 550	3.42	11-3	5.50	18-1
765 to 800	4.53	14-11	7.91	26-0

[1]For single-phase systems use the highest voltage available.

[2]For single-phase lines off three phase systems, use phase-to-phase voltage of the system.

[3]The 46.1 to 72.5 kV phase-to-ground 3-3 (ft-in) distance contains a 1-3 (ft-in) electrical component and a 2-0 (ft-in) inadvertent movement component while the 72.6 to 121 kV phase-to-ground 3-2 (ft-in) distance contains a 2-0 (ft-in) electrical component and a 1-0 (ft-in) inadvertent movement component.

11

11.I.04 When de-energizing lines and equipment operated in excess of 600 volts, and the means of disconnecting from electric energy is not visibly open or visibly locked and tagged out, provisions a through g below are required. > *In addition, requirements in Section 12 apply.*

a. The equipment or section of line to be de-energized shall be clearly identified and shall be isolated from all sources of voltage.

b. Notification and assurance from the GDA shall be obtained that:

(1) All switches and disconnects through which electric energy may be supplied to the particular section of line or equipment to be worked have been de-energized;

(2) All switches and disconnects are plainly tagged and/or locked indicating that persons are at work; and

(3) All switches and disconnects capable of being rendered inoperable are rendered inoperable.

c. After all designated switches and disconnects have been opened, rendered inoperable, and tagged and/or locked, visual inspections shall be conducted to ensure that equipment or lines are de-energized.

d. Protective grounds shall be applied on the disconnected equipment or lines to be worked on. > See Section 11.I.07.

e. Guards or barriers shall be erected as necessary to adjacent energized lines.

f. When more than one crew requires the same line or equipment to be de- energized, a prominent tag and lock for each crew shall be placed on the line or equipment by the Authorized Individual(s) holding the clearance(s) on said equipment or line.

g. Upon completion of work on de-energized lines or equipment, each Authorized Individual holding a clearance shall determine that all employees in the crew are clear and request a release of the clearance. The protective grounds installed will be removed. Authorized Individual will report to the GDA that all tags and locks protecting the crew may be removed.

11.I.05 When opening or closing a disconnect switch or circuit breaker on a power transmission/distribution line, exposure to potential explosion shall be limited. Safe operating procedures shall be established to minimize the risk of explosion.

11.I.06 When a crew working on a line or equipment can clearly see that the means of disconnecting from electrical energy are visibly open or visibly locked-out, the following provisions are required. > *See Section 12.*

a. Guards or barriers shall be erected as necessary to adjacent energized lines.

b. Upon completion of work on de-energized lines or equipment, each designated person-in-charge shall determine that all employees in the crew are clear that all protective grounds installed by the crew have been removed and shall report to the GDA that all tags and locks protecting the crew may be removed.

11.I.07 Grounding.

a. De-energized conductors and equipment that are to be grounded shall be tested or visually checked by meters or indicators to be de-energized.

b. Requirements as detailed in NEC and NESC for placing and removing protective grounds shall be followed.

c. Grounds shall be placed between the work location and all sources of energy and as close as practicable to the work location, or grounds shall be placed at the work location.

(1) If work is to be performed at more than one location in a line section, the line section must be grounded and short circuited at one location in the line section and the conductor to be worked on shall be grounded at each work location.

(2) The minimum distance in Table 11-3 shall be maintained from ungrounded conductors at the work location.

(3) Where the making of a ground is impractical, or the conditions resulting from it would be more hazardous than working on the lines or equipment without grounding, the grounds may be omitted and the line or equipment worked as energized.

d. Grounds may be temporarily removed only when necessary for test purposes and extreme caution shall be exercised during the test procedures. The lines or equipment from which grounds have been removed shall be considered energized.

e. When grounding electrodes are used, such electrodes shall have a resistance to ground of less than 25 ohms to remove the danger of harm to personnel or permit prompt operation of protective devices (NEC 250).

f. Grounding to tower shall be made with a tower clamp capable of conducting the anticipated fault current.

g. All ground leads shall be _properly sized for_ the anticipated fault current, _but shall never be sized smaller than No. 2 AWG._

11.I.08 Tools.

a. All hydraulic tools that are used on or around energized lines or equipment shall use non-conducting hoses having adequate strength for the normal operating pressures.

b. All pneumatic tools that are used on or around energized lines or equipment shall have non-conducting hoses of adequate strength for the normal operating pressures and have an accumulator on the compressor to collect moisture.

c. Portable metal or conductive ladders shall not be used near energized lines or equipment except in specialized work such as in high voltage substations where nonconductive ladders might present a greater hazard than conductive ladders. Conductive or metal ladders shall be prominently marked as conductive and all precautions shall be taken when used in specialized work.

d. _Conductive pull tape_ or rope shall not be used when working on or near energized parts.

11.I.09 Aerial lift trucks. > _See Sections 18 and 22.M._

a. The aerial device manufacturer shall state in the operator's manual and on the instruction plate whether the aerial device is insulating or non-insulating.

b. Aerial lift trucks shall be grounded or barricaded and considered as energized equipment, or the aerial lift truck shall be insulated for the work being performed. Table 11-1 will be legibly printed on a plate of durable non-conductive material and shall be mounted on the bucket or its vicinity so as to be visible to the operator of the boom.

c. Equipment or material shall not be passed between a pole or structure and an aerial lift while an employee working from the basket is within reaching distance of energized conductors or equipment that are not covered with insulating protective equipment.

d. Only qualified electrical workers may operate aerial lift equipment within the restricted approach boundary distances.

11.I.10 With the exception of equipment certified for work on the proper voltage, mechanical equipment shall not be operated closer to any energized line or equipment than the clearances in Table 11-1 unless:

a. An insulated barrier is installed between the energized part and the mechanical equipment;

b. The mechanical equipment is grounded;

c. The mechanical equipment is insulated; or

d. The mechanical equipment is considered as energized.

11.I.11 Material handling and storage.

a. When hauling poles during the hours of darkness, illuminated warning devices shall be attached to the trailing end of the longest pole.

b. Materials and equipment shall not be stored under energized bus, energized lines, or near energized equipment if it is possible to store them elsewhere. If materials or equipment must be stored under energized lines or near energized equipment, clearance shall be maintained as in Table 11-1 and extraordinary caution shall be exercised in maintaining these clearances when operating equipment or moving materials near such energized equipment.

c. Tag lines shall be of a non-conducting type when used near energized lines.

11.I.12 Before climbing poles, ladders, scaffolds, or other elevated structures, an inspection shall determine that the structures are capable of sustaining the additional or unbalanced stresses to which they will be subjected. Poles or structures that may be unsafe for climbing shall not be climbed until made safe by guying, bracing, or other means.

11.I.13 Before installing or removing wire or cable, action will be taken as necessary to prevent the failure of poles and other structures.

11.I.14 When setting, moving, or removing poles by cranes, derricks, gin poles, A- frames, or other mechanized equipment near energized lines or equipment, precautions shall be taken to avoid contact with energized lines or equipment, except in bare hand, live-line work, or where barriers or protective devices are used.

11.I.15 Unless using protective equipment for the voltage involved, employees standing on the ground shall avoid contacting equipment or machinery working adjacently to energized lines or equipment.

11.I.16 Lifting equipment shall be bonded to an effective ground or it shall be considered energized and barricaded when used near energized equipment or lines.

11.I.17 Pole holes shall not be left unattended or

11

unguarded.

11.I.18 Where necessary to assure the stability of mobile equipment, the location shall be graded and leveled.

11.I.19 When employees are working at two or more levels on a tower, activities shall be conducted such that there is a minimum exposure of employees to falling objects.

11.I.20 Guy lines shall be used to maintain sections or parts of tower sections in position and to reduce the possibility of tipping. Guy lines on towers shall be protected at ground level from accidental contact.

11.I.21 Tower members and sections being assembled shall be adequately supported.

11.I.22 No one shall be permitted under a tower that is in the process of erection or assembly, except as may be required to guide and secure the section being set.

11.I.23 When erecting towers using hoisting equipment adjacent to energized transmission lines, the lines shall be de-energized when practical. If the lines are not de-energized, minimum clearance distances shall be maintained as specified in Table 11-1 and extraordinary caution shall be exercised in maintaining these clearances when operating equipment or moving materials near such energized equipment.

11.I.24 The load line shall not be detached from a tower section until the section is adequately secured.

11.I.25 Except during emergency restoration procedures, tower erection shall be discontinued in high wind or other adverse weather conditions that could make the work hazardous. When work is conducted under such conditions, the hazards and the means for their control shall be delineated in an AHA.

11.I.26 Before stringing operations, a briefing shall be held to discuss the following:

    a. The plan of operation;

    b. The type of equipment to be used;

    c. Grounding devices and procedures to be followed;

    d. Crossover methods to be employed; and

    e. Clearance authorizations that are required.

11.I.27 When there is a possibility of a de-energized conductor being installed or removed coming into accidental contact with an energized circuit or receiving a dangerous induced voltage buildup, the conductor

being installed or removed shall be grounded or provisions made to insulate or isolate the employee.

11.I.28 If an existing line is de-energized, proper clearance authorization shall be secured and the line grounded on both sides of the crossover or the wire being strung or removed shall be considered and worked as energized.

11.I.29 When crossing over energized conductors in excess of 600 volts, ropes, nets or guard structures shall be installed unless provision is made to isolate or insulate the worker or the energized conductor. Where practical the automatic re-closing feature of the circuit-interrupting device shall be made inoperative. In addition, the line being strung shall be grounded on either side of the crossover or considered and worked as energized.

11.I.30 Conductors being strung or removed shall be kept under positive control by tension reels, guard structures, tie lines, or other means to prevent accidental contact with energized circuits.

11.I.31 Guard structure members shall be sound, of adequate dimension and strength, and adequately supported.

11.I.32 Catch-off anchors, rigging, and hoists shall be of ample capacity to prevent loss of the lines.

11.I.33 Reel handling equipment, including pulling and braking machines, shall have ample capacity, operate smoothly, and be leveled and aligned in accordance with the manufacturer's operating instructions.

11.I.34 The manufacturer's load rating shall not be exceeded for stringing lines, pulling lines, sock connections, and all load-bearing hardware and accessories.

11.I.35 Pulling lines and accessories shall be inspected regularly and replaced or repaired when damaged or when dependability may be doubtful.

11.I.36 Conductor grips shall not be used on wire rope unless designed for this application.

11.I.37 Employees shall not be permitted under overhead operations or on cross-arms while a conductor or pulling line is being pulled (in motion).

11.I.38 A transmission clipping crew shall have a minimum of two structures clipped between the crew and the conductor being sagged. When working on bare conductors, clipping and tying crews shall work between grounds at all times; the grounds shall remain intact until the conductors are clipped in, except on dead end structures.

11.I.39 Except during emergency restoration procedures, work from structures shall be discontinued when adverse weather (such as high wind or ice on structures) makes the work hazardous. Stringing and clipping operations shall be discontinued during an electrical storm in the vicinity.

11.I.40 Reliable communications between the reel tender and pulling rig operator shall be provided.

11.I.41 Each pull shall be snubbed or dead ended at both ends before subsequent pulls.

11.I.42 Before stringing parallel to an existing energized transmission line, a determination, by a QP, shall be made to ascertain whether dangerous induced voltage buildups will occur, particularly during switching and ground fault conditions. When there is a possibility that such dangerous induced voltage may exist, the employer shall comply with the provisions of Sections 11.I.42 through 11.I.49 in addition to the provisions of Sections 11.I.25 through 11.I.40 unless the line is worked as energized.

11.I.43 When stringing adjacent to energized lines, the tension stringing method or other methods that preclude unintentional contact between the lines being pulled and any person shall be used.

11.I.44 All pulling and tensioning equipment shall be isolated, insulated, or grounded.

11.I.45 A ground shall be installed between the tensioning reel setup and the first structure to ground each bare conductor, sub-conductor, and overhead ground conductor during stringing operations.

11.I.46 During stringing operations, each bare conductor, sub-conductor, and overhead ground conductor shall be grounded at the first tower adjacent to both the tensioning and pulling setup and in increments so that no point is more than 2 mi (3.2 km) from a ground.

　a. The grounds shall be left in place until conductor installation is complete.

　b. These grounds shall be removed as the last phase of aerial cleanup.

　c. Except for moveable-type grounds, the grounds shall be placed and removed with a hot stick.

11.I.47 Conductors, sub-conductors, and overhead ground conductors shall be grounded at all dead-end or catch-off points.

11.I.48 A ground shall be located at each side and within 10 ft (3 m) of working areas where conductors, sub-

conductors, or overhead ground conductors are being spliced at ground level. The two ends to be spliced shall be bonded to each other. Splicing should be carried out on either an insulated platform or a conductive metallic grounding mat bonded to both grounds. The grounding mat should be roped off and an insulated walkway provided for access to the mat.

11.I.49 All conductors, sub-conductors, and overhead ground conductors shall be bonded to any isolated tower where it may be necessary to complete work on the transmission line.

　a. Work on dead-end towers shall require grounding on all de-energized lines.

　b. Grounds may be removed as soon as the work is completed provided the line is not left open-circuited at the isolated tower at which work is being completed.

11.I.50 When performing work from the structure, clipping crews and all others working on conductors, sub-conductors, or overhead ground conductors shall be protected by individual grounds installed at every workstation.

11.I.51 Before using the live-line bare-hand technique on energized high-voltage conductors or parts, a check shall be made of:

　a. The voltage rating of the circuit on which the work is to be performed;

　b. The clearances to ground of lines and other energized parts of which work is to be performed; and

　c. The voltage limitations of the aerial-lift equipment intended to be used.

11.I.52 Only tools and equipment designed, tested, and intended for live-line bare-hand work shall be used, and such tools and equipment shall be kept clean and dry.

11.I.53 All work shall be personally supervised by a person trained and qualified to perform live-line bare-hand work.

11.I.54 The automatic re-closing feature of circuit interrupting devices shall be made inoperative where practical before working on any energized line or equipment.

11.I.55 Work shall not be performed during electrical storms or when electrical storms are imminent.

11.I.56 A conductive bucket liner or other suitable conductive device shall be provided for bonding the insulated aerial device to the energized line or equipment.

11

a. The employee shall be connected to the bucket liner by conductive shoes, leg clips, or other suitable means; climbers shall not be worn while performing work from an aerial lift.

b. Where necessary, electrostatic shielding for the voltage being worked or conductive clothing shall be provided.

11.I.57 Before the boom is elevated, the outriggers on the aerial truck shall be extended and adjusted to stabilize the truck. The body of the truck shall be bonded to an effective ground or barricaded and considered as energized equipment.

11.I.58 Before moving an aerial lift into the work position, all controls (ground level and bucket) shall be checked and tested to determine that they are in proper working condition.

11.I.59 Electrical insulating components and systems of aerial devices that are rated and used as an insulating device shall be, after a thorough inspection of their condition and cleanliness, tested for compliance with their rating.

a. Tests shall be conducted in accordance with the manufacturer's recommendations.

b. Tests shall be conducted only by QPs who are knowledgeable of the hazards.

11.I.60 All aerial lifts to be used for live-line bare-hand work shall have dual controls (ground level and basket).

a. The basket controls shall be within easy reach of the employee in the basket. If a two-basket lift is used, access to the controls shall be within easy reach from either basket.

b. The ground level controls shall be located near the base of the boom and will permit override operation of equipment at any time.

c. Except in case of an emergency, ground level lift control shall not be operated unless permission has been obtained from the employee in the lift. > See Section *11.I.57.*

11.I.61 Before an employee contacts the energized part to be worked on, the conductive bucket liner shall be bonded to the energized conductor by a positive connection that shall remain attached to the energized conductor until the work on the energized circuit is completed.

11.I.62 The minimum clearances for live-line bare-hand work shall be as specified in Table 11-3.

a. These minimum clearances shall be maintained from all grounded objects and from lines and equipment at a different potential than that to which the insulated aerial device is bonded, unless such grounded objects or other lines and equipment are covered by insulated guards.

b. These distances shall be maintained when approaching, leaving, and when bonded to the energized circuit.

c. When approaching, leaving, or bonding to an energized circuit, the minimum distances in Table 11-3 shall be maintained among all parts of the insulated boom assembly and any grounded parts (including the lower arm or portions of the truck).

d. When positioning the bucket alongside an energized bushing or insulator string, the minimum line-to-ground clearances of Table 11-3 must be maintained among all parts of the bucket and the grounded end of the bushing or insulator string.

e. A minimum clearance table (as in Table 11-3) shall be printed on a plate of durable nonconductive material and mounted in the bucket or in its vicinity so as to be visible to the boom operator.

f. Only insulated measuring sticks shall be used to verify clearance distances.

11.I.63 Handlines between buckets, booms, and the ground are prohibited.

a. Conductive materials more than 36 in (1 m) long shall NOT be placed in the bucket, except for appropriate length jumpers, armor rods, and tools.

b. Non-conductive handlines may be used from line to ground when not supported from the bucket.

11.I.64 The bucket and boom shall not exceed the manufacturer's rated capacity while attempting to lift or support additional load.

11.J Underground Electrical Installations.

11.J.01 Guarding underground openings.

a. Warning signs and rigid barricades shall be promptly placed when covers of manholes, handholes, or vaults are removed.

b. When an employee enters an underground opening the opening shall be protected with a barricade, temporary cover, or other guard appropriate for the hazard.

c. Underground opening guards and warning signs shall be adequately illuminated.

11.J.02 Maintenance holes and unvented vaults shall be treated as, and subject to the requirements of confined spaces. > *See Section 3*3.

11.J.03 Smoking shall be prohibited in maintenance holes and vaults.

11.J.04 When open flames must be used in manholes, ventilation shall be provided.

11.J.05 Before using open flames in maintenance holes or vaults, the holes/vaults shall be tested and found safe or cleared of any combustible gases or liquids.

11.J.06 When underground facilities are exposed (electric, gas, water, telephone, etc., or cables other than the one being worked on), they shall be protected to avoid damage.

11.J.07 Before cutting into a cable or opening a splice, the cable shall be identified and verified to be the proper cable and de-energized.

11.J.08 When working on buried cable or on cable in manholes, metallic sheath continuity shall be maintained by bonding across the opening or by equivalent means.

11.K Work In Energized Substations.

11.K.01 When working in an energized substation, authorization shall be obtained from the GDA before work is begun.

11.K.02 When work is to be done in an energized substation, the following shall be determined:

a. The facilities that are energized, and

b. Any protective equipment and precautions are necessary for the safety of personnel.

11.K.03 Clearance requirements per Section 11.I.03 shall be followed.

11.K.04 Only qualified employees shall perform work on or adjacent to energized control panels.
> *See Sections 11.A.01, 11.B.*

11.K.05 Precautions shall be taken to prevent accidental operation of relays or other protective devices due to jarring, vibration, or improper wiring.

11.K.06 Use of vehicles, gin poles, cranes, and other equipment in unguarded high voltage equipment areas

shall at all times be controlled by qualified employees.
> *See Table 11-1.*

11.K.07 All mobile cranes and derricks shall be effectively grounded when being moved or operated near energized lines or equipment or the equipment shall be considered energized.

11.K.08 When a substation fence must be expanded or removed, a temporary fence affording similar protection, when the site is unattended, shall be provided. Adequate interconnection with ground shall be maintained between temporary fence and permanent fence.

11.K.09 All gates to unattended substations shall be locked except when work is in progress.

11.K.10 When switching gang switches, visual inspection shall be made to ensure all insulators and the switch handle ground is in good condition. Insulating gloves must be worn when operating switch handles.

11.L Communication Facilities.

11.L.01 Employees shall not look into an open wave guide or antenna that is connected to an energized electromagnetic source.

11.L.02 If the electromagnetic radiation level within an accessible area exceeds the levels given in Section 06.F, the area shall be posted with appropriate signs.

11.L.03 When an employee works in an area where the electromagnetic radiation is unknown or could exceed the levels given in Section 06.F, measurements shall be taken to ensure that employee's exposure is not greater than that permitted.

11

THIS PAGE INTENTIONALLY LEFT BLANK

SECTION 12 Control of Hazardous Energy

Table of Contents

12

12.A General. Hazardous energy is any energy, including but not limited to mechanical (e.g., power transmission apparatus, counterbalances, springs, pressure, and gravity), pneumatic, hydraulic, electrical, chemical, nuclear, and thermal (e.g., high or low temperature) energies, that could cause injury to employees. > *See Section 12.B.*

12.A.01 When working on or near any system that produces, uses, or stores hazardous energy, a Hazardous Energy Control Program (HECP) is required.

a. USACE-owned/operated facilities and activities shall comply with ER 385-1-31, The Control of Hazardous Energy Program, and any regional HECP as well as local supplements in lieu of this section.

➤ *Note: When USACE employees are on a site that is controlled by a contractor and are affected by the contractor-managed HECP (e.g., QA's on construction sites, etc.), they shall comply with the contractor's HECP.*

b. On contractor-controlled sites:

(1) The contractor shall develop an HECP in accordance with this Section as well as all requirements of 29 CFR 1910.147, ANSI Z244.1, and ANSI A10.44. This HECP shall be submitted as part of their Accident Prevention Plan (APP) to the GDA for acceptance.

(2) The GDA and the contractor shall fully coordinate all control activities with one another throughout the planning and implementation of these activities. Each shall inform the other of their HECPs and Hazardous Energy Control (HEC) procedures, ensure that their own personnel understand and comply with rules and restrictions of the procedures agreed upon to be used for the job, and ensure that their employees affected by the HEC activity are notified when the procedural steps outlined in the HECP are to be initiated.

(3) HEC procedures shall be submitted to the GDA as part of the AHA for that phase of work. HEC procedures cannot be initiated until these procedures have been accepted by the GDA.

(4) The Prime Contractor, as the Controlling Contractor, is also responsible for the HEC procedures of all their sub-contractors. The prime and the sub-contractors shall fully coordinate all HEC activities with one another throughout the planning and implementation of work. Procedures to be used shall be discussed and coordinated to insure all

contractor, government or public persons are protected from hazardous energy, especially where crossover of contractor programs occur.

c. When contractor work involving hazardous energy will be performed at or on a USACE-operated facility, the following must occur:

(1) Contractors shall submit their HECP to the GDA for acceptance;

(2) HEC procedures shall be submitted to the GDA as part of the AHA for that phase of work. HEC procedures cannot be initiated until these procedures have been reviewed by a person knowledgeable in HEC and accepted by the GDA.

(3) The GDA and the Contractor shall fully coordinate all HEC activities with one another throughout the planning and implementation of these activities. The agreed upon HECP and HEC procedures shall be identified and documented.

(4) Both parties shall ensure that their own personnel understand and comply with rules and restrictions of the procedures agreed upon to be used for the job, and ensure that their employees affected by the HEC activity are notified when the procedural steps outlined in the HECP are to be initiated.

12.A.02 A preparatory meeting and inspection with the GDA and Contractor personnel shall be conducted to coordinate HEC activities. This meeting/inspection shall be documented.

a. Employees shall be trained and tested prior to working on Corps' Facilities where the Corps' HECP is in use to ensure that they are knowledgeable of the procedures.

b. Contractors shall ensure that all of their employees and sub-contractors are trained and knowledgeable in their HECPs.

c. When HEC procedures affect USACE and Contractors, USACE and Contractor authorized personnel will participate to ensure that HEC programs and procedures are in place and coordinated.

12.A.03 Introducing Energy inside Clearance Boundaries. To provide for safe work practices where energy is introduced within boundaries of an existing clearance (e.g., commissioning equipment and/or testing activities, etc.), these activities will be coordinated with and communicated to all affected personnel.

    a. An AHA, by the contractor performing the work, shall be created and implemented for these activities to ensure the integrity of the clearance boundary.

    b. Test procedures shall be provided to the GDA prior to performing these activities.

12.B Hazardous Energy Control Program (HECP).

12.B.01 The HECP shall clearly and specifically outline the scope, purpose, authorization, roles and responsibilities, rules, and techniques to be used for the control of hazardous energy.

12.B.02 The HECP shall include, but not be limited to, the following:

a. HECP procedures: Equipment-specific steps to control each energy source and must include isolating, blocking, verifying and securing systems;

b. Means of coordinating and communicating HEC activities with all site personnel (include contractor, sub-contractor, government, suppliers, public, visitors and any other personnel) to insure continuity of protection;

c. Procedural steps and responsibilities for the placement, removal, and transfer of locks, tags and other control devices;

d. Procedural steps, responsibilities and a means of accounting for placing and removing personal protective grounds;

e. Procedural steps, responsibilities and requirements for testing the system to verify the effectiveness of isolation and control;

f. Coordination (Shift/Schedule Change). Provisions shall be made to ensure total continuity of HEC protection during shift or personnel change;

g. Details of any emergency procedures;

h. Procedural steps and responsibilities for daily inspections (conducted to insure that all requirements of the HECP procedures are being followed and documented) and periodic inspections (shall be documented and shall specify the system where the HEC procedures were inspected, the date of the inspection, the names of employees performing and included in the inspections, and any deficiencies in complying with the HEC procedures); and

i. The means to enforce compliance with the HECP.

12.C Training.

12.C.01 Training applicable to the roles and responsibilities shall be provided to ensure that the purpose and function of the HEC procedures are understood by employees and that employees possess the knowledge and skills required for the safe application, usage, and removal of HEC devices.

12.C.02 When tagout systems are used (only when lockout is not possible), employees shall be trained in the limitations of tags.

12.C.03 Employees shall be retrained in HEC procedures whenever:

    a. There is a change in employee job responsibilities or a change in systems or processes that present a new energy control hazard;

    b. A periodic inspection reveals, or there is reason to suspect the presence of, inadequacies in or deviations from the employee's knowledge or use of HEC procedures;

    c. There is a change in contractor or local HEC procedures.

12.C.04 All training shall be documented. Documentation shall contain: names of employees trained; the time, date, and location of training; the name and qualifications of the trainer.

12.D Energy Isolating Devices and Procedures.

12.D.01 Energy Isolating Devices.

a. Energy isolating devices are mechanical devices that, when utilized or activated, physically prevent the unplanned transmission or release of energy and include, but are not limited to the following:

    (1) A manually operated electrical circuit breaker;

    (2) A disconnect switch;

    (3) A valve, bolted blank flange and bolted slip blinds;

    (4) A block (e.g., a safety block or cribbing).

b. Push-buttons, selector switches, safety interlocks, programmable logic controllers, software programming, and other control circuit type devices shall NOT be used as energy isolating devices.

12

12.D.02 Locks or other positive means control must always be used when the energy isolation involves equipment that is accessible by the public.

12.D.03 All equipment shall be covered by the HEC procedures and all energy sources shall be controlled before performing servicing, maintenance, testing, installation or removal on equipment in which the unexpected energizing, startup, or release of stored energy could occur and cause any of the following: Personal injury, property damage, loss of content, loss of protection, loss of capacity, or harm to the environment.

12.E Locks and Tags.

12.E.01 Systems with energy isolating devices that are capable of being locked out shall be locked out. If an energy isolating device is not capable of being locked out, the HEC procedures shall use tagout providing full personnel protection.

a. All tagout requirements of this regulation and of the HEC procedures shall be complied with;

b. The tag shall be attached to the same location, if possible, that the lock would have been attached. If this is not possible then the tag shall be attached as close a safely possible to the device and in a position that will be immediately obvious to anyone attempting to operate the device, and

c. Additional means (e.g., placement of the tag in a manner that inhibits operation of the energy isolating device, removal of an isolating circuit mechanism, blocking of a control switch, opening of an extra disconnecting device, removal of a valve handle to reduce the likelihood of inadvertent energizing, etc.) shall be employed to provide a level of protection commensurate with that provided by a lock.

d. When tags only must be used (the use of locks is not possible), employees shall be instructed in the following requirements and limitations of tags.

(1) Tags must be legible and understood by all authorized and affected employees and incidental personnel.

(2) Tags and their means of attachment must be made of materials that will withstand the environments encountered in the workplace.

(3) Tags shall be securely attached to energy isolating devices so that they cannot become inadvertently or accidentally detached during use.

(4) Tags shall not be removed without authorization of the authorized employee and shall never be bypassed, ignored, or otherwise defeated.

(5) Tags are essentially warning devices affixed to energy isolating devices and do not provide the physical protection that is provided by a lock; tags may evoke a false sense of security.

12.E.02 LOTO shall be performed only by authorized employees.

12.E.03 All employees affected by the LOTO shall be notified, before and upon completion of, the application and removal of locks or tags.

12.E.04 Locks and tags used for lockout/tagout (LOTO) shall:

a. Be capable of withstanding the environment that they are exposed to for the maximum period of time the exposure is expected;

b. Indicate the identity of the employee applying the device;

c. Be of a unique design or color to readily identify them as belonging to the LOTO program;

d. Not be used for anything other than lockout activities;

e. Identify the person who applied the lock or tag. Locks may have a tag attached with the employee's name and/or photograph which will satisfy this requirement;

f. Locks shall be substantial enough to prevent removal without the use of excessive force or unusual techniques (such as with the use of bolt cutters);

g. Tags shall, in addition, meet all of the following requirements:

(1) Have a standardized (within a project) print and format;

(2) Be constructed and printed so that exposure to weather conditions, ultraviolet (UV) light, wet or damp locations, or corrosive environments will not cause the tag to deteriorate or the message to become illegible;

(3) Be attached by means that are: Non-reusable; Substantial enough to prevent inadvertent or accidental removal; Attachable by hand; Self-locking; Non-releasable, with a minimum unlocking strength of no less than 50 lb (22.6 kg); and have the

basic characteristics of being at least equivalent to a one-piece, all-environment-tolerant nylon cable tie; and

(4) Warn against the hazardous condition resulting from system energization and include wording such as "DANGER - DO NOT START, OPEN, CLOSE, ENERGIZE, OPERATE".

12.E.05 Application and Removal Of Locks and Tags.

a. The authorized employee shall ensure that all energy isolating devices needed to control energy to or within the system are identified and that the system is shut down, isolated, blocked and secured in accordance with HEC procedures.

b. Any system operated by a remotely controlled source will be completely isolated such that it cannot be operated by that or any other source.

c. The authorized employee shall affix lock and tag to each energy isolating device in accordance with the HEC procedures.

d. When there is a possibility of re-accumulation of stored energy to a hazardous level, verification of isolation shall be continued until the energy control procedure is complete.

e. Before starting work on systems that have been locked/tagged out, the authorized individual shall verify that isolation and de-energization of the system have successfully been accomplished.

12.E.06 Personal Protective Grounds. Following the application of locks and/or tags to energy isolating devices, all potentially hazardous stored or residual energy shall be relieved or otherwise rendered safe.

a. Protective grounds shall be identified and accounted for in some manner, as identified in the Contractor's HECP and procedures.

b. The authorized employee (or his designee) is responsible for ensuring the control of residual energy and for placing and removing personal protective grounds in accordance with the Contractor's HECP and procedures.

12.E.07 Before locks or tags are removed and energy restored to the system, the authorized individual shall ensure that the following actions have been taken:

a. The work area has been inspected and all nonessential items (e.g., tools and materials) have been removed from the system, the system components are operationally intact, and all

employees have been safely positioned or removed from the area; and

b. All affected individuals have been notified that the locks or tags are about to be removed.

12.E.08 With the exception of the following conditions, each lock and/or tag shall be removed from each energy-isolating device by the authorized individual or systems operator who applied the device. When this employee is not available, the device(s) may be removed by another individual appointed by, and under the direction of the Contractor Project Manager or Contractor designated authority, provided that the following procedures are complied with:

a. The Contractor ensures that the individual appointed to remove locks and/or tags is knowledgeable of the scope and procedures of the safe clearance;

b. This individual and the requirements for transferring removal authority to him/her from the authorized individual are listed in the hazardous energy control plan;

c. Verification by the Contractor that the authorized employee who applied the device is not at the facility;

d. The Contractor designated authority makes all reasonable efforts to contact the authorized employee to inform him that the locks and/or tags are to be removed; and if a group clearance is involved, then an attempt must be made to have all affected persons sign off on the clearance or they must be contacted by phone. If contact cannot be made, then the lift may be made only after all necessary precautions are taken;

e. The authorized employee, upon returning, must be immediately notified of the lift prior to resuming their work.

12

THIS PAGE INTENTIONALLY LEFT BLANK

SECTION 13 Hand and Power Tools

Table of Contents

13

13.A General.

13.A.01 Power tools shall be of a manufacturer listed by a nationally recognized testing laboratory for the specific application for which they are to be used.

13.A.02 Use, inspection, and maintenance.

a. Hand and power tools shall be used, inspected, and maintained in accordance with the manufacturer's instructions and recommendations and shall be used only for the purpose for which designed. A copy of the manufacturer's instructions and recommendations shall be maintained with the tools.

b. Hand and power tools shall be inspected, tested, and determined to be in safe operating condition before use. Continued daily inspections shall be made to assure safe operating condition and proper maintenance.

c. Hand and power tools shall be in good repair and with all required safety devices installed and properly adjusted. Tools having defects that will impair their strength or render them unsafe shall be removed from service.

13.A.03 Guarding.

a. Power tools designed to accommodate guards shall be equipped with such guards. All guards must be functional.

b. Reciprocating, rotating, and moving parts of equipment shall be guarded if exposed to contact by employees or otherwise create a hazard.

13.A.04 When work is being performed overhead, tools not in use shall be secured or placed in holders.

13.A.05 Throwing tools or materials from one location to another or from one person to another, or dropping them to lower levels, shall not be permitted.

13.A.06 Only non-sparking tools shall be used in locations where sources of ignition may cause a fire or explosion.

13.A.07 Tools requiring heat treating or redressing shall be tempered, formed, dressed, and sharpened by personnel who are experienced in these operations.

13.A.08 The use of cranks on hand-powered winches or hoists is prohibited unless the hoists or winches are provided with positive self-locking dogs. Hand wheels with exposed spokes, projecting pins, or knobs shall not be used.

13.A.09 Hydraulic fluid used in powered tools shall retain its operating characteristics at the most extreme temperatures to which it will be exposed. > *For underground use, see Section 26.D.07.*

13.A.10 Manufacturers' safe operating pressures for hydraulic hoses, valves, pipes, filters and other fittings shall not be exceeded.

13.A.11 All hydraulic or pneumatic tools that are used on or around energized lines or equipment shall have non-conducting hoses of adequate strength for the normal operating pressures.

13.A.12 When fuel-powered tools are used in confined or enclosed spaces, the requirements for concentrations of toxic gases as outlined in Sections 5 and 34 of this manual, shall apply.

13.A.13 Clothing.

a. PPE shall be used as outlined in Section 5 of this manual.

b. Loose and frayed clothing, loose long hair, dangling jewelry (including dangling earrings, chains, and wrist watches) shall not be worn while working with any power tool.

13.A.14 For grounding requirements, see Section 11.

13.A.15 An electrical power control shall be provided on each machine/power tool to make it possible for the operator to cut off the power for the machine/power tool without leaving the point of operation.

13.A.16 On applications where injury to the operator might result if motors were to restart after power failure, provisions shall be made to prevent machines from automatically restarting upon restoration of power.

13.A.17 Floor- and bench-mounted power tools shall be anchored or securely clamped to a firm foundation. Anchoring or securing shall be sufficient to withstand lateral or vertical movement.

13.B Grinding and Abrasive Machinery.

13.B.01 With the exception of the following, abrasive wheels shall be used only on machines provided with safety guards. > *See ANSI B74.2 for descriptions of abrasive wheel types.*

a. Wheels used for internal work while within the work being ground;

b. Mounted wheels, 2 in (5 cm) and smaller in diameter, used in portable operations;

c. Types 16, 17, 18, 18R, and 19 cones and plugs and threaded hole pot balls where the work offers protection or where the size does not exceed 3 in (7.6 cm) in diameter by 5 in (12.7 cm) long;

d. Type 1 wheels not larger than 2 in (5 cm) in diameter and not more than ½ in (1.2 cm) thick, operated at peripheral speeds less than 1800 surface-feet per minute (ft/min) (9.1 surface-m/s) when mounted in mandrels driven by portable drills;

e. Type 1 reinforced wheels not more than 3 in (7.6 mm) in diameter and ¼ in (6 mm) in thickness, operating at peripheral speeds not exceeding 9500 surface-ft/min (48.3 surface-m/s), if safety glasses and face shield protection are worn.

13.B.02 Tongue guards on bench/stand grinders shall be adjustable to within ¼ in (6 mm) of the constantly decreasing diameter of the wheel at the upper opening.

13.B.03 Grinders shall be supplied with power sufficient to maintain the spindle speed at safe levels under all conditions of normal operation.

13.B.04 Work or tool rests shall not be adjusted while the grinding wheel is in motion.

13.B.05 Work/tool rests on power grinders shall not be more than 1/8 in (3 mm) distance from the wheel.

13.B.06 Abrasive wheels shall be closely inspected and ring-tested before mounting. Cracked or damaged grinding wheels shall be destroyed.

13.B.07 Grinding wheels shall not be operated in excess of their rated safe speed.

13.B.08 Floor stand and bench-mounted abrasive wheels used for external grinding shall be provided with safety guards (protective hoods).

a. The maximum angular exposure of the grinding wheel periphery and sides shall be not more than 90°, except that when work requires contact with the wheel below the horizontal plane of the spindle the angular exposure shall not exceed 125°; in either case, the exposure shall begin not more than 65° above the horizontal plane of the spindle.

b. Safety guards shall be strong enough to withstand the effect of a bursting wheel.

13.C Power Saws and Woodworking Machinery.

13.C.01 Woodworking machinery shall be operated and maintained in accordance with ANSI 01.1.

13.C.02 Guarding.

a. Circular saws shall be equipped with guards that automatically and completely enclose the cutting edges, splitters, and anti kickback devices.

b. Portable power-driven circular saws shall be equipped with guards above and below the base plate or shoe.

(1) The upper and lower guards shall cover the saw to the depth of the teeth, except for the minimum arc required to permit the base to be tilted for bevel cuts and for the minimum arc required to allow proper retraction and contact with the work, respectively.

(2) When the tool is withdrawn from the work, the lower guard shall automatically and instantly return to the covering position.

c. Blades of planers and jointers shall be fully guarded and have cylindrical heads with throats in the cylinder.

d. Band saw blades shall be fully enclosed except at the point of operation.

13.C.03 Automatic feeding devices shall be installed on machines whenever possible. Feeder attachments shall have the feed rolls or other moving parts covered or guarded so as to protect the operator from hazardous points.

13.C.04 The operating speed shall be permanently marked on circular saws more than 20 in (50.8 cm) in diameter or operating at over 10,000 peripheral ft/minute (min) (50.8 peripheral m/s).

a. Saws shall not be operated at a speed other than that marked on the blade.

b. When a marked saw is re-tensioned for a different speed, the marking shall be corrected to show the new speed.

13.C.05 Radial arm power saws shall be equipped with an automatic brake.

13.C.06 The table of radial arm or swing saws shall extend beyond the leading edge of the saw blade.

13.C.07 Radial arm power saws shall be installed in such a manner that the cutting head will return to the starting position when released by the operator. All swing cutoff and radial saws or similar machines that are drawn across a table shall be equipped with limit stops to prevent the leading edge of the tool from traveling beyond the edge of the table.

13.C.08 Each hand-fed crosscut table saw and each hand-fed circular ripsaw shall have a spreader to

13

prevent the material from squeezing the saw or being thrown back on the operator.

13.C.09 Operating procedures.

a. Band saws and other machinery requiring warm-up for safe operation shall be permitted to warm up before being put into operation whenever the temperature is below 45°F (7°C).

b. A push-stick, block, or other safe means shall be used on all operations close to high-speed cutting edges.

c. The use of cracked, bent, or otherwise defective parts such as saw blades, cutters, or knives is prohibited.

d. A brush shall be provided for the removal of sawdust, chips, and shavings on all woodworking machinery.

e. Power saws shall not be left running unattended.

13.D Pneumatic Power Tools.

13.D.01 Safety clips or retainers shall be installed and maintained on pneumatic impact (percussion) tools to prevent attachments from being accidentally expelled.

a. All hoses exceeding ½-in (1.3 cm) inside diameter shall have a safety device at the source of supply or branch line to reduce pressure in case of hose failure.

b. Compressed air pressure and volume shall be regulated according to manufacturer's rating for the tool.

13.D.02 Pressure shall be shut off and exhausted from the line before disconnecting the line from any tool or connection.

13.D.03 A safety lashing shall be provided at connections between tool and hose and at all quick makeup type connections.

13.D.04 Hoses shall not be used for hoisting or lowering tools.

13.D.05 Airless spray guns of the type which atomize paints and fluids at high pressures [1,000 lb (453.5 kg) or more, per square inch] shall be equipped with automatic or visible manual safety devices which will prevent pulling of the trigger to prevent release of the paint or fluid until the safety device is manually released. In lieu of the above, a diffuser nut that will prevent high-pressure velocity release while the nozzle tip is removed plus a nozzle tip guard that will prevent the tip from coming into contact with the operator, or other equivalent protection may be provided.

13.D.06 Impact wrenches shall be provided with a locking device for retaining the socket.

13.E Explosive-Actuated Tools.

13.E.01 Explosive-actuated (powder-actuated) tools shall meet the design requirements of ANSI A10.3.

13.E.02 Only qualified operators shall operate explosive-actuated tools. A qualified operator is one who has:

a. Been trained by an authorized instructor (one who has been trained, authorized, and provided an authorized instructor's card by the tool manufacturer or by an authorized representative of the tool manufacturer);

b. Passed a written examination provided by the manufacturer of the tool; and

c. Possesses a qualified operator's card supplied by the manufacturer and issued and signed by both the instructor and the operator.

13.E.03 Each tool shall be provided with the following:

a. A lockable container with the words "POWDER-ACTUATED TOOL" in plain sight on the outside and a notice reading "WARNING - POWDER-ACTUATED TOOL TO BE USED ONLY BY A QUALIFIED OPERATOR AND KEPT UNDER LOCK AND KEY WHEN NOT IN USE" on the inside;

b. Operator's instruction and service manual;

c. Power load and fastener charts;

d. Tool inspection record; and

e. Service tools and accessories.

13.E.04 Inspection and testing.

a. Daily inspection, cleaning, and testing shall be performed as recommended by the manufacturer.

b. Explosive-actuated tools shall be tested, in accordance with the manufacturer's recommended procedure, each day before loading to see that safety devices are in proper working condition.

c. Explosive-actuated tools shall be inspected, thoroughly cleaned, and tested after each 1,000 fastenings.

13.E.05 Explosive-actuated tools and the charges shall be secured at all times to prevent unauthorized possession or use.

13.E.06 Explosive-actuated tools shall not be loaded until just before the intended firing time. Neither loaded nor empty tools are to be pointed at any employees. Hands shall be kept clear of the open barrel end.

13.E.07 The use of explosive-actuated tools is prohibited in explosive or flammable atmospheres.

13.E.08 Fasteners shall not be driven:

a. Into soft or easily penetrable materials unless they are backed by a material that will prevent the fastener from passing through to the other side;

b. Into very hard or brittle material, such as cast iron, hardened steel, glazed or hollow tile, glass block, brick, or rock;

c. Into concrete unless the material thickness is at least three times the penetration of the fastener shank; or

d. Into spalled concrete.

13.E.09 The tool operator shall wear appropriate PPE, to include eye protection, hard hats, safety shoes and hearing protection as required. > See Section 5.

13.E.10 If the powder-actuated tool misfires, the employee shall wait at least 30 seconds, then try firing again. If the tool will not fire after a second attempt, the employee shall wait at least another 30 seconds before removing the faulty cartridge. The faulty cartridge shall be placed in water until disposal. Disposal shall follow manufacturer's instructions.

13.F Chainsaws.

13.F.01 Chainsaws shall have an automatic chain brake or kickback device.

13.F.02 The idle speed shall be adjusted so that the chain does not move when the engine is idling.

13.F.03 See Section 5 for proper PPE.

13.F.04 Chainsaws will not be fueled while running, while hot, or near an open flame. Saws will not be started within 10 ft (3 m) of a fuel container.

13.F.05 The operator will hold the saw with both hands during all cutting operations.

13.F.06 A chainsaw must never be used to cut above the operators' shoulder height.

13.F.07 See Section 31 for tree maintenance and removal requirements.

13.G Abrasive Blasting Equipment.

13.G.01 Hose and hose connections shall be designed to prevent build up of static electricity.

13.G.02 Connections and nozzles shall be designed to prevent accidental disengagement. All connections shall be equipped with safety lashings. > See Sections 20.A.16 and 20.A.17.

13.G.03 Nozzle attachments shall be of metal and fit on the outside of the hose. A deadman-type control device shall be provided at the nozzle to cut off the flow if the operator loses control of hose. A support shall be provided on which the nozzle may be mounted when it is not in use.

13.G.04 Additional requirements on abrasive blasting are in Sections 5 and 6.

13.H Power-Driven Nailers and Staplers.

13.H.01 This section applies to hand-held electric, combustion or pneumatically-driven nailers, staplers, and other similar equipment (referred to as "nailers" in this section) which operate by ejecting a fastener into the material to be fastened when a trigger, lever, or other manual device is actuated. This does not apply to common spring-loaded "staple guns".

13.H.02 Nailers shall have a safety device on the muzzle to prevent the tool from ejecting fasteners unless the muzzle is in contact with the work surface. The contact trip device or trigger shall not be secured in an "on" position.

13.H.03 Nailers shall be operated in a way to minimize the danger to others and the operator from ricochets, air-firing, and firing through materials being fastened.

a. Except when used for attaching sheet goods (sheathing, sub-flooring, plywood, etc.) or roofing products, nailers shall be operated with a sequential trigger system that requires the surface contact trip device to be depressed before the firing trigger can be activated and that limits ejection to one nail per trigger pull before resetting.

b. When used for sheet goods and roofing materials, nailers may be operated in the contact trip mode (bump or bounce-nailing) only as allowed by the manufacturer. This mode may only be used when the operator has secure footing, such as on a work platform, floor or deck, and shall not be used when the operator is on a ladder, beam, or similar situations where the operator's balance and/ or reach may be unstable.

13.H.04 Workers that use nailers shall wear appropriate PPE, to include eye protection, hard hats, safety shoes and hearing protection as required. > See Section 5.

13.H.05 When clearing a nail jam or performing maintenance on the nailer, the air hose shall be disconnected. > Use proper Hazardous Energy Control procedures per Section 12.

13

THIS PAGE INTENTIONALLY LEFT BLANK

SECTION 14 Material Handling, Storage and Disposal

Table of Contents

14

14.A Material Handling.

14.A.01 Employees shall be trained in and shall use safe lifting techniques. > See *Section 6.K.*

14.A.02 Requirements for PPE are covered in Section 5.

14.A.03 Material handling devices shall be available and used for the material handling needs of an activity.

14.A.04 Whenever heavy or bulky material is to be moved, the material handling needs shall be evaluated in terms of weight, size, distance, and path of movement. The following hierarchy shall be followed in selecting a means for material handling:

a. Elimination of material handling needs via engineering solutions;

b. Movement by mechanical device (e.g., lift truck, overhead crane, or conveyor);

c. Movement by manual means with handling aid (e.g., dollie or cart); or

d. Movement using safe lifting techniques. > See NIOSH, *"Work Practices Guide for Manual Lifting"*.

14.A.05 Materials will not be moved over or suspended above personnel unless positive precautions have been taken to protect the personnel from falling objects.

14.A.06 Where the movement of materials may be hazardous to persons, taglines or other devices shall be used to control the loads being handled by hoisting equipment. These devices shall be nonconductive when used near energized lines.

14.A.07 Banding or strapping shall not be used as rigging to hoist loads of bundled materials.

14.B Material Hoists.

14.B.01 Material hoists shall be designed to raise and lower materials during construction, alteration, or demolition. It is not applicable to the temporary use of permanently installed elevators used as material hoists. They shall be constructed and installed in accordance with the requirements of ANSI A10.5.

14.B.02 Material hoist towers, masts, guy or braces, counterweights, drive machinery supports, sheave supports, platforms, supporting structures, and accessories shall be designed by a licensed engineer.

14.B.03 Hoist towers shall be erected and dismantled only under the direct supervision of a qualified individual.

14.B.04 A copy of the hoist operating manual shall be available for each hoist on site.

14.B.05 Material hoists and hoist tower systems shall be inspected in accordance with the manufacturer's recommendations.

a. Prior to initial use and each time after the tower is extended, all parts of the tower or mast, cage, bucket, boom, platform, hoisting machine, guy, and other equipment shall be inspected by a Qualified Person (QP) to ensure compliance with the manufacturer's inspection guidelines and ANSI A10.5.

b. Prior to initial use on a USACE project, and monthly thereafter, a periodic inspection shall be conducted by a QP. Periodic inspections shall cover those items specified by the manufacturer.

c. A GDA shall be notified at least 24 hours prior to any of the above inspections and may wish to accompany the contractor's inspector.

d. Pre-operational inspections (start-up procedures) shall be conducted by the operator prior to every operation (shift) of the hoist.

14.B.06 Before a hoist is placed in service and every 4 months thereafter, a car arresting device test shall be performed.

a. For rope-supported cars, the test shall be conducted in the following manner:

(1) Pull a loop in the lifting rope and attach the test rope to each side of the loop above the bucket or platform;

(2) Raise the platform or bucket to allow the load to be supported by the test rope; and

(3) Cut the test rope to allow the load to fall and activate the car-arresting device.

b. For car suspension other than rope supported, the test shall be conducted by creating an over speed condition of the car.

c. Structural components shall be inspected for damage after the test and before the hoist is placed in operation again.

14.B.07 Maintenance and repairs.

a. Replacement parts for load bearing or critical components shall be either obtained from or certified by the equipment manufacturer.

b. Maintenance and repairs shall be conducted in accordance with the manufacturer's procedures.

14.B.08 Landings and runways.

a. Landing platforms and runways that connect the hoist way or tower to a structure shall be designed and constructed to sustain the maximum intended load without failure.

b. Floors or platforms that may become slippery shall have slip-resistant surfaces.

c. When workers may be exposed to falling objects, overhead protection, composed of 2 in (5 cm) planking or equivalent, shall be provided.

d. A barricade shall be provided at the open ends of each landing. The barricade shall extend a minimum distance of 6 ft (1.8 m) laterally along the outer edge of the landing from each side of the hoist way, shall extend from the floor a distance of at least 3 ft (0.9 m), and shall be of #19 US gauge wire or the equivalent, with openings not exceeding ½-in (1.2 cm).

e. All hoist way entrances shall be protected by substantial gates or bars that shall guard the full width of the landing entrance. Gates shall be not less than 66 in (167.6 cm) in height, with a maximum under clearance of 2 in (5 cm), and shall be located not more than 4 in (10 cm) from the hoist way line. Gates of grille, lattice, or other open work shall have openings of not more than 2 in (5 cm).

f. Material shall not be stored on landing platforms or runways.

14.B.09 Whenever a slack line condition occurs, the proper seating of the rope in the sheaves and on the drum shall be checked prior to further operations.

14.B.10 Riding on material hoists or other hoisting equipment not meant for personnel handling is prohibited.

14.B.11 While hoisting equipment is in operation, the operator shall not perform any other work and shall not leave his/her position at the controls until the load has been safely landed or returned to ground level.

14.B.12 Not more than one cage or bucket shall be operated at the same time by any one hoisting machine or operator.

14.B.13 Operating rules shall be established and posted at the operator's station of the hoist. Such rules shall include signal system and allowable line speed for various loads. Rules and notices shall be posted on the car frame or crosshead in a conspicuous location, including the statement "NO RIDERS ALLOWED."

14.B.14 Air-powered hoists shall be connected to an air supply of sufficient capacity and pressure to safely operate the hoist. Pneumatic hoses shall be secured by some positive means to prevent accidental disconnection.

14.C Material Storage.

14.C.01 All material in bags, containers, bundles, or stored in tiers shall be stacked, blocked, interlocked, and limited in height so that it is stable and secured against sliding or collapse.

a. Material shall be stacked as low as practical and in no case higher than 20 ft (6 m) unless otherwise specified in this Section.

b. Storage of flammable and combustible materials is covered in Section 9.

c. Storage of hazardous and toxic agents is covered in Section 6.

d. Storage of compressed gas cylinders is covered in Section 20.D.03.

14.C.02 Materials that could become damaged or affected by exposure to the elements shall be adequately covered or stored indoors.

14.C.03 Materials shall not be stored in areas that would interfere with other normal operations.

14.C.04 Materials shall not be stored directly under power lines unless safe clearance/distance from all materials to the power line is achieved. Documentation shall be in an AHA.

14.C.05 Material storage shall be in compliance with manufacturer's recommendations.

14.C.06 Materials stored inside buildings under construction shall not be placed within 6 ft (1.8 m) of any hoistway or floor opening, or within 10 ft (3 m) of an exterior wall that does not extend above the materials stored.

14

14.C.07 Accessways shall be kept clear.

14.C.08 Unauthorized persons shall be prohibited from entering storage areas. All persons shall be in a safe position while materials are being loaded or unloaded from railroad cars, trucks or barges.

14.C.09 Material shall not be stored on scaffolds, work platforms, or runways in excess of the standards in Section 22.

14.C.10 Materials stored in bins or hoppers that could create an engulfment hazard shall be evaluated and comply with the confined space requirements in Section 33.

14.C.11 Noncompatible materials shall be segregated in storage.

14.C.12 Storage of lumber.

a. Storage of lumber during construction shall be in sections containing a maximum of 1 million board feet with at least a 10 ft (3 m) clearance from buildings.

b. Lumber shall be supported on stable sills and shall be stacked level, stable, and self-supporting.

c. Reusable lumber shall have all nails withdrawn before it is stacked for storage.

d. Lumber piles shall not exceed 20 ft (6 m) in height; lumber to be handled manually shall not be stacked more than 16 ft (4.8 m) high.

14.C.13 Storage of bagged materials.

a. Bagged materials shall be stacked by stepping back the layers and cross-keying the bags at least every 10 bags high.

b. Bags of cement and lime shall not be stacked more than 10 high without setback, except when restrained by walls of appropriate strength.

c. The bags around the outside of the stack shall be placed with the mouths of the bags facing the center of the stack.

d. During unstacking, the top of the stack shall be kept nearly level and the necessary setback maintained.

14.C.14 Storage of brick.

a. Brick shall be stacked on an even, solid surface.

b. Bricks stacks shall not be more than 7 ft (2.1 m) high. When stacked loose brick reaches a height of 4 ft (1.2 m), it shall be tapered back 2 in (5 cm) in every 1 ft (0.3 m) of height above the 4 ft (1.2 m) level.

c. Unitized brick (brick securely gathered into large standard packages and fastened with straps) shall not be stacked more than three units high.

14.C.15 Storage of floor, wall, and partition block.

a. Blocks shall be stacked in tiers on solid, level surfaces.

b. When masonry blocks are stacked higher than 6 ft (1.8 m), the stack shall be tapered back one-half block per tier above the 6 ft level.

14.C.16 Storage of reinforcing and structural steel.

a. Reinforcing steel shall be stored in orderly piles away from walkways and roadways.

b. Structural steel shall be securely piled to prevent members sliding off or the pile toppling over.

14.C.17 Storage of cylindrical material.

a. Structural steel, poles, pipe, bar stock, and other cylindrical materials, unless racked, shall be stacked and blocked so as to prevent spreading or tilting.

b. Pipe, unless racked, shall not be stacked higher than 5 ft (1.5 m).

c. Either a pyramid or battened stack shall be used.

d. Where a battened stack is used, the outside pile or pole shall be securely chocked. Battened stacks shall be tapered back at least one pile or pole in each tier.

e. Unloading of round material shall be done so that no person is required to be on the unloading side of the carrier after the tie wires have been cut or during the unlocking of the stakes.

14.D Housekeeping.

14.D.01 Work areas and means of access shall be maintained safe and orderly.

a. Sufficient personnel and equipment shall be provided to ensure compliance with all housekeeping requirements.

b. Work areas shall be inspected daily for adequate housekeeping and findings shall be recorded on daily inspection reports.

c. Work will not be allowed in those areas that do not comply with the requirements of this Section.

14.D.02 All stairways, passageways, gangways, and accessways shall be kept free of materials, supplies, and obstructions at all times.

14.D.03 Loose or light material shall not be stored or left on roofs or floors that are not closed in, unless it is safely secured.

14.D.04 Tools, materials, extension cords, hoses, or debris shall not cause tripping or other hazards.

14.D.05 Tools, materials, and equipment subject to displacement or falling shall be adequately secured.

14.D.06 Empty bags having contained lime, cement, and other dust-producing material shall be removed periodically as specified by the GDA.

14.D.07 Form and scrap lumber and debris shall be cleared from work areas and accessways in and around building storage yards and other structures.

14.D.08 Protruding nails in scrap boards, planks, and timbers shall be removed, hammered in, or bent over flush with the wood at the time it is disassembled.

14.D.09 Storage and construction sites shall be kept free from the accumulation of combustible materials.

a. Weeds and grass shall be kept down.

b. A regular procedure shall be established for the cleanup of the areas as specified by the GDA.

c. Rubbish, brush, long grass, or other combustible material shall be kept from areas where flammable and combustible liquids are stored, handled, or processed.

14.D.10 Accumulation of liquids, particularly flammable and combustible liquids, on floors, walls, etc., is prohibited. All spills of flammable and combustible liquids shall be cleaned up immediately.

14.E Debris Nets.

14.E.01 When used with personnel safety nets, debris nets shall be secured on top of the personnel safety net but shall not compromise the design, construction or performance of the personnel nets.

14.E.02 A competent person (CP) shall determine and document the size, weight and height of fall of potential falling debris. The debris netting shall have a mesh of the size and strength sufficient to contain the expected debris without penetration when properly supported.

14.E.03 Materials, scraps, equipment, tools and debris that have fallen into the net shall be removed as soon as possible from the net and at least before the next work shift.

14.E.04 Nets and debris shall be protected from sparks and hot slag resulting from welding and cutting operations.

14.E.05 Inspection of debris nets.

a. Debris nets shall be inspected by a CP in accordance with the manufacturer's recommendations.

b. Inspections shall be conducted after installation, at least weekly thereafter, and following any alteration, repair or any occurrence that could affect the integrity of the net system. Inspections shall be documented and maintained on site.

c. Defective nets shall not be used; defective components shall be removed from service.

d. When welding or cutting operations occur above the nets, frequency of inspections shall be increased in proportion to the potential for damage to the nets.

14.F Material Disposal.

14.F.01 Waste material and rubbish shall be placed in containers or, if appropriate, in piles.

a. All containers holding waste material, piles, or stacked material shall be labeled as a waste.

b. Waste material shall be piled or stacked so to prevent engulfment or material avalanche and away from any traffic areas or walkways.

14.F.02 Waste materials and rubbish shall not be thrown down from a height of more than 6 ft (1.8 m), unless the following are complied with:

a. The materials or rubbish are dropped through an enclosed chute constructed of wood or equivalent material. Chutes for debris shall be enclosed, except for openings equipped with closures at or about floor level for the insertion of materials. The openings shall not exceed 4 ft (1.2 m) in height measured along the wall of the chute. Openings shall be kept closed when not in use.

b. When debris cannot be handled by chutes, the area into which the material is dropped shall be enclosed with barricades not less than 42 in (1.1) in height. Barricades shall be positioned to keep personnel from all debris landing areas. Signs warning of the hazard of falling material shall be posted at all debris landing areas and at each level exposed to falling debris.

14.F.03 Burning requirements are found in Section 9.

14.F.04 Separate covered, self-closing, nonflammable/non-reactive containers shall be provided for the collection of garbage, oily, flammable, and dangerous wastes.

14

a. The containers shall be labeled with a description of the contents.

b. The contents shall be properly disposed of daily.

14.F.05 Hazardous material waste (i.e., vehicle and equipment oils and lubricants, containers and drums for solvents, adhesives, etc.) shall be collected, stored, and disposed of in accordance with Section 06.B.03, Federal, State, and local requirements.

SECTION 15 Rigging

Table of Contents

15

15.A General.

15.A.01 Inspection and use.

a. Rigging equipment shall be inspected as specified by the manufacturer, by a Competent Person (CP), before use on each shift as necessary during its use to ensure that it is safe. The CP must have training and experience equivalent to, or be under the supervision of a Qualified Rigger (QR) as defined in Appendix Q.

b. Defective rigging shall be removed from service.

c. The use, inspection and maintenance of rigging equipment shall be in accordance with the rigging equipment manufacturer. Rigging equipment shall not be loaded in excess of its working load limit (WLL).

d. Rigging equipment, when not in use, shall be removed from the immediate work area and properly stored and maintained in a safe condition.

15.A.02 Hoist rope shall not be wrapped around the load.

15.A.03 All eye splices shall be made in an approved manner per ASME B30.9.

15.A.04 When hoisting loads, a positive latching device shall be used to secure the load and rigging (e.g., self-closing or self-locking hooks, an alloy anchor type shackle with a bolt, nut and retaining pin, screw-pin shackle, etc). > See Section 15.E.07.

15.A.05 Custom fabricated grabs, hooks, clamps, or other lifting accessories (e.g., equalizing beams, lifting or spreader beams, etc.) for such units as modular panels, prefabricated structures, and similar materials shall be designed by an Registered Professional Engineer (RPE), marked to indicate the WLL and shall be proof-tested before initial use, to 125% of their WLL.

15.A.06 Structural and mechanical lifting devices shall be designed, tested and used in accordance with ASME B30.20, *Below the Hook Lifting Devices*.

15.B Personnel Qualifications.

15.B.01 Any worker engaged in the duties and performance of rigging shall be a Qualified Rigger (QR). Employers must determine and designate in writing the QRs and the specific rigging tasks for which they are qualified and provide to the GDA for acceptance.

> *Note: The term "rigger" or "Qualified Rigger (QR)" in this manual refers to the function performed, and in no way relates to the worker's job classification or position.*

a. Each QR may have different credentials or experience. A QR is a person that :

(1) Has extensive knowledge, training and experience sufficient to calculate loads, load weights, safe capacities and apply other safe rigging principles and procedures;

(2) Demonstrates the ability to utilize rigging materials and principles, and;

(3) Is capable of safely inspecting and performing rigging operations.

b. In addition, a QR must:

(1) Be at least 18 years of age;

(2) Be able to communicate effectively with the crane operator, the lift supervisor, signal person and affected personnel on site;

(3) Have basic knowledge and understanding of equipment-operating characteristics, capabilities, and limitations and one whose competence in this skill has been demonstrated through training and experience satisfactory to management personnel.

15.B.02 A QR shall also be able to demonstrate knowledge and proficiency to appropriate management personnel in the following:

a. Personnel roles and responsibilities;

b. Site preparation (terrain, environment);

c. Rigging equipment and materials;

d. Safe Hoisting Equipment operating procedures;

e. Principles of safe rigging;

f. Environmental hazards (includes overhead interferences);

g. Rigging and handling the load;

h. Identification of hoisting-related hazards;

i. The associated hazards when employee is required to be in the fall zone to handle a load.

15.C Multiple Lift Rigging (MLR) ("Christmas Tree Rigging"). USACE allows multiple lift rigging practices for the purpose of erecting/placing structural steel ONLY.

15.C.01 Strict compliance with this section and 29 CFR 1926.753 Subpart R shall be mandated.

15.C.02 A lift using a MLR Assembly is considered a critical lift. It requires a carefully detailed, written critical lift plan per Section 16.H. In addition, all details and requirements of this section are required to be addressed:

a. Identifying all multi-lift hazards on the job site;

b. Beam list;

c. Determining load capacity;

d. Determining weight of a member;

e. Proper crane hand signals;

f. Safety rules for MLR;

g. Seven-foot rule;

h. Safe route/path of load and crane;

i. Power line issues;

j. Crane requirements;

k. Marking centerlines;

l. Use of tag line;

m. Qualifications and/or certifications of the operator(s) and rigger(s) to be performing these operations;

n. Rigging equipment: wire rope slings, hooks & shackles;

o. Clean lay-down area;

p. Cribbing;

q. Storage/staging;

r. Wind/environmental limits; and

s. Personal protective equipment.

15.C.03 A lift using a MLR Assembly may only be performed if the following criteria are met:

a. A MLR assembly is used;

b. A maximum of five members are hoisted per lift;

c. Only beams and similar structural members are lifted;

d. All employees engaged in MLR shall be trained in the following:

(1) The nature of the hazards associated with multiple lifts;

(2) The proper procedures and equipment to perform multiple lifts required in this section and as per 29 CFR 1926.753(e).

e. All loads shall be rigged by a QR per Section 15.B;

f. No crane is permitted to be used for multiple lift where such use is contrary to the manufacturer's specifications and limitations;

g. Components of the MLR assembly shall be specifically designed and assembled with a maximum capacity for total assembly and for each individual attachment point. This capacity, certified by the manufacturer or a QR, shall be based on the manufacturer's specifications with a 5:1 safety factor for all components.

h. The total load shall not exceed:

(1) The working load limit (WLL) of the hoisting equipment specified in the hoisting equipment load charts;

(2) The rigging capacity specified in the rigging rating chart.

i. The MLR assembly shall be rigged with members:

(1) Attached at their center of gravity and maintained reasonably level;

(2) Rigged from the top down; and (3) Rigged at least 7 ft (2.1 m) apart.

j. The members on the MLR assembly shall be set from the bottom up.

k. Controlled load-lowering shall be used whenever the load is over the connectors.

15.D Slings.

15.D.01 General. This section applies to slings used in conjunction with load handling equipment (LHE) for

15

hoisting and horizontally moving loads. All slings shall be manufactured, used, inspected and maintained according to ASME B30.9.

a. Inspections.

(1) Slings, all fastenings and attachments shall be visually inspected by a CP each day or shift when in use.

(2) Annual inspections shall be performed by a CP and must be documented. Documentation must be available on site and available to the GDA upon request.

(3) Additional inspections shall be performed during sling use, where service conditions warrant. Damaged or defective slings shall be immediately removed from service.

b. Rigging practices.

(1) All slings shall be hitched in a manner providing control of the load;

(2) Softeners. Sharp edges in contact with slings shall be padded with material of sufficient strength to protect the sling;

(3) Slings shall be shortened or adjusted only by methods approved by the sling manufacturer or a qualified person;

(4) The use of slings will be such that the entire load is positively secured;

(5) In a basket hitch, the load shall be balanced to prevent slippage;

(6) When using a basket hitch, legs of the sling shall contain or support the load from the sides, above the center of gravity, so that the load remains under control;

(7) In a choker hitch, the choke point shall only be on the sling body, never on a splice or fitting;

(8) In a choker hitch, an angle of choke less than 120 degrees shall not be used without reducing the rated load;

(9) Slings shall not be constricted, bunched, or pinched by the load, hook or any fitting;

(10) The load applied to the hook shall be centered in the base (bowl) of the hook to prevent point loading on the hook, unless the hook is designed for point loading;

(11) An object in the eye of a sling is not wider than one-third the length of the eye;

(12) The load shall not be landed on the sling;

(13) A sling shall not be pulled from under the load when load is resting on the sling;

(14) Slings shall not be dragged over abrasive surfaces;

(15) Shock loading is not allowed;

(16) Slings shall not be twisted or kinked.

c. All slings shall be manufactured under ASME B30.9 guidelines and must have an affixed durable permanent identification tag that includes the following as a minimum:

(1) Name or trademark of the manufacturer (country identification only is not acceptable);

(2) Type of material used (synthetic web slings, synthetic round slings or synthetic rope slings only);

(3) WLL for a given type of hitch and configuration;

(4) Number of legs if more than one.

d. Natural fiber rope shall not be used to fabricate slings.

e. Fabricated eye slings or endless loop slings using alloy steel wire rope clips or clamps for hoisting material or lifting are prohibited except where the application precludes the use of prefabricated slings. All slings fabricated using alloy steel wire rope clips or clamps shall be designed by a RPE for the specific application. > See Figures 15-1 and 15-2.

FIGURE 15-1

Wire Rope Clip Spacing

GENERAL NOTE: Correct number of clips for wire rope size shall be used.

NOTES:

    (1) Correct turnback length should be used
    (2) Correct orientation of saddle on live end shall be observed
    (3) Correct spacing of clips should be used
    (4) Correct torque on nuts shall be applied

15

FIGURE 15-2

Wire Rope Clip Orientation

Components

Right Installation

Wrong Installation

15.D.02 Alloy Steel Chain Slings.

a. Only alloy chain Grade 80 or higher shall be used in rigging.

b. Chain shall be visually inspected each day or shift when in use. Inspect chains on an individual link basis. Chains shall be cleaned before they are inspected, as dirt and grease can hide nicks and cracks.

c. Chains shall be removed from service if the following conditions exist:

(1) missing or illegible sling identification;

(2) cracks or breaks;

(3) excessive wear, nicks, or gouges. Minimum thickness of chain links shall not be below the values listed in Table 15-1;

(4) stretched chain links or components;

(5) bent, twisted, or deformed chain links or components;

(6) evidence of heat damage or weld splatter;

(7) excessive pitting or corrosion;

(8) lack of ability of chain or components to hinge (articulate) freely;

(9) other conditions including visible damage that cause doubt as to the continued use of the chain.

d. When used with multiple leg slings, alloy steel chains, hooks, rings, oblong links, pear-shaped links, welded or mechanical coupling links, or other attachments shall have a WLL at least equal to that of the assembly chain.

e. Multiple leg slings shall have the number of legs and lengths identified on the tag. > *See Section 15.D.01.c.*

15.D.03 Wire Rope Slings. Wire rope slings shall be inspected by a CP for the following:

a. Broken wires;

b. Severe localized abrasion or scraping;

c. Kinking, crushing, bird caging or any other damage to the rope structure;

d. Evidence of heat damage;

e. Crushed, deformed, or worn end attachments;

f. Severe corrosion of the rope, and attachments or fittings;

g. Missing or illegible sling identification;

h. Other conditions that cause doubt as to safe use of sling.

TABLE 15-1
Minimum Thickness of Chain Links

Nominal Chain or Coupling Link Size	Minimum Allowable Thickness at any point on link
7/32 in (5.5 mm)	0.19 in (4.80 mm)
9/32 in (7 mm)	0.24 in (6.07 mm)
5/16 in (8 mm)	0.27 in (6.93 mm)
3/8 in (10 mm)	0.34 in (8.69 mm)
1/2 in (13 mm)	0.44 in (11.26 mm)
5/8 in (16 mm)	0.55 in (13.87 mm)
3/4 in (20 mm)	0.69 in (17.45 mm)
7/8 in (22 mm)	0.75 in (19.05 mm)
1 in (26 mm)	0.89 in (22.53 mm)
1-1/4 in (32 mm)	1.09 in (27.71 mm)

15.D.04 Metal Mesh Slings. Metal mesh slings shall be inspected by a CP for the following:

a. Broken weld or brazed joint along the sling edge;

b. Broken wire in any part of the mesh;

c. Reduction in wire diameter of 25% due to abrasion or 15% due to corrosion;

d. Lack of flexibility due to distortion of the mesh;

e. Distortion of the choker fitting so that the depth of the slot is increased by more than 10%;

f. Distortion of either end fitting so the width of the eye opening is decreased by more than 10%;

15

g. A 15% reduction of the original cross-sectional area of metal at any point around the hook opening of end fitting;

h. Excessive pitting or corrosion of fittings; broken or cracked fittings; distortion of either end fitting out of its plane;

i. A sling in which the spirals are locked or without free articulation;

j. Other visible damage that causes doubt as to the strength of the sling.

15.D.05 Synthetic Fiber Rope Slings.

a. Synthetic rope slings shall be inspected by a CP for the following:

(1) Broken or cut fibers, either internally or externally;

(2) Cuts, gouges, abrasions; seriously or abnormally worn fibers;

(3) Powdered fiber or particles of broken fiber inside the rope between the strands;

(4) Variations in size or roundness of strands;

(5) Discoloration or rotting; weakened or brittle fibers;

(6) Excessive pitting or corrosion, or cracked, distorted, or broken fittings;

(7) Kinks;

(8) Melting or charring of the rope;

(9) Other visible damage that causes doubt as to the strength of the rope.

b. Synthetic rope slings shall not be used while frozen. When using synthetic rope slings in chemically active or excessively hot environments, consult with the sling manufacturer or Qualified Person (QP).

c. Synthetic rope slings shall be protected from abrasion by padding where it is fastened or drawn over square corners or sharp or rough surfaces.

d. Do not allow synthetic rope slings to be used in contact with objects or at temperature in excess of 194ºF (90ºC) or below -40ºF (40ºC).

➤ Note: Some synthetic yarns do not retain their breaking strength during long term exposure above 140ºF (60ºC).

e. Eye Splices. All splices shall be made per the rope manufacturer or a QP and in accordance with ASME B30.9.

f. Knots shall not be used in lieu of eye splices.

15.D.06 Synthetic Web Slings.

a. Synthetic Web Slings shall be inspected for the following:

(1) Acid or caustic burns;

(2) Melting or charring of any part of the sling;

(3) Snags, holes, tears, or cuts;

(4) Broken or worn stitches;

(5) Excessive abrasive wear;

(6) Knots in any part of the sling;

(7) Wear or elongation exceeding the amount recommended by the manufacturer;

(8) Excessive pitting or corrosion, or cracked, distorted, or broken fittings;

(9) Other visible damage that causes doubt as to the strength of the sling.

b. Synthetic web slings shall not be allowed to be used in contact with objects or at temperature in excess of 194ºF (90ºC) or below -40ºF (40ºC).

➤ Note: Some synthetic yarns do not retain their breaking strength during long term exposure above 140ºF (60ºC).

15.D.07 Synthetic Round Slings.

a. New slings (before initial use) shall be marked by the manufacturer to show the following, in addition to items required in Section 15.D.01.c:

(1) The core material;

(2) The cover material if different from the core material.

b. Synthetic Round Slings shall be inspected for the following and where any such damage or deterioration is present, remove the sling or attachment from service immediately:

(1)   Missing or illegible sling identification;

(2)   Acid or Caustic burns;

(3)   Evidence of heat damage;

(4)   Holes, tears, cuts, abrasive wear, or snags, that expose the core yarn;

(5)   Broken or damaged core yarns;

(6)   Welding spatter that exposes the core yarns;

(7)   Knots in the round sling body, except for core yarn knots inside the cover;

(8)   Discoloration and brittle or stiff areas on any part of the sling;

(9)   Pitted, corroded, cracked, bent, twisted, gouged, or broken fittings;

(10) Other conditions that cause doubt as to the continued use of the sling.

c. Synthetic round slings shall not be allowed to be used in contact with objects or at temperature in excess of 194°F (90°C) or below -40°F (40°C).

➢Note: Some synthetic yarns do not retain their breaking strength during long term exposure above 140°F (60°C).

15.E   Rigging Hardware (Excludes Reeving Hardware). (Includes all detachable rigging hardware used for load-handling activities). > See also "Rigging Hardware" in Appendix Q. All rigging hardware shall be constructed, installed, used, inspected and maintained in accordance with ASME B30.26.

15.E.01 All rigging hardware shall be inspected for defects prior to use on each shift and periodically as necessary during use to ensure that it is safe.

➢Note: Periodic inspections shall be documented and shall not exceed 1 year. The frequency shall be based on frequency of shackle use, severity of service conditions and nature of load-handling activities. Guidelines: for normal service is yearly; for severe service is monthly to quarterly; and for special service is as recommended by a qualified person. Defective rigging equipment shall be removed from service. Inspections shall be in accordance with the manufacturer's recommendations and at a minimum shall address:

a. Wear greater than 10%;

b. Deformations (straightness, nominal opening tolerances);

c. That manufacturer appropriate connectors are used (i.e., never replace a shackle pin with a bolt).

15.E.02 Rigging hardware shall not be painted once purchased. While the painting of rigging gear for identification is common, USACE considers this an unacceptable practice that constitutes a dangerous condition. Painting of hardware can potentially cover defects creating an unsafe condition.

15.E.03 Drums, sheaves, and pulleys shall be smooth and free of surface defects that may damage rigging. In addition, drums, sheaves, or pulleys having eccentric bores, cracked hubs, spokes, or flanges shall be removed from service.

15.E.04 Connections, fittings, fastenings, and attachments used with rigging shall be of good quality, of proper size and strength, and shall be installed in accordance with recommendations of the manufacturer.

15.E.05 Job hooks, shop hooks and links, makeshift fasteners formed from bolts and rods, and other similar attachments shall not be used.

15.E.06 Shackles. All shackles shall be manufactured according to ASME B30.26.

a. Only shackles marked by manufacturer with name or trademark of manufacturer (country only is not acceptable), WLL and size shall be used. Shackles shall be maintained by the user so as to be legible throughout the life of the shackle.

b. Each new shackle pin shall be marked by manufacturer to show name or trademark of manufacturer and grade, material type or load rating.

c. Shackles shall be inspected visually by the user (or other designated person) prior to each use and periodically.

d. Repairs and/or modifications may only be as specified by the manufacturer. Replacement parts, like pins, shall meet or exceed the original manufacturer's specifications.

e. Shackles shall not be eccentrically (side) loaded or shock loaded.

f. Multiple sling legs shall not be applied to the shackle pin.

15

15.E.07 Hooks. All hooks used for lifting or load handling purposes shall be manufactured according to ASME B30.10. > *See Figure 15-3.*

a. All hooks used for lifting or load handling purposes shall not be used in any other manner.

b. Hooks that show wear exceeding 10% or an increase in the throat opening of 5% (maximum of ¼ in (6mm)), or as recommended by the manufacturer, or any visibly apparent bend or twist from the plane of the hook shall be removed from service.

c. The manufacturer's recommendations shall be followed in determining the WLL of the various sizes and types of specific and identifiable hooks. Any hook for which the manufacturer's recommendations are not available shall be tested to twice the intended safe working load before it is put into use. The employer shall maintain a record of the dates and results of such tests.

FIGURE 15-3

Hooks

SELF-CLOSING TIPLOCK LATCH (EYE HOOK)

SELF-CLOSING TIPLOCK LATCH (SHANK HOOK)

SELF-CLOSING BAIL (EYE HOOK)

SELF-CLOSING FLAPPER LATCH (SHANK HOOK)

SELF-CLOSING FLAPPER LATCH (SWIVEL HOOK)

SELF-LOCKING CLEVIS HOOK (CLOSED)

LAMINATED PLATE HOOK

EYE GRAB HOOK

DOUBLE/ SISTER HOOK CLOSED

d. Open hooks are prohibited in rigging used to hoist loads <u>except for</u> miscellaneous-type hooks (i.e., grab hooks, foundry hooks, sorting hooks, choker hooks, etc). <u>These hooks may be used as long as they are inspected and maintained in accordance with manufacturer's recommendations. The use of these specialty-type hooks shall be identified in the applicable AHA and submitted to the GDA for acceptance.</u> > *See Figure 15-4.*

e. <u>Manufacturer's identification (country only is not acceptable) and WLL shall be forged, cast, or die</u> stamped on a low stress and non-wearing area of the hook.

f. <u>Duplex (sister) hooks shall be loaded equally on both sides unless the hook is specifically designed for single-point loading.</u>

g. <u>If the duplex (sister) hook is loaded at the pinhole instead of at the two saddles, the load applied shall not exceed the WLL that would normally be shared by the two saddles or the WLL of the supporting equipment.</u>

<u>Figure 15-4</u>

Miscellaneous-Type Open Hooks

Throat Opening

Sorting Hook   **Choker Hook**   **Clevis Grab Hook**   **Eye Hook**

15.E.08 Eyebolts, Eye Nuts, Swivel Hoist Rings and Turnbuckles. <u>All eyebolts, eye nuts, swivel hoist rings and turnbuckles shall be manufactured according to ASME B30.26.</u>

a. <u>WLLs</u> shall be in accordance with the manufacturer's recommendation.

b. <u>Each turnbuckle, eye nut and eyebolt shall be marked with name or trademark of the manufacturer (country is not acceptable), size or WLL and grade (for alloy eyebolts). In addition, each swivel hoist ring must also be marked to show torque value (excluding trench cover hoist rings). Markings shall remain legible.</u>

c. <u>This equipment shall be inspected visually before each use by the user (or other designated person) and at least annually to determine condition is safe for use.</u>

d. <u>Turnbuckles shall not be side loaded and shall be rigged and secured to prevent unscrewing during the lift. In addition, end-fittings threads shall be fully engaged in the body threads.</u>

e. <u>Shoulderless eyebolts shall not be loaded at an angle.</u>

15

THIS PAGE INTENTIONALLY LEFT BLANK

SECTION 16 Load Handling Equipment (LHE)

Table of Contents

16

16.A General.

16.A.01 The requirements of this Section are applicable to all load handling equipment (LHE) to include cranes, derricks, hoists and power-operated equipment that can be used to raise, lower and/or horizontally move a suspended load.

> *Exemptions. All requirements of Section 16 apply except as noted below:*

a. Affixed A-frames performing anchor handling or dredge-related operations (ONLY) with a vessel or barge are exempt from Sections 16.B and 16.C; *In addition, see Section 16.L.08 for equipment-specific requirements;*

b. Base-mounted drum hoists used to hoist personnel, guided and non-guided, whether powered by internal combustion engine, electric motor or other prime mover, to include air tuggers) are exempt from Sections 16.B; *In addition, s*ee *Section 16.U for* equipment specific *requirements;*

c. Digger derricks used for utility/pole installation;

d. Vehicle-mounted aerial devices (i.e., Bucket Trucks) - *See Section 22.M* VehicleMounted Elevating and Rotating Work Platforms (Aerial Devices/Lifts) *and also Section 22.L, Elevating Aerial Work Platforms (AWPs);*

e. Hydraulic Excavators, Wheeled/Trackhoe/Backhoe loaders used to hoist loads with rigging are exempt from the requirements in Sections 16.B.02 through 16.B.05 (crane operator certifications) only. Rigger qualifications still apply, per Section 15.B. *See Section 16.S for equipment-specific requirements;*

f. Powered Industrial Trucks (PIT's, i.e., Forklifts)/Telehandlers when configured to hoist and lower (by means of a winch or hook) and horizontally move a suspended (rigged) load are exempt from the requirements in 16.B.02 through 16.B.05 (crane operator certifications) only, UNLESS this equipment is used to hoist/lift personnel. This activity is considered a Critical Lift and as such, requires a physical examination for the operator (per 16.B.05 and additional criteria per Section 16.Q. Rigger qualifications still apply, per Section 15.B. > See Section 16.   Q for equipment-specific requirements;

g. Machinery that hoists by using a come-a-long or chainfall (whether human-, air- or electric- powered, chain or wire-rope type);

h. Operators of equipment with a maximum manufacturer-rated hoisting/lifting capacity of 2,000 pounds (907 kg) or less, are exempt from the operator qualification or certification requirements in Sections 16.B.02 through 16.B.05 only. In addition, this equipment may not be used to hoist personnel;

i. Hoist Operators are exempt from Section 16.B.05, Physical Examination requirements UNLESS this equipment is used to hoist/lift personnel. This activity is considered a Critical Lift and requires a physical examination for the operator. In addition, all Class II operators that will be hoisting personnel shall be trained at a minimum, in the requirements listed in Section 16.T. > *See also Section 16.C.07.b, Note 3 and Section 16.U;*

j. Dedicated drilling rigs;

k. Tree trimming and removal work;

l. Gin poles when used for the erection of communication towers;

m. Helicopter cranes are exempt from Sections 16.B and 16.C;

n. Stacker cranes;

o. Mechanic's Trucks with a hoisting device when used in activities related to maintenance and repair;

p. Material Delivery.

(1) Articulating/knuckle-boom truck cranes that deliver material to a construction site when used to transfer materials from the truck crane to the ground, without arranging the materials in a particular sequence for hoisting.

(2) Articulating/knuckle-boom truck cranes that deliver material to a construction site when the crane is used to transfer building supply sheet goods or building supply packaged materials from the truck crane onto a structure, using a fork/cradle at the end of the boom, but only when the truck crane is equipped with a properly functioning automatic overload prevention device. Such sheet goods or packaged materials include, but are not limited to: sheets of sheet rock, sheets of plywood, bags of cement, sheets or packages of roofing shingles, and rolls of roofing felt.

(3)   This exclusion does not apply when:

(a) The articulating/knuckle-boom crane is used to hold, support or stabilize the material to facilitate a construction activity, such as holding material in place while it is attached to the structure;

(b) The material being handled by the articulating/knuckle-boom crane is a prefabricated component. Such prefabricated components include, but are not limited to: precast concrete members or panels, roof trusses (wooden, cold-formed metal, steel, or other material), prefabricated building sections such as, but not limited to: floor panels, wall panels, roof panels, roof structures, or similar items;

(c) The material being handled by the crane is a structural steel member (for example, steel joists, beams, columns, steel decking (bundled or unbundled) or a component of a systems-engineered metal building.

16.A.02 Certification of Compliance (COC). Contractors shall submit a COC for each piece of LHE prior to being brought on site. The COC shall be submitted to the GDA for acceptance. > See Form 16-1, Certificate Of Compliance.

a. The COC states that the LHE and the rigging equipment meets applicable regulations (to include inspections and tests) as required by the manufacturers and the requirements of this manual. It must be signed by a Competent Person for Crane and Rigging. > See Appendix Q.

b. COC shall be posted on the LHE.

16.A.03 Standard Lift Plan (SLP). All lifts must be planned to avoid situations where the operator cannot maintain safe control of the lift.

a. A written SLP shall be prepared for every lift or series of lifts (if duty cycle or routine lifts are being performed). The SLP shall be developed, reviewed and accepted by all personnel involved in the lift. The SLP shall be maintained on the LHE for the current lift(s) being made. Historical SLPs shall be maintained for a minimum of 3 months.

b. At a minimum, the following shall be addressed or use the non-mandatory Form 16-2, Standard Pre-Lift Plan/Checklist:

(1) Personnel: roles, responsibilities, qualification, public persons or other trade personnel access or affected by lift;

(2) Area Preparation: load handling location and path of travel, blocking/cribbing, overhead lines, ground stability;

(3) LHE Considerations: capacity, configuration, obstructions, inspection, ground support conditions;

(4) Load parameters: weight, center of gravity, radii, and configuration;

(5) Rigging: type, inspection, need for softeners;

(6) Environmental Considerations: wind, storms, precipitation, power lines in area of travel or load swing, counterweight swing area barricaded.

16.A.04 The employer shall comply with all manufacturer's instructions, procedures and recommendations applicable to the operational functions of LHE, including LHE use with attachments. The safe operating speeds or loads shall not be exceeded. When they are not available, the employer shall develop and ensure compliance with all procedures necessary for the safe operation of the equipment and attachments according to:

a. Procedures for the operational controls that must be developed by a Qualified Person (QP).

b. Procedures related to the capacity of the equipment that must be developed and signed by a Registered Professional Engineer (RPE) familiar with the equipment.

16.A.05 When the manufacturer's instructions or recommendations are more stringent than the requirements of this manual, the manufacturer's instructions or recommendations shall apply.

16.A.06. The use of all electronic equipment not necessary to the work activity being performed is prohibited.

16.A.07 LHE shall be shut down before and during fueling operations. Closed systems, with an automatic shut-off that will prevent spillage if connections are broken, may be used to fuel diesel powered equipment left running.

16.A.08 Inspections or determinations of road and shoulder conditions and structures shall be made in advance to assure that clearances and load capacities are safe for the passage or placing of any LHE.

16.A.09 Equipment requirements, as applicable to the type equipment.

a. An operable fuel gage;

b. An operable audible warning device (horn);

c. Adequate rearview mirror or mirrors;

d. Non-slip surfaces on steps;

16

e. A power-operated starting device;

f. Seats must be provided for the operator and all personnel that are required to be in/on equipment;

g. Whenever visibility conditions warrant additional light, all vehicles, or combinations of vehicles, in use shall be equipped with at least two headlights and two taillights in operable condition;

h. Glass in windshields, windows, and doors shall be safety glass. Cracked or broken glass shall be replaced;

i. One (minimum) dry chemical or CO_2 fire extinguisher with a minimum rating of 10B:C installed in the cab or at the machinery housing;

j. All self-propelled LHE, whether moving alone or in combination, shall be equipped with a back-up alarm. > *See Section 18.B.01.*

k. Warning lights, attached to the applicable equipment shall be used as collision avoidance measures for airfield operations. Lighting shall be in accordance with guidance provided by the Federal Aviation Administration (FAA). > *For Airfield Operations, see Section 32.*

16.A.10 Rollover protective structures (ROPS) as required by the manufacturer must be in place and maintained.

16.A.11 The manufacturer's specifications and operating manuals for hydraulic equipment and attachments utilizing quick connect/disconnect systems shall be followed. After completing a switch of attachments, the equipment operator shall take the actions necessary to ensure the quick connect/disconnect system is positively engaged.

16.A.12 All required guarding and safety devices shall be provided, used and maintained:

a. All belts, gears, shafts, pulleys, sprockets, spindles, drums, flywheels, chains, or other reciprocating, rotating, or moving parts of equipment shall be guarded when exposed to contact by persons or when they otherwise create a hazard.

b. All hot surfaces of equipment, including exhaust pipes or other lines, shall be guarded or insulated to prevent injury and fire.

c. Platforms, foot walks, steps, handholds, guardrails, and toe boards shall be designed, constructed, and installed on machinery and equipment to provide safe footing and access ways.

16.A.13 Work Area Control. When there are accessible areas in which the LHE's rotating superstructure (permanently or temporarily mounted) poses a risk of striking or pinching/crushing an employee against another part of the equipment or another object, employees shall be prevented from entering these areas.

16.A.14 Running lines located within 6 ft - 6 in (1.9 m) of the ground or working level shall be guarded or the area restricted by physical barriers to preclude injury.

16.A.15 Maintenance/Repair of LHE.

a. Maintenance, including preventive maintenance and repairs, shall be performed in accordance with the manufacturer's recommendations. Records of maintenance and repairs conducted during the life of a contract shall be made available upon request of the GDA (contractor operators) or the supervisor/leader of the activity/task (government operators).

b. Replacement parts or repairs shall have at least the original design factor; replacement parts for load bearing and other critical parts shall be obtained from the original manufacturer, (if possible) or certified by a RPE knowledgeable in LHE.

c. All LHE shall be shut down and positive means taken to prevent its operation while repairs or manual lubrications are being done.

(1) Equipment designed to be serviced while running are exempt from this requirement.

(2) Control of hazardous energy (lockout/tagout) must be considered during the maintenance and repair of equipment. A Hazardous Energy Control Program and specific isolation procedures shall be identified in the AHA and implemented to ensure the unexpected re-energization of the equipment does not occur. > *See Section 12.*

16.A.16 Parking.

a. Whenever LHE is parked, the parking brake shall be set.

b. LHE parked on an incline shall have the wheels chocked or track mechanisms blocked and the parking brake set.

c. All LHE left unattended at night, adjacent to a highway in normal use or adjacent to construction areas where work is in progress, shall have lights or reflectors, or barricades equipped with lights or reflectors, to identify the location of the equipment.

16.B Personnel Qualifications.

16.B.01 <u>LHE</u> shall be operated only by trained, <u>certified, qualified and designated</u> personnel. Proof of qualification shall be provided by the employer and <u>designation</u> shall be in writing. In addition to fully qualified <u>LHE</u> operators, the following personnel may be designated <u>(in writing)</u> to operate <u>LHE</u> under limited conditions;

a. Trainees under the direct supervision of the designated operator of the crane or hoist;

b. <u>LHE maintenance, inspection and repair personnel are permitted to operate the equipment only where all of the following requirements are met.</u>

(1) <u>The operation is limited to those functions necessary to perform maintenance, inspect the equipment, or verify its performance.</u>

(2) <u>Lifting of loads by these personnel is NOT allowed and they must either</u> operate the equipment:

(a) <u>under the direct supervision of a qualified operator (see Section 16.B.02), OR</u>

(b) <u>must read/review the operator's manual</u> so that they <u>are familiar with the operations, limitation, characteristics and hazards associated with the LHE being inspected, maintained, or repaired.</u>

c. <u>LHE</u> maintenance, inspection and repair personnel <u>covered by this Section are exempt from the crane operator physical requirements identified in Section 16.B.05.</u>

16.B.02 Crane Operator Requirements – General.

<u>a</u>. Prior to the start of a specific activity or task, documentation of operator <u>certifications,</u> qualifications and designations shall be included in the AHA and provided to the GDA (contractor operators) or the supervisor/leader of the activity/task (government operators).

(1) <u>Certification</u> for all crane/hoist operators shall be achieved by successful completion of written and operational testing.

(2) <u>Qualification of all crane/hoist operators shall be made by the employer after a</u> review of the certification documents and an assurance that the operator(s) is familiar <u>with the equipment to be operated (has adequate knowledge of USACE and OSHA</u> crane safety requirements and manufacturer recommendations provided in the crane operator's manual).

(3) <u>The employer then designates the operator(s) in writing for the equipment to be operated.</u>

b. Crane Operators shall be able to communicate effectively with the lift supervisor, rigger(s), <u>signal person(s)</u> and other affected employees on site.

c. Crane operators shall demonstrate their ability to read, write and comprehend in the language of the crane manufacturer's operation and maintenance instruction materials, exhibit acceptable arithmetic skills and load/capacity chart usage and use written manufacturer procedures applicable to the type and <u>configuration</u> of equipment for which <u>qualification</u> is being sought.

16.B.03 Crane Operator <u>Certification, Qualification and Designation.</u> The employer must ensure that, prior to operating any equipment covered under Section 16, <u>the operator of</u> the equipment is covered by Section 16.B.01, or is <u>certified, qualified and designated in writing</u> to operate the equipment in accordance with one of the following options:

a. Option 1. Current certification by a Nationally Accredited Crane Operator Testing Organization.

(1) The operator's certificate must identify the type of equipment on which the operator was certified. <u>Once the operator has obtained the certification, the employer</u> must insure that the operator is qualified to operate a particular piece of equipment for <u>that type and capacity and must designate this in writing.</u>

➢*Note: If no accredited testing agency offers certification examinations for a particular type of equipment, an operator will be deemed <u>certified</u> to operate that equipment if he/she has been certified for the type/capacity that is most similar to that equipment and for which a certification examination is available. <u>Employer qualification <u>and designation</u> on the equipment is still required.</u>*

(2) For a testing organization to be considered accredited to certify operators, it must:

(a) Be accredited by a nationally recognized accrediting agency based on that agency's determination that industry recognized criteria for written and practical testing materials, conditions and administration are being met;

(b) Administer written and practical tests that assess operator applicants regarding necessary knowledge and skills and that provided different levels of certification based on equipment capacity and type;

(c) Have procedures for operators to re-apply and be retested in event operator applicant fails a test or is decertified;

16

(<u>d</u>) Have testing procedures for recertification;

(<u>e</u>) Have accreditation reviewed by the nationally recognized accrediting agency at least every 3 years;

(<u>f</u>) Issue a certification under this option that is portable and is valid for 5 years from date of issuance.

b. Option 2. Qualification by an audited employer program. The employer's qualification of its employee must meet the following requirements:

> Note: This "audited" option was associated with a phase-in period. However, because Industry has not yet met these requirements, OSHA has extended the deadline until 14 Nov 201<u>7</u>, to meet this Option. In lieu of a "Certified auditor that is not an employee of the employer", the employer's qualification of its employees may be performed by a "Qualified Person (QP) that may be an employee of the employer". In addition, the following must be met:

(1) Successful completion of written and practical tests that are either developed by an accredited crane operator testing organization (see Option 1 above) or approved by an auditor (QP) in accordance with the following:

(a) The auditor (QP) is certified to evaluate such tests by an accredited crane operator testing organization (see Option 1 above);

(b) The auditor is not an employee of the employer (see Note above);

(c) The approval must be based on the auditor's determination that the tests meet nationally recognized test development criteria and are valid and reliable in assessing the operator applicants' knowledge and skill needed;

(d) The audit must be conducted in accordance with nationally recognized auditing standards.

(2) The employer program shall be audited within 3 months of the beginning of the program and every 3 years thereafter;

(3) The employer program shall have testing procedures for recertification;

(4) Any significant deficiencies identified by the auditor shall be corrected prior to further qualification of any operators;

(5) Records of audits shall be retained for 3 years and made available to the GDA upon request;

(6) A qualification issued under this option:

(a) Is not portable. Such a qualification meets the requirements of this Section only where the operator is employed by (and operating the equipment for) the employer that issued the qualification;

(b) Is valid for 5 years from date of issuance.

c. Option 3. Qualification by the U.S. Military. An operator who is an employee of the U.S. military is considered qualified if he/she has a current operator certification, qualification and designation issued by the U.S. Military for operation of the equipment. An employee of the U.S. Military is a federal employee of the Department of Defense or Armed Forces and does not include employees of private contractors. This option includes USACE crane, derrick and hoist operators) and is further detailed in Section 16.B.04.

d. Option 4. Licensing by a State or Local Government Entity. A government (state or local) licensing department/office that issues operator licenses for operating equipment covered by this Section is considered a government accredited crane operator testing organization provided the following criteria are met:

(1) The requirements for obtaining the license include assessment and determination via written and operational tests of the operator applicant's knowledge regarding safe operation of the specific type of equipment the individual will operate, including, at a minimum, the knowledge and skills listed in Section 16.B.<u>02</u>;

(2) The testing meets industry recognized criteria for written testing materials, practical examinations, test administration, grading, facilities/equipment and personnel;

(3) The government authority that oversees the examiners has determined that the requirements for Option 4 licensing have been met;

(4) The examiner has testing procedures for recertification designed to ensure that the operator continues to meet the technical knowledge and skills requirements;

(5) A license issued by a government accredited crane operator testing organization:

(a) Meets the operator qualification requirements of this Section for operation of equipment only within the jurisdiction of the government entity; and

(b) Is valid for the period of time stipulated by the licensing department/office but no longer than 5 years.

16.B.04 USACE Operator Certification, Qualification, and Designation.

a. The following options are available for the certification and qualification of USACE operators:

(1) Each crane operator may be trained, tested and certified by a nationally accredited testing organization, (see Section 16.B.03 Option 1); If this option is chosen, USACE is still responsible for ensuring that the operator is qualified to operate a particular piece of equipment (to include, type, capacity and configuration) and must designate this in writing; OR

(2) Each operator can be trained, tested and licensed by a professional source that certifies crane operators as long as the program is audited (see Section 16.B.03, Option 2). This requirement will remain until 14 Nov 2017 whereupon this option will be replaced by one that is required to be audited by a 3rd party certified auditor. If this option is chosen, USACE is still responsible for ensuring that the operator is qualified to operate a particular piece of equipment (to include, type, capacity and configuration) and must designate this in writing, OR

(3) Each operator can be trained, tested and licensed by a USACE designated in-house crane trainer in accordance with USACE National Crane Training Program. If this option is chosen, a qualified person is responsible for ensuring that the operator is qualified to operate a particular piece of equipment (to include, type, capacity and configuration) and must designate this in writing.

b. Certification and qualification under this option is:

(1) Not portable. Such a certification and qualification meets the requirements of this Section only where the operator is employed by (and operating the equipment for) USACE; AND

(2) Is valid for 2 years from date of issuance.

16.B.05 Operator Physical Qualifications/Examination. All crane operators shall be physically qualified to operate the equipment. Physical examinations for operators are required to be conducted every 2 years and any time a condition is observed that may impact safe operation. Written proof, signed by a physician [this term is intended to mean a Medical Doctor (M.D.) or Doctor of Osteopathy (D.O.)] stating that the operator has had a physical examination and meets the medical requirements set forth below shall be submitted to the GDA for acceptance prior to allowing an operator to operate the equipment.

➤ Note: Operators of Hoisting Equipment are exempt from this requirement UNLESS this equipment is used to hoist/lift personnel. > See also Sections 16.A.01.i and 16.U;

a. Operators shall have a current physician's (M.D. or D.O.) certification, dated within the past 2 years, that states the operator meets the following physical qualifications:

(1) Vision of at least 20/30 Snellen in one eye and 20/50 in the other, with or without corrective lenses;

(2) Normal depth perception and field of vision;

(3) Ability to distinguish colors, regardless of position;

(4) Adequate hearing, with or without hearing aid, for the specific operation;

(5) Sufficient strength, endurance, agility, coordination, manual dexterity, and speed of reaction to meet the demands of equipment operation;

(6) No evidence that the operator is subject to seizures or loss of physical control. If evidence of this nature is found, it may be sufficient cause for disqualification. In such cases, specialized medical tests may be required to evaluate these conditions and determine their impact;

(7) No Evidence of physical, emotional or psychological limitations that could result in a hazard to the operator, or that in the opinion of the examiner could interfere with the operator's performance. If evidence of this nature is found, it may be sufficient cause for disqualification. Specialized medical tests may be required to determine these conditions.

b. Deviations from Physical Qualification Requirements.

(1) Deviations from the physical requirements are not necessarily totally disqualifying.

(2) However, where such deviations exist, competent medical and management authorities shall give special consideration to each individual case and may recommend waivers.

(3) Waivers may be approved by the local Safety and Occupational Health office (SOHO) and must be re-issued every 2 years, based on results of

16

operator's medical clearance examination. A copy shall be provided to HQ, SOHO.

(4) Normally, waivers shall not be granted for applicants who have never before established operator qualifications. However, an evaluation on an individual basis shall be made per the above requirements. Any limitations identified shall be noted on the operator's license and license record.

c. Contractor drug testing program. All contractor crane operators shall participate in a drug testing program and have a negative result for a substance abuse test. The level of testing will be in accordance with standard practices for industry or by the agency's random drug testing program. This test will be confirmed by a recognized laboratory service.

d. Government drug testing program. All government (DOD) crane operators, as identified below, shall participate in a drug testing program and have a negative result for a substance abuse test, per AR 600-85, paragraph 5-8 (15). In addition, if an employee is in any other specified Test Designated Position (TDP) in this AR 600-85, he/she must be tested accordingly. The level of testing will be in accordance with by the agency's testing program. This test will be confirmed by a recognized laboratory service:

(1) Crane operators that operate OVERHEAD CRANES (only) with a lifting capacity of 20T or greater, AND

(2) Are in the following job series and are required to operate, inspect, maintain, repair or rig loads for overhead cranes:

(a) WG-5725, Crane Operator;

(b) WG-3359, Instrument Mechanic;

(c) WG-5350, Machinery Mechanic; OR

(d) WK-5401, Industrial Equipment Operator.

16.B.06 Signal Person Qualifications.

a. All signal persons must be qualified by either a third party Qualified Evaluator or the employer's Qualified Evaluator/LHE trainer.

b. Documentation must be provided by the Evaluator and must specify each type of signaling (e.g., hand signals, radio signals, etc.) for which the signal person meets the requirements of this Section.

c. If subsequent actions by the signal person indicate that the individual does not meet the qualification requirement of this Section the employer must not allow the individual to continue working as a signal person until retraining is provided and a re-assessment is made.

d. The qualification means that the Evaluator has assessed the individual's capabilities and has determined that the signal person has met the qualification requirements below:

(1) Know and understand the type of signals used (radio, cell, hand, etc). If hand signals are used, the signal person must know and understand the Standard Method for hand signals;

(2) Be competent in the application of the type of signals used;

(3) Have a basic understanding of crane operation and limitations, including crane dynamics involved in swinging and stopping loads and boom deflection from hoisting loads;

(4) Demonstrate that he/she meets the requirements above through a written and practical test.

e. An assessment by an employer's Qualified Evaluator/LHE trainer is not portable. Other employers are not permitted to use it to meet these requirements.

16.C Classification of USACE LHE and Training of USACE Operators.

➢NOTE: *Operator qualifications/licenses detailed below are only valid provided operator receives refresher training as required below.*

16.C.01 Designated personnel must be qualified to operate a particular Class (i.e., mobile, tower, overhead, etc.) and type (lattice boom, hydraulic boom, etc.) of crane or hoist and the training provided shall be applicable to that Class and type of crane or hoist. The USACE classification of cranes and hoisting equipment and their associated training requirements are identified here. All exams shall meet the applicable parts of Option 3, based on type of equipment.

16.C.02. Class I crane/hoist types:

a. Fixed cab telescopic hydraulic mobile cranes;

b. Swing cab telescopic hydraulic mobile cranes;

c. Lattice boom, truck or crawler cranes;

d. Cab-operated overhead, bridge, gantry, under hung and monorail cranes;

e. Remote-operated (wireless) overhead, bridge, gantry, under hung and monorail cranes over 30T capacity:

> *Exemption: Operators of CONTINUALLY GUIDED loads over 30T are considered Class II operators. As an example, gates that are raised and lowered in a slot and remain in a slot. However, if a gate clears the slot and is freely suspended, then a Class I operator is required).*

f. Hammerhead cranes;

g. Portal cranes;

h. Tower cranes;

i. Derricks post or stiff leg type;

j. Floating or barge-mounted LHE, temporarily or permanently mounted, that requires a Naval Architect Analysis (NAA)/floating load chart per Section 16.L.

16.C.03 Class I operators are qualified to operate, perform preventive maintenance and inspection of this equipment as required;

16.C.04 Class I training must be:

a. Initial: A minimum of 24-hour training with successful completion (passed) written and practical/operational examinations;

b. Biennial (every 24 months) Refresher: A minimum of 8-hour refresher training, with successful completion (passed) of written and practical/operational examination.

> *Note: Grace Period - refresher training is intended to be obtained every 24 months. Understanding that emergencies and other unplanned events can occur that may interrupt the normal scheduling of this training, a 60-day grace period is permitted IF necessary and is dependent upon supervisory approval.*

16.C.05 Class II crane/hoist types:

a. All hard-wired, pendant-mounted operated overhead, bridge and gantry cranes;

b. Under hung;

c. Monorail;

d. Pedestal;

e. Wall-mounted jib cranes.

f. Any remote-operated (wireless) overhead, bridge, gantry, under hung and monorail cranes 30T capacity or less;

g. Base-Mounted Drum Hoists used to Hoist Personnel, Guided and Non-guided Worker's Hoists [Whether Powered by Internal Combustion Engine, Electric Motor or Other Prime Mover (Air Tuggers)].

16.C.06 Class II crane operators are qualified to operate, perform preventive maintenance and inspection of this equipment as required.

16.C.07 Class II training, must be:

a. Initial: A minimum of 2-hour training with successful completion (passed) of written and practical/operational examinations;

b. Biennial (every 24 months) Refresher: A minimum of 1-hour refresher training with successful completion (passed) of written and practical/operational examination.

> *Note 1: Grace Period - Refresher training is intended to be obtained every 24 months. Understanding that emergencies and other unplanned events can occur that may interrupt the normal scheduling of this training; a 60-day grace period is permitted IF necessary and is dependent upon supervisory approval.*

> *Note 2: Exemption of equipment with a maximum manufacturer-rated hoisting/lifting capacity of 2,000 pounds or less (exempt from the requirements in Sections 16.B.02 through 16.B.06 only), See Section 16.A.01.h. It is anticipated that operator of this equipment will review manufacturer's instructions for proper operation however. This equipment shall not be used for hoisting personnel.*

> *Note 3: Operators of Class II cranes/hoisting equipment are exempt from Section 16.B.05, Physical Examination requirements, UNLESS this equipment is used to hoist/lift personnel. See also Sections 16.A.01.i, 16.B.05 and 16.U. This activity is considered a Critical Lift and requires a physical examination for the operator. In addition, All Class II operators that will be hoisting personnel shall be trained at a minimum, in the requirements listed in Section 16.T, 16. U or other applicable equipment-related Section.*

16.C.08 Prior to re-issuance of qualification, crane and hoisting equipment operators must have attended applicable training (initial and refresher) and passed the written and operational examination requirements specified above.

16

16.C.09 Each USACE activity or operating project will maintain a current list of operators, complete crane and hoisting equipment training records for each operator, and a list of all equipment that each operator is qualified to operate.

16.D Inspection Criteria for Load Handling Equipment (LHE).

16.D.01 Inspections of LHE shall be in accordance with this Section, applicable ASME standards, OSHA regulations and the manufacturer's recommendations.

16.D.02 Records of all LHE tests and inspections shall be maintained onsite. Contractors shall make these records readily available upon request and, when submitted, they shall become part of the official project file.

16.D.03 Contractor shall provide the GDA 24-hours notice in advance of any LHE entering the site (prior to inspection/tests) so that observation of the Contractor's inspection process and spot checks may be conducted.

16.D.04 Whenever any LHE is found to be unsafe, or whenever a deficiency that affects the safe operation of the LHE is observed, the affected LHE shall be immediately taken out of service and its use prohibited until unsafe conditions have been corrected.

16.D.05 Cranes, hoists, derricks and other LHE in regular service.

a. Inspection procedures for LHE in regular service are divided into three general classifications based on the intervals at which inspections shall be performed.

b. The intervals depend on the nature of critical components of the LHE and the degree of their exposure to wear, deterioration, or malfunction.

c. The three general types are: Shift, Monthly and Annual.

➤ Note: Monthly inspections are required by OSHA. The items to be inspected and the requirements are the same as those covered by the Shift inspection, therefore monthly inspections will not be addressed separately in this Section but still must be performed.

16.D.06 Shift Inspections. Before every LHE operation (at beginning of each shift) or following a change of operator, a Competent Person (CP) shall, at a minimum, visually inspect the items in accordance with this Section, applicable ASME standards, OSHA regulations and the manufacturer's recommendations. Equipment shall not be used until this inspection demonstrates that no corrective action is required.

a. The shift inspection must be documented and shall include the results of the inspection, name and signature of the CP who conducted the inspection and the date of the inspection.

b. Documentation shall be maintained for a minimum of 12 months, or the life of the contract, whichever is longer.

16.D.07 Annual Inspections shall be performed at least annually, or more frequently if recommended by the manufacturer, or if a load bearing or load controlling part or component has been altered, replaced or repaired. > See Section 16.F.02.b (1).

➤ Note: Adding/removing counterweights is not considered load controlling/load bearing.

a. Annual inspection shall be done by a QP and will include operational testing to determine that the equipment as configured in the inspection is functioning properly.

b. The inspection must be documented and shall include items checked and results of inspection, name and signature of the person who conducted the inspection, and the date and this documentation must be retained until at least the next annual inspection occurs, 12 months, or the duration of the contract, whichever is longer.

c. If any deficiency is identified, an immediate determination shall be made by the QP as to whether the deficiency constitutes a safety hazard. If so, then the equipment shall be removed from service until it has been corrected. If not yet a safety hazard, the QP may determine that the employer shall monitor daily until the deficiency is corrected.

16.D.08 Inspection of cranes, derricks and other LHE not in regular use. Annual inspection shall be performed if the equipment has been idle for 3 months or more. > See Section 16.D.07.

16.D.09 If LHE is involved in an incident or accident, an inspection shall be conducted in accordance with the manufacturer's recommendations. If the manufacturer is no longer available, a RPE shall be consulted and shall determine the level of inspection required.

16.D.10 Running and Standing Wire Rope Inspection.

a. Each Shift. A CP shall perform this inspection each shift by visually inspecting all running ropes, counterweight ropes and load trolley (standing) ropes in accordance with this Section, applicable ASME standards, OSHA regulations and the manufacturer's recommendations. Visual inspection shall concentrate on identifying apparent deficiencies in wire rope (running and standing). Opening of wire rope <u>is prohibited</u> and booming down is not required as part of this inspection.

<u>(1) The shift inspection must be documented and shall include the results of the inspection, name and signature of the CP who conducted the inspection and the date of the inspection.</u>

<u>(2) Documentation shall be maintained for a minimum of 12 months, or the life of the contract, whichever is longer.</u>

b. <u>Annual.</u> At least every 12 months, wire ropes (running and standing) in use on equipment must be inspected by a QP in accordance with this Section, applicable ASME standard, OSHA regulations and the manufacturer's recommendations. Documentation is same as for Shift inspections above.

16.E Safety Devices and Operational Aids. Safety devices and operational aids shall not be used as a substitute for the exercise of professional judgment by the operator.

16.E.01 Safety Devices. The following safety devices are required on all cranes and derricks covered by Section 16 unless otherwise specified.

a. Crane level indicator.

(1) The equipment shall have a crane level indicator that is either built into the equipment or is available on the equipment.

(2) This requirement does not apply to portal <u>overhead or gantry</u> cranes, derricks, floating cranes/derricks and crane/derricks on barges, pontoons, vessels or other means of flotation.

b. Boom stops, except for derricks and hydraulic booms.

c. Jib stops (if jib is attached), except for derricks.

d. Equipment with foot pedal brakes shall have locks, except for portal and floating cranes.

e. Hydraulic outrigger jacks shall have an integral holding device (check valve).

f. Equipment on rails shall have rail clamps and rail stops, except for portal cranes.

g. Horn.

16.E.02 Proper Operation of Safety Devices.

<u>a.</u> Operations shall not begin unless the safety devices listed above are in proper working order.

<u>b.</u> If a safety device stops working properly during operations, the operator shall safely stop operations.

<u>c.</u> Operations shall not resume until the device is again working properly.

<u>d.</u> Alternative measures are not permitted to be used.

16.E.03 Operational Aids.

<u>a.</u> Operations shall not begin unless the listed operational aids are in proper working order except where the employer meets the specified temporary alternative measures. More protective alternative measures specified by the crane manufacturer, if any, shall be followed.

<u>b.</u> If a listed operational aid stops working properly during operations, the operator shall safely stop operations until the temporary alternative measures are implemented or the device is again working properly. If a replacement part is no longer available, the use of a substitute device that performs the same type of function is permitted and is not considered a modification.

<u>c.</u> Category I operational aids and alternative measures. Operational aids listed in this paragraph that are not working properly shall be repaired not later than 7 days after the deficiency occurs.

➤ *Exception: If the employer documents that it has ordered the necessary parts within 7 days of the occurrence of the deficiency, the repair shall be completed within 7 days of receipt of the parts.*

(1) Boom hoist limiting device. TEMPORARY alternative measures (use at least one):

(a) Use a boom angle indicator;

(b) Clearly mark the boom hoist cable, in a visible location to the operator, at a point that will give the operator sufficient time to stop the hoist to keep the boom within the minimum allowable radius. In addition, install mirrors or remote video cameras and displays if necessary for the operator to see the mark;

(c) Clearly mark the boom hoist cable, in a visible location to the spotter, at a point that will give the spotter sufficient time to signal the operator and have the operator stop the hoist to keep the boom within the minimum allowable radius.

16

(2) Luffing jib limiting device. Equipment with a luffing jib shall have a luffing jib limiting device.

(3) Anti two-blocking device (A2B). Anti-two blocking devices shall be installed at all points of two-blocking.

(a) All cranes and derricks shall be equipped with A2B/Hoist-limit device that will disengage the function that is causing the two-blocking or an A2B damage prevention feature (except as noted). They shall be tested and certified functional by a CP prior to operating the crane.

(b) Lattice boom cranes: Lattice boom cranes shall be equipped with an A2B device to stop the load hoisting and boom-down functions before the load block or load contacts the boom tip.

➢*Exception 1 – Duty Cycle: Lattice boom cranes that are used exclusively for duty cycle operations are exempt from A2B equipment requirements. When a lattice boom crane engaged in duty cycle work is required to make a non-duty cycle lift (for example, to lift a piece of equipment), it will be exempt from the A2B equipment requirements if the following procedures are implemented:*

    <u>(i)</u> An international orange colored warning device (flag, tape or ball) is properly secured to the hoist line at a distance of 8 ft to 10 ft (2.4 m to 3m) above the rigging;

    <u>(ii)</u> The signal person acts as a spotter to alert the crane operator with a "STOP" signal when the warning device approaches the boom tip and the crane operator ceases hoisting functions when alerted of this;

    <u>(iii)</u> While the non-duty cycle lift is underway the signal person shall not stand under the load, shall have no duties other than as a signal person, and shall comply with the signaling requirements of this manual.

➢*Exception 2 – Lattice boom cranes with manually operated friction brakes: Lattice boom crane and hoisting equipment with manually activated friction brakes, A2B warning devices may be used in lieu of A2B prevention devices.*

(c) Telescopic boom cranes:

    <u>(i)</u> Telescopic boom cranes shall be equipped with an A2B device to stop the load hoisting function before the load block or load contacts the boom tip and to prevent damage to the hoist rope or other machine components when extending the boom.

    <u>(ii)</u> Telescopic boom cranes that are used exclusively for duty cycle operations shall be equipped with a two-blocking damage prevention feature or warning device to prevent damage to the hoist rope or other machine components when extending the boom.

(d) Floating cranes: Floating cranes may use an A2B alarm system in lieu of a disengaging device unless they are hoisting personnel.

(e) Other cranes used in duty cycle operations, to include clamshell (grapple), magnet, drop ball, container handling, concrete bucket, pile driving and extracting operations, drilled shaft operations (except telescopic boom cranes), <u>dynamic compaction and continuous flight auger</u> <u>drilling</u> are exempt from the requirements for A2B devices.

(f) Temporary alternative measure: clearly mark the cable (so that it can be easily seen by the operator) at a point that will give the operator sufficient time to stop the hoist to prevent two-blocking and use a spotter when extending the boom.

(4) Wind speed indicating device mounted on the crane, in a location where the maximum wind speed can be measured for the lifting activity. In lieu of the above and where wind speed and gusts can be effectively determined, a hand-held anemometer may be used.

<u>d</u>. Category II operational aids and alternative measures. Operational aids listed in this paragraph that are not working properly shall be repaired not later than 30 days after the deficiency occurs.

➢*Exception: If the employer documents that it has ordered the necessary parts within 7 days of the occurrence of the deficiency, and the parts are not received in time to complete the repair in 30 days, the repair shall be completed within 7 days of receipt of the parts.*

(1) Boom angle or radius indicator. The equipment shall have a boom angle or radius indicator readable from the operator's station (does not apply to articulating cranes or digger derricks manufactured before November 8, 2011). Temporary alternative measures: radii or boom angle shall be determined by measuring the radii or boom angle with a measuring device. Calibration and testing of indicators will be performed in accordance with the manufacturer's recommendations.

(2) Jib angle indicator (if equipment has luffing jib; does not apply to articulating cranes). Temporary alternative measures: radii or jib angle shall be determined by ascertaining the main boom angle and then measuring the radii or jib angle with a measuring device.

(3) Boom length indicator (does not apply to articulating cranes) if the equipment has a telescopic boom, except where the load rating is independent of the boom length. Temporary alternative measures: one of the following methods shall be used:

(a) Mark the boom with measured marks to calculate boom length;

(b) Calculate boom length from boom angle and radius measurements; OR

(c) Measure the boom with a measuring device.

(4) Load weighing and similar devices. Equipment shall have at least one of the following: load weighing device, load moment indicator (LMI), rated capacity indicator or rated capacity limiter (does not apply to digger derricks manufactured prior to November 8, 2011). Temporary alternative measures: The weight of the load shall be determined from a reliable source (i.e., load manufacturer), by a reliable calculation method (i.e., calculating a steel beam from measured dimensions and a known per foot weight), or by other equally reliable means. This information shall be provided to the operator prior to the lift.

➤Exception: Overhead and/or mobile LHE used in duty cycle operations are exempt from the requirements for load indicating devices and LMI devices.

(5) Hoist drum rotation indicator if the drum is not visible from the operator's station. Temporary alternative measures: mark the drum and if needed, install mirrors or remote video cameras and displays if necessary for the operator to see the mark.

(6) Outrigger position (horizontal beam extension) sensor/monitor if the equipment has outriggers (required on equipment manufactured after January 1, 2008). Temporary alternative measure: the operator shall verify that the position of the outriggers is correct (in accordance with manufacturer's procedures) before beginning operations requiring outrigger deployment.

16.E.04 All loads shall be determined through one of the following methods. This information must be known or provided to the operator prior to the lift.

a. Load weighing device;

b. Load moment (or rated capacity) indicator;

c. Load moment (or rated capacity) limiter, OR

d. The weight of the load must be determined either from a source recognized by the industry (such as the load manufacturer) or by a calculation method recognized by industry [i.e., calculating a steel beam from measured dimensions and a known per foot weight as determined by a qualified rigger (QR)].

➤Exception: Permanently installed overhead, gantry or other cranes that are used to pick gates (spillway, intake, discharge, etc) from slots have been designed with a reserve capacity and are factory proof tested at 125% of working load limit (WLL). Load cells are highly recommended to determine rigging capacities and overload conditions, but are not required.

16.F Testing.

16.F.01 Written reports of tests, showing test procedures and confirming the adequacy of repairs or alterations, shall be maintained with the crane and hoisting equipment or at the on-site project office.

16.F.02 Operational Testing.

a. A QP shall conduct operational tests in accordance with ANSI/ASME and the manufacturer's recommendations. If the manufacturer has no procedures, the requirements in this Section, as a minimum, must be performed.

b. Operational testing shall be performed:

(1) Before initial use of a crane or hoisting equipment after a load bearing or load controlling part or component, brake, travel component, or clutch (to include securing devices, skids and barges for floating cranes) has been altered, replaced, or repaired.

➤Note: Adding/removing counterweights is not considered load controlling/load bearing.

(2) Every time a crane or hoisting equipment(s) is reconfigured or re-assembled after disassembly (to include booms);

(3) Every time a crane and/or hoisting equipment is brought onto a USACE project; and

(4) Every year during annual inspection.

➤Note: Complete operational testing of the equipment after the replacement of wire rope is not required.

16

However, a limited operational test shall be made prior to putting the equipment back into service.

c. Operational Testing, as a minimum, shall include the following:

(1)   Load lifting and lowering mechanisms;

(2)   Boom lifting and lowering mechanisms;

(3)   Boom extension and retraction mechanisms;

(4)   Swinging mechanisms;

(5)   Travel mechanisms;

(6)   Safety devices;

(7)   Operational aids.

16.F.03 Load Testing. Load testing is considered a Critical Lift. *> See Section 16.H.*

a. Load tests shall be performed under the direction of a QP in accordance with appropriate ASME standards and the manufacturer's recommendations. At a minimum, the load test procedures shall include the following:

(1)   Hoist the test load to ensure that the load is supported by the crane and held by the hoist brake(s) for a minimum of 5 minutes;

(2)   Swing the crane. Insure there are no physical restrictions, the full range of its swing, with the test load;

(3)   Boom the crane up and down within the allowable working radius for the test load. At the maximum radius, hold the load for a minimum of 5 minutes and insure there is no movement of the load;

(4)   Lower the test load and hold the load with the brake(s).

➤*Note: If the manufacturer is no longer in business and procedures are unavailable, a QP familiar with the type of equipment involved shall develop and approve procedures, which as a minimum, shall include those listed above.*

b. Load Testing shall be performed at 100 to 110% of the *ANTICIPATED LOAD* for the specified configuration, **not to exceed** 100% of the manufacturer's load chart at the configuration of the test. The actual anticipated load itself may be used as the test load if approved by the GDA.

c. Load testing shall be performed:

(1) Before initial use of crane or hoisting equipment in which a load bearing or load controlling part or component, brake, travel component, or clutch has been altered, replaced, or repaired, and

➤*Note: Adding/removing counterweights is not considered load controlling/load bearing.*

(2)   Every time a crane or hoisting equipment(s) is reconfigured or re-assembled after disassembly (to include booms);

➤Note: Attaching/detaching a jib, which is an attachment, is not considered "reconfiguring or re-assembling" a crane and so does not require a load test. Installing or stowing the jib must be per manufacturer's recommendations and a competent person shall document this action prior to operation.

(3)   When the manufacturer requires load testing.

(a) The employer shall specifically research, identify and document manufacturer required load-testing frequency for each USACE-owned/operated and/or Contractor-owned/operated crane or hoisting equipment and maintain and/or provide this information to the GDA;

(b) Under conditions (1) and (2) above, a selective load test may be performed (testing only those components that have or may have been affected by the alteration, replacement, or repaired);

(c) The replacement of the rope is specifically excluded from this requirement. However, a limited operational test including actions in Sections 16.F.02.c above, under a normal operating load shall be made prior to putting the equipment back into service.

d. The manufacturer's specifications and limitations applicable to the operation of any crane and hoisting equipment shall be followed. At no time shall a crane or hoisting equipment be loaded in excess of the manufacturer's rating, except overhead and gantry cranes in accordance with ANSI/ASME B30.2 or B30.16. Loads shall not exceed 125% of the rated load for test purposes or planned engineered lifts for overhead and gantry cranes. *> See Section 16.H, Critical Lifts.*

(1)   Where manufacturer's specifications are not available, the limitations assigned to the equipment shall be based on the determinations of a registered engineer competent in this field, and such determinations will be documented and recorded.

(2) Attachments used with crane and hoisting equipment shall not exceed the capacity, rating, or scope recommended by the manufacturer.

e. Written reports that show test procedures and confirm the adequacy of repairs or alterations shall be maintained and provided upon request.

16.G Operation.

16.G.01 All LHE shall have the following documents with them (in the cab, if applicable) at all times they are to be operated:

a. A copy of the operating manual developed by the manufacturer for the specific make and model of equipment.

(1) When not available from a manufacturer, a QP shall establish the ratings and operating limitations (load charts), recommended operating speeds, special hazard warnings, instructions and operators manual, maintenance, testing, and inspection requirements that apply during the use.

(2) Where load capacities are available only in electronic form: in the event of a failure which makes the load capacities inaccessible, the operator must immediately cease operations or follow safe shutdown procedures until the load capacities (in electronic or other form) are available. A printed copy of the load capacities shall be maintained and available.

b. A copy of the load-rating chart (separate or included in the operating manual), shall include:

(1) The LHE make and model, serial number, and year of manufacturer;

(2) Load ratings for all operating configurations, including optional equipment;

(3) Recommended reeving for the hoist line, and

(4) Operating limits in windy or cold weather conditions.

c. A durable load chart with legible letters and figures shall be readily available to the operator at the control station;

d. The crane log book shall be used to record operating hours and all crane inspections, tests, maintenance, and repair. The log shall be updated daily as the crane is used and shall be signed by the operator and supervisor. Service mechanics shall sign the log after conducting maintenance or repairs on the crane;

e. All inspections, test, maintenance and repairs for LHE shall be maintained in the log, the O&M records or equivalent for that piece of equipment.

16.G.02 No modifications or additions that affect the capacity or safe operation of LHE shall be made without the manufacturer's written approval.

a. If such modifications or changes are made, the capacity, operation, and maintenance instruction plates, tags, or decals shall be changed accordingly.

b. In no case shall the original safety factor of the equipment be reduced.

16.G.03 Hoisting wire ropes shall be installed in accordance with ANSI/ASME standards and the equipment manufacturer's recommendations.

a. Overhead and gantry cranes shall have at least two full wraps of wire rope on the drums at all times.

b. All other cranes shall have at least three full wraps (not layers) of wire rope on the drums at all times.

c. The drum end of the wire rope shall be anchored to the drum by an arrangement specified by the crane manufacturer.

16.G.04 Responsibilities.

a. The responsibilities of the operator include, but are not limited to, the following requirements:

(1) The operator shall not engage in any activity that will divert his attention while operating the equipment;

(2) The operator shall not leave the controls while a load is suspended;

(3) Before leaving the LHE unattended, the operator shall:

(a) Land any load, bucket, lifting magnet, or other device;

(b) Disengage the master clutch;

(c) Set travel, swing, boom brakes, and other locking devices;

(d) Put the controls in the "OFF" or neutral position;

(e) Secure the equipment against accidental travel; and

(f) Stop the engine.

16

➢*Exception: When crane operation is frequently interrupted during a shift and the operator must leave the crane. Under these circumstances, the engine may remain running and the* conditions above must be followed (don't have to stop the engine). In addition, the *following conditions shall apply:*

(i) *The operator shall remain adjacent to the equipment and is not engaged in any other duties;*

(ii) *The CP determines that it is safe to do so and implements measures necessary to restrain the boom hoist and telescoping, load, swing and outrigger functions;*

(iii) *The crane shall be located within an area protected from unauthorized entry.*

(4) The operator shall respond to signals from the person who is directing the lift or an appointed signal person. When a signal person is not used in the LHE operation, the operator shall ensure he has full view of the load and the load travel paths at all times the load is rigged to the equipment;

(5) Each operator is responsible for those operations under his direct control. Whenever there is a concern as to safety, the operator shall have the authority to stop and refuse to handle loads until a QP has determined that safety has been assured.

b. The operator, qualified lift supervisor and rigger shall jointly ensure:

(1) The LHE is level and, where necessary, blocked;

(2) The load is well secured and balanced in the sling or lifting device before it is lifted more than a few inches;

(3) The lift and swing path is clear of obstructions and adequate clearance is maintained from electrical sources per Table 16-1; and

(4) All persons are clear of the swing radius of the counterweight and housing.

c. When two or more cranes (tandem lift is a critical lift) or LHE are used to lift one load, the lift supervisor shall be responsible for the following:

(1) Analyzing the operation and instruct all personnel involved in the proper positioning, rigging of the load, and the movements to be made;

(2) Making determinations as necessary to reduce crane (LHE) ratings, load position, boom location,

ground support, and speed of movement, which are required to safely make the lift;

(3) Ensuring that dedicated personnel are present and equipment is functioning properly. All personnel involved with the crane (LHE) operation shall understand the communication systems and their responsibilities.

16.G.05 Communications.

a. A standard signal system shall be used on all LHE (by hand, voice, audible or comparable signals).

(1) Manual (hand) signals may be used when the distance between the operator and signal person is not more than 100 ft (30.4 m). If using hand signals, Standard Method must be used per Figure 16-1 for Mobile Cranes, Figure 16-4 for Overhead and Gantry.

(2) Radio, telephone, or a visual and audible electrically-operated system shall be used when the distance between operator and signal person is more than 100 ft (30.4 m) or when they cannot see each other.

b. A signal person must be used in the following situations:

(1) When the point of operation, load travel, area near or at load placement, is not in full view of the operator;

(2) When the equipment is traveling and the view in the direction of travel is obstructed;

(3) Due to site -specific safety concerns, either the operator or the person handling the load determines that it is necessary.

c. During LHE operations requiring signals, the ability to transmit signals between the operator and signal person shall be maintained. If that ability is interrupted at any time, the operator shall safely stop operations requiring signals until it is reestablished and a proper signal is given and understood.

d. Only one person gives signals to a LHE operator at a time unless an emergency stop signal is given (which may be given by anyone and must be obeyed by the operator).

16.G.06 Riding on loads, hooks, hammers, buckets, material hoists, or other hoisting equipment not meant for personnel handling is prohibited.

16.G.07 When practical and when their use does not create a hazard, tag lines shall be used to control loads.

16.G.08 Whenever a slack line condition occurs, the proper seating of the rope in the sheaves and on the drum shall be checked prior to further operations.

16.G.09 Power Line Clearance During Assembly and/or Disassembly (up to 350 kV). Before assembling or disassembling LHE, the employer must determine if any part of the LHE, load line, or load (including rigging and lifting accessories) could get closer than 20 ft (6 m) to a power line during this process. If so, one of the following requirements must be met:

a. De-energize and ground. Confirm from the utility owner/operator that the line has been de-energized and visibly grounded at the worksite.

b. 20-ft (6 m) clearance. Ensure no part of the LHE, load line or load gets closer than 20 ft (6 m) to the power line by implementing the following:

(1) Conduct a planning meeting with the assembly/disassembly (A/D) director, operator, A/D crew and the other workers who will be in the area. Review location of the power lines and the control measures to prevent encroachment/or electrocution;

(2) If tag lines are used, they must be non-conductive;

(3) In addition, at least one of the following must be in place:

(a) Use of a dedicated spotter who is in continuous contact with the operator;

(b) A proximity alarm set to give operator sufficient warning;

(c) A device that automatically limits range of movement, set to prevent encroachment;

(d) An elevated warning line, barricade or line of signs in view of the operator, equipped with flags or similar high-visibility markings.

c. Table 16-1 clearance.

(1) Determine the line's voltage and minimum clearance distance permitted under Table 16-1.

(2) Determine if any part of the LHE, load line, or load, could get closer that the minimum clearance distance to the power line permitted. If so, the control measures identified in paragraph b (above) shall be implemented.

16.G.10 Power line clearance – equipment operations (all voltages). The employer must identify the work zone

for the LHE in question (work zone is the area 360 degrees around the crane, up to the LHE's maximum working radius). A determination shall be made if any part of the LHE, load line or load (to include rigging and lifting accessories), if operated up to the LHE/crane's maximum working radius in the work zone, could get within 20 ft (6 m) of the power line one of the following must be met:

a. De-energize and ground. Confirm from the utility owner/operator that the power line has been de-energized and visibly grounded at the worksite.

b. Twenty Feet Clearance (20 ft clearance). Ensure no part of the LHE, load line or load gets closer than 20 ft (6 m) to the power line by implementing the following:

(1) Conduct a planning meeting with the site/lift supervisor, signal person/rigger, operator, crew and the other workers who will be in the area. Review location of the power lines and the control measures to prevent encroachment or electrocution.

(2) If tag lines are used, they must be non-conductive;

(3) Erect and maintain an elevated warning line, barricade or line of signs in view of the operator, equipped with flags or similar high-visibility markings, at 20 ft (6 m) from the power line or at a minimum approach distance under Table 16-1.

(4) In addition, at least one of the following must be in place:

(a) Use of a dedicated spotter who is in continuous contact with the operator. The spotter must have a visual aid to assist in identifying the minimum clearance distance (e.g., clearly visible line painted on the ground). The spotter must be positioned to effectively gauge the clearance distance;

(b) A proximity alarm set to give operator sufficient warning;

(c) A device that automatically limits range of movement, set to prevent encroachment.

(d) An insulating link/device installed at a point between the end of the load line (or below) and the load.

c. Table 16-1 clearance.

(1) Determine line's voltage and minimum clearance distance permitted under Table 16-1.

(2) Determine if any part of the equipment, load line, or load, while operating up to the LHE's maximum working radius in the work zone could get closer than the minimum clearance distance to the power line permitted. If so, the control measures

16

identified in paragraph b above shall be implemented.

d. Permanently installed overhead and gantry cranes clearances shall be in accordance with NFPA 70;

e. When working near transmitter/communication towers where the LHE is close enough for an electrical charge to be induced in the LHE or materials being handled, the transmitter must be de-energized or provided with an electrical ground. Taglines, if used, shall be non-conductive.

f. It shall be assumed that all power lines are energized unless the utility owner/operator confirms that the power line has been and will continue to be deenergized and visibly grounded at the worksite.

g. Training. Each operator and crew member assigned to work with the equipment shall have received the following training by a QP:

(1) Procedures to follow in the event there is contact with the power line;

(2) Information regarding the danger of electrocution from the operator simultaneously touching the equipment and the ground;

(3) The importance to the operator's safety of remaining inside the cab except where there is an imminent danger of fire, explosion, or other emergency that necessitates leaving the cab;

(4) The safest means of evacuating LHE that may be energized;

(5) The danger of the potentially energized zone around the LHE;

(6) The need for crew in the area to avoid approaching or touching the LHE and the load;

(7) Safe clearance distance from the power line;

(8) Power lines are presumed to be energized unless the utility owner/operator confirms that the power line is deenergized and visibly grounded;

(9) Power lines are presumed to be uninsulated unless the utility owner/operator or a RPE who is a QP confirms that a line is insulated;

(10) The limitations of an insulating link/device, proximity alarm, and range control (or similar) device if used;

(11) Equipment grounding procedures and the limitations thereof;

(12) Dedicated spotters must be trained to effectively perform their tasks, including the applicable training previously identified herein.

16.G.11 Power line safety - over 350 kV. The requirements of Sections 16.G.09 and 16.G.10 apply to power lines over 350 kV except:

a. For power lines over 350 kV but at or below 1000 kV, wherever the distance "20 feet (6 m)" is specified, the distance "50 feet (15 m)" must be substituted; and,

b. For power lines over 1000 kV, the minimum clearance distance must be established by the utility owner/operator or a RPE who is a QP with respect to electrical power transmission and distribution.

16.G.12 Power Line Safety While Traveling Under or Near Power Lines with NO Load. The employer must ensure that;

a. The boom/mast and its support system are lowered sufficiently to ensure clearances in Table 16-2 are maintained;

b. Effects of speed and terrain on equipment movement (including boom/mast) are considered to ensure clearances in Table 16-2 are maintained;

TABLE 16-1

Minimum Clearance from Energized Overhead Electric Lines

Voltage (nominal, kV, alternating current)	Minimum clearance distance
Up to 50	10 ft (3 m)
51 – 200	15 ft (4.6 m)
201 – 350	20 ft (6 m)
351 – 500	25 ft (7.6 m)
501 – 750	35 ft (10.7 m)
751 – 1000	45 ft (13.7 m)
Over 1,000	(As established by the utility owner/operator or RPE who is a QP with respect to electrical power transmission and distribution).

c. If any part of the LHE, while traveling will get closer than 20 ft (6 m) to the power line, a dedicated spotter who is in continuous contact with the operator is used;

d. When traveling at night, or in conditions of poor visibility, in addition to the above, the employer must ensure that;

(1)   the power lines are illuminated, or alternate methods are used to identify location of power lines;

(2)   a safe path of travel is identified and used.

16.G.13 Physical clearances.

a. Adequate clearance shall be maintained between moving and rotating structures of the LHE and fixed objects to allow the passage of employees without harm. The minimum adequate clearance is 24 in (61 cm).

b. Accessible areas within the swing radius of the rear of the LHE's rotating superstructure, either permanently or temporarily mounted, shall be barricaded to prevent an employee from being struck or crushed.

16.G.14 Crane Mats. Where crane mats are required for a stable, level work surface for crane operations, the matting material shall be in good condition and of adequate thickness, width, and length as to completely support the crane. The mats shall be laid perpendicular to the crane travel path, and shall be placed as close to each other as possible. A spotter shall be used to guide the crane when it moves on the mat surface to prevent the crane from traveling beyond the limit of the crane mats.

16

TABLE 16-2

Minimum Clearance Distance from Energized Overhead Electric Lines While   Traveling with No Load

Voltage (nominal, kV alternating current)	, While traveling - minimum clearance distance
Up to 0.75	4 ft (1.2 m)
.76 – 50	6 ft (1.8 m)
51 – 345	10 ft (3.0 m)
326 – 750	16 ft (4.9 m)
751 – 1000	20 ft (6.1 m)
Over 1,000	(As established by the utility owner/operator or RPE who is a QP with respect to electrical power transmission and distribution).

Note: Environmental conditions like fog, smoke or precipitation may require increased clearances.

16.H Critical Lifts.

16.H.01 When using LHE, the following are identified as critical lifts requiring detailed planning and additional or unusual safety precautions. Critical lifts are defined as:

a. Lifts involving hazardous materials (e.g., explosives, highly volatile substances);

b. Hoisting personnel with LHE;

c. Lifts made with more than one LHE;

d. Lifts where the center of gravity could change;

e. Lifts made when the load weight is 75% of the rated capacity of the LHE load chart or more (not applicable to gantry, overhead or bridge cranes);

f. Lifts without the use of outriggers using rubber tire load charts;

g. Lifts using more than one hoist on the same LHE;

h. Lifts involving Multiple Lift Rigging (MLR) Assemblies or other non-routine or technically difficult rigging arrangements;

i. Lifts involving submerged loads.

➢ *Exception: lifts that were engineered to travel in guided slots throughout the lift and have fixed rigging and/or lifting beams, i.e., intake gates, tailgates/logs);*

j. Lifts out of the operator's view.

➢ *Exception: if hand signals used by a signal person in view of the operator or radio communications are available and in use, load does not exceed two tons AND is determined a routine lift by the lift supervisor;*

k. Load Tests;

l. When land-based LHE mounted on barges, pontoons or other means of flotation are required to travel while lifting the load. > *See Sections 16.L.03 and 16.L.04.*

m. Any lift the operator believes should be considered critical.

16.H.02 Critical lift plans. Before making a critical lift, a critical lift plan shall be developed.

> *See Non-Mandatory, Critical Lift Plan, Form 16-3.*

a. By a CP and shall include the LHE operator, lift supervisor, and the rigger and signed by all involved personnel prior to the lift;

b. For a series of lifts on one project or job, as long as the LHE, personnel, type loads and configuration do not differ;

c. Documented with a copy provided to the GDA for acceptance prior to the lift(s) being made;

d. And shall include, as a minimum:

(1) The specific make and model of each piece of LHE, the line, boom, and swing speeds;

(2) The exact size and weight of the load to be lifted and all LHE and rigging components that add to the weight. The manufacturer's maximum load limits for the entire range of the lift, as listed in the load charts, shall also be specified;

(3) The plan shall specify the lift geometry and procedures, including the LHE position, height of the lift, the load radius, and the boom length and angle, for the entire range of the lift;

(4) Site drawing shall be included to identify placement/location(s) of LHE, adjacent equipment and/or facilities, etc;

(5) The plan shall designate the operator, lift supervisor and rigger and include their qualifications;

(6) The plan will include a rigging plan that shows the lift points and describes rigging procedures and hardware requirements;

(7) The plan will describe the ground conditions, outrigger or crawler track requirements, and, if necessary, the design of mats, necessary to achieve a level, stable foundation of sufficient bearing capacity for the lift;

(8) For floating LHE, the plan shall describe the operating base (platform) condition and any potential maximum list / trim;

(9) The plan will list environmental conditions under which lift operations are to be stopped;

(10) The plan will specify coordination and communication requirements for the lift operation;

(11) For tandem LHE lifts, identify the requirements for an equalizer beam if applicable.

16.I Environmental Considerations.

16.I.01 LHE shall not be operated when wind speeds at the site attain the maximum wind velocity based on the surface/load ratio recommendations of the manufacturer.

a. At winds greater than 20 mph (9 m/s), the operator, rigger, and lift supervisor shall cease all crane operations, evaluate conditions and determine if the lift shall proceed. This determination shall be based on wind calculations per manufacturer's recommendations.

b. The determination to proceed or not shall be documented in the LHE/crane operator's logbook.

16.I.02 Operations performed during weather conditions that produce icing of the LHE or reduced visibility shall be performed at reduced functional speeds and with signaling means appropriate to the situation.

16.I.03 When lightning is observed, all LHE operations shall stop. A determination shall be made as to proximity to operation being performed. (Use a lightning detector or once lightning is seen, count the number of seconds until you hear thunder. Divide number of seconds by 5 to get the distance the lightning is away from you). If lightning is 10 miles away or less, work must stop until 30 minutes after the last audible thunder or visible flash of lightning. Plan work activities according to the latest weather forecast and be prepared to stop operations, until bad weather has safely passed. These actions shall be documented (daily report, crane operator's log book, etc.).

16.I.04 For night operations, lighting adequate to illuminate the working areas while not interfering with the operator's vision shall be provided. > See Section 7.

16.J Lattice, Hydraulic, Crawler-, Truck-, Wheel-, and Ringer-Mounted Cranes.

16.J.01 For required operator aids and indicating devices, see Section 16.E.03.

16.J.02 Boom assembly and disassembly. This operation shall be covered in the AHA and CP shall be identified.

a. The manufacturer's boom assembly and disassembly procedures shall be reviewed by the team before starting the assembly or disassembly. The CP shall be present during assembly/disassembly operations.

b. When removing pins or bolts from a boom, workers shall stay out from under the boom. Sections shall be blocked, cribbed, or otherwise secured to prevent them from falling.

c. Blocking, cribbing and other means of securing shall be confirmed, verified and approved by a CP before assembly/disassembly operations are allowed to proceed.

16.J.03 Outriggers.

a. Anytime outriggers are required to be used, they shall be extended or deployed per the crane manufacturer's load/capacity chart specifications, except for locomotive cranes.

b. When partially extended outriggers are used, the following requirements shall be met:

(1) Crane operation with partially extended outriggers shall only be undertaken if approved by the crane manufacturer;

(2) Outriggers shall be set at equal positions that correspond to the load/capacity charts supplied by the manufacturer for those positions. Only the load chart(s) corresponding to the outrigger positions shall be used for operation;

(3) When situations arise where outriggers must be set at unequal positions that correspond to the load/capacity charts corresponding with the individual quadrants of operation. The manufacturer or QP shall be consulted to determine if the capacity reductions, special operating procedures, or limitations are required;

c. Outrigger floats shall be securely attached to the outriggers.

d. Blocking/pads under outrigger floats shall meet the following requirements:

(1) Sufficient strength to prevent crushing, bending, or shear failure;

(2) Such thickness, width, and length as to completely support the float, transmit the load to the supporting surface, and prevent shifting, toppling, or excessive settlement under load. The blocking area size and thickness shall be based on additional items such as soil conditions, soil type, compaction, liquid limits, underground utilities, crane type and capacity, and having the crane within 1% of level.

16.J.04 Unless the manufacturer has specified an on-rubber rating, mobile cranes shall not pick or swing loads over the side of the crane unless the outriggers are down and properly extended.

16.J.05 Unless recommended against by the manufacturer, crane booms shall be lowered to ground level or secured against displacement by wind loads or other outside forces when not in use. If the manufacturer recommends against this practice, the manufacturer's recommended practice shall be followed.

16.J.06 When pick and carry operations occur (Rough Terrain Cranes), the boom must be centered over the front of the crane, the mechanical swing lock engaged, and the load restrained from swinging.

16.K Portal, Tower, and Pillar Cranes.

16.K.01 All load bearing foundations, supports, and rail tracks shall be constructed or installed as determined by a RPE with knowledge in this area, in accordance with the crane manufacturer's recommendations.

16.K.02 Cranes shall be erected/dismantled in accordance with the manufacturer's recommended procedures, (or if manufacturer procedures are not available, in accordance with procedures developed by a RPE with knowledge in this area).

a. When erected/dismantled, written instructions by the manufacturer and/or RPE and a list of the weights of each component shall be kept at the site.

b. Erection and dismantling shall be performed under the supervision of a QP.

c. An AHA shall be developed and procedures established before the erection/dismantling work commences to insure site-specific needs are considered. The analysis will include:

(1) The location of the crane in relation to other tower cranes, adjacent buildings or towers, overhead power and communication lines, underground utilities;

(2) Foundation design and construction requirements; and

(3) When the tower is erected within a structure, clearances between the tower and the structure and bracing and wedging requirements.

d. Wind velocity at the site at the time of erection/dismantling shall be a consideration as a limiting factor that could require suspending the erection/dismantling operation and shall be as determined by the manufactured or if this data is not available, by a QP.

e. Before crane components are erected, they shall be visually inspected for damage. Dented, bent, torn, gouged or otherwise damaged members shall not be erected.

f. Initially and after each climb, the crane shall be plumbed and then held in the plumbed condition by wedges or other means. Cranes shall be plumbed to a tolerance of 1:500 (1 in:40 ft; 2.4 cm:12 m) unless the manufacturer specifies otherwise.

16.K.03 Pre-operation tests shall be performed when cranes are erected and after each climbing operation, before placing the crane in service. All functional motions, motion limiting devices and brakes shall be properly tested for operation in accordance with the manufacturer's recommended procedures and ANSI/ASME B30.3 or B30.4, as applicable:

a. Crane supports;

b. Brakes and clutches, limit and overload switches, and locking and safety devices; and

c. Load hoisting and lowering, boom hoisting and lowering, and swing motion mechanisms and procedures.

16.K.04 Climbing Procedures. Prior to and during, all climbing procedures (to include inside and top climbing), the employer shall:

a. Comply with all manufacturer prohibitions;

b. Have a RPE verify that the host structure is strong enough to sustain the forces imposed through the braces, brace anchorages and supporting floors;

c. Ensure that no part of the climbing procedure takes place when wind velocity at the crane superstructure exceeds the limit set by the manufacturer or a QP, or 20 mph (9 m/s) at the crane superstructure if no such limit has been set. The characteristics of the gusts should be considered for their effect on the climbing operation; and

d. The operator of a hammerhead tower crane shall be present during climbing or telescoping operations.

16.K.05 Safety devices and operational aids. Operations shall not begin unless the operational aids are in proper working order, except where the employer meets the specified temporary alternative measures. In addition to those listed in 16.E.03, the following shall be provided:

➢ Note: The general requirements, as identified in Section 16.E.03 for Operational aids, do not apply to tower cranes. The devices listed in this Section are required on all tower cranes covered by this subpart, unless otherwise specified.

a. Rail clamps, if used, shall have slack between the point of attachment to the rail and the end fastened to the crane. Rail clamps shall not be used as a means of restraining tipping of a crane display magnitude of load on the hook;

b. Hydraulic system pressure limiting device;

c. The following brakes, which shall automatically set in the event of pressure loss or power failure, are required: hoist brake on all hoists, swing brake, trolley brake, rail travel brake;

d. Deadman control or forced neutral return control (hand) levers;

e. Emergency stop switch at the operator's station;

f. Trolley travel limiting device prevents trolley from running into the trolley end stops;

g. Ambient wind velocity device. This device shall be mounted at or near the top of the crane. A velocity readout shall be provided at the operator's station in the cab, and a visible or audible alarm shall be triggered in the cab and at remote control stations when a preset wind velocity has been exceeded;

h. Hoist line pull limiting device (limits lifted load).

16.K.06 Multiple tower crane jobsites. On jobsites where more than one fixed jib (hammerhead) tower crane is installed, the cranes shall be located such that no crane or its load may come in contact with the structure of another crane. Cranes are permitted to pass over one another.

16.K.07 Weathervaning. Tower cranes required to weathervane when out-of-service shall be installed with clearance for boom (jib) and superstructure to swing through a full 360 degree arc without striking any fixed object or other weathervaning crane. The boom shall be taken in the attitude dictated by its wind area balance. Non-weathervaning boom (jibs) shall be taken in the least favorable attitude. Traveling cranes shall also resist design wind level induced sliding.

16.L Floating Cranes/Derricks, Crane Barges, and Auxiliary Shipboard -Mounted Cranes.

16.L.01 The requirements in this Section are supplemental requirements for floating LHE, pile drivers, drill rigs, man-lifts and land LHE on barges, pontoons, vessels or other means of flotation and auxiliary shipboard mounted cranes, unless otherwise specified.

16.L.02 Design & Construction Standards. The lifting equipment on floating cranes, crane barges and on ships (shipboard cranes) shall be designed and constructed in accordance with one of the following standards:

(a) ANSI/ASME B30.8;

(b) American Bureau of Shipping (ABS) Guide for Certification of Cranes, or

16

(c) American Petroleum Institute (API) Specification 2C.

16.L.03 LHE Manufacturer's Floating Service Load Chart.

a. Manufacturer's Floating Service Load Chart. A LHE Manufacturer's Floating Service Load Chart shall be provided. The Load Chart shall be in accordance with all criteria from the selected standard in Section 16.L.02.

(1) The Floating Service Load Chart shall provide a table of rated load vs. boom angle and radius.

(2) The Floating Service Load Chart shall also provide the maximum allowable machine list and trim associated with the tabular loads and radii provided.

b. Floating Service Load Chart if Manufacturer's Floating Service Load Chart is not available, a floating service load chart may be developed and provided by a qualified RPE, competent in the field of floating cranes. The Load Chart shall:

(1) Be in accordance with all criteria from the selected standard in Section 16.L.02;

(2) Provide a table of rated load vs. boom angle and radius;

(3) Provide the maximum allowable machine list and machine trim associated with the tabular loads and radii provided;

(4) Be stamped by a RPE, qualified and competent in the field of floating cranes. The RPE, competent in the field of floating cranes shall, stamp and certify (sign) that the Naval Architectural Analysis (NAA) meets the requirements of Sections 16.L.03.

16.L.04 Stability During Lift Operation.

a. During lift operations, the stability of the floating LHE, or vessel and shipboard crane shall meet the requirements for "lifting" as set forth in 46 CFR 173.005 through 46 CFR 173.025, over the full range of crane slewing angles.

b. During lift operations, the stability of the floating LHE, or vessel and shipboard crane shall limit floating platform heel and trim such that the resultant LHE list and trim over the full range of LHE slewing angles are within the limits identified in the LHE Floating Service Load Chart.

c. A minimum of 12 in (0.3 m) of freeboard shall be maintained during lift operations, over the full range of crane slewing angles.

d. The entire bottom area of the floating platform shall be submerged for all lifts, over the full range of crane slewing angles.

16.L.05 Floating Service Naval Architectural Analysis (NAA). A NAA shall be provided.

a. The NAA shall evaluate the LHE on the floating platform. The LHE Manufacturer's Floating Service Load Chart (Section 16.L.03) shall be validated for:

(1) The stability during lift operation (Sections 16.L.04.a through d), and

(2) The machine list and trim limits for afloat service. The Load Chart shall be de-rated (reduced) as required to meet the requirements for stability during lift operation and for machine list and trim limits for afloat service.

b. The NAA shall include the full 360° (degree) slewing range of the crane, unless specific slewing angle limits are identified.

c. When deck loads are to be carried while lifting, the NAA shall incorporate the deck loading amount, location and deck load center of gravity, and sail area into the stability analysis.

d. The NAA shall incorporate wind loading, into the heel and list calculations with a minimum wind speed of 40 mph (18 m/s).

e. The NAA shall be stamped/certified by an RPE or qualified Naval Architect/Marine Engineer, competent in the field of floating cranes. The RPE or Naval Architect/Marine Engineer shall stamp and/or certify (sign) that the NAA meets the requirements of Sections 16.L.04, and 16.L.05.

16.L.06 Floating Service Structural Analysis.

a. The floating platform structure shall be adequate for the loads applied from lifting over the full crane slewing range.

b. For vessels which are not built for the application, a structural analysis shall be provided to document the structural adequacy of the floating platform in conjunction with applied LHE loads, for the lift amounts as developed in the NAA. Deck loads and environmental loads shall be applied as part of the structural analysis.

c. Where established floating platform design structural capacities, such as allowable deck loads, are available, these may be used in support of the structural analysis.

d. The structural analysis shall be stamped by an RPE, competent in the field of floating LHE. The RPE shall stamp and certify (sign) that the Floating Service Structural Analysis meets the requirements of Sections 16.L.04 and 16.L.05.

e. The lift amounts developed in the NAA shall be reduced if the structural analysis shows insufficient structural capacity at the NAA loads. The amount of reduction shall be as required for the structural capacity.

16.L.07 Floating Service Load Chart, LHE on Floating Platform. The NAA and Floating Service Structural Analyses shall be used to develop the Floating Service Load Chart.

a. The Floating Service Load Chart will define the lift/radius capacity of the LHE on the specific floating platform.

b. The Floating Service Load Chart shall incorporate any de-ratings required by either the NAA or Floating Service Structural Analysis.

c. An RPE or Naval Architect/Marine Engineer, competent in the field of floating crane/derrick design, shall stamp and/or certify (sign) that the Floating Service Load Chart meets the requirements of Sections 16.L.05 and 16.L.06.

d. The load chart certification may be either:

(1) A floating service load chart developed (de-rated) from the Manufacturer's floating service load chart, or

(2) If no de-rating is required, the Crane Manufacturer's Floating Service Load Chart with separate attached certification document.

e. The Floating Service Load Chart and the Floating Service Naval Architect Analysis shall be submitted to the GDA for acceptance prior to start of work.

f. The Floating Service Load Chart shall be posted in the cab or at the operator's station (if no cab). All other procedures applicable to the operation of the equipment (instructions and operators manual, recommended operating speeds, etc.) shall be readily available on board.

g. The Floating Service Load Chart shall, at a minimum, include the following:

(1) Naval Architect's Notes delineating:

(a) Draft limits;

(b) Deck cargo weight and Vertical Center of Gravity above deck;

(c) Maximum wind speed;

(d) Environmental limits;

(e) Vessel heel and trim limits;

(f) LHE Machine list and trim limits, and

(g) Vessel condition (e.g., dry bilges, watertight integrity, etc.).

(2) The LHE Manufacturer's Floating Service Crane Load Chart.

(3) If de-rating of the Crane Manufacturer's Floating Service Crane Load Chart is required, a separate Floating Service Safe Working Load Chart shall be provided with:

(a) Mode of operation;

(b) Table of hook load, boom elevation angle, lift radius (with list/trim considered);

(c) Maximum Machine List and Trim;

(d) Maximum Floating Platform List and Trim;

(e) LHE configuration, to include boom length, amount of counterweight, parts of wire, and block size.

h. The Floating Service Load Chart shall be programmed into the crane LMI.

i. The Floating Service Load Chart shall remain valid so long as no major modifications are made to the LHE or to the floating platform, as documented by a QP.

16.L.08 Land LHE, derricks and mobile auxiliary LHE mounted on barges, pontoons or other means of flotation.

a. All requirements in Sections 16.L.02 through 16.L.07 shall be applicable for land- LHE, derricks and mobile auxiliary LHE mounted on barges, pontoons or other means of flotation.

b. LHE Mats. The need, type, size and location of LHE mats required shall be determined for the type of LHE on the barge.

c. Means of attachment of LHE shall be shall be provided to prevent shifting during lift operations. The attachment method shall not be used to hold down LHE against overturning moment.

16

16.L.09 LHE Travel.

a. If traveling is required on the barge with no load, the travel area shall be evaluated in the NAA, and identified on the Floating service Load Chart.

b. If traveling is required while lifting the load, the lift shall be deemed a critical lift and a critical lift plan is required.

c. If traveling is required while lifting the load, the requirements in Sections 16.L.02 through 16.L.07 must be satisfied throughout the travel range. The NAA and Structural Analyses shall cover the travel range with load. The travel area shall be evaluated in the in the NAA, and identified on the Floating Service Load Chart.

16.L.10 A-Frame Non-Slewing Anchor Handling Barge/Vessel.

a. A-Frame Non-Slewing anchor handling barge/vessels may be used for anchor handling, low lifting of loads such as anchor buoys/weights, dredge pipe, submerged pipeline and pontoons.

➤*Note: If used for any other lifting application, the work platform will be considered a floating derrick and all other requirements of Section 16 apply.*

b. A-Frame Non-Slewing anchor barge/vessels shall also comply with the following:

(1) All deck surfaces of the pontoon or barge shall be above the water;

(2) Means for limiting the applied load, such as mechanical means or marking the draft of the barge corresponding to the rated load, shall be provided. Calculations shall be available and the barge shall be tested to verify rated load;

(3) A ratchet and pawl shall be provided for releasing the load from the hoisting machinery brake;

(4) An operating manual/procedure shall be available for use by the operator. The operator shall be trained in the anchor handling barge systems operation.

c. If additional external load is superimposed above that which can be hoisted with the onboard hoisting machinery, then a chain stopper shall be used to remove the external load from the A-frame and hoist machinery.

16.L.11 Employer-Made Lift Equipment Used on Barges or Pontoons.

a. If lift equipment is employer-made, it shall not be used unless the employer has documents demonstrating that the load charts and applicable parameters for use meet the requirements of one of the standards identified in Section 16.L.02.

b. All requirements in Sections 16.L.02 through 16.L.07 shall be applicable.

16.L.12 Modifications.

a. Weight and Center of Gravity (CG) changes. Any modifications to the Crane and Floating Platform that result in any of the following changes to the crane and floating platform lightship characteristics shall require a new Naval Architect Analysis, and a new Floating Service Load Chart:

(1) An increase in Vertical CG by more than 2 in (5 cm);

(2) A change in the lightship displacement by more than 3° (degrees), or

(3) A shift in Longitudinal CG of more than 1° of floating platform length.

b. Modifications to the crane that result in changes to the crane lift capacity and/or to the crane machine list and trim limits shall require a new NAA, and a new Floating Service Load Chart.

16.L.13 Overhead Bridge Cranes On Floating Platforms.

a. An overhead bridge crane Naval Architectural Heel and Trim Analysis shall be performed for overhead bridge cranes on floating platforms by a RPE or Naval Architect/Marine Engineer, competent in LHE on floating plant.

(1) The Analysis shall determine the maximum vessel heel and trim that can be generated by use of the bridge crane.

(2) The Analysis shall cover the full longitudinal and transverse motion range of the bridge crane, the crane weight, and the crane full rated load.

(3) If floating platform heel and trim not related to the bridge crane operation is present during the bridge crane operation, the non-related heel and trim shall be included in the Bridge Crane Naval Architectural Heel and Trim Analysis.

(4) A RPE or Naval Architect/Marine Engineer, competent in the field of floating crane/derrick design, shall stamp and/or certify (sign) that the Bridge Crane

Naval Architectural Heel and Trim meets the Analysis requirements of this Section.

b. Bridge Crane Operation at floating platform heel and trim. The bridge crane manufacturer shall verify that the bridge crane may be safely operated at the vessel heel and trim maximums identified by the Bridge Crane Naval Architectural Analysis.

c. Floating Platform heel and trim indication. A heel and trim indicating device shall be provided on all bridge crane equipped floating platforms. The indicating device shall be visible by the bridge crane operator during bridge crane operation.

16.L.14 Use of Elevating Aerial Work Platforms (AWPs) Onboard Floating Platforms.

a. AWPs shall only be operated in accordance with the manufacturer's recommendations for service on floating platforms.

b. AWPs used on floating platforms shall have a secondary set of controls at ground level.

c. AWPs may not be moved on the platform (driven) during operations with personnel onboard the lift unless it is allowed and addressed in the NAA.

d. Floating Platform Heel and Trim.

(1) When an AWP is to be used on a floating platform, the floating platform heel and trim shall remain within the AWP manufacturer's identified limits for floating operation.

(2) The floating platform shall be ballasted as needed to maintain barge heel and trim within the manufacturer's limits for the AWP operation.

e. Verification of Floating Platform Heel and Trim.

(1) Platform heel and trim shall be verified prior to operations with personnel on the AWP.

(2) The secondary set of platform controls shall be utilized to verify platform heel and trim through the intended range of AWP operations. The test shall incorporate weight on the platform at least equal to the personnel and equipment using the AWP.

f. Operations on Floating Platform during AWP operation. No operations on the floating platform that will affect the platform heel and trim beyond the required limits shall be permitted during the use of the AWP.

16.L.15 Near-Maximum Loads. When loads approach the maximum rating of the crane or derrick, the person responsible for the job shall ascertain that the weight of the load has been determined within +/- 10% before it is lifted.

16.L.16 Safety Devices and Operational Aids. In addition to those required by Section 16.E, the following are required:

a. Machine Heel and Trim indicating device. This device shall be located in the crane cab or at the operator's station (if there is no cab);

b. Boom Angle Indicator within clear view of the operator's station;

c. Floating Platform List and Trim indicating device: as a means for the operator to visually determine the heel and trim of the platform as opposed to the crane;

d. Draft Marks - as a means for monitoring both draft and freeboard;

e. Wind speed and direction indicator must be within clear view of the operator's station;

f. Anti two-block device - *See Section 16.E.03.*

16.L.17 Portable Remote Controls. If portable remote controls are used for lifting, the operator shall:

a. be directly aware of the vessel heel and trim and the crane machine heel and trim during lift operations, or

b. be in direct communication with a team member who is directly monitoring vessel heel and trim and the crane machine heel and trim during lift operations.

16.L.18 Inspections. In addition to inspection of the crane/derrick per Section 16.D, inspection of the barge, pontoons, vessel or other means of flotation used to support a land crane/derrick by a CP is required.

a. Each shift: the means used to secure/attach the equipment to the vessel/flotation device shall be inspected for proper condition, to include wear, corrosion, loose or missing fasteners, defective welds and (where applicable) insufficient tension.

b. Monthly: In addition to Section 16.L.08.a, the vessel/means of flotation used shall be inspected for the following:

(1) Taking on water;

(2) Deck load for proper securing;

16

(3) Chain lockers, storage, fuel compartments and battening of hatches for serviceability as a water-tight appliance;

(4) Firefighting and lifesaving equipment in place and functional.

c. If any deficiency is identified, an immediate determination shall be made by a QP as to whether the deficiency constitutes a hazard. If so, the vessel/flotation device shall be removed from service until it has been corrected.

16.L.19 Operations.

a. Operator Lift Planning. Operators shall plan lifts in advance, with particular attention to lift radii & boom angle and machine list & trim. Lift planning shall address the anticipated range of boom angles, LMI response, and expected LMI warning indicators, if any. > See Section 16.L.20.

b. Operators shall monitor the boom tip and the boom angle indicator carefully to ensure that limits of the load chart are not exceeded. The boom angle indicator will respond directly to increasing lift radius resulting from crane trim created by floating platform heel and trim.

c. Operators should be aware that safety devices such as LMIs do not offer protection against loads generated by relative motions between a floating crane and a fixed object to be lifted. The AHA shall address the potential for gross overload and failure mode conditions.

d. Where portable remote controls are used during lifting, the operator shall have procedures to monitor vessel heel and trim and crane machine heel and trim.

e. Whenever practical, crane use during buoy tending shall be limited to lifting the freely suspended buoy clear of the water onto the vessel.

f. Bilges shall be kept as dry as possible to eliminate the adverse effect of free surface (sloshing liquid).

g. Where crane mats are required for a stable, level work surface for crane operations, the matting material shall be in good condition and of adequate thickness, width, and length as to completely support the crane. The mats shall be laid perpendicular to the crane travel path, and shall be placed as close to each other as possible. A spotter shall be used to guide the crane when it moves on the mat surface to prevent the crane from traveling beyond the limit of the crane mats and the NAA.

16.L.20 Standard Lift Plan (SLP).

a. All lifts must be planned to avoid procedures that could result in configurations where the operator cannot maintain safe control of the lift. In addition to the requirements and criteria to be considered in Section 16.A.03 for a written Standard Lift Plan (SLP, nonmandatory Standard Pre-Lift Plan/Checklist, Form 16-2 may be used), the SLP for LHE on floating plant must also consider the following:

b. Lifts shall reflect floating operational parameters such as anticipated boom angles, values for wire leads, unknown load for extractions, and upper limits on crane force.

c. When deck loads are to be carried while lifting, the situation shall be analyzed for modified ratings.

d. When mounted on barges or pontoons, the rated loads and radii of land cranes shall be modified as recommended by the manufacturer or QP. The modification shall be evaluated by the QP specific to the flotation device/platform being used.

e. Load charts in accordance with 16.L.07 shall be posted in the cab or at the operator's station (if no cab). All other procedures applicable to the operation of the equipment (instructions and operators manual, recommended operating speeds, etc.) shall be readily available on board.

f. Procedures to monitor vessel heel and trim and crane machine list and trim, if portable remote controls are used.

16.M Overhead and Gantry Cranes.

16.M.01 The requirements in this Section are supplemental requirements for overhead and gantry cranes whether permanently installed in a facility or not and includes overhead/bridge cranes, semi gantry, cantilever gantry, wall cranes, storage bridge cranes, and others having the same fundamental characteristics whether it travels on tracks, wheels or other means (unless otherwise specified).

16.M.02 All load bearing foundations, anchorages, runways, and rail tracks shall be constructed or installed in accordance with the crane manufacturer's recommendations and ANSI/ASME B30.2 or B30.17, as applicable.

16.M.03 The rated load of the crane shall be plainly marked on each side of the crane.

a. If the crane has more than one hoisting unit, each hoist shall have its rated load marked on it or its load block.

b. Markings on the bridge, trolley, and load block shall be legible from the ground or floor.

16.M.04 <u>Warning device. Except for floor-operated cranes, an alarm or other effective warning signal shall be provided for each crane equipped with a power traveling mechanism.</u>

16.M.05 Clearance shall be maintained between the crane, any structure or object, and any parallel running cranes and cranes operating at different elevations.

16.M.06 Contacts with runway stops or other cranes shall be made with extreme caution. The operator shall do so with particular care for the safety of persons on or below the crane, and only after making certain that any persons on the other cranes are aware of what is being done.

16.M.07 Operators of outdoor cranes shall secure them when leaving.

16.M.08 When the wind-indicating alarm of a cab-operated outdoor crane sounds, crane operations shall be discontinued and the crane shall be prepared and stored for excessive wind conditions.

16.M.09 <u>Hand signals used by signal persons during overhead/gantry crane operations shall be per Figure 16-4.</u>

16.N Monorails and Under Hung Cranes.

16.N.01 Crane runways, monorail tracks, track supports, and track control devices shall be constructed or installed in accordance with the crane manufacturer's recommendations and ANSI/ASME B30.11.

16.N.02 The rated load of the crane shall be plainly marked on each side of the crane.

a. If the crane has more than one hoisting unit, each hoist shall have its rated load marked on it or its load block.

b. Markings on the bridge, trolley, and load block shall be legible from the ground or floor.

16.N.03 <u>Hand signals used by signal persons during monorail/under hung operations shall be per Figure 16-4.</u>

16.O Derricks.

16.O.01 For permanent fixed locations, the following load anchoring data shall be provided to the GDA. For non-permanent installations, this data shall be determined by a QP.

a. Guy derricks.

(1) Maximum horizontal and vertical forces when handling rated loads with the particular guy slope and spacing stipulated for the application, and

(2) Maximum horizontal and vertical forces at the guy when handling rated loads with the particular guy slope and spacing stipulated for the application.

b. Stiffleg derricks.

(1) Maximum horizontal and vertical forces at the mast base when handling rated loads with the particular stiffleg slope and spacing stipulated for the application, and

(2) Maximum horizontal and vertical forces at the stifflegs when handling rated loads with the particular stiffleg arrangement stipulated for the application.

16.O.02 Derrick booms, load hoists, and swinger mechanisms shall be suitable for the derrick work intended and shall be anchored to prevent displacement from imposed loads.

16.O.03 When rotating a derrick, sudden starts and stops shall be avoided and rotational speed shall be such that the load does not swing out beyond the radius at which it can be controlled. A tagline shall be used.

16.O.04 Boom and hoisting rope systems shall not be twisted.

16.O.05 Ropes shall not be handled on a winch head without the knowledge of the operator. When a winch head is being used, the operator shall be within reach of the power unit controls.

16.O.06 When securing the boom, dogs or other positive holding mechanisms on the hoist shall be engaged.

16.O.07 When not in use the derrick boom shall be either:

a. Layed down;

b. Secured to a stationary member as nearly under the head as possible by attachment of a sling to the load block;

c. Lifted to a vertical position and secured to the mast (for guy derricks); or

d. Secured against a stiffleg (for stiffleg derricks).

16.P Handling Loads Suspended from Rotorcraft.

16

16.P.01 Helicopter cranes shall comply with regulations of the Federal Aviation Administration (FAA).

16.P.02 Before each day's operation, a briefing shall be conducted to set forth the plan of operation for the pilot and ground personnel.

16.P.03 Loads shall be properly slung.

a. Tag lines shall be of a length that will not permit their being drawn up into rotors.

b. Pressed sleeve, swedged eyes, or equivalent means shall be used for all freely suspended loads to prevent hand splices from spinning open or wire clamps from loosening.

16.P.04 All electrically operated cargo hooks shall have the electrical activating device so designed and installed as to prevent inadvertent operation.

a. In addition, these cargo hooks shall be equipped with an emergency mechanical control for releasing the load.

b. The hooks shall be tested prior to each day's operation to determine that the release functions properly, both electrically and mechanically.

16.P.05 Every practical precaution shall be taken to provide for the protection of the employees from flying objects in the rotor downwash. All loose gear within 100 ft (30.5 m) of the place of lifting or depositing the load, and all other areas susceptible to rotor downwash, shall be secured or removed.

16.P.06 The helicopter pilot shall be responsible for the size, weight, and manner in which loads are connected to the helicopter. If, for any reason, the helicopter pilot believes the lift cannot be made safely, the lift shall not be made.

16.P.07 When employees are required to work under hovering craft, safe access shall be provided for employees to reach the hoist line hook and engage or disengage cargo slings. Employees shall not work under hovering craft except to hook, unhook, or position loads.

16.P.08 Static charge on the suspended load shall be dissipated with a grounding device before ground personnel touch the suspended load, or protective rubber gloves shall be worn by all ground personnel touching the suspended load.

16.P.09 The weight of an external load shall not exceed the rated capacity.

16.P.10 Hoist wires or other gear, except for pulling lines or conductors that are allowed to "pay out" from a container or roll off a reel, shall not be attached to any fixed ground structure or be allowed to foul on any fixed structures.

16.P.11 When visibility is reduced by dust or other conditions, ground personnel shall exercise special caution to keep clear of main and stabilizing rotors. Precautions shall also be taken to eliminate reduced visibility.

16.P.12 No unauthorized person shall be allowed to approach within 50 ft (15.2 m) of the helicopter when the rotor blades are turning.

16.P.13 Whenever approaching or leaving a helicopter with blades rotating, all employees shall remain in full view of the pilot and keep in a crouched position. Employees shall avoid the area from the cockpit or cabin rearward unless authorized by the helicopter pilot to work there.

16.P.14 There shall be constant reliable communication between the pilot and a designated employee of the ground crew who acts as a signal person during loading and unloading. This signal person shall be distinctly recognizable from other ground personnel. Hand signals used shall be per ASME B30.12.

16.P.15 Good housekeeping shall be maintained in all helicopter loading and unloading areas.

16.Q Powered Industrial Trucks (PITs) /Telehandlers.

16.Q.01 This equipment may only be used to hoist loads if allowed by the equipment manufacturer. If these procedures are unavailable, you are prohibited from performing this function.

16.Q.02 Operations involving the use of PITs to raise personnel and/or using rigging to transport or hoist loads or personnel require different operator skills and considerations than the standard PIT operations performed with this equipment. When PITs are to be used to transport personnel or hoist loads utilizing hooks, eyes, slings, chains, or other rigging the following requirements shall apply:

a. Proper operating procedures in accordance with the equipment manufacturer's operating manual;

b. Written proof of qualifications of equipment operators, riggers, and others involved in the transporting and hoisting operations;

c. Other personnel may also operate this equipment under the specific conditions as identified in Section 16.B.01.

d. Proper use and on site availability of manufacturer's load rating capacities or charts as related to approved attachments;

e. Proper use of rigging, including positive latching devices to secure the load and rigging;

f. Inspection of rigging;

g. Use of tag lines to control the load;

h. Adequate communications, and

i. An AHA specific to the transporting or hoisting operation must be developed and provided to GDA.

16.R Pile Driving Operations.

16.R.01 Pile driving equipment shall be outfitted with a positive and negative restraint device to prevent accidental hammer disengagement (i.e., preventing the hammer from falling or uncontrolled rising out of the lead, as well as preventing contact with head block or sheaves, if so equipped).

a. The contractor shall comply with all manufacturer's instructions, procedures and recommendations applicable to the operational functions of equipment, including its use with pile driving attachments. The safe operating speeds, lifting capacity, stability under load shall not be exceeded. When manufacturer's instructions are not available, the employer shall develop and ensure compliance with all procedures necessary for the safe operation of the equipment and attachments and

(1) Procedures for the operational controls must be developed by a QP.

(2) Procedures related to the capacity of the equipment must be developed and signed by a RPE familiar with the equipment.

b. For contractor installed pile driving attachments to equipment whose original intent was for a different task, (for example an excavator or forklift modified to drive piling) the attachment must be designed by a RPE with experience designing construction equipment, and comply with 16.R.01.(a).

c. The operator of this type of equipment must comply with the requirements of 16.S.03 and must be trained and authorized to operate the pile driving attachment.

d. A Dedicated Pile-Driver is a machine that is designed to function exclusively as a pile-driver. These machines typically have the ability to both hoist the material that will be pile-driven and to pile-drive that material. This type of equipment and the operator must comply with

Sections 16.A through 16.J, 16.L, and 16.R. > See Figures 16-2, Dedicated Pile Driver, and 16-3, Non-Dedicated Pile Driver.

16.R.02 Prior to initiating pile driving or extraction operations, the contractor shall develop a site-specific safety plan. The plan shall identify specific steps for the intended operations, list of hazards, and procedures to minimize or eliminate those hazards. Plans shall include, as a minimum:

a. Identification of utility locations both above and below grade;

b. Designated areas for equipment operations and material storage;

c. Assembly and disassembly sequences for pile driving equipment;

d. Operation of pile driving equipment and handling of pile materials;

e. A geotechnical report identifying subsurface and surface ground conditions;

f. A documented daily inspection requirement to include the hammer, cushion blocks, rigging, fuel lines, pressurized hoses, clamps, welds, hardware, and all other pile driving associated equipment, and

g. Establishment of a controlled work area to prevent access by persons not directly involved in the operation.

16.R.03 With the exception of the pile driver equipment operator (crane/track hoe/forklift), personnel shall not stand under the kicker/spotter or directly under, in front of, or closer than 12 ft (4 m), or greater if manufacturer specifies, of the pile hammer or pile when the pile is being driven.

16.R.04 The crane/track hoe/forklift operator station shall be protected from falling objects.

16.R.05 Cranes and mechanized equipment used only for pile driving and extracting operations (except telescopic boom cranes), are exempt from the requirements for A2B devices. > See Section 16.E.03.c(3).

16.R.06 Guy, outriggers, thrust outs, counter-balances, or rail clamps shall be provided to maintain stability of pile-driver rigs.

16.R.07 Pile-driving leads.

16

a. Pile driving leads shall be assembled using only the approved fasteners and torque values as required by the manufacturer. The leads shall be of adequate size, length, and strength to safely accommodate the weight and length of the pile driving hammer, the pile to be driven, and the position (vertical or on a batter) in which they will be used.

b. Employees shall be prohibited from remaining on leads or ladders while the pile is being driven.

c. Landings on leads shall not be used for storage of any kind.

d. Pile driving leads shall have stop blocks to prevent the hammer from being raised against the head block, if so equipped.

e. Pile driving leads shall be free of projections or snags to minimize damage and personnel safety hazards.

f. A blocking device, capable of supporting the weight of the hammer, shall be provided for placement in the leads under the hammer at all times while employees are working under the hammer.

➢ Exception: Where it is necessary for an employee to momentarily lean through the leads to guide a pile under the hammer, it is not required that the pile hammer be blocked in the leads.

g. A minimum weekly documented inspection of the pile driving leads shall be conducted. If found to be unsafe, or whenever a deficiency that affects the safe use of pile driving leads is observed, they shall be immediately taken out of service and their use prohibited until unsafe conditions have been corrected.

h. Swinging leads shall have fixed ladders or have bracing located such that its configuration will serve as adequate ladder rungs.

i. Fixed leads shall:

(1) Have fixed ladders and if equipped with decked landings, shall have guardrails, intermediate rails, and toe boards. Fixed ladders or stairs shall be provided for access to landings and head blocks.

(2) Be provided with guardrails or Personal Fall Protection Systems, to include Certified Anchorages, to provide fall protection for any workers exposed to falls of 6 ft (1.8 m) or greater, for work over water, over machinery, or over dangerous operations per Section 21.

(3) Have a crane boom tip connection designed by a RPE that is familiar with the ASME B30 standards.

16.R.08 Dogs, on pile-driver hoist drums, that automatically disengage when the load is relieved or the drum is rotated shall be prohibited.

16.R.09 Guards shall be provided across the top of the head block to prevent wire from jumping out of the sheaves.

16.R.10 All pneumatic or steam hose connections to pile-driver hammers, pile ejectors, or jet pipes shall be securely attached with an adequate length of at least ¼ in (0.6-cm) alloy steel chain, having 3,250 lb (1,500 kg) working load limit, or equal strength wire, to prevent whipping if the joint is broken.

16.R.11 Hydraulic/pneumatic/steam line controls shall consist of two shutoff valves, one of which shall be a quick-acting lever type within easy reach of the hammer operator.

16.R.12 Hoisting and moving pile.

a. All employees shall be kept clear when piling is being hoisted into the leads.

b. Hoisting and driving of piling shall be done by use of a closed shackle or other positive attachment that will prevent accidental disengagement of the rigging.

c. Taglines shall be used for controlling unguided piles and free hanging (flying) hammers.

d. Hammers shall be lowered to the bottom of the leads while the pile driver is being moved.

16.R.13 When driving jacked piles, all access pits shall be provided with ladders and bulk headed curbs to prevent material from falling into the pit.

16.R.14 When it is necessary to cut off the tops of driven piles, pile-driving operations shall be suspended except where the cutting operations are located at least twice the length of the longest pile cut-off from the driver.

16.R.15 Pile extraction.

a. If piling cannot be pulled without exceeding the load rating of equipment, a pile extractor shall be used.

b. When pulling piling, the crane shall be equipped with LMI devices (unless the load can be calculated and is within the load rating chart of the crane) and the booms shall not be raised more than 60° above the horizontal. (This requirement does not apply to vibrating-type pulling devices.)

c. Piling shall not be pulled by tipping the crane, releasing the load brake momentarily, and catching the load before the crane has settled.

d. Rigging. When pulling pile, the hook shall have the positive locking safety latch. This latch shall be secured so rigging gear roll will not occur.

16.R.16 Floating pile drivers. > See Section 16.L.

16.S Hydraulic Excavators, Wheel/Track/Backhoe Loaders Used to Hoist Loads with Rigging.

16.S.01 Personnel shall not work in, pass under, or ride in the buckets or booms of excavators in operation.

16.S.02 Hydraulic excavating equipment shall not be used to hoist personnel. The riding of personnel on loads, hooks, hammers, buckets or any other hydraulic excavating equipment attachment is prohibited.

16.S.03 Excavators used with attachments such as drill rigs, pile driving equipment, etc. shall require training specific to that operation for the operator.

16.S.04 Hydraulic excavating equipment may only be used to hoist loads if allowed by the equipment manufacturer. If these procedures are unavailable, you are prohibited from performing this function.

16.S.05 When hydraulic excavating equipment is to be used to hoist loads utilizing hooks, eyes, slings, chains, or other rigging the following requirements shall apply:

a. Operations involving the use of hydraulic excavating equipment and rigging to hoist loads require different operator skills and considerations than the standard excavating operations routinely performed with hydraulic excavating equipment. An AHA specific to the hoisting operation shall be prepared. The AHA shall include, but not be limited to:

(1) Written proof of qualifications of equipment operators, riggers, and others involved in the hoisting operations;

(2) Other personnel may also operate this equipment under the specific conditions as identified in Section 16.B.01.

(3) Operational testing shall be performed as described in Section 16.S.05.b;

(4) Proper operating procedures in accordance with the equipment manufacturer's operating manual;

(5) Proper use and on site availability of manufacturer's load rating capacities or charts;

(6) Proper use of rigging, including positive latching devices to secure the load and rigging;

(7) Inspection of rigging;

(8) Use of tag lines to control the load;

(9) Adequate communications;

(10) Establishment of a sufficient swing radius (equipment, rigging and load); and

(11) Stability of surfaces beneath the hydraulic excavating equipment.

b. An operational test with the selected hydraulic excavating equipment will be performed in the presence of the GDA.

(1) The operational test shall consist of a demonstration that the test load and selected rigging can be safely lifted, maneuvered, controlled, stopped, and landed.

(2) The operational test shall be representative of the complete cycle of the proposed hoisting operation, including configuration, orientation and positioning of the excavating equipment and the use of identical rigging.

(3) The test load shall be equivalent to the maximum anticipated load, but shall not exceed 100% of the manufacturer's load rating capacity for the excavating equipment as configured. Written documentation of the performance of the operational test outlining test procedures and results shall be maintained at the on-site project office.

c. All rigging and rigging operations shall comply with requirements of Section 15.

d. Hooks, eyes, slings, chains or other rigging shall not be attached to or hung from the teeth of a bucket during the transporting or hoisting of a load by hydraulic excavating equipment.

e. After the completion and acceptance of an operational test described in this Section, if repairs, major maintenance or reconfiguration are required to be performed on the hydraulic excavating equipment or attachments, another operational test shall be performed to demonstrate that the completed repairs are satisfactory and that the test load and selected rigging can be safely lifted, maneuvered, controlled, stopped, and landed.

16.S.06 Loads shall be lifted the minimum height necessary to clear the ground or other obstacles and

16

carried as low as possible when the equipment is traveling.

16.S.07 Loads shall not be lifted over personnel.

16.S.08 Adequate clearances shall be maintained from electrical sources.

16.T LHE-Supported Personnel (Work) Platforms.

16.T.01 LHE-supported personnel platforms are only allowed to be used if the crane manufacturer allows personnel lifting to occur on that equipment. In addition, provisions must be made for lowering of the personnel in the event of a (crane) power failure.

16.T.02 Only LHE with power-operated up and down boom hoists and load lines shall be used to support work platforms. The use of machines having live booms is prohibited (i.e., friction cranes). Platforms shall be lowered under power and not by the brake.

16.T.03 If a LHE-supported work platform is determined to be the safest, most practical method of access, the operation shall be deemed a critical lift (per Section 16.H) and meet the following requirements:

a. The person responsible for the lift shall perform an AHA and attest to the need for the operation in writing.

b. The responsible person shall sign the AHA and submit it to the GDA for acceptance.

c. Personnel shall not be hoisted until the GDA has accepted the AHA.

d. Crane supported work platforms may be used for routine access of employees to underground construction via a shaft.

16.T.04 The work platform and suspension system shall be designed and certified by an RPE with knowledge in this area.

a. The work platform (excluding fall protection systems) shall be capable of supporting, without failure, its own weight and at least five times the maximum intended load. Criteria for fall protection systems are contained in Sections 21 and 16.T.10.

b. The suspension system shall be designed to minimize tipping of the platform due to movement of the employees on the work platform.

c. The system used to connect the work platform to the equipment shall allow the platform to remain within 10 degrees of level, regardless of boom angle.

d. All welding of the work platform and its components shall be performed by an AWS D-1 Certified Welder.

16.T.05 LHE-supported work platforms shall meet the following requirements:

a. The scaffold shall be of metal or metal frame construction with a standard guardrail system and shall be enclosed at least from the toeboard to mid-rail with either solid construction material or expanded metal having openings no greater than ½ in (1.2 cm).

b. A grab rail shall be installed inside the entire perimeter of the personnel platform.

c. Access gates, if installed, shall not swing outward and shall be equipped with a device to prevent accidental opening.

d. Headroom shall be provided which allows employees to stand upright in the platform.

e. Employees shall be protected by overhead protection on the personnel platform when the employee(s) are exposed to falling objects.

f. The platform shall be conspicuously posted with a plate or other permanent marking that indicates the weight of the platform and its rated load capacity or maximum intended load.

16.T.06 Rigging.

a. When a wire rope bridle is used to connect the work platform to the load line, each bridle leg shall be connected to a master link or shackle in such a manner to ensure that the load is evenly distributed among the bridle legs.

b. The hook connection to the platform rigging shall be of a type that can be closed and locked to eliminate the hook throat opening and shall be closed and locked when attached. Alternately, an alloy anchor type shackle with a bolt, nut, and retaining pin, in place OR of the screw type, with the screw pin secured from accidental removal may be used.

c. Wire rope, rigging hardware and hooks shall be capable of supporting, without failure, at least five times the maximum intended load.

d. Where rotation-resistant rope is used the slings shall be capable of supporting without failure at least ten times the maximum intended load.

e. Rope sling suspension systems with mechanically spliced flemish eyes, if used, shall be designed with thimbles in all eyes.

f. Bridles and associated rigging for attaching the platform to the hoist line shall be used only for the platform and the employees, their tools and the materials necessary to do the work and shall not be used for any other purpose when not hoisting personnel.

16.T.07 Work Practices.

a. Before employees enter or exit a hoisted personnel platform that is not landed, the platform shall be secured to the structure, unless securing to the structure creates an unsafe condition.

b. The rated load capacity of the platform shall not be exceeded.

c. The number of employees occupying the work platform shall not exceed the number required for the work to be performed.

d. Work platforms shall be used only for employees, their tools and the materials necessary to do their work. Work platforms shall not be used to hoist only materials or tools when not hoisting personnel.

e. Materials and tools for use during a personnel lift shall be secured to prevent displacement. They shall be evenly distributed within the confines of the platform while it is suspended.

f. No lifts shall be made on another of the crane's load lines while personnel are suspended on a platform.

g. Employees (except a designated signal personal) shall keep all parts of the body inside the platform during raising, lowering, and positioning.

h. A CP shall observe the operations while personnel are working from the crane supported work platform.

i. Environmental conditions.

(1) Wind. When wind speed (sustained or gusts) exceeds 20 mph (9 m/s) at the work platform, a QP shall determine if, in light of the wind conditions, if it is safe to lift personnel. If not, the lifting operation shall be terminated.

(2) Other weather and environmental conditions. A QP shall determine if, in light of indications of dangerous weather conditions, or other impending or existing danger, it is safe to lift personnel. If not, the lifting operation shall be terminated.

j. Employees being hoisted shall remain in the continuous sight of, and in direct communication with, the LHE operator or signal person. In situations where direct visual contact with the operator is not possible and the use of a signal person would create a greater hazard for that person, direct communication by radio shall be maintained at all times. The equipment operator shall bring all operations to an immediate stop if radio communications are lost.

k. Taglines shall be used to help control the work platform unless the CP determines that their use creates an unsafe condition.

l. The LHE operator shall remain at the controls at all times with the crane engine running whenever the platform is occupied.

m. Hoisting personnel within 20 ft (6 m) of a power line that is up to 350 kV and hoisting personnel within 50 ft (15.2 m) of a power line that is over 350 kV is prohibited, except for Power Transmission and Distribution Work.

16.T.08 Operational Criteria

a. Hoisting of the personnel platform shall be in a slow, controlled, cautious manner with no sudden movements.

b. Load lines shall be capable of supporting, without failure, at least 7 times the maximum intended load, except where rotation resistant rope is used the lines shall be capable of supporting, without failure, at least 10 times the maximum intended load. The required design factor is achieved by taking the current safety factor of 3.5 and applying the 50% de-rating of the crane capacity.

c. A Qualified Person must determine if the footing is sufficiently firm and stable for the operation. The crane shall be uniformly level within 1 degree of level grade and located on firm footing. LHE equipped with outriggers shall have them all equally deployed to load chart criteria following manufacturer's specifications, as applicable, when hoisting personnel.

d. The total weight of the loaded personnel platform and related rigging shall not exceed 50% of the rated capacity for the radius and configuration of the crane.

e. Only LHE with an A2B device that prevents contact between the load block or overhaul ball and the boom tip, or a system that deactivates the hoisting action before damage occurs shall be used.

f. LHE with variable angle booms shall be equipped with a boom angle indicator readily visible to the operator.

g. LHE with telescoping booms shall be equipped with a device to indicate clearly to the operator, at all times, the boom's extended length, or an accurate determination of the load radius to be used during the lift shall be made prior to hoisting personnel.

h. The load line hoist drum shall have a system or device on the power train, other than the load hoist brake, that regulates the lowering rate of speed of the hoist mechanism (controlled lowering). Free-fall is prohibited.

16.T.09 Trial Meeting, Trial Lift and Inspection.

a. Prior to every trial lift, the LHE operator, signal person, employees to be lifted, and the CP shall attend a pre-lift meeting to review the applicable parts of this manual, the AHA, and the details of this particular lift.

b. A trial lift with the unoccupied work platform loaded at least to the anticipated lift weight shall be made from the ground level, or any other location where employees will enter the platform, to each location at which the work platform is to be hoisted and positioned.

c. The trial lift shall be made immediately prior to each shift in which personnel will be hoisted and must be repeated prior to hoisting employees after the LHE is moved and set up at new location or returned to a previously used location, and when the lift route is changed unless the CP determines that the route change is not significant.

d. The operator shall determine that all systems, controls, and safety devices are activated and functioning properly; that no interferences exist; and that all configurations necessary to reach those work locations will allow the operator to remain under the 50% limit of the equipment's rated capacity.

e. Materials and tools to be used during the actual lift may be loaded in the platform (evenly distributed and secured) for the trial lift.

f. After the trial lift and just prior to hoisting employees, the platform shall be hoisted a few inches and inspected to ensure that it is secure and properly balanced.

g. A visual inspection of the LHE, rigging, work platform, and the crane support base shall be conducted by a CP immediately after the trial lift to determine whether the testing has exposed any defect or produced any adverse effect upon any component or structure.

h. Any defects found during inspection which create a safety hazard shall be corrected before hoisting personnel.

i. If the load rope goes slack, the hoisting system shall be re-inspected to ensure that all ropes are properly seated on drums and sheaves.

16.T.10 Proof Testing

a. At each job site, prior to hoisting employees on the work platform, and after any report or modification, the platform and rigging shall be proof tested to 125% of the platform's rated capacity by holding it in a suspended position for 5 minutes with the proof test load evenly distributed on the platform (this may be done concurrently with the trial lift).

b. After proof testing, a CP shall inspect the platform and rigging. Personnel hoisting shall not be conducted until the CP determines that the platform and rigging have successfully passed the proof test.

16.T.11 Personal Fall Protection.

a. For work over water, see Section 21.O for fall protection versus PFD requirements. Lifesaving equipment and safety skiffs meeting the requirements of this manual shall be available.

b. When NOT working over water, all employees occupying the work platform shall use a properly anchored personal fall protection (arrest or restraint) system. The system shall be attached to an allowed anchorage point/structural member within the platform.

(1) The attachment points to which personal fall arrest or restraint systems are attached on the platform must meet the anchorage requirements in Section 21.

(2) Depending on the type of work to be done and the height of the work platform above a lower surface, all workers shall wear a fullbody harness as part of a fall arrest or fall restraint system. The CP for fall protection on-site will assess each situation and determine which system would best fit the current work requirement and be in accordance with the crane manufacturer's instructions and recommendations. Particular attention should be paid to anchor points and capacities.

(3) Workers working from the platform suspended from LHE are permitted to be tied off to the lower load block or overhaul ball. An AHA shall be developed to details on how work will be safely performed. AHA shall be submitted to the GDA for acceptance.

(4) Anchoring to the load line. A personal fall arrest system is permitted to be anchored to the crane's hook (or other part of the load line). This activity requires a critical lift plan to be developed and implemented, per Section 16.H.01. In addition, the following requirements must be met:

(a) There is no other load on the load line;

(b) A QP has determined that the set-up and rated capacity of the LHE (including the hook, load line and rigging) meets or exceeds the requirements in Section 21. This information shall be placed in/attached to the AHA developed for the activity;

(c) The equipment operator shall be located in or adjacent to the cab, has been informed that the equipment is being used for this purpose, shall remain in contact (verbal, radio, hand signals) with the signal person for the operation and shall remain in direct control of any intended movement of the load line. If the operator is not in the cab, the controls shall be locked/tagged out so that no movement of the load line can occur without his knowledge.

16.T.12 Employees shall not be hoisted unless the following conditions are determined to exist:

a. The load test and proof test requirements are satisfied;

b. Hoist ropes are free of kinks;

c. Multiple part lines are not twisted around one another,

d. The primary attachment is centered over the platform, and

e. The hoisting system is inspected if the load rope is slack to ensure all ropes are properly seated on drums and in sheaves.

16.T.13 Traveling – equipment other than derricks.

a. Hoisting of personnel while the crane is traveling is prohibited, except for equipment that travels on fixed rails or it is demonstrated that there is no less hazardous way to perform the work. This does not apply to rubber-tired equipment.

b. Where employees are hoisted while the equipment is traveling, all of the following criteria must be met:

(1) Crane travel shall be restricted to a fixed track or runway;

(2) Travel shall be limited to the load radius of the boom used during the lift;

(3) The boom must be parallel to the direction of travel, except where it is safer to do otherwise;

(4) A complete trial run shall be performed to test the route of travel before employees are allowed to occupy the platform (this trial run may be performed when the trial lift required in Section 16.T.08 is performed).

16.U Base-Mounted Drum Hoists Used to Hoist Personnel, Guided and Non-Guided Worker's Hoists (Air Tuggers). (Whether Powered by Internal Combustion Engine, Electric Motor or Other Prime Mover).

16.U.01 The use of this equipment to hoist personnel requires the development of a written Standard Operating Procedure (SOP). All personnel involved with the use of this equipment shall assist in the development of this SOP. The SOP shall be maintained for a period of no more than 12 months, at which time it shall be reviewed and changed as necessary. All operators that will be hoisting personnel shall have a physical examination per 16.B.05 and shall be trained at a minimum, in the requirements listed in 16.U. and 16.T. > USACE operators shall also be trained as Class II operators per Section 16.C.05.

16.U.02 This equipment shall meet the applicable requirements for design, construction, installation, testing, inspection, maintenance and operations as required by the manufacturer, to include an 8:1 safety factor for the hoist rope. > See ASSE A10.22.

16.U.03 For operations within the scope of the ASSE A10.22 standard, a base mounted drum hoist (rope-guided) or non-rope guided hoists shall be used when hoisting personnel. The hoist shall be used in accordance with the manufacturer's recommendations for these applications.

16.U.04 The hoist machine shall meet all criteria set forth in ASSE A10.22, Chapter 4.

16.U.05 The operator of the hoist shall be qualified and instructed in the proper operation of the hoisting system, in accordance with manufacturer's recommendations.

16.U.06 The hoist may be used to hoist materials or personnel, but not both simultaneously.

16.U.07 An independent lifeline and a full body harness shall be provided and used by any person being transported. Personal fall protection is not required when fully enclosed baskets are used.

16.U.08 Voice communications shall be maintained between the hoist operator and each landing.

16.U.09 A minimum of two guide ropes (for rope-guided hoists) shall be used when transporting personnel in the cage. Splicing of the hoisting and guide ropes shall not be spliced except for the formation of end terminations.

16.U.10 A sign stating capacity in number of persons and rated loading in pounds shall be posted on the cage.

16.U.11 Inspection and Testing.

a. Visual checks shall be conducted daily prior to use (during use).

b. Inspections (no drop test) shall be conducted weekly when hoist is in continuous operation and before reuse following periods of idleness in excess of one week.

c. Documentation at each job location shall be maintained and kept on file for at least 2 years.

16.U.12 Non-Guided Hoist for Personnel/Air tugger hoist. This equipment may be substituted for a base mounted drum hoist and in addition to the requirements above, must meet the following:

a. Hoist shall be secured in position to prevent moving, shifting or dislodgement;

b. Hoist machine may be operated at cable speeds not to exceed 110 ft/min when transporting personnel on a non-guided worker's hoist;

c. An independent lifeline and a full body harness shall be provided and used by any person being transported by a non-guided hoist. Personal fall protection is not required when fully enclosed baskets are used.

d. Rope grabs (fall prevention devices) for connecting a safety harness to the lifeline shall be of a type that can be attached to or detached from the independent lifeline. They shall be compatible with the lifeline size and type of material being used. Attachment to the lifeline shall be maintained at a point above waist height of the person. Other devices that provide equivalent safety may be used;

e. Minimum wire rope diameter shall be 5/16 inch (7.9mm);

f. Non-guided hoist line shall be weighted as necessary to prevent line run of the hoisting rope under the basket

16

FORM 16-1

Certificate of Compliance for LHE and Rigging

This certificate shall be signed by an official of the company that provides LHE/cranes and rigging gear for any application under this contract.

Contracting Officer's Point of Contact: (Government Designated Representative)	Phone #:
Prime Contractor/Phone #:	Contract Number:
SSHO/QC:	Phone #:
LHE Manufacturer/Type/Capacity:	
LHE Operator(s) Name(s):	

I certify that:

1. The above noted LHE and all rigging gear conform to the EM 385-1-1, applicable OSHA regulations (host country regulations in foreign countries) and applicable ASME standards.

2. The operator(s) noted above has been trained, qualified and designated in accordance with the requirements in Section 16, EM 385-1-1 for the operation of the above noted LHE.

3. The operator(s) noted above has been trained not to bypass safety devices during LHE operations.

4. The operator(s), rigger(s) and company official (staff) are aware that immediate notification to the GDA of any incident or accident involving this equipment is required.

Company Official Signature:	Date:
Company Official Name/Title:	

Post on Crane/LHE.
(In Cab and Contractor's Office for each LHE onto USACE Project/Property)

FORM 16-2

Standard Pre-Lift Crane Plan/Checklist

DATE: ___/___/_____ Job Number: _____ Location: _____

TIME: _____ Completed By (Competent Person):_____

NOTE: Applies to Cranes, Derricks, Hoists and Power-Operated equipment that can be used to hoist, lower and/or horizontally move a suspended load (includes excavators, forklifts, Rough Terrain equipment, etc., when used with rigging).

Crane Considerations		Yes	No
1	Are the lifts within the crane's rated capacities? (based on boom height, radius)		
2	Boom deflections considered?		
3	Have all potential crane boom obstructions been identified?		
4	Have Environmental Considerations been addressed? (Wind, Weather-Lightning)		
5	Have electrical hazards been addressed (Overhead / Underground) - Clearance distances established? - Is a spotter required? - Public Utility contact required?		
6	Crane swing radius properly barricaded and personnel advised of hazards?		

Comments:

Load		Yes	No
1	Weights and Centers of Gravity (COG) have been Determined?		
2	Anything Inside / Outside the loads that could shift during the lift?		
3	Determine if the rigging needs protection from the loads?		
4	All anchor bolts, hold downs, or fasteners have been removed?		
5	Potential for binding – are load cells required to verify the loads are free?		
6	Attachment points rated to take load weight?		
7	Are the loads structurally capable of being lifted? (bending & twisting issues)		
8	Is a critical lift plan required per the EM section 16.H?		

Comments:

16

FORM 16-2 (cont'd)

Standard Pre-Lift Crane Plan/Checklist

Rigging		Yes	No
1	All rigging has been inspected by a Qualified Rigger?		
2	Have sling angles been calculated?		
3	Are shackles correctly sized for the sling eyes?		
4	Are softeners needed?		

Comments:

Personnel		Yes	No
1	The roles, responsibilities and qualifications for personnel have been defined? (Operator, Lift Supervisor, Rigger, Signal Person)		
2	A Pre-Lift meeting has been conducted?		
3	Personnel trained per the EM?		

Comments:

Area Preparation		Yes	No
1	The locations for the load landings has been selected and prepared?		
2	Blocking and or Cribbing is available to set the loads on?		
3	Travel paths have been determined and cordoned off?		
4	Other personnel in the area have been notified of the lifts?		
5	Have ground bearing support questions been addressed?		

Comments:

Crane Operator: _____ Date: _____

Riggers: _____ Date: _____

Signal Person: _____ Date: _____

Others: _____ Date: _____

FIGURE 16-1

Crane Hand Signals

FIGURE 16-1 (Continued)

Crane Hand Signals

FIGURE 16-1 (Continued)

Crane Hand Signals

EXTEND BOOM (Telescoping Boom). One Hand Signal. One fist in front of chest with thumb tapping chest.

RETRACT BOOM (Telescoping Boom). One Hand Signal. One fist in front of chest, thumb pointing outward and heel of fist tapping chest.

16

U.S. Army Corps of Engineers
CRITICAL LIFT PLAN
For use of this form, see EM 385-1-1, Section 16. Proponent agency is Crane HHWG.

Date:	Prepared By:
Location:	USACE District:

A "critical lift" can be defined as any non-routine crane lift requiring detailed planning and additional or unusual safety precautions. Critical lifts include lifts made where the load weight is greater than 75% of the rated capacity of the crane; lifts which require the load to be lifted, swung or placed out of the operator's view (except Change 6 exemption) ; lifts made with more than one crane; lifts involving non-routine or technically difficult rigging arrangement; hoisting personnel with a

A. TOTAL LOAD

1. Load Weight		lbs
2. Wt. of Aux. Block		lbs
3. Wt. of Main Block		lbs
4. Wt. of Lifiting Beam		lbs
5. Wt. of Sling/Shackles		lbs
6. Wt. of Jib/Ext. (erected/stowed)		lbs
7. Wt. of Hoist Rope		lbs
8. Other:		lbs
TOTAL WEIGHT		

Note: Source of load weight (Drawings, Calcs, etc.) must be attached on Page 2.

E. CRANE PLACEMENT (*Mobile Cranes Only*)

1. Maximum Bearing Pressure _____ PSF
Note: Bearing Pressure Calculations must be attached on Page 3.

2. Ground Conditions Suitable for Load? ____ YES / NO
Note: Ground Condition Calculations must be attached on Page 3.

3. High Voltage or Electrical Hazards? ____ YES / NO
Note: If Electrical Hazards are present they must be shown on Page 4.

4. Obstructions to Lift or Swing? ____ YES / NO
Note: If Obstructions are present they must be shown on Page 4.

5. Travel with Load Required? ____ YES / NO

6. Other?

B. CRANE

1. Type of Crane   Mobile Hydraulic Truck
2. Maximum Crane Capacity _____ lbs.
3. Radius (Maximum) _____ ft.
4. Radius (Minimum) _____ ft.
5. Boom Length (Maximum) _____ ft.
6. Boom Length (Minimum) _____ ft.
7. Crane Capacity (Max Radius) _____ lbs.
8. Crane Capacity (Min Radius) _____ lbs.
9. Boom Angle (Maximum) _____ deg.
10. Boom Angle (Minimum) _____ deg.
11. Gross Load of Crane _____ lbs.
12. Lift is _____ % of the Crane's rated capacity
13. If Jib/Ext. is to be used:
    Length _____ ft.
    Offset _____ ft.
14. Rated Capacity of Jib/Ext. _____ lbs

F. OPERATOR QUALIFICATIONS

1. Certified Operator? ____ YES / NO
2. Option? _____
3. Certified for Type, Class & Capacity? ____ YES / NO
4. Designated in writing by emp

G. PRE-LIFT CHECKLIST

	(YES)	N/A	(NO)
1. Crane Inspected			
2. Rigging Inspected			
3. Crane Set-up			
4. Overhead Hazard Check			
5. Swing Check			
6. Counterweight Check			
7. Operator Qualifications			
8. Signal Person Qualifications			
9. Rigger Qualifications			
10. Load Chart in Crane			
11. Load Test			
12. Tag Lines			
13. Wind Conditions			
14. Traffic Hazard Check			
15. Site Control			
16. Signatures			

C. HOIST ROPE

	Main	Aux 1	Aux 2
1. # of Parts			
2. Rope Diamter			
3. Capacity			

D. RIGGING

1. Hitch Type(s) _____
2. No. of Slings: _____ Size: _____
3. Sling Type: _____
4. Sling Assembly Capacity: _____ lbs.
5. Shackle Size(s): _____
6. Shackle Rated Capacity(s) _____ lbs.

H. SIGNATURES

1. Crane Operator _____
2. Rigger _____
3. Signal Person _____
4. Lift Supervisor _____
5. Other _____
6. Other

U.S. Army Corps of Engineers
CRITICAL LIFT PLAN
For use of this form, see EM 385-1-1, Section 15. Proponent agency is Crane HHWG.

LOAD CALCULATIONS

Show here or attach calculations, drawings, etc.

16

U.S. Army Corps of Engineers
CRITICAL LIFT PLAN
For use of this form, see EM 385-1-1, Section 16. Proponent agency is Crane HHWG.

BEARING PRESSURES & GROUND CONDITIONS

Show here or attach calculations, drawings, etc.

U.S. Army Corps of Engineers
CRITICAL LIFT PLAN
For use of this form, see EM 385-1-1, Section 16. Proponent agency is Crane HHWG.

LOAD CHART

Show here or attach load chart

U.S. Army Corps of Engineers
CRITICAL LIFT PLAN
For use of this form, see EM 385-1-1, Section 16. Proponent agency is Crane HHWG.

OPERATOR, RIGGER, SINGAL PERSON QUALIFICATIONS

Show here or attatch operator qualifications

U.S. Army Corps of Engineers
CRITICAL LIFT PLAN
For use of this form, see EM 385-1-1, Section 16. Proponent agency is Crane HHWG.

SITE PLAN

Show here or attach site plan and sequencing

Apr-13

Page 6 of 6

FIGURE 16-2

16

Dedicated Pile Driver, Example

Service
Winch
Line

Impact or
Vibratory
Hammer

Mast

Base Carrier

Lower Guide /
Centralizer

FIGURE 16 - 2, DEDICATED PILE DRIVER (EXAMPLE)

FIGURE 16-3

Non-Dedicated Pile Driver, Example

FIGURE 16 - 3, NON-DEDICATED PILE DRIVER (EXAMPLE)

SECTION 17 Conveyors

Table of Contents

17

17.A General. Conveyor systems shall be constructed and installed in accordance with the manufacturer's recommendations.

17.A.<u>01</u> Inspection, maintenance, and repair. <u>These activities</u> shall be performed in accordance with the manufacturer's recommendations by a Qualified Person (QP). The entire system shall be visually inspected daily before start up.

<u>a</u>. No maintenance shall be performed when a conveyor is in operation except for the following:

(1) If lubrication is to be done while the conveyor is in motion, lubrication points shall be accessible <u>through guard openings which are small enough that fingers cannot</u> <u>reach the hazardous locations.</u> Only trained personnel who are aware of the hazards of the conveyor in motion shall be allowed to lubricate a conveyor that is operating; and

(2) When adjustments or maintenance is required while the conveyor is in operation, only trained personnel who are aware of the hazards shall be permitted to make the adjustment or maintenance. <u>If guards need to be removed for the adjustment or</u> <u>maintenance, the conveyor MUST be locked out</u> <u>prior to removing the guards.</u>

<u>b</u>. Hazardous Energy Control Procedures shall be used <u>for maintenance and servicing other than</u> <u>lubrication which is done without removing guards.</u> > *See Section 12.*

<u>c</u>. Safe access shall be provided to permit inspection, lubrication, repair and maintenance activities.

17.A.<u>02</u> Safety devices.

a. On all conveyors where reversing or runaway are potential hazards or the effects of gravity create a potential for hazardous uncontrolled lowering, anti-runaway devices, brakes, backstops, or other safeguards shall be installed to protect persons from injury and property from damage.

b. Conveyor systems shall be equipped with a time-delay audible and visual warning signal to be sounded immediately before starting of the conveyor. On overland conveyor systems, the devices shall be required only at the transfer, loading, and discharge points and those points where personnel are normally stationed.

<u>c</u>. Safety devices shall be arranged to operate in such a manner that if power failure or a failure of the device occurs a hazardous condition would not result. The safety devices shall be designed to prevent the conveyor from restarting until the safety device is manually reset.

17.A.<u>03</u> All exposed moving machinery parts that present a hazard shall be mechanically or electrically guarded or guarded by location.

a. Nip and shear points shall be guarded.

b. Take-up mechanisms may be guarded as an entity by placing standard railings or fencing, and warning signs, around the area in lieu of guarding each nip and shear point.

c. In the case of a trolley conveyor when mechanical or electrical guarding would render the conveyor unusable, prominent and legible warnings shall be posted in the area or on the equipment and, where feasible, areas barricaded or lines marked on the ground to indicate the hazard area.

d. Guards shall be provided at points where personnel could contact cables, chains, belts, and runaways of exposed bucket conveyors.

e. Unless guarded by location, those sections of chain conveyors that cannot be enclosed without impairing the function shall be provided with warning signs or personnel barriers.

f. Trolley conveyors shall be provided with spill guards, pan guards, or the equivalent if there is a potential for material to fall off the conveyor and endanger personnel or equipment.

g. At transfer, loading, and discharge points, unconfined and uncontrolled free fall of material that may result from flooding, ricocheting, overloading, trajectory, leakage, or a combination thereof, shall be prevented if the material would create a hazard to personnel.

➤ *Note: In the absence of a guard specifically erected to protect personnel, warnings shall be provided to restrict unauthorized personnel from entering such hazardous areas.*

h. At all points along the conveyor, except at points where loads are removed from or placed on a conveyor or where a conveyor discharges to or receives material from another conveyor, provisions shall be made to eliminate the possibility of loads or material being dislodged from the conveyor.

i. The build-up of excess material shall be removed from all points along the conveyor.

17.A.04 Access.

a. Crossovers or underpasses with safeguards shall be provided for passage over or under all conveyors: crossing over or under conveyors is prohibited except where safe passageways are provided.

b. Whenever conveyors pass adjacent to, or over, work areas, roadways, highways, railroads, or other public passageways, protective guards shall be installed. The guards shall be designed to catch and hold any load or material that may fall off or become dislodged from the system.

c. Where conveyors are operated in tunnels, pits, and similar enclosures, ample room shall be provided to allow safe access and operating space for all personnel.

17.A.05 Operating controls.

a. Unless the design, construction, and operation of a conveyor is clearly non-hazardous to personnel, emergency stop buttons, pull cords, limit switches, or similar emergency devices shall be provided at the following locations:

(1) Operator stations;

(2) Loading arms;

(3) Transfer points; and

(4) Other potentially hazardous locations on the conveyor path not guarded by location or guards.

b. Emergency stop buttons shall be red in color, easily identifiable and readily accessible. They shall not be protected with collars or other devices which might make it difficult to activate.

c. Emergency stop devices shall act directly on the control of the conveyor concerned and shall not depend on the stopping of any other equipment. If a multi-conveyor system, the emergency stop shall stop all conveyors that are tied together.

d. Emergency stop devices shall be installed so that they cannot be overridden from other locations.

e. Starting controls shall be GREEN in color and protected from accidental activation.

f. All controls shall be clearly labeled to identify their function.

g. Conveyor controls shall be arranged so that in case of an emergency stop, manual reset or restart is required at the location where the emergency stop was initiated to resume conveyor operations.

17.A.06 Control stations shall be arranged and located so that the operation of the equipment is visible from them.

17.A.07 Gates and switches.

a. Power-positioned gate and switch sections shall be provided with devices that will prevent these sections from falling in case of power failure.

b. Means shall be provided on all gates and switch sections to prevent conveyed material from discharging into the open area created by lifting of the gate or switch.

17.A.08 Counterweights.

a. When counterweights are supported by belts, cables, chains, or similar means, the weights shall be confined in an enclosure to prevent the presence of personnel beneath the counter-weight, or the arrangement shall provide a means to restrain the falling weight in case of failure of the normal counterweight support.

b. When counterweights are attached to lever arms they shall be securely fastened.

17.A.09 When two or more conveying systems are interfaced, special attention shall be given to the interfaced area to ensure the presence of adequate guarding and safety devices.

17.A.10 Hoppers and chutes.

a. All openings to the hopper and chutes shall be guarded to prevent persons from accidentally stepping into them. If guards are not practical, warning signs shall be posted.

b. Dump hoppers having the hopper flush with the floor and which by their use cannot be guarded shall be equipped with grating having a maximum opening of 4 in (10 cm) and heavy enough to withstand any load which may be imposed on it. If the openings in the grating are larger or if no grating is provided, temporary railing shall be placed around ground level hoppers when dumping operation are not in progress. During dumping operation, warning signs shall be placed in conspicuous locations warning personnel of an open pit.

17

17.A.11 Mobile conveyors.

a. Mobile conveyors shall be provided with brakes or other position locking devices for each degree of motion where movement would present a hazard.

b. Mobile conveyors shall be designed to be stationary against runaway and stable against overturning under normal conditions of operation.

c. When an operator is required on a mobile conveyor, a platform or cab shall be provided for his/her protection.

17.A.12 Portable conveyors.

a. The raising and lowering mechanism for the boom of a portable conveyor shall be provided with a safety device that will hold the boom at any rated angle of inclination.

b. Portable conveyors shall be stable so that the conveyor will not topple when used with the manufacturer's rating and in a manner in which it was intended or when being moved.

17.A.13 Screw Conveyors.

a. Screw conveyors shall not be operated unless the conveyor housing completely encloses the conveyor moving elements and power transmission guards are in place, except that if the conveyor must have an open housing as a condition of use, the entire conveyor shall then be guarded by railing, fence, or by location.

b. Feed openings for shovel, front-end loader, or other manual or mechanical equipment shall be constructed in such a way that the conveyor screw is covered by grating. If the nature of the material is such that grating cannot be used, then the exposed section of the conveyor shall be guarded by a railing and warning signs shall be posted.

17.A.14 Conveyors shall be properly grounded before use and all connections, switches and cables shall conform to the National Electric Code (NEC).

17.B Operation.

17.B.01 Conveyor equipment shall be used to convey only those materials for which it was designed and within the rated capacities and speeds.

17.B.02 Flight and apron conveyors shall be "jogged" or hand run through at least one complete revolution at installation to check design clearances prior to running under automatic power.

17.B.03 A conveyor that could cause injury when started shall not be started until all personnel in the area are alerted by a signal or by a designated person that the conveyor is about to start.

17.B.04 When a conveyor that could cause injury when started is automatically controlled or must be controlled from a remote location, an audible warning device shall be provided. The device shall be clearly audible at all points along the conveyor where personnel may be present.

a. The warning device shall be activated by the controller device that starts the conveyor and shall continue for a period of time before the conveyor starts. A flashing light or similar visual warning shall be used with the audible device.

b. If a conveyor system is not exposed to the public, and if function of the system would be seriously hindered or adversely affected by the required time delay or where the intent of the warning may be misinterpreted, clear, concise, and legible warning signs shall be provided and indicate that the system may be started at any time, that danger exists, and that personnel must keep clear. These warnings signs shall be provided along the conveyor at areas that are not guarded or protected by their location.

17.B.05 Before restarting a conveyor that has been stopped because of an emergency, an inspection of the conveyor shall be conducted and the cause of the emergency stop determined.

17.B.06 The area around loading and unloading points shall be kept clear of obstructions that could create a hazard.

17.B.07 Applying a belt dressing or other foreign material to a rotating drive pulley or conveyor belt shall be avoided.

17.B.08 Flight and apron conveyors handling sticky materials that tend to build up shall be cleaned as often as required for safe operation.

17.C Training.

17.C.01 Only trained personnel shall be permitted to operate a conveyor. Training shall include instruction in operation under normal conditions and in emergencies.

17.C.02 Riding on conveyors is prohibited.

17.C.03 Personnel working with or near a conveyor shall be:

a. Instructed as to the location and operation of pertinent stopping devices; and

b. Prohibited from wearing loose or baggy clothing, jewelry or long hair.

17.C.04 Only trained personnel shall track a conveyor belt that must be done while the conveyor is operating.

SECTION 18 <u>Vehicles, Machinery and Equipment</u>

Table of Contents

18

18.A General. The requirements in this Section apply to the operation of all motor vehicles, machinery and mechanized equipment, All-Terrain Vehicles (ATVs), Utility Vehicles (UVs), and other specialty vehicles. Operators must also comply with state and host nation regulations as applicable to the above listed equipment.

18.A.01 Every person operating machinery and mechanized equipment, ATVs, UVs or other specialty vehicles, shall be properly trained (as described in this Section), qualified (license/certificate/permit) and designated by the employer in writing to operate such equipment.

18.A.02 Every person operating a motor vehicle, machinery and mechanized equipment, ATV, UV, or other specialty vehicles, shall possess, at all times while operating such vehicle/equipment, a license/permit (proof of qualification) valid for the equipment being operated. Licensing requirements will be as per Service regulation for military personnel and State regulations for civilian personnel, to include contractors. The operator must present the license/permit to the GDA upon request. Failure to do so will result in the immediate prohibition of the operator to operate motor vehicles.

➤ Note 1: USACE vehicle/equipment operators: In lieu of a license/permit for each piece of equipment, an Operator Equipment Qualification Record (OF Form 348 or similar type of documentation) may be maintained on file at the employee's project office for all USACE vehicle/equipment operators.

➤ Note 2: Government personnel may be required to carry the OF 346, Motor Vehicle Operator's License and Driving Record on military bases in addition or in lieu of a state driver's license (check local bases for requirements).

18.A.03 Inspections, tests, maintenance, and repairs.

a. Inspections, tests, maintenance and repairs shall be conducted by a qualified person in accordance with the manufacturer's recommendations.

b. Before initial use, vehicles not otherwise inspected by State or local authorities, shall be inspected by a qualified mechanic and found in safe operating condition and in compliance with all required published vehicle safety standards. This one-time inspection shall be documented and available for inspection on the work site.

c. When dump trucks are brought onto a USACE job site, they shall be inspected and found in compliance with the requirements of this Section before they are placed in service. This inspection shall be documented on a checklist.

d. All vehicles/equipment shall be inspected on a scheduled maintenance program.

e. Prior to each use, but not more often than daily, vehicles/equipment shall be checked by the operator to assure that the following parts, equipment, and accessories (as applicable) are in safe operating condition and free of apparent damage that could cause failure while in use:

(1) Service brakes, including trailer brake connections;

(2) Parking system (hand brake);

(3) Emergency stopping system (brakes);

(4) Tires;

(5) Horns;

(6) Steering mechanism;

(7) Coupling devices;

(8) Seat belts;

(9) Operating controls;

(10) Safety devices (e.g., back-up alarms and lights, fire extinguishers, first-aid kits, etc.), and

(11) Accessories including lights, reflectors, windshield wipers and defrosters where such equipment is necessary.

f. Inspection, test, repair, and maintenance records shall be maintained at the site available on request to the GDA.

18.A.04 Vehicles/equipment not meeting safe operating conditions shall be immediately removed from service, its use prohibited until unsafe conditions have been corrected, and re-inspected before being placed in service again.

18.A.05 Whenever visibility conditions warrant additional light, all vehicles or combinations of vehicles, in use shall be equipped with:

a. Two headlights, one on each side in the front;

b. At least two red taillights and one red or amber stoplight on each side of the rear;

c. Directional signal lights (both front and back); and

d. Three emergency flares, reflective markers, or equivalent portable warning device.

18.B Guarding and Safety Devices.

18.B.01 Reverse signal (back-up) alarm.

a. All self-propelled construction and industrial equipment, <u>dump trucks and cargo trucks, whose trailer/body permanently block the view to the rear,</u> whether moving alone or in combination, shall be equipped with a back-up alarm.

➤ *Note: Equipment designed and operated so that the operator is always facing the direction of motion does not require a back-up alarm.*

b. Back-up alarms shall be audible and sufficiently distinct to be heard above the surrounding noise level.

c. Alarms shall operate automatically upon commencement of backward motion. Alarms may be continuous or intermittent (not to exceed 3-second intervals) and shall operate during the entire backward movement.

<u>d.</u> Commercial cargo vehicles such as pick-up trucks, utility cargo/tool trucks, and flat-bed cargo trucks intended for use on public highways with a normally clear view through the rear window are not required to have back-up alarms. If the view to the rear is temporarily obstructed by a load or permanently blocked by a utility/tool box or other modification, then a signal person <u>may be used, if the value outweighs the risk as determined by an AHA. In lieu of a signal person, a back-up alarm</u> must be installed.

<u>e.</u> The removal or disabling of any back-up alarm is strictly prohibited.

18.B.02 A warning device shall be provided where there is danger to persons from moving equipment, swinging loads, buckets, booms or similar. <u>A signal person may be used in lieu of a warning device if the value outweighs the risk, as determined by an AHA.</u>

18.B.03 Guarding.

a. All belts, gears, shafts, pulleys, sprockets, spindles, drums, flywheels, chains, or other reciprocating, rotating, or moving parts of equipment shall be guarded when exposed to contact by persons or when they otherwise create a hazard.

b. All hot surfaces of equipment, including exhaust pipes or other lines, shall be guarded or insulated to prevent injury and fire.

c. All equipment having a charging skip shall be provided with guards on both sides and open end of the skip area to prevent persons from walking under the skip while it is elevated.

d. Platforms, foot walks, steps, handholds, guardrails, and toe boards shall be designed, constructed, and installed on machinery and equipment to provide safe footing and access ways.

e. Equipment shall be provided with suitable working surfaces of platforms, guardrails, and hand grabs when attendants or other employees are required to ride for operating purposes outside the operator's cab or compartment. Platforms and steps shall be of nonskid material.

f. Substantial overhead protection shall be provided for the operators of forklifts and similar material handling equipment. *> See also Section 18.G.29.*

18.B.04 Brake systems.

a. All vehicles, except trailers having a gross weight of 5,000 lb (2,268 kg) or less, shall be equipped with service brakes and manually-operated parking brakes.

b. Service and parking brakes shall be adequate to control the movement of, to stop, and to hold the vehicle under all conditions of service.

c. Service brakes on trailers and semi-trailers shall be controlled from the driver's seat of the prime mover.

d. Braking systems on every combination of vehicles shall be so designed as to be in approximate synchronization on all wheels and develop the required braking effort on the rear-most wheels first. The design shall also provide for application of the brakes by the driver of the prime mover from the cab. Exceptions to this are vehicles in tow by an approved tow bar hitch.

18.B.05 Fuel tanks shall be located in a manner that will not allow spills or overflows to run onto engine, exhaust, or electrical equipment.

18.B.06 Exhaust or discharges from equipment shall be so directed that they do not endanger persons or obstruct the view of the operator.

18.B.07 A safety tire rack, cage, or equivalent protection shall be provided and used when inflating, mounting, or dismounting tires installed on split rims, or rims equipped with locking rings of similar devices. *> See Section 18.G.22.*

18.B.08 No guard, safety appliance, or device shall be removed from machinery or equipment, or made ineffective, except for making immediate repairs, lubrications, or adjustments, and then only after the

18

equipment has been de-energized and Hazardous Energy Control Program (lockout/tagout procedures) implemented. All guards and devices shall be replaced immediately after completion of repairs and adjustments and before power is turned on. *> See Section 12.*

18.B.09   Seat belts and anchorages meeting the requirements of 49 CFR 571 shall be installed and worn in all motor vehicles (installation and usage on buses is optional).

a. Two-piece seat belts and anchorages for construction equipment shall comply with applicable Federal specifications or Society of Automotive Engineers (SAE) Standard J386.

b. All construction equipment equipped with seat belts must have the seat belts worn by the operator, unless specified otherwise in the manufacturer's operating manual and justified in an AHA and accepted in writing by the GDA.

18.B.10 All high-lift PITs shall be equipped with overhead guards that meet the structural requirements defined in ANSI/ASME B56.1.

18.B.11 Suitable protection against the elements, falling or flying objects, swinging loads, and similar hazards shall be provided for operators of all machinery or equipment. Glass used in windshields or cabs shall be safety glass.

18.B.12 Falling object protective structures (FOPS).

a. All bulldozers, tractors, or similar equipment used in clearing operations shall be provided with guards, canopies, or grills to protect the operator from falling and flying objects as appropriate to the nature of the clearing operations.

b. FOPS for other construction, industrial, and grounds-keeping equipment will be furnished when the operator is exposed to falling object hazards.

c. FOPS will be certified by the manufacturer or a licensed engineer as complying with the applicable recommended practices of SAE Standards J231 and J1043.

18.B.13 Rollover Protective Structures (ROPS).

a. In addition to the requirements of Sections 18.B.09 and 18.B.11, seat belts and ROPS shall be installed on:

(1)   Crawler and rubber-tire tractors including dozers, push and pull tractors, winch tractors, and mowers;

(2)   Off-the-highway self-propelled pneumatic-tire earth movers (i.e., trucks, pans, scrapers, bottom dumps, and end dumps);

(3)   Motor graders;

(4)   Water tank trucks having a tank height less than the cab; and

(5)   Other self-propelled construction equipment such as front-end loaders, backhoes, rollers, and compactors.

b. ROPS are not required on:

(1)   Trucks designed for hauling on public highways;

(2)   Crane-mounted dragline backhoes;

(3)   Sections of rollers and compactors of the tandem steel-wheeled and self-propelled pneumatic-tired type that do not have an operator's station;

(4)   Self-propelled, rubber-tired lawn and garden tractors and side-boom pipe laying tractors operated solely on flat terrain (maximum 10° slope; 20° slope permitted when offloading from a truck) not exposed to rollover hazards; and

(5)   Cranes, draglines, or equipment on which the operator's cab and boom rotate as a unit.

c. ROPS may be removed from certain types of equipment when the work cannot be performed with the ROPS in place and when ROPS removal is justified and delineated in an AHA and accepted in writing by the GDA.

d. The operating authority shall furnish proof from the manufacturer or certification from a licensed engineer that the ROPS complies with applicable SAE Standards (i.e., J167, J1040, J1042, J1084, and J1194).

e. ROPS shall also be acceptable if they meet the criteria of any State that has a Department of Labor-approved OSHA program or meets Water and Power Resources Service requirements.

f. The following information permanently affixed to the ROPS is acceptable in lieu of a written certification:

(1)   Manufacturer's or fabricator's name and address;

(2)   ROPS model number, if any; and

(3) Machine make, model, or series number that the structure is designed to fit.

g. Field welding on ROPS shall be performed by welders who are certified, per Section 10.A.07.

18.B.14 All points requiring lubrication during operation shall have fittings so located or guarded to be accessible without hazardous exposure. > *See also Section 12.*

18.B.15 All machinery or equipment and material hoists operating on rails, tracks, or trolleys shall have positive stops or limiting devices either on the equipment, rails, tracks, or trolleys to prevent overrunning safe limits.

18.B.16 Under the following circumstances, long-bed end-dump trailers used in off-road hauling should be equipped with a rollover warning device. The device should have a continuous monitoring display at the operator station to give the operator a quick and easily read indicator and audible warning of an unsafe condition:

a. The material being dumped is subject to being stuck or caught in the trailer rather than exiting the bed freely, and

b. The dumpsite cannot be maintained in a nominally level condition (lateral slope less than 1° - 2°).

18.C Operating Rules.

18.C.01 General. For the purpose of this paragraph, a government-owned motor vehicle is any vehicle (government-owned; POV or Rental Car if being used while on-duty in lieu of government-owned vehicle) used to transport Government employees.

a. Operators of Government and Contractor motor vehicles being used on USACE projects may only use cellular telephones with hands-free devices while the vehicle is in motion.

(1) Prior to using a hand-held cellular phone, drivers shall find a safe place to bring their vehicle to a stop.

(2) Text messaging by the operator is strictly prohibited while operating motor vehicles.

b. The use of any other portable headphones, earphones, or other listening devices (except for hands–free cellular phones) while operating Government or contractor motor vehicles on USACE projects is prohibited. > *See AR 190-5.*

c. Operators of government-owned motor vehicles (whether government- or contractor- operated, GOGO or GOCO) shall not eat, drink alcohol, or smoke while the vehicle is in motion.

d. GPS Systems.

(1) GPS systems shall be mounted within the vehicle so that they do not create sight hazards for the operator.

(2) Programming of GPS systems while driving is prohibited.

(3) The use of non-mounted GPS systems may only be used by the vehicle operator while the vehicle is in a stopped position.

18.C.02 Defensive Driving. The principles of defensive driving shall be practiced. Operators (government and contractor) of government-owned vehicles shall complete Defensive Driver Training initially and every four years thereafter. Contractor operators of government-owned vehicles shall provide documentation of completion of a suitable Defensive Driving Course to the GDA initially and upon request.

18.C.03 Seat belts shall be installed and worn per Section 18.B.09. Buses are exempt from this requirement.

18.C.04 At all times, the operator must have the vehicle under control and be able to bring it to a complete stop within a safe stopping distance.

18.C.05 Vehicles may not be driven at speeds greater than the posted speed limit, with due regard for weather, traffic, intersections, width and character of the roadway, type of motor vehicle, and any other existing condition.

18.C.06 Headlights shall be on from sunset to sunrise, during fog, smoke, rain, or other unfavorable atmospheric conditions, and at any other time when there is not sufficient light for the vehicle to be seen or the operator to see on the highway at a distance of 500 ft (150.4 m), unless local regulations prohibit.

18.C.07 Vehicles shall not be driven on a downgrade with gears in neutral or clutch disengaged.

18.C.08 Railroad crossings and drawbridges.

a. Upon approaching a railroad crossing or drawbridge, vehicles shall be driven at such a speed as to permit stopping before reaching the nearest track or the edge of the draw bridge and shall proceed only if the course is clear.

b. Vehicles transporting 15 or more persons, explosives, or flammable or toxic substances shall

18

stop at railroad crossings and drawbridges and shall not proceed until the course is clear, except at a railroad crossing or drawbridge protected by a traffic officer or a traffic signal giving a positive indication for approaching vehicles to proceed.

18.C.09 Vehicles shall not be stopped, parked, or left standing on any road, or adjacent thereto, or in any area in a manner as to endanger the vehicle, other vehicles, or personnel using or passing that road or area. Operator will ascertain safest exit path before exiting vehicle.

18.C.10 Vehicles shall not be left unattended until the motor has been shut off, the key removed (unless local regulations prohibit), parking brake set, and gear engaged in low, reverse, or park.

18.C.11 Vehicles carrying loads that project beyond the sides or rear of the vehicle shall carry a red flag, not less than 144 in^2 (929 cm^2), at or near the end of the projection. At night or when atmospheric conditions restrict visibility, a warning light shall be used in lieu of the red flag. Drivers will assure the load does not obscure vehicle lights and/or reflectors.

18.C.12 Employees shall not be permitted to get between a towed vehicle and towing vehicle except when hooking or unhooking.

18.C.13 No vehicle or combination of vehicles hauling unusually heavy loads or equipment shall be moved until the driver has been provided with the required permits, the correct weights of the vehicles and load, and a designated route to be followed.

18.C.14 When maneuvering or performing back-up operations, operators will take the applicable precautions outlined in Section 08.B.04. If a signal person or spotter is not used, operators will walk behind their vehicle to view the area for possible hazards before performing back-up operations with their vehicle.

18.C.15 When a bus, truck, or truck-trailer combination is parked or disabled on a highway or the adjacent shoulder, yellow flashing lights and other traffic warning devices (e.g., cones, flags, signs, etc.) per 49 CFR 571.5 shall be used during the daytime and reflectors, flares, electric lights or other effective means of identification shall be displayed at night.

18.C.16 Loading vehicles.

a. Drivers of trucks and similar vehicles shall leave the cab while the vehicle is being loaded when they are exposed to danger from suspended loads or overhead loading equipment, unless the cab is adequately protected.

b. Vehicles shall not be loaded in a manner that obscures the driver's view ahead or to either side or which interferes with the safe operation of the vehicle.

c. The load on every vehicle shall be distributed, chocked, tied down, or secured. Loads shall be covered when there is a hazard of flying/falling dirt, rock, debris, or material. Tail gates shall not be removed without implementing a positive means to prevent material from falling out of the back of the vehicle and may be done only with the acceptance of the GDA.

18.C.17 Maintenance Vehicles. All maintenance vehicles that are used at USACE recreational areas (or projects) shall be provided with two 28 in (0.7 m) day glow/highvisibility orange traffic cones. Vehicle operators that operate maintenance vehicles in USACE recreational areas shall place a cone in front and behind the vehicle when parked, remove and place in vehicle prior to departure.

18.D Transportation Of Personnel.

18.D.01 The number of passengers in passenger-type vehicles shall not exceed the number that can be seated.

18.D.02 Trucks used to transport personnel shall be equipped with a securely anchored seating arrangement, a rear end gate, and guardrail. Steps or ladders, for mounting and dismounting, shall be provided.

18.D.03 All tools and equipment shall be guarded, stowed, and secured when transported with personnel.

18.D.04 No person will be permitted to ride with arms or legs outside of a vehicle body, in a standing position on the body, on running boards, seated on side fenders, cabs, cab shields, bed of the truck, or on the load.

18.D.05 All vehicles transporting personnel during cold or inclement weather shall be enclosed. Passengers shall be protected from inclement weather elements.

18.D.06 Explosives, flammable materials (excepting normal fuel supply), or toxic substances may not be transported in vehicles carrying personnel.

18.D.07 Vehicles transporting personnel shall not be moved until the driver has ascertained that all persons are seated and the guardrails and rear end gates are in place or doors closed.

18.D.08 Getting on or off any vehicle while it is in motion is prohibited.

18.D.09 All motor vehicles shall be shut down prior to and during fueling operations. > *See Section 18.G.10.*

18.E Motor Vehicles (for Public Roadway Use).

18.E.01 For the purposes of the Section, a motor vehicle is defined as a sedan, van, SUV, truck, motorcycle, or other mode of conveyance intended for use on public roadways. This includes construction equipment that is driven on public highways. Other types of equipment such as machinery and mechanized equipment, ATVs, UVs and other specialty vehicles are addressed later in this Section.

18.E.02 Every motor vehicle shall have:

a. An operable speedometer;

b. An operable fuel gage;

c. An operable audible warning device (horn);

d. An adequate rearview mirror or mirrors;

e. A power-operated starting device;

f. A windshield equipped with an adequate windshield wiper;

g. An operable defrosting and defogging device;

h. Non-slip surfaces on steps; and

i. Cabs, cab shields, and other protection to protect the driver from the elements and falling or shifting materials;

➢ *Note: Items f through i do not apply to motorcycles. Gloves, a DOT-approved motorcycle helmet with full faceshield or goggles, sturdy footwear, long sleeved shirt or jacket, long trousers, full fingered gloves, and high-visibility garments (bright color for day and retroreflective for night), shall be worn at all times while operating or riding as a passenger on motorcycles.*

18.E.03 Glass in windshields, windows, and doors shall be safety glass. Any cracked or broken glass shall be replaced.

18.E.04 All buses, trucks, and combinations of vehicles with a carrying capacity of 1.5 tons (1,360.8 kg) or over, when operated on public highways, shall be equipped with emergency equipment required by State laws but not less than:

a. One red flag not less than 12 in^2 (77.4 cm^2) with standard and three reflective markers that shall be available for immediate use in case of emergency stops;

b. Two wheel chocks for each vehicle or each unit of a combination of vehicles;

c. At least one 2A:10B:C fire extinguisher (at least two properly rated fire extinguishers are required for flammable cargo).

18.E.05 All rubber-tired motor vehicles shall be equipped with fenders, and tires shall not extend beyond fenders. Mud flaps may be used in lieu of fenders whenever motor vehicle equipment is not designed for fenders.

18.F Trailers.

18.F.01 All towing devices used on any combinations of vehicles shall be structurally adequate for the weight drawn and shall be properly mounted.

18.F.02 A locking device or double safety system shall be provided on every fifth-wheel mechanism and tow bar arrangement to prevent the accidental separation of towed and towing vehicles.

18.F.03 Every trailer shall be coupled with safety chains or cables to the towing vehicle. Such chain or cable shall prevent the separation of the vehicles in case of tow bar failure.

18.F.04 Trailers equipped with power brakes shall be equipped with a breakaway device that effectively locks the brakes in the event the trailer separates from the towing vehicle.

18.F.05 All vehicle/equipment operators required to pull a trailer must be properly trained, evaluated, qualified and designated to perform this operation.

18.G Machinery And Mechanized Equipment.

18.G.01 For the purposes of the Section, machinery and mechanized equipment is defined as mobile, stationary, self-propelled or towed equipment intended for use on construction sites or industrial sites. This equipment is NOT intended for operation on public highways. Equipment such as dump trucks, cargo trucks, and other vehicles that may also travel on public roadways must also meet the requirements of Section 18.E.

18.G.02 Before any machinery or mechanized equipment is placed in use, it shall be inspected and tested in accordance with the manufacturer's recommendations and requirements of this manual.

a. Inspections will be documented on either a manufacturer-, government-supplied or contractor-

18

generated checklist. The Competent Person (CP) is required to sign the checklist designating that it meets the manufacturer's recommendations and requirements of this manual.

b. All checklists will be submitted to the GDA upon completion of the inspection and will become a part of the project file.

c. All safety deficiencies noted during the inspection shall be corrected prior to the equipment being placed in service at the project.

d. Re-inspection. Subsequent re-inspections will be conducted at least annually thereafter. Any time the machinery or mechanized equipment is removed and subsequently returned to the project (other than equipment removed for routine off-site operations as part of the project), it shall be re-inspected and recertified prior to use.

e. The Contractor shall provide the GDA ample notice in advance of any equipment entering the site so that the Contractor's inspection process may be observed and so that spot checks may be conducted.

18.G.03 No modifications or additions that affect the capacity or safe operation of machinery or equipment shall be made without the manufacturer's written approval.

a. If such modifications or changes are made, the capacity, operation, and maintenance instruction plates, tags, or decals shall be changed accordingly.

b. In no case shall the original safety factor of the equipment be reduced. > See Section 18.G.30.

18.G.04 Daily/shift inspections and tests.

a. All machinery and equipment shall be inspected daily (when in use) to ensure safe operating conditions. The employer shall designate CPs to conduct daily inspections and tests. These inspections and tests shall be documented by the CP to include as a minimum, the date, name of the inspector; specific items inspected, and "PASS/FAIL" indication. Copies of the inspections will be provided to the GDA upon request.

b. Tests shall be made at the beginning of each shift during which the equipment is to be used to determine that the brakes and operating systems are in proper working condition and that all required safety devices are in place and functional.

18.G.05 Whenever any machinery or equipment is found to be unsafe, or whenever a deficiency that affects the safe operation is observed, the equipment shall be immediately taken out of service and its use prohibited until unsafe conditions have been corrected.

a. A tag indicating that the equipment shall not be operated, and that the tag shall not be removed, shall be placed in a conspicuous location on the equipment. Where required, lockout procedures shall be used. > See Section 12.

b. The tag shall remain in its attached location until it is demonstrated to the individual dead-lining the equipment that it is safe to operate.

c. When corrections are complete, the machinery or equipment shall be retested and re-inspected before being returned to service.

18.G.06 Machinery and mechanized equipment shall be operated only by designated, qualified personnel.

a. Machinery or equipment shall not be operated in a manner that will endanger persons or property nor shall the safe operating speeds or loads be exceeded.

b. Getting off or on any equipment while it is in motion is prohibited.

c. Machinery and equipment shall be operated in accordance with the manufacturer's instructions and recommendations.

d. The use of headphones for entertainment purposes (e.g., radio, CD, music, books, etc.,) while operating equipment is prohibited except for communication directly related to operating the machinery or equipment.

e. The use of cell phones or any other electronic device that may cause distraction is prohibited while operating equipment.

f. All operator training and evaluation shall be conducted by persons who have the knowledge, training, and experience to train the equipment operators and evaluate their competence.

(1) These examiners may not license themselves, but instead, must be licensed by another qualified examiner.

(2) All qualification/licensing of equipment operators by examiners must include, at a minimum, requirements of this Section, the manufacturer's instructions and recommendations as well as observation of a practical operating examination on the equipment.

18.G.07 When the manufacturer's instructions or recommendations are more stringent than the requirements of this manual, the manufacturer's instructions or recommendations shall apply.

18.G.08 Inspections or determinations of road and shoulder conditions and structures shall be made in advance to assure that clearances and load capacities are safe for the passage or placing of any machinery or equipment.

18.G.09 Equipment requirements.

a. An operable fuel gage;

b. An operable audible warning device (horn);

c. Adequate rearview mirror or mirrors;

d. Non-slip surfaces on steps;

e. A power-operated starting device;

f. Seats or equal protection must be provided for each person required to ride on equipment (unless standing is permitted by the equipment manufacturer);

g. Whenever visibility conditions warrant additional light, all vehicles, or combinations of vehicles, in use shall be equipped with at least two headlights and two taillights in operable condition;

h. All equipment with windshields shall be equipped with powered wipers. Vehicles that operate under conditions that cause fogging or frosting of windshields shall be equipped with operable defogging or defrosting devices. Glass in windshields, windows, and doors shall be safety glass. Cracked or broken glass shall be replaced;

i. Mobile equipment, operating within an off-highway job site not open to public traffic, shall have a service brake system and a parking brake system capable of stopping and holding the equipment while fully loaded on the grade of operation.

j. It is recommended that heavy-duty hauling equipment have an emergency brake system that will automatically stop the equipment upon failure of the service brake system. This emergency brake system should be manually operable from the driver's position.

18.G.10 Mechanized equipment shall be shut down before and during fueling operations. Closed systems, with an automatic shut-off that will prevent spillage if connections are broken, may be used to fuel diesel powered equipment left running.

18.G.11 Bulldozer and scraper blades, end-loader buckets, dump bodies, and similar equipment shall be either fully lowered or blocked when being repaired or when not in use. All controls shall be in a neutral position, with the engines stopped and brakes set, unless work being performed on the machine requires otherwise.

18.G.12 Stationary machinery and equipment shall be placed on a firm foundation and secured before being operated.

18.G.13 All mobile equipment and the areas in which they are operated shall be adequately illuminated while work is in progress.

18.G.14 Equipment powered by an internal combustion engine will not be operated in or near an enclosed area unless adequate ventilation is provided to ensure the equipment does not generate a hazardous atmosphere.

18.G.15 All vehicles that will be parked or are moving slower than normal traffic on haul roads shall have a yellow flashing light or four-way flashers visible from all directions.

18.G.16 No one shall be permitted in the truck cab during loading operations except the driver, and then only if the truck has a cab protector. > *See also Section 18.C.16.a.*

18.G.17 All machinery or equipment operating on rails, tracks, or trolleys (except railroad equipment) shall be provided with substantial track scrapers or track clearers (effective in both directions) on each wheel or set of wheels.

18.G.18 Steering or spinner knobs shall not be attached to the steering wheel unless the steering mechanism prevents road reactions from causing the steering handwheel to spin. When permitted, the steering knob shall be mounted within the periphery of the wheel.

18.G.19 Safeguards (i.e., bumpers, railings, tracks, etc.,) shall be provided to prevent machinery and equipment operating on a floating plant from going into the water.

18.G.20 The controls of loaders, excavators, or similar equipment with folding booms or lift arms shall not be operated from a ground position unless so designed.

18.G.21 Personnel shall not work in, pass under, or ride in the buckets or booms of loaders in operation.

18.G.22 Tire service vehicles shall be operated so that the operator will be clear of tires and rims when hoisting operations are being performed. Tires large enough to require hoisting equipment will be secured from

18

movement by continued support of the hoisting equipment unless bolted to the vehicle hub or otherwise restrained. > *See also Section 18.B.07.*

18.G.23 Each bulldozer, scraper, dragline, crane, motor grader, front-end loader, mechanical shovel, backhoe, and other similar equipment shall be equipped with at least one dry chemical or CO_2 fire extinguisher with a minimum rating of 10-B:C.

18.G.24 Fill hatches on water haul vehicles shall be secured or the opening reduced to a maximum of 8 in (20.3 cm).

18.G.25 Maintenance and repairs.

a. Maintenance, including preventive maintenance, and repairs shall be in accordance with the manufacturer's recommendations and shall be documented. Records of maintenance and repairs conducted during the life of a contract shall be made available upon request of the GDA.

b. All machinery or equipment shall be shut down and positive means taken to prevent its operation while repairs or manual lubrications are being done. Equipment designed to be serviced while running are exempt from this requirement.

c. All repairs on machinery or equipment shall be made at a location that will protect repair personnel from traffic.

d. Heavy machinery, equipment, or parts thereof that are suspended or held apart by slings, hoist, or jacks also shall be substantially blocked or cribbed before personnel are permitted to work underneath or between them.

18.G.26 Dump trucks.

a. All dump trucks shall be equipped with a physical holding device to prevent accidental lowering of the body while maintenance or inspection work is being done.

b. All hoist levers shall be secured to prevent accidental starting or tripping of the mechanism.

c. All off-highway end-dump trucks shall be equipped with a means (plainly visible from the operator's position while looking ahead) to determine whether the dump box is lowered.

d. Trip handles for tailgates on all dump trucks shall be arranged to keep the operator in the clear.

18.G.27 Parking.

a. Whenever equipment is parked, the parking brake shall be set.

b. Equipment parked on an incline shall have the wheels chocked or track mechanisms blocked and the parking brake set.

c. All equipment left unattended at night, adjacent to a highway in normal use or adjacent to construction areas where work is in progress, shall have lights or reflectors, or barricades equipped with lights or reflectors, to identify the location of the equipment.

18.G.28 Towing.

a. All towing devices used on any combination of equipment shall be structurally adequate for the weight drawn and securely mounted.

b. Persons shall not be permitted to get between a towing vehicle and the piece of towed equipment until both have been completely stopped with all brakes set and wheels chocked on both vehicle and equipment.

18.G.29 Powered Industrial Trucks (PITs)/Forklifts and Telehandlers. All PITs and telehandlers shall meet the requirements of design, construction, stability, inspection, testing, maintenance, and operation (as defined in ANSI/ASME B56.1).

➢ *Note: When PITs or Telehandlers are configured to hoist and lower (by means of a winch or hook and/or with rigging) and horizontally move a suspended load, refer to Sections 16.A.01 and 16.Q.*

a. All PITs, lift trucks, stackers, and similar equipment shall have the rated capacity posted on the vehicle so as to be clearly visible to the operator. When the manufacturer provides auxiliary removable counterweights, corresponding alternate rated capacities also shall be clearly shown on the vehicle. The ratings shall not be exceeded.

b. Only trained, qualified/certified and designated operators shall be permitted to operate a PIT. Qualification shall be in writing via a license, permit or other documentation.

(1) Training must be both classroom and practical operation and in accordance with OSHA Standard 29 CFR 1910.178. It must be on the same type of truck the operator uses on the job.

(2) The employer must certify that the operator has been trained and evaluated as required by the standard. The certification shall include the name of

the operator, the date of the training, the date of the evaluation, and the identity of the person(s) performing the training or evaluation.

(3) Refresher training in relevant topics shall be conducted at least once every three (3) years including an evaluation of each powered industrial truck operator's performance. In addition, refresher training shall be provided to the operator when the operator:

(a) has been observed to operate the vehicle in an unsafe manner;

(b) has been involved in a mishap;

(c) has received an evaluation that reveals that the operator is not operating the truck safely;

(d) is assigned to drive a different type of truck; or

(e) a condition in the workplace changes in a manner that could affect safe operation of the truck.

c. When a PIT is left unattended, load engaging means shall be fully lowered, controls shall be neutralized, power shall be shut off, and brakes shall be set. Wheels shall be blocked if the truck is parked on an incline.

d. An overhead guard shall be used as protection against falling objects. It should be noted that an overhead guard is intended to offer protection from the impact of small packages, boxes, bagged material, etc., representative of the job application, but not to withstand the impact of a falling capacity load.

e. Dock board or bridge plates shall be properly secured before they are driven over. Dock board or bridge plates shall be driven over carefully and slowly and their rated capacity shall never be exceeded.

f. Under all travel conditions the PIT shall be operated at a speed that will permit it to be brought to a stop in a safe manner.

g. On all grades the load and load engaging means shall be tilted back if applicable, and raised only as far as necessary to clear the road surface.

h. When ascending or descending grades in excess of 10%, loaded PITs shall be driven with the load upgrade.

i. Multi-purpose machines, material handling equipment (i.e. Rough-Terrain Forklifts, Lulls, etc.), and construction equipment used to lift loads suspended by rigging equipment shall:

(1) Have proof or authorization from the manufacturer that the machine is capable of making lifts of loads suspended by rigging equipment;

(2) Demonstrate that the equipment is properly configured to make such lifts, and

(3) The machine/equipment must be equipped with a load chart.

j. Contractor must provide certification that the operator is trained, qualified and designated for the operation of the machine (multi-purpose, material handling and construction equipment) being utilized to lift loads suspended by rigging equipment.

18.G.30 Floating Equipment. All equipment placed or operating on barges, pontoons, vessels or other means of flotation must be evaluated by a Qualified Person (QP) for safe placement, transport and operating conditions. At a minimum, the evaluation shall include: proper operating procedures per the manufacturer; stability and structural assessment of equipment and barge/pontoon; if required, where and how the equipment will be secured to address positively secured positioning of the equipment (no movement/tipping), and environmental restrictions.

(1) If the QP determines that the equipment can safely operate under the anticipated conditions, within the manufacturer's operating procedures, the evaluation shall be documented in writing by the QP in the AHA and provided to GDA prior to work beginning.

(2) If the equipment cannot safely operate under the anticipated conditions, within the manufacturer's operating procedures, or the QP determines that it is not safe to do so, then the use of this equipment in this capacity is not allowed.

(3) If there are no manufacturer's operating procedures, an RPE with knowledge and experience with this type of equipment must develop the safe operating procedures. The QP can then perform the evaluation of the equipment and barge/pontoon. This evaluation shall be documented in writing by the QP in the AHA and provided to GDA prior to work beginning.

➤ Note: If this equipment is mechanized equipment used in conjunction with rigging to lift a load, it is considered Load Handling Equipment. > See Section 16.L.

18.H Drilling Equipment.

18.H.01 Applicability. The requirements of this Section are in addition to other requirements identified in Section 18 and are applicable to rock, soil, and concrete drilling operations.

18.H.02 Drilling equipment shall be operated only by qualified (training, evaluation and experience) personnel who are designated by their respective employer to operate subject equipment.

a. The drilling equipment shall be operated, inspected, and maintained as specified in the manufacturer's operating manual.

b. A copy of the manual will be available at the job site.

18.H.03 AHA Development. Prior to initiating rock, soil, and/or concrete drilling operations, the contractor shall develop an AHA for the intended operations. AHA shall include, as a minimum:

a. Location of all overhead electrical lines/hazards;

b. Location of any possible unexploded ordnance or hazardous agents in the soil;

c. Location of utilities both above and below grade;

d. Designated areas for equipment operations and material storage;

e. Assembly and disassembly sequences for rock, soil, and concrete drilling equipment;

f. Operation of rock, soil, and concrete drilling equipment and handling of associated materials;

g. A geotechnical survey report identifying subsurface and surface ground conditions. The findings of this survey and the controls for all potential hazards shall become a part of the AHA;

h. A hard copy of the Safety Data Sheet (SDS) for the drilling fluids, if required;

i. The AHA meets the requirements of Section 01.A.14 or 01.A.15, and

j. AHA shall be reviewed at the preparatory meeting, when the plan has been completed.

18.H.04 Training. Members of drilling crews shall be provided training based on the equipment operating manual and the AHA. This training shall include, at a minimum:

a. The operation, inspection, and maintenance of the equipment;

b. The safety features and procedures to be used during operation, inspection, and maintenance of the equipment; and

c. Overhead electrical line and underground hazards.

18.H.05 Drilling equipment shall be equipped with two easily accessible emergency shutdown devices, one for the operator and one for the helper.

a. Only one emergency shutdown switch is required on a pier -hole rig.

b. Rigs must be shut down before any helpers enter a barricaded area.

c. Auger heads must be in the hole or a cover placed over the hole before workers enter the barricaded area.

➢ *Note: If infeasible due to type of drill equipment being used, a risk assessment shall be performed by a Competent Person (CP), and documented in the AHA as to why this requirement is not practical. Identification of additional precautions and/or controls shall be identified to insure an equal level of safety is being accomplished.*

18.H.06 Clearance from electrical sources shall be as specified in Table 11-1.

a. Drilling equipment shall be posted with signs warning the operator of electrical hazards.

b. The equipment operator shall assure proper clearance before moving equipment. Clearance shall be monitored by a spotter or by an electrical proximity warning device.

18.H.07 Moving equipment.

a. Before drilling equipment is moved, the travel route shall be surveyed for overhead and terrain hazards, particularly overhead electrical hazards.

b. Earth drilling equipment shall not be transported with the mast up. The exception is movement of the equipment required in drilling a series of holes, such as in blasting, if the following conditions are satisfied:

(1) Movement is over level, smooth terrain;

(2) The path of travel has been inspected for stability and the absence of holes, other ground hazards, and electrical hazards;

(3) The travel distance is limited to short, safe distances; and

(4) Travel with mast up may only be performed according to manufacturer's recommendations and/or specification.

18.H.08 Equipment set-up.

a. Equipment shall be set-up on stable ground and maintained level. Cribbing shall be used when necessary.

b. Outriggers shall be extended per the manufacturer's specifications.

c. When drilling equipment is operated in areas with the potential for classification as a confined space, the requirements of Section 34 shall be followed.

18.H.09 When drilling equipment is parked or disabled on a highway or the adjacent shoulder, yellow flashing lights and other traffic warning devices (cones, flags, signs, etc) per 49 CFR 571.5 shall be used during the daytime and reflector, flares, electric lights or other effective means of identification shall be displayed at night.

18.H.10 Equipment operation.

a. Weather conditions shall be monitored. Operations shall cease during electrical storms or when electrical storms are imminent. > *See Sections 01.E.*

b. Drill crewmembers shall not wear loose clothing, jewelry, or equipment that might become caught in moving machinery. High visibility vests used on drilling rigs, if required, must be of the break-away type.

c. Auger guides shall be used on hard surfaces. If infeasible due to type of drill rig being used, a risk assessment shall be performed by a CP, and documented in the AHA as to why this requirement is not feasible. Identification of additional precautions and/or controls shall be identified to insure an equal level of safety is being accomplished).

d. The operator shall verbally alert employees and visually ensure employees are clear from dangerous parts of equipment before starting or engaging equipment.

e. The discharge of drilling fluids shall be channeled away from the work area to prevent the ponding of water.

f. Hoists shall be used only for their designed intent and shall not be loaded beyond their rated capacity. Steps shall be taken to prevent two-blocking of hoists.

g. The equipment manufacturer's procedures shall be followed if rope becomes caught in, or objects get pulled into, a cathead.

h. Drill rods shall not be run or rotated through rod slipping devices. No more than 1 ft (0.3 m) of drill rod column shall be hoisted above the top of the drill mast. Drill rod tool joints shall not be made up, tightened, or loosened while the rod column is supported by a rod-slipping device.

i. Dust shall be controlled. When there is potential for silica exposure, the requirements contained in Section 06.N shall be implemented.

j. Augers shall be cleaned only when the rotating mechanism is in neutral and the auger stopped. Long-handled shovels shall be used to move cutting from the auger.

k. Open boreholes shall be capped and flagged. Open excavations shall be barricaded.

l. Means shall be provided to guard against employee contact with the auger (e.g. guard around the auger; barricade around the perimeter of the auger; electronic brake activated by a presence-sensing device).

➢ *Note: If infeasible due to type of drill equipment being used, employees must maintain a safe, clear distance while the drilling equipment is operating. Only when the drill has stopped rotating, the controls returned to the neutral position, and a clear signal has been given by the operator and understood by the helper that it is safe, shall the employee proceed to approach the drill. A risk assessment shall be performed by the CP, and documented in the AHA as to why this requirement is not practical. Identification of additional precautions and/or controls shall be identified to insure an equal level of safety is being accomplished.*

m. The use of side-feed swivel collars on drill rods are restricted to those collars that are retained by either a manufacturer-designed stabilizer or a stabilizer approved by a professional engineer.

18.I All Terrain Vehicles (ATVs). ATVs are vehicles intended for off-road use that travel on four low pressure tires with a seat designed to be straddled by the operator and should not be confused with utility vehicles. > *See Section 18.J.*

18.I.01 Every ATV operator shall have completed a nationally-recognized accredited ATV training course (such as provided by the Specialty Vehicles Institute of America or by inhouse resources that have been certified as trainers by an accredited organization) prior to operation of the vehicle.

a. The operator must pass an operating skills test prior to being allowed to operate an ATV. Proof of

18

completion of this training shall be made available to the GDA upon request.

b. The in-house trainer, certified by an accredited organization, must perform at least 1 training session every 3 years to maintain certification. If the accrediting agency requires the trainer to return for refresher training to maintain certification, this shall be in addition to the 1 training session taught every 3 years.

18.I.02 All ATVs shall be equipped with:

a. An adequate audible warning device (horn) at the operator's station in operable condition (if determined necessary for the work being performed); and

b. Brake lights in operable condition (regardless of light conditions).

c. Operable rear view mirror(s).

18.I.03 Whenever visibility conditions warrant the need for additional light, all vehicles or combinations of vehicles in use, shall be equipped with at least two headlights and two taillights in operable condition.

18.I.04 The manufacturer's recommended payload/passenger limitations shall not be exceeded at any time.

18.I.05 Gloves and a DOT-approved motorcycle helmet with full-face shield or goggles shall be worn at all times while operating ATVs. When required for operators, passengers shall wear an approved motorcycle helmet with full faceshield or goggles.

18.I.06 ATVs will not be driven on public roadways except to cross the roadway, and may only be driven on public roadways at designated crossing points or with a road guard (no paved road use unless allowed by the manufacturer).

18.I.07 Only ATVs with four or more wheels may be used.

18.I.08 A copy of the operator's manual will be kept on the vehicle and protected from the elements (if practicable).

18.I.09 Tires shall be inflated to the pressures recommended by the manufacturer.

18.I.10 ATVs shall be equipped with mufflers.

18.I.11 All ATVs shall be equipped with spark arresters.

18.J Utility Vehicles. For the purposes of the Section, utility vehicles are defined as specialty vehicles designed to perform off-road utility tasks such as passenger and cargo transportation (e.g., rangers, rhino, m-gators, gators, mules, etc.) and shall not be confused with ATVs. > *See Section 18.I.*

18.J.01 Utility vehicle operators shall be trained.

a. They must be familiar with the use of all controls and understand proper moving, stopping, turning and other operating characteristics of the vehicle.

b. Operators must review all training materials provided by the manufacturer for the specific vehicles, and training should be in accordance with appropriate manufacturer recommendations. At a minimum, training shall be documented and shall address:

(1) Basic riding tips from the manufacturer's published literature for each vehicle;

(2) Reading terrain;

(3) Climbing hilly terrain;

(4) Descending a hill;

(5) Traversing a slope;

(6) Riding through water;

(7) Cargo carriers and accessories;

(8) Loading and unloading;

(9) Troubleshooting;

(10) Proper preventative maintenance (i.e., oil levels, tire pressure requirements and scheduled maintenance requirements according to the manufacturer's guidelines).

18.J.02 A copy of the operator's manual shall be kept on the vehicle at all times and protected from the elements.

18.J.03 Utility vehicles shall be equipped with:

a. An adequate audible warning device (horn), in operable condition, at the operator's station; and

b. Brake lights in operable condition regardless of light conditions.

c. Operable rear view mirror(s).

18.J.04 Whenever visibility conditions warrant additional light, all vehicles, or combinations of vehicles, in use shall be equipped with at least two headlights and two taillights in operable condition, a yellow flashing light or equivalent.

18.J.05 Occupancy in utility vehicles is limited to manufacturer designated seating that has built-in seat belts. Passengers may not ride in the vehicles back cargo area unless the vehicle is otherwise equipped.

> Note: When used for emergency response, medical litters may be placed in the back cargo area but must be secured as described in Section 18.J.07.

18.J.06 The manufacturer's recommended load carrying capacity, personnel capacity, or maximum safe vehicle speed shall not be exceeded at any time.

18.J.07 Cargo items will be secured as necessary to prevent movement/tipping. All loads over 50 lbs (22.7 kg) - to include medical litters - must be securely strapped to cargo tiedowns in the rear and to the cargo shelf in the front.

18.J.08 Manufacturer-installed safety equipment will be maintained in working order and used in compliance with the requirement of this regulation and in accordance with manufacturer's recommendations.

18.J.09 Seat belts and anchorages meeting the requirements of 49 CFR Part 571 (DOT, Federal Motor Vehicle Safety Standards) shall be installed in all utility vehicles and will be worn by operators and passengers.

18.J.10 Operators and passengers shall wear goggles at all times when a utility vehicle, not equipped with a windshield, is in motion.

18.J.11 Utility vehicles will not normally be driven on public roadways except to cross the roadway, and will only be driven on a public roadway at designated crossing points or with a road guard.

18.J.12 Utility vehicles that are allowed to operate outside a controlled work area and/or on public roads will meet the minimum vehicle safety standards in accordance with 49 CFR 571.5, to include ROPs, seat belts, and placement of "Slow Moving Vehicle" emblems where required.

18.J.13 When not equipped with ROPS, operators and passengers of utility vehicles will wear approved head protection (helmet) that at a minimum conforms to DOT 218 standards or equivalent and protective goggles or face shield.

18.K Specialty Vehicles. For the purposes of the Section, specialty vehicles are defined as all other vehicles not meeting any of the definitions above and may include cargo or personnel carriers or custom vehicles (i.e., Taylor-Dunn/Cushman, golf carts, Segway-type vehicles, snow machines, etc.).

18.K.01 A driver qualification and training program specific to the specialty vehicle shall be established.

18.K.02 An AHA/SOP that includes at a minimum, the safe operations, limits of operational work areas, required PPE and vehicle safety equipment requirements shall be established for the use of all specialty vehicles.

18.K.03 Whenever visibility conditions warrant additional light, all vehicles, or combinations of vehicles, in use shall be equipped with at least one headlight and one taillight in operable condition.

18.K.04 The manufacturer's recommended load carrying capacity, personnel capacity, and maximum safe vehicle speed shall not be exceeded at any time.

18.K.05 Specialty vehicles shall not be used for other than their manufactured purpose. Manufacturer-installed safety equipment will be maintained in working order and used in compliance with the requirement of this regulation and in accordance with manufacturer's recommendations.

18.K.06 Cargo items will be secured as necessary to prevent movement/tipping.

18.K.07 Specialty vehicles shall not be operated on unimproved surfaces.

18.K.08 For Segway HT, the minimum head protection standard is an approved bicycle helmet.

18.K.09 A snow machine is any vehicle designed to travel over ice and snow using mechanical propulsion in conjunction with skis, belts, cleats, or low-pressure tires.

a. All state and local laws and regulations shall be observed. Snow machines may be used on public roadways only where authorized by state and local regulations or in an emergency.

b. Operator training for snow machines will include:

(1) Hand signals;

(2) Riding positions;

(3) Towing of a sled;

(4) Surface conditions and types (e.g. snow, ice, tundra, etc.);

18

(5) Proper apparel while riding;

(6) Dangers to avoid.

c. The following minimum equipment is required on all snow machines:

(1) Brakes that will work under normal driving conditions and when loading;

(2) A throttle in which, when released by hand, will return engine speed to idle, close the carburetor, and disengage the clutch;

(3) A rear snow flap to deflect material or objects thrown by the track;

(4) A protective shield over all moving parts;

(5) Reflectors on the sides or side cowling (must meet Society of Automotive Engineers Standards);

(6) A rigid drawbar that is no longer than 10 ft (30 m) when towing;

(7) Operable rear view mirror(s).

d. When working from snow machines, two machines are the minimum (the buddy system). When working more than five miles from support base, a track vehicle for support will be used to support the operation.

e. Passengers are not authorized on personal snow machines (snowmobiles) except in case of an emergency (i.e., a broken-down machine).

SECTION 19 Floating Plant and Marine Activities

Table of Contents

19

19.A General.

19.A.01 Floating plant inspection and certification.

a. All floating plant regulated by the USCG shall have required USCG documentation that is current before being placed in service. A copy shall be posted in a public area on board the vessel. A copy of any USCG Form 835 issued to the vessel in the preceding year shall be available to the GDA and a copy shall be on board the vessel.

b. All dredges and quarter boats not subject to USCG inspection and certification or not having a current ABS classification shall be inspected in the working mode annually by a marine surveyor accredited by the National Association of Marine Surveyors (NAMS) or the Society of Accredited Marine Surveyors (SAMS) and having at least 5 years experience in commercial marine plant and equipment.

(1) All other plant shall be inspected before being placed in use and at least annually by a qualified person.

(2) The inspection shall be documented, a copy of the most recent inspection report shall be posted in a public area on board the vessel, and a copy shall be furnished to the GDA upon request.

(3) The inspection shall be appropriate for the intended use of the plant and shall, as a minimum, evaluate structural condition and compliance with NFPA 302.

c. Periodic inspections and tests shall assure that a safe operating condition is maintained.

d. Records of inspections shall be maintained at the site and shall be available to the GDA.

e. Floating plant found in an unsafe condition shall be taken out of service and its use prohibited until unsafe conditions have been corrected.

19.A.02 Personnel qualifications.

a. Officers and crew shall be in possession of a current, valid USCG license, which shall be posted in a public area on board the vessel, or correctly endorsed document as required by the USCG.

b. Government operators shall be licensed or certified in accordance with the requirements outlined in ER 385-1-91. A qualified individual designated as the USACE Command's marine licensing official will perform licensing and certification in accordance with the requirements of ER 385-1-91.

c. Officers and crew of government floating plant shall be licensed and/or documented by the USCG when the plant is subject to one or more of the following criteria:

(1) The vessel is inspected and certified by USCG in accordance with EP 1130-2-500, Appendix L;

(2) The vessel is normally engaged in or near a channel or fairway in operations that restrict or affect navigation of other vessels and is required by law to be equipped with radio-telephones of the 156-162 band frequency; or

(3) Floating plant is engaged in the transfer of oil or hazardous material in bulk.

d. A USCG Radar Observers endorsement on licenses is required for Operators of Uninspected Towing Vessels and Masters and Pilots on radar-equipped vessels 26 ft (7.9 m) or more in length. Endorsements must be issued from a USCG-approved training facility.

19.A.03 Severe weather precautions.

a. Where floating plant, boats or other marine activities may be endangered by severe weather (including sudden and locally severe weather, storms, high winds, hurricanes, and floods) plans shall be made for removing or securing plant and evacuation of personnel in emergencies. > See Section 01.E. This plan shall be part of the APP and shall include at least the following:

(1) A description of the types of severe weather hazards the plant may potentially be exposed to and the steps that will be taken to guard against the hazards;

(2) The time frame for implementing the plan (using as a reference the number of hours remaining for the storm to reach the work site if it continues at the predicted speed and direction), including the estimated time to move the plant to safe harbor after movement is started;

(3) The name and location of the safe location(s);

(4) The name of the vessel(s), type, capacity, speed, and availability that will be used to move any non-self-propelled plant;

(5) River/tide gage readings at which floating plant must be moved away from dams, river structures, etc., to safe areas;

(6) Method for securing equipment if not moved.

b. Extended movement of floating plant and tows shall be preceded by an evaluation of weather reports and conditions by a responsible person to ascertain that safe movement of the plant and tow can be accomplished.

c. Work or task orders shall be preceded by an evaluation of weather reports and conditions by a responsible person to ascertain that safe working conditions exist and safe refuge of personnel is assured.

d. USCG approved personal flotation devices (PFDs) - Types I, II, III, or V - shall be worn by all personnel on decks exposed to severe weather, regardless of other safety devices used. USCG-approved Type V automatic inflatable PFDs rated for commercial use may be worn by workers on USACE sites per Section 05.J.02.

e. A sufficient number of vessels of adequate size and horsepower, each designed, outfitted, and equipped for towing service, shall be available at all times to move both self- and non-self-propelled plant against tides, current, and winds during severe weather conditions.

f. Contractors working in an exposed marine location shall monitor the National Oceanic and Atmospheric Administration (NOAA) marine weather broadcasts and use other commercial weather forecasting services as may be available.

g. The floating plant shall be capable of withstanding whatever sea conditions may be experienced in the work area during the time period the work is being performed (i.e., seaworthiness, or good "sea keeping" qualities).

19.A.04 Emergency planning.

a. Plans shall be prepared for response to marine emergencies such as fire, sinking, flooding, severe weather, man overboard, hazardous material incidents, etc. (Fire: USCG-approved fire plans meet this requirement). > See Section 01.E.

b. A station bill, setting forth the special duties and the duty station of each crewmember for various emergencies, shall be prepared and posted in conspicuous locations throughout the vessel.

c. Each crewmember shall be given a written description of, and shall become familiar with, his/her emergency duties and shall become familiar with the vessel's emergency signals.

d. "Abandon ship/boat" and "person overboard" procedures shall include instructions for mustering personnel.

e. On all floating plant that have a regular crew or on which people are quartered, the following drills shall be held at least monthly during each shift (unless the vessel is required, under USCG regulations, to be drilled more frequently): abandon ship/boat drills, fire drills, and person overboard or rescue drills.

(1) The first set of drills shall be conducted within 24 hours of the vessel's occupancy or commencement of work.

(2) Where crews are employed or quartered at night, every fourth set of drills shall be at night; the first set of night drills shall be conducted within the first 2 weeks of the vessel's occupancy.

(3) Drills shall include, where appropriate, how to handle a pump shell or pipe rupture or failure within the hull (proper shutdown procedures, system containment, etc.) and how to handle leaks or failures of the hull or portions of it (what compartments to secure, how to handle power losses, pulling spuds to move to shallow water, etc.).

f. Person overboard or rescue drills shall be held at least monthly at boat yards, locks, dams, and other locations where marine rescue equipment is required.

g. Emergency lighting and power systems shall be operated and inspected at least monthly to ensure proper operation.

(1) Internal combustion engine driven emergency generators shall be operated under load for at least 2 hours each month.

(2) Storage batteries for emergency lighting and power systems shall be tested at least once every 2 months.

h. A record of all drills and emergency system checks, including any deficiencies noted in equipment and corrective action taken, shall be made in the station log.

19.A.05 Equipment requirements.

a. Fenders shall be provided to prevent damage and sparking and to provide safe areas for workers exposed to pinching situations caused by floating equipment.

b. Axes or other emergency cutting equipment shall be sharp and provided in accessible positions on all towing vessels for use such as freeing lines. On other floating plant (i.e., work barges, and floating cranes) emergency cutting equipment shall be provided in accessible positions.

c. Signal devices shall be provided on all vessels to give signals required by the navigation rules applicable to the waters on which the vessel is operated.

d. All controls requiring operation in cases of emergency (i.e., boiler stops, safety valves, power switches, fuel valves, alarms, and fire extinguishing systems) shall be located so that they are protected against accidental operation but are readily accessible in an emergency.

e. Electric lights used on or around gasoline and oil barges or other marine locations where a fire or explosion hazard exists shall be explosion-proof or approved as intrinsically safe.

f. General alarm systems shall be installed and maintained on all floating plant where it is possible for either a passenger or crewman to be out of sight or hearing from any other person.

(1) Where general alarm systems are used they shall be operated from the primary electrical system with standby batteries on trickle charge that will automatically furnish the required energy during an electrical-system failure.

(2) A sufficient number of signaling devices shall be placed on each deck so that they can be distinctly heard/seen above the normal background noise at any point on the deck.

(3) All signaling devices shall be so interconnected that actuation can occur from at least one strategic point on each deck.

g. Smoke alarms are required for all living quarters on floating plant; smoke alarms, if wired, should use the same electrical system as that of the electrical alarms.

h. For floating plant with internal combustion engines, marine quality listed CO monitors shall be installed and maintained in all enclosed occupied spaces (crew quarters, pilot houses, etc.).

i. All doors shall be capable of being opened from either side and provided with positive means to secure them in both the open and closed position.

j. Escape hatches and emergency exits shall be marked on both sides with letters, at least 1 in (2.5 cm) high, stating "EMERGENCY EXIT - KEEP CLEAR."

k. Each prime mover (engine, turbine, motor) driving a dredge pump shall be capable of being stopped by controls remote from the prime mover locations.

l. Shore power receptacles shall have a grounding conductor to prevent potential difference between the shore and the vessel.

m. All 120-, 208-, and 240-volt systems in toilet/shower spaces, galley, machinery spaces, weather deck, exterior, or within 3 ft (0.9 m) of any sink shall be grounded and fitted with Ground Fault Circuit Interrupter (GFCI) protection.

(1) Cord connected equipment used in any of the above areas shall be connected to an outlet with GFCI protection.

(2) Ground-fault protected receptacles shall be conspicuously marked "GFCI PROTECTED".

n. Where appropriate, vessels should have watertight compartments readily identified and properly maintained in a watertight condition (i.e., sealable doors in place and fully functional). Penetrations shall be maintained in a watertight condition.

o. All reciprocating, rotating and moving parts of winch gears and other equipment shall be properly guarded.

19.A.06 Fuel systems and fuel transfers. The provisions of the Oil Pollution Act of 1990, as amended, shall apply to floating plant operations as applicable.

a. Gauge glasses or try cocks shall not be installed on fuel tanks or lines unless they meet the requirements of 46 CFR 58.50-10.

b. A shutoff valve shall be installed at the fuel tank connection: arrangement shall be made for operating this valve from outside the compartment in which the tank is located and from outside the engine compartment and outside the house bulkheads at or above the weather deck of the vessel.

c. A shutoff valve shall be installed at the engine end of the fuel line unless the length of the supply pipe is 6 ft (1.8 m) or less.

d. All carburetors on gasoline engines shall be equipped with a backfire trap or flame arrestor.

e. All carburetors, except down-draft type, shall be provided with a drip pan, with flame screen, that is continuously emptied by suction from the intake manifold or by a waste tank.

f. Fuel and lubricant containers and tanks shall be diked, curbed or controlled by other means complying with USCG requirements to contain the tank contents in case of leakage in accordance with 46 CFR 98.30-15, and 33 CFR 155.320.

g. Fuel oil transfers for floating plant shall be in accordance with the provisions of USCG regulations, 33 CFR 155, and/or 33 CFR 156. For uninspected vessels, USCG regulations in 33 CFR 156.120 and 33 CFR 155.320 for fuel coupling devices and fuel oil discharge containment apply.

h. All decks, overheads, and bulkheads, serving as fuel oil tank boundaries shall indicate the tank boundary with contrasting paint and be labeled "FUEL OIL TANK - NO HOT WORK".

19.A.07 Safe practices.

a. Obstructing cables/lines that cross waterways between floating plant or between plant and mooring shall be clearly marked.

b. On floating plant where people are quartered, one person shall be on watch at all times to guard against fire and provide watch person service. In lieu of a watch person, an automatic fire detection and fire and emergency warning system(s) may be used.

c. Provisions shall be made to prevent accumulation of fuel and grease on floors and decks and in bilges.

d. Swimming and/or diving shall be prohibited for all personnel, except certified divers in the performance of their duties, unless necessary to prevent injury or loss of life.

e. Wading is permitted only when there are no severe underwater hazards such as sudden drop-offs, heavy surf above 3 ft (1 m), dangerous aquatic life, etc. Personnel wading shall wear an approved PFD and shall be monitored by personnel who are nearby and equipped to conduct a rescue if needed. Wading shall be discontinued when the person's feet cannot easily touch bottom, regardless of depth.

f. A person in the water shall be considered as a person overboard and appropriate action shall be taken.

g. When barriers or blanks are installed in piping systems as a lock-out procedure, positive means (such as protruding handles) shall be used to easily recognize their presence. Barriers shall be marked (including name of installer, name of inspector, and date of installation) and accounted for prior to installation and subsequent to removal.

h. Deck loading will be limited to safe capacity. Loads will be secured and holdbacks or rings will be provided to secure loose equipment during rough weather.

i. Deck openings and other fall hazards not addressed by Section 19.C shall be protected in accordance with Section 21.

j. Safeguards such as barriers, curbs, or other structures shall be provided to prevent front-end loaders, bulldozers, trucks, backhoes, track hoes, and similar operating equipment on floating equipment from falling into the water. Whenever this equipment is operating on deck, deck surfaces of floating plant shall remain above water and the entire bottom area of a floating plant shall remain submerged

k. Projection and tripping hazards shall be removed, identified with warning signs, or distinctly marked with safety yellow.

l. Deck cargo carried on fuel barges shall be placed on dunnage.

m. When two or more pieces of floating plant are being used as one unit, they shall be securely fastened together to prevent openings between them or the openings shall be covered or guarded.

n. When three or more floating plant are configured for stationary work, a competent person shall identify any openings between decks of stationary vessels or vessels and other structures that create fully enclosed water areas (duck ponds) into which personnel can fall. If such openings are detected, means shall be taken to protect personnel from the hazard.

(1) When practical, duck pond protection will consist of guardrails, nets or other physical barriers to prevent employees from falling into the openings.

(2) When physical barriers are not practical, ladders and life rings shall be installed in each enclosed water area to allow personnel to self-rescue. Ladders may be a rigid type or Jacob's ladder, and must be securely anchored to the vessel or structure. Life rings shall have a sufficient length of rope to allow them to float on the water surface and the rope shall be securely anchored to the vessel. The number and placement of ladders and life rings shall be sufficient so that the maximum swimming distance to them is no more than 25 ft (7.9 m). Ladders and life rings may be retracted during reconfiguration or movement of plant.

o. Anchor points shall be clearly identified and shall be inspected prior to applying a load or putting cables under tension. Anchor points not structurally sound shall be cut out, removed, and/or welded over to preclude usage. Visual checks and "all clear" warnings shall be made prior to tensioning cables.

p. Provisions shall be made to protect persons being transported by water from the elements.

q. Plant fleeting areas will be designated in which all idle plant shall be moored. Such areas shall have warning buoys, signs, and lights in prominent locations.

r. The Contractor or, for Government-conducted operations, the GDA, shall provide information to the local USCG Office identifying the marine activity and hazards.

s. Open or pelican hooks may be used for lifting anchor buoys.

t. Mechanical means such as securing pins shall be used to hold spuds safely in place before transiting from one site to another.

19.A.08 Work Inside Confined and Enclosed Spaces in Ships and Vessels. > *See Section 34.B.*

19.A.09 When there is a potential for marine activities to interfere with or damage utilities or other structures, including those underwater, a survey shall be conducted to identify the utilities or structures in the work area, analyze the potential for interference or damage, and recommend steps to be taken to prevent the interference or damage.

19.A.10 Ventilation.

a. Motor vessels or boats powered by internal combustion engines having electric spark ignition systems or having auxiliary engines of this type in cabins, compartments, or confined spaces shall be equipped with an exhaust fan(s) for ventilating engine space and bilges.

b. At least two ventilators fitted with fans capable of ventilating each machinery space and fuel tank compartment, including bilges, shall be provided to remove any flammable or explosive gases, except those vessels constructed with the greater portions of the bilges open or exposed to the natural atmosphere at all times.

➢Note: *this requirement does not apply to diesel engines.*

c. Other compartment spaces within a vessel, not covered in this Section, may be naturally vented.

d. Living spaces, including the galley, shall be adequately ventilated in a manner suitable to the purpose of the space.

e. For launches and motorboats having diesel power plants not equipped with fans, ventilating shall be by natural draft through permanently open inlet and outlet ducts extending into the bilges. Inlet and exhaust ducts shall be equipped with cowls or exhaust heads.

f. For launches, motorboats (survey boats), and skiffs having deck-mounted internal combustion engines (such as generators, jigger pumps) and not equipped with fans, exhaust piping shall be located away from personnel spaces to minimize CO infiltration in the work space.

g. Vent and ventilator requirements.

(1) Fans shall be rated for Class I hazardous locations and located as remotely from potential explosive areas as practical. > *See Section 11.H.*

(2) The vent intake shall extend to within 1 ft (0.3 m) of the bottom of the compartment.

(3) Means shall be provided for stopping fans in ventilation systems serving machinery components and for closing doorways, ventilators, chases, and annular spaces around tunnels and other openings from outside these spaces in case of fire.

h. Engines shall not be started until the engine space and bilges have been ventilated to remove fuel vapor.

19.A.11 The most current, pertinent information published by the USCG regarding aids to navigation shall be maintained aboard self-propelled vessels 26 ft (7.9 m) or more in length.

19.B Access.

19.B.01 General.

a. Means of access shall be properly secured, guarded, and maintained free of slipping and tripping hazards. > *See Section 24.*

b. Non-slip surfaces shall be provided on working decks, stair treads, ship ladders, platforms, catwalks, and walkways, particularly on the weather side of doorways opening on deck.

c. Double rung or flat tread type Jacob's ladders shall be used only when no safer form of access is practical.

When in use, they shall hang without slack and be properly secured.

d. Vertical ladders shall comply with ASTM F1166-95a.

e. Ladders shall not be climbed by more than one person at a time between the same set of rails.

19.B.02 Access to/from vessels.

a. Safe means for boarding or leaving a floating plant shall be provided and guarded to prevent persons from falling or slipping thereon. Walking on rip-rap should be avoided where practical.

b. A stairway, ladder, ramp, gangway, personnel hoist or other safe means of access shall be provided at personnel points of access with breaks of 19 in (48.2 cm) or more in elevation.

c. Ramps for access of equipment and vehicles to or between vessels shall be of adequate strength, be provided with sideboards, and be well maintained.

d. Gangways and ramps shall be:

(1) Secured at one end by at least one point on each side with lines or chains to prevent overturning;

(2) Supported at the other end in such a manner to carry them and their normal load during use in the event they slide off their supports;

(3) Placed at an angle no greater than that recommended by the manufacturer; and

(4) Provided with a standard guardrail (toe boards are optional depending on their usefulness and the hazard involved).

19.B.03 Access on vessels.

a. Vertical access shall be provided between various decks by means of stairs, ramps, or vertical ladders installed in accordance with ASTM F1166.

b. Employees shall not be permitted to pass fore and aft, over, or around deck loads unless there is a safe passage.

c. If cargo or materials are stored on deck of barges, scows, floats, etc., the outboard edge shall not be used as a passageway unless at least 2 ft (0.6 m) of clearance is maintained.

d. Vessel loads shall be limited so that access and passageways in use will remain above the waterline. Decks and passageways shall not be used for access if submerged or subject to constant breaking waves, except in an emergency.

19.B.04 Emergency access.

a. Vessels, except those easily boarded from the water, shall be equipped with:

(1) At least one portable or permanent ladder of sufficient length to allow a person to self-rescue by boarding the ladder from the water, and

(2) Other methods or means designed to assist in the rescue of an incapacitated person overboard.

b. Two means of escape shall be provided for normal work, assembly, sleeping, and messing areas on floating plants.

c. Means of access shall be maintained as safe and functional.

19.B.05 Access on floating pipelines.

a. Floating pipelines used as access ways shall be equipped with a walkway and handrail on at least one side.

b. Walkways shall be at least 20 in (50.8 cm) wide and anchored to the pipeline.

c. PFDs must be worn at all times by anyone on pipelines. > See Section 05.J.

d. When walkways and handrails are not provided (i.e., the pipeline is not intended for access), the pipeline shall be barricaded at both ends to prevent access by any person.

19.C Marine Fall Protection Systems.

19.C.01 On decks or work surfaces 6 ft (1.8 m) or more above the main deck or 6 ft or more above adjacent vessel decks, docks, or other hard surfaces, Railing Type A or Type B, as described in Section 19.E., or bulwarks, coamings, or other structures meeting the height and strength requirements of these railing systems shall be provided except as excluded in Sections 19.C.03 and 19.C.04.

19.C.02 Deck edge toe boards not less than 3.5 in (8.8 cm) high for Type A and 2 in (5 cm) high for Type B railings shall be provided when the railings are used for fall protection. Toe boards shall meet the strength requirements in Section 21.F.01.f. Scuppers and/ or drainage holes may be installed as needed as long as the top edge of the toeboard is intact and the strength requirements are retained.

19.C.03 Personal fall protection systems meeting the requirements of Section 21.I may be used when railing systems are not installed.

19.C.04 Railing systems and personal fall protection systems are not considered feasible on the main deck of vessels that perform duty cycle material loading and unloading operations from barges, scows or other vessels alongside.

19.D Main Deck Perimeter Protection. New vessels built or purchased for USACE use shall meet these requirements upon delivery or prior to first use.

19.D.01 Main deck perimeter protection systems are intended to provide protection against falling overboard. Main deck perimeter protection is required on all manned vessels, except where excluded in Section 19.D.05. Unmanned vessels do not require perimeter protection, however, fall protection shall be provided where the vessel configuration and operation exposes personnel to falls onto a hard surface from vertical distances greater than 6 ft (1.8 m). The design parameters for the different types of main deck railing systems listed in this Section are in Section 19.E unless otherwise noted.

a. Manned vessels are vessels that operate with crews, or quartered personnel, or that have work areas that are occupied by assigned personnel during normal work activities.

b. Unmanned vessels are typically those that carry cargo such as materials, supplies, equipment, or liquids, and do not have personnel on board except during loading and unloading and during short term operations such as tie-down, inspections, etc.

19.D.02 Manned vessels over 26 ft (7.9 m) in length operating in unprotected or partially protected waters (as defined in 46 CFR) shall have Type B Railings provided around the deck edge, except where excluded in Section 19.D.05.

19.D.03 Manned vessels over 26 ft (7.9 m) in length operating in rivers or protected waters shall have Type B or Type C Railings provided around the deck edge, except where excluded in Section 19.D.05.

19.D.04 Type D Grab rails shall be provided on all manned vessels in the following instances:

a. On deckhouses or other similar permanent structures more than 48 in (1.2 m) from deck edge rail systems;

b. On deck houses or similar permanent structures that are within 8 ft (2.5 m) of the deck edge in areas where the deck edge rail has been omitted or may be

temporarily removed in accordance with Section 19.D.05.

19.D.05 The following are main deck areas where perimeter protection may be omitted or temporarily removed:

a. Deck perimeter rails may be omitted from deck work areas specifically intended for line handling, working over the side of the vessel, load handling operations and designated boarding areas. Railings in these areas may obstruct work or access and present additional hazards such as pinch points against railings. Such deck edge areas may include those for line handling, fleeting scows, mooring vessels, towing, pile driving activities, and handling or placing of construction materials and equipment pipelines, and anchors.

b. Deck Perimeter rails may be omitted from main deck areas where the overall walkway width is less than 2 ft (0.6 m) between deck structures/permanent equipment and the deck edge.

c. Removable perimeter rail sections may be installed in areas where activities such as working over the side of the vessel or loading operations are not normally performed. These rails shall be maintained in place when vessel operations do not include activity in these areas or during periods of tie-up or inactivity.

19.D.06 When deck-edge perimeter protection is not present, standard operating procedures, AHAs, or other documents shall be developed to address the hazards involved. These documents shall be reviewed by all crew during initial orientation and at regular intervals afterward. The following operational procedures shall be followed:

a. PFD's must be worn by personnel in areas where deck perimeter protection is not present. Such areas may be used by crew to transit or access areas of the boat, but when doing so, all other requirements of this Section must be met. Areas where railings are removed shall be blocked off from access by a suitable barrier, or shall be clearly marked as PFD- required areas by signage, deck markings, or other means;

b. Continuous sight and verbal/radio contact shall be maintained between personnel in the non-protected deck perimeter areas and the vessel operator or a designated crew member who is in sight and verbal/radio contact with the operator, and who will monitor the workers in the area;

c. A safety skiff or equivalent rescue vessel shall be readily available throughout the duration of these activities in accordance with Section 05.K.

19.D.07 Boats with length 26 ft (7.9 m) or less shall be provided with integrated combinations of two or more of the below listed items to provide continuous perimeter protection around the vessel: Cockpits; Coamings; Handholds; Toe Rails; Life Rails; Deck Rails; Stern Rails and Bow Rails. The installations shall be in accordance with either ABYC Standards or ISO Standard 15085, as demonstrated by a manufacturer's certificate, label or other documentation.

19.E Marine Railing Types.

19.E.01 Allowable types of railings on vessels (A, B, C, & D) are identified below. Specific requirements for the vessel types and areas where each may be used are delineated in Sections 19.G and 19.H. > *See Appendix F.*

19.E.02 Railing Type A: Two-Tier Rigid Fall Protection Rail. This railing is comprised of rigid vertical stanchions and two rigid horizontal tiers in accordance with Section 21.F.01. Minimum top rail height is 42 in +/- 3 in (106.6 cm +/- 7.6 cm) and the lower horizontal tier is at half height.

19.E.03 Railing Type B: Three-Tier Marine Rigid or Tensioned Railing. This railing is comprised of rigid vertical stanchions and three rigid or tensioned horizontal tiers. The following parameters apply:

a. Clear spacing between tiers shall be no greater than 9 in (22.8 cm), 15 in (38 cm) and 15-in respectively. The 9-in space is closest to the deck surface. Minimum height from deck to the top tier may not be less than 39 in (99 cm).

b. The 9-in, 15-in and 15-in tier spacing above may not be exceeded.

c. The bottom tier may be omitted in way of deck fittings or in order to facilitate line handling. The space resulting from the removed lower tier may not extend more than 2 ft (0.6 m) beyond either side of the deck fitting.

d. Vertical stanchions may be pipe or structural sections. Horizontal tiers may be constructed from rigid (pipe or structural sections) or non-rigid (wire rope or chain) components, or from combinations of these components. Non-rigid tiers must be tensioned with turnbuckles or similar components.

e. Railings may be either fixed or removable in sections. All vertical stanchions must be adequate to withstand a 200 lbs (60.9 kg) load applied horizontally at the top of the stanchion. Stanchion spacing may not exceed 8 ft (2.4 m).

f. Pipe or structural section rail components shall be sized appropriately to meet the performance criteria of Section 21.F.01.

g. Chain or wire rope together with all connecting fittings shall have minimum breaking strength of 4,000 lbs (1814.3 kg).

h. Chain or wire rope horizontal tiers shall be tensioned so that:

(1) There is no slack;

(2) Sag does not exceed 1/4 in (.62 cm) at any point between stanchions, and

(3) The lowest point from deck to the top of the upper rail may not be less than 39 in (1 m) at any point between the stanchions. Tensioned railing tiers shall not deflect more than 1 in (2.5 cm) under a load of 200 lbs (60.9 kg).

i. Solid bulwarks or coamings providing equal perimeter protection to a height of 39 in (1 m) may also be provided. Bulwarks may be constructed of structural plate and shapes. Bulwarks must meet all strength/deflection/open spacing requirements presented above for railings.

19.E.04 Railing Type C: Non-Tensioned Railings and Flexible or Swing-Away Railings shall consist of rigid vertical stanchions with horizontal non-tensioned chain, wire rope or rigid tiers that clip to the verticals.

a. Non-Tensioned Railings shall consist of horizontal tiers constructed from chain, wire rope, pipe or structural sections or combinations of these components. Vertical stanchions shall be pipe or structural sections. Vertical support spacing shall not exceed 8 ft (2.4 m).

b. Flexible or Swing-Away Rails shall consist of chain or wire rope tensioned vertical support lines with non-tensioned chain, wire rope or clip-on rigid horizontal tiers. Vertical support line spacing shall not exceed 6 ft (1.8 m).

c. Pipe or structural section rail components shall be sized appropriately to meet the performance criteria of Section 21.F.01. Chain or wire rope together with all connecting fittings shall have minimum breaking strength of 4,000 lbs (1800 kg).

d. For Non-Tensioned Railings and Flexible or Swing-Away Railings, sag of horizontal tiers shall not exceed 3 in (10 cm) between vertical supports.

e. Non-Tensioned Railings and Flexible or Swing-Away Railings shall be configured with four or more horizontal tiers. The number of horizontal tiers shall be sufficient to meet the following requirements:

(1) Effective clear spacing between the deck and bottom tier shall be no greater than 9 in (22.8 cm).

(2) Effective clear spacing between all tiers above the bottom tier shall be no greater than 15 in (38.1 cm).

(3) Effective minimum height from deck to the top tier may not be less than 39 in (1 m).

f. The effective tier spacing identified above includes the effect of the increased spacing associated with sag in the tiers, applied either up or down. Clear spacing measurements shall be made with the railing tiers spread to form the largest opening.

g. Railing height is reduced by the amount of sag in the tiers. Railing minimum height shall be measured at the lowest point in the rail.

h. The bottom tier may be omitted in way of deck fittings or in order to facilitate line handling. The space caused by the removed lower tier may not extend more than 2 ft (0.6 m) beyond either side of the deck fitting.

i. The top tier may not deflect to a height less than 39 in (1 m) above the deck under a force of 200 lbs (60.9 kg), applied vertically. In addition, the top tier may not deflect more than 12 in (30.4 cm) horizontally under a force of 200 lbs applied horizontally.

j. Tensioning springs in the vertical support lines, if provided, must be of the compression with drawbar type.

19.E.05 Railing Type D: Grab Rails are railing sections mounted to deckhouse sides or to the sides of other permanent structures.

a. Grab rail height shall match the height of the deck top rail/tier. Where there is no top rail near the grab rail, grab rail height shall be 39 in (1 m).

b. Grab rail strength shall be adequate to withstand a 200 lb (60.9 kg) load applied in any direction.

c. Grab rails shall be sized dimensionally comparable to 1.5 in (3.8 cm) pipe. Clear distance between the rail and house side may not be less than 3 in (7.6 cm).

19.F Launches, Motorboats and Skiffs.

19.F.01 Crew requirements.

a. In the following circumstances a qualified employee shall be assigned to assist with deck duties:

(1) When extended trips including overnight trips are made from the work site;

(2) When conditions of navigation make it hazardous for an operator to leave the wheel while underway;

(3) When operations being performed, other than tying-in, require the handling of lines;

(4) When operating at night or during inclement weather;

(5) When towing; or

(6) While a vessel is transporting crew or passengers.

b. A qualified employee is any individual who has established, to the satisfaction of the operator of the vessel that he/she is physically and mentally capable of adequately performing the deck duties to which he/she may be assigned.

19.F.02 Personnel and cargo requirements.

a. The maximum number of personnel and weight that can safely be transported shall be posted on all launches, motorboats, and skiffs. The number of personnel (including crew) shall not exceed the number of PFDs aboard.

b. Each boat shall have sufficient room, freeboard, and stability to safely carry the cargo and number of persons allowed with consideration given to the weather and water conditions in which it will be operated.

c. Launches, motorboats and skiffs less than 20 ft (6 m) in length shall meet 33 CFR 183 requiring level floatation after flooding or swamping.

d. All open cabin launches or motorboats shall be equipped with "kill (dead man) switches".

19.F.03 Fire protection.

a. The minimum number and rating of fire extinguishers that shall be carried on all launches and motorboats, including outboards, are shown in Table 19-1:

b. All launches and motorboats having gasoline or liquid petroleum gas power plants or equipment in cabins, compartments, or confined spaces shall be equipped with a built-in automatic CO_2 fire extinguishing system meeting the requirements of 46 CFR 25.30-15.

TABLE 19-1

Fire Extinguisher Requirements for Launches/Motorboats

Length	Extinguisher
Less than 26 ft (7.9 m)	One 1-A:10-B:C
26 ft (7.9 m) or more	Two 1-A:10-B:C

19.F.04 Float Plans. Float plans shall be prepared by the operator of a launch or motorboat when engaged in surveying, patrolling, or inspection activities that are remote and are expected to take longer than 4 hours or when the operator is traveling alone. The plan shall be filed with the boat operator's supervisor and shall contain the following, as a minimum:

a. Vessel information (make/model or local identifier);

b. Personnel on-board;

c. Activity to be performed;

d. Expected time of departure, route, and time of return;

e. Means of communication (adequate means of communication shall be provided).

19.F.05 All motorboat operators shall complete and document the following training:

a. A boating safety course meeting the criteria of the USCG Auxiliary, National Association of Safe Boating Law Administrators (NASBLA), or equivalent;

b. Motorboat handling training, based on the type of boats they will operate, provided by qualified instructors (in-house or other). Operators must pass a written and operational test;

c. Current USCG licensed personnel are exempt from the boating safety training, but they shall complete the written exam and operational test;

d. Government employees shall complete a USACE-approved 24-hour initial boating safety course and refresher as prescribed in ER 385-1-91.

19.F.06 USACE launches, motorboats, skiffs and boat trailers shall be inspected, tested, repaired and maintained in accordance with ER 385-1-91 and the manufacturer's recommendations.

a. Inspection shall be conducted by a qualified person (QP), documented and retained for a period of 5 years.

b. Boats and boat trailers shall be inspected:

(1) Prior to each use, and

(2) Periodically, in accordance with manufacturer's recommendations and USACE requirements.

19.G Dredging.

19.G.01 Prior to repair or maintenance on the pump, suction or discharge lines below the water line, or within the hull, the ladder (or drag arm) shall be raised (above the waterline) and positively secured. This provision is in addition to the normal securing of hoisting machinery. Blank or block plates shall also be set in suction or discharge lines as appropriate.

19.G.02 Dredge pipelines that are floating or supported on trestles shall display appropriate lights at night and in periods of restricted visibility in accordance with USCG regulations and 33 CFR 88.15.

19.G.03 Submerged and floating dredge pipeline.

a. Submerged pipeline and any anchor securing the pipeline shall rest on the channel bottom where a pipeline crosses a navigation channel. The depth of the submerged pipeline will be provided to the USCG for publication.

(1) Whenever buoyant or semi-buoyant pipeline is used, the dredge operator will assure that the pipeline remains fully submerged and on the bottom. Whenever it is necessary to raise the pipeline, proper clearances shall be made and maintained and the entire length of the pipeline will be adequately marked.

(2) Submerged pipelines shall be marked in accordance with local USCG requirements and as approved by the GDA.

(a) Unless otherwise specified by the USCG, submerged pipelines are considered to require special marks and shall have a USCG-approved flashing yellow light.

(b) Indicators, such as signs or buoys that state "DANGER SUBMERGED PIPELINE" will be placed at the beginning and end of the pipeline. In addition, indicators are required

(c) Beginning in areas which reduce the charted depth by more than 10%, and, as a minimum, every 1000 ft (304.8 m) to clearly warn of the pipeline length and course.

(d) If barges or other vessels are used to anchor the beginning and/or end of the submerged pipeline, they shall be lighted in accordance with 33 CFR 88.13.

(e) Within a navigation channel, each end of the pipeline shall be identified with a regulatory marker buoy.

(f) Lengths of submerged pipeline located outside of the navigation channel, which reduce the charted depth by more than 10 percent, will be identified with high visibility buoys marked with 360 degree visibility retro-reflective tape, such as orange neoprene buoys, placed at an interval not to exceed 500 ft (152.4 m) to clearly show the pipeline length and course.

(3) Routine inspections of the submerged pipe shall be conducted to ensure anchorage.

(4) All anchors and related material shall be removed when the submerged pipe is removed.

b. Floating pipeline is any pipeline that is not anchored on the channel bottom. Pipelines shall not be permitted to fluctuate between the water surface and the channel bottom.

c. Pipelines shall be marked with the owner's name for positive identification in the event of loss (adrift) or damage to vessels operating in the area.

19.G.04 Dredges shall be designed so that a failure or rupture of any of the dredge pump components, including dredge pipe, shall not cause the dredge to sink. Data or plans supporting this capability must be available to the GDA upon request.

19.G.05 Mobilization, demobilization, and relocation of dredges, support barges, support tenders, tugs, and heavy equipment shall be by qualified persons under the direct supervision of a responsible individual.

19.G.06 Hopper dredges shall offer a safe means and process to load and unload personnel.

19.G.07 Any dredge that has a dredge pump below the waterline shall have a bilge alarm or shutdown interface.

19.G.08 Covers of "stone boxes" shall be secured with at least two positive means when the boxes are working under positive pressure.

19.G.09 Dredge disposal sites.

a. Drinking water. An adequate supply of drinking water shall be provided at all dredge disposal sites. Cool water shall be provided during hot weather. Portable drinking dispensers shall comply with Section 2 of this manual.

b. Toilet facilities. Toilet facilities shall be provided in accordance with and meet the requirements of Section 2 of this manual.

c. Medical and first-aid requirements. All disposal area watchmen shall be certified in first aid and CPR in accordance with Section 03. At least one 16-unit first-aid kit complying with ANSI Z308.1 shall be provided onsite at all times. The first-aid kit shall be protected from the environment.

d. Amphibious excavators will only be operated in accordance with the manufacturer's operating instructions. A copy of the operator's manual will be readily available on the equipment.

e. Lighting. Lighting shall be provided as required by Section 7 of this manual. The minimum lighting level in the vicinity of the disposal site shelter (dump shack) shall be 5 foot-candles.

f. Disposal site shelters (Dump Shacks).

(1) Disposal site shelters (dump shacks) shall be provided as a means of protecting personnel from inclement weather and environmental hazards. The shelter shall be of a size to accommodate a minimum of four workers. The shelter shall have adequate seating for the workers, heating equipment, water cooler, and space to store all hands tools and personal protective equipment. The shelter shall be weather tight with operable windows and screens for ventilation.

(2) All electrical systems shall comply with the NEC. All flexible electrical cords shall be hard usage or extra-hard usage. All frayed, patched, oil-soaked or worn shall be taken out of service.

(3) Portable generators used for lighting shall comply with the requirements of Section 11 of this manual and shall be located downwind of shelters.

(4) Fossil fuel heating is prohibited.

(5) All rigid insulation shall be covered with a non-combustible material to prevent accidental ignition.

(6) All shelters shall be equipped with a minimum of one multi-purpose fire extinguisher.

19.H Scows and Barges.

19.H.01 Scows dumping in open ocean waters should be equipped with remote opening devices to preclude the transfer of personnel between the vessels.

19.H.02 A safe means for transferring personnel between the towing vessels and scow shall be provided in accordance with Section 19.B.02.

19.H.03 The Contractor shall identify general and site-specific adverse weather and sea conditions (e.g., currents) under which the towing of scows or cargo barges is prohibited.

19.H.04 All barges and scows that are used as deck cargo barges shall comply with 46 CFR 174.010 through 174.020 for intact stability of deck cargo barges.

19.H.05 Personal fall protection devices or other fall protection as listed in Sections 21 and 19.C shall be used on all scows and open barges to prevent personnel transiting between the stern and bow of the vessel from falling into the hopper or falling off the side of the vessel to structures (e.g. dock, vessels) located 6 ft (1.8 m) or more below.

19.I Navigation Locks and Vessel Locking.

19.I.01 Smoking, open flames, or other ignition sources shall be prohibited on lock structures within 50 ft (15.2 m) of vessels containing hazardous cargos of flammable or other hazardous materials ("Red Flag" vessels) during approach and lockage.

a. When construction, maintenance, and other non-navigational related activities are taking place on or adjacent to the lock structure, the Lock Master will relay information to supervisory personnel in these activities regarding the approach and passage of Red Flag vessels.

b. The Lock Master or Work Crew supervisor may suspend hot work at their discretion during the approach and passage of Red Flag vessels.

c. Prior to the start of work on these activities, the Work Crew Supervisor will establish safe zones that maintain at least the minimum 50 ft (15.2 m) required distance between Red Flag vessels and sources of ignition such as hot work and smoking areas.

(1) The minimum distance shall be calculated vertically and horizontally throughout a lock chamber when the chamber is pumped out for maintenance.

(2) These zones shall be marked, barricaded, or otherwise designated so personnel can easily distinguish them.

(3) The location of and restricted activities within these zones shall be included in the activity AHA and discussed with workers prior to start of work.

19.I.02 Pleasure and commercial recreational craft shall not be locked through a lock chamber with Red Flag vessels.

19.I.03 Lockage Of Red Flag Vessels.

a. Simultaneous lockage of two Red Flag Vessels or tows or simultaneous lockage of another vessel or tow carrying non-dangerous cargoes and vessel or tow carrying dangerous cargoes, shall not be permitted when river traffic in the approach to a lock is light.

b. When the river approach to a lock is congested, simultaneous lockage of the aforementioned vessels or tows, other than pleasure craft, shall be permitted provided:

(1) The first vessel or tow entering and the last vessel or tow exiting are secured before the other enters or leaves;

(2) Any vessel or tow carrying dangerous cargoes is not leaking; and

(3) All masters involved have agreed to the joint use of the lock chamber.

19.I.04 Vessels with flammable or highly hazardous cargo will be passed separately from all other vessels. Hazardous materials are described in 49 CFR 171; flammable materials are defined in the National Fire Code of the NFPA.

THIS PAGE INTENTIONALLY LEFT BLANK

SECTION 20 Pressurized Equipment and Systems

Table of Contents

20.A General

20.A.01 Inspections and Tests - General.

a. Pressurized equipment and systems shall be inspected and performance tested before being placed in service AND after any repair or modification.

b. <u>Frequency</u>. Unless State or local codes specify more frequent inspection, temporary or portable pressurized equipment and systems shall be inspected at intervals of not more than 6 months and permanent installations shall be inspected at least annually.

c. <u>New pressure vessels.</u> Inspections of pressure vessels prior to being placed in service shall be in accordance with the ASME "*Boiler and Pressure Vessel Code*".

d. <u>In-service pressure vessels</u>. Inspections of pressure vessels shall be in accordance with the National Board of Boiler and Pressure Vessel Inspectors (NBBI), "*National Board Inspection Code.*"

e. <u>Qualified Inspectors.</u> Inspections and tests will be performed by personnel qualified in accordance with the ASME Code or the NBBI.

20.A.02 Hydrostatic testing <u>of In-Service Pressure Vessels</u>.

a. Unless otherwise specified by State or local codes, hydrostatic testing of <u>in-service</u>, unfired pressured vessels shall be performed:

<u>(1)</u> After any repairs or modifications <u>that may affect the integrity of the system, or</u> <u>its ability to maintain stored pressure, as determined by the qualified inspector, and</u>

<u>(2)</u> In accordance with the manufacturer's recommendations, and/or a qualified inspector's recommendations after consultation with the manufacturer, which may include:

<u>(a)</u> When vessels are installed;

<u>(b)</u> When vessels are placed in service after lay-up;

<u>(c)</u> Every 3 years, (starting at the time of installation);

<u>(d)</u> If the vessel shows any rust or other deterioration; and/or

<u>(e)</u> When conditions found during inspections warrant tests.

b. The following unfired vessels are exempt from this requirement:

(1) Vessels designed for a maximum allowable pressure not exceeding 15 psi (103.4 kPa);

(2) Vessels having an internal volume of 5 ft^3 (0.14 m^3) or less and a maximum pressure of 100 psi (689.4 kPa);

(3) Compression tanks containing water under pressure not exceeding 100 psi (689.4 kPa) and temperatures not exceeding 200°F (93.3°C);

(4) Compression tanks containing water and fitted with a permanent air charging line subject to pressures not exceeding 15 psi (103.4 kPa) and temperatures not exceeding 200°F (93.3°C);

(5) Fire extinguishers. > *See Section 9.*

(6) For vessels with inspection doors (such as oil-filled (governor) pressure tanks), hydrostatic tests need only be <u>performed on</u> repaired, modified, or deteriorated tanks. Inspections to determine deterioration will be made every 2 years for external condition and every 4 years for internal condition.

20.A.03 Records of the inspections and tests shall be available for review on request. A certificate shall be posted and maintained near the vessel controls prior to operation of the equipment.

20.A.04 Testing using Pressurized Gases/Air.

a. Tests for structural integrity or leaks using pressurized gases, such as air, are prohibited, except for:

(1) Testing of bulk petroleum, oil, and lubricant (POL) storage tanks under API standards, or

(2) Testing when permitted by all applicable manufacturers' specifications or when specified by an applicable code.

b. Testing with pressurized air or gases must be conducted within the limits of the specific codes or standards specified by the manufacturer's recommendations using detailed test procedures that have been prepared by a Competent Person (CP), submitted <u>to</u> and accepted by the GDA. A CP shall be responsible for supervision of the testing procedures and all workers performing the testing shall be knowledgeable of the procedures, hazards and controls. Quality assurance/control measures shall assure strict enforcement of all requirements.

c. If interim or final acceptance testing is anticipated to occur 2 or more months after the initial pipe or system installation preparatory meeting, a supplemental preparatory meeting shall be held immediately prior to the testing to review the test procedures and AHA.

20.A.05 Any pressurized equipment or system found to be in an unsafe operating condition shall be tagged "UNSAFE PRESSURIZED SYSTEM - DO NOT USE" at the controls and its use shall be prohibited until the unsafe conditions have been corrected.

20.A.06 Pressurized equipment and systems shall be operated and maintained only by qualified, designated personnel.

20.A.07 The normal operating pressure of pressurized equipment and systems shall not exceed the design pressure.

20.A.08 No safety appliance or device shall be removed or made ineffective, except for making immediate repairs or adjustments, and then only after the pressure has been relieved and the power shut off using proper lockout/tagout procedures. > *See Section 12.*

20.A.09 Repairs or adjustments to equipment or systems under pressure require a written safe clearance procedure.

20.A.10 The discharge from safety valves, relief valves, and blowoffs shall be located so that it is not a hazard to personnel.

20.A.11 Master valves and controls shall be either located or equipped to permit operation from the floor level or they shall be provided with safe access.

20.A.12 A pressure gauge shall be provided on all pressurized equipment and systems and shall be in good operational condition.

20.A.13 Safety and relief valves shall be provided on all pressurized equipment and systems.

a. A safety relief valve setting not more than 10% over working pressure is recommended. In no case shall the safety relief valve setting be higher than the maximum allowable pressure of the receiver or the system.

b. No valve shall be placed between the pressure vessel or generating equipment and a safety or relief valve or between the safety or relief valve and the atmosphere.

c. Adjustments and settings of safety relief valves must be made by a qualified mechanic with equipment

designed for valve adjustment. Valves shall be sealed after adjustment.

d. In the event that the pressure registers above the maximum allowable working pressure on the gauge without the safety or relief valve operating, the pressure gauge shall be checked immediately. If such check indicates that the safety or relief valve is inoperative, the equipment shall be removed from service until the safety or relief valve has been adjusted or replaced.

20.A.14 Piping shall meet requirements of the ASME B31.

20.A.15 Pressurized manual equipment, subject to whipping or rotation if released, shall be provided with an automatic shut-off or control of the dead-man type.

20.A.16 Except where automatic shutoff valves are used, safety lashings or suitable double action locking devices shall be used at connections to machines of high pressure hose lines and between high pressure hose lines.

20.A.17 Connections with high pressure hoses must be secured with a safety lashing/whip check:

a. Safety lashings shall consist of two metal hose clamps connected by a flexible lacing: the metal hose clamps shall be attached to the hose ends separate from the quick makeup connection;

b. The flexible lacing shall be suitably strong cables, chains, or wires. Wires or pins through the quick makeup connection are not acceptable for use as safety lashings.

20.A.18 All pressurized cylinders, actuating booms, outriggers, or other load supporting appliances shall be equipped with pilot check valves, holding valves, or positive mechanical locks to prevent movement in case of failure in the pressure system. Replacement of pressure system fittings shall be with new parts equivalent to the manufacturer's standards.

20.B Compressed Air and Gas Systems.

20.B.01 Standards.

a. Air receivers shall be constructed in accordance with the ASME "*Code for Unfired Pressure Vessels.*"

b. All safety valves used shall be constructed, installed, tested, and maintained in accordance with the ASME "*Code for Unfired Pressure Vessels.*"

20.B.02 Access and guarding.

a. Compressors and related equipment shall be located to provide safe access to all parts of the equipment for operation, maintenance, and repairs.

b. Safety appliances, such as valves, indicating devices, and controlling devices, shall be constructed, located, and installed so that they cannot be readily rendered inoperative by any means, including the elements.

20.B.03 Air hose, pipes, valves, filters, and other fittings shall be pressure rated by the manufacturer and this pressure shall not be exceeded. Defective hose shall be removed from service.

20.B.04 Hose shall not be laid over ladders, steps, scaffolds, or walkways to create a tripping hazard.

20.B.05 Compressed air for cleaning.

a. The use of compressed air for blowing dirt from hands, face, or clothing is prohibited.

b. Compressed air shall not be used for other cleaning purposes except where reduced to less than 30 psi (206.8 kPa) and then only with effective chip guarding and PPE (face shield and safety glasses). This 30 psi requirement does not apply for concrete forms, mill scale, and similar cleaning purposes.

20.B.06 When used on tools and equipment such as track drills, all airlines exceeding 0.5 in (1.2 cm) inside diameter shall have a safety device at the source of supply or branch line to reduce pressure in case of hose failure.

20.B.07 Governors.

a. A speed governor, independent of the unloaders, shall be installed on all air compressors except those driven by electrical induction or electrical synchronized motors.

b. If the air compressor is engine or turbine driven, an auxiliary control to the governor shall be installed to prevent racing when the unloader operates.

20.B.08 Every air compressor shall automatically stop its air-compressing operation before the discharge pressure exceeds the maximum working pressure allowable on the weakest portion of the system.

a. If this automatic mechanism is electrically operated, the actuating device shall be so designed and constructed that the electrical contact or contacts cannot lock or fuse in a position that will cause the compressor to continue its operation.

b. An air bypass and alarm may be used as an alternative.

20.B.09 Provisions shall be made to exclude flammable materials and toxic gases, vapors, or dusts from the compressor and compressor intake and to prevent steam, water, or waste being blown or drawn into a compressor intake.

20.B.10 No valve shall be installed in the air intake pipe to an air compressor with an atmospheric intake.

20.B.11 The air discharge piping from the compressor to the air receiver shall be at least as large as the discharge opening on the air compressor.

20.B.12 A stop valve shall be installed between the air receiver and each piece of stationary utilization equipment at a point convenient to the operator, and a stop valve shall be installed at each outlet to which an air hose may be attached.

20.B.13 If a stop valve is installed between the compressor and the receiver, spring-loaded safety valves shall be installed between the air compressor and the stop valve.

a. The capacity of safety valves shall be sufficient to limit pressure in the air discharge piping to 10% above the working pressure of the piping.

b. Stop valves should be of the gate type. If a globe valve is used, it shall be installed so that the pressure is under the seat and that the valve will not trap condensation.

20.B.14 Provisions shall be made in compressed air and gas systems for expansion and contraction and to counteract pulsation and vibration.

20.B.15 Piping shall be equipped with traps or other means for removing liquid from the lines.

20.B.16 Air discharge piping shall be installed to eliminate possible oil pockets.

20.B.17 Installation and location of air receivers.

a. Air receivers shall be installed so that all drains, hand holes, and manholes are accessible.

b. Air receivers should be supported with sufficient clearance to permit a complete external inspection and to avoid corrosion of external surfaces.

c. Air receivers shall not be buried underground or located in inaccessible places.

d. The receiver should be located to keep the discharge pipe as short as possible.

e. The receiver should be located in a cool place to facilitate condensation of moisture and oil vapors.

20.B.18 A drain valve shall be installed at the lowest point of every air receiver for the removal of accumulated oil and water.

20.B.19 Automatic traps may be installed in addition to drain valves.

20.B.20 The drain valve on the air receiver shall be opened and the receiver drained often enough to prevent the accumulation of excessive liquid in the receiver.

20.B.21 No tool change or repair work shall be done until the stop valve in the air line supplying the equipment is closed.

20.B.22 Soapy water or any suitable non-toxic, non-flammable solution may be used for cleaning the system.

20.B.23 Hose and hose connections used for connecting compressed air to utilization equipment shall be designed for the pressure and service to which they are subjected and utilized in accordance with the manufacturer's specifications.

20.C Boilers and Systems.

20.C.01 Provisions of the ASME "*Boiler and Pressure Vessel Code*" shall apply in the construction, operation, maintenance, and inspection of steam boilers and pressure vessels.

20.C.02 Inspection.

a. Inspections shall be made to assure that all safety devices affecting operation of the firing equipment are installed in such a location that they cannot be isolated from the heat source by the closing of a valve.

b. Boilers that have undergone major structural repairs or that have been relocated during the 12 calendar months for which certification has been made shall be re-inspected and a new certificate posted before being put into operation.

20.C.03 When any boiler is being placed in service or restored to service after repairs to control circuits or safety devices, an operator shall be in constant attendance until controls have functioned through several cycles or for a period of 24 hours whichever is greater. A report of the operating test shall be provided

to the GDA and include the following specific information: time, date, and duration of test; water pressure at boiler; boiler make, type, and serial number; design pressure and rated capacity; gas pressure at burner; flue gas temperature at boiler outlet; and the surface temperature of the boiler jacket. All indicating instruments shall be read and recorded at half-hour intervals.

20.C.04 Fusible plugs shall be provided on all boilers, other than those of the water tube type.

a. Replacement of fusible plugs shall coincide with the inspections recommended by the ASME *Boiler and Pressure Vessel Code.*

b. When necessary to replace fusible plugs between inspections, a written report covering the circumstances and providing make and heat number of plugs removed and inserted shall be forwarded to the responsible boiler inspector.

20.C.05 All boilers shall be equipped with water columns, gauge glass, and try cocks approved by a nationally-recognized testing laboratory.

a. Gauge glasses and water columns shall be guarded.

b. When shutoffs are used on the connections to a water column, they shall be of an approved locking or sealing type.

20.C.06 All boilers shall be equipped with blowoff cocks or valves approved by a nationally-recognized testing laboratory. The blowoff line shall be arranged so that leakage can be observed by the operator.

20.D Compressed Gas Cylinders.

20.D.01 Compressed gas cylinders shall be visually inspected in accordance with 49 CFR 171 through 179, CGA C6, and CGA C8.

20.D.02 All Government-owned cylinders shall be color coded and the gas contained identified by name in accordance with Military Standard (MIL-STD) 101B.

20.D.03 Storage. > *See also Section 20.D.10.*

a. Cylinders shall be stored in well-ventilated locations.

b. Cylinders containing the same gas shall be stored in a segregated group. Empty cylinders shall be labeled as empty and stored in the same manner.

c. Cylinders in storage shall be separated from flammable or combustible liquids and from easily ignitable materials (such as wood, paper, packaging materials, oil, and grease) by at least 40 ft (12 m) or by a fire resistive partition having at least a 1-hour rating.

d. Cylinders containing oxygen or oxidizing gases shall be separated from cylinders in storage containing fuel gases by at least 20 ft (6 m) or by a fire resistive partition having at least a 1-hour rating.

e. Areas containing hazardous gas in storage shall be appropriately placarded.

➢Exception: If it is reasonably anticipated that gas will be drawn from the cylinders within 24 hours, they are considered "in service" and these storage requirements do not apply.

20.D.04 Smoking shall be prohibited wherever cylinders are stored, handled, or used.

20.D.05 Cylinders shall be protected from physical damage, electric current, and extremes of temperature. The temperature of cylinders shall not be allowed to exceed 125°F (51.7°C).

20.D.06 Cylinders containing oxygen and acetylene (or other fuel gas) shall not be taken into confined spaces.

20.D.07 Cylinder valves and valve caps.

a. Cylinder valves shall be closed when cylinders are in storage, in transit, not in use, or empty.

b. Cylinder valve caps shall be in place when cylinders are in storage, in transit, or whenever the regulator is not in place.

20.D.08 All compressed gas cylinders in service shall be secured in substantial fixed or portable racks or hand trucks.

20.D.09 Compressed gas cylinders transported by crane, hoist, or derrick shall be securely transported in cradles, nets, or skip pans, and never directly by slings, chains, or magnets, unless the cylinder manufacturer's handling instructions specifically allows for handling cylinders otherwise.

20.D.10 Compressed gas cylinders shall be secured in an upright position at all times, except when being hoisted (except acetylene cylinders, which shall never be laid horizontally). Horizontal storage configurations

approved for transportation are permitted for cylinders other than acetylene.

20.D.11 Valve wrench or wheel shall be in operating position when cylinder is in use.

a. Valves shall be opened slowly.

b. Quick closing valves on fuel gas cylinders shall not be opened more than 1 1/2 turns.

20.D.12 Cylinders shall be used only for their designed purpose of containing a specific compressed gas.

20.D.13 Cylinders shall be refilled only by qualified persons.

20.D.14 Cylinders shall be handled in a manner that will not weaken or damage the cylinder or valve.

20.D.15 If the movement can be accomplished safely, leaking cylinders shall be moved to an isolated location out of doors, the valve shall be cracked and the gas shall be allowed to escape slowly.

a. Personnel and all sources of ignition shall be kept at least 100 ft (30 m) away.

b. Instrumentation should be used to assure protection of personnel from health and flammability hazards.

c. The cylinder shall be tagged "DEFECTIVE", after the gas has escaped.

20.D.16 Cylinders containing different gases shall not be bled simultaneously in close proximity of each other.

20.D.17 Bleeding of cylinders containing toxic gases shall be accomplished in accordance with environmental regulations, and in accordance with a government accepted APP and AHA specifically addressing the bleeding of compressed gas cylinders, and only under the direct supervision of qualified personnel.

20.D.18 Oxygen cylinders and fittings shall be kept away from oil or grease.

a. Cylinders, cylinder valves, couplings, regulators, hose, and apparatus shall be kept free from oil or greasy substance and shall not be handled with oily hands or gloves.

b. Oxygen shall not be directed at oily surfaces, greasy cloths, or within a fuel oil or other storage tank or vessel.

20.D.19 Oxygen and fuel gas pressure regulators, including their related gauges, shall be in proper working order while in use.

SECTION 21 Fall Protection

Table of Contents

21.A General. The requirements of this Section are applicable to all Government and Contractor work forces when their employees are working at heights, exposed to fall hazards and/or using fall protection equipment. Every Contractor and USACE owned/operated permanent facility is responsible for establishing, implementing and managing a fall protection program.

21.A.01 Fall Protection Threshold.

a. The fall protection threshold height requirement is 6 ft (1.8 m) for ALL work covered by this manual, unless specified differently below, whether performed by Government or Contractor work forces, to include steel erection activities, systems-engineered activities (prefabricated) metal buildings, residential (wood) construction and scaffolding work.

b. For all USACE-owned/operated permanent facilities with open-sided floors, platforms or unprotected edges 4 ft (1.2 m) or more above adjacent floor or ground level, *see Section 24.A.01.d.*

➤ *Note 1: Floating Plant and Vessels are excluded from these requirements except where specifically cited in Sections 19.D and 19.E.*

➤ *Note 2: For fall protection requirements in excavations, see Section 25.A.02.*

➤ *Note 3: The Terms "CP" And "QP" in this section refer to Competent Person for fall protection and Qualified Person for Fall Protection respectively. > See Sections 21.B.02, 21.B.03 and Appendix Q.*

21.A.02 Workers exposed to fall hazards shall be protected from falling to a lower level by the use of standard guardrails (see Section 21.F.01.b), work platforms, temporary floors, safety nets, engineered fall protection systems, personal fall arrest systems, or the equivalent, in the following situations:

a. Whenever workers are exposed to falls from unprotected sides or edges, access ways, fixed ladders over 20 ft (6 m) in height, unprotected roof edge or floor openings, holes and skylights, unstable surfaces, leading edge work, scaffolds, formwork, work platforms, re-bar assembly, steel erection and engineered metal buildings;

b. For access ways or work platforms over water, machinery, or dangerous operations;

c. When installing or removing sheet piles, h-piles, cofferdams, or other interlocking materials from which workers may fall 6 ft (1.8 m) or more;

➤ *Note: The use of sheet pile stirrups as a fall protection method is prohibited.*

d. Where there is a possibility of a fall from any height onto dangerous equipment, into a hazardous environment, or onto an impalement hazard;

e. For steel erection activities, when connectors are working at the same connecting point, they shall connect one end of the structural member before going out to connect the other end. The connectors shall always be 100% tied off.

21.A.03 The order of control measures (the hierarchy of controls) to abate fall hazards or to select and use a fall protection method to protect workers performing work at heights shall be:

a. Elimination: Remove the hazard from work areas or change task, process, controls or other means to eliminate the need to work at heights with its subsequent exposure to fall hazards (i.e., build roof trusses on ground level and then lift into place or design change by lowering a meter or valve at high locations to a worker's level). This control measure is the most effective;

b. Prevention (passive or same-level barrier): isolate and separate fall hazards from work areas by erecting same level barriers such as guardrails, walls, covers or parapets;

c. Work platforms (movable or stationary): use scaffolds, scissor lifts, work stands or aerial lift equipment to facilitate access to work location and to protect workers from falling when performing work at high locations. > See Section 22.S;

d. Personal Protective Systems and Equipment: Use of fall protection systems, including (in order of preference): restraint, positioning, or personal fall arrest. All systems require the use of full body harness, connecting means and safe anchorage system.

e. Administrative Controls: Introduce new work practices that reduce the risk of falling from heights, or to warn a person to avoid approaching a fall hazard (i.e., warning systems, warning lines, audible alarms, signs or training of workers to recognize specific fall hazards).

21.A.04 When using stilts, working from raised platforms, or floors above a walking/working surface that exposes workers to a fall of 6 ft (1.8 m) or more in areas protected by guardrails, the height of the guardrail must be raised accordingly to maintain a protective height of 42 in (107 cm) above the stilt, raised platform, floors, or work stands.

21.A.05 During construction activities, fall protection is required for employees exposed to fall hazards while conducting inspection, investigation or assessment work.

21.A.06 Prior to start of construction or after construction work is complete, fall protection is required when conducting inspection, investigation or assessment work WITHIN 6 ft (1.8 m) from an unprotected edge of a roof. An AHA shall be developed and reviewed by a CP for this activity and submitted for GDA review and acceptance. > See Figure 21-1.

21.A.07 Prior to start of construction or after construction work is complete, fall protection may not be required when conducting inspection, investigation or assessment work MORE THAN 6 ft (1.8 m) away from an unprotected edge of a roof. An AHA shall be developed and reviewed by a CP for this activity and submitted for GDA review and acceptance. > See Figure 21-1.

21.A.08 During maintenance evolutions (i.e., inspecting or maintaining HVAC or other equipment on roofs), fall protection is required when conducting inspection and investigation work.

Figure 21-1
Control Zone/Safe Zone Fall Protection

FP is required in the Control Zone when conducting inspection, investigation or assessment work of roofs

6 FT.

CONTROL ZONE

Access to safe zone by stairs or a hatch

SAFE ZONE

FP may not be required in the safe zone when conducting roof inspection and investigation work

CONTROL ZONE

Safe access via 100% transition zone (dark area) using ladder

UNPROTECTED ROOF EDGE

21.B Roles and Responsibilities.

21.B.01 Fall Protection Program Manager (Program Administrator per ANSI Z359.2). The Program Manager is responsible for the overall development, implementation, monitoring and evaluation of the Fall Protection Program. This person can also function as a QP, CP, CP trainer, QP trainer and/or competent rescue trainer if so trained. The Program Manager shall:

a. Be trained appropriately, as described in Section 21.C;

b. Advise and provide guidance for managers, employees and others on all matters pertaining to their Fall Protection Program;

c. Establish all duties and responsibilities required by the Fall Protection Program and assign them to individuals who are trained and qualified to perform them;

d. Verify personnel are provided with resources to accomplish their responsibilities;

e. Establish and implement a procedure to identify and eliminate or control new and existing fall hazards;

f. Ensure the proper development and implementation of the fall protection and prevention plan (written Fall Protection Procedures, per ANSI Z359.2) and rescue plan (written Rescue Procedures, per ANSI Z359.2).

g. Provide/ensure appropriate level of training is received by End Users (Authorized Persons per ANSI Z359.2), CP, QP, and others as required;

h. Participate in investigation of all mishaps (near misses, incidents or accidents) related to falls from heights (personally or by designation of persons qualified to perform the investigation);

i. Measure and evaluate the effectiveness of the Fall Protection Program by conducting periodic program evaluations and making improvements as necessary.

21.B.02 Qualified Person for Fall Protection. The QP is responsible for technical support of the Fall Protection Program. The QP shall:

a. Have advanced understanding and knowledge of the requirements, equipment and systems, physical sciences, and engineering principles that affect equipment and systems for fall protection and rescue;

b. Be qualified to select proper fall protection and rescue equipment;

c. Supervise the design, selection, installation and inspection of certified anchorages and horizontal lifelines;

d. Be trained to the applicable level, as described in Section 21.C.

21.B.03 Competent Person for Fall protection. The CP is responsible for the immediate supervision, implementation and monitoring of the Fall Protection Program. The CP shall:

a. Be trained to the applicable level, as described in Section 21.C;

b. Conduct a fall hazard survey to identify all fall hazards before End Users are exposed to those hazards;

c. Identify, evaluate and impose limits on the workplace activities to control fall hazard exposures and swing falls and communicate all limitations to all employees authorized to utilize the fall protection system;

d. Have the authority to stop the work immediately if it is determined to be unsafe and take prompt corrective measures to mitigate fall hazards;

e. Prepare, update, review and approve fall protection and prevention plans as directed by the Program Manager.

f. Review procedures as workplace activities change to determine if additional practices, procedures or training need to be implemented;

g. Ensure a rescue plan has been developed for all activities;

h. Specify in the fall protection and prevention plan, the fall protection systems, anchorage locations, connecting means, body supports and other equipment that End Users are required to use when exposed to a fall hazard;

i. Supervise the selection, installation, use and inspection of non-certified anchorages;

j. Verify End Users who work at heights are trained and authorized to do so;

k. Review, periodically and as needed, fall protection and prevention plan/rescue plan and procedures, to insure the End User is adequately informed about the fall protection and prevention plan/rescue plan and procedures for workplace activities;

l. Ensure prompt rescue of End Users can be accomplished via the rescue plan and procedures to be used;

m. Participate in investigation of all mishaps related to falls from heights;

n. Ensure all damaged or deployed fall protection equipment, is removed from service immediately;

o. Inspect all fall protection equipment at the frequency required by the manufacturer.

21.B.04 End User. The End User shall have understanding of workplace activities and follow the policy and procedures and the instructions of the CP regarding the use of fall protection and rescue systems and equipment. >*See Section 21.C for training requirements.* The End User shall:

a. Bring all unsafe or hazardous conditions or actions that may cause injury to them or others, to the attention of the CP;

b. Properly use, inspect, maintain, store and care for their fall protection equipment and systems;

c. Inspect all fall protection equipment or damage or defects, prior to each use. End User shall notify the CP of those problems and shall not use that equipment.

21.B.05 Competent Rescuer. The Competent Rescuer is responsible for anticipating the potential for planned rescue and ensuring effective rescue plan/procedures and methods are in place before End Users starts any work at heights. This function may be performed by local emergency services, in-house professionals, competent or qualified persons or contractor services. In addition, they shall:

a. Be trained appropriately so they have a working knowledge through experience and training of current fall protection and planned rescue regulations, standards, equipment and systems. > See Section 21.C for all training requirements;

b. Prepare, update, review and approve the rescue plan and procedures before End Users start work at heights;

c. Verify all Authorized Rescuers have been adequately trained and are proficient at performing rescue;

d. Identify resources necessary to conduct safe, effective rescue from heights and verify those resources are available for a prompt rescue;

e. Know the hazards associated with rescue from heights and how to mitigate these hazards within the area of rescue;

f. Verify the rescue equipment is protected against damage;

g. Verify rescue plans, procedures, and performances are, at a minimum, evaluated annually and any deficiencies have been corrected.

21.B.06 Authorized Rescuer. The Authorized Rescuers is responsible for performing and/or assisting in workplace rescues for personnel suspended in, or attached to fall protection systems. They shall:

a. Through experience and training, have a working knowledge of and experience in the selection, use, storage and care of all equipment necessary to perform a rescue;

b. Inspect the rescue equipment according to procedures developed by the Competent Rescuer and

ensure it is protected, in proper working condition, and safe for rescue use;

c. Trained to the appropriate level and shall be aware of the hazards that may endanger the rescuer during rescue operations. >*See Section 21.C for Authorized Rescuer training requirements.*

21.C Training.

21.C.01 Training of all personnel involved in the Fall Protection Program – The Program Manager, QPs, CPs, End Users, Authorized and Competent Rescuers, as well as any associated fall protection trainers – shall be as described in ANSI/ASSE Z359.2, Minimum Requirements for a Comprehensive Managed Fall Protection Program, and shall conform to ANSI/ASSE Z490.1, Criteria for Accepted Practices in Safety, Health and Environmental Training. The refresher for all personnel involved in the fall protection program shall also be in accordance with requirements prescribed in ANSI/ASSE Z359.2 standard.

21.C.02 Fall Protection Program Manager Training. Training for Program Managers shall be conducted by a CP Trainer or QP Trainer.

a. Program Managers shall have a working knowledge of current fall protection regulations, requirements, standards, equipment and systems. Training shall cover the items prescribed in ANSI/ASSE Z359.2 standard.

b. For USACE-owned and/operated permanent facilities, Program Managers shall complete refresher training annually, by participating in at least one (1) hour of fall protection and rescue-related informational meetings and/or training.

21.C.03 Qualified Person for Fall Protection. A QP shall be trained by a QP Trainer in proper inspection, assembly and use of all fall protection equipment and systems that they encounter in their work as a QP. The frequency and duration of training that a QP requires to remain proficient in that role varies with the amount and types of fall protection work for which that person is responsible.

a. QPs are responsible for performing various duties that may be critical to the life and health of other workers. Training shall include those items in ANSI /ASSE Z359.2 standard, and shall include hands-on use of all types of equipment and systems used in locations where End Users work, to include: inspecting the systems prior to use; installing systems; analyzing structures and verifying that fall protection systems are properly installed; determining component compatibility; estimating free fall distances; determining total required clearance; dismantling systems storing equipment and common hazards associated with each system component.

b. For USACE-owned/operated permanent facilities, the refresher training requirement for the QPs is to stay current with fall protection and rescue knowledge by participating in at least one (1) hour annually of fall protection and rescue-related training and/or informational meetings.

21.C.04 Competent Person for Fall protection. CP shall be trained by a Competent Person trainer or a Qualified Person Trainer (see ANSI/ASSE Z359.2).

a. Currently, CPs shall have been trained to the level necessary to safely perform their duties.

➢ *Note: Eighteen (18) months from the effective date of this manual, acceptable Competent Person for Fall Protection training shall be a MINIMUM of 24 hours, with a combination of formal classroom training and practical applications. All training shall be documented.*

b. For USACE-owned/operated permanent facilities, the refresher training requirement for the CPs is to stay current in fall protection and rescue knowledge by participating in at least two (2) hours annually of fall protection and rescue-related training and/or informational meetings.

21.C.05 End User. Each worker who might be exposed to fall hazards from heights, shall be trained before using fall protection equipment by a CP, who is qualified in delivering fall protection training to the workers in the safe use of fall protection systems/equipment and the recognition of fall hazards related to their use, including:

a. The nature of fall hazards in the work area;

b. The correct procedures for erecting, using, dismantling, inspecting, maintaining, and storing fall protection equipment;

c. The application limits, free fall distance, total fall distance and clearance requirements of fall protection systems and equipment;

d. Rescue equipment and procedures;

e. Hands-on training and practical demonstrations;

f. Proper anchoring and tie off techniques;

g. All applicable requirements from this Section.

h. Refresher training shall be provided as necessary for the end users in the following situations:

(1) Changes in the fall protection program render previous training obsolete;

(2) Changes in fall protection or rescue equipment render previous training obsolete;

(3) Inadequacies in an employee's performance indicate a lack of knowledge or skill;

(4) A condition in the workplace changes in a manner that could affect the safe use of the fall protection equipment.

i. For USACE-owned/operated permanent facilities, the refresher training for end users shall be provided a minimum of one (1) hour annually to stay current with fall protection and rescue requirements.

21.C.06 Competent Rescuer. The Competent Rescuer shall be trained by a Competent Rescue Trainer (see ANSI/ASSE Z359.2). The training shall include:

a. Safe use of all types of equipment and systems used for rescue including inspection of the systems prior to use, installation, component compatibility, descent control, backup systems, dismantling, storage and the common hazards associated with each system;

b. Practical demonstrations on how to properly select, inspect, anchor, assemble and use the fall protection and rescue equipment used;

c. For USACE-owned/operated permanent facilities, the refresher training for Competent Rescuers shall be provided a minimum of one (1) hour annually to stay current with fall protection and rescue requirements.

21.C.07 Authorized Rescuer. The Authorized Rescuer shall be trained by a Competent Rescuer (see ANSI/ASSE Z359.2). The training shall:

a. Be received before exposure to a fall hazard or a potential rescue event;

b. Include practical demonstrations on how to properly select, inspect, anchor, assemble, disassemble, store and use the fall protection and rescue equipment used.

c. Include and demonstrate before-use inspection of rescue equipment and systems.

d. For USACE-owned/operated permanent facilities, the refresher training for authorized rescuers shall be provided a minimum of one (1) hour annually to stay current with fall protection and rescue requirements.

21.C.08 Documentation. Training and evaluations for fall protection and rescue training shall be documented and retained for the current and previous training program and shall include: trainer/evaluator's name, student's name, training or evaluation organization's name (if external), dates/times of training and evaluations, course objectives, content of training program, performance of student based on observation of physical demonstrations of skill or on exercises.

21.D Fall Protection Program.

21.D.01 If a Contractor will have personnel working at heights and/or exposed to fall hazards, a Fall Protection and Prevention Plan shall be developed and submitted to the GDA for review and acceptance as part of their Accident Prevention Plan (APP). This plan may be developed by either the CP or QP. If the plan includes fall protection components or systems requiring direction, supervision, design calculations or drawings by a QP, the name, qualifications and responsibilities of the QP shall be addressed. It shall describe, in detail, the specific practices, equipment and control methods used to protect workers from falling to lower levels. This plan shall be updated as conditions change, at least every six months and shall include:

a. Duties and responsibilities. Identify CPs and QPs and their responsibilities and qualifications;

b. Description of the project or task performed;

c. Training requirements to include safe use of fall protection equipment;

d. Anticipated hazards and fall hazard prevention and control;

e. Rescue plan and procedures;

f. Design of anchorages/fall arrest and horizontal lifeline systems:

(1) It is realized that the provision of fall protection for the first person up for establishing anchorages ONLY would be difficult. In this situation, fall protection may not be required. After anchorages are installed, fall protection is required.

(2) The contractor shall identify all locations where anchorages need to be established, and detail in the Fall Protection and Prevention Plan and AHA how work will be performed safely.

g. Inspection, maintenance and storage of fall protection equipment;

h. Incident investigation procedures;

i. Evaluation of program effectiveness, and

j. Inspection and oversight methods employed.

21.D.02 Each Government-owned facility shall develop a written Fall Protection Program if they have personnel working at heights. The facility shall also develop a Site Specific Fall Protection and Prevention Plan and conduct a fall hazard survey, prepare survey report at existing buildings or structures, and comply with the program elements and requirements as identified in this section.

21.E Controlled Access Zones. The use of Controlled Access Zone as a fall protection method is prohibited.

21.F Fall Protection Systems.

21.F.01 Standard Guardrail Systems.

a. For marine and floating plant guardrail systems, see Sections 19.C, D and E.

b. A standard guardrail shall consist of:

(1) Toprails, midrails, and posts, and shall have a vertical height of 42 +/- 3 in (106.6 cm +/- 7.6 cm) from the upper surface of the toprail to the floor, platform, runway, or ramp level;

(2) Midrails shall be erected halfway between the toprails and the floor, platform, runway, or ramp;

(3) The ends of the toprails and midrails shall not overhang the terminal posts except where such overhang does not create a projection hazard;

(4) Toe-boards shall be provided on all open sides/ends at locations where persons are required or permitted to pass or work under the elevated platform or where needed to prevent persons and material from falling from the elevated platform.

c. Strength requirements: toprails and midrails shall be designed to meet the following requirements:

(1) Toprail shall be capable of withstanding, without failure, a force of at least 200 lb (0.9 kN) applied within 2 in (5 cm) of the top edge, in any outward or downward direction, at any point along the top edge;

(2) When the force described in (1), above, is applied in a downward direction, the top edge of the top rail shall not deflect more than 3 in (7.6 cm) nor to a height less than 39 in (99 cm) above the walking/working level;

(3) Midrails, screens, mesh, intermediate vertical members, solid panels, and equivalent structural members shall be capable of withstanding, without failure, a force of at least 150 lb (666 N) applied in any downward or outward direction at any point along the midrail or other member;

(4) Guardrail systems shall be so surfaced as to prevent injury to a worker from punctures or lacerations and to prevent snagging of clothing.

d. Minimum construction materials for standard guardrail components. The following are minimum requirements used for underlineconstructing guardrail systems. The employer is responsible for designing a complete system and assembling these components in accordance with this Section.

➤ Note 1: Synthetic or natural fiber ropes shall not be used as toprails or midrails.

➤ Note 2: Wood railing components shall be minimum 1,500 lb-ft/in^2 fiber (stress grade) construction grade lumber.

(1) Wood railings:

(a) Toprails: Constructed of at least 2-in x 4-in (5-cm x 10-cm) lumber;

(b) Midrails: Constructed of at least 1-in x 6-in (2.5-cm x 15.2-cm) lumber; and,

(c) Posts: Constructed of at least 2-in x 4-in (5-cm x 10-cm) lumber spaced not to exceed 8 ft (2.4 m) on centers.

(2) Pipe railings:

(a) Toprails and midrails: At least 1 ½ in (3.8 cm) nominal diameter (schedule 40 steel pipe); and

(b) Posts: At least 1½ in (3.8 cm) nominal diameter (schedule 40 steel pipe) spaced not more than 8 ft (2.4 m) on centers.

(3) Structural steel railings:

(a) Toprails and midrails: At least 2-in x 2-in x 3/8 in (5 cm x 5 cm x .9 cm) angles, and,

(b) Posts: At least 2-in x 2-in x 3/8-in (5 cm x 5 cm x .9 cm) angles spaced not more than 8 ft (2.4 m) on centers.

(4) Steel Cable (Wire Rope) railings:

(a) Toprail and midrail: ¼ in (6.25 mm) steel cable, flagged every 6 ft (1.8 m) with high visibility material, may be used if tension is maintained to provide not more than 3 in (7.5 cm) deflection, in any direction from the center line, under a 200 lb (0.89 kN) load;

(b) Support posts shall be located to ensure proper tension is maintained;

(c) Perimeter safety cables shall meet the criteria and requirements for guardrail systems. If the perimeter safety cables are used by the workers as a method of attaching a lanyard to the cables they shall meet the requirements of Horizontal Lifeline System (see Section 21.I.08.d.(2).

e. Commercial, off-the-shelf (COTS), engineered guardrail systems may be used instead of constructing a system with the materials above. If so, the portable guardrail system (webbing, straps, etc) must be designed and engineered to meet the same requirements in this section. The employer is still responsible for insuring the system used is approved, completed, installed and used as designed.

f. Toe-boards.

(1) Toe-boards shall be 3½ in (8.75 cm) in vertical height and shall be constructed from 1-in x 4-in (2.5-cm x 10.1-cm) lumber or the equivalent.

(2) Toe-boards shall be securely fastened in place and have not more than ¼ in (0.6 cm) clearance above floor level.

(3) Toe-boards shall be made of any substantial material, either solid or with openings between adjacent pieces not greater than 1 in (2.5 cm).

(4) Where material is piled to such a height that a standard toe-board does not provide protection, paneling or screening from floor to toprail or midrail shall be provided.

(5) Toe-boards shall be able to withstand, without failure, a force of 50 lbs (0.22 kN) applied in any outward or downward direction at any point along the toe-board.

21.F.02 Guardrails receiving heavy stresses from workers trucking or handling materials shall be provided additional strength by using heavier stock, closer spacing of posts, bracing, or by other means.

21.F.03 When guardrails are used at hoisting areas, a minimum 6 ft (18. m) of guardrail shall be erected on each side of the access point through which materials are hoisted.

21.F.04 A gate or removable guardrail section may be used as long as it meets the standard guardrail height 42 +/- 3 in (106.6 +/- 7.6 cm) and is secured across the opening between the guardrail sections when hoisting operations are not taking place.

21.F.05 Existing parapet walls. In order for parapet walls to be considered adequate fall protection systems, they shall have a height of 42 in +/- 3 in (1 m +/- 7.6 cm) unless it is an EXISTING parapet walls with a height of less than 42 in (1 m). If so, the EXISTING parapet wall may be used as a compliant fall protection system if the vertical height is a minimum of 30 in (76 cm) or more plus width that equals to 48 in (1.2 m). > See Figure 21-2.

equivalent methods (e.g., red or orange "X"). Workers must be made aware of the meaning for color coding and equivalent methods.

21.G Covers.

21.G.01 Install covers on any hole 2 in (5.1 cm) or more in its least dimension on walking/working surfaces such as floors, roofs or other openings.

21.G.02 Covers shall be capable of supporting, without failure, at least twice the weight of the worker, equipment and material combined.

21.G.03 Covers shall be secured when installed, clearly marked with the word "HOLE", "COVER" or "Danger, Roof Opening-Do Not Remove" or color-coded or

FIGURE 21-2

Existing Parapet Wall Used as a Fall Protection System

Any combination of 30 in (76 cm) or more in height plus width that equals 48 in (1.2 m) or more is acceptable.

21.H Safety Net Systems for Fall Protection.

➢ *Debris nets are addressed in Section 14.E Housekeeping.*

21.H.01 Safety nets shall be installed as close under the work surfaces as practical but in no case more than 30 ft (9.1 m) below such work surface. Nets shall be hung with sufficient clearance to prevent contact with the surfaces or structures below. Such clearance shall be determined by impact load testing. When nets are used on bridges, multi-story buildings or structures, the potential fall area from the walking/working surface to the net shall be unobstructed.

a. The maximum size of the mesh openings shall not exceed 36 in^2 (230 cm^2), nor be longer than 6 in (15 cm) on any side.

b. The border rope or webbing shall have a minimum breaking strength of 5,000 lb (22.2 kN).

21.H.02 Nets shall extend outward from the outermost projection of the work surface as shown in Table 21-1.

21.H.03 Operations requiring safety net protection shall not be undertaken until the net(s) is in place and has either been tested without failure per a. and b. below, or complies with c. below.

a. Safety nets and safety net installations shall be tested in the suspended position immediately after installation under the supervision of QP and in the presence of the GDA and before being used as a fall protection system; whenever relocated, after major repair; and when left at one location, at not more than 6 month intervals.

b. The test shall consist of dropping into the net a 400 lb (180 kg) bag of sand, not more than 30 in+/- 2 in (76.2 cm +/- 5 cm) in diameter, at least 42 in (106.6 cm) above the highest working/walking surface at which workers are exposed to fall hazards. Means must be taken to ensure the weight can be safely retrieved after the test is conducted.

c. If a QP can demonstrate in writing that it is unreasonable to perform the drop- test, the QP shall certify in writing that the net and installation (to include anchorages) is in compliance with all requirements for acceptance by the GDA. The certification must include an identification of the net and net installation, the date that it was determined, and the signature of the QP making the determination and certification. The certification shall remain at the job-site.

TABLE 21-1

Safety Net Distances

Vertical Distance from Working Level to Horizontal Plane of Net	Minimum Required Horizontal Distance of Outer Edge of Net from Edge of Working Surface
Up to 5 ft (up to 1.5 m)	8 ft (2.5 m)
5 ft up to 10 ft (1.5 m up to 3.1 m)	10 ft (3.1 m)
more than 10 ft (more than 3.1 m)	13 ft (4 m)

21.H.04 Shackles and hooks used in safety net installations shall be made of forged steel.

21.H.05 When used with safety nets, debris nets shall be secured on top of the safety net but shall not compromise the design, construction, or performance of the safety nets.

21.H.06 Materials, scrap pieces, equipment, and tools that have fallen into the safety net shall be removed as soon as possible and at least before the next work shift.

Safety nets shall be protected from sparks and hot slag resulting from welding and cutting operations.

21.H.07 Inspection of safety nets.

a. Safety nets shall be inspected by a CP in accordance with the manufacturer's instructions and recommendations.

b. Inspections shall be conducted immediately after installation, at least weekly thereafter, and following any alteration, repair, or any occurrence that could affect the integrity of the net system. Inspections shall be documented.

c. If any welding or cutting operations occur above the net(s), noncombustible barriers shall be provided. The frequency of inspections shall be increased in proportion to the potential for damage to the nets.

d. Defective nets shall not be used. Defective components shall be removed from service and replaced.

21.I Personal Fall Protection Systems.

21.I.01 Personal fall protection equipment and systems (to include fall arrest, positioning and restraint) shall be used when a person is working at heights and exposed to a fall hazard.

21.I.02 Inspection of personal fall protection equipment. Personal fall protection equipment shall be inspected by the End User prior to each use to determine that it is in a safe working condition. A CP shall inspect the equipment at least once semi-annually and whenever equipment is subjected to a fall or impacted. Inspection by the CP shall be documented. Defective or damaged equipment shall be immediately removed from service and replaced. Inspection criteria shall include:

a. Harnesses, lanyards, straps and ropes: Check all components for cuts, wear, tears, damaged threads, broken or torn stitching, discoloration, abrasions, burn or chemical damage, ultraviolet deterioration and missing markings and/or labels.

b. Hardware: Check all components for signs of wear, cracks, corrosion and deformation.

21.I.03 Personal fall protection equipment shall be used, inspected, maintained and stored in a safe place in accordance with manufacturer's instructions and recommendations or as prescribed by the CP.

21.I.04 Selection of personal fall protection equipment shall be based on the type of work being performed; the work environment; the weight, size, and shape of the worker; the type and position/location of anchorage; and the required length of the lanyard.

21.I.05 Personal Fall Arrest System (PFAS) consists of full body harness, connecting means, and an anchorage system.

> Note: All PFAS shall meet the requirements contained in ANSI Z359, Fall Protection Code, to include fall restraint and positioning systems.

a. PFAS are generally certified for users within the capacity range of 130 to 310 lbs (59 to 140.6 kg) including the weight of the worker, equipment and tools.

(1) Workers shall not be permitted to exceed the 310 lbs (140.6 kg) limit unless permitted in writing by the manufacturer.

(2) For workers with body weight less than 130 lbs (59 kg), a specially designed harness and also a specially designed energy absorbing lanyard shall be utilized which will properly deploy if this person was to fall.

b. When stopping a fall, PFAS shall:

(1) Limit maximum arresting force on the body of the employee to 1,800 lbs (8.0 kN) when used with a full body harness;

(2) Be rigged such that a worker can neither free fall more than 6 ft (1.8 m) nor contact any lower level or other physical hazard in the path of the fall. The free fall distance of 6 ft (1.8 m) can be exceeded if the proper energy absorbing lanyard is used.

c. When designing new PFAS, the QP shall attempt to minimize fall distances including free fall distances and arrest forces. > See Figure 21-3. If it is necessary to increase free fall distances and arrest forces in order to accommodate existing and new structures or provide mobility to end users:

(1) Only the QP shall make this determination; and

(2) The maximum arrest force shall be kept below 1,800 lbs (8.0 kN).

FIGURE 21-3

Calculating Fall Distance

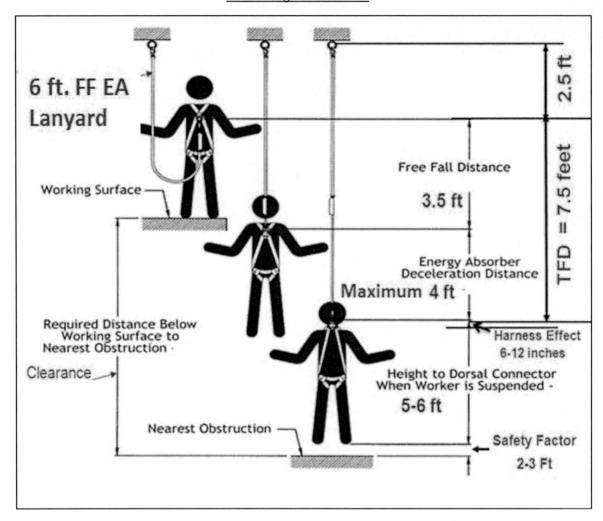

21.I.06 PFAS – Body Support.

a. Full Body Harness. PFAS require the use of a full-body harness. The use of body belts is prohibited.

(1) Only full body harnesses meeting the requirements of ANSI Z359 are acceptable. Full body harnesses labeled to meet the requirements of the ANSI A10.14 shall not be used.

(2) The fall arrest attachment point on the full body harness shall be integrally attached and located at the wearer's upper back between the shoulder blades (dorsal D-ring).

➢ Note: A frontal D-ring attachment point integrally attached to wearer's full body harness and located at the sternum, can be used for fall arrest (i.e., used with a ladder climbing device), provided the free fall distance does not exceed 2 ft (0.6 m) and the maximum arresting force does not exceed 900 lbs (4 kN).

(3) All full body harnesses shall be equipped with Suspension Trauma Preventers such as stirrups, relief steps, or similar in order to provide short-term relief from the effects of orthostatic intolerance.

b. Lineman's equipment (electrically rated harnesses). The full body harness used around high voltage equipment or structures shall be an industry designed "linemen's fall protection harness" that will resist arc flash and shall meet ASTM F887 and ANSI Z359 and the equipment must bear a label or similar stating such.

21.I.07 PFAS – Connecting Means. Connecting subsystems may include energy absorbing lanyards (shock absorbing lanyards) with snap hooks or carabiners at each end, self-retracting <u>devices (SRDs)</u>, and/or fall arrestors (rope grabs).

<u>a</u>. Lanyards - General. Lanyards shall be made of ropes, straps or webbing made from synthetic materials. Energy absorbing lanyards, (including rip stitch/tearing and deforming lanyards) shall be capable of sustaining a minimum tensile load of 5,000 lbs (22.2 kN). The maximum length of single or "Y" lanyards used in fall arrest shall not exceed 6 ft (1.8 m).

(<u>1</u>) The 6 ft (1.8 m) Free Fall (FF) energy absorbing lanyard shall only be used when the tie-off point is above the dorsal D-ring creating a FF distance of less than 6 ft. <u>The energy absorber shall have an average arrest force of 900 lbs (4 kN) and a maximum deployment distance of 4 ft (1.2 m). > See ANSI Z359.13, Par 3.1.8.1.</u>

(<u>2</u>) When an anchor point is below the dorsal D-ring, a FF distance greater than 6 ft (1.8 m) is created. For these situations, a 12 ft (3.6 m) FF energy absorbing lanyard shall be used in accordance with manufacturer's instructions and recommendations. <u>The energy absorber shall have an average arrest force of 1,350 lbs (6 kN) and the maximum deployment distance of 5 ft (1.5 m). > See ANSI Z359.13, Par 3.1.8.2.</u>

➤*Note: A 12 ft (3.6 m) FF energy absorbing lanyard does not refer to the lanyard length. Instead it refers to a FF that is greater than 6 ft (1.8 m) up to 12 ft which is created by the anchor point being located below the dorsal D-ring. The maximum length of the lanyard used shall not exceed 6 ft. > <u>See Figure 21-4</u>.*

FIGURE 21-4

<u>6 ft Free Fall and 12 ft Free Fall Energy Absorbing Lanyard Labels</u>

Warning: Maximum User Weight 130-310 lbs.

6ft.   900lbs.
Maximum   Maximum
Free Fall   Arresting Force
Read Instructions Before Use

Warning: Maximum User Weight 130-310 lbs.

12ft.   1350lbs.
Maximum   Maximum
Free Fall   Arresting Force
Read Instructions Before Use

(3) The 6 ft (1.8 m) and 12 ft (3.6 m) FF energy absorbing lanyards shall meet the requirements of ANSI Z359.13 Standard.

➤*Note: Lanyards shall not be looped back over or through an object and then attached back to themselves unless permitted by the manufacturer.*

b. <u>"Y" Lanyards</u>. When using lanyard with two integrally connected legs for 100% tie-off, attach only the snap hook at the center of the lanyard shall be attached to the fall arrest attachment element of the harness (D-ring).

(1) The two legs of the lanyard and the joint between the legs shall withstand a force of 5,000 lbs (22.2 kN).

(2) When one leg of the lanyard is attached to the anchorage, the unused leg of the lanyard shall not be attached to any part of the harness except to attachment points specifically designated by the manufacturer for this purpose.

(<u>3</u>) The 6 ft (1.8 M) FF "Y" lanyard shall only be used when the tie-off point is above the dorsal D-ring height and when the FF distance is less than 6 ft.

(<u>4</u>) When the tie-off point is located below the dorsal D-ring, the FF distance is greater than 6 ft (1.8 m) so a 12 ft (3.6 m) FF "Y" lanyard may be used.

➤*Note: A 12 ft (3.6 m) FF energy absorbing "Y" lanyard does not refer to the lanyard length. Instead it refers to a FF that is greater than 6 ft (1.8 m) up to 12 ft which is created by the anchor point being located below the dorsal D-ring. The maximum length used shall not exceed 6 ft.*

(<u>5</u>) The maximum arrest force on the body shall not exceed 1800 lbs (8 kN).

(<u>6</u>) The 6 ft (1.8 m) and 12 ft (3.6 m) FF energy absorbing "Y" lanyards shall meet ANSI/ASSE Z359.13 standard.

➤*Note: <u>Effective 2 years from date of publication, all energy absorbers used shall be equipped with a deployment indicator.</u>*

<u>c</u>. Hardware (connecting components).

(<u>1</u>) Snap hooks and carabiners shall be self-closing and self-locking, capable of being opened only by at least two consecutive deliberate actions. Snap hooks and carabiners having minimum gate strength of 3,600 lbs (16 kN) <u>in all directions</u>, per ANSI Z359.12 shall be used.

(<u>2</u>) Snap hooks and carabiners shall have a minimum tensile strength of 5,000 lbs (22.2 kN); D-rings, O-rings, snap hooks and carabiners shall be <u>capable of withstanding a tensile load of 5,000 lbs.</u>

(<u>3</u>) Connectors, adjusters, <u>and any buckles used as</u> <u>adjusters</u> shall be <u>capable of withstanding a</u> <u>minimum tensile load of 3,372 lbs (15 kN) and shall</u> <u>be made of</u> drop forged, pressed or formed steel, or made of equivalent materials; shall have corrosion resistant finish; and all surfaces and edges shall be smooth to prevent damage to interfacing parts of the system.

(<u>4</u>) All connecting components used in PFAS shall be compatible and shall be used properly.

<u>d</u>. Self Retracting <u>Devices (SRDs). The SRDs shall</u> <u>meet the requirements of the ANSI/ASSE Z359.14</u> <u>standard.</u>

(<u>1</u>) A Self-retracting lanyard (SRL) <u>is a device</u> <u>mounted or anchored such that the arrest distance</u> <u>shall not exceed 2 ft (60 cm), and the average arrest</u> <u>force shall not exceed 1,350 lbs (6 kN) or a</u> <u>maximum peak force of 1,800 lbs (8 kN). The SRL</u> <u>is only</u> used for vertical applications.

(<u>2</u>) An SRL with leading edge capability (SRL-LE) <u>is designed for applications where during use, the</u> <u>device is not necessarily mounted or anchored</u> <u>overhead and may be at foot level and where the</u> <u>possible free fall distance from the edge is up to 5 ft</u> <u>(1.5 m) and the average arrest distance shall not</u> <u>exceed 4.5 ft (1.37 m). The device is equipped with</u> <u>an energy absorber to withstand impact loading of</u> <u>the line with a sharp or abrasive edge during fall</u> <u>arrest and for controlling fall arrest forces on the</u> <u>worker.</u>

➤ <u>Note: Effective 2 years from date of publication, all</u> <u>SRDs used shall be equipped with visual indicator.</u>

<u>e</u>. Fall arrestors (rope grabs) designed to be used with a vertical lifeline and ladder climbing devices (rope, cable or <u>rail</u>) shall be approved by the manufacturer for such use. Fall arresters shall have a minimum ultimate strength of 3,600 lbs (16 kN).

➤ <u>Note</u>: For vertical lifelines or ladder climbing devices, use <u>the automatic</u> fall arrestors that move in one direction only.

<u>21.I.08 PFAS - Anchorage System</u>. The anchorage system consists of the anchorage (the rigid part of the building, facility, structure or equipment) and the anchorage connector.

a. Anchorages used for attaching the PFAS shall be independent of any anchorage used to support or suspend platforms. They shall be capable of supporting at least 5,000 lbs (22.2 kN) per worker attached or designed by a QP for twice the maximum arrest force on the body.

b. Anchorage connectors are used to tie the PFAS to the anchorage and shall be capable of withstanding without breaking 5,000 lbs (22.2 kN) load per worker attached.

<u>c. Steel cable/wire rope guardrails may not be used</u> <u>as a Horizontal Life Line (HLL) unless designed and</u> <u>approved by a QP.</u>

➤ <u>Note</u>: Do not use electric conduits, utility pipes, ductwork or unstable points as anchorages for PFAS.

<u>d</u>. Lifelines.

(<u>1</u>) Vertical lifeline (VLL). A VLL shall have a minimum tensile strength of 5,000 lbs (22.2 kN) attached to a <u>single overhead anchorage</u>. Each worker shall be attached to a separate lifeline system.

(<u>2</u>) Horizontal lifeline (HLL).

(<u>a</u>) Locally manufactured HLLs are not acceptable unless they are custom designed for limited or site specific applications by a Registered Professional Engineer (RPE) who is also qualified in designing HLL systems.

(<u>b</u>) Commercially manufactured HLLs shall be designed, installed, certified and used under the supervision of QP only, as part of a complete fall arrest system. The CP may (if deemed appropriate by QP), supervise the assembly, disassembly, use and inspection of the HLL systems, under the direction of the QP.

(<u>c</u>) The design shall include drawings, required clearance, instructions on proper installation, and use procedures, proof testing reports and inspection requirements.

(<u>d</u>) All HLL anchorages shall be designed by a RPE who is also qualified in designing HLL systems. > See ANSI/ASSE Z359.6.

(<u>e</u>) The design of all HLLs shall be reviewed and accepted by the GDA as part of the Fall Protection and Prevention Plan.

21.I.09 Positioning System. A positioning system <u>uses some of the same equipment as a fall protection system (i.e., a harness, etc.), however, a positioning system used alone does not constitute fall protection.</u>

a. A positioning system shall not be used as a primary fall arrest system. While positioning (working with both hands free), a person shall use a separate system that provides backup protection from a fall.

b. System requirements. Positioning System shall:

(1) Be rigged such that a worker cannot free fall more than 2 ft (0.6 m);

(2) Be secured to an anchorage capable of supporting at least twice the potential impact load of a worker's fall or 3,000 lbs (13.3 kN), whichever is greater;

(3) <u>Ensure workers achieve 100% tie-off during use;</u>

(4) The attachment points on the full body harness used in the positioning system shall be located on the sides or on the front of the harness.

21.I.10 Restraint Systems.

a. <u>Consideration shall be made for use of fall restraint over fall arrest.</u> Fall restraint systems prevent the user from reaching an area where a free fall could occur by restricting the length of the lanyard or by other means.

b. The anchorage strength requirement for restraint systems shall be 3,000 lbs (13.3 kN) or designed by a QP for two times the foreseeable force.

c. Restraint systems can be used only on <u>flat or low-sloped surfaces (</= 18.4° or 4:12 slope).</u>

21.J Ladder-Climbing Devices (LCDs). A LCD is a sleeve or cable/rope attached to a fixed ladder over 20 ft (6 m) in length.

21.J.01 Anchorage strength for LCDs shall be a minimum of 3,000 lbs (13.3 kN).

21.J.02 The connector between the front D-ring of the harness and the ladder cable, rope or sleeve shall be 9 in (20 cm) long.

21.J.03 The free fall distance when using a LCD shall not exceed 2 ft (0.6 m).

21.J.04 There shall be 100% transition at the top of the LCD for safe access to above work surface or roof.

➢ *Note: Do not install LCDs on ladders that have ¾ in (1.9 cm) rungs (off-the-shelf-ladders) unless the ladders are designed to withstand the fall forces.*

21.K Scaffolds, <u>Work Platforms and Elevating/Aerial Devices.</u>

21.K.01 Scaffolds shall be equipped with a standard guardrail per 21.F.01 or other fall protection systems.

21.K.02 For workers erecting and dismantling scaffolds, an evaluation shall be conducted by a CP to determine the feasibility and safety of providing fall protection if fall protection is not feasible. An AHA detailing rationale for infeasibility of use of fall protection shall be submitted and accepted by the GDA.

21.K.03 Suspended scaffolds.

a. Single point or two point suspended scaffold: In addition to railings, workers shall also be tied off to an independent vertical lifeline using a full body harness.

b. Other suspended scaffolds (e.g. catenary, float, needle-beam, Boatswain chairs): PFAS is required and workers shall be tied off to an independent vertical lifeline using a full body harness.

c. A risk assessment shall be performed when persons are supported on a multi-point adjustable suspended scaffold to evaluate the effectiveness and feasibility of the use of PFAS. Results shall be documented in the AHA for the activity being performed. > *See 21.I.05.*

21.K.04 <u>Self-Propelled</u> Elevating Work Platforms (Scissor Lifts), <u>per ANSI A92.6.</u>

<u>a.</u> Scissor lifts shall be equipped with standard guardrails.

<u>b.</u> In addition to the guardrail provided, the scissor lift shall be equipped with anchorages meeting the ANSI Z359 Fall Protection Code.

➢ <u>*Note: Scissor lifts not equipped with anchorages are prohibited.*</u>

<u>c.</u> A restraint system shall be used in addition to guardrails. <u>The lanyards, to include lanyards with built-in shock absorbers, used with the restraint system shall be sufficiently short</u> to prohibit workers from climbing out of, or being ejected from the platform.

<u>d.</u> <u>The use of a self-retracting device (SRD) is prohibited unless permitted by the SRD manufacturer and used in accordance with manufacturer's instructions.</u>

e. Workers are prohibited from climbing on or over the guardrails.

21.K.05 Aerial Work Platforms: Boom Supported Platforms (per ANSI A92.5) and Vehicle Mounted Rotating and Elevating Aerial Devices (per ANSI A92.2).

a. Workers shall be anchored to the basket or bucket in accordance with manufacturer's specifications and instructions (anchoring to the boom may only be used when allowed by the manufacturer and permitted by the CP).

b. Lanyards used shall be sufficiently short to prohibit worker from climbing out of basket.

c. Lanyards with built-in shock absorbers are acceptable.

d. Self-retracting devices are not acceptable.

e. Tying off to an adjacent pole or structure is not permitted unless a safe device for 100% tie-off is used for the transfer.

21.K.06 Manually Propelled Elevating Work Platforms (per ANSI/SIA A92.3). > *See Section 22.C.06 for Mobile Scaffolds.*

a. The platform shall be equipped with standard guardrails.

b. If the platform is equipped with anchorages meeting the ANSI Z359, a restraint system shall be used in addition to the guardrails.

c. Lanyards used with the restraint system shall be sufficiently short to prohibit workers from climbing out of, or being ejected from the platform.

d. Lanyards with built-in shock absorbers are acceptable.

e. Self retracting devices are **not** acceptable.

f. The platform shall not be occupied when moved and at no time will workers be allowed to climb on or over the guardrails. > *See Figure 21-5.*

FIGURE 21-5

Typical Examples of Manually Propelled Elevating Aerial Platforms

Example #1   Example #2   Example #3

21.L Warning Line System (WLS).

21.L.01 A WLS may ONLY be used on floors, or flat or low-sloped roofs (between 0-18.4° or less than 4:12 slope) during construction work and shall be erected around all sides of the work area.

21.L.02 A WLS shall consist of wires, rope or chains 34-39 in (0.9-1.0 m) high with supporting stanchions. WLS shall be flagged at not more than 6 ft (1.8 m) intervals with a high visibility material.

21.L.03 The wire, rope or chains shall have a minimum tensile strength of 500 lbs (2.2 kN) and after being attached to the stanchions shall be capable of supporting without braking, the loads applied to the stanchions.

21.L.04 Stanchions shall be capable of resisting without tipping a force of 16 lbs (71 N) applied horizontally against the stanchions 30 in (76.2 cm) above the walking/working surface, perpendicular to the warning line and in the direction of the roof floor or platform edge. The line consisting of wire rope or chains shall be attached at each stanchion in such a way that the pulling on one section of the line will not result in a slack being taken up in adjacent sections before the stanchion tips over.

21.L.05 Working within the WLS does not require fall protection. No worker shall be allowed in the area between the roof or floor edge and the WLS without fall protection. Fall protection is required when working outside the WLS.

21.L.06 Roofing Work.

a. For roofing work on flat roofs, the WLS shall be erected not less than 6 ft (1.8 m) from the edge.

b. When roofing work is conducted on low sloped roofs (less than 4:12), or when using mechanical equipment or when work is performed by other trades (i.e., mechanical contractor performing work on equipment located on roofs, etc), the WLS shall be erected not less than 15 ft (4.5 m) from the unprotected side or edge.

21.L.07 A Designated Area is used as a fall protection method during maintenance work (i.e., inspecting or maintaining HVAC equipment) on roofs. The requirement for the Designated Area is identical to WLS. In addition, a 100% transition is required from the access point on the roof to the Designated Area. > See Figure 21-6.

21.M Safety Monitoring System (SMS). The use of a SMS as a fall protection method is prohibited.

Figure 21-6
Designated Area

100% transition from the ladder to the designated area

HVAC Unit

6 ft minimum

- Used on roofs during maintenance work – i.e., inspecting or maintaining HVAC equipment - (NOT roofing work)
- Similar to warning line system for construction (21.L)

21.N Rescue Plan and Procedures. The employer is required to provide prompt rescue to all fallen workers.

21.N.01 A rescue plan shall be prepared and maintained when workers are using fall protection equipment.
> *See ANSI Z359.2, Written Rescue Procedures.*

21.N.02 The plan shall contain provisions for self-rescue and assisted rescue of any worker who falls including rescue equipment. If other methods of rescue are planned (i.e. a jurisdictional public or Government emergency rescue agencies), it shall be indicated in the rescue plan including how to contact and summon the agency to the mishap site.

21.N.03 Personnel conducting rescue shall be trained accordingly.

21.N.04 If required, anchorages for self-rescue and assisted–rescue shall be identified, selected, and documented in Site-Specific Fall protection and Prevention Plan. Anchorages selected for rescue shall be capable of withstanding static loads of 3,000 lbs (13.3 kN) or five times the applied loads as designed by a QP.

21.N.05 Workers using fall protection equipment shall have an assigned safety person (spotter) also known as the "buddy system", who will be within visual/verbal range to initiate rescue of the fallen worker if required.

21.N.06 Rescue equipment used for self-rescue or assisted-rescue (i.e. SRL with rescue capability) shall meet ANSI Z359.4 and Z359.14.

21.O Working Over or Near Water (piers, wharves, quay walls, barges, aerial lifts, crane-supported work platforms, etc). PFDs are required for all work over or near water unless detailed below. > *See Figure 21-7*.

➢ *Note 1: All USACE and contractor workers, to include divers, shall comply with the requirements below.*
➢ *Note 2: If utilizing PFDs with full body harness, the full body harness shall be worn under the PFD. The type of PFD used shall not interfere with proper use of a full body harness and lanyard.*

21.O.01 When continuous fall protection is used, without exception, to prevent workers from falling into the water, the employer has effectively removed the drowning hazard and PFDs are not required.

FIGURE 21-7
Fall Protection (FP) vs. Personal Flotation Device
(PFD) Use When Working Over or Near Water

> _Note_: When using safety nets as fall protection, USCG-approved PFDs are usually required, unless rationale is provided in AHA.

21.O.02 When working over or near water and the distance from walking/working surface to the water's surface is 25 ft (7.6 m) or more, workers shall be protected from falling by the use of a fall protection system and PFDs are not required.

21.O.03 When working over or near water where the distance from the walking/working surface to the water's surface is less than 25 ft (7.6 m) AND the water depth is less than 10 ft (3.05 m), fall protection shall be required and PFDs are not required.

21.O.04 When working over water, PFD, lifesaving equipment and safety skiffs meeting the requirements of this EM shall be used <u>as required.</u>

21.O.05 When working from/in machinery (mechanically operated equipment), aerial lift equipment or other movable work platforms/cranes directly over water AND the depth of the water is at least 10 ft (3 m) deep, fall protection is not required however, PFDs are required.

<u>21.O.06 When there are hazards from currents, intakes, dangerous machinery or equipment, or barges, etc., fall protection shall be required regardless of the fall distance and PFDs are not required.</u>

21.P Other Engineered Fall Protection Systems.

21.P.01 Commercially available engineered/<u>integrated</u> systems are recognized as effective fall protection and may be used. These are systems that are not addressed in Paragraph 21.<u>F</u>.

21.P.02 Commercially available engineered/<u>integrated</u> systems shall be designed, installed, certified and used only under the supervision of QP and used per manufacturer instructions and recommendations. The CP may (if deemed appropriate by a QP), supervise the assembly, disassembly, use and inspection of the engineered system, under the direction of the QP.

21.P.03 The design shall include drawings, required clearance, instructions on proper installation, use and inspection requirements. These systems shall be reviewed and accepted by the GDA as part of the Fall Protection and Prevention Plan.

THIS PAGE INTENTIONALLY LEFT BLANK

SECTION 22 Work Platforms and Scaffolding

Table of Contents

22

22.A General. This Section establishes safety requirements for the construction, operation, maintenance and use of work platforms and scaffolding used in construction alteration, demolition, operations and maintenance of buildings and other structures. It does not apply to permanently installed scaffolds or platforms.

22.A.01 Scaffolding and work platforms shall be erected, used, inspected, tested, maintained, and repaired in accordance with:

a. For non-mechanized equipment - ANSI A10.8, *Scaffolding Safety Requirements,* or the Scaffolding, Shoring, and Forming Institute's *Code of Safe Practices,* and the manufacturer's operating manual.

b. For mechanized equipment - the manufacturer's operating manual, a copy of the manual shall be available at the work site.

22.A.02 Work platforms and scaffolding shall comply with fall protection (FP) and appropriate access requirements of Sections 21 and 24.

a. All requirements of this Section shall be applied to work platforms and means of access.

b. Standard railings and handrails for stairs shall be in compliance with the requirements of Sections 24.C and 24.E.

c. Standard guardrails shall be in compliance with Section 21.F.01.

(1) Cross bracing is acceptable in place of a midrail when the crossing point of two braces is between 20 in (0.5 m) and 30 in (0.8 m) above the work platform.

(2) Cross bracing is acceptable as a toprail when the crossing point of two braces is between 38 in (0.97 m) and 48 in (1.3 m) above the work platform.

(3) The end points at each upright shall be no more than 48 in (1.3 m) apart.

(4) Cross bracing shall not be used for both a midrail and top rail.

d. Personal FP devices shall be in compliance with Section 21.I;

e. Safety (FP) nets shall be in compliance with the requirements of Section 21.H.

f. Ladders used to access scaffolds and work platforms shall be in compliance with the requirements of this Section and Section 24.B.

22.A.03 Prior to commencing any activity that requires work in elevated areas, all provisions for access and fall protection shall be delineated in the Site-Specific Fall Protection and Prevention Plan and Activity Hazard Analysis (AHA), per Section 21.D, and accepted by the GDA for the activity. For specific guidance related to erecting and disassembling scaffolds, see Section 21.K.

22.A.04 The following hierarchy and prohibitions shall be followed in selecting appropriate work platforms.

a. Scaffolds, platforms, or temporary floors shall be provided for all work except that which can be performed safely from the ground or similar footing.

b. Ladders may be used as work platforms only when allowed by Section 24.B.

c. Ladder jacks, lean-to, and prop-scaffolds are prohibited.

d. Emergency descent devices shall not be used as working platforms.

22.A.05 Work platforms and scaffolds shall not be erected or used in the immediate vicinity of power lines or electrical conductors until such are insulated, de-energized, or otherwise rendered safe against accidental contact. >*See Section 11.F.*

22.B Scaffolds (excludes Elevating Aerial Work Platforms). >*See Section 22.L.*

22.B.01 An AHA shall be prepared by the contractor performing the work and submitted to the GDA prior to erection. The AHA will address all of the following elements, if applicable. If not applicable, reasoning shall be provided.

a. Site conditions (ground conditions, overhead utilities, etc.);

b. Identity of specific type of scaffolding to be used;

c. Scaffold dimensions to include height, width, depth and length;

d. Load calculation for the anticipated work load and wind loading;

e. The name of the Competent Person (CP) for Scaffolding, and

f. The method of marking or barricading to be used per 22.B.21.

22.B.02 Erection, moving, dismantling, or altering of scaffolding shall be under the supervision of a CP for Scaffolding.

a. A CP for scaffolding must have a documented, minimum of 8-hours of scaffold training to include training on the specific type of scaffold being used (e.g. Mast-Climbing, Adjustable, Tubular Frame, etc.).

b. The training must include:

(1) Assessment of the base material the scaffold will be erected upon;

(2) Load calculations for materials and personnel;

(3) Erection and dismantling; or,

(4) Training must meet the training requirements in the applicable ANSI standard. >See Section 21.B.04.

22.B.03 When scaffolding is in use, they will be inspected daily by the CP, prior to each shift. The inspection will be recorded on the daily safety inspection required by Section 01.A.13 and on the scaffold tag.

22.B.04 Scaffolding that has been hoisted after configuration or assembly shall be re-inspected by a CP before initial use and again after each hoisting. This inspection will be documented on the scaffold inspection tag.

22.B.05 A scaffold tagging system shall be used. All scaffolds are tagged by the CP. Tags shall:

a. Include name and signature of the CP;

b. Include dates of initial and all daily inspections;

c. Be readily visible, legible, and made from materials that will withstand the elements;

d. Include wording that states one of the following:

(1) Scaffold is complete and safe to use;

(2) Scaffold is incomplete, not ready for use and reasoning, or

(3) Scaffold is incomplete and unsafe to use.

22.B.06 Anyone involved in erecting, disassembling, moving, operating, using, repairing, maintaining or inspecting a scaffold shall be trained by a CP to recognize any hazards associated with the work in question. Proof of training shall be maintained on site and made available to the GDA upon request.

22.B.07 Where persons are required to work or pass under a scaffold, a screen (consisting of No. 18 gauge US Standard wire ½ in (1.2 cm) mesh or the equivalent) shall be provided between the toeboard and the guardrail and extending over the entire opening; or access to the potential impact area below shall be restricted.

22.B.08 Capacities.

a. Scaffolds and their components shall meet the requirements contained in ANSI A10.8 or other applicable ANSI standard and be capable of supporting without failure at least 4 times the maximum anticipated load.

b. Direct connections to roofs and floors, and counterweights used to balance adjustable suspension scaffolds, shall be capable of resisting at least 4 times the tipping moment imposed by the scaffold operating at the rated load of the hoist, or 1.5 times (minimum) the tipping moment imposed by the scaffold operating at the stall load of the hoist, whichever is greater.

22.B.09 Design.

a. The dimensions of the members and materials used in the construction of various working platforms or scaffolds shall conform to the sizes shown in the ANSI A10.8 tables.

b. Factory-fabricated scaffolds and components shall be designed and fabricated in accordance with the applicable ANSI standard. When there is a conflict between the ANSI standard and this manual concerning the design or fabrication of factory-fabricated scaffolds, the ANSI standard shall prevail.

c. Load-carrying timber members shall be a minimum of 1,500 lb-f/in^2 (10,342kPa) (stress grade) construction grade lumber.

(1) All dimensions are nominal sizes (except where rough sizes are noted) as provided by Voluntary Product Standard DOC PS20, published by NIST of the US Department of Commerce.

(2) Where rough sizes are noted, only rough or undressed lumber of the size specified will satisfy minimum requirements.

(3) Lumber shall be reasonably straight-grained and free of shakes, checks, splits, cross grains, unsound knots or knots in groups, decay and growth characteristics, or any other condition that will decrease the strength of the material. > For planking, see Section 22.B.15.

d. When scaffolds are wrapped with tarps, poly enclosures, or similar materials; wind calculations will be calculated by a Qualified Person (QP) to determine the strength and placement of the ties.

22.B.10 Supporting members and foundations shall be of sufficient size and strength to safely distribute loading.

a. Supporting members shall be placed on a firm, smooth foundation that will prevent lateral displacement.

b. Unstable objects such as barrels, boxes, loose bricks, or concrete blocks shall not be used as supports.

c. Vertical members (i.e., poles, legs, or uprights) shall be plumb and securely braced to prevent swaying or displacement.

22.B.11 The design and construction or selection of solid wood planking and platform for means of access shall be based upon either the number of persons for which they are rated or the uniform load distribution to which they will be subjected, whichever is the more restrictive.

22.B.12 Scaffolds shall be plumb and level unless engineered and designed to contour as the structure does.

22.B.13 Scaffolds (other than suspended scaffolds) shall bear on base plates upon mudsills or other adequate firm foundation.

22.B.14 Working levels of work platforms shall be fully planked or decked.

22.B.15 Planking.

a. All wood planking shall be selected for scaffold plank use as recognized by grading rules established by a recognized independent inspection agency for the species of wood used.

b. The maximum permissible spans for 2-in x 10-in (5-cm x 25.4-cm) (nominal), shall be 8 ft (2.4 m) or 2-in x 9-in (5-cm x 22.8-cm) (rough) solid sawn wood planks shall be 10 ft (3 m).

c. Fabricated planks and platforms may be used in lieu of solid sawn wood planks. Maximum spans for such units shall be as recommended by the manufacturer.

d. Planking shall be secured to prevent loosening, tipping, or displacement and supported or braced to prevent excessive spring or deflection. Intermediate

beams shall be provided to prevent dislodgement of planks due to deflection. > *See Section 24.A.04.*

e. Each platform on all working levels of scaffolds shall be fully planked or decked between the front uprights and the guardrail supports as follows:

(1) Each platform unit (e.g. scaffold plank, fabricated plank, fabricated deck, or fabricated platform) shall be installed so that the space between adjacent units and the space between the platform and the uprights is no more than 1 in (2.5 cm) wide, except where the employer can demonstrate that a wider space is necessary (e.g., to fit around uprights when side brackets are used to extend the width of the platform).

(2) Where the employer makes the demonstration as described in 22.B.15.e.(1), the platform shall be planked or decked as fully as possible and the remaining open space between the platform and the uprights shall not exceed 9 ½ in (24.1 cm).

f. When planking is lapped in a long run, each plank shall lap its supports at least 12 in (30.4 cm). Scaffold planks shall extend over their end supports not less than 6 in (15.2 cm) (unless the planking is manufactured with restraining hooks or equivalent means of preventing movement) or more than 12 in (30.4 cm). Work surfaces shall be properly lapped or securely fastened to the scaffold.

g. Where the ends of planks abut each other to form a flush floor, the butt joint shall be at the centerline of a pole and abutted ends shall rest on separate bearers.

h. The front edge of all platforms shall not be more than 14 in (36 cm) from the face of the work, unless guardrail systems are erected along the front edge and/or personal fall arrest systems are used; the maximum distance from the face for plastering and lathing operations is 18 in (46 cm).

i. Planking shall be supported or braced to prevent excessive spring or deflection and secured and supported to prevent loosening, tipping, or displacement.

j. When a scaffold materially changes its direction, the platform planks shall be laid to prevent tipping.

(1) The planks that meet the corner bearer at an angle shall be laid first (unless hook-on fabricated planks are used), and extend over the diagonally placed bearer far enough to have a good safe bearing, but not far enough to involve any danger from tipping, and;

(2) The planking running in the opposite direction at an angle shall be laid so as to extend over and rest on the first layer of planking.

k. Planks shall be maintained in good condition. When cracks exceed 1.5 times the width of the board, the plank will not be used. Planks with notches deeper than 1/3 the width of the plank will not be used. Planks with saw kerfs shall not be used.

22.B.16 When moving platforms to the next level, the existing platform shall be left undisturbed until the new bearers have been set to receive the platform planks.

22.B.17 Materials shall not be stored on scaffolds or runways in excess of supplies needed for that shift.

22.B.18 Access.

a. An access ladder or equivalent safe access shall be provided.

b. Where a built-in ladder is part of a scaffold system, it shall conform to the requirements for ladders. > See Section 24.B.

c. Climbing of braces is prohibited.

d. When hook-on or attachable ladders are used on a supported scaffold more than 20 ft (6 m) in height, they shall have rest platforms every 20 ft or fall protection will be used. If scaffold platforms are used as rest platforms they will be arranged so the climber must exit to a platform before climbing the next section of ladder. When end frames are used for access they will conform to the ladder standard and not exceed 20 ft without FP.

e. Hook-on or attachable ladders shall be specifically designed for use with the type of scaffold and they shall be positioned so as not to tip the scaffold.

f. When erecting or dismantling welded frame scaffolds, the end frames may be used as access provided the horizontal members are not more than 22 in (55.9 cm) apart.

g. The minimum clear length of the rungs shall be 16 in (40.7 cm).

h. The distance from the supporting surface to the first step of a ladder, stair, or frame designed to be climbed shall not exceed 2 ft (61 cm).

i. Ladder access points shall be protected by an inward swinging gate or chain guard.

22.B.19 Where the scaffold height exceeds four times the minimum scaffold base dimension (and including the width added by outriggers, if used), the scaffold shall be secured to the wall or structure.

a. The first vertical and horizontal tie shall be placed at this point.

b. Vertical ties shall be repeated at intervals not greater than 26 ft (7.9 m) with the top tie placed no lower than four times the base dimension from the top of the scaffold.

c. Horizontal ties shall be placed at each end and at intervals not greater than 30 ft (9.1 m).

d. When more stringent means of securing the scaffold are recommended by the manufacturer or an RPE, the more stringent requirements shall be followed.

22.B.20 When scaffolds are to be partially or fully enclosed, a QP shall verify the adequacy of the number, placement, and strength of ties attaching the scaffold to the structure, taking into consideration wind loads and weather.

22.B.21 When vehicles or mobile equipment are used or allowed adjacent to scaffolding, substantial stop logs or barricades shall be installed.

a. The use of a ground guide is recommended for this equipment, however, if it is demonstrated that barricades are not feasible or are not required based on distance, a ground guide shall be used.

b. Ground guides shall not be exposed to potential falling objects from the scaffold or the equipment.

c. Hanging scaffolds are exempt unless the CP determines that vehicles or mobile equipment could pose a hazard to safe operation.

22.B.22 The use of brackets on scaffolds shall be prohibited unless the tipping effect is controlled.

22.B.23 Use of the following types of scaffolding is permitted if they are designed and constructed in accordance with ANSI A10.8:

a. Outrigger scaffolds;

b. Needle beam scaffolds;

c. Interior hung scaffolds;

d. Bricklayer's square scaffolds;

e. Float/ship scaffolds;

f. Boatswain's scaffolds;

g. Window jack scaffolds;

h. Carpenter's bracket scaffolds, and

i. Form scaffolds.

22.B.24 Other types of scaffolding not included in ANSI A10.8 may be approved by the GDA provided the design is approved by a Registered Professional Engineer (RPE) or it meets a nationally recognized design standard.

22.C Metal Scaffolds and Towers.

22.C.01 Scaffold components made of dissimilar metals shall not be used together unless a CP has determined that galvanic action will not reduce the strength of any component to a level below that required by Section 22.B.09.

22.C.02 The sections of metal scaffolds shall be securely connected and all braces shall be securely fastened.

22.C.03 A ladder or stairway shall be provided for access and shall be affixed or built into all metal scaffolds and so located that, when in use, it will not have a tendency to tip the scaffold.

22.C.04 Tube and coupler scaffolds.

a. Tube and coupler scaffolds shall have posts, runners, and bracing of nominal 2 in (5-cm) (outside diameter) steel tubing or pipe: other structural metals, when used, must be designed to carry an equivalent load. The size of bearers (outside diameter) and the spacing of posts shall meet the requirements contained in ANSI A10.8.

b. Tube and coupler scaffolds shall be limited in heights and working levels to those permitted in ANSI A10.8. Drawings and specifications for tube and coupler scaffolds that exceed the limitations in ANSI A10.8 shall be designed by a RPE.

c. All tube and coupler scaffolds shall be constructed to support four times the maximum intended loads, as set forth by ANSI A10.8 or as specified by a RPE (with knowledge in structural design).

d. Runners shall be erected along the length of the scaffold and shall be located on both the inside and the outside posts at even heights.

(1) When tube and coupler guardrails and midrails are used on outside posts, they may be used in lieu of outside runners. If guardrail systems are removed

to other levels, extra runners shall be installed to compensate.

(2) Runners shall be interlocked to form continuous lengths and coupled to each post.

(3) The bottom runners shall be located as close to the base as possible.

(4) Runners shall be placed not more than 6 ft - 6 in (1.9 m) on center.

e. Bearers.

(1) Bearers shall be installed transversely between posts.

(2) When coupled to the post, the inboard coupler shall bear directly on the runner coupler. When coupled to the runners, the couplers shall be kept as close to the post as possible.

(3) Bearers shall extend beyond the posts and runners and shall provide full contact with the coupler.

f. Bracing across the width of the scaffold shall be installed at the ends of the scaffold at least every fourth level vertically and repeated every third set of posts horizontally.

(1) Such bracing shall extend diagonally from the outer post or runner at this level upward to the inner post or runner at the next level.

(2) Building ties shall be installed adjacent to bracing.

g. Longitudinal diagonal bracing across the inner and outer rows of poles shall be installed at approximately a 45° angle in both directions from the base of the end post upward to the extreme top of the scaffold.

(1) Where the longitudinal length of the scaffold permits, such bracing shall be repeated beginning at every fifth post.

(2) On scaffolds where the length is shorter than the height the longitudinal bracing shall extend diagonally from the base of the end posts upward to the opposite end posts and then in alternating directions until reaching the top of the scaffold.

(3) Where conditions preclude the attachment of bracing to the posts, it may be attached to the runners.

22.C.05 Metal frame scaffolds.

a. Spacing of tubular welded panels or frames shall be consistent with the loads imposed.

b. Scaffolds shall be properly braced by cross, horizontal, or diagonal braces (or combination of these) to secure vertical members together laterally, and the cross braces shall be of such length as will automatically square and align vertical members so that the erected scaffold is always plumb, square, and rigid. All brace connections shall be made secure.

c. Scaffold legs shall be set on adjustable bases or plain bases placed on mudsills or other foundations adequate to support the maximum rated loads.

d. Frames shall be placed one on top the other with coupling or stacking pins to provide vertical alignment of the legs.

e. Where uplift may occur, panels shall be locked together vertically by pins or other equivalent suitable means.

f. Drawings and specifications for all frame scaffolds over 125 ft (38.1 m) in height above the base plates shall be designed by a RPE.

22.C.06 Manually propelled mobile scaffolds, including mobile work stands, such as "baker scaffolds".

a. All wheels and casters on rolling scaffolds shall have a positive locking device, securely fastened to the scaffold, to prevent accidental movement.

b. All casters or wheels shall be locked when a scaffold is occupied.

c. The force necessary to move the mobile scaffold shall be applied as close to the base as practical and provision shall be made to stabilize the tower during movement from one location to another.

d. Rolling scaffolds shall be used only on firm, level, and clean surfaces.

e. Free-standing mobile scaffold working platform heights shall not exceed three times the smallest base dimension.

f. No person shall be allowed to ride on manually propelled scaffolds unless all of the following conditions exist:

(1) The ground surface is within 3° of level and free from pits, holes, or obstructions;

(2) The minimum dimension of the scaffold base (when ready for rolling) is at least one-half of the height and outriggers, if used, are installed on both sides of staging;

(3) The wheels are equipped with rubber or similar resilient tires; and

(4) All tools and materials are secured or removed from the platform before the scaffold is moved.

22.D Wood Pole Scaffolds. > See 29 CFR 1926.452(a).

22.E Suspended Scaffolds.

22.E.01 Suspended scaffolds are scaffolds that are suspended from anchorage points/hoists that allow the scaffold to move up and down as needed for work to be performed. Suspended scaffolds shall be designed, constructed, operated, inspected, tested, and maintained as specified in the operating manual for the device.

22.E.02 Inspections.

a. Suspended scaffold systems shall be inspected prior to being placed in service to determine that the system conforms to this manual and the manufacturer's specifications.

b. Before the scaffold is used, direct connections shall be evaluated by a CP who shall confirm, based on the evaluation, that the supporting surfaces are capable of supporting the loads imposed.

c. Each hoist shall be inspected by a CP before use, after every installation and re-rigging in accordance with the manufacturer's specifications. A trial operation will be done by the operator alone after every installation.

d. Connection and anchorage systems of suspended scaffold shall be inspected at the beginning of each shift.

e. All wire ropes, fiber and synthetic ropes, slings, hangers, hoists, rigging, fall protection equipment, platforms, anchorage points and their connections, and other supporting parts shall be inspected before every installation, daily thereafter, and periodic while the scaffold is in use.

f. Governors and secondary brakes for powered hoists shall be inspected and tested per the manufacturer's recommendations: at the minimum, inspections shall be made annually.

(1) Inspections and tests shall include a verification that the initiating device for the secondary braking operates as intended.

(2) A copy of the latest inspection and test report shall be maintained on the job site.

g. Records of inspections conducted while the unit is at the work site shall be maintained at the work site.

22.E.03 Only personnel trained in the use of the suspended work platform shall be authorized to operate it. Anyone involved in erecting, disassembling, moving, operating, using, repairing, maintaining or inspecting a suspended scaffold shall be trained by a CP to recognize any hazards associated with the work in question. Proof of training shall be maintained on site and made available to the GDA upon request. Training shall include:

a. Reading and understanding the manufacturer's operating manual and any associated rules and instructions, or training by a QP on the contents on these documents, and

b. Reading and understanding all decals, warnings, and instructions on the device.

22.E.04 All parts of all suspended scaffolds shall have a minimum safety factor of 4. A minimum safety factor of 6 is required for support ropes.

22.E.05 Support ropes.

a. Support ropes shall be attached at the vertical centerline of the outrigger and the attachment shall be directly over the hoist machine.

b. Support ropes shall be vertical for their entire length. The scaffold shall not be swayed nor the support ropes fixed to any intermediate points to change the original path of travel.

c. Support ropes shall have the fixed end equipped with a proper size thimble and secured by eye splicing or equivalent means. Free ends shall be brazed or secured to prevent fraying.

d. The wire rope for traction hoists shall be of such length that the operator may descend to the lowest point of travel without the end of the wire rope entering the hoist. Where the wire rope is inadequate for the lowest descent, provision shall be made to prevent the hoist from running off the wire rope.

e. On winding drum type hoists, running ends of suspension ropes shall be attached by positive means to the hoisting drum and at least four wraps of the rope shall remain on the drum at all times.

f. Support ropes shall be capable of resisting chemicals or conditions to which they are exposed.

g. No welding, burning, riveting, or open flame work shall be performed on any platform suspended by fiber or synthetic rope.

h. Defective or damaged rope shall not be used as lifelines or suspension lines. The repairing of wire rope is prohibited.

22.E.06 All suspension scaffold support devices such as outrigger beams, cornice hooks, parapet clamps, or similar devices shall:

a. Be made of mild steel, wrought iron, or materials of equivalent strength;

b. Be supported by bearing blocks;

c. Rest on surfaces capable of supporting the reaction forces imposed by the scaffold hoist operating at its maximum rated load; and

d. Be secured against movement by tiebacks installed at right angles to the face of the building whenever possible and secured to a structurally sound portion of the building. Tiebacks shall be equivalent in strength to the hoisting rope.

22.E.07 Outrigger beams.

a. Outrigger beams shall be made of structural metal and shall be restrained to prevent movement.

b. The inboard ends of outrigger beams shall be stabilized by bolts or other direct connections to the floor or roof deck, or they shall have their inboard ends stabilized by counterweights, except mason's multiple point adjustable suspension scaffold outrigger beams shall not be stabilized by counterweights.

c. Before use, direct connections shall be evaluated by a CP who shall affirm that the supporting surfaces are capable of supporting the loads to be imposed. Mason's multiple point adjustable suspension scaffold connections shall be designed by a RPE experienced in scaffold design.

d. Counterweights shall be made of non-flowable solid material, shall be secured to the outrigger beams by mechanical means, and shall not be removed until the scaffold is disassembled.

e. Outrigger beams shall be secured by tiebacks equivalent in strength to the suspension ropes. Tiebacks shall be secured to a structurally sound portion of the building or structure and shall be installed parallel to the centerline of the beam.

f. Outrigger beams shall be provided with stop bolts or shackles at both ends.

g. When channel iron beams are used in place of I-beams, the channels shall be securely fastened together with the flanges turned outward.

h. Outrigger beams shall be installed with all bearing supports perpendicular to the beam centerline.

i. Outrigger beams shall be set and maintained with the web in a vertical position.

j. Where a single outrigger beam is used, the steel shackle or clevises with which the wire ropes are attached to the beam shall be placed directly over the hoisting machines.

22.E.08 Hoisting machines

a. Hoisting machines shall be of a type tested and listed by a nationally recognized testing laboratory.

b. Each hoist shall contain a name plate(s) containing:

(1) Manufacturer's name;

(2) Maximum load rating;

(3) Identification number; and

(4) Wire rope specifications.

c. Powered hoists shall be electric-, air-, hydraulic-, or propane-powered. Gasoline-powered hoists are prohibited.

d. All powered hoists shall be equipped with speed reducers and shall be provided with a primary brake and a secondary brake.

(1) The primary brake shall automatically engage whenever power is interrupted or whenever the operator ceases to apply effort;

(2) The secondary brake shall stop and hold the hoist under over speed or abnormal conditions. All secondary brakes shall be periodically tested under simulated conditions in accordance with the manufacturer's recommendations.

e. Each powered hoist shall have its own separate control.

(1) If the control is of the push-button type, it shall be constant pressure;

(2) If the control is of the fixed-position type, it shall have provision for automatic locking when in the off position, or shall be guarded against accidental actuation; and

(3) If the control is of the lever type, it may be of the constant pressure type or of the fixed-position type.

f. Manual operation of powered hoists may be provided if the hoist is designed so that not more than one person per hoist is required to perform this operation.

(1) During manual operation, a means shall be provided to make the prime mover inoperative.

(2) Instruction shall be provided advising personnel to disconnect the power source before using a manual crank.

g. Manually-operated hoists.

(1) Manual operation shall provide a means to prevent rapid handle movement or fast un-spooling. Mechanisms used to allow fast un-spooling during the erection process shall not be in place on the scaffold.

(2) In the event a controlled descent device is used, it shall not bypass the secondary brake.

(3) All winding drum hoists shall be provided with a driving pawl and a locking pawl that automatically engages when the driving pawl is released.

(4) Gripping-type hoists shall be designed so that the hoist is engaged on the suspension rope at all times, including all travel actuations of the operating lever.

(5) Each winding drum hoist shall be provided with a positive means of attachment of the suspension hoist. The drum attachment shall develop a minimum of four times the rated capacity of the hoist.

(6) Each hoist shall require a positive crank force to descend.

22.E.09 Working surfaces.

a. Light metal platforms, when used, shall be of a type tested and listed by a nationally recognized testing laboratory.

b. Ladder-type platforms are prohibited.

c. Planking.

(1) Planking shall be composed of not less than nominal 2-in x 10-in (5-cm x 25.4-cm) unspliced planks, cleated together on the underside, starting 6 in (15.2 cm) from each end at intervals not to exceed 4 ft (1.2 m).

(2) The planking shall not extend beyond the hangers more than 12 in (30.4 cm). A bar or other effective means shall be securely fastened to the platform at each end to prevent its slipping off the hanger.

(3) The span between hangers for planked platforms shall not exceed 8 ft (2.4 m).

d. Beam platforms <u>are prohibited</u>.

22.E.10 Suspended scaffolds shall be guyed, braced, guided, or equipped with tag line to prevent swaying.

22.E.11 Two-point suspension scaffolds.

a. Two-point suspension scaffold platforms shall not be less than 20 in (50.8 cm) or more than 36 in (91.4 cm) wide. The platform shall be securely fastened to the hangers by U-bolts or by other equivalent means.

b. The hangers of two-point suspension scaffolds shall be made of mild steel, or equivalent materials, having a cross sectional area capable of sustaining four times the maximum rated load and shall be designed with a support for a standard railing.

c. Two-point suspension scaffolds shall be securely lashed to the structure. Window cleaner's anchors shall not be used.

d. The platform on every two-point suspension scaffolds shall be of the light metal or planking.

e. Two-point suspension scaffolds shall not be joined by bridging.

f. Two-point suspension scaffold platforms, when in use, shall be level within 1 in (2.5 cm) for every 1 ft (0.3 m) of platform length.

22.E.12 Mason's multiple-point adjustable suspension scaffolds.

a. When employees on the scaffold are exposed to overhead hazards, overhead protection equivalent in strength to 2 in (5-cm) planking shall be provided on the scaffold not more than 9 ft (2.7 m) above the platform, laid tight and extending the entire width of the scaffold.

b. The scaffold shall be capable of sustaining a load of 50 psf (2,394 Pa) and shall not be overloaded.

c. The platform shall be suspended by wire ropes from overhead outrigger beams.

22.E.13 Stonesetters' multiple-point adjustable suspension scaffolds <u>shall be designed and used in accordance with ANSI A10.8.</u>

22.E.14 Working capacities.

a. On suspension scaffolds designed for a working load of 500 lb (226.8 kg), no more than two employees shall be permitted to work at one time.

b. On suspension scaffolds with a working load of 750 lb (340.2 kg), no more than three people shall be permitted to work at one time.

22.F Hanging Scaffolds.

22.F.01 A hanging scaffold is a scaffold/work platform that is hung from a location (such as a lock gate) for work to be performed and that remains stationary until it is then repositioned with a crane/hoisting device. Hanging scaffolds shall be designed by a RPE competent in structural design. Scaffold performance and components shall meet or exceed those for general scaffolds and platforms found in ANSI A10.8-2001. > *See Figure 22-1.*

22.F.02 Hanging scaffolds shall meet the following requirements:

a. The scaffold shall be securely fastened to a vertical structure (i.e. wall, lock gate, etc.) by hooks over a secured structural supporting member, bolt-on brackets, or other secure attachment. The maximum span between secure attachments is 8 ft (2.4 m). Fasteners shall be of adequate size to achieve design strength of scaffold.

b. The scaffold must be secured against an uplift force equal to two times the weight of the scaffold and its rated load by means of hooks, brackets, or other secure attachments designed and placed to counteract uplift.

c. The scaffold shall have a secondary attachment method to secure it against falling if the primary attachment fails. This should be a flexible attachment, such as wire rope or chain, designed to withstand a minimum of five (5) times the weight of the scaffold and its rated load. The secondary attachment shall be connected to an anchor point of the same load rating or greater.

d. The scaffold shall have only one working level. Working platform decks shall be slip resistant and securely attached to the scaffold frame. The maximum width, front to back, of decks is 42 in (106.6 cm).

Grating used for deck surfaces shall have a maximum width opening between bars small enough to prevent the rigging components used (slings, chains) from entering.

FIGURE 22-1

Hanging Scaffold

e. Standard guardrails systems meeting the requirements of Section 21.F.01 shall be installed on all open sides and ends of the platform.

f. The scaffold shall be conspicuously posted with a plate or other permanent marking that indicates:

  (1) Weight of the scaffold;

  (2) Number of personnel it was designed for;

  (3) Rated weight capacity;

(4) Specific structure(s) it was designed to be attached to – this may be a code or other form of identification when designed for a number of different structures with similar structural attachment points;

(5) Name of the RPE who designed the scaffold; and

(6) Date of manufacture.

g. Hanging scaffolds designed to also function as crane- or other load handling equipment- (LHE-) supported personnel work platforms shall meet the requirements of Section 16.T. This includes scaffolds that require a person to stand/ride on the platform while the initial attachment to the structure is made.

h. The space between the platform deck edge and the face of the vertical structure shall not be more than 14 in (35.6 cm). Prior to use on each jobsite application, the CP shall determine if this space constitutes a hazard by being large enough to allow tools or objects to fall on workers below or, if LHE rigging may enter and entangle in the space. In these situations, the space shall be closed or blocked to remove the hazard.

22.F.03 Testing

a. Prior to initial use and after any modification of the structural members or secure attachment points, the platform shall be proof tested to 125% of its rated capacity. The test shall take place on a structure the scaffold was designed for or a test structure with similar support member characteristics.

b. Prior to use on each jobsite or placement location, hanging scaffolds shall be performance tested to 100% of the maximum intended load for the expected work. This test shall be performed with the scaffold attached to the structure in the work location.

22.F.04 Operations

a. Scaffolds and their attachments shall be inspected by a CP prior to initial use on a worksite, before use on each work shift, and regularly during use until they are removed.

b. Workers shall use properly selected and anchored personal fall protection when accessing and working on hanging scaffolds. Personal FP system components shall meet the requirements of Section 21.I.05. No part of a hanging scaffold shall be used as an anchor point for personal FP.

c. The number of workers on the platform shall not exceed the number listed on the scaffold.

d. Ladders may not be used on hanging scaffolds, except as a means of access from above the deck. Ladders used for access must meet the requirements of Section 24.B.

e. Hanging scaffolds shall be coated or painted to minimize corrosion of the components. Storage between uses shall be designed to minimize damage to the scaffold.

22.G Form and Carpenter's Bracket Scaffolding.

22.G.01 Scaffolds shall be constructed of wood, steel, or aluminum members with known strength characteristics and be designed to support a minimum load of 25 lbs/ft^2 (1.054 kg/m^2).

22.G.02 No more than two persons shall occupy any given 8 ft (2.4 m) span of a bracket scaffold at any one time. Tools and materials shall not exceed 75 lbs (34 kg) in addition to person(s) occupying the area.

22.G.03 A guardrail or other form of fall protection is required for all open edges when a fall of 6 ft or greater exists (1.8 m) or, when other hazards exist below the platform.

22.G.04 Figure-four scaffolds shall be constructed as follows:

a. Spacing shall be not more than 8 ft (2.4 m) on centers and scaffold shall be constructed from sound lumber.

b. The bracket ledger shall consist of two pieces of 1-in x 6-in (2.5-cm x 15.2-cm) or heavier material nailed on opposite sides of the vertical form support. Ledgers shall project not more than 3 ½ ft (1 m) from the outside of the form support and shall be braced and secured to prevent tipping or turning.

c. The knee or angle brace shall intersect the ledger at least 3 ft (.9 m) from the form at an angle of approximately 45 degrees, and the lower end shall be nailed to a vertical support.

d. The platform shall consist of two or more scaffold planks that extend at least 6 in (15.2 cm) beyond the ledgers at each end unless secured to the ledgers. When planks are secured to the ledgers (nailed or bolted) a wood filler strip shall be used between the ledgers. Unsupported projecting ends of planks shall be limited to an overhang of 12 in (30 cm).

e. The maximum permissible spans for planking shall be in conformance with ANSI A10.8 and be consistent with allowable bearer loads.

22.G.05 Metal brackets or scaffold jacks that are an integral part of the form shall be securely bolted or welded to the form. Folding-type brackets shall be either bolted or secured with a locking-type pin when extended for use.

22.G.06 Clip-on or hook-over brackets may be used on form work provided the form walers are bolted to the form or secured by snap ties or tie-bolts extending through the form and securely anchored. In addition, carpenter bracket scaffolds may be attached by:

a. A bolt extending through to the opposite side of the structural wall;

b. A metal stud attachment device;

c. Welding; or

d. Hooking over a secured structural supporting member.

22.G.07 Metal brackets shall be spaced not more than 8 ft (2.4 m) on centers.

22.G.08 Scaffold planks shall be either bolted to the metal brackets or be of such length that they overlap the brackets at each end by at least 6 in (15.2 cm). Unsupported projecting ends of scaffold planks shall be limited to a maximum overhang of 12 in (30.4 cm).

22.G.09 The maximum permissible spans for planking shall be consistent with allowable bearer loads.

22.G.10 Folding-type metal brackets, when extended for use, shall be either bolted or secured with a locking-type pin.

22.G.11 Wooden bracket form scaffolds shall be designed in accordance with Table 22-1 and shall be an integral part of the form panel.

22.G.12 Brackets shall consist of a triangular shaped frame made of wood with a cross-section not less than 2-in x 3-in (5-cm x 7.6-cm) or of 1-1/4-in x 1-1/4-in x 1/8-in (3.1-cm x 3.1-cm x 0.3-cm) structural angle iron.

22.G.13 The minimum design for wooden scaffolds criteria shall be in accordance with Table 22-1.

22.G.14 Scaffold planks shall be either nailed or bolted to the runners or be of such length that they overlap the ledgers at each end by at least 6 in (15.2 cm). Unsupported projecting ends of scaffold planks shall be limited to a maximum overhang of 12 in (30.4 cm).

22.G.15 The maximum permissible spans for planking shall be consistent with allowable bearer loads.

22

TABLE 22-1

Form Scaffolds

(Minimum Design Criteria for Wooden Bracket Form Scaffolds)

Members	Dimensions
Bracket uprights	2 x 4 in or 2 x 6 in (5 x 10.1 cm or 5 x 15.2 cm)
Bracket support ledgers	2 x 6 in (5 x 15.2 cm)
Maximum bracket width	3 ft 6 in (1 m)
Bracket braces	1 x 6 in (2.5 x 15.2 cm)
Guardrail post	2 x 4 in (5 x 10.1 cm)
Guardrail height	36 to 45 in (91.4 to 114.3 cm)
Midrail	1 x 6 in (2.5 x 15.2 cm)
Toeboards	1 x 6 in (2.5 x 15.2 cm)
Bracket upright spacing	8 ft (2.4 m) (on centers)

SECTION 22 Work Platforms and Scaffolding

Form Scaffolds

(Minimum Design Criteria for Light-Duty Figure-Four Form Scaffolds)

Members	Dimensions
Bracket uprights	2 x 4 in or 2 x 6 in (5 x 10.1cm or 5 x 15.2cm)
Bracket outrigger ledgers	(2) 1 x 6 in (2.5 x 15.2 cm)
Bracket braces	(2) 1 x 6 in (2.5 x 15.2 cm)
Maximum length of ledgers	3 ft 6 in (1 m) (unsupported)
Bracket upright spacing	8 ft (2.4 m) (on centers)

22.H Horse Scaffolds.

22.H.01 Horses shall not be constructed or arranged more than two tiers or 10 ft (3 m) in height: scaffolds shall be 5 ft (1.5 m) or less in height and 5 ft (1.5 m) or more in width. When tiered heights exceed 6 ft (1.8 m), FP shall be used.

22.H.02 The members of horse scaffolds shall not be less than those specified in Table 22-2.

TABLE 22-2

Minimum Dimensions for Horse Scaffold Members

Members	Dimensions
Horizontal members of bearers	3 x 3.9 in (7.6 x 10 cm)
Legs	2 x 3.9 in (5 x 10 cm)
Longitudinal brace between legs	1 x 5.9 in (2.5 x 15 cm)
Gusset brace at top of legs	1 x 7.9 in (2.5 x 20 cm)
Half diagonal braces	2 x 3.9 in (5 x 10 cm)

22.H.03 Horse scaffolds shall be spaced not more than 5 ft (1.5 m) for medium duty and not more than 8 ft (2.4 m) for light duty.

22.H.04 When arranged in tiers, each horse scaffold shall be placed directly over the horse scaffold in the tier below. The legs shall be nailed or otherwise secured to the planks to prevent displacement or thrust and each tier shall be cross braced.

22.H.05 Weakened or defective components shall not be used.

22.I Pump Jack Scaffolds.

22.I.01 Pump jack scaffolds shall be designed for a minimum working load of 500 lbs (226.8 kg) and not more than two (2) workers shall be allowed on the scaffold at one time.

22.I.02 Pump jack brackets, braces, and accessories shall be fabricated from metal plates and angles and installed in accordance with the manufacturer's recommendations. Installation and operational manuals shall be maintained onsite and made available upon request of the GDA.

22

22.I.03 The standing platform shall be fully decked and the planking secured. Platforms thicker than 2 in (5.08 cm) shall not be overlapped.

22.I.04 The minimum width of a standing platform shall be 18 in (45.7 cm) and the work bench shall be 12 in (30.4 cm).

22.I.05 All materials on the work bench shall be secured from falling.

22.I.06 Pump jack scaffolds shall be provided with a guardrail system as specified by the manufacturer. Personal fall arrest systems may be used in lieu of guardrails.

22.I.07 When a workbench is used at an approximate height of 42 in (1.06 m), the top rail may be eliminated if the workbench is fully decked, if the workbench is secured, and if it is capable of withstanding 200 lbs (90.7 kg) force in any direction.

22.I.08 Workbenches shall not be used as a standing platform.

22.I.09 A ladder shall be provided for access to the platform.

22.I.10 All poles shall be supported by sills or other foundations adequate to support the load.

22.I.11 Poles.

a. Pole lumber shall be 2-in x 4-in (5-cm x 10.1-cm) stock, of Douglas fir, or equivalent, straight-grained, clear, free of cross-grain, shakes, large loose or dead knots, and other defects that might impair strength.

b. Wood poles shall not exceed 30 ft (9.1 m) in height; and spacing cannot exceed 7 ft (2.1 m).

c. Metal poles shall not exceed 50 ft (15.2 m) in height unless the design is approved by an RPE. The spacing of metal poles in excess of 7 ft (2.1 m) must also be determined by an RPE.

d. When poles are constructed of two continuous lengths they shall be of 2-in x 4-in (5-cm x 10.1-cm) (kiln dried straight grain fir) or equivalent, spiked together with the seam parallel to the pump jack, and with 10d common nails, 12 in (30.4 cm) center-to-center, staggered uniformly from opposite outside edges.

e. 4-in by 4-in (10.1 cm by 10.1 cm) wood poles may not be spliced to increase the length of any individual member.

f. Poles shall be secured to the wall by triangular bracing, or equivalent, at the bottom, top, and other points to provide a maximum vertical spacing of not more than 10 ft (3 m) between braces. Each brace shall be capable of supporting a minimum of 225 lbs (102 kg) tension or compression.

g. When wood scaffold planks are used as platforms, poles used for pump jacks shall not be spaced more than 10 ft (3 m) on center. When fabricated platforms are used that comply with all other provisions of this Section, pole spacing may exceed 10 ft on center if permitted by the manufacturer.

h. Poles shall not be placed closer than 10 ft (3.04 m) of power lines or electrical conductors until such are insulated, de-energized, or otherwise rendered safe against contact. > See Table 11-1.

22.I.12 Brackets.

a. Each pump jack bracket shall have two positive gripping mechanisms to prevent any failure or slippage.

b. For the pump jack bracket to pass bracing already installed, an extra brace shall be used approximately 4 ft (1.2 m) above the one to be passed until the original brace is reinstalled.

22.J Adjustable Scaffolds.

22.J.01 Adjustable scaffolds shall be designed and constructed in accordance with ANSI/SIA A10.8.

22.J.02 A copy of the user's manual shall be kept on site at all times.

22.J.03 Adjustable scaffolds will be secured to the structure in accordance with the manufacturer's user manual.

22.J.04 Safe access.

a. If portable ladders are used they will be removed every time the platform is raised or lowered, repositioned to ensure that the 4:1 ratio is maintained, and secured to prevent movement.

b. When stair towers are used for access to adjustable scaffolds the difference between the two elevations will be 2 ft (.6 m) or less.

c. Self-retracting lanyard, if allowed by the manufacturer, can be used to provide FP when climbing the tower. > See also Section 21.

d. On towers over 20 ft (10.7 m), rest platforms will be provided at not more than 20 ft intervals.

22.J.05 The leveling of adjustable scaffold will be accomplished by using leveling jacks.

22.J.06 When bridges are used on a single tower it will be done in strict compliance with the manufacturer's recommendations.

22.J.07 Ratchet driven winding drum hoist shall be equipped with a driving pawl and a locking pawl. The locking pawl must automatically engage when the driving pawl is released.

22.J.08 All crank-driven winding drum hoists shall employ a positively actuated locking pawl that engages the drive train of the hoist and is actuated by reverse descending movement of the crank handle. This mechanism shall not be rendered inoperative by outside contamination.

22.J.09 Every winding drum shall contain not less than three wraps of the suspension wire rope at the lowest point of hoist travel.

22.J.10 Each hoist shall be provided with positive wire rope attachments. Wire rope attachments shall develop a minimum of 80% of the wire rope breaking strength. Wire rope termination methods shall be according to the manufacturer's recommendation. U-type wire rope clips shall not be used as a wire rope termination method.

22.J.11 The wire rope shall be capable of supportable at least six (6) times the scaffold's design load.

22.J.12 Employers shall instruct and supervise their employees in the safe use of the adjustable scaffolding provided and shall supply them with all of the manufacture's instructional material.

22.J.13 Personnel shall not work on scaffolds during storms, high winds or other adverse weather conditions.

22.K Load Handling Equipment (LHE) – Supported Personnel Work Platforms. > *See Section 16.T.*

22.L Elevating Aerial Work Platforms (AWPs).

22.L.01 All elevating aerial work platforms (AWPs) shall be designed and constructed in accordance with ANSI/SIA A92.3, ANSI/SIA A92.5, and ANSI/SIA A92.6, as appropriate.

22.L.02 AWPs shall be operated, inspected, and maintained as specified in the operating manual for the equipment.

a. AWPs shall comply with requirements of this Section and Section 18.G.

b. Records of inspections conducted while the unit is at the work site shall be maintained at the work site.

c. Height-to-base width ratio of the scaffold during movement is 2:1 or less, or per manufacturer's instructions.

d. All elevating AWPs shall have the manufacturer's operating manual readily available on the equipment.

e. AWPs will not be operated unless the access door or chains are in the closed position.

f. Fall protection shall be used in accordance with Section 21.K of this manual.

g. Climbing of the rails is prohibited.

22.L.03 All boom-supported AWPs shall be equipped with an alarm, or other suitable warning device, at the platform. The alarm shall be in operable condition and shall automatically activate when the machine base is more than 5° out of level in any direction.

22.L.04 All AWP operators shall have training that includes both general as well as equipment specific familiarization before being allowed to operate this equipment. Training shall be documented.

22.L.05 Before operating the AWP the operator shall:

a. Survey the work area for loose or soft ground, ditches, drop-offs or holes, bumps and floor obstructions, debris, overhead obstructions, ground and elevated energy sources, and other possible hazards;

b. Ensure the AWP is on a firm, level surface;

c. Ensure the AWP is loaded in accordance with the manufacturer's specifications;

d. Ensure that outriggers and/or stabilizers are used if required by the manufacturer;

e. Ensure that, if the vehicle is on wheels, the wheels are locked or chocked; and

f. Ensure that the fall restraint system is connected.

22.L.06 These AWPs shall not be used by persons working on energized electrical wiring and/or equipment.

22.L.07 AWPs shall only be operated from the ground position in an emergency (rescue), for maintenance, or when unoccupied.

22.L.08 Lift controls will be located below the guardrail height. When lift controls are not located below the guardrail height an aftermarket guard will be installed.

22.M Vehicle-Mounted Elevating and Rotating Work Platforms (Aerial Devices/Lifts).

22.M.01 Vehicle-mounted elevating and rotating work platforms (aerial lifts, to include articulating boom platforms/lifts (knuckle boom lifts), trailer-mounted boom lifts) shall be designed and constructed per ANSI/SIA A92.2.

22.M.02 Vehicle-mounted elevating and rotating work platforms shall be operated, inspected, tested, and maintained as specified in the operating manual for that piece of equipment.

a. Vehicle-mounted elevating and rotating work platforms shall also comply with requirements in Sections 18.G and 21.

b. Records of inspections conducted while the unit is at the work site shall be maintained at the work site.

c. All aerial devices shall have manufacturer's operating manual readily available in or on the vehicle.

d. If the unit is considered rated, and used as an insulating device, copies of the electrical insulating components and system tests conducted while the unit is at the work site shall be maintained at the work site.

e. All required safety decals, labels and signs shall be in place and readable.

22.M.03 Only personnel trained in the use of the vehicle-mounted elevating and rotating work platform shall be authorized to operate it. Training shall consist of:

a. Reading and understanding the manufacturer's operating manual and any associated rules and instructions, or training by a QP on the contents on these documents; and

b. Reading and understanding all decals, warnings, and instructions on the vehicle-mounted elevating and rotating work platform.

22.M.04 Transporting.

a. Aerial lift trucks, to include cherry pickers, shall not be moved when the boom is elevated in a working position with personnel in the basket except for equipment that is specifically designed for this type of operation. When manufacturers allow mobile operation, the worksite shall be inspected for:

(1) Untamped earth fills (soft ground);

(2) Ditches;

(3) Drop-offs and floor obstructions;

(4) Debris;

(5) Overhead obstructions and electrical conductors;

(6) Weather conditions, and

(7) The presence of unauthorized persons.

b. Before moving an aerial lift, the boom(s) shall be inspected to see that it is properly cradled and outriggers are in stowed positions, except as provided in a, above.

c. Aerial ladders shall be secured in the lower traveling position by the locking device on top of the truck cab and the manually operated device at the base of the ladder before the truck is moved for highway travel.

22.M.05 Operating practices. The manufacturer's instruction for control station operation must be followed (e.g. primary versus secondary; upper versus lower).

a. Brakes shall be set and outriggers, when used, shall be positioned on pads or a solid surface.

b. Wheel chocks shall be installed before using an aerial lift on an incline.

c. Lift controls shall be tested each day prior to use to ensure safe working condition.

d. Lift controls will be located below the guardrail height. When lift controls are not located below the guardrail height, an after-market guard will be installed.

e. Boom and basket load limits specified by manufacturer shall not be exceeded.

f. Articulating boom and extensible boom platforms, primarily designed as personnel carriers, shall have both platform (upper) and lower controls.

(1) Upper controls shall be in or beside the platform within easy reach of the operator.

(2) Lower controls shall provide for overriding the upper controls.

(3) Controls shall be plainly marked as to their function.

(4) Lower level controls shall not be operated unless permission has been obtained from the employee in the lift except in case of emergency. This practice shall be documented in the applicable AHA.

g. Climbers (spikes) shall not be worn while performing work from an aerial lift.

h. The insulated portion of an aerial lift shall not be altered in any manner that might reduce its insulating value.

i. Occupants shall always stand firmly on the floor of the basket and shall not sit or climb on the edge of the basket or use planks, ladders, or other devices for a work position.

22.N Mast Climbing Work Platforms.

22.N.01 Mast Climbing work platforms (MCWPs) shall be erected, used, inspected, tested, maintained, and repaired in accordance with ANSI A92.9, the IPAF/SAIA Safe Use Guidelines for Mast Climbing Work Platforms (henceforth referred to as 'IPAF/SAIA') and the manufacturer's recommendations as outlined in the operating manual, henceforth referred to as 'manual'.

22.N.02 A pre-use inspection will be performed prior to erecting the work platform, according to requirements set out in IFPA/SAIA and the operator's manual.

a. An overhead inspection will be done to ensure that the MCWP will not come in contact with any obstructions while moving up or down the mast. Special attention will be given to high voltage conductors. Once the voltage of the line(s) is established, the minimum safe approach distance in Table 11-1 will be used.

b. An inspection of the ground will be done to ensure that there are no obstacles around the MCWP and in the path of travel (if the unit is on a mobile chassis) such as holes, drop-offs, debris, ditches, or soft fill. For static and mobile units, compaction will be sufficient to support the static and live loads for the configuration. The perimeter around the base of the unit, matching the length and width of the platform area above, shall be identified as restricted access by use of danger signs, tape, fences, or other suitable means.

c. Daily maintenance and inspections will be performed and documented by a CP per Section 22.B.03. Copies will be maintained on the job site.

22.N.03 Only designated and trained users shall operate the MCWP. Training records shall be maintained for at least 3 years and maintained on-site. All personnel on the MCWP shall be trained per Section 22.N.14 below.

22.N.04 The MCWP will not be raised on uneven or sloped surfaces unless outriggers are used to level the MCWP and the ground is suitable to support the load.

22.N.05 MCWPs shall be raised only in accordance with manufacturer's recommended free standing height and outrigger requirement, and loading recommendations. All outriggers shall be as per manufacturer's recommendation. The unit shall be level before raising the platform (mast should be plumb and level before vertical movement of platform).

➤ Note: Not all Mast Climbing Work Platforms are designed with freestanding capability. Check the machine and manual to see if the machine being operated has a freestanding height.

22.N.06 If the unit is on a powered chassis, the MCWP must be lowered to its lowest position prior to being moved. Additionally, all material and tools must be removed from the platform, the outriggers must be fully extended and open and the jacks must be raised no more than 1 in (2.5 cm) from the ground. When moved into its new working position, the unit must be set up and leveled again before it is elevated. The work platform shall remain horizontal within 2 degrees during normal movement of the platform.

22.N.07 A MCWP, with platform elevated or personnel on the platform, shall not be driven. The manufacturer's instructions shall be followed when moving a MCWP to determine the safe mast height for ground conditions, ground slope, and overhead obstructions.

22.N.08 MCWPs will be properly tied to the building (or structure) according to manufacturer's guidelines unless it is designed to be freestanding. A QP shall demonstrate the correct anchoring method based on tensile, shear and torsion forces as advised by the manufacturer and with respect to the strength of the structure to be tied to, following all relevant requirements on installation from the anchor manufacturer's data.

22.N.09 No ladders or structures of any kind will be used to increase the size or working height of platform unless specifically designed by the manufacturer for the intended use and all fall hazards have been controlled.

22.N.10 Access.

a. Climbing of braces and guardrails is prohibited. When access ladders, including masts designed as ladders, exceed 20 ft (6 m) in height, positive fall protection shall be used.

b. All access gates shall either close automatically or be electronically interlocked to prevent operation of the MCWP unless they are closed. Chains or ropes shall not be used as access gates.

c. Prior to use at elevations of 20 ft (6 m) or more, an emergency egress plan will be developed to evacuate workers from a MCWP that gets caught in an elevated position 20 ft or more above the ground. If that plan includes descending the mast, all employees working on the MCWP will be provided fall arrest equipment and will be trained in its use.

22.N.11 The MCWP shall not be raised in windy or gusty conditions.

a. The operation manual shall be followed to determine maximum in-service wind speed conditions. A copy of the operator's manual shall be available on the job site.

b. Loads and forces shall be accounted for and followed per manufacturer's instructions.

22.N.12 MCWPs shall not be altered or modified in any way, unless approved by the manufacturer, and performed by a QP.

22.N.13 Only authorized personnel (users and operators) shall use the MCWP.

22.N.14 Training. Personnel will be trained and familiarized by a QP (Qualified by either a manufacturer or an Industry recognized training course) before using and/or operating MCWPs. Anyone involved in erecting, disassembling, moving, operating, using, repairing, maintaining or inspecting a MCWP shall be trained by a QP to recognize any hazards associated with the work in question. Proof of training shall be made readily available on site. Operator training shall meet the following:

a. All training must be per the ANSI 92.9 standard and IPAF/SAIA guidelines.

b. All non-user trained personnel (i.e., building inspectors, consultants, etc.) that may need to be on the MCWPs shall have as a minimum, safety/hazard awareness training, and be escorted by a trained user while on the scaffold.

22.N.15 A damaged or malfunctioning machine shall not be used. Operation of damaged equipment shall be discontinued until the unit is repaired.

22.N.16 MCWPs shall be equipped with a permanently installed device on the work platform to switch off the work platform and secure it from unauthorized use.

22.N.17 Planking and decking shall follow the guidelines set forth in Section 22.B.15 and 29 CFR 1926.451.

22.N.18 Guarding.

a. All open sides of the platform shall be equipped with a guardrail which can be securely fastened in place. Guardrails shall be secured per the manufacturer's instructions and shall withstand, without failure, a force of 300 lbs, applied in any outward or downward direction.

b. If the MCWP is erected towards a wall and the distance is more than 14 in (0.36 m), a guardrail shall be required. The maximum distance between wall and platform may increase to 18 in (0.46 m) for plastering and lathing operations. When it is possible to have a horizontal distance between the wall and platform of not more than 14 in (.36 m), then a guardrail is not necessary.

c. Any MCWP with a travel speed of more than 15 fpm shall include a mast guard around at least 3 sides of the mast. The guard shall provide protection from not more than 1 in (2.5 cm) above the platform floor to a minimum height of 6 ½ ft (1.98 m) above the platform floor, and shall have no opening larger than 1 in2 (2.5 cm2).

22.N.19 Annual inspection. An annual inspection will be performed in accordance with the manufacturer's guidelines but no later than 13 months from the date of the prior inspection. The inspection shall be performed by a QP on the specific make and model of MCWP. A copy of the inspection shall be maintained on site with the owner's manual.

22.O Roofing Brackets.

22.O.01 Roofing brackets shall be secured by nailing in addition to the pointed metal projections. Nails will be driven into a rafter or beam; not just into the decking. Fasteners will be selected in accordance with the manufacturer's recommendations.

22.O.02 When it is impractical to nail brackets, rope supports shall be used. When rope supports are used, they shall consist of first-grade manila rope, ¾ in (1.9 cm) diameter or equivalent.

22.P Stilts.

22.P.01 Stilts shall not be used on scaffolds.

22.P.02 Surfaces on which stilts are used shall be flat and free of pits, holes, obstructions, debris and other tripping or slipping hazards.

22.P.03 Stilts shall be properly maintained. Any alteration of the equipment shall be approved by the manufacturer.

22.P.04 Stilts shall not be used on stairs. When used adjacent to stairs or ramps where a fall to a different level could occur, guardrails (as defined in Section 21.F.01.b) or other fall protection shall be provided (increased in height by an amount equal to the height of the stilts).

22.P.05 Employees shall be trained in the proper use of stilts.

22.P.06 When using stilts exposes workers to a fall of 6 ft (1.8 m) or more in areas protected by guardrails, the height of the guardrails must be raised accordingly to maintain a protective height of 42 in (107cm) above the stilt. > See Section 21.A.04.

22.Q Turbine Maintenance Platforms (TMPs). A TMP is type of scaffold unique to hydropower Operations and Maintenance that incorporates aspects of both suspended scaffolds and hanging scaffolds. These TMPs are assembled in the draft tube below the turbine where they are physically attached to the structure. Some TMPs must be assembled below the turbine at the draft tube door level and raised into position and may also be required to be close to the turbine blades such that the TMP must wrap around the turbine hub. This applies to vertical access turbines where the TMP is assembled under the runner.

➢ Note: This Section does not apply to standard off-the-shelf applications of scaffolds designed and used in accordance with ANSI A.10.

22.Q.01 Design.

a. TMPs shall be designed and/or certified by a RPE. Existing TMPs shall be certified prior to the next use. There is a grace period of 6 months from the effective date of this manual.

b. TMPs shall be designed to support their own weight plus 4 times the maximum intended load.

c. A data plate will be attached or the documentation showing the design will be readily available on-site. The RPE will be listed on the drawings and calculations for the platform and not on the data plate. Data, when used, will include the following:

(1) Descriptive name indicating intended usage;

(2) Assembled weight of TMP;

(3) Total maximum live load, pounds;

(4) Total maximum distributed live load (psf);

(5) Date of fabrication;

(6) Name of fabricator;

(7) Any load restrictions or usage limitations.

d. If wire rope is used to either support the platform after installation or to raise the platform while occupied, the wire rope shall have a safety factor of 6.

e. Deflections in structural members and structural systems under appropriate service load combinations shall not impair the serviceability of the structure.

f. If hooks are used to support the platform in its final position, they will be designed with a positive means of securing them to prevent the hooks from being disengaged.

g. The decking/platform shall be designed so that the space between adjacent obstacles or structures and the space between the platform is no more than 9.5 in (24.1 cm) wide, except where the user can demonstrate that a wider space is necessary. Where gaps exceed 9.5 in, needed FP measures shall be evaluated in accordance with Section 21.

h. The working surfaces shall be slip-resistant.

22.Q.05 Testing. Immediately after fabrication and after any modification of the structural members, the platform shall be proof tested to 100% of its rated capacity. The test may take place in the fabricator's shop or other location provided the supports and connections are also tested to 100%. The full rated load shall be statically applied for a minimum of 15 minutes. Following the load test, the TMP shall be inspected for plastic deformation, fracture, and 100% of welds shall receive Non-Destructive Inspection.

22.Q.06 Assembly/Disassembly.

a. An AHA shall be developed for the process of installing and removing TMPs. Fall protection, working over water, and fire protection will be addressed in the AHA along with any other hazards the workers identify. The AHA will be reviewed immediately prior to the start of work with the entire crew.

b. The TMP will be positively attached prior to use. Platform components shall be supported and secured such that each component is stable in all anticipated load conditions. When attachment points are welded they will be either welded by an AWS certified welder or a pull test will be done in accordance with the RPE specifications.

c. Raising and lowering the platform, when occupied by personnel, will only be done with rated grip hoists or other lifting equipment rated for lifting personnel. Chain falls will not be used to lift personnel unless an independent FP system is used.

22.Q.07 Visual inspections shall be done daily in accordance with Section 22.B.03.

22.Q.08 Training.

a. Employees that install and/or remove TMPs shall be trained on how to properly assemble, install and the removal of the specific type of TMP. > *See Section 22.B.06.*

b. FP training shall be done IAW Section 21.

22.R Forklift-/Powered Industrial Truck (PIT) – Mounted Work Platforms.

22.R.01 Forklifts/PITs will not be used to support work platforms unless there is no other practical method. If a rough terrain (RT) forklift must be used, all the conditions in this Section must be met.

22.R.02 The manufacturer must specifically allow this specific machine to lift personnel. The operator's manual shall be maintained at the work site on the forklift.

22.R.03 The manufacturer's platform specifications shall be maintained on site and those specifications must reference ASME B56-6.

a. A data plate may be used in lieu of the manufacturer's specifications if it references ASME B56.6.

b. If the platform is not manufactured by, or for, the company that manufactures the forklift, a letter must be obtained from the forklift manufacturer that states the machine is compatible with the platform design. This letter must be kept on site and a copy provided to the GDA.

22.R.04 The platform must be securely attached to the lifting carriage and forks.

22.R.05 The lifting carriage and forks must be secured from pivoting forward.

22.R.06 If the truck is equipped with a rotator, the rotator must be deactivated.

22.R.07 Personnel shall be protected from moving parts while in their normal working positions.

22.R.08 Overhead protection shall be provided as necessary for the operating conditions.

22.R.09 The lifting operation shall be done smoothly throughout the entire range of the lift.

22.R.10 All lift limiting devices and latches, if so equipped, shall be functional.

22.R.11 A firm footing will be verified by the operator before lifting personnel.

22.R.12 A fall restraint system shall be used in accordance with Section 21 and personnel will maintain a firm footing on the platform at all times.

22.R.13 The platform shall not be tilted forward or rearward.

22.R.14 The platform shall be lowered to the ground level for personnel to enter and exit.

22.R.15 The operator shall remain at the controls whenever personnel are elevated.

22.R.16 The forklift shall not be moved horizontally while occupied.

22.R.17 Before elevating personnel, forklift travel controls must be in neutral and the parking brake set.

22.R.18 The operator shall verify that the mast or boom travel is vertical and will not operate on a slope unless the RT forklift is level.

22.R.19 The operator shall verify that the path of the platform travel is clear of hazards, such as electrical wires, overhead obstructions, scaffolding, storage racks, and other obstacles.

22.R.20 Before elevating personnel, the work area must be marked to warn of work by elevated personnel.

22.R.21 Driving a forklift equipped with a personnel work platform in a raised position or with personnel on the platform is forbidden.

22.R.22 Before raising or lowering the platform, the operator shall alert the personnel on the platform and then move the platform smoothly and with caution as requested by the occupants.

22.R.23 The combined weight of the platform, load, and personnel shall not exceed one-third of the capacity at the related load center position as indicated on the information plate(s) of the RT forklift truck.

22.S Work Stands (Portable Work Platforms).

22.S.01 Work stands shall be designed in accordance with either ANSI A14.2 (aluminum) or ANSI A14.5 (plastic/fiberglass). > See Figure 22-2.

22.S.02 Work stands shall not have a working height exceeding 4 ft (1.2 m).

22.S.03 The load rating shall be clearly and legibly marked and the work stand shall not be loaded beyond the manufacturer's rated capacity. The maximum intended load includes the worker and all tools and supplies.

22.S.04 When work stands are used adjacent to stairs or ramps where a fall to a different level could occur, guardrails (as defined in 21.F.01.b) or other fall protection shall be provided (increased in height by an amount equal to the height of the work stand. > *See Section 21.A.04.*

22.S.05 Work stands shall inspected for visible defects on a daily basis and shall be maintained with no structural damage.

22.S.06 Job-built work stands are not allowed. Saw horses shall not be used as work stands.

FIGURE 22-2

Work Stands (Portable Work Platforms), Examples

3 ft Fiberglass Work Stand

2 ft Aluminum Work Stand

3 ft Aluminum Work Stand

4 ft Aluminum Work Stand

22.T Trestle Ladder Scaffolds.

22.T.01 Scaffold platforms must be placed no higher than the second-highest rung or step of the ladder supporting the platform.

22.T.02 All ladders used in step, platform and trestle ladder scaffolds must:

a. Meet or exceed 29 CFR 1926 Subpart X.
➢NOTE: job-made ladders are not permitted.

b. Be prevented from slipping by how they are placed, fastened, or equipped.

22.T.03 Scaffolds must not be bridged one to another.

22.T.04 Climbing and Working Locations. The user shall climb or work with the body near the middle of the step or rung. Higher than the step or rung indicated on the label marking the highest standing level of a ladder. The user shall not step or stand on:

a. A ladder top cap or the top step of the step or trestle ladder, or the bucket or pail shelf of a self-supporting ladder.

b. The rear braces of a self-supporting ladder, unless designed and recommended for that purpose by the manufacturer.

c. The top step of the extension section of an extension trestle ladder.

d. The top cap or top step of a combination ladder when it is used as a self-supporting ladder.

FIGURE 22-3

Trestle Ladder Scaffolds, Examples

Example #1

Example #2

Example #3

Example #4

THIS PAGE INTENTIONALLY LEFT BLANK

SECTION 23 Demolition, Renovation and Re-Occupancy

Table of Contents

23

23.A General. The process of demolishing or renovating a structure can be completed in several ways. The terms "renovation", "structural demolition", "soft demolition" and "mechanical demolition" should be understood within the context of this section. > *See Appendix Q for definitions.*

23.A.01 Demolition and renovation activities shall be performed in accordance with ANSI Standard A10.6, Safety Requirements for Demolition.

a. Prior to initiating demolition or renovation activities, the following survey and plan shall be accomplished. > *See lead and asbestos requirements in Section 06.C.*

(1) Engineering Survey. An engineering survey by a Registered Professional Engineer (RPE) shall be performed of the structure to determine the structure layout, the condition of the framing, floors, walls, the possibility of unplanned collapse of any portion of the structure (any adjacent structure where employees or property may be exposed shall be similarly checked), and the existence of other potential or real demolition hazards.

➢ *Note: The engineering survey is not required for soft demolition or renovation activities as long as no load-bearing structure will be removed or demolished.*

(2) Demolition/Renovation Plan. A demolition plan developed by a RPE and shall be submitted to the GDA. Plan shall be based on the engineering, lead and asbestos surveys and shall intend for the safe dismantling and removal of all building components and debris. This plan is required for all demolition and renovation activities and shall include, but is not limited to, the following basic elements: schedule; scope of work being accomplished; description of work methods, equipment, job site and key personnel; site preparation; Waste Management Plan to include Asbestos-Containing Materials (ACM)/Other Regulated Material (ORM) Abatement Plan; Site Restoration Plan and other requirements specified in a Statement of Work or as directed by the Contracting Officer (KO).

b. All employees engaged in demolition/renovation activities shall be instructed in the plan so that they may conduct their work activities in a safe manner.

23.A.02 Electric, gas, water, steam, sewer, and other service lines affected as a result of project work shall be shut off, capped, or otherwise controlled inside and outside the building line before demolition is started.

a. In each case, any utility company that is involved shall be notified in advance.

b. The Contractor shall provide the GDA and the Contractor's designated authority with an engineering drawing (e.g., site plans, utility plans) that indicates the location of all service lines and the means for their control.

c. If it is necessary to maintain any power, water, or other utilities during renovation, such lines shall be temporarily relocated and protected.

d. It shall be the responsibility of the facility owner to identify and field verify the point or points for disconnection and de-energizing electrical components and electrical service lines. > *See Sections 11 and 12.*

(1) The Contractor must confirm that the disconnection or de-energizing has been performed prior to the start of the demolition process.

(2) De-energized electrical service shall be secured via a lock-out method and field verified by the contractor, per Section 12 and their HEC Program.

e. If the project includes the abandonment or demolition of existing gas lines, ensure that the existing lines are accurately located and the procedures and installations for removal or replacement are accomplished in accordance with applicable sections of 29 CFR 1926.850.

f. If the project includes fire suppression systems, the owner shall provide to the GDA confirmation or verification that the Chemical Fire Suppression (CFS) system has been deactivated and that the chemical has been removed from the system prior to the start of the renovation/demolition process. If the CFS system is found to be active after demolition has begun, the contractor shall immediately cease work and notify the GDA. The contractor shall take no action to abate or remove the CFS system or components.

23.A.03 It shall be determined if any hazardous building materials, hazardous chemicals, gases, explosives, flammable materials, or dangerous substances have been used in any building construction, pipes, tanks, or other equipment on the property.

a. When such hazards are identified, testing shall be conducted to determine the type and concentration of the hazardous substance and test results shall be provided to the GDA and the Contractor's designated authority.

b. Such hazards shall be controlled or eliminated before demolition is started.

c. If Hazardous Materials (HAZMAT) are found on the project site or location after demolition has begun, the contractor shall immediately cease work and notify the GDA. The contractor shall take no action to abate or remove the HAZMAT without GDA approval.

23.A.04 All ACM and ORMs shall be removed from structures in accordance with all federal and state laws before renovation/demolition begins.

a. ACM/ORM shall be taken to a controlled landfill or other licensed disposal facility;

b. Construction and Debris (C&D) shall be taken to a general waste landfill; and

c. Recyclable materials shall be taken to a recycle yard or retained by the GOV.

23.A.05 When employees work within a structure to be demolished that has been damaged by fire, flood, explosion, or other cause, the walls or floor shall be shored or braced IAW the Engineering Survey and Plan required by Section 23.A.02.

23.A.06 Work progression.

a. Except for cutting holes in floors for chutes, holes through which to drop materials, preparation of storage space, and similar preparatory work, the demolition of floors and exterior walls shall begin at the top of the structure and proceed downward.

b. Each story of exterior wall and floor construction shall be removed and dropped into the storage space before commencing the removal of exterior walls and floors on the next story below.

23.A.07 Potential hazards due to the fragmentation of glass shall be considered and controlled for all persons inside and outside of the demolition site.

23.A.08 Mechanical equipment shall not be used on floors on working surfaces unless such floors or surfaces are of sufficient strength to support the imposed load.

23.A.09 Employee entrances to multistory structures being demolished shall be protected by sidewalk sheds, canopies, or both.

a. Protection shall be provided from the face of the building for a minimum of 8 ft (2.4 m).

b . All such canopies shall be at least 2 ft (0.6 m) wider than the building entrances or openings (1 ft (0.3 m) wider on each side), and shall be capable of sustaining a load of 150 psi (1,034.2 kPa).

23.A.10 Only those stairways, passageways, and ladders designated as means of access to the structure shall be used.

a. The designated means of access shall be indicated on the demolition plan. Other access ways shall be indicated as not safe for access and closed at all times.

b. The stairwell shall be covered to protect workers from falling debris at a point no less than two floors below the floor on which work is being performed.

c. Access to a floor where work is in progress shall be through a separate lighted, protected passageway.

23.A.11 During demolition, continuing inspections by a Competent Person (CP) shall detect hazards resulting from weakened or deteriorated floors, walls, or loosened material. No employee shall be permitted to work where such hazards exist until they are corrected by shoring, bracing, or other means. The frequency of inspections will be identified in the blasting/renovation plan.

23.A.12 Debris Removal.

a. Walls, or sections of masonry, shall not be permitted to fall upon the floors of the building in such masses as to exceed the safe carrying capacities of the floors.

b. Any chute opening into which debris is dumped shall be protected by a guardrail 42 in (1.1 m) above the floor or other surface on which personnel stand to dump the material. Any space between the chute and the edge of openings in the floors through which it passes shall be covered.

c. When debris is dropped through openings in the floors without chutes, the openings and the area onto which the material is dropped shall be enclosed with barricades not less than 42 in (1.1 m) high and not less than 6 ft (1.8 m) back from the projected edge of the opening above.

(1) Signs warning of the hazard of falling materials shall be posted at each side of the debris opening at each floor.

(2) Debris removal shall not be permitted in lower areas until debris handling ceases on the floors above.

d. All material chutes, or sections thereof, at an angle of more than 45° from the horizontal shall be enclosed, except for openings equipped with closures at or about floor level for the insertion of materials.

(1) The openings shall not exceed 48 in (1.2 m) in height measured along the wall of the chute.

(2) Such openings, when not in use, shall be kept closed at all floors below the top floor.

e. A substantial gate shall be installed in each chute at or near the discharge end. A competent employee shall be assigned to control operation of the gate and the backing and loading of trucks.

f. When operations are not in progress, the area surrounding the discharge end of a chute shall be closed.

g. Where material is dumped from mechanical equipment or wheelbarrows, a toe board or bumper, not less than 4 in (10 cm) thick and 6 in (15 cm) high, shall be attached at each chute opening.

h. Chutes shall be designed and constructed of such strength as to eliminate failure due to impact of materials or debris loaded therein.

i. The storage of waste and debris on any floor shall not exceed the allowable floor loads.

j. In buildings having wood floor construction, the floor joists may be removed from not more than one floor above grade to provide storage space for debris provided falling material is not permitted to endanger the stability of the structure.

(1) When wood floor beams serve to brace interior walls or freestanding exterior walls, such beams shall be left in place until other support can be installed to replace them.

(2) Floor arches, to an elevation of not more than 25 ft (7.6 m) above grade, may be removed to provide storage area for debris provided such removal does not endanger the stability of the structure.

(3) Storage space into which material is dumped shall be blocked off, except for openings for the removal of materials. Such openings shall be kept closed when material is not being removed.

(4) Floor openings shall have curbs or stop-logs to prevent equipment from running over the edge.

(5) Any opening cut in a floor for the disposal of materials shall be not longer in size than 25% of the aggregate of the total floor area, unless the lateral supports of the removed flooring remain in place. Floors weakened or otherwise made unsafe by demolition shall be shored to carry safely the intended imposed load for demolition.

23.A.13 Debris Disposal.

a. Debris generated by demolition or contained within the facility or found within the defined work perimeter of the facility or project shall be removed from the site as waste material, to include ACM and ORM. Debris shall be separated according to type of disposal that is required.

b. The disposal site, whether Government furnished, private, or commercial shall be approved by the GDA

prior to Notice to Proceed. Contractor shall provide to the GDA documentation that confirms the disposal location, the type of debris, and quantities of each type.

23.A.14 Wall Removal.

a. Masonry walls, or sections of masonry, shall not be permitted to fall upon the floors of the building in such masses as to exceed the safe carrying capacities of the floors.

b. No wall section that is more than 6 ft (1.8 m) in height shall be permitted to stand without lateral bracing, unless such wall was designed and constructed to stand without such lateral support and is in a condition safe enough to be self-supporting. No wall section shall be left standing without lateral bracing any longer than necessary for removal of adjacent debris interfering with demolition of the wall.

➤ *Exception: For wall sections that are designed and constructed to stand without lateral support, an exception may be allowed*.

c. Employees shall not be permitted to work on the top of a wall when weather constitutes a hazard.

d. Structural or load-supporting members on any floor shall not be cut or removed until all stories above such a floor have been demolished and removed. This shall not prohibit the cutting of floor beams for the disposal of materials or for the installation of equipment, providing the requirements of in this Section are met.

e. Floor openings within 10 ft (3 m) of any wall being demolished shall be planked solid, except when employees are kept out of the area below.

f. In buildings of skeleton-steel construction, the steel framing may be left in place during the demolition of masonry. Where this is done, all steel beams, girders, and structural supports shall be cleared of all loose material as the masonry demolition progresses downward.

g. Walls that serve as retaining walls to support earth or adjoining structures shall not be demolished until such earth has been braced or adjoining structures have been underpinned. > *See Section 23.B.04.*

h. Walls shall not be used to retain debris unless capable of safely supporting the imposed load.

23.A.15 Floor Removal.

a. Before demolishing any floor, debris and other material shall be removed from the immediate work location and other adjacent floor areas.

(1) Planks not less than 2-in x 10-in (5-cm x 25.4-cm) in cross section, full sized

undressed, shall be provided for and shall be used by employees to stand on while breaking down floor areas between beams/joists.

(2) Such planks shall be so located as to provide a safe support for personnel should the joists between the beams collapse.

(3) Straddle space between planks shall not exceed 16 in (40.6 cm).

b. Safe walkways, not less than 18 in (45.7 cm) wide, formed of wood planks not less than 2 in (5 cm) thick or of equivalent strength, shall be provided and used by personnel when necessary to enable them to reach any point without walking upon exposed beams.

c. Stringers of ample strength shall support the flooring planks. The ends of such stringers shall be supported by floor beams or girders.

d. Planks shall be laid together over solid bearings with the ends overlapping at least 1 ft (0.3 m).

e. When floors are being removed, employees shall not be allowed in the area directly underneath. The area shall be barricaded to prevent access and signed to warn of the hazard.

23.A.16 Steel Removal.

a. When a floor, or any portion of a floor, has been removed, planking shall be provided for the workers razing/dismantling the steel framing.

b. Steel construction shall be dismantled column-by-column and tier-by-tier (columns may be in two-story lengths).

c. Any structural member being dismembered shall not be overstressed.

23.B Structural Demolition.

23.B.01 General. Removal of a facility may include the structure as well as any related appurtenances: fences, parking areas and associated lights, roadways and access from roadways, sidewalks and stairs associated with access, pads, patios, and paved lay-down areas, utilities, underground storage tank (UST)/above ground storage tank (AST), poles, interior and exterior equipment associated with the facility, interior and exterior equipment within the designated perimeter of the facility.

23.B.02 All operations involving the use of load handling equipment (LHE) shall meet Section 16 to include: Certificated of Compliance; documented personnel qualifications (operators, riggers, signal persons, others); LHE inspections, operational and load tests and certifications; and standard lift plan. If the manufacturer of the equipment does not allow the equipment to be utilized as planned, you are prohibited from performing this function.

23.B.03 No personnel shall be working within the structure once the structural demolition process has begun. Before structural demolition can begin, abatement of ACM and other regulated materials shall be done.

23.B.04 Structural demolition may include any or all of these features prior to demolition:

a. Removal of universal waste prior to the start of facility removal;

b. Partial demolition to expose the structure frame;

c. Soft demolition.

23.B.05 Mechanical Demolition.

a. All motorized equipment used on a project shall meet requirements of the EM 385-1-1, as well as applicable OSHA requirements. In addition, see National Demolition Association's *Demolition Safety Manual,* Chapter 7.0 for further information on equipment safety.

b. No person shall be permitted in any area that can be affected by demolition when mechanical demolition is being performed. Only those persons necessary for the operations shall be permitted in this area at any other time.

c. Dust abatement measures will be used to suppress dust during demolition.

d. Operators are required to wear respirators per Section 05.

e. A demolition ball shall be used ONLY if it has been approved by GDA. If the use of a demolition ball is approved:

(1) The weight of the demolition ball shall not exceed 50% of the crane's rated load, based on the length of the boom and the maximum angle of operation at which the demolition ball will be used, or it shall not exceed 25% of the nominal breaking strength of the line by which it is suspended, whichever is less;

(2) The crane boom and load line shall be as short as possible;

(3) The ball shall be attached to the load line with a swivel-type connection to prevent twisting of the load line and shall be attached by positive means so that the weight cannot be accidentally disconnected.

(4) Continued on-going inspections by the CP shall be made as the demolition work progresses to detect hazards resulting from weakened or deteriorated floors or walls, or loosened material. No employee shall be permitted to work where such hazards exist until they are corrected by shoring, bracing, or other effective means.

23

THIS PAGE INTENTIONALLY LEFT BLANK

SECTION 24 Safe Access

Table of Contents

24

24.A General.

24.A.01 Safe access shall be provided to work areas and where danger exists of workers falling through floor, roof, or wall openings, or from platforms, runways, ramps, fixed stairs, <u>ladders, or for rope access.</u>

a. A stairway, ladder, ramp, or personnel hoist shall be provided where there is a break of 19 in (48.2 cm) or more in a route of access.

b. Means of access constructed of metal shall not be used for electrical work or where the potential exists to contact electrical conductors.

c. Means of access between levels shall be kept clear to allow free passage of workers. If work is performed in an area that restricts free passage, a second means of access shall be provided.

d. For all government-owned/operated facilities, every open-sided floor or platform 4 ft (1.2 m) or more above adjacent floor or ground level shall be guarded by a guardrail system (or equivalent) along all open sides (except where there is an entrance to a ramp, stairway or fixed ladder). The guardrail system shall be provided with a toeboard when necessary. > *See Section 21.F.01.*

24.A.02 An AHA, accepted by the GDA for the activity in which means of access are to be used, shall delineate the following:

a. The design, construction, and maintenance of the means of access, and

b. Erection and dismantling procedures of scaffolds, including provisions for providing fall protection (FP) during the erection or dismantling when the erection or dismantling involves work at heights. > *See Sections 21.K.02 and 22.A.03.*

24.A.03 Job-made means of access shall be designed to support, without failure, at least four times the maximum intended load and shall be constructed according to Section 22 of this manual.

24.A.04 Means of access shall not be loaded beyond the maximum intended load for which it was designed or beyond its manufacturer's rated capacity. When loaded, planking and decking shall not deflect more than 1/60 the span length.

24.A.05 The width of accessways shall be determined by the purpose for which they are built, shall be sufficient to provide safe passage for materials and movement of personnel and (except for ladders) shall not be less than 18 in (45.7 cm).

24.A.06 Accessways shall have overhead protection equal to 2 in (5 cm) solid planking whenever work is performed over them or if personnel are exposed to hazards from falling objects.

24.A.07 Accessways shall be inspected daily.

a. The walkway must be free of tripping hazards, obstructions and cannot impede or restrict the travel of personnel. In addition, accessways shall be kept free of ice, snow, grease and mud or any other environmental hazards.

b. Where accessways are slippery, abrasive material shall be used to assure safe footing.

c. All obstructions or projections into an access way shall be removed or conspicuously marked. Obstructions or projections that are sharp, pointed or that may cause lacerations, contusions, or abrasions shall be covered with protective material.

d. Accessways, including their accessories that become damaged or weakened shall not be used. These defective items shall be repaired or replaced.

24.A.08 When moving platforms to the next level, the old platform shall be left undisturbed until the new bearers have been set to receive the platform planks.

24.A.09 Safe Roof Access.

a. Platforms, level and guarded shall be provided at the landing area on the roof.

b. Crawling boards.

(1) Crawling boards shall be not less than 10 in (25 cm) wide and 1 in (2.5 cm) thick, having cleats 1 in x 1.5 in (2.5 cm x 3.75 cm).

(2) Cleats shall be equal in length to the width of the board and spaced at equal intervals not to exceed 24 in (60 cm).

(3) Nails shall be driven through and clinched on the underside. Screws may be used in lieu of nails.

(4) Crawling boards shall be secured and extend from the ridge pole to the eaves when used with roof construction, repairs, or maintenance.

(5) A firmly fastened lifeline of at least ¾ in (2 cm) diameter rope, or equivalent, shall be strung beside each crawling board for a handhold.

c. Access paths shall be erected as follows:

(1) Points of access, material handling areas and storage areas shall be connected to the work area by a clear access path formed by two warning lines.

(2) When the path to a point of access is not being used, one of the following shall be used:

(a) A rope, wire, or chain, equal in strength and height to the warning line, shall be placed across the path at the point where the path intersects the warning line erected around the work area, or

(b) The path shall be offset such that a person cannot walk directly into the work area.

24.B Ladders. *> See also Sections 22.S, Work Stands (Portable Work Platforms) and 22.T, Trestle Ladder Scaffolds.*

24.B.01 The construction, installation, and use of ladders shall conform to ANSI/American Ladder Institute (ALI) A14 series standards as applicable. The load rating shall be clearly and legibly marked on all ladders.

24.B.02 Every ladderway, floor opening or platform shall be guarded by a standard railing with standard toe-board (when exposure exists to falling materials), on all exposed sides (except at entrance to opening). The passage through the railing shall be provided with either a guardrail or shall be offset so that a person cannot walk directly into the opening. The guarding shall meet the strength requirements of Section 21.F.01. Swing gates are preferred over chain gates.

24.B.03 Length of ladders.

a. All portable ladders shall be of sufficient length and shall be placed so that workers will not stretch or assume a hazardous position.

b. Portable ladders, used as temporary access, shall extend at least 3 ft (0.9 m) above the upper landing surface.

(1) When a 3 ft (0.9 m) extension is not possible, a grasping device (such as a grab rail) shall be provided to assist workers in mounting and dismounting the ladder.

(2) In no case shall the length of the ladder be such that ladder deflection under a load would, by itself, cause the ladder to slip from its support.

c. The length of stepladders shall not exceed 20 ft (6 m).

d. For portable ladders:

(1) The length of single ladders or individual sections of ladders shall not exceed 30 ft (9 m).

(2) Two-section extension ladders shall not exceed 48 ft (14.6 m).

(3) Multi-section extension ladders (over two-sections) shall not exceed 60 ft (18 m) in length.

e. When splicing of side rails is required to obtain the required length, the resulting side rail must be at least equal in strength to a one-piece side rail made of the same material.

24.B.04 Width of ladders.

a. The minimum clear distance between the sides of individual-rung/step ladders shall be 16 in (40.6 cm).

b. The minimum clear distance between side rails for all portable ladders shall be 12 in (30.4 cm).

24.B.05 Spacing of rungs, cleats, and steps on ladders.

a. On portable ladders, spacing of rungs shall be 12 in (30.4 cm) on center and uniform, except for job-made ladders where the spacing shall be 10 in (25.4 cm) to 14 in (35.5 cm).

b. On step stools, spacing shall be not less than 8 in (20.3 cm) or more than 12 in (30.4 cm) apart, as measured from their centerlines.

24.B.06 Ladders shall be surfaced so as to prevent injury to an worker from punctures or lacerations and to prevent snagging of clothing.

24.B.07 Wooden ladders shall not be coated with any opaque covering, except for identification or warning labels that may be placed on only one face of a side rail.

24.B.08 Portable ladders shall have slip-resistant feet.

24.B.09 The rungs and steps of portable metal ladders shall be corrugated, knurled, dimpled, coated with skid-resistant materials, or otherwise treated to minimize slipping.

24.B.10 A metal spreader bar or locking device shall be provided on each stepladder to hold the front and back sections in an open position.

24.B.11 Set-up of ladders.

a. Ladders shall not be placed in passageways, doorways, drives, or any locations where they may be displaced by any other work unless protected by barricades or guards.

b. Portable ladders shall be used at such a pitch that the horizontal distance from the top support to the foot of the ladder will not be greater than ¼ the vertical distance between these points.

c. Wooden job-made ladders, with spliced rails, shall be used at an angle such that the horizontal distance is 1/8 the length of the ladder.

d. Ladders shall be secured by top, bottom, and intermediate fastenings, as necessary, to hold them rigidly in place and to support the loads that will be imposed upon them.

e. The steps or rungs of all ladders shall be set to provide at least 7 in (17.7 cm) toe space from the inside edge of the rung to the nearest interference.

f. The top of a non-self supporting ladder shall be placed with the two rails supported equally, unless the ladder is equipped with a single support attachment.

g. Step-across distance. The step-across distance from the nearest edge of ladder to the nearest edge of equipment or structure shall be not more than 12 in (30.5 cm) or less than 2-1/2 in (6.4 cm).

24.B.12 Use of ladders.

a. Ladders shall be restricted to their intended use. Three points-of-contact (*see Appendix Q*) shall be maintained at all times when ascending or descending ladders.

b. Ladders shall be inspected for visible defects on a daily basis and after any occurrence that could affect their safe use. Broken or damaged ladders shall be immediately tagged "DO NOT USE", or with similar wording, and withdrawn from service until restored to a condition meeting their original design.

c. Ladders shall not be moved, shifted, or extended while occupied.

d. Ladders shall not be loaded beyond the maximum intended load for which they were designed and tested, or beyond the manufacturer's rated capacity (includes the worker and all the tools and supplies carried).

e. Ladders shall not be climbed by more than one person at a time between the same set of rails.

f. Portable ladders used as means of access to ascend and descend to a work location do not require fall protection, however only light work for short periods of time shall be performed on portable ladders.

No work requiring lifting of heavy materials or substantial exertion shall be done from ladders.

g. When ladders are the only means of access to or from a working area for 25 or more workers, or when a ladder is to serve simultaneous two-way traffic, double-cleated ladders shall be used.

h. The top or top step of a stepladder, shall not be used, as a step unless it has been designed to be so used by the manufacturer (e.g., platform ladders).

i. Ensure latches are in place before climbing an extension ladder.

j. Keep loose tools off the steps and top platform.

k. Modifications to manufactured ladders in order to adapt the ladder to specific or special use shall only be performed using a design approved by a RPE. These ladders shall meet the applicable ANSI A14 series standard.

24.B.13 Job made wooden ladders will be made in accordance with ANSI A14.4.

24.B.14 Single-rail ladders shall not be used. Three-legged ladders may be used for specific tasks, if accepted by the GDA.

24.B.15 The use of ladder climbing devices shall be in accordance with Section 21.J.

24.B.16 Articulated ladders are allowed if they meet ANSI A14.2 standard.

24.B.17 Any ladder accessory, including but not limited to, ladder levelers, ladder stabilizers or stand-off devices, or ladder straps or hooks, that may be installed or used in conjunction with ladders must be installed and used per manufacturer's instructions.

24.C Handrails.

24.C.01 A standard handrail shall be of construction similar to a standard guardrail (*see Section 21.E.01*) except that it is mounted on a wall or partition and does not include a midair.

24.C.02 Handrails shall have smooth surfaces along the top and both sides.

24.C.03 Handrails shall have an adequate handhold for anyone grasping it to avoid falling.

24.C.04 Ends of handrails shall be turned into the supporting wall or partition or otherwise arranged so as to not constitute a projection hazard.

24.C.05 The height of handrails shall be not more than 38 in (86.3 cm) nor less than 34 in (76.2 cm) from upper surface of handrail to surface of tread, in line with face of riser or to surface of ramp. Existing installations need not be modified if they meet the building code that was in effect at the time the facility was built.

24.C.06 All handrails and railings shall be provided with a clearance of approximately 3 in (7.6 cm) between the handrail or railing and any other object.

24.D Floor, Wall, and Roof Holes and Openings.

24.D.01 Floor and roof holes/openings are any that measure over 2 in (51 mm) in any direction of a walking/working surface which persons may trip or fall into or where objects may fall to the level below. > *See Section 21.*G.

> ➢ *Note: Skylights located in floors or roofs are considered floor or roof hole/openings.*

24.D.02 All floor, roof openings or hole into which a person can accidentally walk or fall through shall be guarded either by a railing system with toeboards along all exposed sides or a load-bearing cover. When the cover is not in place, the opening or hole shall be protected by a removable guardrail system or other fall protection system, or shall be attended when the guarding system has been removed. > *See Sections 21.F and 21.G.*

24.D.03 All floor and roof holes through which equipment, materials, or debris can fall shall be covered.

24.D.04 Conduits, trenches, and manhole covers and their supports, when exposed to vehicles or equipment, shall be designed to carry a truck rear axle load of 2 times the maximum anticipated load.

24.D.05 Every hatchway and chute floor opening shall be guarded by a hinged floor-opening cover. The opening shall be barricaded with railings so as to leave only one exposed side. The exposed side shall be provided either with a swinging gate or offset so that a person cannot walk into the opening. When operating conditions require the feeding of material into a hatchway or chute opening, protection shall be provided to prevent a person from falling through the opening.

24.D.06 Wall openings 30 in (76 cm) or more in height and 18 in (48 cm) or more in width from which a fall could occur shall be protected with a standard guardrail or equivalent. A toeboard shall be provided where the bottom of the wall opening, regardless of width, is less than 4 in (10.1 cm) above the working surface. > *See Section 21.F.01.*

24.D.07 An extension platform outside a wall opening onto which materials can be hoisted for handling shall have a standard railing that meets criteria in Section 21.F.01 of this manual. However, one side of an extension platform may have removable railings to facilitate handling materials, if appropriate fall protection is used.

24.D.08 Roof openings and holes shall be provided with covers, guardrail systems or warning lines systems on all exposed sides.

a. Roofing material, such as roofing membrane, insulation or felts, covering or partly covering openings or holes, shall be immediately cut out. No hole or opening shall be left unattended unless covered according to Section 21.G.

b. All covers for openings shall be identified in accordance with Section 21.G.

c. Non-load-bearing skylights shall be guarded by a load-bearing skylight screen, cover, or railing system along all exposed sides.

d. Workers are prohibited from standing/walking on skylights.

24.E Stairways.

24.E.01 On all structures 20 ft (6 m) or more in height, stairways shall be provided during construction.

a. Where permanent stairways are not installed concurrently with the construction of each floor, a temporary stairway shall be provided to the work level.

b. Alternatives to the use of stairways shall be addressed in the AHA and shall be acceptable to the GDA.

24.E.02 Requirements for stairways.

a. Temporary stairways shall have landings not less than 30 in (76.2 cm) in the direction of travel and extend at least 22 in (55.8 cm) in width at every 12 ft (3.6 m) or less of vertical rise.

b. Stairs shall be installed between 30° and 50° from horizontal.

c. Risers shall be of uniform height and treads of uniform width.

24.E.03 Metal pan landings and metal pan treads, when used, shall be secured in place and filled with concrete, wood, or other material at least to the top of each pan.

24

24.E.04 Wooden treads shall be nailed in place.

24.E.05 Every flight of stairs with four or more risers or rising more than 30 in (76.2 cm) shall have standard stair railings (defined below) or standard handrails, unless omitted by design.

a. On stairways less than 44 in (111.7 cm) wide having both sides enclosed, at least one standard handrail shall be installed, preferably on the right descending side.

b. On stairways less than 44 in (111.7 cm) wide having one side open, at least one standard stair railing shall be installed on the open side.

c. On stairways less than 44 in (111.7 cm) wide having both sides open, one standard stair railing shall be installed on each side.

d. On stairways more than 44 in (111.7 cm) wide, but less than 88 in (223.5 cm) wide, one standard handrail shall be installed on each enclosed side, and one standard stair railing installed on each open side.

e. On stairways more than 88 in (223.5 cm) wide, one standard handrail shall be installed on each enclosed side, one standard stair railing on each exposed side, and a standard handrail in the middle of the stairway.

24.E.06 Standard stair railing shall be installed around all stairwells.

a. The height of stair rails shall be 42+/- 3 in (1 m +/- 8 cm) from the upper surface of the top rail to surface of tread in line with face of riser at forward edge of tread. Existing installations need not be modified. Existing installations need not be modified.

b. Midrails, screens, mesh, intermediate vertical members, or equivalent intermediate structural members shall be provided between the toprail and the stairway steps.

(1) Midrails shall be located at a height midway between the top edge of the stairway system and the stairway steps.

(2) Screens or mesh, when used, shall extend from the toprail to the stairway steps and along the entire opening between rail supports.

(3) Intermediate vertical members, when used, shall be not more than 19 in (48.2 cm) apart.

(4) Other structural members, when used, shall be installed in such a manner that there are no openings in the stair rail system that are more than 19 in (48.2 cm) wide.

24.E.07 Doors or gates opening onto a stairway shall have a platform; and swinging of the door shall not reduce the width of the platform to less than 20 in (50.8 cm).

24.E.08 Spiral stairways shall not be permitted, except for special limited usage and secondary access where it is not practical to provide a conventional stairway.

24.E.09 Three points of contact shall be maintained at all times when ascending or descending spiral stairs, ship stairs, or alternating tread stairs. Three point contact means that either both hands and one foot, or both feet and one hand are in contact with the climbing device at all times.

24.F Ramps, Runways and Trestles.

24.F.01 Ramps, runways, and platforms shall be as flat as conditions will permit. Where the slope exceeds 1 ft:5 ft (0.3 m:1.5 m), traverse cleats shall be applied to the working surface.

24.F.02 Vehicle ramps, trestles, and bridges on which foot traffic is permitted shall be provided with a walkway and guardrail outside the roadway. The roadway structures shall be provided with wheel guards, fender logs, or curbs not less than 8 in (20.3 cm) high placed parallel and secured to the sides of the runway.

24.F.03 All locomotive and gantry crane trestles that extend into or pass over a work area, except where a crane is hoisting between rails, shall be decked solid with not less than 2 in (5 cm) planking, or the equivalent, for the full length of the extension into the working area.

24.F.04 When used in lieu of steps, ramps shall be provided with cleats to ensure safe access.

24.G Personnel Hoists and Elevators.

24.G.01 Design, construction, installation or erection, operation, inspection, testing, and maintenance of personnel hoists and elevators shall be in accordance with the manufacturer's recommendations and the applicable ANSI standard.

a. Track-guided personnel hoist systems and structures that are temporarily installed inside or outside buildings during construction, alteration, or demolition shall be in compliance with ANSI A10.4;

b. Rope-guided personnel hoist systems that are temporarily erected during construction, alteration, or demolition shall be in compliance with ANSI A10.22;

c. Non-guided personnel hoist systems that are temporarily erected during construction, alteration, or demolition shall be in compliance with ANSI A10.8 and

ANSI A10.22. (An air-tugger hoist, or the equivalent meeting the criteria in section 4.2 of ANSI A10.22, may by substituted for a base-mounted hoist).

d. Elevators operating in permanent hoistways on the permanent guide rails for handling personnel during construction shall be in compliance with ANSI/ASME A17.1

e. A copy of the manufacturer's manual covering construction, installation or erection, operation, inspection, testing, and maintenance and a copy of the applicable ANSI standard shall be available on site.

f. Personnel hoists and elevators shall comply with applicable requirements from section 16 of this manual.

24.G.02 Personnel hoists used in bridge tower construction shall be approved by a registered engineer and erected under the supervision of a RPE competent in this field.

24.H Safe Practices for Rope Access Work. If rope access work is to be performed, a Rope Access Work Plan and accompanying procedures must be developed and submitted to the GDA for acceptance.

24.H.01 Climbing equipment.

a. Ropes: Used as working line and safety line shall be made of synthetic fiber with a nominal breaking strength of at least 5400 lbs (24 kN) when new. The working lines and safety lines shall be specifically designed and intended for life safety use. Additionally, elasticity (elongation) of both lines shall be limited to 7% with a load of 540 lbs applied.

b. Carabiners and snap hooks: Used for climbing (life support) shall have at least two consecutive, deliberate actions to prepare the gate for opening and shall be rated at 5,000 lbs (22.2kN) and shall meet the ANSI/ASSE Z359 Fall Protection Code. Gates shall be rated at 3600 lbs (16kN). Rope snaps and snap hooks shall be self-closing and self-locking. The use of rope thimbles when attaching rope snaps is recommended to prevent rope fraying.

c. Pulleys/Rope Sleeves: Anti-friction devices are also recommended to prevent rope damage.

d. Rope Blocks/Brakes: Used to make the work safer and requires less hands to control heavy loads. When handling limb removal ropes, ground personnel should not wrap the rope around their hands or waist and keep the rope away from their feet to prevent entanglement.

e. Climbers PPE: Appropriate footwear, long pants, work shirt with a minimum 4 in (10.2 cm) sleeve length, eye protection, face shield, hearing protection during chainsaw usage, hard hat with chin strap or ANSI Z89.1 approved climbers helmet (vented or non-vented), and fingerless gloves such as mechanics gloves. When the air temperature exceeds 85 °F (29 °C), climbers should carry a water supply with them.

f. All equipment shall be inspected prior to each use and maintained and used in accordance with manufacturer instructions.

g. Employees shall be properly trained in the use of all equipment.

h. Ropes shall not be used to lower limbs or raise equipment.

i. Sharp tools such as hand saws shall be sheathed when not in use.

j. Tools used for de-barking, cavity work, cabling, bark tracing, shall be carried in a bag or belt designed for such use, and not carried in pockets or placed in boots.

k. Climbers Saddle: Climbers belts/saddles are only meant to be used as a suspension scaffold/equipment. In addition to the saddle a fall arrest system is required. Belts shall be equipped with leg straps or seats to take pressure off of the climbers back.

l. Climbing ropes shall not be spliced to effect repair.

m. Ropes shall be coiled and piled, or shall be suspended, so that air can circulate through the coils to aid in drying.

n. Wet ropes shall not be used for electrical work.

o. Ropes shall be inspected before and after each use.

p. Harnesses and other personal fall protection equipment used in rope access shall meet the ANSI Z359/ASSE Z359, *Fall protection Code.*

q. If descender devices are used, they shall allow a controlled descent taking into consideration the weight of the worker, the length of the descent, considerations for safety and the need for stopping along the working line for the purpose of hands free work.

24.H.02 General Practices.

a. Safety, Secondary, Belay or Backup Line(s).

(1) Safety, Secondary, Belay or Backup line(s) or other appropriate fall arrest devices shall be used in addition to the main line (working line) unless the employer can demonstrate that the second line or other fall arrest devices would create a greater hazard or otherwise would not be feasible. > *See paragraph 24.H.02.a(2).*

(2) Safety, Secondary, Belay or Backup line(s) shall not be used alone for tree climbing. The use of a secondary line (safety line) may pose additional risks and increased difficulties. Careful consideration to the impact of secondary line use should be considered before making a decision on use in tree climbing operations.

(3) Where a safety line is used in conjunction with the working line, each line shall have its own separate anchor and shall be separately fixed to the worker's harness. This does not preclude both lines being attached to a single harness attachment point.

(4) The safety line shall be connected to the sternal or dorsal D-ring of the full body harness.

(5) When using safety line, the maximum free fall distance shall not exceed 6 ft (1.8 m) and the maximum arrest force shall not exceed 1,800 lbs (8 kN).

b. Employer shall insure that anchors have been evaluated in order to ensure that overall system safety factors can be met.

c. Before adopting rope access techniques for a particular job, the Competent Person (CP) for Rope Access shall perform risk assessment and develop a written safety analysis report and submit it as part of the Rope Access Work Plan to GDA for acceptance. The safety analysis report shall include consideration of the various rope access alternatives available and their respective access advantages and hazards. In particular, attention shall be given to the following aspects:

(1) Ability of the suspended person to safely use materials, equipment or tools necessary for the work and whether the reaction from any tool may place the person at risk;

(2) Whether the work may loosen material which could become a hazard to the worker or others;

(3) Whether the time required for the work at any one location will be such that there may be unacceptable levels of risk;

(4) Whether it would be possible to quickly rescue workers that are using rope access techniques from any position they could be expected to enter.

d. The contractor shall make provision for prompt rescue or self rescue and for emergency services.

e. The Rope Access Worker shall:

(1) Have a working understanding of the employer's Rope Access Work Plan and all applicable policy and procedures;

(2) Adjust, inspect, maintain, care for, and properly store rope access equipment;

(3) Inspect and verify the integrity of anchor systems and components;

(4) Recognize worksite hazards and notify the Rope Access Supervisor of any such hazard;

(5) Be capable of identifying work zones and job hazard analyses;

(6) Understand and communicate any written or verbal warnings;

(7) Be familiar with rescue procedures and systems used by the employer, and assist in the performance of rescue from rope access systems;

(8) Utilize appropriate personal protective equipment as designated by the Rope Access Supervisor;

(9) Follow the Competent Person (CP) for Rope Access directions or, where appropriate pursuant to the requirements of the Safe Practices Document, the Rope Access Lead Technician's directions regarding the work to be performed;

(10) Notify the CP for Rope Access if assigned.

SECTION 25 Excavation and Trenching

Table of Contents

25

25.A General. The requirements of this Section are applicable to all Government and contractor work forces when their employees are performing excavation or trenching activities.

25.A.01 Excavation/Trenching Plan. An Excavation/Trenching Plan and/or Activity Hazard Analysis (AHA) will be prepared by the Competent Person (CP) for Excavation or a Registered Professional Engineer (RPE), submitted and accepted by the GDA prior to beginning operations.

a. For excavations or trenches greater than 5 ft (1.5 m) in depth, both an Excavation/Trenching plan and AHA are required;

b. For excavations/trenches less than 5 ft (1.5 m) in depth, or made entirely in stable rock, an AHA is required (See Sections 1 and 25.A.01.a) and the Excavation/Trenching plan is optional;

c. The Excavation/Trenching Plan shall include, at a minimum;

(1) Activity Hazard Analysis (AHA). The AHA shall include required information per Section 1 and in addition:

(a) For all piping activities, include workers' increased exposure during connection activities (i.e. bent over, kneeling);

(b) Methods and locations for egress;

(c) Identification and credentials of the CP for Excavation;

(d) Documentation that examination of the ground by the CP provides no indication of a potential cave-in.

(2) Rescue plan and procedures (*See Section 25.B.02*). A rescue plan shall be prepared and maintained when workers are working at depths in excess of 5 ft (1.5 m);

(3) Diagram or sketch of the area where the work is to be done, with adjacent and nearby structures shown;

(4) Projected maximum depth of the excavation;

(5) Projected soil type and method of testing to determine soil type;

(6) Planned method of shoring, sloping and/or benching;

(7) Planned method for confined space entry, trench access and egress and atmospheric monitoring processes;

(8) Location of utility shut offs (if required);

(9) Proposed methods for preventing damage to overhead utility lines, trees designated to remain, and other man-made facilities or natural features designated to remain within or adjacent to the construction rights-of-way;

(10) Plan for management of excavated soil/asphalt/concrete;

(11) Plan for traffic control;

(12) Digging permits (Excavation permits). All underground lines/utilities (communication lines, water, fuel, electric lines) shall be located and protected from damage or displacement.

(a) Utility companies and other responsible authorities shall be contacted to locate and mark the locations and, if they so desire, direct or assist with protecting the underground installations.

(b) The Contractor shall obtain a "Digging Permit" (excavation permit) from Base Civil Engineers or other authority having jurisdiction prior the initiation of any excavation work. Requests for the permits will be processed through the GDA.

(13) Certification of UXO clearance. Where excavations are to be performed in areas known or suspected to contain explosives, unexploded munitions, or military ordnance, surface and subsurface clearance by qualified explosive ordnance disposal (EOD) personnel shall be accomplished prior to excavation work;

(14) For Cofferdams: Controlled flooding plan, fall protection, access/egress and evacuation procedures.

25.A.02 Excavation Testing and Documentation. > *See Table 25-1.*

a. When workers will be in or around an excavation, a CP for Excavation shall inspect the excavation, the adjacent areas, and protective systems daily. Inspections shall also be completed: before each work shift, throughout the work shifts as dictated by the work being done; after every rainstorm; when fissures, tension cracks, sloughing, undercutting, water seepage, bulging at the bottom or similar conditions occur; when there is a change in size, location or placement of the spoil pile; where there is any indication or change in adjacent structures; and after other events that could increase hazards (e.g., snowstorm, windstorm, thaw, earthquake, etc.).

b. The CP shall be able to demonstrate:

(1) Training, experience, and knowledge of soil analysis, use of protective systems, and requirements of this Section and 29 CFR 1926 Subpart P;

(2) Ability to detect conditions that could result in cave-ins, failures in protective systems, hazardous atmospheres, and other hazards including those associated with confined spaces; and

(3) The authority to take prompt corrective measures to eliminate existing and predictable hazards and stop work when required.

c. When persons for the purpose of inspection/testing will be in or around an excavation that is between 6 ft (1.8 m) and 20 ft (6.1 m) deep, that has vertical face leading edge fall exposure (sides have not been laid back), or that contains hazards (e.g., impalement hazards, hazardous substances), they shall be provided with fall protection per Section 21.

➤ *Exception: The Designated CP for Excavation may exempt the use of fall protection for inspectors/supervisors provided those individuals are not exposed to hazards within 24 in (0.6 m) of edges, the excavation contains no additional hazards and the individual(s) stay a minimum of 24 in (0.6 m) from the excavation's edge.*

d. Testing for soil classification shall be of an approved method: pocket penetrometer, plasticity/ wet thread test or visual test and shall be conducted at a minimum of once prior to the start of each work shift or, if conditions warrant, as described in Section 25.A.02.a.

e. All testing for soil classification shall be determined by the CP, documented, and maintained for the life of the project (i.e., QC daily reports, excavation inspection log, etc.). > *See Table 25-1.*

f. If evidence of a situation that could result in possible cave-ins, slides, failure of protective systems, hazardous atmospheres, or other hazardous condition is identified, exposed workers shall be removed from the hazard and all work in the excavation stopped until all necessary safety precautions have been implemented.

g. In locations where oxygen deficiency or gaseous conditions are known or suspected, in excavations 4 ft (1.2 m) or greater in depth, air in the excavation shall be tested prior to the start of each shift or more often

if directed by the GDA. A log of all test results shall be maintained at the work site. > *See Sections 5 and 6.*

25.A.03 Protective systems. Protective systems shall have the capacity to resist without failure all loads that are intended or could reasonably be expected to be applied or transmitted to the system.

a. The sides of all excavations in which employees are exposed to danger from moving ground shall be guarded by a support system, sloping or benching of the ground, or other equivalent means.

b. Excavations less than 5 ft (1.5 m) in depth and which a CP examines, determines and documents that there is no potential for cave-in do not require protective systems, however, a fixed means of egress shall be provided.

c. Sloping or benching of the ground shall be in accordance with Section 25.C.

d. Support systems shall be in accordance with Section 25.D.

e. Protective systems shall have the capacity to resist without failure all loads that are intended or could reasonably be expected to be applied to the system.

f. Shoring shall be used for unstable soil or depths greater than 5 ft (>1.5 m) unless benching, sloping, or other acceptable plan is implemented by the Contractor and accepted by the GDA.

25.A.04 Stability of adjacent structures.

a. Except in stable rock, excavations below the level of the base of footing of any foundation or retaining wall shall not be permitted unless:

(1) A support system, such as underpinning, is provided to ensure the stability of the structure and to protect employees involved in the excavation work or in the vicinity thereof; or

(2) A RPE has approved the determination that the structure is sufficiently removed from the excavation so as to be unaffected by the excavation and that the excavation will not pose a hazard to employees.

b. If the stability of adjoining buildings or walls is endangered by excavations, shoring, bracing, or underpinning designed by a qualified person shall be provided to ensure the stability of the structure and to protect employees.

c. Sidewalks, pavements, and related structures shall not be undermined unless a support system is

25

provided to protect employees and the sidewalk, pavement, or related structure.

25.A.05 Where it is necessary to undercut the side of an excavation, overhanging material shall be safely supported.

25.A.06 Protection from water.

a. Diversion ditches, dikes, or other means shall be used to prevent surface water entering an excavation and to provide good drainage of the area adjacent to the excavation.

b. Employees shall not work in excavations in which there is accumulated water or in which water is accumulating unless the water hazards posed by accumulation is controlled.

(1) Freezing, pumping, drainage, and similar control measures shall be planned and directed by a RPE. Consideration shall be given to the existing moisture balances in surrounding soils and the effects on foundations and structures if it is disturbed.

(2) When continuous operation of ground water control equipment is necessary, an emergency power source shall be provided. Water control equipment and operations shall be monitored by the CP to ensure proper operation.

25.A.07 Protection from falling material.

a. Employees shall be protected (by scaling, ice removal, benching, barricading, rock bolting, wire mesh, or other means) from loose rock or soil that could create a hazard by falling from the excavation wall: special attention shall be given to slopes that may be adversely affected by weather, moisture content, or vibration.

b. Materials, such as boulders or stumps, that may slide or roll into the excavation shall be removed or made safe.

c. Excavated material shall be placed at least 2 ft (0.6 m) from the edge of an excavation or shall be retained by devices that are sufficient to prevent the materials from falling into the excavation. In any case, material shall be placed at a distance to prevent excessive loading on the face of the excavation.

25.A.08 Mobile equipment and motor vehicle precautions.

a. When vehicles or mobile equipment are used or allowed adjacent to an excavation, substantial stop logs or barricades shall be installed. The use of a ground guide is recommended.

b. Workers shall stand away from vehicles being loaded or unloaded to avoid being struck by spillage or falling materials.

c. Excavating or hoisting equipment shall not be allowed to raise, lower, or swing loads over or adjacent to personnel in the excavation without substantial overhead protection. Personnel shall maintain a safe distance from hoisting operation until the load has been placed.

➤ *Note: Any equipment used to hoist loads, with the use of rigging attached to the equipment (to include excavators, forklifts, etc.) shall be considered "load handling equipment (LHE) or hoisting equipment" and as such, shall follow the requirements in Section 16.*

d. Employees exposed to public vehicular traffic shall be provided with, and shall wear, high visibility apparel as per Section 05.F.

25.A.09 Employees shall not be permitted to work on the faces of sloped or benched excavations at levels above other employees except when employees at lower levels are adequately protected from the hazard of falling material or equipment.

25.A.10 When operations approach the location of underground utilities, excavation shall progress with caution until the exact location of the utility is determined. Workers shall be protected from the utility and the utility shall be protected from damage or displacement.

25.A.11 Employees entering excavations classified as confined spaces, or that otherwise present the potential for emergency rescue (i.e., bell-bottom pier holes or similar), shall wear rescue equipment and maintain communication with the (confined space) attendant. > *See Section 34.*

25.B Safe Access.

25.B.01 Protection shall be provided to prevent personnel, vehicles, and equipment from falling into excavations. Protection shall be provided according to the following hierarchy. > *See Appendix Q for definitions of Perimeter Protection: Class I, Class II, and Class III.*

a. If the excavation is exposed to members of the public or vehicles or equipment, then Class I perimeter protection is required.

b. Class II perimeter protection is the minimum protection required if the excavation does not meet the requirements for Class I perimeter protection but is:

(1) Routinely exposed to employees, and

(2) Is deeper than 6 ft (1.8 m) or

(3) Contains hazards (e.g., impalement hazards, hazardous substances).

c. When workers are in the zone between the warning barricades/ flagging and the excavation, they shall be provided with fall protection as specified in Section 21. > See Section 25.A.02.c for exception.

d. If the excavation does not meet the requirements for either Class I or Class II perimeter protection, then Class III perimeter protection is the minimum protection required.

25.B.02 Rescue Plan and Procedures. The employer is required to provide prompt rescue to all buried workers.

a. A written rescue plan shall be prepared by the CP or a RPE, submitted and accepted by the GDA prior to beginning operations and maintained when workers are working at depths of over 5 ft (1.5 m).

b. The plan shall contain provisions for self-rescue and assisted rescue of any worker who is buried during a cave-in including rescue equipment. If other methods of rescue are planned (i.e. by a jurisdictional, public or Government emergency rescue agencies), it shall be indicated in the rescue plan including how to contact and summon the agency to the mishap site.

c. Personnel conducting rescue shall be trained accordingly.

25.B.03 All wells, calyx holes, pits, shafts, etc., shall be barricaded or covered.

25.B.04 Excavations shall be backfilled as soon as possible. Upon completion of exploration and similar operations, test pits, temporary wells, calyx holes, etc., shall be backfilled immediately.

25.B.05 Walkways or bridges shall be provided with standard guardrails (as defined in Section 21.F.01) where people or equipment are required or permitted to cross over excavations.

25.B.06 Where personnel are required to enter excavations/trenches over 4 ft (1.2 m) in depth, sufficient stairs, ramps, or ladders shall be provided to require no more than 25 ft (7.6 m) of lateral travel.

a. At least two means of exit shall be provided for personnel working in excavations. Where the width of the excavation exceeds 100 ft (30.4 m), two or more means of exit shall be provided on each side of the excavation.

b. When access to excavations in excess of 20 ft (6 m) in depth is required, ramps, stairs, or mechanical personnel hoists shall be provided.

25.B.07 Ramps. > See Sections 24.B. and 24.F.

a. Ramps used solely for personnel access shall be a minimum width of 4 ft (1.2 m) and provided with standard guardrails. > See Section 21.F.01.

b. Ramps used for equipment access shall be a minimum width of 12 ft (3.6 m). Curbs not less than 8-in x 8-in (20.3-cm x 20.3-cm) timbers, or equivalent protection, shall be provided. Equipment ramps shall be designed and constructed in accordance with accepted engineering practice.

25.B.08 Ladders used as access ways shall extend from the bottom of the excavation to not less than 3 ft (0.9 m) above the surface.

25.C Sloping and Benching.

25.C.01 Sloping or benching of the ground shall be in accordance with one of the systems outlined below. > See 29 CFR 1926, Subpart P, Appendix B).

a. Allowable configurations and slopes. For excavations less than 20 ft (6 m) in depth, the maximum slope shall be 34° measured from the horizontal (1-1/2 horizontal to 1 vertical). These slopes shall be excavated to form configurations that are in accordance with the slopes shown for Type C soil. > See also Section 25.A.03 and 29 CFR 1926, Subpart P, Appendices A and B and Figure 25-1.

b. Determination of slopes and configurations using classification of soil and rock deposits. > See Section 25.A.03 and 29 CFR 1926, Subpart P, Appendix A. All excavations less than 20 ft (6m) in depth which have vertically lowered portions shall be shielded or supported to a height at least 18 in (.5 m) above the top of the vertical side with a maximum allowable slope of 1-1/2:1. Maximum allowable slopes and allowable configurations for sloping and benching systems, shall be determined in accordance with the conditions and requirements set forth in 29 CFR 1926, Subpart P, Appendices A and B. > See also Figure 25-1.

c. Designs using other tabulated data. The design shall be selected from and be in accordance with written tabulated data, such as charts and tables approved by a RPE. At least one copy of the tabulated data shall be maintained at the job site during excavation. The tabulated data shall include:

(1) Identification of the parameters that affect the selection of a sloping or benching system drawn from the data;

(2) Identification of the limits of use of the data, to include the magnitude and configuration of slopes determined to be safe;

(3) Explanatory information as may be necessary to aid the user in correctly selecting a protective system from the data; and

(4) The identity of the RPE who approved the data.

d. Design by a RPE. The sloping or benching systems was not created using Options a, b or c above but is instead, approved by a RPE. At least one copy of the design shall be maintained at the job site during excavation. Designs shall be in writing and include:

(1) The magnitudes and configurations of the slopes that were determined to be safe for the particular excavation, and

(2) The identity of the RPE who approved the design, including name, address, telephone, fax and email address.

25.D Support Systems.

25.D.01 Support systems (including shield systems and other protective systems) shall be in accordance with one of the following systems:

a. Designs Using Manufacturer's Tabulated Data. Designs drawn from manufacturer's tabulated data shall be in accordance with all specifications, limitations, and recommendations issued or made by the manufacturer.

(1) Deviation from the specifications, recommendations, and limitations are only allowed after the manufacturer issues specific written approval.

(2) A copy of the manufacturer's specifications, recommendations, and limitations (and the manufacturer's approval to deviate from these, if required) shall be in written form and maintained at the job site during excavation.

b. Designs using other tabulated data. Designs shall be selected from and be in accordance with tabulated data (such as tables and charts). At least one copy of the tabulated data shall be maintained at the job site during excavation. The tabulated data shall include:

(1) Identification of the parameters that affect the selection of the protective system drawn from such data,

(2) Identification of the limits of use of the data, and

(3) Explanatory information as may be necessary to aid the user in correctly selecting a protective system from the data, and

(4) The identity of the RPE who approved the data, including name, address, telephone, fax and email address.

c. Designed by a RPE. At least one copy of the design shall be maintained at the job site during excavation. Designs shall be in writing and include:

(1) A plan indicating the sizes, types, and configurations of the materials to be used in the protective system, and

(2) The identity of the RPE who approved the design, including name, address, telephone, fax and email address.

25.D.02 Materials and equipment used for protective systems.

a. Materials and equipment shall be free from damage or defects that might impair their proper function.

b. Manufactured materials and equipment shall be used and maintained in a manner consistent with the recommendations of the manufacturer and in a manner that will prevent employee exposure to hazards.

c. When material or equipment is damaged, a CP shall examine the material or equipment and evaluate its suitability for continued use.

25.D.03 Installation and removal of support systems. > *See Figures 25-1 through 25-3.*

a. Members of support systems shall be securely connected together to prevent sliding, falling, kickouts, or other predictable failure.

b. Support systems shall be installed and removed in manners that protect employees from cave-ins, structural collapses, or from being struck by members of the support system.

c. Individual members of a support system shall not be subjected to loads exceeding those for which they were designed to withstand.

d. Before temporary removal of individual members, additional precautions shall be taken to ensure the safety of employees, such as installing other structural members to carry the loads imposed on the support system.

e. Removal shall begin at and progress from the bottom of the excavation. Members shall be released slowly as to note any indication of possible failure of the remaining members or possible cave-in of the sides of the excavation.

f. Backfilling shall progress together with the removal of support systems from excavations.

g. For trench excavations: excavation material shall be permitted to a level not greater than 2 ft (.6 m) below the bottom of the members of a support system, only if the system is designed to resist the forces calculated for the full depth of the trench, and there is no indication while the trench is open of a possible loss of soil from behind or below the bottom of the support system.

25.D.04 Shield systems.

a. Shield systems shall not be subjected to loads exceeding those that the system was designed to withstand.

b. Shields shall be installed in a manner to restrict lateral or other hazardous movement of the shield in the event of the application of sudden lateral loads.

c. Employees shall be protected from the hazard of cave-ins when entering or exiting the area protected by shields.

d. Employees shall not be allowed in shields when shields are being installed, removed, or moved vertically.

e. For shield systems used in trench excavations: excavations of earth material to a level not greater than 2 ft (.6 m) below the bottom of the shield shall be permitted, only if the shield is designed to resist the forces calculated for the full depth of the trench, and there is no indications while the trench is open of a possible loss of soil from behind or below the bottom of the shield.

25.D.05 Additional requirements for trenching.

a. Installation of support systems shall be closely coordinated with excavations of trenches.

b. Bracing or shoring of trenches shall be carried along with the excavation.

c. Backfilling and removal of trench supports should progress together from the bottom of the trench. Jacks or braces shall be released slowly and, in unstable soil, ropes shall be used to pull out the jacks or braces from above after personnel have cleared the trench. > *See Figure 25-3.*

d. Excavation of material to a level no greater than 2 ft (0.6 m) below the bottom of the members of a trench support system (including a shield) shall be permitted, only if the system is designed to resist the forces calculated for the full depth of the trench and there are no indications while the trench is open of a possible loss of soil from behind or below the bottom of the support system.

25.E Cofferdams.

25.E.01 If overtopping of the cofferdams by high water is possible, design shall include provisions for controlled flooding of the work area.

25.E.02 If personnel or equipment are required or permitted on cofferdams, standard railings, or equivalent protection, shall be provided.

25.E.03 Walkways, bridges, or ramps with at least two means of rapid exit, with standard guardrails (as defined in Section 21.F.01), shall be provided for personnel and equipment working on cofferdams.

25.E.04 A plan (including warning signals) for evacuation of personnel and equipment in case of emergency and for controlled flooding shall be developed and posted.

25.E.05 Cofferdams located close to navigable shipping channels shall be protected from vessels in transit.

25

TABLE 25-1

Soil Classification

Soil Type	Criteria	Other Considerations
Stable Rock	Natural solid mineral that can be excavated with vertical sides and remain intact while exposed.	
Type A	Cohesive soil with an unconfined compressive strength of 1.5 tons per square foot (tsf) (144 kPa) or greater.	Can not be Type A if soil is: 1) fissured; 2) subject to vibration from heavy traffic, pile driving, etc.; 3) previously disturbed; 4) part of sloped, layered system where layers dip into excavation on a slope of 4H:1V or greater; or 5) subject to other factors requiring it to be classified as less stable material.
Type B	Cohesive soil with an unconfined compressive strength greater than 0.5 tsf (48 kPa) but less than 1.5 tsf (144 kPa).	Type B soil can also be: 1) granular cohesionless soils such as angular gravel, silt, silt loam, sandy loam, and in some cases, silty clay loam and sandy clay loam; 2) previously disturbed soils except those which would otherwise be classed as Type C soil; 3) soil that meets the requirements of Type A, but is fissured or subject to vibration; 4) dry rock that is not stable; or 5) part of sloped, layered system where layers dip into excavation on a slope of 4H:1V , but only if the soil would otherwise be classed as Type A.
Type C	Cohesive soil with an unconfined compressive strength of 0.5 tsf (48 kPa) or less.	Type C soil can also be: 1) granular soils including gravel, sand, and loamy sand; 2) submerged soil or soil from which water is freely seeping; 3) submerged rock is not stable; or 4) part of sloped, layered system where layers dip into excavation on a slope of 4H:1V or steeper. <u>Can NOT be benched!</u>

NOTE: Soil classification must be determined by a Competent Person, per section 25.A.02

FIGURE 25-1
Sloping and Benching

Simple Slope - Type C Soil

Vertical-Sided
Lower Portion - Type C Soil

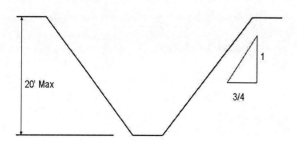

Simple Slope – General - Type A Soil*

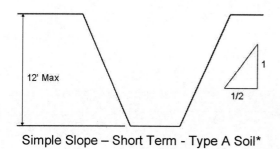

Simple Slope – Short Term - Type A Soil*

Simple Bench -Type A Soil*

Multiple Bench - Type A Soil*

Unsupported Vertically Sided Lower Portion -
Maximum 8 Feet in Depth - Type A Soil*

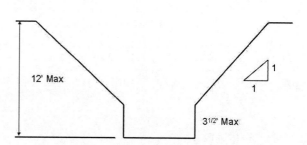

Unsupported Vertically Sided Lower Portion –
(Maximum 12 Ft In Depth) - Type A Soil*

25

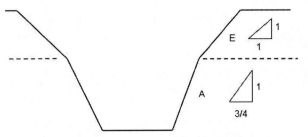

Excavations Made In Layered Soils - B over A*

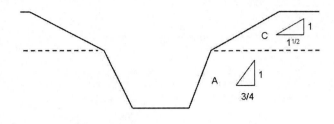

Excavations Made In Layered Soils - C over A*

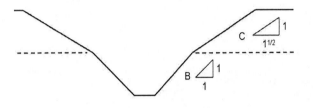

Excavations Made In Layered Soils - C over B*

* Requires the approval and identity of a Registered Professional Engineer if paragraph(s) 25.C.01.c or 25.C.01.d are used to determine design of sloping/benching system(s).

FIGURE 25-2
Trench Shields

18" MAX.

VERTICAL RAIL

HYDRAULIC CYLINDER

VERTICAL SPACING

4' MAX.

2' MAX.

Aluminum Hydraulic Shoring

FIGURE 25-3
Trench Jacks

Pneumatic/hydraulic Shoring

SECTION 26 Underground Construction (Tunnels), Shafts and Caissons

Table of Contents

26

26. General. This section applies to the construction of underground tunnels, shafts, chambers, and passageways. This section also applies to cut-and-cover excavations which are both physically connected to ongoing underground construction operations within the scope of this section, and covered in such a manner as to create conditions characteristic of underground construction.

26.A.01 Access and Egress.

a. Access to all underground openings shall be controlled to prevent unauthorized entry.

b. Unused access ways or other openings shall be tightly covered or fenced off and shall be posted with warning signs indicating "KEEP OUT" or similar language.

c. Completed or unused sections of underground structures shall be barricaded.

d. See Section 34 of this manual for confined space requirements.

26.A.02 Every location of underground construction shall have a check-in/check-out system that will ensure that above-ground personnel can determine the identification of all underground personnel.

26.A.03 Oncoming shifts shall be informed of any hazardous occurrences or conditions that have affected or might affect employee safety, including liberation of gas, equipment failures, earth or rock slides, cave-ins, flooding, fires, or explosions.

26.A.04 Communications.

a. In situations where unassisted voice communication is inadequate, power-assisted means shall be used to provide communication among workers and support personnel.

b. At least two effective means of communication (at least one of which shall be voice communication) shall be provided in all shafts that are being developed or used either for personnel access or for hoisting.

c. Powered communication systems shall operate on an independent power supply and shall be installed so that the use of or disruption of any one phone or signal location will not disrupt the operation of the system from any other location.

d. Communication systems shall be tested upon initial entry of each shift to the underground and as often as necessary thereafter to ensure proper operation.

e. Any employee working alone underground, who is both out of range of natural unassisted voice communication and not under observation by other persons, shall be provided with effective means to communicate the need for and to obtain emergency assistance. Employees working alone shall be required to check in with their supervisor at least once an hour.

26.A.05 Emergency rescue plans and equipment.

a. Plans for rescuing personnel who might become injured or incapacitated while underground or in a shaft or caisson shall be developed.

(1) Plans shall be incorporated in either the APP or the AHA and posted at the job site.

(2) Plans shall be periodically reviewed with all affected personnel so that they maintain a working knowledge of emergency responsibilities and procedures.

(3) Emergency plans shall be drilled on a periodic basis to ensure their efficacy.

b. Emergency equipment specified in the emergency plan shall be provided within 15 minutes of each portal or shaft entry. Inspections and workability tests of the equipment shall be made and documented monthly.

c. When a shaft is used as a means of egress, arrangements shall be made for power-assisted hoisting capability to be readily available in an emergency, unless the regular hoisting means can continue to function during a power failure.

d. Hoisting devices used for emergencies shall be designed so that the load hoist drum is powered in both directions of rotation and so that the brake is automatically applied upon power release or failure.

e. Self-rescuing/emergency respirators shall be immediately available to all employees at workstations in underground areas where they may be trapped by smoke or gas. > *See Section 05.G.*

f. At least one designated person shall be on duty above ground whenever personnel are underground.

(1) The designated person shall be responsible for keeping an accurate count of employees' underground and securing immediate aid in case of emergency.

(2) The designated person shall not be given other responsibilities that could affect his emergency response duties.

g. Each worker underground shall have an acceptable portable hand lamp or cap lamp in his work area for emergency use, unless natural light or an emergency lighting system provides adequate illumination for escape.

26.A.06 Rescue teams.

a. On job sites where less than 25 persons are underground at one time, provisions shall be made for at least one five-person rescue team to be either on the job site or within 30-minutes travel time from the underground entry point. This rescue team may be provided by local emergency response services.

b. On job sites where 25 or more persons are underground at one time, provisions shall be made for at least two five-person rescue teams. One rescue team shall be on the job site or be within 30-minutes travel time from the underground entry point, and the other rescue team shall be within 2-hours travel time. These rescue teams may be provided by local emergency response services.

c. Rescue team members shall be qualified in rescue procedures, the use and limitations of breathing apparatus, and the use of firefighting equipment. Qualifications shall be reviewed not less than annually.

d. On job sites where flammable or noxious gases are encountered or anticipated in hazardous quantities, rescue team members shall practice donning and using SCBA monthly.

e. Rescue teams shall be kept informed of conditions at the job site with may impact their response.

26.A.07 In addition to the requirements of Section 5, personnel in wet underground areas shall wear rubber boots (and rain gear, as necessary).

26.A.08 First aid facilities.

a. A fully equipped first aid station and emergency transportation shall be provided at each underground construction project regardless of the number of persons employed.

b. If an underground construction project has multiple portals, a first aid station shall be provided at each portal or entry shaft or shall be so located between them that the distance from the station to each portal/entry shaft is less than 5 mi (8 km) and travel time less than 15 minutes.

26.A.09 Electrical and lighting.

a. All electrical systems used in hazardous locations must be approved for that location. > *See Section 11.H.*

b. Lighting circuits shall be installed on one side of the tunnel near the spring line and shall be mounted on insulators at each point of suspension.

c. Light fixtures shall be nonmetallic and weatherproof and mounted in a manner that provides safe clearance for personnel and equipment.

d. Only portable lighting equipment that is approved for the hazardous location shall be used within:

(1) Storage areas, or

(2) 50 ft (15.2 m) of any underground heading during explosives handling.

26.A.10 Inspections, testing and documentation.

a. A program for testing all rock bolts for tightness shall be established. The frequency of testing shall be determined by rock conditions and the distance from vibration sources.

b. The employer shall examine and test the roof, face, and walls of the work area at the start of each shift and frequently thereafter.

c. Ground conditions along underground haulways and accessways shall be inspected by a Competent Person (CP) as frequently as necessary to maintain safe passage.

d. All drilling and associated equipment to be used during a shift shall be inspected before each shift by a CP.

e. Drilling areas shall be inspected for hazards before drilling operations are started.

f. A CP shall inspect haulage equipment before each shift.

g. Whenever defects affecting safety or health are identified, the defects shall be corrected before activities are initiated or continued.

26.A.11 Protection from falling material.

a. A CP shall inspect the roof, face and walls of the work area at the start of each shift and as often as necessary to determine the stability of the tunnel. > *See 29 CFR 1926.800(o)(3)(i)(A).*

b. Portal openings and access areas shall be guarded by shoring, fencing, head walls, shotcreting, or other equivalent means to ensure safe access of employees and equipment. Adjacent areas shall be scaled or otherwise secured to prevent loose soil or rock from endangering the portal and access areas.

c. Ground stability in hazardous subsidence areas shall be ensured by shoring or filling in, or by erecting barricades and posting warning signs to prevent entry.

d. Loose ground in underground areas that might be hazardous to employees shall be taken down, scaled, or supported.

e. Rock masses separated from the main mass by faults, joints, or fractures shall be secured by rock

26

bolting or other suitable means or shall be removed. The means of securing shall be designed by a foundation engineer, an engineering geologist, or other qualified person.

f. Anchored chain-link fabric or other method approved by the GDA shall be provided on rock faces subject to spalling.

g. Where tunnels are excavated through earth or shale, any excavation above or adjacent to portal areas shall be sloped to the angle of repose or held in place by ground supports. When undercutting occurs on these slopes (whether due to erosion or other causes) the overhanging material shall be promptly removed.

h. Where the need is indicated, a protective shelter shall be provided at each underground portal to protect persons and equipment from the hazards of falling rock or other material. The protective shelter shall project at least 15 ft (4.5 m) out from the portal.

i. Ice or snow buildup on rock faces or earth slopes that create a hazard shall be promptly removed.

26.A.12 Tunneling in soil.

a. Where tunnels are excavated by conventional methods, the excavation shall not be extended more than 24 in (60.9 cm) ahead of ground supports; where continuous mining machines are used for tunnel excavation, the excavation shall not be extended more than 48 in (121.8 cm) ahead of ground supports.

b. Under no circumstances shall persons be permitted to work in unsupported sections of the tunnels.

c. All voids in back of ground supports shall be filled, blocked, braced, or treated to prevent further cave-ins.

d. Where liner plate is not used for tunnel support, 2 in (5 cm) wire mesh or chain-link fabric shall be installed over the crown section, extending down to the spring line on each side of the tunnel and secured in place.

26.A.13 Ground support systems.

a. Torque meters and/or torque wrenches shall be used where rock bolts are used for ground support.

b. Frequent tests shall be made to determine if bolts meet the required torque. The test frequency shall be determined by rock conditions and distance from vibration sources.

c. Rock bolt support systems shall be designed by a foundation engineer, geologist, geotechnical engineer, mining engineer or other qualified Registered Professional Engineer (RPE). Suitable protection shall be provided for employees exposed to the hazard of loose ground while installing ground support systems.

d. Support sets shall be installed so that the bottoms have sufficient anchorage to prevent ground pressures from dislodging the support base of the sets. Lateral bracing shall be provided between immediately adjacent sets to provide added stability.

e. Damaged or dislodged ground supports shall be repaired or replaced. Whenever possible, new supports shall be installed before removing the damaged supports.

f. A shield or other type of support shall be used to maintain a safe travel way for personnel working in dead-end areas ahead of any support replacement operation.

26.A.14 Material handling equipment.

a. Powered mobile haulage equipment shall have audible warning devices to inform personnel to stay clear. The operator shall sound the warning device before moving the equipment and whenever necessary during travel.

b. All vehicles and mobile equipment required to move in and out of underground construction areas shall have a revolving, flashing amber light, mounted so as to be visible in all directions. The flashing light shall be on whenever a vehicle or mobile equipment is in operation.

c. Haulage equipment shall be equipped with two headlights at both ends, a backup light, and an automatic backup alarm.

d. Conveyors used to transport muck from tunnels shall be installed, guarded, and maintained as required by Section 17. Fire extinguishers or equivalent protection shall be provided at the head and tail pulleys of underground belt conveyors and at 300 ft (91.4 m) intervals along the belt line.

e. No person shall ride haulage equipment unless it is equipped with seating for each passenger and passengers are protected from being struck, crushed, or caught between other equipment or surfaces.

f. When dumping cars by hand, the car dumps shall be provided with tie-down chains or bumper blocks to prevent cars from overturning.

g. Where narrow-gage railroads are used for haulage, the tracks shall be secured to prevent shifting. No "humping" of mine dump cars shall be permitted.

h. Whenever rails serve as a return for a trolley circuit, both rails shall be bonded at every joint and cross-bonded every 200 ft (60.9 m).

i. Mine dump cars shall be equipped with automatic safety couplings, and cradle cars shall be equipped with a positive locking device to prevent accidental dumping.

j. Berms, bumper blocks, safety hooks, or equivalent means shall be provided to prevent over-travel and overturning of haulage equipment at dumping locations.

k. Bumper blocks or equivalent shall be provided at all track dead ends.

26.A.15 Vehicles not directly involved in work shall be kept away from portals and separated from construction activities.

26.A.16 A caution sign reading "BURIED LINE" (or similar wording) shall be posted where air lines or other utility lines are buried or otherwise hidden by water or debris.

26.A.17 Where underground openings are located adjacent to sources of water with potential for causing flooding in the underground work area, measures shall be taken to ensure that the underground area cannot be flooded.

26.B Hazardous Classifications.

26.B.01 Underground construction operations shall be classified in accordance with the following.

a. Underground construction operations shall be classified as potentially gassy operations if either:

(1) Air monitoring discloses 10% or more of the lower explosive limit (LEL) for methane or other flammable gases measured at 12 in +/- 0.25 in (30.4 cm +/- 0.6 cm) from the roof, face, floor, or walls for a period of more than 24 hours; or

(2) The history of the geological area or geological formation indicates that 10% or more of the LEL for methane or other flammable gas is likely to be encountered.

b. Underground operations shall be classified as gassy operations if:

(1) Air monitoring discloses 10% or more of the LEL for methane or other flammable gases measured at 12 in +/- 0.25 in (30.4 cm +/- 0.6 cm) from the roof, face, floor, or walls for three consecutive days; or

(2) There has been an ignition of methane or other flammable gases emanating from the strata that indicates the presence of such gases; or

(3) The underground construction operation is both connected to an underground work area that is currently classified as gassy and is also subject to a continuous course of air containing the flammable gas concentration.

26.B.02 Underground construction gassy operations may be downgraded to potentially gassy operations when air monitoring results remain under 10% of the LEL for methane or other flammable gases for 3 consecutive days.

26.B.03 Requirements for gassy operations.

a. Only equipment approved for the hazardous location and maintained in suitable condition shall be used in gassy operations.

b. Mobile diesel-powered equipment used in gassy operations shall be approved in accordance with the requirements of 30 CFR 36 by MSHA and State regulations and shall be operated in accordance with these requirements and the manufacturer's instructions.

c. Each entrance to a gassy operation shall be prominently posted with signs notifying all entrants of the gassy classification.

d. Smoking shall be prohibited in all gassy operations and the employer shall be responsible for collecting all personal sources of ignition, such as matches and lighters, from all persons entering a gassy operation.

e. A permit is required and a fire watch shall be maintained when hot work is performed. > See Section 9.

f. Once an operation has been classified as gassy, all activities in the affected area (except those in (1) through (3), below) shall be discontinued until the operation either is in compliance with all gassy operation requirements or has been downgraded to potentially gassy:

(1) Activities related to the control of the gas concentration;

(2) Installation of new equipment, or conversion of existing equipment, to comply with subparagraph (1), above; and

(3) Installation of above-ground controls for reversing the air flow.

26.C Air Monitoring, Air Quality Standards, and Ventilation.

26.C.01 Air monitoring requirements.

a. Air monitoring devices shall be inspected, calibrated, maintained, and used in accordance with the manufacturer's instructions. Back-up monitoring devices shall be maintained in calibrated and working condition at the worksite. > See Section 6.

b. When air monitoring is required "as often as necessary", the CP shall determine which substances

26

to monitor and how frequently to monitor. Such determination shall be based on:

(1) The location of the job site and proximity to fuel tanks, sewers, gas lines, old landfills, coal deposits, and swamps;

(2) The geology of the job site, particularly the soil types and their permeability;

(3) Any history of air contaminants in nearby job sites or any changes in air quality monitored during a previous shift; and

(4) Work practices and job site conditions (use of diesel engines, explosives, or fuel gas, ventilation characteristics, visible atmospheric conditions, decompression of the atmosphere, welding, cutting, or hot work, etc.).

c. A record (including location, date, time, substance, monitoring results, and name of person conducting the test) of all air quality tests shall be maintained at the job site.

d. The atmosphere in all underground work areas shall be tested as often as necessary to assure that the atmosphere at normal atmospheric pressure contains at least 19.5% oxygen and no more than 22% oxygen.

e. The atmosphere in all underground work areas shall be tested quantitatively for CO, nitrogen dioxide, hydrogen sulfide, and other toxic gases, dusts, vapors, mists, and fumes as often as necessary to ensure that the PEL are not exceeded.

f. The atmosphere in all underground work areas shall be tested quantitatively for methane and other flammable gases as often as necessary to determine whether action is to be taken under 26.C.02.f-h and to determine whether an operation is to be classified gassy or potentially gassy under 26.B.01.

g. The atmosphere in all underground work areas shall be tested as often as necessary to ensure that the ventilation requirements of Section 26.C.03-05 are met.

h. If diesel-engine or gasoline-engine driven ventilating fans or compressors are used, an initial test shall be made of the inlet air of the fan or compressor, with the engine operating, to ensure that the air supply is not contaminated by engine exhaust.

i. When rapid excavation machines are used, a continuous flammable gas monitor shall be operated at the face with the sensor(s) placed as high and close to the front of the machine's cutter head as possible.

j. Operations that meet the criteria for potentially gassy or gassy operations shall be subjected to the following monitoring:

(1) Tests for oxygen content shall be conducted in all affected work areas and work areas immediately adjacent to such areas at least at the beginning and midpoint of each shift;

(2) When using rapid excavation machines, continuous automatic flammable gas monitoring equipment shall be used to monitor the air at the heading, on the rib, and in the return air duct. The continuous monitor shall signal the heading and shut down electric power in the affected underground work area, except for acceptable pumping and ventilation equipment, when 20% or more of the LEL for methane or other flammable gases is encountered.

(3) A manual flammable gas monitor shall be used as needed, but at least at the beginning and midpoint of each shift, to ensure that the limits prescribed in 26.B 01 and 26.C.01.d and f are not exceeded. In addition, a manual electrical shut down control shall be provided near the heading.

(4) Local gas tests shall be made prior to and continuously during any welding, cutting, or other hot work.

(5) In underground operations driven by drill-and-blast methods, the air in the affected area shall be tested for flammable gas prior to re-entry after blasting and continuously when employees are working underground.

26.C.02 Air quality standards.

a. Whenever air monitoring indicates the presence of 5 ppm or more of hydrogen sulfide, a test shall be conducted in the affected underground work areas, at least at the beginning and midpoint of each shift, until the concentration of hydrogen sulfide has been less than 5 ppm for 3 consecutive days.

b. Whenever hydrogen sulfide is detected in an amount exceeding 10 ppm, a continuous sampling and indicating hydrogen sulfide monitor shall be used to monitor the affected work areas.

c. Employees shall be informed when a concentration of 10 ppm hydrogen sulfide is exceeded.

d. The continuous sampling and indicating hydrogen sulfide monitor shall be designed, installed, and maintained to provide a visual and aural alarm when the hydrogen sulfide concentration reaches 10 ppm to signal that additional measures might be necessary to maintain hydrogen sulfide exposure below the PEL.

e. When the competent person determines, on the basis of air monitoring results or other information, that air contaminants may be present in sufficient quantities to be dangerous to life, the employer shall:

(1) Prominently post a notice at all entrances to the underground area to inform all entrants of the hazardous condition, and

(2) Ensure that the necessary precautions are taken.

f. Whenever 5% or more of the LEL for methane or other flammable gases is detected in any underground work area or in the air return, steps shall be taken to increase ventilation air volume or otherwise control the gas concentration, unless operations are conducted in accordance with the potentially gassy or gassy operation requirements: such additional ventilation controls may be discontinued when gas concentrations are reduced below 5% of the LEL.

g. Whenever 10% or more of the LEL for methane or other flammable gases is detected in the vicinity of welding, cutting, or other hot work, such work shall be suspended until the concentration of such flammable gas is reduced to less than 10% of the LEL.

h. Whenever 20% or more of the LEL for methane or other flammable gases is detected in any underground work area or in the return:

(1) All employees, except those necessary to eliminate the hazard, shall be immediately withdrawn to a safe location above ground; and

(2) Electrical power, except for acceptable pumping and ventilation equipment, shall be cut off to the area endangered by the flammable gas until the concentration of such gas is reduced to less than 20% of the LEL.

i. When ventilation has been reduced to the extent that hazardous levels of methane or other flammable gas may have accumulated, all affected areas shall be tested after ventilation has been restored and before any power, other than for acceptable equipment, is restored or work is resumed and shall determine whether the atmosphere is within flammable limits.

j. Whenever the ventilation system has been shut down with all employees out of the underground area, only competent persons authorized to test for air contaminants shall be allowed underground until the ventilation has been restored and all affected areas have been tested for air contaminants and declared safe.

26.C.03 Ventilation.

a. Fresh air shall be supplied to all underground work areas in sufficient quantities to prevent dangerous accumulation of dusts, fumes, mists, gases, or vapors.

b. Mechanical ventilation shall be provided in all underground work areas except where it is demonstrated that natural ventilation provides the necessary air quality through sufficient air volume and airflow.

(1) Ventilation and exhaust systems for tunnel excavation shall be of sufficient capacity to maintain an adequate supply of uncontaminated air at all points in the tunnel.

(2) The supply of fresh air shall not be less than 200 CFM (94.4 L/s) each employee underground plus that necessary to operate the equipment.

(3) The linear velocity of air flow in all underground work areas shall be at least 30 ft/min (0.15 m/s) where blasting or rock drilling is conducted or where there are other conditions likely to produce dusts, fumes, vapors, or gases in harmful quantities.

(4) The direction of mechanical airflow shall be reversible.

(5) Ventilation doors shall be designed and installed so that they remain closed when in use, regardless of the direction of airflow.

c. Following blasting, ventilation systems shall exhaust smoke and fumes to the outside atmosphere before work is resumed in affected areas.

d. Potentially gassy or gassy operations shall have ventilation systems installed which are constructed of fire-resistant materials and have acceptable electrical systems, including fan motors.

e. Gassy operations shall be conducted with controls for reversing the airflow of ventilation systems located above ground.

f. In potentially gassy or gassy operations, wherever mine-type ventilation systems using an offset main fan installed on the surface are used, they shall be equipped with explosion-doors or a weak-wall having an area at least equivalent to the cross sectional area of the airway.

g. Air that has passed through underground oil- or fuel-storage areas shall not be used to ventilate work areas.

26.C.04 When drilling rock or concrete, appropriate dust control measures shall be taken to maintain dust levels within safe limits.

26.C.05 Internal combustion engines, except diesel-powered engines on mobile equipment, are prohibited underground.

26.C.06 Mobile diesel-powered equipment used underground in atmospheres other than gassy operations shall be either approved by MSHA (30 CFR 36), or shall be demonstrated to be fully equivalent to

26

such MSHA-approved equipment, and shall be operated in accordance 30 CFR 36.

26.D Fire Prevention and Protection.

26.D.01 Fire Prevention and Protection Plans.

a. For every underground construction project, a Fire Prevention and Protection Plan shall be developed and implemented. The plan shall detail:

(1) The specific work practices to be implemented for preventing fires;

(2) Response measures to be taken in case of fire to control and extinguish the fire;

(3) Equipment required;

(4) Personnel requirements and responsibilities; and

(5) Requirements for daily and weekly fire prevention and protection inspections.

b. Fire prevention and protection plans shall be incorporated in either the APP or the AHA and posted at the job site.

c. Fire prevention and protection plans shall be reviewed with all affected personnel as often as is necessary for them to maintain a working knowledge of emergency responsibilities and procedures.

d. Plans shall be drilled as often as is necessary to ensure their efficacy.

26.D.02 Fire extinguishers.

a. Fire extinguishers shall be provided and maintained in accordance with the requirements of Section 9.

b. Fire extinguishers (or equivalent protection) shall be provided and maintained at each portal and shaft entry, within 100 ft (30.4 m) of the advancing face of each tunnel, and at locations containing combustible materials.

c. A fire extinguisher of at least 4A:40B:C rating or other equivalent extinguishing means shall be provided at the head pulley and tail pulley of underground belt conveyors.

26.D.03 Open flames/fires and smoking.

a. Open flames and fires are prohibited in all underground construction operations except as permitted for welding, cutting, and other hot work operations.

b. Smoking may be allowed only in areas free of fire and explosion hazards.

c. Readily visible signs prohibiting smoking and open flames shall be posted in areas having fire or explosion hazards.

26.D.04 Heating devices used in tunnels shall be approved for such locations by a nationally-recognized testing laboratory.

26.D.05 Gasoline shall not be taken, stored, or used underground.

26.D.06 Acetylene, LP-Gas, and methyl acetylene propadiene stabilized gas may be used underground only for welding, cutting, and other hot work. No more than the amount necessary for work during the next 24-hour period shall be permitted underground.

26.D.07 Only fire-resistant hydraulic fluids approved by a nationally-recognized authority or agency shall be used in hydraulically actuated underground machinery and equipment unless the machinery or equipment is protected by a fire suppression system or a multi-purpose fire extinguisher rated for sufficient capacity for the type and size of hydraulic equipment involved (but at least 4A:40B:C).

26.D.08 Storage of flammable and combustible materials.

a. Not more than a 1-day supply of diesel fuel may be stored underground.

b. Oil, grease, and diesel fuel stored underground shall be kept in tightly sealed containers in fire-resistant areas at least 300 ft (91.4 m) from underground explosive magazines and at least 100 ft (30.4 m) from shaft stations and steeply inclined passageways.

c. Flammable or combustible materials shall not be stored above ground within 100 ft (30.4 m) of any access opening to any underground operation unless they are located as far as practical from the opening and either a fire-resistant barrier of not less than a 1-hour rating is placed between the stored material and the opening.

d. Electrical installations in underground areas where oil, grease, or diesel fuel are stored shall be used only for lighting fixtures.

e. Lighting fixtures in storage areas or within 25 ft (7.6 m) of underground areas where oil, grease, or diesel fuel are stored shall be approved for Class I, Division 2 locations > *See Section 11.H.*

26.D.09 The piping of diesel fuel from the surface to an underground location is permitted only if:

a. Diesel fuel is contained at the surface in a tank whose maximum capacity is no more than the amount required to supply the equipment serviced by the underground fueling station for a 24-hour period;

b. The surface tank is connected to the underground fueling station by an acceptable pipe or hose system controlled at the surface by a valve, and at the shaft bottom by a hose nozzle (nozzle shall not be of the latch-open type);

c. The pipe is empty at all times except when transferring diesel fuel from the surface tank to a piece of equipment in use underground; and

d. Hoisting operations in the shaft are suspended during refueling operations if the supply piping in the shaft is not protected from damage.

26.D.10 Any structure located underground or within 100 ft (30.4 m) of an opening to the underground shall be constructed of material having a fire-resistance rating of at least 1 hour.

26.D.11 Oil-filled transformers shall not be used underground unless they are located in a fire-resistant enclosure and surrounded by a dike to contain the contents of the transformers in event of a rupture.

26.D.12 Noncombustible barriers shall be installed below welding or burning operations in or over shaft or raise.

26.E Drilling.

26.E.01 Drilling machines. > See also Section 18.

a. Employees shall not be allowed on a drill mast while the drill bit is in operation or the drill machine is being moved.

b. When drill machines are being moved from one drilling area to another, drill steel, tools, and other equipment shall be secured and the mast placed in a safe position.

c. Drills on columns shall be anchored firmly before drilling is started and shall be retightened frequently.

d. Accessible areas within the swing radius of the rear of the equipment's rotating superstructure, either permanently or temporarily mounted, shall be barricaded to prevent an employee from being struck or crushed by the crane and hoisting equipment.

e. Jumbos.

(1) Safe access shall be provided to all working levels of drill jumbos.

(2) Jumbo decks and stair treads shall be designed to be slip-resistant and secured to prevent accidental displacement.

(3) Only employees assisting the operator shall be allowed to ride on jumbos, unless the jumbo meets the requirements for adequate seating arrangements that protect passengers from being struck, crushed, or caught between equipment or surfaces, and has safe access.

(4) Employees working under jumbo decks shall be warned whenever drilling is about to begin.

(5) On jumbo decks over 10 ft (3 m) in height, guardrails, which are removable, or equal protection shall be provided on all open sides, excluding access openings of platforms, unless an adjacent surface provides equivalent fall protection.

(6) Stair access to jumbo decks wide enough to accommodate two persons if the deck is over 10 ft (3 m) in height.

(7) Receptacles or racks shall be provided for drill steel stored on jumbos.

(8) The employer shall provide mechanical means for lifting drills, roof bolts, mine straps, and other material to the top decks of jumbos over 10 ft (3 m) in height.

26.E.02 Scaling bars shall be available at scaling operations and shall be maintained in good conditions at all times. Blunted or severely worn bars shall not be used.

26.E.03 Blasting holes shall not be drilled through blasted rock (muck) or water.

26.E.04 Before commencing the drill cycle after a blast, the face and any remaining blasting holes shall be examined for misfires that, if found, shall be removed.

26.E.05 Employees in a shaft shall be protected either by location or by suitable barriers if powered mechanical loading equipment is used to remove muck containing unfired explosives.

26.F Shafts.

26.F.01 All wells or shafts over 5 ft (1.5 m) in depth that employees must enter shall be supported by lagging, piling, or casing of sufficient strength to withstand shifting of the surrounding earth.

a. The full depth of the shaft shall be supported by casing or bracing except where the shaft penetrates into solid rock having characteristics that will not change because of exposure as determined by a CP or a Qualified Geotechnical Engineer.

(1) Where the shaft passes through earth into solid rock or through solid rock into earth and where there is potential for shear, the casing or bracing shall extend at least 5 ft (1.5 m) into the solid rock.

(2) When the shaft terminates in solid rock, the casing of bracing shall extend to the end of the shaft or 5 ft (1.5 m) into the solid rock, whichever is less.

b. The casing or bracing shall extend 42 in +/- 3 in (106.6 cm +/- 7.6 cm) above ground level, except that the minimum casing height may be reduced to 12 in

26

(30.4 cm) provided that a standard railing is installed, that the ground adjacent to the top of the shaft is sloping away from the shaft collar to prevent entry of liquids, and that effective barriers are used to prevent mobile equipment operating near the shaft from jumping over the 12 in (30.4 cm) barrier.

26.F.02 After blasting operations in shafts, a competent person shall inspect the walls, ladders, timbers, blocking, and wedges to determine if they have loosened. Where found unsafe, corrections shall be made before shift operations are started.

26.F.03 No employee shall be permitted to enter an unsupported auger-type excavation in unstable material for any purpose. In such cases, necessary clean-out shall be accomplished without entry.

26.F.04 There shall be two safe means of access in shafts at all times: this may include the ladder and hoist.

26.G Hoisting. Hoistways may be used to hoist materials or personnel, but not both simultaneously.

26.G.01 A warning light suitably located to warn employees at the shaft bottom and subsurface shaft entrances shall flash whenever a load is being moved in the shaft, except in fully enclosed hoistways.

26.G.02 Whenever a hoistway is not fully enclosed and employees are at the shaft bottom, conveyances or equipment shall be stopped at least 15 ft (4.5 m) above the bottom of the shaft and held there until the signalman at the bottom of the shaft directs the operator to continue lowering the load; except that the load may be lowered without stopping if the load or conveyance is within full view of a bottom signalman who is in constant voice communication with the operator.

26.G.03 Before maintenance, repairs, or other work is commenced in a shaft served by a cage, skip, or bucket, the operator and other employees shall be informed and given suitable safety precautions. A sign warning that work is being performed in the shaft shall be installed at the shaft collar, at the operator's station, and at each underground landing.

26.G.04 Any connection between the hoisting rope and the cage or skip shall be compatible with the type of wire rope used for hoisting.

26.G.05 Spin-type connections, where used, shall be maintained in a clean condition and protected from foreign matter that could affect their operation.

26.G.06 Cage, skip, and load connections to the hoist rope shall be made so that the force of the hoist pull, vibration, misalignment, release of lift force, or impact will not disengage the connection. Moused or latched open-throat hooks do not meet this requirement.

26.G.07 When using wire rope wedge sockets, means shall be provided to prevent wedge escapement and to ensure that the wedge is properly seated.

26.H Caissons.

26.H.01 In caisson work in which compressed air is used and the working chamber is less than 11 ft (3.3 m) in length, whenever such caissons are at any time suspended or hung while work is in progress so that the bottom of the excavation is more than 9 ft (2.7 m) below the deck of the working chamber, a shield shall be erected for the protection of the workers.

26.H.02 Shafts shall be subjected to a hydrostatic test, at which pressure they shall be tight. The shaft shall be stamped on the outside shell about 12 in (30.4 cm) from each flange to show the safe working pressure.

26.H.03 Whenever a shaft is used, it shall be provided, where space permits, with a safe, proper, and suitable staircase for its entire length, including landing platforms (not more than 20 ft (6 m) apart). Where this is impractical, ladders not more than 20 ft (6 m) high shall be installed with each section offset from adjacent sections and a guarded landing provided at each offset.

26.H.04 All caissons having a diameter or side greater than 10 ft (3 m) shall be provided with a man lock and shaft for the exclusive use of employees.

26.H.05 In addition to gauges in the locks, an accurate gauge shall be maintained on the outer and inner side of each bulkhead. These gauges shall be accessible at all times and kept in accurate working order.

26.H.06 In caisson operations where employees are exposed to compressed air working environments, the requirements of Section 26.I shall be complied with.

26.I Compressed Air Work.

26.I.01 All safety requirements for compressed air work will be carefully detailed in a Compressed Air Work Plan that shall be included as a part of the Accident Prevention Plan or AHA.

26.I.02 The Compressed Air Work Plan shall include the following considerations:

a. Requirements for a medical lock and its operation;

b. An identification system for compressed air workers;

c. Communications system requirements;

d. Requirements for signs and recordkeeping;

e. Special compression and decompression requirements;

f. Man lock and decompression chamber requirements;

g. Requirements for compressor systems and air supply;

h. Ventilation requirements;

i. Electrical power requirements;

j. Sanitation considerations;

k. Fire prevention and fire protection considerations, and

l. Requirements for bulkheads and safety screens.

26.I.03 Work in compressed air environments shall be performed in compliance with the requirements of 29 CFR 1926.803.

26.J Underground Blasting. A Blasting Plan must be developed and submitted for this work. > *See also Section 29.*

26.J.01 Explosives.

a. Dynamite used in tunnel blasting shall be Fume Class 1. Fume Class 2 and Fume Class 3 explosives may be used if adequate ventilation is provided.

b. Storage of explosives, blasting agents, and detonators in tunnels or underground work areas shall be prohibited.

c. Trucks used for the transportation of explosives underground shall have the electrical system checked weekly to detect any failures that may constitute an electrical hazard. A written record of such inspections shall be kept on file and available for review. The installation of auxiliary lights on truck beds that are powered by the truck's electrical system shall be prohibited.

d. Explosives or blasting agents, not in original containers, shall be placed in a suitable container when transported manually. Detonators, primers, and other explosives shall be carried in separate containers when transported manually.

26.J.02 Blasting circuits.

a. All underground blasts fired by external power shall be by a power blasting switch system.

b. Blasting power circuits shall be separate and distinct from, and kept clear of, other power and lighting circuits and pipes, rails, and other conductive material (excluding earth) to prevent explosives initiation or employee exposure to electric current.

c. Sectioning switches or equivalent shall be installed in the firing line at 500-ft (150.4 m) intervals.

26.J.03 Loading.

a. Prior to loading, all power, water, and air lines shall be disconnected from the loading jumbo and power lines, including lighting circuits, shall be moved back a minimum of 50 ft (15.2 m).

b. The loading area shall be illuminated a minimum 10 ft-candles (107.6 lx) by floodlights located 50 ft (15.2 m) from the face. If additional illumination is needed, the loading crew shall be provided with head lamps approved by the United States Bureau of Mines.

c. Equipment used for pneumatic placement of non-cap-sensitive blasting agents shall be designed for that purpose and shall be grounded while in use.

26.J.04 Blasting.

a. The person in charge of blasting shall be the last to leave the blast area, shall see that no one remains in the blast area, and shall operate the sectioning switches in the firing line while proceeding out of the blast area.

b. No persons shall enter the tunnel blast area until the ventilation system has cleared the heading of harmful gases, smoke, and dust.

c. After each blast, the underground supports in the blast area shall be inspected and secured as necessary work is resumed. Rock surfaces shall be inspected, scaled, and if required, provided with shoring, bracing, rock bolts, shotcrete, or chain-link fabric, before mucking is started. Rock bolts within 100 ft (30.4 m) of a blast shall be tested after each blast before drilling for the next round begins.

d. The muck pile shall be wet down prior to mucking and kept wet during mucking operations.

26.J.05 Blasting in excavation work under compressed air.

a. When detonators or explosives are brought into an air lock, no employee (except the blaster, lock tender, and employees necessary for transport) shall be permitted to enter the air lock; no other material, supplies, or equipment shall be locked through with the explosive materials.

b. Detonators and explosives shall be taken separately into pressure working chambers.

c. All metal pipes, rails, air locks, and steel tunnel lining shall be electrically bonded and grounded at or near the portal or shaft. Such pipes and rails shall be cross-bonded at not less than 1000-ft (304.8-m) intervals throughout the length of the tunnel. In addition, each low air supply pipe shall be grounded at its delivery end.

d. The explosive suitable for use in wet holes shall be water resistant and shall be Fume Class 1.

e. When tunnel excavation in rock face is approaching mixed face, and when tunnel excavation is in mixed face, blasting shall be performed with less explosive per drilled hole and with less dimension in hole spacing and to the free face. Advance drilling shall be performed as tunnel excavation in rock face approaches mixed face to determine the nature and extent of rock cover and the remaining distance ahead to soft ground.

26

THIS PAGE INTENTIONALLY LEFT BLANK

SECTION 27 Concrete, Masonry, <u>Roofing</u> and Residential Construction

Table of Contents

27

27.A General. The fall protection threshold height requirement is 6 ft (1.8 m) for ALL work covered by this Section, unless specified differently below, whether performed by Government or Contractor work forces, to include residential (wood) construction and scaffolding work. > *See Section 21.*

27.A.01 Construction loads shall not be placed on a structure or portion of a structure unless the employer determines, based on information from a person who is qualified in structural design, that the structure or portion of the structure is capable of supporting the loads.

27.A.02 Employees shall not be permitted to work above or in positions exposed to protruding reinforcing steel, fasteners, or other impalement hazards unless provisions have been made to control the hazard.

27.A.03 Working under loads.

a. No employee shall be permitted to work under concrete buckets, bundled material loads, or other suspended loads.

b. Elevated concrete buckets and loads shall be routed, to the extent practical, to minimize the exposure of workers to hazards associated with falling loads or materials from the loads. Vibrator crews shall be kept out from under concrete buckets suspended from cranes of cableways.

c. Riding on concrete buckets or other suspended loads shall be prohibited.

27.A.04 Based on hazard evaluations conducted by supervisors, employers shall identify and select, and each affected employee shall use, personal protective equipment (PPE) and safety equipment that will provide appropriate protection for the work being performed. All PPE (i.e., for eyes, face, head and extremities, protective clothing, respiratory devices and protective shields and barriers) shall be provided, used, and maintained in a sanitary and reliable condition whenever the hazard dictates. > *See 29 CFR 1910.132.*

27.B Concrete.

27.B.01 Equipment.

a. Bulk storage bins, containers, or silos shall have conical or tapered bottoms with mechanical or pneumatic means of starting the flow of material.

b. Concrete mixers equipped with 1 yd³ (0.8 m³) or larger loading skip shall be equipped with a mechanical device to clear the skip of material and shall have guardrails installed on each side of the skip.

c. Handles on bull floats used where they may contact energized electrical conductors shall be constructed of nonconductive material or insulated with a nonconductive sheath whose electrical and mechanical characteristics provide equivalent protection.

d. Powered and rotating concrete troweling machines that are manually guided shall be equipped with a control switch that will automatically shut off the power whenever the operator removes his/her hands from the equipment handles.

e. Concrete pumping systems using discharge pipes shall be provided with pipe supports designed for 100% overload.

f. Handles of concrete buggies shall not extend beyond the wheels on either side of the buggy.

g. Concrete buckets equipped with hydraulic or pneumatically operated gates shall have positive safety latches or similar safety devices installed to prevent premature or accidental dumping. The buckets shall be designed to prevent material from accumulating on the top and sides of the bucket.

h. Sections of tremies and similar concrete conveyances shall be secured with wire rope (or equivalent material) in addition to the regular couplings or connections.

27.B.02 Structural and reinforcing steel for walls, piers, columns, and similar vertical structures shall be supported and/or guyed to prevent overturning or collapse. Support systems for reinforcing steel that are independent of other form or shoring support systems shall be designed by a Registered Professional Engineer (RPE).

a. Connections of equipment used in plumbing-up shall be secured.

b. The turnbuckles shall be secured to prevent unwinding while under stress.

c. Plumbing-up guys and related equipment shall be placed so that employees can get at the connection points.

d. Plumbing-up guys shall be removed only under the supervision of a Competent Person (CP).

e. Measures shall be taken to prevent unrolled wire mesh from recoiling.

27.B.03 Post-tensioning operations.

a. No employee (except those essential to the post-tensioning operations) shall be permitted to be behind jacks or end anchorages during post-tensioning operations.

b. Signs and barriers shall be erected to limit employee access to the post-tensioning area during tensioning operations.

27.C Formwork and Shoring.

27.C.01 Formwork, shoring, and bracing shall be designed, fabricated, erected, supported, braced, and maintained so that it will safely support all vertical and lateral loads that might be applied until such loads can be supported by the structure.

27.C.02 Planning and design.

a. The planning and design of formwork and shoring shall be in accordance with provisions of American Concrete Institute (ACI) Publication 347.

b. The design of the shoring shall be prepared by a QP (designer) and the Erection and Removal Plan for Formwork and Shoring shall be submitted for review to the GDA. The erected shoring shall be inspected by an engineer qualified in structural design.

c. The manufacturer's specifications for fabricated shoring systems shall be available at the job site during job planning and execution.

27.C.03 Base support.

a. Supporting ground or completed construction upon which formwork and shoring is to be placed shall be of adequate strength to carry the vertical and lateral loads to be imposed.

b. Sills for shoring shall be sound, rigid, and capable of carrying the maximum intended load.

c. Base plates, shore heads, extension devices, or adjustment screws shall be in firm contact with the footing sill and form material and when necessary, shall be secured to them.

27.C.04 Splices shall be designed and constructed to prevent buckling and bending.

27.C.05 Diagonal bracing shall be provided in vertical and horizontal planes to provide stiffness and to prevent buckling of individual members.

27.C.06 Inspection.

a. Shoring equipment shall be inspected prior to erection to determine that it is as specified in the shoring design. Any equipment found to be damaged shall not be used.

b. Erected shoring equipment shall be inspected immediately prior to, during, and immediately after the placement of concrete. Any shoring equipment that is found to be damaged, displaced, or weakened shall be immediately reinforced or re-shored.

27.C.07 Re-shoring shall be provided to safely support slabs and beams after stripping or where such members are subjected to superimposed loads due to construction.

27.C.08 Fabricated shoring shall not be loaded beyond the safe working load recommended by the manufacturer.

27.C.09 Single post shores.

a. Wherever single post shores are used in more than one tier, the layout shall be designed and inspected by an RPE qualified in structural design.

b. Single post shores shall be vertically aligned and spliced to prevent misalignment.

c. When shoring is at an angle, sloping, or when the surface shored is sloping, the shoring shall be designed for such loading.

d. Adjustment of single post shores to raise formwork shall not be made after concrete is in place.

e. Fabricated single post shores and adjusting devices shall not be used if heavily rusted, bent, dented, re-welded, or have broken welds or other defects; if they contain timber, they shall not be used if timber is split, cut, has sections removed, is rotted, or otherwise structurally damaged.

f. All timber and adjusting devices to be used for adjustable timber single post shores shall be inspected before erection.

g. All nails used to secure bracing or adjustable timber single post shores shall be driven home and the point of the nail bent over if possible.

h. For stability, single post shores shall be horizontally braced in both the longitudinal and transverse directions.

27

(1) Single-post shores shall be adequately braced in two mutually perpendicular directions at the splice level.

(2) Each tier shall also be diagonally braced in the same two directions.

(3) Bracing shall be installed as the shores are erected.

(4) Each post (near the slab perimeter) shall be secured during assembly and dismantling/re-shoring to prevent the post from "fall out".

27.C.10 Tube and coupler shoring.

a. The material used for the couplers shall be of a structural type such as drop-forged steel, malleable iron, or structural grade aluminum. Gray cast iron shall not be used. No dissimilar metals shall be used together.

b. Couplers shall not be used if they are deformed, broken, or have defective or missing threads on bolts, or other defects.

c. When checking the erected shoring towers with the shoring design, the spacing between posts shall not exceed that shown on the layout and all interlocking of tubular members and tightness of couplings shall be checked.

27.C.11 Tubular welded-frame shoring.

a. All locking devices on frames and braces shall be in good working order, coupling pins shall align the frame or panel legs, pivoted cross braces shall have their center pivot in place, and all components shall be in a condition similar to that of original manufacture.

b. When checking the erected shoring frames with the shoring design, the spacing between towers and cross brace spacing shall not exceed that shown in the design and all locking devices shall be closed.

c. Devices for attaching external lateral stability bracing shall be fastened to the legs of the shoring frames.

27.C.12 Vertical slip forms.

a. Vertical slip forms shall be planned and designed by an RPE.

b. The steel rods or pipe on which the jacks climb or by which the forms are lifted shall be designed specifically for that purpose. Such rods shall be braced where not encased in concrete.

c. Jacks and vertical supports shall be positioned in such a manner that the vertical loads are distributed equally and do not exceed the capacity of the jacks.

d. The jacks or other lifting devices shall be provided with mechanical dogs or other automatic holding devices to provide protection in case of failure of the power supply or the lifting mechanism.

e. Lifting shall proceed steadily and uniformly and shall not exceed the predetermined safe rate of lift.

f. Lateral and diagonal bracing of the forms shall be provided to prevent excessive distortion of the structure during the jacking operation.

g. During jacking operations, the form structure shall be maintained in line and plumb.

h. All vertical lift forms shall be provided with scaffolding or work platforms completely encircling the area of placement.

27.C.13 Removal of formwork.

a. Forms and shores (except those on slab or grade and slip forms) shall not be removed until the individual responsible for forming and/or shoring determines that the concrete has gained sufficient strength to support its weight and all superimposed loads. Such determination shall be based on one of the following:

(1) Satisfaction of conditions stipulated in the plans and specifications for removal of forms and shores, or

(2) Concrete testing (in accordance with ASTM standard test methods) indicates that the concrete has achieved sufficient strength to support its weight and superimposed loads.

b. Re-shoring shall not be removed until the concrete being supported has attained adequate strength to support its weight and all loads placed on it.

27.D Precast Concrete Operations.

27.D.01 Precast Concrete operations shall be planned and designed by a RPE. Precast Concrete Plans and designs shall include detailed instructions and sketches indicating the prescribed method of erection and shall be submitted to the GDA for review.

27.D.02 Precast concrete members shall be adequately supported to prevent overturning or collapse until permanent connections are complete.

27.D.03 Lifting inserts and hardware.

a. Lifting inserts which are embedded or otherwise attached to tilt-up precast concrete members shall be capable of supporting at least two times the maximum intended load applied or transmitted to them.

b. Lifting inserts which are embedded or otherwise attached to precast concrete members, other than tilt-up members, shall be capable of supporting at least four times the maximum intended load applied or transmitted to them.

c. Lifting hardware shall be capable of supporting at least five times the maximum intended load applied or transmitted to the lifting device.

27.D.04 No employee shall be permitted under precast concrete members being lifted or tilted into position except employees required for the erection of those members.

27.E Lift-Slab Operations.

27.E.01 Lift-slab operations shall be planned and designed by an RPE. Lift-Slab Plans and designs shall include detailed instructions and sketches indicating the prescribed method of erection and shall be submitted to the GDA for review.

27.E.02 Jacking equipment.

a. The manufacturer's rated capacity shall be legibly marked on all jacks and shall not be exceeded.

b. All jacking equipment such as threaded rods, lifting attachments, lifting nuts, columns and other members that transmit loads to the jacks shall be capable of supporting at least two and one-half times the load being lifted.

c. Jacks shall be designed and installed so that they will not continue to lift when overloaded.

d. All jacks shall have a positive stop to prevent over-travel.

e. Hydraulic jacks used in lift-slab construction shall have a safety device that will cause the jacks to support the load in any position if the jack malfunctions.

27.E.03 Jacking operations.

a. When it is necessary to provide a firm foundation, the base of the jack shall be blocked or cribbed. Where there is a possibility of slippage of the metal cap of the jack, a wood block shall be placed between the cap and the load.

b. The maximum number of manually-controlled jacks on one slab shall be limited to 14, and in no event shall the number be too great to permit the operator to maintain the slab level within specific tolerances.

c. Jacking operations shall be synchronized to ensure even and uniform lifting of the slab.

d. During lifting, all points of the slab support shall be kept within ½ in (1.2 cm) of that needed to maintain the slab in a level position.

(1) If leveling is automatically controlled, a device shall be installed which will stop the operation when the ½ in (1.2 cm) leveling tolerance is exceeded.

(2) If leveling is manually controlled, such controls shall be located in a central location and attended by a trained operator while lifting is in progress.

e. No one shall be permitted under the slab during jacking operations.

27.F Masonry Construction. > See also Standard Practice for Bracing Masonry Walls under Construction, by the Council for Masonry Wall Bracing.

27 F.01 Prior to the beginning of the erection of any structural masonry, a Masonry Bracing Plan shall be submitted to the GDA for review and acceptance. The plan will include the identification of the site and project and will be signed and dated by the Qualified Person(QP) responsible for its preparation and modifications. The plan shall include the following information, as applicable to the particular project:

a. The sequence of erection activity, developed in coordination with the controlling contractor that includes the following:

(1) Material deliveries;

(2) Material staging and storage; and

(3) Coordination with other trades and construction activities.

b. A description of the bracing selection and placement procedures, including the following:

(1) Site preparation;

(2) Restricted Zone perimeters;

(3) Supportive calculations;

(4) Stability considerations requiring temporary bracing;

(5) Terminus point; and

(6) Connections.

c. Activity Hazard Analysis (AHA) in accordance with Section 1 of this manual;

d. A list of the QPs and CPs; and

e. A description of the procedures that will be utilized in the event of rescue or emergency response.

27.F.02 A restricted zone shall be established whenever a masonry wall is being constructed. The restricted zone is created to keep masons and other tradesmen away from a wall under construction when winds exceed critical velocities until the wall is completely tied into the rest of the structure. The restricted zone shall:

a. Be established prior to the start of construction on the wall;

b. Be equal to the height of the wall being constructed plus 4 ft (1.2 m), and shall run the entire length of the wall;

c. Be established on the side of the wall that will be not be scaffolded;

d. Be restricted to entry only by employees actively engaged in constructing the wall; no other employees shall be permitted to enter the zone;

e. Be evacuated during the initial period of construction when wind speeds exceed 20 mph;

f. Be evacuated during the intermediate period of construction when wind speeds exceed 35 mph;

g. Remain in place until the wall is adequately supported to prevent overturning and to prevent collapse unless the height of the wall is over 8 ft (2.4 m), in which case the restricted zone shall remain in place until the requirements of this Section 27.F.02 have been met.

h. For multi-story structures, the restricted zone shall be determined by a QP.

27.F.03 All masonry walls over 8 ft (2.4 m) in height shall be adequately braced to prevent overturning and to prevent collapse unless the wall is adequately supported so that it will not overturn or collapse. The bracing shall remain in place until permanent supporting elements of the structure are in place.

27.F.04 Each employer having workers in the restricted zone shall monitor the wind speed continuously while the work is in progress and evacuate employees as required above.

a. Wind speeds shall be 3-second gust speeds.

b. Instrument methods shall accurately measure wind speed to +/- 2 mph and instruments shall be properly maintained.

27.F.05 The CP shall inspect unsupported masonry walls, including the wall bracing system, for visible defects at the beginning of each shift and after any occurrence that could affect the structural integrity of the wall or wall bracing system.

27.F.06 Any damaged or weakened brace element shall be repaired or replaced before work is permitted in the restricted zone in the vicinity of the damaged brace or weakened brace element. A CP shall supervise the repairs.

27.F.07 A structural engineer, familiar with the work being performed, shall design the repairs to the wall. Repairs shall not be performed without the approval of the project structural designer of record.

27.F.08 Scaffolds for masonry construction workers shall not be used to provide temporary lateral support of masonry walls.

27.F.09 Cleanouts shall be on the side of the masonry wall opposite to the scaffolding.

27.F.10 Fall protection shall be provided to masonry workers exposed to falls of 6 ft (1.8 m) or more. > See Section 21.

27.G Roofing.

27.G.01 Before work begins, a CP for Fall Protection shall complete a daily inspection of each job site. The CP for Fall Protection, designated by management, shall be capable of identifying existing predictable fall hazards and has the authority to take prompt corrective action to eliminate them. Hazards shall be eliminated by engineering methods and if this cannot be accomplished, guarding to isolate the hazard from the exposed employees shall be implemented. In no case shall warnings or instructions be used as a substitute for elimination of hazards by engineering means or guarding.

27.G.02 Prior to the start of work, a structural analysis of the roof shall be conducted by a QP to assure that the load capacity of the roof deck will not be exceeded.

27.G.03 Where the work presents a potential hazard to the public, the Contractor shall set up and maintain barricades with proper postings to alert public to the hazards in accordance with ANSI D6.1. Applicable statutes and local regulations shall be examined and the more restrictive requirements shall be followed.

27.G.04 Work on the roof shall be halted during severe weather such as strong winds, electrical storms, icing conditions, heavy rain, or snow as soon as practical.

27.G.05 The employer shall establish emergency plans and fire prevention plans. All employees shall be trained in accordance with these plans.

27.G.06 Roof openings and holes shall be protected in accordance with Section 24.

27.G.07 In the construction, maintenance, repair, and demolition, of roofs, fall protection systems shall be provided which will prevent personnel from slipping and falling from the roof and prevent personnel on lower levels from being struck by falling objects in accordance with Section 21.

27.G.08 On all roofs greater than 16 ft (4.8 m) in height, a hoisting device, stairways, or progressive platforms shall be furnished for supplying materials and equipment.

27.G.09 Roofing materials and accessories that could be moved by the wind, including metal roofing panels, which are on the roof and unattached, shall be secured when wind speeds are greater than, or are anticipated to exceed, 10 mph (16.1 km/h).

27.G.10 Access to roofs and sections of roofs shall comply with Sections 22 and 24.

27.G.11 Materials may not be stored within 6 ft (1.8 m) of the roof edge unless guardrails are erected at the roof edge. Materials that are to be piled, stacked, or grouped shall be stable and self-supporting.

27.G.12 Proper PPE shall be worn by all personnel working with hot materials during roofing work. > See also 06.D.02.d.

27.H Residential Construction.

27.H.01 All wood used for residential construction shall meet applicable building codes and design criteria. Wood used for temporary work platforms and/ or fall protection must be inspected for compliance with Sections 21 and 22, as structural lumber from the site may not meet the requirements for protective systems.

27.H.02 Hand and power tools shall be equipped and used in accordance with the requirements of Section 13.

27.H.03 Raising Walls.

a. Before manually raising framed walls that are 10 ft (3 m) or more in height, temporary restraints such as cleats on the foundation/floor system or straps on the wall bottom plate shall be installed to prevent inadvertent horizontal sliding or uplift of the framed wall bottom plate.

b. Anchor bolts alone shall not be used for blocking or bracing when raising framed walls 10 ft (3 m) or more in height.

27.H.04 Employees shall not work from or walk on top plates, joists, rafters, trusses, beams or other structural members until they are securely braced and supported.

27.H.05 Truss Support Plate. Where a truss support plate is used during the installation of trusses, it shall be constructed of a 2-in x 6-in (5 cm x 15.2 cm) plank laid flat, secured linearly to a 2-in x 6-in plank laid on edge, supported with 2-in x 4-in (5.4 x 10.2 cm) wood members (legs) spaced no more than 6 ft (1.8 m) on center and attached to diagonal bracing adequately secured to support its intended load. All material dimensions are minimum and nominal.

27.H.06 Trusses installed without a ridge beam or other horizontal structural connection shall be connected temporarily to each other and to a secured end gable by a minimum of one 1-in x 4-in (2.5 cm x 10.2 cm) plank face-nailed to every rafter on each slope of the truss. The number of planks shall be sufficient to protect against wind-related collapse of the truss rows.

27.H.07 During construction, proper work platforms such as scaffolds and decks, in accordance with Section 22 shall be used. Walking on plates, beams, joists, and other members more than 6 ft (1.8 m) above the ground or floor is prohibited unless workers meet the fall protection practices outlined in Section 21.

27

THIS PAGE INTENTIONALLY LEFT BLANK

SECTION 28 <u>Steel Erection</u>

Table of Contents

28

28.A General. The fall protection threshold height requirement is 6 ft (1.8 m) for ALL work covered by this manual, unless specified differently below, whether performed by Government or Contractor work forces, to include steel erection activities and systems-engineered activities (prefabricated) metal buildings. > *See Section 21.*

28.A.01 Construction loads shall not be placed on a structure or portion of a structure unless the employer determines, based on information from a person who is qualified in structural design, that the structure or portion of the structure is capable of supporting the loads.

28.A.02 Employees shall not be permitted to work above or in positions exposed to protruding reinforcing steel, fasteners, or other impalement hazards unless provisions have been made to control the hazard.

28.A.03 No employee shall be permitted to work under bundled material loads or other suspended loads. Riggers securing lower loads to multi-lift rigging assemblies and workers setting suspended structural components such as beams, trusses, and precast members are excluded from this requirement. In these cases, work controls should be used to minimize the time spent directly under loads.

28.B Structural Steel Assembly.

28.B.01 Prior to beginning the erection of any structural steel, a Steel Erection Plan shall be submitted to the GDA for review and acceptance. The plan will include the identification of the site and project; and will be signed and dated by the Qualified Person (QP) responsible for its preparation and modification. This plan shall include the following information, as applicable to the particular project.

a. The sequence of erection activity, developed in coordination with the Controlling contractor that includes the following:

(1) Material deliveries;

(2) Material staging and storage; and

(3) Coordination with other trades and construction activities.

b. A description of the crane and derrick selection and placement procedures, including the following:

(1) Site preparation;

(2) Path for overhead loads; and

(3) Identification of any lifts classified as critical lifts, requiring separate plans.

(4) If load handling equipment (LHE) other than crane or derrick (e.g., All-Terrain Forklifts, Powered Industrial Trucks, etc.) is used, it must be used in accordance with the manufacturer's instructions. If LHE is used with rigging, see also Section 16.

c. A description of steel erection activities and procedures, including the following:

(1) Stability considerations requiring temporary bracing and guying;

(2) Erection bridging terminus point;

(3) Anchor rod (anchor bolt) notifications regarding repair, replacement and modifications;

(4) Columns and beams (including joists and purlins);

(5) Connections;

(6) Decking; and

(7) Ornamental and miscellaneous iron.

d. A description of the fall protection procedures that will be used;

e. A description of the procedures that will be used to comply with this section including;

(1) Activity hazard analysis in accordance with Section 1 of this manual;

(2) A certification for each employee who has received training for performing steel erection operations as required by 29 CFR 1926.761;

(3) A list of the QPs and CPs; and

(4) A description of the procedures that will be utilized in the event of rescue or emergency response.

28.B.02 Steel erection activities include:

a. Hoisting, laying out, placing, connecting, welding, burning, guying, bracing, bolting, plumbing, and rigging structural steel, steel joists and metal buildings;

b. Installing metal decking, miscellaneous metals, ornamental iron, and similar materials; and

c. Moving point-to-point while performing these activities.

28.B.03 Refer to 29 CFR 1926.750 (b)(2) for a list of activities that are covered (but may not normally be considered) and that occur during and are a part of steel erection activities.

28.B.04 Written notifications. Before authorizing the commencement of steel erection, the Controlling contractor shall ensure that the steel erector is provided with the following written notifications:

a. The concrete in the footings, piers, and walls has attained, on the basis of an appropriate ASTM standard test method of field-cured samples, either 75% of the intended minimum compressive design strength or sufficient strength to support the loads imposed during steel erection.

b. Any repairs, replacements, and modifications to the anchor bolts were conducted in accordance with contract specifications and/or project structural engineer of record.

c. A steel erection contractor shall not erect steel unless it has received written notification that the concrete in the footings, piers and walls has attained, on the basis of an appropriate ASTM standard test method of field-cured samples, either 75% of the intended minimum compressive design strength or sufficient strength to support the loads imposed during steel erection.

d. Both steel and concrete contractors will keep a copy of this written notification on-site.

28.B.05 Site layout. The Controlling contractor shall ensure that the following is provided and maintained:

a. Adequate access roads into and through the site for the safe delivery and movement of derricks, cranes, trucks, other necessary equipment, and the material to be erected; and means and methods for pedestrian and vehicular control.

➤ Exception: This requirement does not apply to roads outside of the construction site.

b. An adequately compacted, properly graded, drained area readily accessible to the work with adequate space for the safe storage of materials and the safe operation of the erector's equipment.

c. Pre-planning of overhead hoisting operations. All hoisting operations in steel erection shall be pre-planned.

28.B.06 Load Handling Equipment (LHE) and rigging. All applicable requirements of Sections 15 and 16 apply to this Section.

28.B.07 Inspection of LHE (cranes, hoists, etc). A CP shall visually inspect LHE being used in steel erection activities prior to each shift as per Section 16.D.

28.B.08 Deficiencies. If any deficiency is identified on the LHE, an immediate determination shall be made by the CP as to whether the deficiency constitutes a hazard.

a. If the deficiency constitutes a hazard, the LHE shall be removed from service until the deficiency has been corrected.

b. The operator shall be responsible for the operations under his/her's direct control. Whenever there is any doubt as to safety, the operator shall have the authority to stop and refuse to handle loads until safety has been assured.

28.B.09 A Qualified Rigger shall inspect the rigging prior to each shift.

28.B.10 The headache ball, hook, or load shall not be used to transport personnel.

28.B.11 LHE may be used to hoist employees on a personnel platform when all applicable provisions of Section 16.T have been met.

28.B.12 Safety latches on hooks shall not be deactivated or made inoperable.

28.B.13 Structural steel assembly.

a. Structural stability shall be maintained at all times during the erection process.

b. The following additional requirements shall apply for multi-story structures:

(1) The permanent floors shall be installed as the erection of structural members progresses, and there shall be not more than eight stories between the erection floor and the upper-most permanent floor, except where the structural integrity is maintained as a result of the design.

(2) At no time shall there be more than four floors or 48 ft (14.6 m), whichever is less, of unfinished bolting or welding above the foundation or uppermost permanently secured floor, except where the structural integrity is maintained as a result of the design.

28.B.14 Walking/working surfaces.

a. Shear connectors and other similar devices.

(1) Tripping hazards. Shear connectors (such as headed steel studs, steel bars, or steel lugs), reinforcing bars, deformed anchors or threaded studs shall not be attached to the top flanges of beams, joists, or beam attachments so that they project vertically from or horizontally across the top flange of the member until after the metal decking, or other walking/working surface, has been installed.

(2) Installation of shear connectors on composite floors, roofs, and bridge decks. When shear connectors are used in construction of composite floors, roofs, and bridge decks, employees shall lay out and install the shear connectors after the metal decking has been installed, using the metal decking as a working platform.

b. Bracing.

(1) When deemed necessary by a CP, temporary erection bracing equipment shall be installed in conjunction with the steel erection process to ensure the stability of the structure.

(2) When used, bracing equipment shall be in place and properly installed before the structure is loaded with construction material such as loads of joists, bundles of decking, or bundles of bridging.

(3) Bracing equipment shall be removed only with the approval of a CP.

c. Metal decking - Hoisting, landing, and placing of metal decking bundles.

(1) Bundle packaging and strapping shall not be used for hoisting unless specifically designed for that purpose.

(2) If loose items such as dunnage, flashing, or other materials are placed on the top of metal decking bundles to be hoisted, such items shall be secured to the bundles.

(3) Bundles of metal decking on joists shall be landed in accordance with Section 28.B.26.

(4) Metal decking bundles shall be landed on framing members so that enough support is provided to allow the bundles to be unbanded without dislodging the bundles from the supports.

(5) At the end of the shift or when environmental or jobsite conditions require, metal decking shall be secured against displacement.

(6) Roof and floor holes and openings. Metal decking at roof and floor holes and openings shall be installed as follows:

(a) Framed metal deck openings shall have structural members turned down to allow continuous deck installation except where not allowed by structural design constraints or constructability.

(b) Roof and floor holes and openings shall be decked over or protected in accordance with Section 24.

(c) Metal decking holes and openings shall not be cut until immediately prior to being permanently filled with the equipment or structure needed or intended to fulfill its specific use and that meets the strength requirements of Section 24, or shall be immediately covered or guarded.

28.B.15 Installation of metal decking.

a. Metal decking shall be laid tightly and secured upon placement to prevent accidental movement or displacement. A maximum of 3,000 ft^2 (278.7 m^2) may be laid before securing.

b. During initial placement metal-decking panels shall be placed to ensure full support by structural members.

28. B.16 Derrick floors.

a. A derrick floor shall be fully decked and/or planked and the steel member connections completed to support the intended floor loading.

b. Temporary loads placed on a derrick floor shall be distributed over the underlying support members so as to prevent local overloading of the deck material.

28. B.17 Column anchorage.

a. General requirements for erection stability.

(1) All columns shall be anchored by a minimum of four anchor rods or anchor bolts.

(2) Each column anchor rod or anchor bolt assembly, including the column-to-base plate weld and the column foundation, shall be designed to resist a minimum eccentric gravity load of 300 lbs (136.2 kg) located 18 in (45.7 cm) from the extreme

outer face of the column in each direction at the top of the column shaft.

(3) Columns shall be set on level finished floors, pre-grouted leveling plates, leveling nuts, or shim packs. If shim packs are used, they must be used at the direction of a qualified person.

(4) All columns shall be evaluated by a CP to determine whether guying or bracing is needed; if guying or bracing is needed, it shall be installed.

b. Repair, replacement or field modification of anchor rods or anchor bolts.

(1) Anchor rods or anchor bolts shall not be repaired, replaced, or field-modified without the approval of the project structural engineer of record.

(2) Prior to the erection of a column, the Controlling Contractor shall provide written notification to the steel erector if there has been any repair, replacement, or modification of the anchor rods or anchor bolts of that column.

28.B.18 Beams and columns.

a. During the final placing of solid web structural members, the load shall not be released from the hoisting line until the members are secured with at least two bolts per connection (of the same size and strength as shown in the erection drawings) drawn up wrench-tight or the equivalent as specified by the project structural engineer of record, except as specified in Section 28.B.19.

b. A CP shall determine those pieces that require more than two bolts in each end before the piece is released from the crane. Column erection splices shall be completely bolted prior to adding more than two floors.

28.B.19 Diagonal bracing. Solid web structural members used as diagonal bracing shall be secured by at least one bolt per connection drawn up wrench-tight or the equivalent as specified by the project structural engineer of record.

28.B.20 Double connections.

a. Double connections at columns and/or at beam webs over a column. When two structural members on opposite sides of a column web, or a beam web over a column, are connected sharing common connection holes, at least one bolt with its wrench-tight nut shall remain connected to the first member unless a shop-attached or field-attached seat or equivalent connection device is supplied with the member to secure the first member and prevent the column from being displaced. *> See Figures 28-1 and 28-2.*

b. If a seat or equivalent device is used, the seat (or device) shall be designed to support the load during the double connection process. It shall be adequately bolted or welded to both a supporting member and the first member before the nuts on the shared bolts are removed to make the double connection.

28.B.21 Column splices. Each column splice shall be designed to resist a minimum eccentric gravity load of 300 lbs (136.2 kg) located 18 in (45.7 cm) from the extreme outer face of the column in each direction at the top of the column shaft.

28.B.22 Perimeter columns. Perimeter columns shall not be erected unless:

a. The perimeter columns extend a minimum of 48 in (121.9 cm) above the finished floor to permit installation of perimeter safety cables prior to erection of the next tier, except where constructability does not allow.

b. The perimeter columns have holes or other devices in or attached to perimeter columns at 42-45 in (106.6-114.3 cm) above the finished floor and at the midpoint between the finished floor and the top cable to permit installation of perimeter safety cables except where constructability does not allow.

28.B.23 Open web steel joists.

a. Except as provided in paragraph 28.B.23.b(2) below, where steel joists are used and columns are not framed in at least two directions with solid web structural steel members, a steel joist shall be field-bolted at the column to provide lateral stability to the column during erection. For the installation of this joist:

(1) A vertical stabilizer plate shall be provided on each column for steel joists. The plate shall be a minimum of 6-in x 6-in (15.2-cm x 15.2-cm) and shall extend at least 3 in (7.6 cm) below the bottom chord of the joist with a 13/16-in (2.1-cm) hole to provide an attachment point for guying or plumbing cables.

(2) The bottom chords of steel joists at columns shall be stabilized to prevent rotation during erection.

(3) Hoisting cables shall not be released until the seat at each end of the steel joist is field-bolted, and each end of the bottom chord is restrained by the column stabilizer plate.

28

FIGURE 28-1

Controlling Risk for Double Connections in Steel Erection (Side View)

FIGURE 28-2

Double Connection with Seat to Support First Section while Second Section is Being Installed

b. Where constructability does not allow a steel joist to be installed at the column:

 (1) An alternate means of stabilizing joists shall be installed on both sides near the column and shall:

  (a) Provide stability equivalent to Section 28.B.23.a (1) above,

  (b) Be designed by a QP,

  (c) Be shop installed, and

  (d) Be included in the erection drawings.

 (2) Hoisting cables shall not be released until the seat at each end of the steel joist is field-bolted and the joist is stabilized.

c. Where steel joists at or near columns that span 60 ft (18.3 m) or less, the joist shall be designed and erected by either:

 (1) Installing bridging or otherwise stabilizing the joist prior to releasing the hoisting cable or,

 (2) Releasing the cable without having a worker on the joist.

d. Where steel joists at or near columns span more than 60 ft (18.3 m), the joists shall be set in tandem with all bridging installed unless an alternative method of erection, which provides equivalent stability to the steel joist, is designed by a QP and is included in the site-specific Steel Erection Plan.

e. A steel joist or steel joist girder shall not be placed on any support structure unless such structure is stabilized.

f. When steel joist(s) are landed on a structure, they shall be secured to prevent unintentional displacement prior to installation.

g. No modification that affects the strength of a steel joist or steel joist girder shall be made without the approval of the project structural engineer of record.

h. Field-bolted joists.

(1) Except for steel joists that have been pre-assembled into panels, connections of individual steel joists to steel structures in bays of 40 ft (12.1 m) or more shall be fabricated to allow for field bolting during erection.

(2) These connections shall be field-bolted unless constructability does not allow.

i. Steel joists and steel joist girders shall not be used as anchorage points for a fall arrest system unless written approval to do so is obtained from a QP.

j. A bridging terminus point shall be established before bridging is installed.

28.B.24 Attachment of steel joists and steel joist girders.

a. Each end of "K" series steel joists shall be attached to the support structure with a minimum of two 1/8-in (0.3-cm) fillet welds that are 2 in (5 cm) long, or with two 1/2-in (1.2cm) bolts, or the equivalent.

b. Each end of "LH" and "DLH" series steel joists and steel joist girders shall be attached to the support structure with a minimum of two1/4-inch (0.6-cm) fillet welds 2 in (5 cm) long, or with two 3/4-in (1.9-cm) bolts, or the equivalent.

c. Except as provided in paragraph d below, each steel joist shall be attached to the support structure, at least at one end on both sides of the seat, immediately upon placement in the final erection position and before additional joists are placed.

d. Panels that have been pre-assembled from steel joists with bridging shall be attached to the structure at each corner before the hoisting cables are released.

28.B.25 Erection of steel joists.

a. Both sides of the seat of one end of each steel joist that requires bridging under Tables 28-1 and 28-2 shall be attached to the support structure before hoisting cables are released.

b. For joists over 60 ft (18.2 m), both ends of the joist shall be attached as specified in Section 28.B.24 and the provisions of Section 28.B.26 are met before the hoisting cables are released.

c. On steel joists that do not require erection bridging under Tables 28-1 and 28-2, only one employee shall be allowed on the joist until all bridging is installed and anchored.

d. Employees shall not be allowed on steel joists where the span of the steel joist is equal to or greater than the span shown in Tables 28-1 and 28-2 in accordance with Section 28.B.26.

e. When permanent bridging terminus points cannot be used during erection, additional temporary bridging terminus points are required to provide stability.

28.B.26 Erection bridging.

a. Where the span of the steel joist is equal to or greater than the span shown in Tables 28-1 and 28-2, the following shall apply:

(1) A row of bolted diagonal erection bridging shall be installed near the mid-span of the steel joist,

(2) Hoisting cables shall not be released until this bolted diagonal erection bridging is installed and anchored, see Figure 28-1, and

(3) No more than one employee shall be allowed on these spans until all other bridging is installed and anchored.

b. Where the span of the steel joist is over 60 ft (18.2 m) through 100 ft (30.4 m), the following shall apply:

(1) All rows of bridging shall be bolted diagonal bridging,

(2) Two rows of bolted diagonal erection bridging shall be installed near the third points of the steel joist,

(3) Hoisting cables shall not be released until this bolted diagonal erection bridging is installed and anchored, and

(4) No more than two employees shall be allowed on these spans until all other bridging is installed and anchored.

c. Where the span of the steel joist is over 100 ft (30.4 m) through 144 ft (43.9 m), the following shall apply:

(1) All rows of bridging shall be bolted diagonal bridging,

(2) Hoisting cables shall not be released until all bridging is installed and anchored, and

(3) No more than two employees shall be allowed on these spans until all bridging is installed and anchored.

28

d. For steel members spanning over 144 ft (43.9 m), the erection methods used shall be in accordance with Sections 28.B.18 through 28.B.22.

e. Where any steel joist specified in paragraph b above or Section 28.B.26.a-c is a bottom chord-bearing joist, a row of bolted diagonal bridging shall be provided near the support(s). This bridging shall be installed and anchored before the hoisting cable(s) is released.

f. When bolted diagonal erection bridging is required by this section, the following shall apply:

(1) The bridging shall be indicated on the erection drawing;

(2) The erection drawing shall be the exclusive indicator of the proper placement of this bridging;

(3) Shop-installed bridging clips, or functional equivalents, shall be used where the bridging bolts to the steel joists, *see Figures 28-3, 28-4 and 28-5*;

(4) When two pieces of bridging are attached to the steel joist by a common bolt, the nut that secures the first piece of bridging shall not be removed from the bolt for the attachment of the second; and

(5) Bridging attachments shall not protrude above the top chord of the steel joist.

28.B.26 Landing and placing loads.

a. During the construction period, the employer placing a load on steel joists shall ensure that the load is distributed so as not to exceed the carrying capacity of any steel joist.

b. Except for paragraph d below, no construction loads are allowed on the steel joists until all bridging is installed and anchored and all joist-bearing ends are attached.

c. The weight of a bundle of joist bridging shall not exceed a total of 1,000 lbs (454 kg). A bundle of joist bridging shall be placed on a minimum of three steel joists that are secured at one end. The edge of the bridging bundle shall be positioned within 1 ft (0.3 m) of the secured end.

d. No bundle of decking may be placed on steel joists until all bridging has been installed and anchored and all joist bearing ends attached, unless all of the following conditions are met:

(1) The employer has first determined from a QP and documented in a site-specific Steel Erection Plan that the structure or portion of the structure is capable of supporting the load,

(2) The bundle of decking is placed on a minimum of three steel joists,

(3) The joists supporting the bundle of decking are attached at both ends,

(4) At least one row of bridging is installed and anchored,

(5) The total weight of the bundle of decking does not exceed 4,000 lbs (1816 kg), and the edge of the construction load shall be placed within 1 ft (0.3 m) of the bearing surface of the joist end.

28.C Systems-Engineered Metal Buildings.

28.C.01 All of the requirements of the previous section apply to the erection of systems-engineered metal buildings except Sections 28.B.17 (column anchorage) and 28.B.23 (open web steel joists).

a. Each structural column shall be anchored by a minimum of four anchor rods or anchor bolts.

b. Rigid frames shall have 50% of their bolts or the number of bolts specified by the manufacturer (whichever is greater) installed and tightened on both sides of the web adjacent to each flange before the hoisting equipment is released.

c. Construction loads shall not be placed on any structural steel framework unless such framework is safely bolted, welded, or otherwise adequately secured.

d. In girt and eave strut-to-frame connections, when girts or eave struts share common connection holes, at least one bolt with its wrench-tight nut shall remain connected to the first member unless a manufacturer-supplied, field-attached seat or similar connection device is present to secure the first member so that the girt or eave strut is always secured against displacement.

e. Purlins and girts shall not be used as an anchorage point for a fall arrest system unless written approval is obtained from a QP for Fall Protection.

f. Purlins may only be used as a walking/working surface when installing safety systems after all permanent bridging has been installed and fall protection is provided.

g. Construction loads may be placed only within a zone that is within 8 ft (2.4 m) of the centerline of the primary support member.

h. Both ends of all steel joists or cold-formed joists shall be fully bolted and/or welded to the support structure before:

(1) Releasing the hoisting cables,

(2) Allowing an employee on the joists, or

(3) Allowing any construction loads on the joists.

28.C.02 Falling object protection.

a. Securing loose items aloft. All materials, equipment, and tools, which are not in use while aloft, shall be secured against accidental displacement.

b. Protection from falling objects other than materials being hoisted shall be provided. The Controlling contractor shall bar other construction processes below steel erection unless overhead protection for the employees below is provided.

28.C.03 Controlled Decking Zones (CDZ) are not permitted.

TABLE 28-1

Erection Bridging for Short Span Joists

JOIST	SPAN	JOIST	SPAN
8K1	NM	22K6	36-0
10K1	NM	22K7	40-0
12K1	23-0	22K9	40-0
12K3	NM	22K10	NM
12K5	NM	22K11	NM
14K1	27-0	24K4	36-0
14K3	NM	24K5	38-0
14K4	NM	24K6	39-0
14K6	NM	24K7	43-0
16K2	29-0	24K8	43-0
16K3	30-0	24K9	44-0
16K4	32-0	24K10	NM
16K5	32-0	24K12	NM
16K6	NM	26K5	38-0
16K7	NM	26K6	39-0
16K9	NM	26K7	43-0
18K3	31-0	26K8	44-0
18K4	32-0	26K9	44-0
18K5	33-0	26K10	49-0
18K6	28-0	26K12	NM
18K7	NM	28K6	40-0
18K9	NM	28K7	43-0
18K10	NM	28K8	44-0
20K3	32-0	28K9	45-0
20K4	34-0	28K10	49-0
20K5	34-0	28K12	53-0
20K6	36-0	30K7	44-0
20K7	39-0	30K8	45-0
20K9	39-0	30K9	45-0
20K10	NM	30K10	50-0
22K4	34-0	30K11	52-0

28

TABLE 28-1 (Continued)

Erection Bridging for Short Span Joists

JOIST	SPAN	JOIST	SPAN
22K5	28-0	30K12	54-0
10KCS1	NM	22KCS2	36-0
10KCS2	NM	22KCS3	40-0
10KCS3	NM	22KCS4	NM
12KCS1	NM	22KCS5	NM
12KCS2	NM	24KCS2	39-0
12KCS3	NM	24KCS3	44-0
14KCS1	NM	24KCS4	NM
14KCS2	NM	24KCS5	NM
14KCS3	NM	26KCS2	39-0
16KCS2	NM	26KCS3	44-0
16KCS3	NM	26KCS4	NM
16KCS4	NM	26KCS5	NM
16KCS5	NM	28KCS2	40-0
18KCS2	28-0	28KCS3	45-0
18KCS3	NM	28KCS4	53-0
18KCS4	NM	28KCS5	53-0
18KCS5	NM	30KCS3	45-0
20KCS2	36-0	30KCS4	54-0
20KCS3	39-0	30KCS5	54-0
20KCS4	NM		
20KCS5	NM		

NM=Diagonal bolted bridging not mandatory for joists under 40 ft (12.1 m).

TABLE 28-2

Erection Bridging for Long Span Joists

JOIST	SPAN	JOIST	SPAN
18LH02	33-0	28LH05	42-0
18LH03	NM	28LH06	46-0
18LH04	NM	28LH07	54-0
18LH05	NM	28LH08	54-0
18LH06	NM	28LH09	NM
18LH07	NM	28LH10	NM
18LH08	NM	28LH11	NM
18LH09	NM	28LH12	NM
20LH02	33-0	28LH13	NM
20LH03	38-0	32LH06	47-0 THROUGH 60-0
20LH04	NM	32LH07	47-0 THROUGH 60-0
20LH05	NM	32LH08	55-0 THROUGH 60-0
20LH06	NM	32LH09	NM THROUGH 60-0
20LH07	NM	32LH10	NM THROUGH 60-0
20LH08	NM	32LH11	NM THROUGH 60-0
20LH09	NM	32LH12	NM THROUGH 60-0
20LH10	NM	32LH13	NM THROUGH 60-0
24LH03	28-0	32LH14	NM THROUGH 60-0
24LH04	39-0	32LH15	NM THROUGH 60-0
24LH05	40-0	36LH07	47-0 THROUGH 60-0
24LH06	45-0	36LH08	47-0 THROUGH 60-0
24LH07	NM	36LH09	57-0 THROUGH 60-0
24LH08	NM	36LH10	NM THROUGH 60-0
24LH09	NM	36LH11	NM THROUGH 60-0
24LH10	NM	36LH12	NM THROUGH 60-0
24LH11	NM	36LH13	NM THROUGH 60-0
		36LH14	NM THROUGH 60-0
		36LH15	NM THROUGH 60-0

28

NM = diagonal bolted bridging not mandatory for joists under 40 feet (12.1 m).

FIGURE 28-3

Illustrations of OSHA Bridging Terminus Points

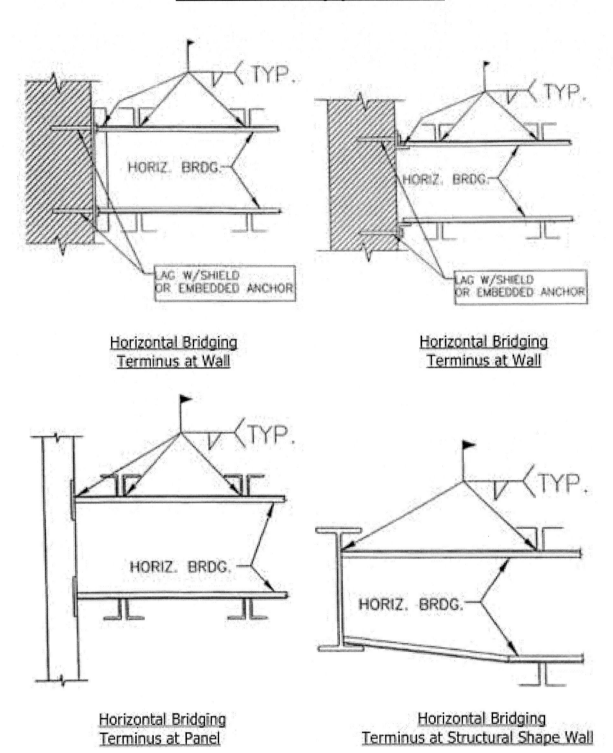

Horizontal Bridging
Terminus at Wall

Horizontal Bridging
Terminus at Wall

Horizontal Bridging
Terminus at Panel

Horizontal Bridging
Terminus at Structural Shape Wall

FIGURE 28-3 (Continued)
Illustrations of OSHA Bridging Terminus Points

Horizontal Bridging Terminus at Structural Shape with Optional "X-Bridging"

Bolted Diagonal Bridging Terminus at Wall

Bolted Diagonal Bridging Terminus at Wall

Bolted Diagonal Bridging Terminus at Wall

<u>FIGURE 28-3 (Continued)</u>

Illustrations of OSHA Bridging Terminus Points

<u>Joists Pair Bridging
Terminus Point</u>

<u>Joists Pair Bridging
Terminus Point with Horizontal Truss</u>

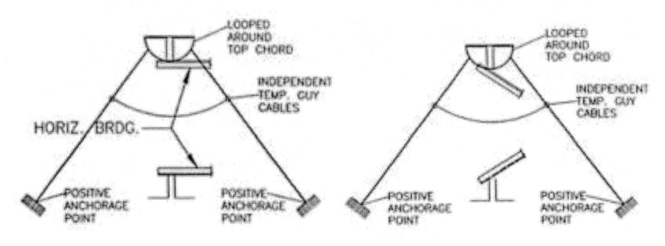

<u>Horizontal Bridging
Terminus Point
Secured By Temporary Guy Cables</u>

<u>Diagonal Bridging
Terminus Point
Secured by Temporary Guy Cables</u>

FIGURE 28-4

Clip End Connection

FIGURE 28-5

Staggered (High/Low Connection)

Guidelines for Complying with OSHA Steel Erection Standard, Paragraph §1926.757(a)(10) and §1926.757(c)(5).

THIS PAGE INTENTIONALLY LEFT BLANK

SECTION 29 Blasting

Table of Contents

29

29.A General. This section applies to blasting activities performed by DA civilians or under DA contract with the use of commercial explosives on non-military lands/installations. For all other blasting activities, *see Section 01.G.*

29.A.01 Prerequisites.

a. An Explosives Safety Site Plan (ESSP), approved by DoD Explosives Safety Board (DDESB), IAW DA Pam 385-64 and DA Pam 385-65, is required prior to the placement of explosives on site or the start of explosives-related operations.

b. Permission in writing shall be obtained from the GDA before explosive materials are brought onto the job site. Periodic replenishment of approved supplies does not require written approval.

c. A Blasting Plan shall be developed by the contractor, submitted and accepted by the GDA prior to the placement of explosives on site or the start of any explosives-related operations. As a minimum, it shall include the following:

(1) List the names, qualifications, and responsibilities of personnel involved with explosives;

(2) The Contractor's requirements for handling, transportation, and storage of explosives; employee training programs and certifications; types of explosives; schedule of activities and loading procedures; detailed blasting schedule; explosives transportation route; safety signals methods and locations; danger area clearance; methods for securing the site; seismograph, vibration and damage control; test shots, post-blast inspection and misfire procedures; provisions for disposal of explosives, blasting agents, unused and associated material; and post-blast ventilation requirements;

(3) Public relations requirements before and after blasting (e.g. community communication, protection of structures and personnel).

29.A.02 The transporting, handling, storage, and use of explosives, blasting agents, and blasting equipment shall be directed and supervised by a person of proven experience and ability in blasting operations in accordance with ANSI A10.7; 29 CFR 1910.109; 29 CFR 1926, Subpart U; 27 CFR 555; the manufacturers, the Institute of Makers of Explosives (IME), and, where applicable, DoD 6055.9M.

29.A.03 All persons working with explosives shall be in good physical condition and be able to understand and give written and verbal orders.

29.A.04 Warning signs shall be provided at points of access to blasting area.

29.A.05 Operations involving the handling or use of explosive materials shall be discontinued and personnel moved to a safe area during the approach or progress of a thunderstorm or dust storm; controls will be established to prevent accidental discharge of electric blasting caps from extraneous electricity.

29.A.06 Blasting operations near overhead power lines, communications lines, utility services, or other structures shall not be carried on until the operators and/or owners have been notified and measures for safe control have been taken.

29.A.07 All loading and firing shall be directed and supervised by one designated person.

29.A.08 A positive system to detect and measure the probability of lightning or massive static electrical discharges shall be used.

29.A.09 Before adopting any system of electrical firing, a thorough survey shall be made for extraneous currents and all dangerous currents shall be eliminated before any holes are loaded.

29.A.10 Blasts using electric detonators shall be fired with an electric blasting machine or a properly designed power source.

a. Blasts using non-electric detonators shall be fired by a blasting machine or starting device prescribed by the manufacturer.

b. When blasting near radar or radio transmission facilities or near electrical energy sources where testing has shown that RF energy or stray electrical current may present a hazard to electrical blasting, an approved non-electrical initiation system shall be employed.

c. When electric detonators are used, leg wires shall be short circuited (shunted) until connected into the circuit for firing.

29.A.11 Detonating cord shall be initiated by non-electric detonator (cap and fuse), electric detonator, shock tube detonator or gas initiated detonator in accordance with the manufacturer's recommendation.

29.A.12 Delay electric detonators, non-electric delay detonators, detonating cord connectors, or sequential blasting machines shall be used for all delayed blasts; the practice shall conform to the manufacturer's recommendations.

29.A.13 Blasting machines.

a. Blasting machines shall be operated, maintained, tested, and inspected as prescribed by the manufacturer.

b. Blasting machines shall be tested prior to use and periodically thereafter as prescribed by the manufacturer.

c. Blasting machines shall be secured and accessible only to the blaster; only the blaster shall connect the leading wire to the machine.

29.A.14 When energy for blasting is taken from power circuits, the voltage shall not exceed 550 volts. The wiring controlling arrangements shall conform to the following (see Figures 29-1 and 29-2):

a. The blasting switch shall be an ungrounded UL (or other nationally-recognized testing laboratory) listed, enclosed, externally operated double-pole double-throw switch that, when locked in the open position, will shunt the firing lines.

b. A grounded switch shall be installed between the blasting switch and the power circuit at a distance not less than 15 ft (4.5 m) from the blasting switch.

c. A lightning gap of at least 15 ft (4.5 m) shall be provided between the two switches; the gap connection shall be made by cable, plug, and receptacle.

29.A.15 The cable between switches shall be disconnected and both switches shall be locked in the open position immediately after firing the shot.

29.A.16 Keys to the switches shall remain in the possession of the blaster at all times.

29.A.17 Insulated solid core wires of an appropriate gage in good condition shall be used for all lines.

29.A.18 Sufficient firing line shall be provided to permit the blaster to be located at a safe distance from the blast.

29.A.19 Mechanized equipment (including drills) shall not be operated within 50 ft (15.2 m) of a loaded hole.

➤ *Exception: Mechanized equipment may be permitted to operate within 50 ft (15.2 m) of a loaded hole when placing blasting mats or back covering.*

29.A.20 The use of black powder is prohibited.

29.A.21 All refuse from explosive loading such as empty boxes, paper, and fiber packing shall not be used again for any purpose, but shall be destroyed by burning at an approved location.

29.A.22 Storage of explosives.

a. The storage of explosives shall be in accordance with requirements of the Bureau of Alcohol, Tobacco, and Firearms (as outlined in 27 CFR 555, Subpart K) or the State in which they are stored.

b. An accurate running inventory of all explosives and blasting agents stored at the project shall be maintained: two copies shall be maintained - one at the magazine and one in a facility which is at least 50 ft (15.2 m) from the magazine.

29.A.23 Security of Explosives.

a. Area shall be guarded to control access to the explosives and ensure no tapping with explosives during non-working times.

b. Explosive materials shall not be abandoned.

29.B Transportation of Explosive Materials.

29.B.01 Transportation of explosives by the following modes shall be in accordance with the prescribed federal regulations and the applicable state requirements.

a. Transportation of explosive materials over public highways shall be in accordance with DOT requirements.

b. Marine transportation of explosive materials shall be in accordance with USCG requirements.

c. Transportation of explosive materials by aircraft shall be in accordance with FAA requirements.

29.B.02 Vehicles used for transportation of explosive materials shall not be loaded beyond their rated capacity and the explosive materials shall be secured to prevent shifting of load or dislodgment from the vehicle; when explosive materials are transported by a vehicle with an open body, a magazine or closed container shall be securely mounted on the bed to contain the cargo.

29

SECTION 29 Blasting

FIGURE 29-1

Power Firing Systems for Series and Parallel Series Firing (No Arcontroller)

FIGURE 29-2

Recommended Installation of Shooting Station and Accessory Arrangement for Using AR Controller

29.B.03 Vehicles transporting explosive materials shall display all placards, lettering, and/or numbering required by DOT.

29.B.04 Explosive materials and blasting supplies shall not be transported with other materials or cargoes. Blasting caps (including electric) shall not be transported in the vehicle or conveyance with other explosives unless the conditions of 49 CFR 177.835(g) are met.

29.B.05 Personnel.

a. Vehicles for transportation of explosive materials shall be in the charge of and operated by a person who is physically fit, careful, reliable, able to read and understand safety instructions, and not under the influence of intoxicants or narcotics.

b. Only the authorized driver and a properly trained helper shall be permitted to ride on any conveyance transporting explosive materials or detonators.

29.B.06 Vehicles used in the transportation of explosives shall be substantially constructed, in good repair, and shall have tight beds to prevent explosives from falling from the vehicle. The ends and sides of vehicles shall be high enough to prevent containers from falling off.

29.B.07 Explosives shall not be exposed to sparking metal during transportation. When steel or part steel bodies are used, non-sparking cushioning materials shall separate the containers of explosives from the metal.

29.B.08 No spark-producing tools, carbides, oils, matches, firearms, electric storage batteries, flammable substances, acids, or oxidizing or corrosive compounds shall be carried in the bed or body of any vehicle transporting explosive materials.

29.B.09 Vehicles transporting explosive materials shall be equipped with one or more fire extinguishers having a rating of 10-B:C and placed at strategic points.

a. The extinguishers shall be of a type listed by a nationally- recognized testing laboratory and shall be ready for use.

b. The driver will be trained in the use of the extinguisher.

29.B.10 A vehicle containing explosive materials shall not be taken into a garage or repair shop, parked in congested areas, or stored at any time in a public garage or similar building.

29.B.11 Vehicles transporting explosive materials shall be operated with extreme care. Full stops shall be made at approaches to all railroad crossings and main highways, and the vehicles shall not proceed until it is known that the way is clear.

29.B.12 No vehicle shall be refueled while explosive materials are on the motor vehicle except in an emergency.

29.B.13 Persons employed in the transportation, handling, or other use of explosive materials shall not smoke or carry on their persons or in the vehicle, matches, firearms, ammunition, or flame-producing devices.

29.B.14 Provision shall be made for safe transfer of explosive materials to magazine vessels including substantial ramps or walkways free of tripping hazards.

29.B.15 Vehicles transporting explosive materials shall not be left unattended.

29.B.16 The hoist operator shall be notified before explosive materials are transported in a shaft conveyance.

29.B.17 Explosive materials shall be hoisted, lowered, or conveyed in a powder car. No other materials, supplies or equipment shall be transported in the same conveyance at the same time.

29.B.18 No person shall ride in any shaft conveyance transporting explosive materials. Loading and unloading shall be accomplished only when the conveyance is stationary.

29.B.19 No explosive materials shall be transported on any locomotive. At least two car lengths shall separate the locomotive from the powder car.

29.B.20 No explosive materials shall be transported on a man haul trip.

29.B.21 The car or conveyance containing explosive materials shall be pulled, not pushed, whenever possible.

29.B.22 The powder car or conveyance built for transporting explosive materials shall bear a reflectorized sign with a sharply contrasting background on each side with the word "EXPLOSIVES" in letters not less than 4 in (10.1 cm) in height.

29.C Handling of Explosive Materials.

29.C.01 There shall be no smoking, open lights, or fire of any kind within 50 ft (15.2 m) of any area where

29

explosives are being handled. No source of ignition, except necessary means to light fuses or fire electric detonators, shall be permitted in an area containing loaded holes.

29.C.02 Containers of explosive materials shall be opened only with non-sparking tools or instruments. Metal cutters may be used for opening fiberboard boxes, paper bags or plastic tubes.

29.C.03 Explosive materials shall be removed from containers only as they are needed for immediate use.

29.C.04 Explosive materials and detonators or primers shall be separated and taken to the blasting area in original containers, Type 3 Magazines, or containers prescribed by 49 CFR 177.835.

29.C.05 Primers shall not be made up in excess of immediate need for holes to be loaded.

29.C.06 Primers shall not be made up in or near magazines or excessive quantities of explosive materials.

29.C.07 After loading of a blast is completed, all excess explosive materials and detonators shall be removed to a safe location or returned at once to the storage magazines, observing the same rules as when being conveyed to the blasting area.

29.C.08 The quantity of explosive materials taken to an underground loading area shall not exceed the amount estimated to be necessary for the blast.

29.C.09 Detonators and explosive materials shall be taken separately into pressure working chambers.

29.D Electromagnetic Radiation.

29.D.01 Blasting operations or storage of electrical detonators shall be prohibited in vicinity of operating RF transmitters or other RF producing devices except where the clearances in ANSI C95.4 can be maintained.

29.D.02 When necessary to perform blasting operations at a distance less than those shown in ANSI C95.4 tables, an approved non-electric initiation system shall be used.

29.D.03 Mobile radio transmitters, which are less than 100 ft (30.4 m) away from electric blasting caps in other than original containers, shall be de-energized and effectively locked, except in blasting areas where a non-electric initiation system as described in Section 29.A.11 is used.

29.E Vibration and Damage Control.

29.E.01 Blasting operations in or adjacent to cofferdams, piers, underwater structures, buildings, structures, or other facilities shall be carefully planned with full consideration for all forces and conditions involved.

29.E.02 Prior to initiation of vibration controlled blasting operations, a written plan for monitoring the operations shall be established.

29.E.03 When appropriate, owners, occupants, and the public shall be notified of the nature of blasting operations to be undertaken and controls to be established.

29.E.04 Where vibration damage may occur, energy ratios and peak particle velocities shall be limited in accordance with state requirements or the requirements in Table 29-1, whichever is more stringent. When any recording indicates either energy ratio or peak particle velocity limits have been exceeded, blasting shall be suspended and the designated authority (Government and Contractor) shall be immediately notified; blasting shall not be resumed until the probable cause has been determined and corrective measures taken.

29.E.05 Where required by State regulations, scaled distances shall be determined before each shot and included in the records. Scaled distances shall not exceed limitations set by the State.

29.E.06 Air blast pressure exerted on structures resulting from blasting shall not exceed 133 dB (0.013 psi).

29.E.07 The monitoring, recording, and interpreting of vibrations shall be by qualified personnel. Records and interpretations shall be furnished to the GDA.

TABLE 29-1

Energy Ratio and Peak Particle Velocity Formula

The maximum total energy ratio (ER) shall be limited to 1.0, calculated as follows:

$$ER = (3.29FA)^2$$

where:
F = frequency in cycles per second
A = amplitude in inches

The total energy ratio is equal to the arithmetic sum of the energy ratios in the 3 mutually perpendicular planes of motion in the vertical and horizontal directions at any one instant of time.

The maximum total peak particle velocity (PV) shall be limited to 1.92, calculated as follows:

$$PV = A/t$$

where:
A = amplitude in inches
t = time in seconds

The total peak particle velocity is equal to the vector sum of the particle velocities in the 3 mutually perpendicular planes of motion in the vertical and horizontal directions any one instant of time.

29

29.F Drilling and Loading.

29.F.01 All drill holes shall be sufficiently large enough to freely allow for the insertion of the explosives.

29.F.02 Drilling shall not be done in an area already blasted until remaining "bootlegs" are examined for unexploded charges and the total area has been examined to make sure that there are no unexploded charges remaining.

a. Never insert a drill, pick, or bar into bootlegs even if examination fails to disclose explosives.

b. When misfires have occurred and drilling must be done in an area where undetonated holes may exist, holes shall not be drilled where there is danger of intersecting a misfired hole.

c. All drilling necessary to neutralize misfires must be done under the supervision of a competent person who has a working knowledge of the explosive materials involved and is familiar with the conditions under which the misfired holes were drilled, loaded, primed, and initiated, and is familiar with the drilling equipment capabilities that will be used during the neutralization.

29.F.03 Drilling and loading operations shall not be carried on in the same area. Drilling shall be separated from loaded holes by at least the depth of the loaded hole but in no case less than 50 ft (15.2 m).

29.F.04 No person shall be allowed to deepen drill holes that have contained explosives or blasting agents.

29.F.05 Holes shall not be drilled so that they disturb or intersect a loaded hole.

29.F.06 See Section 18.H for earth drilling requirements.

29.F.07 The loading or loaded area shall be kept free of any equipment, operations, or persons not essential to loading; no vehicle traffic shall be permitted over loaded holes; the blast site shall be guarded or barricaded and posted with danger signs to restrict unauthorized entry.

29.F.08 No holes shall be loaded except those to be fired in the next round of blasting; after loading, all remaining explosive materials and detonators shall be immediately returned to an authorized magazine; no explosive materials or loaded holes shall be left unattended at the blast site at any time.

29.F.09 Loading of sprung or jet-pierced holes shall be prohibited until it is established that the hole has cooled sufficiently to allow loading.

29.F.10 No explosive shall be loaded or used underground in the presence of combustible gases or combustible dusts unless the conditions of use have been thoroughly identified and accepted, in writing, as safe by a competent person qualified by a thorough knowledge of the factors to be evaluated or by the written permission of the authority having jurisdiction where an authority exercises jurisdiction.

29.F.11 Cartridges shall be primed only in the number required for a single round of blasting.

29.F.12 No detonator shall be inserted in explosive materials which do not have a cap well without first making a hole in the cartridge with a non-sparking punch of proper size, or the appropriate pointed handle of a cap crimper.

29.F.13 Cartridges shall be seated by even steady pressure only.

29.F.14 Tamping shall be done with wood rods without exposed metal parts. Non-sparking metal connectors may be used for joint poles. An approved plastic tamping pole may also be used.

29.F.15 Springing boreholes.

a. A borehole shall never be sprung when it is adjacent to or near a hole that is loaded.

b. Flashlight batteries shall never be used as a power source to replace a blasting machine when springing boreholes.

29.F.16 Use of detonating cord.

a. Detonating cord shall be handled and used with the same respect and care given other explosives. Care shall be made to avoid damaging or severing cord during and after loading and hooking-up.

b. When using a detonating cord down line, after the primer is loaded in the hole, the detonating cord shall be cut from the supply reel before loading the rest of the charge.

c. Detonating cord connections shall be positive in accordance with recommended methods. Knot or other cord-to-cord connections shall be made only with detonating cord in which the explosive core is dry.

d. All detonating cord trunk lines and branch lines shall be free of loops, sharp kinks, or angles that direct the cord back toward the oncoming line of detonation.

e. When connecting a detonator to detonating cord, the detonators shall be taped or otherwise attached securely along the side or the end of the detonating cord, with the end of the detonator containing the explosive charge pointing in the direction in which the detonation is to proceed.

f. Detonators for firing the trunk line shall not be brought to the loading area nor attached to the detonating cord until everything else is in ready for the blast.

29.F.17 The blaster shall keep an accurate, up-to-date record of explosives, blasting agents, and blasting supplies used in a blast.

29.F.18 Loaded holes shall be stemmed to the collar with non-combustible material.

29.F.19 All loaded holes or charges shall be checked and located and all detonating cord connections shall be inspected before firing the blast.

29.F.20 All charges shall be covered with blasting mats or back covered before firing where blasting may cause injury or damage by flying rock or debris. Where mats are used, care shall be taken to protect electric blasting circuits.

29.G Wiring.

29.G.01 In any blast using electric detonators, all blasting caps shall be from the same manufacturer.

29.G.02 Wiring.

a. Bus wires shall be single solid wires of sufficient current carrying capacity.

b. The insulation on all firing lines shall be adequate and in good condition.

29.G.03 The number of electric blasting caps in a circuit shall not exceed the capacity of blasting machine or power source.

29.G.04 A power circuit used for firing electric detonators shall not be grounded.

29.G.05 Whenever the possibility exists that a leading wire might be thrown onto a live power source by the force of the explosion, care shall be taken to see that the total length of wires is kept too short to contact the source or that the wires are securely anchored to the ground. Alternatively, de-energize the live power until it is certain during the post blast inspection that the lines have not crossed. If these requirements cannot be met, a non-electric system shall be used.

29.G.06 The manufacturer's shunt shall not be removed from the cap leg wires until the cap is connected to the lead line or to another cap in preparation for the assembly of two or more caps into a series circuit or when the cap is to be tested.

29.G.07 No lead wire shall be connected to the circuit until it has been grounded to dissipate any static charge.

29.G.08 The circuit, including all caps, shall be tested with an approved blasting instrument (blasting galvanometer, blasting ohmmeter, blaster's ohmmeter, or blaster's multimeter) before being connected to a firing line.

29.G.09 No firing line shall be connected to a blasting machine or other power source until the shot is to be fired. The firing line shall be checked with an approved blasting instrument before being connected to the blasting machine or other power source.

29.G.10 When a single series of caps is to be fired, or a number of series of caps is to be fired as a series-in-parallel circuit, the resistance of the circuit shall be checked with an approved blasting instrument.

29.G.11 For series-in-parallel circuits, each series shall have the same resistance.

29.G.12 Each series circuit shall be separately tested for two readings:

a. To ensure that the series is complete; and

b. To ensure that each series shows the same resistance and that this resistance is as close to the calculated resistance for such a series of caps as the testing instrument will read. If the first reading shows a series to be incomplete, the faulty cap or connection shall be located and corrected. If the second reading shows incorrect resistance, the cause shall be found and corrected.

29.H Firing.

29.H.01 Prior to the firing of a shot, all persons in the danger area shall be warned of the blast and ordered to a safe distance from the area. Blasts shall not be fired until it is certain that every person has retreated to a safe distance and no one remains in a dangerous location.

29.H.02 Prior to the firing of a shot, a competent flag person shall be posted at all access points to danger areas.

29.H.03 Prior to the firing of a shot, drill boats and other vessels shall be moved a safe distance from the danger area.

a. Prior to and while the drill boat or vessel is being moved from the danger area, a series of short signals by horn or whistle similar to the usual navigation warning signals shall be given.

b. No blast shall be fired while any vessel under way is closer than 1,500 ft (457.2 m) to the underwater blasting area. Those on board vessels or craft moored or anchored within 1,500 ft must be notified before a blast is fired.

c. No blast shall be fired closer than 250 ft (76.2 m) to a boat or vessel containing an explosive magazine; personnel engaged in drilling operations on another drill boat within 500 ft (152.4 m) shall leave the drill frames for cover if any holes have been loaded.

d. No blast shall be fired while any swimming or diving is in progress near the blasting area.

e. Whenever a drill boat is moved from the drilling setting, all loaded under water holes shall be fired.

29.H.04 Safety signals.

a. All blasting operations shall use the following safety signals:

(1) WARNING SIGNAL - a one-minute series of long audible signals 5 minutes prior to blast signal;

(2) BLAST SIGNAL - a series of short audible signals 1 minute prior to the shot; and

(3) ALL CLEAR SIGNAL - a prolonged audible signal following the inspection of blast area.

b. The safety signals shall be given by use of a compressed air whistle, a horn, or equivalent means, and shall be clearly audible at the most distant point in the blast area. The boat whistle on a drill boat shall not be used as a blasting signal.

c. The code for safety signals and warning signs and flags shall be posted at all access points.

d. Employees shall be made familiar with the signals and instructed accordingly.

29.H.05 The person making leading wire connections shall fire the shot. All connections shall be made from the borehole back to the source of firing current and the leading wire shall remain shorted and not be connected to the blasting machine or other source of current until the charge is to be fired.

29.H.06 After firing an electric blast, the leading wires shall be immediately disconnected from the power source and shunted.

29.H.07 When firing a circuit of electric blasting caps, care shall be exercised to ensure that an adequate quantity of delivered current is available in accordance with the manufacturer's recommendations.

29.I Post-Blast Procedures.

29.I.01 Immediately after blast has been fired, the firing line shall be disconnected from the blasting machine or power source. Power switches shall be locked open. Atmospheres in confined areas shall be tested and/or ventilated after blast.

29.I.02 An inspection shall be made by the blaster to determine that all charges have been exploded. All wires shall be traced and search made for unexploded cartridges.

29.I.03 Other persons shall not be allowed to return to the area of the blast until an "all clear" signal is given.

29.I.04 Loose pieces of rock and other debris shall be scaled down from the sides of the face of excavation and the area made safe before proceeding with the work.

29.I.05 Misfires.

a. Misfires shall be handled under the direction of the blaster. The blaster shall determine the safest method for handling the hazards of misfires (some misfires may require consultation with the supplier or manufacturer of the explosive material).

b. When a misfire is declared, the blaster shall wait 1-hour before inspecting the site and provide proper safeguards for excluding all employees, except those necessary to do the work, from the danger zone.

c. No other work shall be done except that necessary to remove the hazard of the misfire. Only those employees necessary to do the work shall remain in the danger zone.

d. No drilling, digging, or picking shall be permitted until all misfire holes have been detonated or the blaster has approved that work can proceed.

e. Based on contractor experience, a secondary/dual initiation system to prevent misfires should be considered.

29.J Underwater Blasting.

29.J.01 A blaster shall conduct all blasting operations. No shot shall be fired without his approval.

29.J.02 Loading tubes and casings of dissimilar metals shall not be used because of possible electric transient currents from galvanic action of the metals and water.

29.J.03 Only water-resistant blasting caps and detonating cords shall be used for all marine blasting. Loading shall be done through a non-sparking metal loading tube when necessary.

29.J.04 Blasting flags shall be displayed.

29.J.05 The storage and handling of explosive materials aboard vessels used in underwater blasting operations shall be according to provisions in Sections 29.A and 29.C.

29.J.06 When more than one hole is loaded to be fired underwater, a steel shot line shall be anchored and floated over the row of loaded holes.

a. The detonation down line from each loaded hole shall be tied to the steel line and the loose end shall be tied to the detonation trunk line.

b. After the trunk line fires, the steel shot line shall be inspected for misfires. Misfires shall be handled in accordance with the requirements of Section 29.I.05.

29.J.07 When drilling near or adjacent to a loaded hole, drilling shall be limited to vertical holes only. Drilling shall be separated from loaded holes by the depth of water plus the depth of the loaded hole.

a. If a solid casing or drill mast - vertically plumbed with an inclinometer - is extended from the barge and firmly seated on bedrock, the distance between a loaded hole and one being drilled shall be 1/3 the depth of the hole, with a minimum of 8 ft (2.4 m) between the loaded hole and the one being drilled.

b. Drilling shall be halted to check alignment with an inclinometer every 4 ft (1.2 m) of hole depth.

29

THIS PAGE INTENTIONALLY LEFT BLANK

SECTION 30 Diving Operations

Table of Contents

30

30.A General. All USACE diving operations, both government and contractor shall be performed in accordance with this manual. Failure to meet these requirements will be cause for rejection or cessation of operations.

30.A.01 Unless otherwise delegated in this section, requests for waivers or variance to the requirements of this section must be made in accordance with Appendix D of this manual through the local Designated Dive Coordinator (DDC) or the Alternate Dive Coordinator (ADC) acting on their behalf.

30.A.02 Diving shall not be used as a work method if the work objective can be more safely and efficiently accomplished by another means, including but not limited to, using Remotely Operated Vehicles (ROV's), and/or camera systems, or by dewatering the work area so work may be accomplished in the dry.

30.A.03 Surface-Supplied Air (SSA) shall be used whenever possible in accordance with the practical constraints of the diving operations.

30.A.04 Live boating will not be used without prior specific acceptance by the DDC.

30.A.05 Training documentation shall be in compliance with the OSHA Diving Standards 29 CFR 1910.410 and shall show that dive team members, including dive tenders, have successfully completed training to the appropriate level (e.g., SSA diver's certificate, surface supplied mixed-gas diver certificate). Copies of all dive-related training certificates are required. Such training shall be provided by:

a. A commercial diving school, military school, Federal school (e.g., USACE), or an Association of Commercial Diving Educators (ACDE) accredited school;

b. An in-house training program that meets the requirements contained in ANSI/ACDE-01, or in the Association of Diving Contractors International (ADCI) Consensus Standards;

c. Training for Scientific Divers using compressed air (SCUBA or SSA), shall be in compliance with 29 CFR 1910.410 and shall meet the above requirements or the training guidelines in the Standards for Scientific Diving published by the American Academy of Underwater Scientists (AAUS).

30.A.06 Proof of certification (a diploma and/or official transcript) as a commercial working diver from an accredited commercial dive school and other dive-related training certificates (e.g. chamber operator, saturation diver, etc.) are required as proof of a dive team member's certification and/or experience. An ADCI card or similar certification from an internationally recognized commercial diving organization may be substituted as proof of training for divers demonstrating more than five (5) years of diving experience within the six (6) years preceding beginning of dive operations.

30.A.07 Contractors shall provide dive-log evidence that each dive team member has training and experience consistent with the performance requirements of the scope of work.

a. As a minimum, each diver, back-up diver, and dive team supervisor shall have at least 1 year of commercial experience in the applicable position.

b. Divers shall have completed at least 4 working dives with similar decompression techniques as in the dive plan, using the particular diving techniques and equipment. Divers shall demonstrate that at least 1 of the 4 qualification dives was performed in the last 9 months prior to the start of dive operations.

c. Dive tenders must have previous experience and training as a dive tender.

30.A.08 Each dive team member shall have current certification in first aid and CPR from the American Red Cross (ARC), the American Heart Association (AHA), or from an organization whose training adheres to the standards of the International Liaison Committee on Resuscitation, or from a Licensed Physician (LP).

a. Additionally, each dive team member shall have current certification in the use of emergency oxygen systems, and, if provided on the dive site, the use of Automated External Defibrillators (AEDs).

b. All classes shall contain a hands-on component and cannot be taken online. Evidence of this will be a photocopy of the certificates. The certificate(s) shall state the date of issue and length of validity.

➢ *Note: Training in the use of emergency oxygen systems shall be specific to underwater diving and shall meet the requirements of a nationally recognized training organization such as Divers Alert Network (DAN), Professional Association of Diving Instructors (PADI), National Association of Underwater Instructor s (NAUI), the YMCA or other recognized sources.*

30.A.09 Divers shall receive an annual diving physical according to ADCI or similar standards preferably by a hyperbaric physician (MD or DO) or other licensed physician knowledgeable in the physiology of diving.

a. A "Fit to Dive" statement that each diver has been medically examined within the previous 12 months and has been determined fit and approved to dive shall be signed and signature stamped by the examining physician.

<u>b</u>. The DDC will maintain a file of physician <u>"Fit to Dive"</u> <u>statement</u> for all USACE <u>qualified</u> divers.

<u>c</u>. Contractors shall submit physician's <u>"Fit to Dive"</u> <u>statement</u> to the DDC in accordance with Section 30.A.1<u>3</u>.

<u>d.</u> After any serious diving-related injury or illness <u>such</u> <u>as an over-pressurization</u> injury <u>and/or decompression</u> <u>illness,</u> divers shall be re-examined by <u>a</u> <u>hyperbaric</u> physician <u>and be re-certified as "Fit to Dive"</u>.

30.A.<u>10</u> Divers will wait at least 12 hours before flying after any dive. This interval should be extended to 24 hours following multiple days of repetitive dives.

30.A.<u>11</u> When diving at altitudes of 1000 ft (304.8 m) or more of elevation above sea level, dive supervisors shall use appropriate high altitude decompression tables that compensate for the increased elevation.

30.A.<u>12</u> Contract diving operations will be monitored and/or inspected by personnel qualified as USACE Dive Inspectors. Individual USACE Dive teams shall be inspected during operations at least once annually by the DDC, ADC and/or Dive Safety Representative (DSR).

a. Qualified Dive Inspectors shall hold current USACE training certification as Dive Inspector, Diver/ Dive Supervisor, Dive Safety Administrator, or Dive Coordinator. All USACE personnel used as dive inspectors must be approved by the DDC prior to performing inspector duties.

➢ *Note: Use of trained monitors/inspectors with other credentials will be considered on a case-by-case basis and may be approved in writing by the DDC and HQUSACE Program Manager (PM) for Diving Safety.*

b. Inspectors shall conduct on-site monitoring/ inspections of contractor dive sites during pre-dive conference, equipment inspection, and initial dives. Monitoring <u>should</u> be continuous for the duration of the contract dive activity <u>but may be</u> intermittent, as determined by the DDC based on an evaluation of the job complexity and degree of hazards.

30.A.<u>13</u> The following documents are required for all Contractor diving operations. All documents will be reviewed and found acceptable by two of the following: DDC/ADC/DSR, prior to start of diving operations. Contractors shall submit the documents <u>to the DDC</u> through the Contracting Officer <u>(KO)</u>. Additional documentation may be required depending on the scope of the diving operation:

a. Safe Practices Manual; > *See Section 30.A.<u>15</u>.*

b. Dive Operations Plan(s); > *See Section 30.A.<u>16</u>.*

c. AHA to cover all aspects of the job; > *See Section 30.A.<u>17</u>.*

d. Emergency Management Plan; > *See Section 30.A.<u>18</u>.*

e. Dive Personnel Qualifications. > *See Sections 30.A.<u>05</u> – <u>30.A.09</u>.*

➢ *Note: The above review requirement is that two USACE Qualified Personnel independently evaluate the documents prior to acceptance. The ADC may substitute for either the DDC or DSR in the review and/or acceptance process if these personnel are not available at the time of review.*

30.A.<u>14</u> A Dive Operations Plan, AHA, emergency management plan, and personnel list with qualifications will be developed for each separate diving operation.

<u>a</u>. These documents will be submitted to the DDC <u>through the KO</u> for review, and found acceptable, prior to commencement of diving operations and will be at the diving location at all times. Each of these documents will become a part of the project file.

<u>b</u>. Potential high-hazard conditions, such as penetration diving, contaminated environment diving, dives outside the no decompression limits, and in areas where differential pressure entrapment hazards exist, will be specifically addressed in the <u>Dive</u> <u>Operations Plan and AHA</u> when they are anticipated as part of the diving operation.

<u>c. Diving in contaminated water is prohibited for all</u> <u>USACE projects unless</u> supporting documentation is <u>provided that demonstrates that divers and topside</u> <u>personnel are not exposed to, or will be protected</u> <u>from, known or potential contamination hazards that</u> <u>would pose a chronic or acute health risk.</u>

<u>(1) All divers and topside personnel shall be</u> <u>trained, equipped and resourced to dive in</u> <u>contaminated water.</u>

<u>(2) The dive plan shall be accepted by the GDA</u> <u>within 10 business days prior to dive operations and</u> <u>shall specifically address the areas below in</u> <u>accordance with the</u> *U.S. Navy Guidance For Diving* *In Contaminated Waters,* SS521-AJ-PRO-010 <u>located at the U.S. Navy SEA 00C3 website:</u>

<u>(a) Types of contaminants and Category (CAT 1, 2,</u> <u>3, 4). Additional hazard scenarios and control</u>

measures shall be considered for surface, mud-line/sediment, rainfall, points of discharge, and vertical and bottom water contamination (i.e., a diver walking/crawling/working including swim fin action that stirs up bottom sediments);

(b) Levels of protection and protective equipment;

(c) Contaminated water diver and topside personnel training and qualifications;

(d) Sources of information used to determine water quality;

(e) Dive Station Decontamination Procedures for Divers and Topside Personnel;

(f) Medical evaluation support and post dive monitoring;

(g) Hazardous waste minimization and disposal.

30.A.15 Safe Practices Manual. Contractors and USACE Districts/Labs with in-house dive teams shall develop and maintain a safe practices manual that encompasses their entire diving program. The safe practices manual shall be available at all times to the Government representative and all dive team members at each diving location. The safe practices manual shall include, as a minimum, the following:

a. Dive safety procedures and checklists;

b. Assignments and responsibilities of dive team members;

c. Equipment certifications, procedures, and inspection checklists;

d. Emergency procedures for fire, equipment failure, adverse weather conditions, and medical illness or injury and specific procedures for:

(1) Entrapped or fouled diver including fouled umbilical (suction and entanglement/debris);

(2) Actions upon loss of vital support equipment;

(3) Actions upon loss of gas supply;

(4) Action upon loss of communication;

(5) Lost diver plan (SCUBA Operations only);

(6) Injured diver plan;

(7) Actions upon discovery of fire;

(8) Diver blow up/over rapid ascent to surface;

(9) Diver loss of consciousness; and

(10) Injury/illness of member of surface crew with diver in the water.

e. Procedures for internal safety inspections (frequency, checklists, etc.);

f. A complete copy of OSHA, 29 CFR 1910, Subpart T, and a statement of the employer's policy for ensuring compliance with the standard;

g. The appropriate U.S. Navy Table(s), including as a minimum:

(1) U.S. Navy Table of No-Decompression Limits and Repetitive Group Designation for No-Decompression Air Dives;

(2) U.S. Navy Residual Nitrogen Timetables for Repetitive Air Dives;

(3) U.S. Navy Standard Air Decompression Table.

h. A sample of the diving log sheets to be used;

i. A sample of the repetitive dive worksheets or equivalent (dive profile method) to be used;

j. An outline of the fitness for duty (including medical) requirements for dive team members, and

k. An outline of administrative and record-keeping procedures.

30.A.16 Dive Operations Plan. This plan is a general overview of all tasks to be performed, dive modes and equipment, site access, etc. Complex projects involving more than one work task, location, and/or dive team require task-specific dive plans as part of the overall Dive Operations Plan. As a minimum, the Dive Operations Plan will contain the following: a. Date of dive plan submission;

b. Name and contact information for diving supervisor preparing the dive plan;

c. Names and duties of on-site dive team members, including diving supervisor;

d. List of diving equipment to be used;

e. Type of diving platform to be used;

f. Detailed description of the mission; Identify how/if work will be divided into separate tasks or phases of work;

g. Date(s), time(s), duration, and location of operation;

h. Diving mode used (SCUBA, SSA, and snorkeling) including a description of the backup air supply, as required;

i. Nature of work to be performed by the divers, including tools used and materials to be handled or installed;

j. Anticipated surface and underwater conditions, to include visibility, temperature, currents, etc. Thermal protection will be considered as appropriate;

k. Maximum single dive bottom time for the planned depth of dive for each diver. Altitude adjustments to dive tables will be calculated for dives made at altitudes of 1000 ft (304.8 m) or more above sea level;

l. Identification of topside assistance/support to the dive team (i.e., crane operator, lock operator, etc.);

m. Means of direct communication between the dive site and the DDC, project office, the lockmaster or USACE project manager, and the contracting officer (if applicable);

n. Plans submitted for Contractor operations shall also include the name of Contractor (and diving subcontractor if applicable), Contract number, and names and contact information for key personnel.

➢ Note: The dive plan will include the following statement: "If for any reason the dive plan is altered in mission, depth, personnel, or equipment, the DDC will be contacted in order to review and accept the alteration prior to actual operation."

30.A.17 Activity Hazard Analysis (AHA). An AHA represents the dive team's best effort to anticipate and mitigate or prevent the adverse effects of equipment failure, extreme weather and environmental conditions, or other hazardous/unexpected situations.

a. AHA's shall address risk to personnel, property and to impacts to the overall USACE mission. When required, a new AHA shall be conducted to reflect changes in site conditions, operational changes, etc.

b. Each AHA will be job specific and address each phase of work, to include the hazards associated with flying after diving.

c. For USACE dive teams, a Risk Assessment Code (RAC) shall be applied to all underwater diving activities, with residual risk being approved by the appropriate level of command.

d. Hazardous Energy Control (HEC) procedures in accordance with Section 12 of this manual and procedures for dealing with differential pressures will be included if appropriate.

(1) If HEC procedures are required for the diving operation, the diving supervisor will visually check all lockout/tagout and other control procedures/devices to assure they are in place and redundant where possible prior to the commencement of the diving operation.

(2) A copy of any clearances/permits to be issued to deal with identified hazards will be attached to the AHA.

e. Some dives may be sufficiently complex to warrant several separate analyses.

f. The AHA will be covered in detail at the pre-dive conference.

30.A.18 Emergency management plan. An emergency management plan will be prepared for each dive operation. The minimum content of the plan will be as follows:

a. Location and phone number of nearest operational recompression chamber if not located at the dive site and the Divers Alert Network (DAN) phone number (919-684-9111);

b. Location, directions to and phone number(s) of nearest hospital(s) or available physicians capable of treating dive injuries;

c. Location and phone number of nearest USCG Rescue Coordination Center, where appropriate;

d. Description of an emergency victim transport plan including phone numbers of appropriate emergency transport services;

e. Procedures and phone numbers or other means of communications to activate emergency services at the facility where the work is being performed;

f. Diver rescue procedures conducted by the dive team, including responsibilities of team members, best location(s) where injured divers may be removed from the water, and best location(s) for performing first aid/stabilization prior to emergency medical assistance arrival.

30

30.A.19 Prior to the initial work on each dive operation, a Pre-Dive Conference shall be held with key personnel designated by the DDC to discuss the Dive Operations plan, AHA, and Emergency Management Plan and any modifications needed. For contractor operations, the pre-dive conference will also be attended by the USACE dive inspector or DDC and a representative of the Contractor with sufficient authority to implement any changes required by the USACE diving inspector or coordinator.

30.A.20 Prior to each dive, the entire dive team will be briefed in detail on the following (as a minimum):

a. Description of mission and location, including drawings and/or photographs pertinent to the mission and equipment and materials that are to be installed as part of the mission;

b. Description of diving apparatus/equipment and craft to be used;

c. Maximum working depth with estimated bottom times and water temperatures;

d. Names and duties of personnel on the team (when possible, incorporate at least one person on the dive that has previously performed the same or similar mission);

e. Discussion of AHA; and

f. Emergency procedures.

30.A.21 Upon completion of each diving operation or at the conclusion of each day, a dive team debriefing shall be conducted by the dive supervisor. At the debriefing divers are advised of the location of the nearest recompression chamber (if not located on site), the phone number for DAN or local dive medical facility, and cautioned on the limitations of their post dive activities including repetitive dives, traveling to higher altitude, and flying.

30.A.22 If for any reason the dive mission is altered:

a. Minor to moderate revisions to the accepted dive plan will be reviewed and accepted by the DDC or ADC prior to continuing the operation. These revisions may include differences in time, date, dive team members, work methods/tools used, and other changes that do not affect overall risk. This review may be conducted electronically or verbally and confirmed in writing after completion of the dive operation.

b. Major changes or those which modify high-risk activities, such as modifying pressure differential and hazardous energy controls, adding penetration diving, changing dive equipment modes (i.e. from SCUBA to

SSA), discovery of unexpected contaminated diving conditions, etc. require a two-person review as outlined in Section 30.A.13.

c. For contract operations, the project superintendent or the dive supervisor shall submit/request the revised plan through the GDA for DDC acceptance.

30.A.23 All diving activities shall be conducted with full knowledge and close coordination with the GDA and on-site authorities such as the dive inspector, lockmaster/ project manager, etc.

30.A.24 For each diver and dive, the following dive log information, as a minimum, shall be recorded and maintained at the dive location:

a. Full name;

b. Date, time and location of dive;

c. Maximum depth and bottom time;

d. Surface interval between dives;

e. Breathing medium and type of equipment used;

f. Group classification at the beginning and end of each interval and repetitive dive worksheet;

g. Underwater and surface conditions;

h. Depth(s) and duration(s) of any decompression stops;

i. Date and time of last previous dive if it occurred in the last 24 hours;

j. Name of Dive Supervisor(s) during dive;

k. General description of work performed; and

l. For dives outside the no-decompression limits, deeper than 100 ft salt water (fsw) (30.5m), or using mixed-gas, include depth-time and breathing-gas profiles and decompression tables (including any modifications).

30.A.25 For each dive in which decompression sickness and/or pulmonary barotraumas is suspected or symptoms are evident, the following information shall be recorded and maintained:

a. Descriptions of signs and symptoms (including depth and time of onset);

b. Description and results of treatment; and

c. Name, address, and phone number of attending physician.

30.A.26 Prior to the dive, the Dive Supervisor shall assure, as a minimum, the following pre-dive checks are performed:

a. Breathing air tanks contain sufficient air supply to perform the required work (i.e., standby air tanks are on site and full to the necessary capacity);

b. All diving equipment shall be checked for proper function prior to diver entry;

c. All necessary safety equipment specified herein is on site and functioning properly;

d. Lockout/tagout procedures are followed;

e. When applicable, crane signals are reviewed and radio communication with the crane operator is functioning properly;

f. When applicable, welding or cutting procedures are clearly reviewed, the proper welder polarity is set, and precautions have been taken to ensure that electrocution will not occur;

g. When applicable, blasting procedures are clearly reviewed and precautions have been taken to ensure unplanned/unscheduled blasts will not occur;

h. A pre-dive briefing shall be given that includes, but is not limited to, the accident management plan, AHA, equipment checklist, diving logs, diving conditions, and diving procedures;

i. When applicable, manbaskets used for diver access shall be inspected and load tested prior to use, and a Critical Lift Plan shall be submitted per Section 16.H and Section 30.B.06).

30.A.27 Copies of the dive logs shall be submitted to the DDC after completion of the dive operation. For USACE dive teams, these records shall be maintained on file for two years.

30.B Diving Operations.

30.B.01 Staging areas, where the fully suited and equipped diver enters the water, shall be selected and configured based on a hazard analysis that includes an examination of:

a. Ease of diver access to the water;

b. Hazards to diver (currents, equipment, etc.) in route from surface to work area;

c. Ability of standby diver to access the water immediately and to reach the diver quickly;

d. If used as the topside dive team station, the ability to protect topside members and the standby diver from weather, operational, and other hazards;

e. Whether topside equipment can be stowed safely and function properly;

f. If diver entry to water is remote from the staging area, the standby diver shall be placed at the water entry or immediately accessible to it.

30.B.02 All Dive teams shall be manned in accordance with the criteria established in Appendix G.

30.B.03 A standby diver will be provided whenever a diver(s) is in the water to serve as immediate emergency assistance to the primary diver(s).

a. Untethered SCUBA divers, working in "buddy" pairs, shall have one tethered standby diver at the surface for each pair.

b. A standby diver will deploy only after the dive supervisor assesses the situation and instructs him/her to do so.

c. The standby diver shall be fully equipped to dive and immediately available the entire time the diver is in the water.

(1) The standby shall don all specific gear (suits, harnesses, and equipment) they will wear/use and test all for proper operation before the primary diver leaves the surface.

(2) With the exception of Appendix G, Table G-3, the stand-by diver shall not assume other work responsibilities, other than communications, as required, with the diver.

(3) All gear shall be maintained operational and ready for immediate use for the duration of the dive. If any of the tested gear is exchanged or replaced during the dive, it shall be donned and tested by the standby.

d. The standby diver shall be dressed appropriately for the water and air temperature and remain fully suited up with helmet/mask ready for immediate donning from the time the primary diver leaves the surface until reaching the work area/working depth. The standby may remove the portions of his or her gear needed to prevent heat/cold stress and prevent fatigue. If the AHA identifies a need for the standby diver to remain fully dressed to deploy, it will address measures that

30

will be taken to control these hazards (i.e., standby in water at surface). Any gear that has been removed must be maintained ready for immediate donning and use, accessible to the standby at the entry to the water.

e. If configuration of the surface staging area prevents safe, immediate entry of the standby into the water, the standby diver will be placed in the water fully dressed prior to the primary diver leaving the surface, and remain at the surface ready for deployment if needed.

30.B.04 Dive operations that require surface decompression as an integral part of the dive operation shall have a trained competent person (CP)/operator, whose sole purpose is to attend to the chamber operation.

a. In dive operations where the chamber is required for emergency, first aid, or used for other unexpected recompression events, a team member with other team duties (tender, console operations, etc.) not diving during the current dive may serve as the chamber operator so long as he is specifically trained and competent in hyperbaric chamber operations. If used for the latter purpose, all diving shall be suspended during the chamber operations.

b. Whenever a chamber is on site, the chamber CP/operator shall be capable of communicating with a diving physician.

c. Divers completing a recompression dive will remain within 60 minutes drive time from a fully operable and staffed recompression chamber for a minimum of 2 hours after completing the recompression dive.

30.B.05 Dive operations will be conducted in full coordination with external operations and processes that may impact the safety of the dive.

a. When the operation of machinery or release of hazardous energy will affect the diver or dive team safety, the dive supervisor will develop a HECP. > *See Section 12.* When diving at a facility with an existing HECP, the dive supervisor will review the facility's plan and establish positive control procedures with the facility leader.

b. When water traffic, land-based traffic, industrial operations, heavy equipment operation, or other operations exist that present a hazard to the diver or dive team, the dive supervisor shall coordinate with the controlling authorities to minimize the hazards. This shall include coordination with the USCG, as required, for establishing a safety zone.

30.B.06 Crane operations conducted to support diving operations shall follow the requirements of Section 16 of this manual.

a. All working dives requiring communications between the divers and topside to direct crane load movements, etc., shall be performed in SSA mode.

b. The crane operator will take direction from the tender or supervisor directly in communication with the diver.

c. Crane operations where the load is placed or removed while a diver is underwater shall be considered Critical Lifts and the diver/load director will participate in the Critical Lift Plan development as outlined in Section 16.H.

d. If divers are required to perform rigging duties, they must be a qualified rigger and meet the personnel qualifications listed in Section 15.B.

30.B.07 When dives will take place in an area or facility where potential or actual pressure differentials exist (i.e., locks, dams, spillways, powerhouses, etc.), the dive supervisor will develop specific plans and procedures, in coordination with the facility operator, to prevent diver exposure to pressure differentials. The plans and procedures shall be site-specific and include the following:

a. Identification of all potential exposure points (gate sills, valve openings, holes, etc.);

b. Means for identifying whether control structures/mechanisms are fully in place (measurements of stop gates and openings, valve indicators, etc.);

c. Methods for checking pressure differential openings (observing current/water flow, remote testing of opening area with objects (rope, sandbags, cinders, etc.);

d. Route diver will take from staging area to work area with specific designs to prevent diver and umbilical from uncontrolled pressure differential openings;

e. Procedures for immediate emergency pressure equalization or reduction, if possible, and

f. Procedures for emergency diver extraction or rescue due to pressure differential exposure, including standby diver deployment precautions.

30.B.08 Underwater Welding and Burning Operations.

a. Underwater welding and burning shall be limited to SSA mode only.

b. Equipment configuration and procedures shall be in accordance with the *U.S. Navy Underwater Cutting & Welding Manual*, S0300-BB-MAN-010.

c. Divers performing underwater welding and burning operations shall be equipped with the following as a minimum:

(1) A rubber or neoprene dive suit in good condition that provides electrical insulation to the diver;

(2) Insulating gloves with a cuff that, as a minimum, reaches and fully covers the wrist;

(3) A welding/burning eye shield attached to the dive helmet with appropriate shade for the conditions at the working area.

30.C SCUBA Operations.

30.C.01 SCUBA diving operations shall not be conducted:

a. At depths greater than 100 ft (30.5 m);

b. On dives outside the no-decompression limits unless a dual lock, multi-place, recompression chamber (capable of recompressing diver at the surface to a depth equivalent to 165 ft (50.3 m) of sea water) is available at the dive location and is immediately available for use, a trained competent operator is on site, and the chamber is of sufficient size to accommodate the diver as well as an inside tender;

c. Against currents exceeding one knot;

d. In enclosed or physically confining spaces;

e. Using closed circuit or semi-closed circuit SCUBA;

f. In visibility less than 3 ft (0.9 m) unless line tended with diver/surface two-way voice communications;

g. In areas where pressure differentials exist and it cannot be positively verified that all potential leaks have been eliminated;

h. When the diver does not have direct access to the surface.

30.C.02 Specific operational requirements for SCUBA operations are as follows:

a. The minimum sized SCUBA tank allowed as primary air is a standard 80 ft^3 aluminum tank pressurized to at least 2,700 PSI at the beginning of dive operations.

(1) Divers shall terminate their dive so that they reach the surface with a minimum tank pressure of 500 PSI.

(2) Each diver shall be equipped with a minimum 30 ft^3 bailout bottle for emergency use pressurized to at least 90 percent of its working PSI rating and equipped with a separate 1st and 2nd stage regulator. An "octopus" is not considered to be an alternate air source.

b. Each diver shall be equipped with a buoyancy compensation device (BCD) having a manually activated inflation source, an oral inflation device, and an exhaust valve.

c. Each SCUBA diver shall be equipped with a submersible cylinder pressure gauge capable of being monitored by the diver during the dive.

d. Each SCUBA diver shall be equipped with a weight belt or assembly capable of quick release.

e. Each SCUBA diver shall be equipped with a depth gauge and knife.

f. SCUBA air cylinders shall comply with the following requirements:

(1) Air cylinders of seamless steel or aluminum that meet DOT 3AA and DOT 3AL specifications are approved for used on USACE projects;

(2) Each cylinder used on USACE projects must have identification symbols stamped into the shoulder of the tank; and

(3) SCUBA tanks used on USACE projects must be visually inspected internally at least annually and hydrostatically tested at least once every 5 years in accordance with DOT and the CGA regulations; hydrostatic test dates will be stamped into the shoulder of each tank.

g. A timekeeping device shall be used for recording diving times for all SCUBA diving operations. When two-way voice communications are not used, each dive supervisor and diver shall have a timekeeping device. When two-way voice communications are used, the dive supervisor, at a minimum shall have a timekeeping device.

h. Each tethered SCUBA diver shall wear a safety harness with a positive buckling device, attachment point for the safety line, and a lifting point to distribute the pull force of the line over the diver's body while maintaining the body in a heads-up vertical position when unconscious or inert.

30

30.D Surface Supplied Air (SSA) Operations.

30.D.01 SSA operations shall not be conducted at depths greater than 190 ft (57.9 m) except that dives with bottom times of 30 minutes or less may be conducted to depth of 220 ft (67 m). Exceptional exposure dives, as defined by the US Navy Diving Manual, shall not be conducted except in emergency lifesaving situations. USACE in-house SSA operations shall not exceed a depth of 110 ft (33.5 m) unless a waiver is requested by the DDC and approved by the HQUSACE Dive Safety Program Manager.

30.D.02 SSA equipment components shall be a type specifically designed to be used in diving support systems.

30.D.03 A recompression chamber shall be available for all SSA operations when diving outside the decompression limits, utilizing mixed gas, and/or when diving at or deeper than 100 ft (30.5 m) is planned.

  a. Under these conditions, a dual lock, multi-place, recompression chamber (capable of recompressing a diver at the surface to a depth equivalent to 165 ft (50.3 m) of sea water) must be available at the dive location and immediately available for use.

  b. The chamber must be of sufficient size to accommodate the diver as well as an inside tender, and a trained chamber operator must be immediately available.

  c. Sufficient oxygen shall be available to complete chamber operations.

30.D.04 A bell shall be used for dives with an in-water decompression time greater than 120 minutes, unless heavy gear is worn or diving is conducted in physically confining spaces.

30.D.05 Minimum specific operational requirements for SSA diving operations are as follows:

  a. Each diver shall be continuously tendered while in the water, with one diver per tender, regardless of depth. The tender shall not perform any other duties outside of tending the diver except as allowed by Appendix G;

  b. An underwater tender/diver shall be stationed at the immediate underwater point of entry when any overhead obstruction limiting direct access to the surface is present and/or penetration diving is conducted or in enclosed or physically confining spaces;

  c. Each diving operation shall have a primary breathing air supply sufficient to support divers for the duration of the planned dive, including decompression;

  d. Each diver must have a reserve breathing supply available that can be turned on immediately by the diver in the event of loss of air. The reserve breathing air supply shall be of sufficient capacity to recover the diver and complete emergency recompression (if required) in the event of loss of primary air but no less than 30 ft^3 (0.85 m^3). Heavy-gear diving is exempted from these provisions because the gear carries its own reserve;

  e. Each dive location shall have a reserve breathing air supply integral or in-line with the primary air source sufficient to safely terminate the dive and recover the diver(s) in the event of loss of the primary air supply;

  f. For dives deeper than 100 ft (30.5 m) or outside the no decompression limits and using heavy gear, a spare air supply hose, to replace the diver's air hose should it become damaged, shall be available to the standby diver. An in-water support stage shall be provided to divers in water when using heavy gear, regardless of depth;

  g. Electronic communication systems with an external speaker shall be incorporated so the entire dive team can monitor communications.

    (1) Communications devices shall be tested prior to each dive, maintained in an operable condition, and protected from damage during use and storage IAW the manufacturer's recommendations.

    (2) All dive operations will be terminated in a safe, orderly fashion using line-pull signals if voice communications are lost.

    (3) Defective electronic communication equipment shall not prevent a standby diver from deploying in an emergency if the dive supervisor determines it is safe for the diver to deploy and line-pull signals are used.

30.E Mixed-Gas Diving Operations.

30.E.01 A dual lock, multi-place, recompression chamber with a trained, competent operator shall be available and ready for use at the dive location for any mixed-gas dive. Sufficient oxygen shall be available to complete chamber operations. At extreme depth, mixed gas diving can only be done if:

  a. A bell is used at depths greater than 220 ft (67 m) or when the dive involves in- water decompression time of greater than 120 minutes (except when heavy gear is worn or when diving in physically confining spaces), or

b. A closed bell is used at depths greater than 300 ft (91.4 m), except when diving is conducted in physically confining spaces.

30.E.02 Each diving operation shall have a primary breathing gas supply sufficient to support divers for the duration of the planned dive, including decompression.

30.E.03 Each diving operation shall have a reserve breathing gas supply integral or in-line with the primary air source sufficient to safely recover the diver(s) in the event of failure of the primary breathing gas supply.

30.E.04 When heavy gear is worn:

a. An extra breathing gas hose capable of supplying breathing gas to the diver in the water shall be available to the standby diver, and

b. An in-water stage shall be provided to divers in the water.

30.E.05 An in-water stage shall be provided for divers without access to a bell for dives deeper than 100 ft (30.4 m) or outside the no-decompression limits.

30.E.06 When a closed bell is used, one dive team member in the bell shall be available and tend the diver in the water.

30.E.07 Oxygen Enriched Air.

a. The use of "Oxygen Enriched Air" (OEA) such as Nitrox (EANx) breathing mixtures by USACE in-house dive teams requires the specific initial approval of the HQUSACE Dive Safety Program Manager prior to the first use of such equipment. Requests for approval will be accompanied by a written program that identifies training, certification, and procedures for OEA use. Use of OEA by Contractors requires approval by the local DDC.

b. Navy or NOAA Nitrox Dive Tables or other decompression tables designed specifically for the OEA mixture being used shall be followed without exception.

c. The use of OEA/Nitrox is considered mixed gas diving and requires a decompression chamber on site and ready for use.

30.E.08 Contractors must provide evidence of training and experience with OEA breathing mixtures prior to actual diving operations.

30.E.09 OEA breathing mixture shall be analyzed/tested by the diver to assure proper mix prior to each use. No more than 40% OEA is allowed for normal diving operations. Higher OEA concentrations are allowable for in-water decompression at shallow safety stops.

30.E.10 Use of Surface Decompression with Oxygen (SUR-D-O2) and/or 100% oxygen in-water decompression by trained and certified dive teams, shall only be authorized as a decompression methodology upon submittal of an oxygen-specific decompression plan and schedule, and only with the expressed written approval of the District Dive Coordinator or alternate.

30.F Equipment Requirements.

30.F.01 Equipment modifications, repairs, tests, calibrations, or maintenance shall be recorded by means of a tagging or logging system, and include the date and nature of work performed and the name of the individual performing the work.

30.F.02 Air compressor systems used on-site as a direct source to supply air to SSA divers (Direct Source Compressors) shall be equipped with a volume tank with a check valve on the inlet side, a pressure gauge, a relief valve, and a drain valve.

30.F.03 Direct Source compressors shall be of sufficient capacity to overcome any line loss or other losses and deliver a minimum 4.5 ft^3 (2.1 l/s), actual, or a delivery amount (cfm) as set by the helmet manufacturer, to each diver at the maximum diving depth.

30.F.04 All air compressor intakes shall be located away from/upwind of areas containing exhaust or other contaminants.

a. All shall be equipped with appropriate in-line air purifying absorbent beds and/or filters inserted into the supply line to assure breathing air quality.

b. Oil-lubricated compressors containing a petroleum or potential CO-producing lubricant for the air pressurization pistons will not be used.

c. All monitor/alarm systems shall be so designed with a visual and/or audio alarm and placed so that the dive supervisor will be made aware of the hazardous conditions.

d. Direct Source compressors shall be equipped specifically for their intended use and shall have a suitable approved means to regulate the pressure and a low air pressure alarm in the system. In addition, they will have a Carbon Monoxide (CO) monitor with alarm in the following situations:

(1) The compressor is powered by an internal combustion engine,

30

(2) Compressors used in close proximity to internal combustion engines that may/will be running during dive operations (boat motors, generators, cranes, etc.). Air intake pipes shall be placed away from/upwind of the exhaust source;

(3) Fueling a compressor during operation shall not be allowed.

30.F.05 Air compressor systems will be tested by means of sampling at the connection to the distribution system.

a. All air compressors with a working pressure greater than 500 psi will be tested every six months by an accredited testing laboratory.

b. Compressors with a working pressure less than 500 psi may be tested in-house with documentation every six months and must be tested by an accredited testing laboratory every two years. Lab accreditation shall be from NIST/NVLAP, American Association of Laboratory Accreditation (A2LA – for environmental or calibration) or similar recognized accreditation.

c. Purchased air must be certified by the supplier that it has been tested and meets the standards below.

d. A copy of the certificate of analysis showing the breathing air meets the minimum acceptable criteria shall be provided to the GDA.

e. Air purity standards are as follows:

(1) Air shall not contain a level of carbon monoxide greater than 10 ppm;

(2) Air shall not contain a level of carbon dioxide greater than 1,000 ppm;

(3) Air shall not contain a level of oil mist greater than 5 mg/m3;

(4) Air shall not contain a level of hydrocarbons other than methane greater than 25 ppm; and

(5) Air shall not contain a noxious or pronounced odor.

30.F.06 Breathing supply hoses.

a. Breathing air supply hoses shall be suitable for breathing gas service or shall be specifically manufactured for SSA use. Hoses shall have a maximum allowable working pressure equal to or greater than supply pressure plus 150 psi.

b. Breathing air supply hoses shall have connectors made of corrosion resistant materials and have a

working pressure at least equal to the working pressure of the hose to which they are attached: connectors must not be able to become accidentally disengaged.

c. Umbilicals shall be marked, beginning at the divers end, in 10 ft (3 m) increments to 100 ft (30.5 m) and in 50 ft (15.2 m) increments thereafter. > See Table 30-1. USACE in-house dive teams shall use the following umbilical marking system found in the ADCI Consensus Standard 006 in order to assure consistency and interoperability:

d. Umbilicals shall have a nominal breaking strength of 1000 lb (453.6 kg) and shall be made of kink resistant materials.

e. Hoses must be tested prior to being placed into initial service and after any repair, modification, or alteration, and at least every 12 months to 1.5 times the working pressure. Umbilical assemblies shall be tensile tested at the same time intervals by subjecting each hose-to-fitting connection to a 200 lb axial load.

f. When breathing gas hoses are not in use, their open ends must be closed by capping.

g. The umbilical assembly used for the standby diver must be of sufficient length to reach the primary diver at the furthest distance he can proceed from the dive station or beyond.

h. Umbilicals shall be carefully tended to maintain them and the diver clear of hazards such as propellers (including those of ROV's) or intakes present in the diving zone, so that the diver or umbilical cannot be drawn into them.

30.F.07 SSA and mixed-gas helmets and masks shall have a non-return valve at the attachment between the helmet or mask and hose which will close readily and also have an exhaust valve.

a. Helmets and masks shall have a minimum ventilation rate capacity of 4.5 ft³ (2.1 L/s) (actual) at the depth at which they are operated.

b. The use of Jack Brown masks is prohibited on SSA operations unless it incorporates electronic communication and a means of incorporating a diver carried bailout system.

TABLE 30-1
Umbilical Markings

Distance (from diver's end)	Marking
10 ft [3 m]	one white band
20 ft [6.1 m]	two white bands
30 ft [9.2 m]	three white bands
40 ft [12.2 m]	four white bands
50 ft [15.2 m]	one yellow band
60 ft [18.3 m]	1 yellow/1 white
70 ft [21.3 m]	1 yellow/2 white
80 ft [24.4 m]	1 yellow/3 white
90 ft [27.4 m]	1 yellow/4 white
100 ft [30.5 m]	1 red band
150 ft [45.7 m]	1 red/1 yellow
200 ft [61 m]	2 red bands
250 ft [76.2 m]	2 red/1 yellow
300 ft [91.5 m]	3 red bands

➢ *Note: For each 50 ft (15.2 m) thereafter the sequence continues by increasing the number of red bands at each even increment of 100 ft (30.5 m). In cases where the umbilical color matches an above band color, a reasonable substitute may be used (contrasting outline on same-color tape, contrasting diagonal pattern, replacement with color not used above).*

30.F.08 SSA and mixed-gas helmets and masks must be capable of supporting a reserve breathing supply which can be immediately turned on by the diver in event of loss of air.

30.F.09 SSA and mixed-gas helmets and masks must be capable of supporting a two-way or four-way diver-surface communication system.

30.F.10 Weights and harnesses. Unless heavy gear is worn, each tethered diver shall wear a <u>divers</u> safety harness with a positive buckling device, attachment point for the safety line, and a lifting point to distribute the pull force of the line over the diver's body while maintaining the body in a heads-up vertical position when unconscious or inert.

30.F.11 The following emergency and first aid equipment shall be located at all dive sites:

a. A first aid kit meeting the requirements of Section 3;

b. An oxygen resuscitation system <u>shall contain a pocket mask with O$_2$ inlet, non-rebreather mask, demand inhalator and/or demand resuscitator</u> capable of delivering oxygen for a minimum of 30 minutes <u>at 15 lpm or</u> until emergency medical assistance can be administered; and

c. A stokes litter or backboard, <u>equipped with at least four body straps and snap buckles, a head block and have</u> flotation capability.

30.F.12 When diving from vessels, International alpha code and recreational dive flags with a minimum dimension of 23 in (58.4 cm) will be displayed a minimum of 3 ft (0.9 m) above the working surface at the dive location during diving operations. When diving from surfaces other than vessels in areas capable of supporting marine traffic, a rigid replica of the international code flag "A" at least 3 ft (1 m) in height shall be displayed at the dive location in a manner which allows all-round visibility, and shall be illuminated during night diving operations.

30

30.F.13 Hand-held power tools shall be tested and certified to be safe for underwater use. These tools shall be de-energized at the surface before being placed into or retrieved from the water and shall not be supplied with power until requested by the diver.

30.F.14 The use of one-atmosphere suits (e.g., Newt Suits) requires the specific approval of the MSC DDC and FOA DDC prior to the use of such equipment.

30.G Scientific Snorkeling.

30.G.01 Scientific snorkeling will be conducted only with prior acceptance of the DDC.

30.G.02 Scientific snorkeling will be allowed only for environmental assessments such as fish surveys, stream surveys, and the like. It will not be used for structural inspections or other work.

30.G.03 An on-site snorkeling team shall be made up of no less than two persons: snorkeler, and observer/assistant. Additional site personnel may be required by the DDC or Safety Office DSR based on site hazards and conditions. Snorkeling team plans and procedures shall be developed and enacted by a team supervisor who is qualified and experienced in scientific snorkeling.

30.G.04 Quality assurance for contractor snorkeling operations will be provided by USACE certified Diving Inspectors or qualified USACE scientific snorkelers.

30.G.05 Scientific snorkeling will only be done on the surface of the water. No diving of any kind is permitted.

a. Untethered scientific snorkeling will NOT be allowed in waters deeper than 5 ft (1.5 m), in bodies of water that a snorkeler cannot wade across, or anywhere a pressure differential may exist.

b. Scientific snorkeling in open waters greater than 5 feet deep may be allowed by the local DDC based on an acceptable AHA and compliance with all of the following:

(1) The snorkeler shall be tethered with a harness and a maximum of 40 ft (12.2 m) of floating line;

(2) The tether must be constantly tended from the shore or boat;

(3) The snorkeler must wear a device providing a minimum of 15.5 lbs (7 kg) of positive buoyancy (Type III PFD, fully inflated snorkeling vest, etc.), and

(4) There are no potential tether entanglement hazards in the snorkeling area (overhanging branches, surface stumps, rocks, etc.).

30.G.06 All snorkelers and observers/assistants will be certified as skin divers (snorkelers) or open water divers by a nationally-recognized organization (e.g., Professional Association of Diving Instructors (PADI), National Association of Underwater Instructors (NAUI), etc.) or the U.S. Forest Service Snorkel Safety Program.

30.G.07 An observer/assistant will accompany each untethered snorkeler either along the shore or in a boat and be within 50 ft (15.2 m) of the snorkeler at all times.

a. Two untethered snorkelers in the same body of water may act as observer/ assistant for each other if they remain within 50 ft (15.2 m) of each other.

b. Non-snorkeling observer/assistants shall wear a PFD and be equipped with a throw bag and/or ring buoy with at least 70 ft (21.3) of line, and must be capable of performing a rescue on the specific snorkeler(s) in an emergency.

30.G.08 Areas of extreme water velocity and turbulence will be avoided especially those immediately upstream from debris jams or bedrock outcrops.

30.G.09 Snorkelers will be provided with appropriate thermal protection.

30.G.10 Employees will be determined medically fit by a licensed physician (DO or MD) prior to snorkeling. This certification shall be signed by a physician familiar with sports medicine, and state that each snorkeler is physically and medically fit to perform snorkeling activities according to commonly accepted sports medicine guidelines. The Contractor shall submit such certification to the GDA for acceptance.

30.G.11 All snorkeling team members shall be certified in first aid and CPR. Certification shall be in accordance with most recent Emergency Cardiovascular Care (ECC) guidelines, and/or American Heart Association or ARC standards.

30.G.12 A first aid kit meeting the requirements of Section 3 will be available at each location where snorkeling is being performed. A means of securely transporting an unconscious person, such as a litter or stretcher, shall be provided when snorkeling is conducted in areas inaccessible to vehicles or boats.

30.G.13 A means of communication capable of contacting emergency services must be available at locations where snorkeling is performed.

30.G.14 Each snorkeler will be equipped with <u>a Dive Equipment Manufacturer's Association (DEMA) rated</u> professional grade mask, <u>fins,</u> snorkel <u>and snorkeling vest.</u>

30.G.15 A snorkeling protocol will be developed and included in the project file. It will contain as a minimum, the following:

  a. An AHA for each specific snorkeling mission. Particular detail will be given to currents and other environmental considerations;

  b. Records for snorkeling activities will be maintained and will include as a minimum:

    <u>(1)</u> Snorkeler's annual physician certifications;

    <u>(2)</u> AHAs, and

    <u>(3)</u> A snorkeling plan that is based on the requirements of Section 30.A.1<u>5</u>.a-e. Contractors shall submit these to the GDA for acceptance by the DDC/SOH Dive Safety Officer a minimum of 10 days prior to start of work.

30.G.16 Snorkelers will wear apparel which provides appropriate <u>protection</u> from environmental <u>conditions.</u> The apparel must include fins or other appropriate foot protection.

30

THIS PAGE INTENTIONALLY LEFT BLANK

SECTION 31 Tree Maintenance and Removal

Table of Contents

31

31.A General. The references used in this section are: ANSI Z133, American National Standard for Arboricultural Operations – Safety Requirements; 29 CFR Part 1910 OSHA General Industry; 29 CFR 1910.269, Electrical Power Generation, Transmission, and Distribution; ANSI A300, American National Standard for Tree Care Operations – Tree, Shrub, and Other Woody Plant Management – Standard Practices; ANSI/SIA A92.2, American National Standard for Vehicle-Mounted Elevating and Rotating Aerial Devices.

31.A.01 Tree felling and maintenance shall be performed IAW a Tree Felling and Maintenance Program that has been developed by/under the direction of a qualified tree worker and in accordance with references above and this Section. This Program shall be submitted to the GDA for acceptance prior to work being performed.

a. The services of other licensed or credentialed professionals may be necessary to properly address the required maintenance to be performed and/or hazards that may be encountered.

b. Examples of credentialed professionals include but are not limited to: TCIA-accredited Tree Care Company, Certified Arborist, Licensed Tree Expert, Certified Tree Care Safety Professional (CTSP), Certified Crane Operator, Rigger or Signalperson, or Certified Utility Safety Professional (CUSP).

31.A.02 Personal protective equipment (PPE), as outlined in this section, shall be required when there is a reasonable probability of injury or illness that can be prevented by such protection.

a. A hardhat and eye protection should be worn for all tree maintenance and removal operations.

b. Training shall be provided in the use, care, maintenance, and proper fitting of PPE. > *See also Section 05.*

31.A.03 Working near electrical equipment and systems. > *See Section 11 and 29 CFR 1910.269.*

a. Employees working in the proximity of electrical equipment or conductors shall consider them to be energized.

b. A qualified tree worker shall make a visual inspection to determine whether an electrical hazard exists before climbing or performing any work in or on a tree.

(1) If electrical lines or equipment cannot be safely avoided, arrangements shall be made with the power company to mitigate the electrical hazard. Mitigation options should include de-energizing, testing, isolating and grounding the electrical conductors by the power company as well as all safe OSHA-compliant and practical work methods.

(2) The qualified tree worker and designated power company representative shall confirm that protective ground(s) have been installed as close to the work to be performed to prevent hazardous differences in electric potential.

c. Only a qualified line-clearance tree trimmer or line-clearance trainee under the direct supervision of a qualified person (QP) for electrical hazards shall be assigned to work in close proximity to electrical hazards.

➢ *Note: Qualified line-clearance tree trimmers should be certified by the employer according to OSHA in 29 CFR 1910.269.*

d. There shall be a second qualified line-clearance tree trimmer or line-clearance tree trimmer trainee within normal voice communication during the clearing operations aloft under the following conditions:

(1) When the line-clearance tree trimmer or line-clearance tree trimmer trainee must approach any closer than 10 ft (3 m) to any conductor or electrical apparatus energized in excess of 750 volts;

(2) When branches or limbs being removed cannot first be cut (with a pole pruner/pole saw) sufficiently clear of the equipment or conductors so as to avoid contact; or

(3) When roping is required to remove branches or limbs from such equipment or conductors.

e. Line-clearance tree trimmers and trainees shall maintain the distances from energized conductors as specified in Table 11-3. All other tree workers shall maintain a minimum separation distance of 10 ft (3 m) or greater according to Table 11-1.

f. Aerial devices that are electrically rated above the electrical voltages of adjacent power lines are exempt from the 10 ft (3 m) rule, and can follow Table 11-3 if operators have been electrically qualified. Operators shall be instructed that insulated aerial devices do not protect them from other potentially fatal electric paths to the ground, such as paths through trees, guy wires, or from phase-to- phase contact.

g. Electrically rated aerial devices shall be tested yearly with approved test methods and equipment, in accordance with ANSI/SIA A92.2.

31.A.04 Equipment.

a. Equipment shall be inspected, maintained, repaired, and used in accordance with manufacturers' instructions.

b. Employees shall be instructed in the safe and proper use of all equipment provided to them.

c. *See Section 21 for Climbing Equipment Requirements.*

31.A.05 Climbing lines shall not be used to lower limbs or other parts of trees or to raise or lower equipment, with the exception of hand tools.

31.A.06 Tool handles shall be used when raising and lowering tools.

31.A.07 Tools used for cabling, bark tracing, cavity work, etc., shall be carried in a bag, belt, or sheath designed to hold tools and not put in the pockets or stuck in the top of a boot.

31.A.08 Elevating Aerial Work Platforms (AWPs).

a. AWPs shall be provided with fall protection anchor(s) meeting design requirements of the ANSI/SIA A92.2 on which to secure an approved system of personal fall protection (e.g., full body harness with an energy-absorbing lanyard), which shall be worn by the operator(s) whenever aloft.

b. The operator may use a climber's belt and lanyard in place of a full body harness if he/she intends to transfer from the AWP to the tree. The employee shall be secured to the tree prior to removing the lanyard attached to the basket. Under no circumstances shall the employee perform any work while secured to both the tree and the basket.

c. See Section 21.H for all other fall protection requirements.

31.B Tree Climbing.

31.B.01 Tree Climbing Techniques.

a. All tree work operations above a height of 12 ft (3.6 m), whether there are electrical hazards or not, shall require a second worker in the area. If climbing is being performed, the second worker shall also be a qualified climber, capable and knowledgeable of rescue techniques, including self rescue.

b. Use of Rope Access techniques should only be used where other means of accessing the tree or undertaking the work, such as aerial devices or pole saws, are not practical. > See Section 24 for recommended rope climbing equipment, techniques, and safety practices.

31.B.02 The climber shall inspect the tree and surrounding area for hazards and perform a risk assessment of the tree and work site. Some issues to be considered are: power lines, tree hangers or broken and dead branches, entanglement with adjacent or downed trees, shape and lean of the tree, tree damage from wind, lightning, disease, location of septic lines and tanks and other potential at-grade or below-grade utilities that could be impacted.

a. Debris and other objects shall be removed from beneath the climber whenever possible.

b. Weather conditions shall be assessed as well as location of adjacent structures. Adverse weather conditions may include lightning and thunderstorms in the area.

31.B.03 Where climbing is required, tree crews shall have a secondary climber who could assist in a rescue if necessary OR the crew shall be working in proximity to nearby crews with a climber who could assist in a rescue.

31.B.04 A climber shall have available a climbing line and at least one other means of being secured, on their person at all times (e.g., climbing line and a work positioning lanyard, etc.).

a. The climber shall be tied in with an approved type of climbing line and safety saddle while ascending the tree, including when using climbing spurs/gaffs.

b. The climber shall be tied in once the work begins and shall remain tied in until the work is completed and he or she has returned to the ground.

c. The climber shall be secured when repositioning the climbing line.

d. Work may be performed while standing on a ladder only when the worker is tied in or secured as required.

31.B.05 The climbing line shall be passed around the trunk of the tree as high above the ground as possible using branches with a wide crotch to prevent any binding of the safety line. The crotch selected for tying should be directly above the work area, or as close to such a position as possible, but located in such a way that a slip or fall would swing the climber away from any electrical conductor. The line shall be passed around the main leader or an upright branch, using the limb as a stop. Feet, hands, and ropes shall be kept out of tight V-shaped crotches.

> Exception: Palms and other trees with similar growth characteristics that will not allow a climbing line to move freely.

31.B.06 The climber shall tie a stopper knot (e.g., figure-eight knot) in the end of the line, particularly when the climber will be working at heights greater than half the length of the climbing line, to prevent pulling the climbing line accidentally through the climbing hitch and possibly falling.

31.B.07 If it is necessary to re-crotch the climbing line in the tree, the climber shall re-tie in or use the safety strap before releasing the previous tie.

31.B.08 The climber working from a stem or spar without a suitable natural crotch shall select tie-in points or a tie-in method that positively prevent the climbing line from sliding down or up, or off the stem during climbing operations.

a. Placing a climbing line around a stem in an area without a lateral limb is not acceptable unless the climbing line is cinched or choked around the stem or runs through a double-wrapped or adjustable false crotch, which is secured/cinched around the stem.

31

b. The tie-in point selected shall be able to withstand the forces being applied during the pruning/removal operation.

31.B.09 Climbers shall not carry tools in their hands while climbing. Chainsaws and tools shall be raised and lowered one at a time by means of a line, except when working from an aerial-lift device or during topping or removing operations.

31.B.10 Chainsaws used aloft shall be secured against falling. Climbers may attach chainsaws weighing less than 15 lbs (6.8 kg) to themselves by means of a saw lanyard.

31.B.11 Climbers shall carry a hand saw. When carried aloft, the hand saw shall be carried in a scabbard attached to the safety saddle.

31.B.12 Climbing of dead and dying trees shall only be performed where no other safe and feasible alternative exists for removal of the tree. Climbers shall not trust the capability of a dead branch to support his/her weight. If possible, dead branches should be broken off on the way up and hands and feet should be placed on separate limbs.

31.B.13 Climbing with tree spurs on live trees that are being pruned or otherwise maintained is generally not allowed, in accordance with tree care management standards found in ANSI A300.

a. Tree spurs used for thick bark trees shall have longer gaffs, such as 2 ¾ in (7 cm). Gaff lengths of 1 ¾ in (4.5 cm) are intended only for pole climbing.

b. Gaff lengths shall be suitable for the tree being climbed.

31.B.14 Climbing techniques. The climber may apply a variety of climbing techniques, but they must be approved by the GDA.

a. Climbing without the use of tree spurs may be required.

b. The most commonly used arborist rope climbing technique is the "Advancing the Rope and Body Thrusting/Alternate Lanyard Technique".

c. If the climber can remain near the trunk of the tree, he may use both the belt lanyard/flip line and the Rope Advance (lifeline) technique. Otherwise, a single line access is permitted. If a lifeline (Access Line) cannot be set in the tree, then the use of two flip lines may be used.

d. The use of auto-locking belay devices or tree climber's hitches is both permitted.

e. Climbers shall not ascend above their tie in point. Tie-in points shall be well above the climber to prevent an uncontrolled pendulum swing in the event of a slip.

f. Once in the tree, climbers shall be tied off at two points while working or using the chainsaw, (this includes the primary support of the access line or climbing line, and secondary support with a second climbing line or the flip line/lanyard/buck strap).

(1) Climbers may ascend or descend from the tree using only the access line by using approved single rope techniques.

(2) Once the worker is at the tie-in point, a secure climbing system shall be installed.

(3) The climber shall disconnect from the access line only when a new tie in point has been established.

g. Use of the three-point contact climbing is recommended if possible. Climbers may use ground personnel to help pull them up the tree.

h. Tree climbers shall be medically cleared every 2 years by a licensed healthcare provider for unlimited tree climbing. The examination will have an emphasis on identifying and providing mitigating factors for prior heat/cold injuries, the ability to work at heights on uneven surfaces, and any environmental allergens. Additionally it will ensure that there are no medical conditions or medications which could affect balance, the ability to communicate with others, level of consciousness, extremity sensation, fine motor movement, gross motor movement, or the ability to physically lift or lower oneself.

31.C Felling.

31.C. 01 Prior to felling operations, the employee shall consider the associated hazards that may include, but are not limited to:

a. Tree size (e.g., able to fit in landing zone);
b. Selected direction of fall;
c. Felling path obstacles to avoid or clear;
d. Vines or interlocking limbs;
e. Species and shape of tree;
f. Lean of tree;
g. Loose limbs, hangers, broken tops, chunks, or other overhead material;
h. Wind force and direction;
i. Decay, cavities, or weak spots throughout the tree;
j. Location of any electrical conductors or other wires;
k. Tree cables, bracing, lightning protection, or other tree hardware;
l. Size and terrain characteristics or limitations of work area;
m. Potential for flying debris from tree impact;
n. Adequate retreat path;
o. Evidence of bees or wildlife habitation in tree;
p. Poisonous plants, water hazards;
q. Ability to control access to work site;
r. Authority to remove tree;
s. Quality of wood fiber in hinge area;
t. Root mass stability;
u. Ice or snow load;
v. Throw-back or bounce-back potential;
w. Potential for spring poles;

x. Lodged trees or dead snags in area;
y. Access to tools or resources required for task;
z. Lightning damage;
aa. Barber chair potential;
bb. Foreign objects, nails, wire fence, concrete, etc. in the tree.

31.C.02 Prior to felling operations, the work area shall be cleared to permit safe working conditions and an escape route shall be planned. Workers shall ensure that homes and structures are evacuated where trimming and felling operations are in close proximity.

31.C.03 Felling paths shall be at least twice the distance as the height of the tree (due to limbs and debris being thrown after hitting the ground. Where this distance cannot be maintained, limbing may be required. Power lines may also need to be dropped or de-energized.

31.C.04 Each worker shall be instructed as to exactly what he is to do. All workers not directly involved in the operation shall be kept clear of the work area.

31.C.05 Before starting to cut, the chainsaw operator shall be sure of his footing and must clear away brush, fallen trees, and other materials that might interfere with cutting operations.

31.C.06 A notch and backcut shall be used in felling trees over 5 in (12.7 cm) in diameter (measured at breast height). No tree shall be felled by "slicing" or "ripping" cuts.

a. The two cuts that form the notch shall meet at a point called the apex, and shall not cross that point or go beyond the point where they meet.

b. The notch cut used shall be a conventional notch, an open-face notch, or a Humboldt notch.

c. Notches shall be 45 degrees or greater and large enough to guide the fall of the tree or trunk.

d. Notch depth should not exceed one-third the diameter of the tree. The hinge width should be 80 percent of the tree's diameter, as measured at the hinge.

e. Saw cuts made to form the notch and back cut shall leave suitable amounts of hinge wood to adequately control the directional fall of the tree.

f. With a conventional notch or Humboldt notch, the back cut shall be 1 to 2 in (2.5 to 5 cm) above the apex of the notch to provide an adequate platform to prevent kickback of the tree or trunk. With an open-face notch (greater than 70 degrees), the back cut should be at the same level as the apex of the notch.

31.C.07 If sections of the tree are to be removed, sections shall be limited in lengths to one-third of the distance to the nearest structure [e.g. If the tree is 30 ft (9 m) from the structure, sections shall be no more than 10 ft (3m)].

> Note: The discretion of the chainsaw operator must be used. In some instances it may be safer to fell a large trunk away from the structure rather than to remove it in small sections, especially where the tree has grown very close to the house or structure. If this is done, a tag line shall be used to help guide the direction of the fall along with the use of proper notch and backcut.

31.C.08 The chainsaw operator shall work from the uphill side whenever possible. Tag lines may be used to help guide the direction of the fall provided the workers on the tag line are well clear of the fall path, such as twice the distance of the fall area.

31.C.09 Just before the tree of limb is ready to fall, an audible warning shall be given to all those in the area. All persons shall be safely out of range when the tree falls.

31.C.10 If there is danger that the trees being felled may fall in the wrong direction or damage property, wedges, block and tackle, rope, or wire cable (except when an electrical hazard exists) shall be used. All limbs shall be removed from trees to a height and width sufficient to allow the tree to fall clear of any wires and other objects in the vicinity.

31.C.11 Special precautions shall be taken when roping rotten or split trees due to the potential for falling in an unexpected direction even though the cut is made on the proper side.

31.C.12 Persons shall be kept back from the butt of a tree that is starting to fall.

31.D Brush Removal and Chipping.

31.D.01 Brush and logs shall not be allowed to create a hazard at the work site.

31.D.02 Employees working with a brush chipper shall be trained in its safe operation. The chipper shall be operated in accordance with the manufacturer's recommendations.

31.D.03 Brush chippers.

a. Rotary drum and disk-type tree or brush chippers not equipped with a mechanical in-feed system shall be equipped with an in-feed hopper not less than 85 in (2.2 m) (the sum of the horizontal distance from the chipper blade out along the center of the chute to the end of the chute and the vertical distance from the chute down to the ground).

b. Rotary drum and disk-type tree or brush chippers not equipped with a mechanical in-feed system shall have a flexible anti-kickback device installed in the in-feed hopper for the purpose of protecting the operator and other persons in the machine area from the hazards of flying chips and debris.

c. Disk-type tree or brush chippers equipped with a mechanical in-feed system shall have a quick stop and reversing device on the in-feed. The activating mechanism for the quick stop and reversing device shall be located across from the top, along each side of, and as close as possible to the feed end of the in-feed hopper and within easy reach of the operator.

d. The feed chute or feed table of a chipper shall have sufficient height on its side members to prevent operator contact with the blades or knives during normal operation.

e. Bush chippers shall be equipped with a discharge chute of sufficient length or design to prevent contact with the blade.

f. Brush chippers shall be equipped with a locking device on the ignition system to prevent unauthorized starting of the equipment.

g. Brush chipper cutting bars and blades shall be kept sharp, properly adjusted, and otherwise maintained in accordance with the manufacturer's recomm-endations.

h. Trailer brush chippers detached from trucks shall be chocked or otherwise secured.

i. All workers feeding brush into chippers shall wear eye protection. Loose clothing, gauntlet-type gloves, rings, and watches shall not be worn by workers feeding the chipper.

j. Employees shall never place hands, arms, feet, legs, or any other part of the body on the feed table when the chipper is in operation or the rotor is turning. Push-sticks (of material that can be consumed by brush chipper) or long branches shall be used to feed shorter material into the chipper.

k. Brush chippers shall be fed from the side of the centerline, and the operator shall immediately turn away from the feed table when the brush is taken into the rotor. Chippers shall be fed from the curbside whenever possible.

l. Material such as stones, nails, sweepings, etc. shall not be fed into brush chippers.

m. The brush chipper discharge chute or cutter housing cover shall not be raised or removed while any part of the chipper is turning or moving.

31.E Other Operations and Equipment.

31.E.01 Pruning and trimming.

a. Pole pruners, pole saws, and similar tools shall be equipped with wood or nonmetallic poles. Actuating cords shall be of a non-conducting material.

b. Pole pruners and pole saws shall be hung securely in a vertical position with the sharp edges away from employees. They shall not be hung on utility wires or cables or left overnight in trees.

c. When necessary, warning shall be given by the worker in the tree before a limb is dropped.

d. A scabbard or sheath shall be hooked to the climbing belt to carry a handsaw when not in use.

e. A separate lowering/rigging line shall be attached to limbs that cannot be dropped safely or are too heavy to be controlled by hand. The lowering/rigging line should be held by workers on the ground end of the rope. Use of the same crotch for both the climbing line and the lowering/rigging line shall be avoided.

f. Cut branches shall not be left in trees overnight.

g. A service line shall be installed for operations lasting overnight or longer and shall be used to bring the climbing line back into position at the start of the next day's work.

31.E.02 Limbing and bucking.

a. Chainsaw cut-resistant leg protection shall be worn by the chainsaw operator for all chainsaw operations on the ground.

b. When more than one worker is limbing or bucking a tree, each shall be positioned and their duties organized so that the actions of one worker will not create a hazard for any other worker.

c. Branches bent under tension shall be considered hazardous.

d. Chainsaws should be operated away from the vicinity of the legs and feet. Natural barriers, such as limbs between the saw and the body, should be employed where possible, while ensuring proper balance. While operating a chainsaw, the preferred working position is on the uphill side of the work.

e. The tree worker shall block the log to prevent rolling when necessary. Before bucking or limbing wind-thrown trees, precautions shall be taken to prevent the root ball or butt log from striking a worker.

f. When bucking, wedges shall be used as necessary to prevent binding of the guide bar or chain.

g. The worker shall make sure of firm footing before and during limbing and bucking. The worker shall not stand on loose chunks or logs that will roll when the cut is complete.

31.E.03 Stump removal.

a. Stump cutters shall be equipped with enclosures or guards that effectively protect the operator.

b. When flush cutting stumps with a chainsaw, all persons assisting the chainsaw operator shall wear the same level of PPE that is required of the chainsaw operator.

31.E.04 Cabling.

a. Branches that are to be cabled shall be brought together to the proper distance by means of a block and tackle, a hand winch, a rope, or a rope with a come-along.

b. No more than two persons shall be in a tree working at opposite ends during cabling installation.

c. In general, if an old cable system is being replaced, the old system should not be removed until after the new system is installed.

d. When the block and tackle is released, workers in trees shall be positioned off to one side in order to avoid injury in case the lag hooks pull out under the strain.

e. Ground persons shall not stand under the tree when cable is being installed.

31.E.05 Topping/Lowering Limbs.

a. Workers performing topping operations shall ensure the trees can stand the strain of topping procedures; if not, some other means of lowering the branches shall be used.

b. If large limbs are lowered in sections, the worker in the tree shall be above the limb being lowered.

31.E.06 Trucks.

a. A steel bulkhead or equivalent protection shall be provided to protect the occupants of vehicles from load shifts.

b. Logs or brush shall be securely loaded onto trucks in such a manner as not to obscure taillights or brake lights and vision, or to overhang the side.

c. In order to avoid the hazard of spontaneous combustion or the production of undesirable products, wood chips shall not be left in trucks for extended periods.

31.E 07 Power saws.

a. When used by a climber aloft, chainsaws weighing more than 15 lbs (6.8 kg) shall be supported by a separate line crotched in the tree. Where there are no lateral branches on which to crotch a separate support line, a false crotch shall be used.

b. Use of hydraulic or electric power saws is permissible. Corded electrical power saws or other corded electric tools shall not be used in the vicinity of overhead power lines.

c. The engine shall be started and operated only when all co-workers are clear of the saw and then in accordance with the manufacturer's recommendations and instructions.

d. The operator will shut off the saw when carrying it over slippery surfaces, through heavy brush, and when adjacent to personnel. The saw may be carried running (idle speed with the brake set) for short distances (less than 50 ft (15.2 m)) as long as it is carried to prevent contact with the chain or muffler.

e. All saws shall be equipped with a clutch, chain brake (gas only), throttle trigger latch, stop switch, rear hand guard, chain catcher, vibration damper, spark arrestor, and muffler.

f. Chainsaw chains shall be kept sharp and properly adjusted.

g. Chainsaws shall be operated per Section 13.F.

h. Additional PPE for chainsaw use includes chaps, safety boots, and hearing protection. Hearing protection may not be needed on hydraulic saws.

i. Gas-powered chainsaws shall be equipped with a control that will return the saw to idling speed when released.

j. A chainsaw shall not be left running while a climber is ascending, descending or moving any considerable lateral distance in the tree.

31.E.08 Chopping tools.

a. Chopping tools that have loose or cracked heads or splintered handles shall not be used.

b. Chopping tools shall never be used while working aloft.

c. Chopping tools shall be swung away from the feet, legs, and body, using the minimum power practical for control.

d. Chopping tools shall not be driven as wedges or used to drive metal wedges.

e. All edged tools and blades shall be properly sheathed when not in use.

31.E.09 Cant hooks, tongs, and carrying bars.

a. Hooks shall be firmly set before applying pressure.

b. Workers shall be warned and shall be in the clear before logs are moved.

c. The points of hooks shall be at least 2 in (5 cm) long and shall be kept sharp.

d. Workers shall stand to the rear and uphill when rolling logs.

31.E.10 Wedges and chisels.

a. Wedges and chisels shall be properly pointed and tempered.

b. Only wood, plastic, or soft metal wedges shall be used with power saws.

c. Wood-handled chisels should be protected with a ferrule on the striking end.

31

THIS PAGE INTENTIONALLY LEFT BLANK

SECTION 32 Airfield and Aircraft Operations

Table of Contents

32

32.A General.

32.A.01 The following safety requirements shall be in addition to the airfield's safety requirements. When an airfield has safety requirements that differ from those of this Section, the more stringent requirements shall prevail.

32.A.02 Construction Safety and Phasing Plan (CSPP) and a Safety Plan Compliance Document (SPCD). Prior to the performance of any work upon or around an airfield, a CSPP and a SPCD will be prepared by a Competent Person (CP). The CSPP will follow the guidelines found in the most current edition of Federal Aviation Administration (FAA) Advisory Circular AC No: 150/5370-2F, Operational Safety on Airports During Construction.

a. The CSPP and SPCD shall be reviewed and accepted by the GDA. The GDA will ensure the airfield's appropriate FAA Regional or District Office is notified of the construction and will provide the FAA a copy of the CSPP and SPCD.

b. The Airfield Manager shall review and accept the CSPP and SPCD no later than 14 days prior to beginning work.

c. Ensure prompt submittal of a Notice of Proposed Construction or Alteration (FAA Form 7460-1) for conducting an aeronautical study of potential obstructions such as tall equipment (cranes, concrete pumps, etc.), stock piles, and haul routes. One form may be filed describing the entire construction area and maximum equipment height or a separate form can be filed for each potential obstruction. In the former case, a separate form must be filed for any object beyond or higher than the originally evaluated area/height.

d. The GDA and Airfield Manager shall be informed in writing of proposed revisions to the approved CSPP and SPCD.

e. The GDA shall keep the airport operator informed so that a Notice to Airmen (NOTAM) can be issued to reflect hazardous conditions or changes to the CSPP.

32.A.03 Unless a runway is closed by the airfield operator and properly marked, it shall not be used for purposes other than aircraft operation without permission of the GDA.

32.A.04 All paved surfaces, such as runways, taxiways, and hardstands, shall be kept clean at all times, particularly with regards to stones and other small objects that might damage aircraft propellers or jet aircraft. Sweeping operations shall be performed by truck mounted vacuum sweeper capable of regenerative air sweeping and water to minimize dust generation. When possible, magnetic bar assemblies should be attached to vehicles and used to pick up ferrous metal foreign object debris (FOB).

32.A.05 When mobile equipment is not actively being utilized to perform work on an airfield, it shall be removed to a location(s) that is approved by the GDA and at a minimum distance required by the GDA (plus any additional distance necessary to ensure the safety of airfield operations) from the runway centerline and outside the Runway Safety Area (RSA), the Obstacle Free Zone, and the Runway Object Free Area of active runways.

32.A.06 Excavations.

a. Open trenches or excavations are not permitted within the RSA while the runway is open or on the Taxiway Surface Area while the taxiway is open. If possible, backfill trenches before the runway or taxiway is opened. If the runway or taxiway must be opened before excavations are backfilled, cover the excavations appropriately. Covering for open trenches must be designed to allow the safe operation of the heaviest aircraft operating on the runway across the trench without damage to the aircraft.

b. Construction contractors must prominently mark open trenches and excavations at the construction site with red or orange flags, as approved by the airport operator, and light them with red lights during hours of restricted visibility or darkness.

c. Lights must be red, either steady burning or flashing, and must meet the luminance requirements of the State Highway Department. Lights must be mounted on barricades and spaced at no more than 10 ft (3 m). Lights must be operated between sunset and sunrise and during periods of low visibility whenever the airport is open for operations. They may be operated by photocell, but this may require that the contractor turn them on manually during periods of low visibility during daytime hours.

32.A.07 Nothing shall be placed upon the landing areas without authorization of the GDA.

32.A.08 All vehicle access shall be at an entry control point (ECP) and approved by the Airfield Manager. Effective control of vehicles required to enter or cross aircraft movement areas shall be maintained as directed by the Airfield Manager.

a. Training must be provided to vehicle drivers and equipment operators to ensure compliance with the airport operator's vehicle rules and regulations. Specific training should be provided to those vehicle operators providing escorts. See AC 150/5210-20, Ground Vehicle Operations on Airports, for information on training and records maintenance requirements.

b. Vehicles other than those that routinely traverse any portion of the AOA under the control of ATC, which are not escorted by a vehicle in constant two-way radio communication with ATC and properly equipped and authorized to operate in the AOA, must be provided with a flag on a staff attached to the vehicle so that the flag will be readily visible.

c. At airports without air traffic control facilities, flags must be provided on all vehicles.

d. The flag must be at least a 3-ft by 3-ft (0.9-m by 0.9-m) square having a checkered pattern of international orange and white squares at least 1 ft (.3 m) on each side.

32.A.09 Those landing areas hazardous to aircraft shall be submitted to the Air Field manager for a FAA NOTAM on displaced threshold or other changes on non use or caution (unless otherwise directed by the GDA).

a. During daylight, areas shall be outlined with highly reflective barricades, lights, signs, and/or orange or red flags, spaced in accordance with AC 150/5370-2F and as approved by the airfield manager. The flags will be at least 20-in by 20-in (.5-m by .5-m), with diagonal plastic stiffeners.

b. During periods of darkness, areas shall be outlined with battery-operated, low-intensity omni directional red flashing lights spaced in accordance with AC 150/5370-2F and as approved by the airfield manager.

c. Lights must be red, either steady burning or flashing, and must meet the luminance requirements of the State Highway Department. Lights must be mounted on barricades and spaced at no more than 10 ft (3 m) and must be operated between sunset and sunrise and during periods of low visibility whenever the airport is open for operations. They may be operated by photocell, but this may require that the contractor turn them on manually during periods of low visibility during daytime hours.

32.A.10 When work is to be performed at an airfield where flying is controlled, permission to enter a landing area shall be obtained from the control tower operator every time entry is required, unless the landing area has been closed by the airfield operator and marked as hazardous in accordance with Section 32.A.09.

a. All vehicles which operate in landing areas shall be identified by means of a checkered flag on a staff attached to, and flying above, the vehicle. The flag shall be 3 ft (0.9 m) square and consist of a checkered pattern of international orange and white squares of 1 ft (0.3 m) on each side.

b. All other equipment and materials in the landing area shall be marked as specified in Section 32.A.09.

32.A.11 When working in landing areas, work shall be performed so as to leave that portion of the landing area that is available to aircraft free from hazards, including holes, piles, or material, and projecting shoulders that might damage an airplane tire. Each vehicle, piece of equipment, or work crew shall be equipped with a two-way radio capable of maintaining communications with the air traffic control tower while performing work in landing areas.

32.A.12 No equipment, materials or contractor plant shall be placed upon or within a safety precaution area without approval of the GDA.

32.A.13 All equipment and materials in a safety precaution area shall be marked as specified in Section 32.A.09.a-c. If an object in a safety precaution area projects above the approach-departure clearance surface or above the transitional surface, the object shall be marked with a red light.

32.A.14 Prohibitions.

a. No use of tall equipment (e.g., cranes, concrete pumps, etc.) unless an FAA Form 7460-1 determination letter is issued for such equipment.

b. No use of open-flame welding or torches unless fire safety precautions are provided and the airport operator has approved their use.

c. No use of electrical blasting caps on or within 1,000 ft (300 m) of the airport property.

d. No use of flare pots within the AOA.

32.B Aircraft.

32.B.01 All non-military aircraft shall be registered, certified in the appropriate category and maintained in accordance with the airworthiness standards of the FAA. (If used OCONUS, and not prohibited by other regulation such as ER 95-1-1, registration, certification and maintenance in accordance with the standards of a comparable governing body of foreign or international authority may be substituted for those of the FAA.)

32.B.02 All contract pilots or pilots of chartered aircraft shall hold at least a commercial pilot certificate with instrument rating. All pilots of non-military aircraft shall possess ratings to comply with the FAA Regulation governing the aircraft and operations involved.

32.B.03 All non-military aircraft shall be equipped with a two-way radio.

32.B.04 All non-military flight operations shall be in accordance with the FAA rules governing conduct for the specific operation (i.e., 14 CFR 133, 14 CFR 135 and 14 CFR 91).

32.B.05 All military flight operations shall be conducted under appropriate DOT/DOD regulations.

32.B.06 All USACE-owned aircraft will use approved Government Flight Representatives' (GFRs) approved procedures as outlined in AR 95-20 and AR 95-1. GFRs are appointed in accordance with AR 95-20.

32

THIS PAGE INTENTIONALLY LEFT BLANK

SECTION <u>33</u> Hazardous Waste Operations and Emergency Response (HAZWOPER)

Table of Contents

33

SECTION 33 Hazardous Waste Operations and Emergency Response (HAZWOPER)

33.A General.

33.A.01 This Section applies to:

a. Hazardous waste site operations performed under the Comprehensive Environmental Response, Compensation, Liability Act (CERCLA) or Resource Conservation and Recovery Act (RCRA) as specified by OSHA in 29 CFR 1910.120 and 29 CFR 1926.65 (a) (1) (i), (ii) and (iii) (e.g., site investigations, remedial action construction, treatment process operation, and maintenance at: Formerly Used Defense Sites (FUDS) projects, Installation Restoration Program (IRP) projects, Base Realignment and Closure (BRAC) projects, Formerly Used Sites Remedial Action Program (FUSRAP) projects, U.S. Environmental Protection Agency (EPA) Superfund projects, and hazardous waste site cleanup operations performed under the civil works program).

b. Facilities or construction projects holding RCRA Treatment Storage and Disposal (TSD) permits as specified by OSHA in 29 CFR 1910.120 and 29 CFR 1926.65 (a) (1) (iv).

c. Facilities or construction projects where emergency response as specified by OSHA in 29 CFR 1910.120 and 29 CFR 1926.65 (a) (1) (v) may be required.

33.B Site Safety and Health Plan (SSHP).

33.B.01 Hazardous waste site cleanup operations require development and implementation of a SSHP that shall be attached to the Accident Prevention Plan (APP) as an appendix. Information from the APP should not be duplicated in the SSHP.

a. The APP/SSHP shall address all occupational safety and health hazards associated with site operations.

b. Contracted work on the projects shall be performed in compliance with the APP/SSHP.

c. Hazardous waste operations performed by Government personnel do not require development of an APP, but do require a Project Safety and Health Plan and a SSHP in compliance with Section 01.A.09 and local safety and health policies for in-house activities. All activities shall comply with the written SSHP.

d. Changes and modifications to the SSHP are permitted and shall be made in writing with the knowledge and concurrence of the local Safety and Health Manager (SHM) and accepted by the GDA.

e. A SSHP is not required for contracts where the site has been fully characterized and there is no known OR anticipated potential for employee contamination-related exposures during the tasks being performed.

f. If the work meets the criteria in Section 33.B.01.e and the tasks being performed are limited in scope (e.g., mowing, routine maintenance, or utility checks of existing equipment as part of long-term maintenance or site management), an abbreviated APP as described in Section 01.A.12.e may be used in lieu of a full APP.

33.B.02 The SSHP shall cover the following in project-specific detail. General information adequately covered in the APP (introduction, site background, SOH organization and lines of authority, general site control and layout and general site safety procedures, logs, reports and inspections) need not be duplicated. Section 06.E Ionizing Radiation shall be used to develop appropriate sections of the SSHP for HTRW projects involving radioactive isotopes.

a. Site description and contamination characterization - a description of the contamination with the exposure potential to adversely affect safety and occupational health and likely to be encountered by the on-site work activities;

b. Activity Hazard Analysis (AHA). An AHA shall be developed for each task/operation to be performed per Section 01.A.13. The AHA shall account for all hazards (classic safety, chemical, physical, biological, ionizing radiation) likely to be encountered while performing the work;

c. Staff organization, qualifications, and responsibilities per Section 33.C;

d. Training, general and project-specific per Section 33.D;

e. Personal Protective Equipment (PPE). PPE used to protect workers from site-related hazards (construction safety and health and contaminant-related) shall comply with requirements specified in Section 5;

f. Medical surveillance. Certification of medical surveillance program participation shall be appended to the SSHP and shall include: employee name, date of last examination, and name of examining physician(s) and shall be per Section 33.E. The required written physician's opinion shall be made available upon request to the GDA;

g. Exposure monitoring/Air sampling program. Exposure monitoring and air sampling shall be performed to determine if the PPE provides adequate protection and to evaluate worker exposure to site-related contaminants and hazardous substances used in the cleanup process. Project-specific exposure monitoring/air sampling requirements shall comply with requirements specified Section 6;

h. Heat and cold stress. The procedures and practices for protecting workers from heat and cold stress shall comply with Section 06.J;

i. Standard operating safety procedures (SOPs), engineering controls, and work practices. SOPs, engineering controls and work practices shall be addressed for the following as appropriate:

(1) Site rules/prohibitions (e.g., buddy system, eating/drinking/ smoking restrictions, etc.);

(2) Work permit requirements (e.g., radioactive work, excavation, hot work, confined space, etc.);

(3) Material handling procedures (e.g., soil, liquid, radioactive materials, spill contingency);

(4) Drum/container/tank handling (e.g., opening, sampling, overpacking, draining, pumping, purging, inerting, cleaning, excavation and removal, disassembly and disposal, spill contingency);

(5) Comprehensive AHA of treatment technologies employed at the site;

j. Site control measures. Work zones shall be established so that on-site activities do not spread contamination. The site shall be set up so that there is a clearly defined exclusion zone (EZ) and a clearly defined support zone (SZ) with a contamination reduction zone (CRZ) as a transition between the EZ and SZ;

k. Personal hygiene and decontamination. A personal hygiene and decontamination station shall be set up in the CRZ for personnel to remove contaminated PPE and to wash when exiting the EZ;

l. Equipment decontamination. An equipment decontamination station shall be set up in the CRZ for equipment to be decontaminated when exiting the EZ;

m. Emergency equipment and first aid. The equipment and personnel required for first aid and CPR shall comply with the requirements in Section 3. Emergency equipment required to be on-site shall have the capacity to respond to project-specific emergencies. Site emergencies may require (but should not be limited to) PPE and equipment to control fires, leaks and spills, or chemical (contaminant or treatment process) exposure;

n. Emergency response and contingency procedures. Emergency Response Procedures shall be developed that address the following:

(1) Pre-emergency planning. An agreement shall be established between the Contractor (or the GDA for in-house work), local emergency responders, and the servicing emergency medical facility that specifies the responsibilities of on-site personnel, emergency response personnel, and the emergency medical facility in the event of an onsite emergency;

(2) Personnel and lines of authority for emergency situations;

(3) Criteria and procedures for emergency recognition and site evacuation (e.g., emergency alarm systems, evacuation routes and reporting locations, site security);

(4) Decontamination and medical treatment of injured personnel;

(5) A route map to emergency medical facilities and phone numbers for emergency responders;

(6) Criteria for alerting the local community responders.

33.C Responsibilities.

33.C.01 The Safety and Health Manager (SHM) must meet the qualifications and fulfill the responsibilities stated below for all hazardous waste operations. The SHM, dependent upon the contaminant-related hazards on the project, shall be a Certified Industrial Hygienist (CIH), Certified Safety Professional (CSP) or Certified Health Physicist (CHP).

a. The SHM shall have 3 years of experience managing SOH at hazardous waste site cleanup operations.

b. The SHM shall enlist the support of SOH professionals with appropriate education and experience when working on sites with multiple hazards (i.e., chemical, safety, ionizing radiation).

c. The SHM shall be responsible for the following actions:

(1) Developing, maintaining, and overseeing implementation of the SSHP;

(2) Visiting the project as needed to audit the effectiveness of the SSHP;

(3) Remaining available for project emergencies;

33

SECTION 33 Hazardous Waste Operations and Emergency Response (HAZWOPER)

(4) Developing modifications to the SSHP as needed;

(5) Evaluating occupational exposure monitoring/air sampling data and adjusting SSHP requirements as necessary;

(6) Serving as a QC staff member;

(7) Approving the SSHP by signature.

33.C.02 Site Safety and Health Officer (SSHO). The SSHO is required at HTRW operations.

a. The SSHO shall have a minimum 1 year experience implementing SOH procedures at cleanup operations and shall meet 29 CFR 1910.120/29 CFR 1926.65 requirements for 40-hour initial and 8-hour supervisor training and, maintain 8-hour refresher training requirements. In addition, for supervision of safety and health at projects involving intrusive activities, the SSHO shall meet the qualifications specified in Section 01.A.17. b. Intrusive activities include, but are not limited to, drilling, demolition, and excavation.

b. The SSHO shall have training and experience to conduct exposure monitoring/air sampling and select/adjust protective equipment use.

c. The SSHO shall have the authority and is responsible for the following actions:

(1) Being present anytime cleanup operations are being performed to implement the SSHP;

(2) Inspecting site activities to identify SOH deficiencies and correct them;

(3) Coordinating changes/modifications to the SSHP with the SHM, site superintendent, and contracting officer; and

(4) Conducting project-specific training.

33.D Training. Personnel shall comply with the following general and project-specific training requirements:

33.D.01 General training. General training requirements apply to project personnel exposed to contaminant-related SOH hazards. General training must comply with the following requirements:

a. 40-hour off-site HTRW site instruction. Off-site instruction shall comply with the 40-hour training requirements in OSHA standards 29 CFR 1910.120 and 29 CFR 1926.65.

(1) Instructor qualifications: Personnel responsible for planning and teaching/facilitating the 40-hour training course shall be thoroughly knowledgeable of the 40-hour training topics specified by OSHA in 29 CFR 1910.120 and 29 CFR 1926.65 and shall possess the knowledge and experience to instruct on each of the topics. Instructors shall retain qualifications for teaching on organizationally relevant 40-hour training safety and occupational health topics by regularly attending and participating in formal industrial hygiene or safety related courses, seminars and conferences. Five (5) days of training over a 5-year period is required.

(2) 40-hour training course outline for HTRW operations. 40-hour training courses shall cover the following topics in a manner that is relevant to organizational operations:

(a) Names of personnel and alternates responsible for site safety and health;

(b) Safety, health and other hazards;

(c) Use of personal protective equipment;

(d) Work practices by which employees can minimize risks from hazards;

(e) Safe use of engineering controls and equipment to minimize exposure to hazards;

(f) Medical surveillance implemented for the protection of employees;

(g) Decontamination procedures for personnel and equipment;

(h) Emergency response plan development and implementation for site work;

(i) Confined space hazards and awareness;

(j) Spill containment.

(3) Computer-based interactive 40-hour training. Computer-based interactive training is acceptable as long as the following criteria are met:

(a) The course shall cover each of the topics required by OSHA for cleanup operations 40-hour training. > *See Section 33.D.01.a (2);*

(b) Students shall be able to ask questions and receive answers in a timely manner from a qualified instructor with hazardous waste site cleanup safety and health experience;

(c) Students shall participate in 16-hours of hands-on exercises to demonstrate equipment use and procedural proficiency.

b. Three (3)-Days On-the-Job-Training (OJT). In addition to the classroom training, the training shall include 3 days of OJT (in field) experience under the direct supervision of a trained, experienced supervisor.

c. 8-hour annual refresher training. Refresher training shall comply with the requirements in OSHA standards 29 CFR 1910.120 and 29 CFR 1926.65. USACE employees shall comply with local district hazardous waste refresher training policies.

(1) The 8-hour refresher training course outline for HTRW operations shall cover the topics identified in Section 33.D.01.a (2) above. Refresher training courses shall cover those topics in a manner that is relevant to organizational operations and shall address hazards that were encountered in the previous year:

(2) Computer-based interactive 8-hour refresher training. Computer based interactive training is acceptable as long as the criteria identified in Section 33.D.01.a (3) above are met.

d. Supervisory training. On-site supervisors shall comply with the 8-hour supervisory training requirements in OSHA standards 29 CFR 1910.120 and 29 CFR 1926.65.

33.D.02 Project-specific training. Training specific to other sections of this manual, OSHA standards applicable to site work and operations, and site specific hazards relevant to onsite contamination shall be provided to workers before on-site work begins. When relevant, assure that workers are made aware of contaminant-related hazards by use of a site specific map.

33.D.03 DOT and DOD training is required for all persons who prepare DOT shipping papers (including hazardous waste manifests), label, package and/or mark containers for purposes of transportation. Training shall be documented and employees should be issued an appointment letter by their command. > See EP 415-1-266 and DOD 4500.9-R.

33.E Medical Surveillance. All personnel performing on-site work that will result in exposure to contaminant-related SOH hazards shall be enrolled in a medical surveillance program that complies with OSHA standards 29 CFR 1910.120 (f) and 29 CFR 1926.65 (f).

33.E.01 Certification of medical surveillance program participation shall be appended to the SSHP. The certification shall include: employee name, date of last examination, and name of examining physician(s).

33.E.02 The required physician's written opinion shall be made available upon request to the GDA.

33.E.03 All medical records shall be maintained in accordance with 29 CFR 1910.1020.

33.E.04 USACE employees must comply with medical requirements in ER 385-1-40, Appendix B.

33.E.05 Should any unforeseen hazard become evident during the performance of work, the SSHO shall bring such hazard information to the attention of the SHM and the GDA (both verbally and in writing) for resolution as soon as possible. In the interim, necessary action shall be taken to reestablish and maintain safe working conditions.

33.F RCRA TSD Facilities. Requirements specified in 29 CFR 1910.120 and 29 CFR 1926.65(p), and the terms of the facility RCRA permit shall be complied with for operations at TSD facilities.

33.G Facility or Construction Project Emergency Response. Projects using, storing, or handling hazardous substances and whose employees will be engaged in emergency response operations shall comply with 29 CFR 1910.120 (q) and 29 CFR 1926.65 (q) (a) (1) (v) when a hazardous substance release may result in exposure causing adverse affects to the health or safety of employees.

➢ Exception: Projects that will evacuate their employees from the danger area when an emergency occurs, and do not permit any of their employees to assist in handling the emergency, (if they provide an Emergency Response Plan in accordance with 29 CFR 1910.38(a) and 29 CFR 1926.35).

33.G.01 If applicable, the site manager shall develop and implement an Emergency Response Plan that addresses the following items:

a. Operations. Identify operations requiring use of hazardous substances;

b. Pre-emergency planning with local emergency responders. Describe emergency response agreements, including roles and responsibilities, made with local emergency responders for hazardous material response, fire, rescue, emergency medical care, and security and law enforcement;

c. Personnel roles, lines of authority, training, and communication. Describe key personnel roles, command structure/lines of authority and

33

communications requirements for responding to site-specific hazardous substance releases;

d. Emergency recognition and prevention. Identify the likely emergency scenarios for the project and how employees can expect to identify and recognize emergency scenarios;

e. Safe distances and places of refuge. Select safe places of refuge to be used in emergency situations, identify these locations in the ERP, and require employees to report to selected places of refuge during emergencies;

f. Site security and control. Describe how the facility will be secured and describe access to the site controlled during emergencies;

g. Evacuation routes and procedures. Describe and map out evacuation routes to safe places of refuge and any special safety and health procedures employees must follow while evacuating the facility;

h. Decontamination. Develop and describe plans and procedures for decontaminating personnel if/when they come in contact with leaking hazardous substances;

i. Emergency medical treatment and first aid. Explain how emergency medical treatment and first aid will be provided in the event of a hazardous substance spill;

j. Emergency alerting and response procedures. Describe how personnel will be alerted in the event of a hazardous substance spill, and how facility personnel must respond after emergency alerting procedures are initiated;

k. Critique of response and follow-up. Describe how lessons learned from emergency response will be documented and used to improve future emergency response actions;

l. PPE and emergency equipment. Describe the PPE and emergency response equipment that will be available for use by response personnel at the facility;

m. Emergency Response Team. Designate a facility-specific Emergency Response Team. Describe the team's emergency responsibilities for interacting with local emergency response providers (i.e., where the facility team's responsibilities end and the local response providers begin);

<u>33</u>.G.02 Personnel training requirements. At a minimum, Emergency Response Team personnel at the project shall be trained to the "First Responder Operations Levels" specified in 29 CFR 1910.120

(q)(6)(ii). Response above and beyond defensive requires additional training and highly qualified supervision under 29 CFR 1910.120(q) and 29 CFR 1926.65(q) and must be specified on a project specific basis.

<u>33</u>.G.03 Emergency Response Team responsibilities. The Emergency Response Team shall, at a minimum, respond in a defensive manner to hazardous substance releases at the facility or construction project using the equipment and procedures specified in the emergency response plan for defensive response. The Emergency Response Team shall only provide response services beyond defensive if qualified and only according the procedures specified in the facility or construction project-specific Emergency Response Plan.

SECTION 34 Confined Space Entry

Table of Contents

34

34.A General.

34.A.01 Confined Spaces – Non-Marine Facilities. Confined space (CS) work performed in permanent, fixed facilities and/or performed on construction sites shall be performed in accordance with this Section, 29 CFR 1910.146 and ANSI Z117.1. This section does not regulate underground construction work (tunneling) as a confined space. > *See Section* 26.

34.A.02 USACE-conducted CS work activities on or in a watercraft or vessel of any kind and/or associated with vessel repair and maintenance operations are covered in Section 34.B.

34.A.03 The definitions for CS that are applicable to all CSs, during operations, maintenance and construction are listed in Appendix Q, Definitions.

34.A.04 Confined Space Identification. Facilities and job sites shall assign a Safety Supervisor or Confined Space Competent Person (CSCP) to identify all CSs and determine entry rules and requirements. > *See Figure 34-1.*

a. On USACE facilities, all fixed permit-required CS (PRCS) shall be labeled as a PRCS. With the approval of the local Safety Office (SOHO), the CSCP may exclude from labeling those confined spaces that pose little or no hazard, (i.e., a navigation lock), but meet the strict definition of a permit-required confined space (PRCS).

b. On construction sites and/or during O&M activities, all fixed PRCS shall be labeled as a danger. PRCS that are created as part of construction work shall be labeled and have a barrier to restrict entry. All Non Permit-Required Confined Spaces (NPRCS) created as part of construction and/or O&M activities are not required to be labeled.

c. If activities in a NPRCS (i.e., welding), create or have a potential to create a hazardous atmosphere, that space shall be declared a PRCS.

d. All previously identified CSs shall be identified in writing to any contract personnel prior to the beginning of work if they are required to enter and/or work in this area.

(1) The contract documents shall list any known hazards and controls in the CS.

(2) If it is known that work to be conducted inside a CS would create a possible hazardous atmosphere, the contractor shall be notified prior to beginning work and shall be required to follow the requirements for PRCS.

(3) All entry into an identified or contractor-created PRCS shall be coordinated with the GDA and site security or emergency personnel before each entry.

e. For work conducted on military installations, the CSCP or designer shall coordinate with the installation CS program manager/team to identify all CSs and determine any specific installation requirements for entry.

34.A.05 Confined Space Entry (CSE) Procedures.

a. PRCS Entry Procedures. Entry into PRCSs shall comply with the requirements of 29 CFR 1910.146.

b. NPRCS Entry Procedures:

(1) There are no entry requirements if the space does not contain or have the ability to contain an atmospheric hazard capable of causing death or physical harm.

(2) If a NPRCS has an environment being controlled by permanent ventilation system and/or has an isolation barrier, then entry requires: continual air monitoring; the use of audible/visual alarms for failure of the ventilation system or isolation barrier; and training for the employees in visual contact with the CS and those working in the CS on the proper rescue procedures to be used shall be required. The alarm shall be capable of notifying both the entrants and rescue personnel. This shall be documented and written in the CSE Plan.

c. PRCS Permit. The CSCP shall complete or review and sign the completed PRCS permit (see Form 34-1 for non-mandatory example) and shall be responsible for enforcing the use of PRCS permits for entry into all PRCSs at the facility/site.

FIGURE 34-1

Confined Space Identification Flow Chart

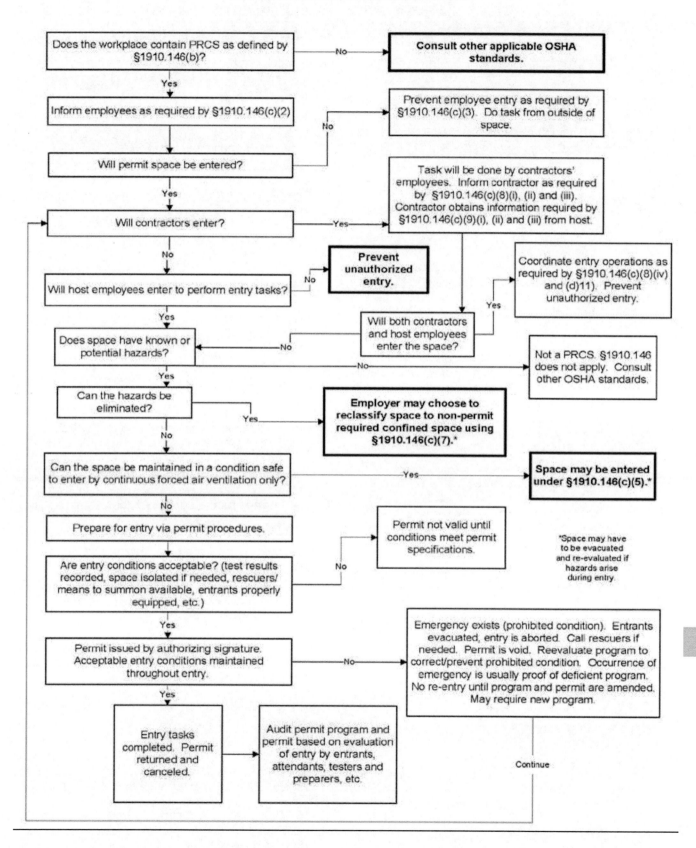

34

d. At the end of the work task where a PRCS was entered, there shall be an after action review by all parties on procedures used and if improvement can be gained. For USACE operations, this review should include safety personnel for the site, and any security or emergency responders. For contract operations, this review should include GDA and any security or emergency responders on site.

34.A.06 CSCP/Safety Supervisor Responsibilities.

a. Identification and Labeling. The CSCP shall identify and label all PRCSs as noted in Section 34.A.04.b.

b. The CSCP shall develop and implement an activity/site-specific Confined Space program. The program shall contain and adequately address the CS program elements of 29 CFR 1910.146 and those defined in this section.

c. It is the responsibility of the site supervisor or project manager to ensure all entries into a CS are completed in a safe and protective manner. The procedures shall be documented in a CS program which is part of the APP or Project Safety and Health Plan.

d. Coordination with local emergency responders. The CSCP shall coordinate with local emergency responders to determine if they are capable of a timely (5 minutes) rescue from the specific CS. If the local emergency responders do not have the appropriate rescue capability, the rescue capability should be developed on-site.

e. Review CS program and all past entries annually.

34.A.07 CS Program Elements. The CS program shall address each of the following elements with facility-/site-specific detail:

a. Identification and Labeling. Describe the process for identifying a work area as a CS and rationale used for classifying the type of CSs. Describe labeling and enforcement procedures that will assure personnel do not enter CSs in an unauthorized fashion;

b. CS hazard identification. Describe the hazards in the CS and all potential hazards that may be created by potential work in the CS, any permanent air monitoring, physical isolation identification, or permanent ventilation;

c. Safe CSE conditions. Describe the practices and procedures that will be followed to assure that CSs will be entered safely. Procedures and practices shall include but are not limited to the following:

(1) NPRCSs. Describe any monitoring and employee training that will assure non- permit

conditions are maintained and that employees entering the NPRCS understand how to maintain a safe working environment while working in it. Describe the potential atmospheric and/or physical hazards that are present in the CS and the necessary controls for these hazards, necessary training requirements of entrants and workers within visual contact.

(2) PRCSs. At a minimum, describe how each of the elements below will be enforced at each PRCS:

(a) Entry permit (See Form 34-1 34-2 for example) completion, review, processes, signature authority, and maintenance procedures for all PRCS. The entry supervisor or manager shall be required to sign all permits daily before entry;

(b) Acceptable entry conditions;

(c) Observation by the authorized entrant of monitoring or testing in PRCSs;

(d) Isolation and/or any alarms for physical hazards or atmospheric hazards of the PRCSs;

(e) Purging, inerting, flushing or ventilating the PRCS as necessary to eliminate or control atmospheric hazards;

(f) Installation of barriers to protect entrants from external hazards;

(g) Monitoring requirements and procedures used to verify that acceptable entry conditions are maintained for the duration of the authorized entry;

d. Equipment (and equipment maintenance procedures) to be used for CSE at the facility/site. All equipment shall be calibrated and functionally tested before each entry in accordance with the manufacturer's instructions. Equipment shall include the following at a minimum:

(1) Appropriate atmospheric testing and monitoring equipment necessary to assure safe entry and that safe entry conditions are maintained;

(2) Ventilation equipment to assure maintenance of safe entry conditions;

(3) Communication equipment for constant contact between the attendant and the entrants and means of communication to the emergency personnel;

(4) Personal Protective Equipment (PPE) necessary in the event that engineering controls and work practices do not adequately protect entrants;

(5) Lighting equipment for entry;

(6) Barriers and shields to keep unauthorized entrants out of the CS during entry;

(7) Ladders or other equipment necessary for entrant access and egress;

(8) Rescue and emergency equipment needed to remove entrants in the event of an emergency. Particular emphasis shall be placed on the use and implementation of appropriate self-rescue procedures and equipment;

(9) Any other equipment necessary for safe entry into or rescue from CSs;

e. Procedures for evaluating PRCS conditions when entry is conducted. Address each of the following in facility/site-specific detail:

(1) Atmosphere conditions required to be maintained during entry to ensure safe entry;

(2) At a minimum, test the PRCS atmosphere for the following in the order specified:

(a) Oxygen (before and continual while entrant is in the PRCS);

(b) Combustible gases and vapors; and

(c) Toxic gases and vapors.

f. Policies and procedures to assure that at least one attendant is immediately available outside the PRCS during entry operations to monitor the conditions of the space, to communicate with entrants, and to respond to emergencies;

g. Designate by name, personnel at the facility/site with active roles in CSE and their responsibilities for PRCS entry. All permits shall be signed by each employee entering the CS, the CSCP, attendant and a responsible entry supervisor;

h. Document procedures and agreements with local emergency responders for notifying emergency services of a pending entry and summoning rescue and emergency services for rescuing PRCS entrants;

i. Document a facility/site procedure for preparing, issuing, using and canceling PRCS entry permits;

j. Document procedures for coordinating with employees from outside organizations who will be participating in PRCS entry. The coordination shall include the type of CS, the known hazards, safety procedures, PPE and debrief following the entry;

k. Document procedures for concluding an entry after entry operations have been completed;

l. Develop procedures for reviewing PRCS entries and documenting lessons learned from them; and

m. Establish a policy to review cancelled, expired or revoked permits to modify the PRCS entry procedures annually.

n. Establish a policy to review the CS program annually.

34.A.08 Employee Training. All employees entering PRCS or NPRCS, authorized attendants, supervisors and managers, and workers within visual contact of the CS shall be trained to understand the requirements of the facility/site-specific CSE Program and procedures and emergency retrieval procedures.

a. Initial CS training. All entrants, authorized attendants, and supervisor or managers shall receive an initial CS training course that includes hands-on practical exercise with all the equipment; rescue exercise; and completing the CS permit. The training shall include, as a minimum: the roles and responsibilities in conducting an entry; specialized training on the use, calibration, and maintenance of monitoring, communications, and retrieval equipment; the hazards of the entry and the control of the hazards of the entry.

b. Before each activity requiring entry into a CS, the entrant, authorized attendants, supervisor/managers, and workers in close proximity, shall review the entry procedures, the use of the air monitoring, PPE, and retrieval equipment. Emergency responders shall be invited to the training review. If it has been over a year since the initial training, a rescue exercise shall be part of the training review.

c. Training shall be documented and include a roster of those attending and topics discussed.

34.A.09 Rescue and Emergency Services. The CSCP shall develop or establish rescue and emergency services for PRCS entry. Emergency responders shall be notified of the training and at least annually, or immediately prior to each entry, shall have participated in an emergency response drill for retrieval of an employee or dummy from the CSs.

34

FORM 34-1

Confined Space Entry Permit {PRIVATE}

Location of Work: _____

Description of Work (Purpose): _____

Authorized Attendants: _____

_____

Authorized Entrants: _____

_____

Entry Date: _____ Entry Time: _____

Outside Contractors: _____

Isolation Checklist (Safe Clearance):

    Blanking and/or Disconnecting _____

    Electrical _____

    Mechanical _____

    Other _____

Hazardous Work:

    Burning _____

    Welding _____

    Brazing _____

    Open Flame _____

    Other _____

Hazards Expected:

    Corrosive Materials _____

    Hot Equipment _____

    Flammable Materials _____

    Toxic Materials _____

    Drains Open _____

    Cleaning (Ex: chemical or water lance) _____

    Spark Producing Operations _____

    Spilled Liquids _____

    Pressure Systems _____

Other _____

Vessel Cleaned:

    Deposits _____

Method _____
Inspection _____
Neutralized with _____

Fire Safety Precautions: _____
_____

Personal Safety:
    Ventilation Requirements _____
    Respirators _____
    Life Lines and Harness _____
    Lighting _____
    Communications _____
    Buddy   System ____
    Name of Attendant _____

Atmospheric Gas Tests:

	Tests Performed	Location	Reading
Example:	(Oxygen)	_____	(19.5%)
Example:	(Flammability)	_____	(< 10% LFL)
	_____	_____	
	_____	_____	
	_____	_____	

Remarks: _____
_____

Test Performed By: _____
                                      Signature
Time: _____

Authorizations:
    Entry Supervisor: _____
    Safety Supervisor/Qualified Person: _____

Emergency Phone Numbers:
    Fire Department _____
    Ambulance _____
    Hospital _____
    Doctor _____

Permit Expires: _____

34

34.B Confined and Enclosed Spaces on Ships and Vessels (defined as any watercraft). The following applies only to ship and vessel repair and maintenance, not operational ship and vessel activities. > *See Section 19; See Appendix Q for CS definitions.*

34.B.01 All spaces on a vessel or ship or floating plant that could be considered a "Potential Confined Space", shall be posted as a "Potential Confined Space".

a. If the potential CS has an oxygen deficient atmosphere, the space shall be labeled "Not Safe for Workers".

b. If the potential CS has an oxygen-enriched atmosphere, the space shall be labeled "Not Safe for Workers – Not Safe for Hot Work".

c. If the potential CS contains a flammable gas or vapor at 10% or higher than the lower explosive limit (LEL) for the gas, then the space shall be labeled "Not Safe for Workers – Not Safe for Hot Work".

d. If the CS contains a potential atmosphere that is toxic, corrosive, or irritants that exceed the OEL, the space shall be labeled "Not Safe for Workers".

e. An inventory of these spaces shall be maintained in the pilot house and the land-based office.

34.B.02 Before and during entry into the types of spaces listed below, the Competent Person for Confined Spaces in ships and vessels (CPCSSV) shall test for oxygen content, flammability, and toxicity. These tests and all entries shall be recorded on an entry form or in an entry log which will be reviewed by the GDA. At a minimum, the entry log or form shall have the time and date, monitoring device type, model, serial number, and calibration date, and the name of the individual doing the testing.

a. Unventilated CSs that have been closed up or freshly painted;

b. CSs that have contained or do contain combustible or flammable liquids or gases;

c. CSs that have contained or do contain toxic, corrosive, or irritant liquid, gases, or solids.

34.B.03 Testing Requirements.

a. If the testing determines the oxygen is below 19.5% or above 23.5%, or the lower explosive limit (LEL) of 10% is exceeded, or other toxic substances are measured, then the space should be thoroughly ventilated and appropriate PPE used for entry as directed by the CPCSSV. Entry is prohibited when the LEL is greater than 10% unless it is required for emergency rescue.

b. Air monitoring shall be continuous during entry into the confined space if the oxygen level is not between 19.5% and 23.5% or ventilation was required to lower the explosive limit to below 10% of the LEL.

c. Air testing for toxic, corrosive, or irritant chemicals shall be made using a calibrated direct reader that provides a reading at a minimum of 50% of the OEL. If the reading is over the OEL, then the space shall be ventilated until the value is below the OEL and/or entry shall be made with appropriate PPE.

d. Before hot work is completed in a confined space with toxic, corrosive, or irritating chemicals, the CPCSSV shall conduct an evaluation to confirm the hot work will not create a toxic, corrosive, or irritant atmosphere. This evaluation shall be documented and signed by the CPCSSV. During the entry the air shall be continually monitored.

e. Air sampling shall be conducted at the ventilation discharge point if there is anyone in the area or if the discharge is a semi-enclosed or enclosed area.

34.B.04 Entry Precautions.

a. No hot work will be completed adjacent to flammable chemicals unless the area is well ventilated and continually tested.

b. No ignition source shall be taken into an area of flammable chemicals unless the area is well ventilated and continually tested.

34.B.05 Training.

a. Anyone required to enter a potential confined space shall be trained when the hazards change or annually, whichever is sooner. The training shall include discussion of the hazards of the space, including the symptoms of any hazardous materials; the controls, including blanking and ventilation; the warnings if the controls fail; personal protective equipment required; and emergency procedures.

b. The training on the emergency procedures shall include an exercise on retrieving a person from the confined space.

c. This training shall be documented on a certificate that includes the date of training, name of individual trained, the trainer, and the topics covered. The training certificate shall be available for GDA review.

APPENDIX A Minimum Basic Outline for Accident Prevention Plans

1. **Accident Prevention Plan (APP) - General.** An APP is a safety and health policy and program document that is contract- or job- specific. It is an integral part of the planning process. > *See Section 01 and 01.A.12.*

a. The APP shall interface with the employer's overall safety and health program. Any portions of the overall safety and health program that are referenced in the APP shall be included as appropriate.

b. The APP shall be submitted to the GDA for acceptance prior to work starting.

   (1) Understanding that the APP is submitted prior to work starting and that some project-specific information is not yet known (e.g., subcontractors to be used, type of fall protection to be used at a certain point in time, specific cranes or other load handling equipment (LHE) to be brought on site, etc.), the known information shall be provided and additional information added at each preparatory phase/meeting along with the appropriate Activity Hazard Analyses (AHAs).

   (2) A copy of the contractor's project-specific, accepted APP shall be available on the work site. > *See ANSI/ASSE A10.38 for programmatic issues.*

2. **Abbreviated APP.** In lieu of a fully-developed APP, for Limited-Scope Service, Supply and R&D Contracts (e.g. grass mowing, park attendant, rest room cleaning, etc.), the Contracting Officer (KO) and local Safety and Occupational Health Office (SOHO) may allow an Abbreviated APP to be developed and submitted for acceptance.

a. The non-mandatory Abbreviated APP Form, Form A-1 (or similar) may be used to insure each area of required information has been provided.

b. This APP is a short-version APP that can be used on low-risk, limited-scope contracts. > *See 01.A.12.e, and Appendix A, paragraph 3.k.*

c. Each sub-contractor shall be provided a copy of the APP by the prime contractor and be required to comply with it.

3. **APP Format.** The following areas are typically addressed in an APP, but besides being job-specific, the APP shall also address any unusual or unique aspects of the contract or job for which it is written. The non-mandatory Accident Prevention Plan (APP) Checklist, Form A-2 (or similar), may be used to insure each area of required information has been provided. > *See ANSI A10.33 for multi-employer projects.*

a. Signature Sheet: Include title, signature, and phone number of the following:

   (1) Plan preparer (Qualified Person (QP), Competent Person (CP), Corporate safety staff person, QC) and their qualifications;

   (2) Plan must be approved by company/corporate officers authorized to obligate the company;

   (3) Plan concurrence (e.g., Chief of Operations, Corporate Chief of Safety, Corporate Industrial Hygienist, project manager or superintendent, project safety professional, project QC). Contractors shall provide concurrence of other applicable corporate and project personnel.

b. Background Information. List the following:

   (1) Contractor;

   (2) Contract number;

   (3) Project name;

   (4) Brief project description, description of work to be performed, location (map), equipment to be used, anticipated high risk activities, and

   (5) Major phases of work anticipated.

   (6) Within these major phases of work identified, activities [includes Definable features of Work (DFOWs) and tasks] to be performed that will require an AHA shall be specifically highlighted. This information can then be used by QC, QA and Safety personnel to track AHA submittals. The AHAs for these activities, tasks of DFOWs are NOT submitted at this time (AHAs created/submitted at this time would not be activity- specific as they are intended to be). > *See Sections 01.A.14 and 01.A.15.*

c. Statement of Safety and Health Policy. Provide a copy of current corporate/company Safety and Health Policy Statement, detailing commitment to providing a safe and healthful workplace for all employees. The Contractor's written safety program goals, objectives, and accident experience goals for this contract shall also be provided.

d. Responsibilities and Lines of Authority. Provide the following:

   (1) A statement of the employer's ultimate responsibility for the implementation of his SOH program for his own employees, all sub-contractors

and all others on the worksite (includes the strict enforcement of the program).

(2) Identification and accountability of personnel responsible for safety at both corporate and project level. Contracts specifically requiring safety or industrial hygiene personnel shall include a copy of their resumes. Qualifications shall be in accordance with Section 01.A.17.

➤*Note: Only official OSHA 30-Hour cards will be accepted or, if equivalent training is provided, appropriate instructor qualifications. > See also Section 01.A.17.i, Exception 2.*

(3) If equivalent training to the OSHA 30-hour classes is being presented as qualification, the training shall have covered the following areas:

(a) OSH Act/General Duty Clause;

(b) 29 CFR 1904, Recordkeeping;

(c) Subparts C, CC, D, E, F, K and M of OSHA;

(d) Rigging, load handling equipment (LHE), welding and cutting, scaffolding, excavations, concrete and masonry, demolition, health hazards in construction, materials handling, storage and disposal, hand and power tools, motor vehicles, mechanized equipment, marine operations, steel erection, stairways and ladders, confined spaces or any others that are applicable to the work being performed;

(4) The names of CP(s) and/or QP(s) and proof of competency/qualification to meet specific OSHA CP/QP requirements must be attached. The local SOHO will review the qualifications for acceptance;

(5) Requirements and details of the employer's Risk Management Process;

➤*Note: USACE uses the Activity Hazard Analysis (AHA) as part of a total risk management process. Contractors and other individual employer's may use the AHAs or their own version [Job Safety Analyses (JSAs), Job Hazard Analyses (JHAs), or similar Risk Management assessment tools]. These documents are considered equivalent to, and acceptable substitutes for, the USACE's AHA provided the data collected is the same as that required by the AHA.*

(6) Requirements for initial activity-specific AHAs to be submitted and accepted at preparatory meetings, prior to work being performed;

(7) Requirements that no work by the Contractor

shall be performed unless a designated CP/SSHO is present on the job site;

(8) Policies and procedures regarding non-compliance with safety requirements (to include disciplinary actions for violation of safety requirements) should be identified;

(9) Lines of authority;

(10) Provide written company procedures for holding managers and supervisors accountable for safety.

e. Subcontractors and Suppliers. If applicable, provide procedures for coordinating SOH activities with other employers on the job site:

(1) Identification of subcontractors and suppliers. If not known at the time of initial APP submittal, the contractor shall include the following statement in their initial APP: "The subcontractors for the following DFOWs/activities are not known at this time, but additional information will be submitted to the APP for acceptance prior to the start of any activities listed";

(2) Safety responsibilities of subcontractors and suppliers.

f. Training.

(1) Requirements for new hire SOH orientation training at the time of initial hire of each new employee.

(2) Requirements for mandatory training and certifications that are applicable to this project (e.g. explosive actuated tools, confined space entry, crane operator, underwater diver, vehicle operator, HAZWOPER training and certification, PPE, etc.) and any requirements for periodic retraining/recertification.

(3) Procedures for periodic safety and health training for supervisors and employees.

(4) Requirements for emergency response training.

g. Safety and Health Inspections.

(1) Specific assignment of responsibilities for a minimum daily jobsite SOH inspection during periods of work activity: Who will conduct (e.g., SSHO, PM, QC, supervisors, employees – depends on level of technical proficiency needed to perform said inspections), proof of inspector's training/qualifications, when inspections will be conducted, procedures for documentation, deficiency tracking system, and follow-up

procedures;

(2) Any external inspections/certifications that may be required (e.g. USCG).

h. Mishap Reporting and Investigation. The Contractor shall identify means to provide the following:

(1) Exposure data (man-hours worked);

(2) Mishap reports, investigations, and documentation. Report all accidents per the requirements covered in Section 01.D. Mishaps shall be reported as soon as possible but not more than 24 hours afterwards to the KO/COR. The contractor shall report, thoroughly investigate, and analyze all mishaps occurring incidentally to an operation, project or facility for which this manual is applicable. Implement corrective actions as soon as reasonably possible and provide notice to the KO/COR when corrective actions are completed;

i. Plans, Programs and Procedures, required by this manual. Based on a risk assessment of contracted activities and on mandatory OSHA compliance programs, the Contractor shall address all applicable SOH risks and associated compliance plans.

(1) Include a project-specific compliance plan, as applicable to the work being performed, and as identified below. The plans shall incorporate project-wide procedures to control hazards to which the employees of all project employers may be exposed.

(2) These procedures shall be coordinated with all project employers and shall include project-specific, project-wide emergency response and evacuation procedures, PPE requirements, recordkeeping and reporting requirements, and training requirements.

(3) The plans shall be prepared prior to the start of any work activities on the job site (as much as the information can be known at that point in time). The plans shall be updated throughout the life of the project to include changes in personnel, equipment, conditions, etc. Additional revisions shall be incorporated as necessary to reflect changing site conditions, construction methods, personnel roles and responsibilities and construction schedules.

(4) No activity (DFOW) shall be started on site until the APP is revised and submitted to the GDA for acceptance, with the site-specific plans, programs and procedures required to complete the project. Using the EM 385-1-1 as a guide, plans, programs, procedures (assessments and evaluations) may include but not be limited to:

- Fatigue Management Plan (01.A.20);

- Emergency Plans (01.E);

- Site Sanitation/Housekeeping Plan (02.B);

- Medical Support Agreement (03.A.01; 03.A.03);

- Blood-borne Pathogen Program (03.A.05);

- Exposure Control Plan (03.A.05);

- Automatic External Defibrillator (AED) Program (03.B.04);

- Site Layout Plan (04.A);

- Access/Haul Road Plan (04.B);

- Hearing Conservation Program (05.C);

- Respiratory Protection Plan (05.G);

- Health Hazard Control Program (06.A);

- Hazard Communication Program (06.B.01);

- Process Safety Management Program (06.B.04);

- Lead Compliance Plan (06.C.02 & specifications);

- Asbestos Abatement Plan (06.C.03 & specifications);

- Radiation Safety Program (06.F);

- Abrasive Blasting Procedures (06.I.01);
- Heat Stress Monitoring Plan (HSMP) (06.J.02);

- Cold Stress Monitoring Plan (CSMP) (06.J.04)

- Indoor Air Quality Management (06.L);

- Mold remediation Plan (06.L.04);

- Chromium (VI) Exposure Evaluation (06.M);

- Crystalline Silica Evaluation (06.N.02);

- Lighting Plan for Night Operations (07.A.06);

- Traffic Control Plan (08.C.05);
- Fire Prevention Plan (09.A.01);

- Wild Land Fire Management Plan (09.L);

- Arc Flash Hazard Analysis (11.B);

- Assured Equipment Grounding Control Program (AEGCP) (11.D.05, Appendix E);

- Hazardous Energy Control Program & Procedures (12.A.01);

- Standard Pre-Lift Plan–Load Handling Equipment (16.A.03);

- Critical Lift Plan – <u>Load Handling Equipment</u> (16.H);

- Naval Architectural Analysis – Load Handling Equipment (Floating) (16.L);

- <u>Floating Plant Inspection and Certification (19.A.01)</u>;

- <u>Severe Weather Plan for Marine Activities</u> (19.A.03);

- <u>Emergency Plan for Marine Activities (19.A.04)</u>;

- Man overboard/Abandon Ship <u>Procedures</u> (19.A.04);

- Float Plan for <u>Launches, Motorboats, and Skiffs</u> (19.F.04);

- Fall Protection and Prevention Plan (21.D);

- Demolition/<u>Renovation</u> Plan (to include engineering survey) (23.A);

- <u>Rope Access Work Plan (24.H)</u>;

- Excavation/Trenching Plan (25.A.01);

- Fire Prevention and Protection Plan for Underground construction (26.D.01);

- Compressed Air <u>Work</u> Plan <u>for Underground Construction</u> (26.I.01);

- Erection and Removal plan for Formwork and Shoring (27.C);

- PreCast Concrete Plan (27.D.01);

- Lift-Slab Plans (27.E);

- Masonry Bracing Plan (27.<u>F</u>.01);

- Steel Erection Plan (<u>28.B</u>);

- <u>Explosives Safety Site Plan (ESSP) (29.A)</u>;

- Blasting Plan (29.A; <u>26.J</u>);

- Dive Operations Plan (30.A.<u>14</u>, 30.A.<u>16</u>);

- <u>Safe Practices Manual for Diving Activities (30.A.15)</u>

- <u>Emergency Management Plan for Diving (30.A.18)</u>

- Tree Felling and Maintenance Program (31.A.01);

- <u>Aircraft/Airfield Construction Safety & Phasing Plan (CSPP) (32.A.02)</u>;

- <u>Aircraft/Airfield Safety Plan Compliance Document (SPCD) (32.A.02)</u>;

- Site Safety and Health Plan for HTRW (<u>33</u>.B);
- <u>Confined Space Entry Procedures (34.A.05);</u>
- Confined Space Program (34.A.06).

j. Risk Management Process (AHAs). Detailed project-specific hazards and controls shall be provided by AHAs for each activity <u>(DFOW). No work will begin on an activity (DFOW) until the initial AHA has been accepted by the GDA addressing the project-specific hazards. > See Section 01.A.14 and 01.A.15.</u>

➤*Note: USACE uses the Activity Hazard Analysis (AHA) as part of a total risk management process. Contractors and other individual employer's may use the AHAs or their own version [Job Safety Analyses (JSAs), Job Hazard Analyses (JHAs), or similar Risk Management assessment tools]. These documents are considered equivalent to, and acceptable substitutes for, the USACE's AHA provided the data collected is the same as that required by the AHA.*

(1) <u>The AHA defines the work sequence, anticipated hazards, conditions, equipment, materials, personnel and the control measures to be implemented to eliminate or reduce each hazard to an acceptable level of risk, and the Risk Assessment Code for each step.</u>

(2) <u>Once this process has occurred, an overall RAC shall be assigned to the activity, based on the highest RAC assigned to an individual step.</u>

(3) <u>Acceptance of risk. The residual risk is that which remains after controls have been applied. This residual risk must be communicated to the proper authority for acceptance in order to proceed with the activity.</u>

(4) <u>Before beginning each work activity/DFOW, the *Contractor performing that work activity* shall prepare the initial AHA, which will include a RAC for that activity.</u>

(5) <u>No work will begin on the activity until the initial AHA has been accepted by the GDA addressing the activity-specific hazards.</u>

(6) <u>AHA's are intended to be created by the contractor field crews/workers performing the work, with the assistance of others (SSHO, QC, Superintendent, etc) as needed. They are living documents and are intended to be created in the field and updated (by the workers) as needed.</u>

(7) <u>The AHA shall be reviewed and modified as necessary to address changing site conditions, operations, or change of CP(s)/QP(s).</u>

(a) If a new CP/QP (not on the original list) is added, the list shall be updated (an administrative action not requiring an updated AHA). The new person shall acknowledge in writing that he or she has reviewed the AHA and is familiar with current site safety issues.

(b) If the initial RAC increases due to a change made to the AHA by the workers, the AHA shall be resubmitted to GDA for acceptance prior to work proceeding.

(c) Changes to or updates of an AHA that do not increase the RAC are not required to be resubmitted for acceptance by the GDA.

(8) Workers/crews shall have in their possession the current AHA that reflects current site conditions, personnel, equipment, control measures, etc while the work is being performed.

(9) The AHA shall be used by the contractor and USACE personnel to assure work is being performed consistent with the AHA. In the event that the work is not being conducted in a safe manner, the contractor and/or the USACE shall stop the unsafe work being conducted until it is in compliance with this manual, APP and the AHA or the APP/ AHA is revised and accepted by the GDA, if necessary. > *See Section 01.A.14.*

(10) Once the activity has been completed, the AHA shall be available and kept on file on site for the length of the contract.

k. Abbreviated APP for Limited-Scope Service, Supply And R&D Contracts. If service, supply and R&D contracts with limited-scopes are awarded, the contractor may submit an abbreviated APP in lieu of a full APP. The abbreviated APP shall address the following areas at a minimum. If other areas of the EM 385-1-1 are pertinent to the contract, the contractor must assure these areas are addressed as well. The non-mandatory Abbreviated APP Form, Form A-01 (or similar) may be used to insure each area of required information has been provided.

(1) Title, signature, and phone number of the plan preparer.

(2) Background Information to include:
  (a) Contractor;
  (b) Contract number;
  (c) Project name;
  (d) Brief project description,

➢*Note: The project description shall provide a means to evaluate the work being done (see AHA requirements in 01.A.14), associated hazards*

involved *and a RAC assigned to each. The overall RAC for the activity must be determined (based on highest task RAC) and accepted at the appropriate level in order for work to proceed.*

  (e) Description of work to be performed, and
  (f) Location of work being performed, to include a map.

(3) Statement of Safety and Health Policy detailing their commitment to providing a safe and healthful workplace for all employees.

(4) Responsibilities and Lines of Authorities – to include a statement of the employer's ultimate responsibility for the implementation of his SOH program; Identification and accountability of personnel responsible for safety at all levels to include designated site safety and health officer (SSHO) and associated qualifications. The District SOHO will be asked to review the qualifications for acceptance.

(5) Training - new hire SOH orientation training at the time of initial hire of each new employee and any periodic retraining/recertification requirements.

(6) Procedures for job site inspections - assignment of responsibilities and frequency.

(7) Procedures for reporting man-hours worked and reporting and investigating any mishaps required by Section 01.D.

(8) Emergency Planning. Employees working alone shall be provided an effective means of emergency communication. This may be cellular phone, two-way radio or other acceptable means. The selected means of communication must be readily available and must be in working condition.

(9) Drinking Water provisions, toilet and washing facilities.

(10) First Aid and CPR training (at least two employees on each shift shall be qualified/certified to administer first aid and CPR) and provision of first aid kits (types/size).

(11) Personal Protective Equipment (PPE).

  (a) Work Clothing - Minimum Requirements. Employees shall wear clothing suitable for the weather however minimum requirements for work shall be short-sleeve shirt, long pants (excessively long or baggy pants are prohibited) and leather work shoes. If analysis determines that safety-toed (or other protective) footwear is necessary (i.e., mowing, weedeating, chainsaw use, etc), they shall be worn.

(b) Eye and Face Protection. Eye and face protection shall be worn as determined by an analysis of the operations being performed, however, all involved in chainsaw use, chipping, stump grinding, pruning operations, grass mowing, weedeating and blowing operations shall be provided safety eyewear (Z87.1) as a minimum.

(c) Hearing Protection. Hearing protection must be worn by all those exposed to high noise activities (to include grass mowing and trimming, chainsaw operations, tree chipping, stump grinding and pruning).

(d) Head Protection. Hard hats shall comply with ANSI Z89.1 and shall be worn by all workers when a head hazard exists, per Section 05.D.

(e) High Visibility Apparel shall comply with ANSI/ISEA 107, Class 2 requirements at a minimum and shall be worn by all workers exposed to vehicular or equipment traffic.

(f) Protective Leg chaps shall be worn by all chainsaw operators.

(g) Gloves of the proper type shall be worn by persons involved in activities that expose the hands to cuts, abrasions, punctures, burns and chemical irritants.

(h) If work is being performed around water and drowning is a hazard, PFDs must be provided and worn as appropriate.

(12) Machine Guards and safety devices. Power tools/equipment must have appropriate guards and safety devices in place and operational.

(13) Hazardous Substances. When any hazardous substances are procured, used, stored or disposed, a Hazard Communication Program must be in place and MSDSs (SDSs) shall be available at the worksite. Employees shall have received training in hazardous substances being used. When the eyes or body of any person may be exposed to corrosives, irritants or toxic chemicals, suitable facilities for quick drenching or flushing of the eyes and body shall be provided within 10 seconds of the worksite.

(14) Traffic control shall be accomplished in accordance with DOT's MUTCD.

(15) Control of Hazardous Energy (Lockout/ Tagout). Before an employee performs any servicing or maintenance on any equipment where the unexpected energizing or startup of the equipment could occur, procedures must be in place to ensure adequate control of this energy. *> See Section 12.*

(16) High hazard activities should not be encountered on these types of jobs. If they are (i.e., driving/operating equipment on slopes, working from/in boats, etc), a determination shall be made by the KO and local SOH Office as to whether an abbreviated APP is applicable. If so, they shall be fully addressed in the APP. AHAs are required on work activities which include high hazard activities.

U.S.Army Corps of Engineers
Safety Inspection Checklist
Abbreviated Accident Prevention Plan

Date of Inspection

Location (Plant or Facility)	Contract Number
Contractor Name	Project Name
Inspector Name (Print)	Inspector Signature

This checklist serves as a guide only. It does not replace or eliminate the need to comply with the requirements set forth in Engineering Manual 385-1-1, Safety and Health Requirements Manual, dated XX September 2014.The references included In this checklist correspond to the applicablesections of EM 385-1-1.

If service, supply and R&D contracts with limited scopes are awarded, the contractor may submit an abbreviated Accident Prevention Plan. This APP shall address the following areas at a minimum. If other areas of the EM 385-1-1 are pertinent to the contract, the contractor must assure these areas are addressed as well.

Item Description	Yes	No	N/A	Remarks (Any NO or N/A Item)
. Signature sheet				
. Includes the name, signature, and title of the Plan Preparer (Qualmed person, i.e. corporate safety staff person, QC)				
. Includes the name, signature,and tiUe of the Plan Approver {e.g. owner, company president, regional vice presiden				
. Includes the name{s), signature(s), and title{s) for Plan concurrence (provide concurrence of other applicable corporate and project personnel(contractor))				
.Background information				
. Includes the Contractor Name.				
. Includes the Contract Number.				
. Includes the Project Name.				
. Includes the Brief Project Description.				
. Includes the Location of the Project {map).				
. Includes a means to evaluate the work being done (see AHA requirements in 01.A.13) and associated hazards involved.				
. Addresses the identified hazards involved and the control measures to be taken.				
. Statement of Safety and Health Policy detailing their commitment providing a safe and healthfulworkplace for all employees.				
Responsibilities and Lines of Authorities				
Includes the identification and job responsibilities of personnel responsible for safety - at both corporate and project level - including their resumes.				
Includes the lines of authority.				
Training- new hire SOH orientation training at the time of initial hire of each new employee and any periodic retraining/recertification requirements				
Procedures for job site inspections - assignment of responsibilities and frequency				

ESO Checklist A-01,Sep 14

U.S.Army Corps of Engineers
Safety Inspection Checklist
Abbreviated Accident Prevention Plan

Item Description	Yes	No	N/A	Remarks (Any NO or N/A item)
7.Procedures for reporting man-hours worked and reporting and investigating any accidents as soon as possible but not more than 24 hours afterwards to the Contracting Officer/Representative (CO/COR)				
8.Emergency Planning. Employees working alone shall be provided an effective means of emergency communication. This may be cellular phone, two-way radio or other acceptable means. The selected means of communication must be readily available and must be in working condition.				
9.Drinking Water provisions, toilet and washing facilities.				
10.First Aid and CPR training (at least two employees on each shift shall be qualified/certified to administer first aid and CPR) and provision *of* first aid kit (types/size).				
11.Personal Protective Equipment				
a. Work Clothing - Minimum Requirements. Employees to wear clothing suitable for the weather; minimum requirements for work shall be short-sleeve shirt, long pants (excessively long or baggy pants are prohibited) and leather work shoes. If AHA determines safety-toed (or other protective) footwear is necessary (i.e., mowing, weed eating, chain saw use, etc), they shall be wom.				
b.Eye and Face Protection. Eye and face protection shall be worn as determined by an analysis of the operations being performed HOWEVER, all involved in chain saw use, chipping,stump grinding, pruning operations, grass mowing, weed eating and blowing operations shall be provided safety eyewear (Z87.1) as a minimum.				
c. Hearing Protection. Hearing protection must be worn by all exposed to high noise activities {includes grass mowing/trimming, chainsaw operations, tree chipping, stump grinding and pruning)				
d.Head Protection. Hard hats shall comply with ANSIZ89.1 and shall be wom by all workers when a head hazard exists. At a minimum, hard hats shall be worn when performing activities identified in {b) above				
e.High Visibility Apparel shall comply with ANSI/ISEA 107, Class 2 requirements at a minimum and shall be worn by all workers exposed to vehicular or equipment traffic.				
f.Protective Leg chaps shall be wom by all chainsaw operators.				
g. Gloves of the proper type shall be worn by persons involved in activities that expose the hands to cuts,abrasions, punctures, bums and chemicalirritants.				
h. If work is being performed around water and drowning is a hazard, PFD's must be provided and worn as appropriate.				
12.Machine Guards and safety devices. Lawn maintenance equipment must have appropriate guards and safety devices in place and operational.				

CESO Checklist A-01,Sep 14

U.S.Army Corps of Engineers
Safety Inspection Checklist
Abbreviated Accident Prevention Plan

Date of Inspection

Item Description	Yes	No	N/A	Remarks (Any NO or N/A Item)
3. Hazardous Substances. When any hazardous substances are rocured, used, stored or disposed, a hazard communication rogram must be in effect and MSDSs shall be available at the orksite. Employees shall have received training in hazardous ubstances being used. When the eyes or body of any person may e exposed to corrosives, irritants or toxic chemicals, suitable acilities for quick drenching or flushing of the eyes and body shall be rovided within 10 seconds of the worksite.				
4. Traffic control shall be accomplished in accordance with DOrs 1UTCD.				
5. Control of Hazardous Energy (Lockout/Tagout). Before an mployee perfonns any servicing or maintenance on any equipment here the unexpected unergizing or startup of the equipment could ccur, procedures must be in place to ensure adequate control of				
6. Driving, working on (i.e., working with equipmenUmowers) while n slopes, working from/in boats/skiffs, etc shall also be considered nd dealt with accordingly.				

ther Remarks

Form A-02
U.S. Army Corps of Engineers
Accident Prevention Plan Checklist

Date of Inspection	

Location (Plant or Facility)	Contract Number
Contractor Name	Project Name
Inspector Name (Print)	Inspector Signature

This checklist serves as a guide only, it does not replace or eliminate the need to comply with the requirements set forth in Engineering Manual 385-1-1, Safety and Health Requirements Manual, dated XX Sept 2014. The references included in this checklist correspond to the applicable sections of EM 385-1-1.

Item Description	Yes	No	N/A	Remarks (Any NO or N/A item)
1. Signature sheet				
a. Includes the name, signature, and title of the Plan Preparer (*Qualified person, i.e. corporate safety staff person, QC*)				
b. Includes the name, signature, and title of the Plan Approver (*e.g. owner, company president, regional vice president*) (HTRW activities require approval of a Certified Industrial Hygienist, a Certified Safety Professional may approve the plan for operations involving UST removal where contaminants are known to be petroleum, oils, or lubricants).				
c. Includes the name(s), signature(s), and title(s) for Plan Concurrence (provide concurrence of other applicable corporate and project personnel (contractor)) (*e.g. Chief of Operations, Corporate Chief of Safety, Corporate Industrial Hygienist, project manager or superintendent, project safety professional, project QC.*)				
2. Background information				
a. Includes the Contractor Name.				
b. Includes the Contract Number.				
c. Includes the Project Name.				
d. Includes the Brief Project Description.				
e. Includes the Location of the Project (map).				
f. Includes the Contractor Accident Experience (*Copy of OSHA 300*				
g. Includes the Listing of Phases of Work and Hazardous Activities Requiring an Activity Hazard Analyses (AHA).				
3. Statement of Safety and Health Policy. Includes a copy of the corporate safety policy. (*In addition to the corporate policy statement, a copy of the corporate safety program may provide a portion of the information required by the accident prevention*				
4. Responsibilities and Lines of Authorities				
a. Includes the identification and job responsibilities of personnel responsible for safety - at both corporate and project level – including their resumes.				
b. Includes the lines of authority.				

CESO Form A-02 Sep 13

Form A-02
U.S. Army Corps of Engineers
Accident Prevention Plan Checklist (cont'd)

Date of Inspection

Item Description	Yes	No	N/A	Remarks (Any NO or N/A item)
. Training				
. Includes the list of subjects to be discussed with employees at afety indoctrination.				
. Includes the list of mandatory training and certifications pplicable to this project (*e.g., explosive actuated tools, confined pace entry, crane operator, diver, vehicle operator, HAZWOPER aining and certification, PPE*) and any requirements for periodic etraining / recertification.				
. Includes the identity requirements for emergency response aining.				
. Includes the outline requirements (*who attends, when given, ho will conduct, etc.*) for supervisory and employee safety				
. Safety and Health Inspections				
. Includes the name(s) of individual(s) responsible for conducting afety inspections. (*e.g., PM, safety professional, QC, supervisors, mployees*)				
Includes proof of inspector's training / qualifications.				
Indicates when inspections will be conducted.				
Furnished sample forms upon which inspections will be corded.				
Indicates deficiency tracking system and follow-up procedures.				
Includes the names of competent and / or qualified person(s) nd proof of competency / qualification to meet specific OSHA ompetent / qualified person(s) requirements.				
Includes any external inspections / certifications which may be quired. (*e.g., US Coast Guard*)				
Safety and Health Expectations, Incentive Programs, and ompliance				
Includes the company's written safety program goals, objectives, nd accident experience goals.				
Includes a brief description of the company's safety incentive ograms (*if any*).				
Includes the policies and procedures regarding noncompliance ith safety requirements (to include disciplinary actions for olation of safety requirements).				
Includes the written company procedures for holding managers nd supervisors accountable for safety.				
Mishap Reporting				
The plan identifies how, when, and who shall complete the xposure data (man-hours worked).				
The plan identifies how, when, and who shall complete mishap vestigations, reports, and logs.				
The plan identifies how, when, and who shall make immediate otification of major mishaps.				

ESO Form A-02 Sep 13

Based on a risk assessment of contracted activities and on mandatory OSHA compliance programs, the Contractor shall address all applicable occupational risks and compliance plans. Using the EM 385-1-1 as a guide, plans may include but not be limited to:

Item Description	Yes	No	N/A	Remarks (Any NO or N/A item)
9. Plans (Programs, Procedures) required by the Safety Manual				
a. Fatigue Management Plan (01.A.20)				
b. Emergency response plans:				
(1) Procedures & Test (01.E.01)				
(2) Spill Plans (01.E.01, 06.A.02)				
(3) Fire Fighting Plan (01.E.01; 19.A)				
(4) Posting of Emergency Telephone Numbers (01.E.05)				
(5) Man overboard/abandon ship (19.A.04)				
(6) Medical Support. Outline on-site medical support and off-site medical arrangements including rescue and medical duties for those employees who are to perform them, and the name(s) of on-site Contractor personnel trained in first aid and CPR. A minimum of two employees shall be certified in CPR and first-aid per shift/site (Section 03.A; 03.D)				
c. Plan for prevention of alcohol and drug abuse (01.C.02)				
d. Site Sanitation Plan (Section 02.B)				
e. Medical Support Plan, (03.A.01; 03.A.06; 03.D)				
f. Bloodborne Pathogen Plan (03.A.05)				
g. Exposure Control Plan (03.A.05)				
h. Site Layout Plan (04.A)				
i. Access/Haul road Plan (04.B)				
j. Hearing Conservation Program (05.C)				
k. Respiratory Protection Plan (05.G)				
l. Health Hazard Control Program (06.A)				
m. Process Safety Management Plan (06.B.04)				
n. Lead Abatement Plan (06.C & Specs)				
o. Asbestos Abatement Plan (06.C & Specs)				
p. Radiation Safety Program (06.F)				
q. Abrasive Blasting Plan (06.I)				
r. Heat/Cold Stress Monitoring Plan (06.J)				
s. Indoor Air Quality Management Plan (06.L)				
t. Mole Remediation Plan (06.L.04)				
u. Chromium (VI) Exposure Evaluation (06.M)				
v. Crystalline Silica Assessment (06.N)				
w. Lighting Evaluation (07.A)				
x. Lighting Plan for Night Operations (07.A.09)				

Form A-02
U.S. Army Corps of Engineers
Accident Prevention Plan Checklist (cont'd)

Date of Inspection

Based on a risk assessment of contracted activities and on mandatory OSHA compliance programs, the Contractor shall address all applicable occupational risks and compliance plans. Using the EM 385-1-1 as a guide, plans may include but not be limited to:

Item Description	Yes	No	N/A	Remarks (Any NO or N/A item)
. Plans (Programs, Procedures) continued.				
. Traffic Control Plan (08.C.05)				
. Fire Prevention Plan (09.A.01)				
a. Wild Land Fire Management Plan (09.L)				
b. Arc Flash Hazard Analysis (11.B)				
c. Assured Equipment Grounding Control Program (AEGCP), 11.D.05, App D)				
d. Hazardous Energy Control Plan, (12.A.01)				
e. Standard Pre-Lift Plan (LHE) (16.A.03, 16.L.15)				
. Critical Lift Plan – LHE (16.H)				
g. Naval Architectural Analysis (16.L)				
h. Contingency Plan for Severe Weather (19.A.03)				
. Man Overboard/Abandon Ship (19.A.04)				
. Float Plan (19.F.04)				
k. Fall Protection Program, (21.D);				
. Demolition/Renovation Plan (to include engineering survey), 23.A.02)				
m. Rope Access Program, (24.H.02)				
n. Excavation/Trenching Plan, (25.A.01)				
o. Underground construction fire prevention and protection Plan, 26.D.01)				
p. Compressed Air Plan, (26.I.01)				
q. Formwork and Shoring Erection and Removal plan, (27.C)				
. PreCast Concrete Plan, (27.D)				
s Lift. slab plans, (27.E)				
. Masonry Bracing Plan, (27.F.01)				
u. Steel Erection Plan, (28.B)				
v. Explosives Safety Site Plan (ESSP) (29.A)				
w. Blasting Plan, (29.A; 26.J)				
x. Underwater Dive Operations Plan, (30.A.14, 16,)				
y. Tree Felling/Maintenance Program, (31.A)				
z. Aircraft/Airfield Construction Safety & Phasing Plan, (32.A.02)				
aa. Site Safety and Health Plan (HTRW), (33.B)				
bb. Confined Space Entry Program, (34.A.06, 07)				
. Risk Management Processes. Detailed project-specific azards hall be identified and controls provided via Activity Hazard				

ESO Form A-02 Sep 13

Other Remarks:

CESO Form A-02 Sep 13

APPENDIX B Emergency Operations

1. Safety and Health Requirements. During emergency operations, it is extremely important that safety and occupational health (SOH) requirements are implemented. Personnel often perform unusual, difficult, hazardous tasks while in a challenging environment, and these conditions may increase risk and the potential for accidents. Additionally, resources are in short supply, and the loss of any resource to a mishap reduces the USACE ability to respond.

a. The SOH of USACE employees, Contractors, and members of the public exposed to USACE activities will be a primary concern during all USACE emergency operations. SOH Offices (SOHO) shall provide the necessary input to their Emergency Management counterparts to ensure that planning for SOH concerns (including hazard and risk analysis) is addressed prior to and during emergency operations.

b. Contract Requirements. SOH program requirements shall be included in all Government and contract operations. FAR Clause 52.236-13 shall be included in contracts and memoranda of agreement/understanding (MOAs/MOUs) for emergency operations and recovery assistance.

c. Accident Prevention Plan (APP) and Activity Hazard Analyses (AHAs). In addition to the APP already submitted by the Controlling Contractor, activity-specific AHAs shall be developed and submitted to the on-site USACE SOH professional for review and acceptance prior to beginning any operation (debris removal, tree removal, blue-roof activities, leaners and hangers, etc.). Once accepted, the AHA is considered a living/field document that is intended to be updated in the field by the field crews so that it constantly reflects current equipment, personnel, conditions, PPE, etc. GDA acceptance of changes made to an AHA is not necessary as long as changes do not increase original risk assessment code (RAC) level for the activity, as long as requirements are being met and a copy is made available upon request.

d. Structural Demolition. For structural demolition activities, consideration shall be given to combine like-structures under a common engineering survey and demolition plan, see Section 23.A.01.a. For example, single-story residential structures that would pose no hazards to neighboring structures or personnel could be demolished using a common engineering survey and demolition plan, whereas multiple-story structures or others that would pose risks to personnel or other structures would have individual surveys and plans per Section 23.A.01.

2. Initial Response. A qualified SOH professional shall be immediately alerted of the disaster and shall be included in the planning and execution of response and recovery efforts. This individual shall assess SOH issues and shall assure precautions are taken prior to deployment of personnel. Issues to consider include: sanitation, drinking water, power supply, living quarters, driving conditions, environmental conditions, and health issues.

3. Staffing. SOHO in the Geographic District experiencing the disaster will be temporarily staffed with additional safety, industrial hygiene, and medical personnel as necessary to ensure a comprehensive SOH program is administered for all emergency operations. If a Recovery Field Office (RFO) is established, SOH staffing is usually accomplished by use of SOH functional planning and response teams (PRT). If a RFO is not established, the Geographic District shall establish an emergency operations safety office (minimum staffing to include a safety manager and administrative support person) dedicated totally to emergency operations. Also, each Emergency Field Office established shall have a minimum of one SOH professional.

a. Medical personnel shall provide medical assistance, assessments, and advice to USACE management and employees.

b. SOH personnel shall: manage safety and health aspects of emergency operations; provide advice on SOH issues; provide SOH technical oversight for USACE employees, other Federal employees engaged in fulfilling the Corps' mission, and quality assurance for Contractor employees.

c. Prime Contractors for emergency operations are required to have as a minimum a full-time, qualified SOH professional on-site. Qualifications of the SOH professional shall be provided to the GDA for review and acceptance. Additional Contractor personnel may be required as determined by the GDA.

4. Qualifications of Government Employees.

a. All Government employees reporting for emergency recovery operations shall meet the medical requirements in the current All Hazards OPORD (currently 2012-11) and shall have a current medical clearance in ENGLink. This requirement shall be confirmed upon arrival during the check-in process.

b. Employees with known pre-existing non-work-related medical conditions such as uncontrolled diabetes, cardiovascular or pulmonary problems, back conditions, pregnancy or hypertension shall not deploy to emergency operations sites unless specific medical clearance is provided by the USACE medical provider in conjunction with their personal physician(s) indicating their current medical condition will not jeopardize their health or their ability to fully perform their duty assignments at deployment sites.

c. Employees may be returned to their duty station if during the course of duty they experience health problems that may endanger their well-being.

d. Employees shall be notified that pharmacies and medical services may be limited at the emergency operations site.

5. Mobilization of USACE Personnel. USACE personnel will be provided the following prior to departing their <u>home</u> duty station for emergency operations:

a. PPE <u>consisting of, at a minimum</u>, head, eye and foot protection appropriate for the hazards of the field activities that they will perform <u>(additional PPE that may be necessary will be provided at the emergency operations site)</u>, and

b. Immunizations appropriate for their field exposure (follow-up immunizations will be the responsibility of each employee's home duty station). Deploying USACE personnel shall <u>obtain the immunizations as required by the current All Hazards OPORD. The USACE personnel will </u>update their immunization data in ENGLink before departing their home station, <u>provide a copy to a USACE nurse for verification</u>, and carry with them their immunization record (USPHS Form 731) <u>or immunization record</u> which provides, type of immunization with lot and manufacture, date of immunization, and name and credential of provider.

6. Safety Orientation. SOH in-briefings and orientation shall be conducted as personnel arrive at the emergency area and prior to beginning work activities.

7. Communications.

a. Two-way radios, cellular phones, computers <u>and</u> facsimile machines shall be used as needed to establish and enhance communications. > *See Section 18.C.01.*

b. SOH programs, documents, signs, tags, instructions, etc., shall be communicated to employees and the public in a language they understand.

8. Duty Schedule.

a. During the first 2 weeks of an emergency response operation extended work hours are allowed. Supervisors shall monitor employees for signs of stress-related health problems and seek medical assistance as appropriate.

b. For operations lasting longer than 2 weeks, USACE and contractor employees shall not work in excess of 84 hours per week. The duty hours an employee would be required to work during emergency operations are 12 hours per day, 7 days a week. Work and travel time must allow for 8 hours continuous rest between each work shift.

c. Employees <u>who are working 12 hours per day, 7 days a week </u>shall be provided the opportunity for 24 hours of rest after working 14 days and 48 hours of rest after working 21 days. Employees shall be required to take at least 24 hours off for rest after a continuous <u>30-</u>day period of work <u>during normal non-duty days (Saturday or Sunday)</u> and shall be required to take at least 24 hours every 2 weeks thereafter. Supervisors shall monitor employees for signs of stress-related health problems and seek medical assistance as appropriate.

9. Machinery and Mechanized Equipment.

> *See Sections 16 and 18.*

a. Inspection of equipment is critical as mobilization can be extremely short and equipment may not be up to USACE safety standards. Whenever feasible, contract specifications shall provide adequate mobilization time to allow equipment to be inspected and brought up to USACE standards. Equipment not meeting the requirements of this manual will not be used.

b. Trucks hauling debris on public highways shall have physical barriers (covers and either tail gates or chain link fencing) to preclude debris from falling from the truck. <u>Tail gates or chain link fencing shall cover the full area at the rear of the dump body.</u>

(1) Back-up alarms shall be provided.

(2) The need for rollover warning devices shall be considered for long-bed end dump trucks.

(3) Sideboards shall not be added to trucks to increase their capacity unless specific design specifications are provided to Contractors as part of the scope of work. Single or double boards added to trailers designed for normal operation with the additional boards are permitted. <u>Where sideboards</u>

are permitted, the tail gate or chain link fencing shall extend to cover the full area of the rear of the vehicle.

(4) Trees, to include leaners and hangers, shall be cut into manageable size to place in the bed of a truck. All loads shall be secured so that any debris, dust-like emission, aggregate (gravel), soil, or stump cannot be ejected during transport to the final reduction site. After final reduction, tarping systems that prevent workers from being exposed to fall hazards greater than 6 ft (1.8 m) shall be required. All loads leaving the reduction site shall be secured and tarped.

c. Prior to operation, Contractors shall develop written safe operating procedures (SOPs) for each brush chipper, shredder, and/or grinder.

(1) SOPs shall incorporate the manufacturer's recommendations for safe operation of this equipment as well as the use of an exclusion zone (EZ) and fire prevention efforts.

(2) Operations and maintenance manuals for chippers, grinders, and shredders shall be kept on-site.

(3) A minimum 200 ft (61.0 m) EZ is required for authorized persons during operation of chippers, shredders, and grinders unless documentation or actual practice indicates otherwise. Signs shall be placed at 200 ft (61.0 m) identifying the EZ.

(4) The public shall be kept a minimum of 300 ft (91.4 m) from all chipper operations.

(5) Unauthorized personnel shall not enter the EZ while the chipper is in operation.

(6) Front-end loaders, skid steers, knuckle booms, and other equipment working in debris reduction areas or feeding grinders, shredders or chippers shall provide protection to the operator as required in Section 18.

(7) Whenever chipper operations are shut down for any significant length of time (e.g., overnight or when the chipper will be left unattended), equipment walls, crevice drums, cutter heads and hammers, and drive mechanisms shall be cleared of all combustible materials by blowing, washing, and wetting down.

(8) Any material contaminated by leakage of hydraulic fluids, oils, or fuel shall be immediately removed. Leakage shall be minimized through preventive maintenance.

(9) Because piles of chipped wood are susceptible to spontaneous combustion, fire controls such as segregation, separation, and adequate water supply shall be used.

d. The number of workers in proximity to loaders, trucks, and other equipment shall be the minimum necessary to accomplish the job.

(1) In restricted areas or areas with reduced access or visibility, special precautions will be taken to ensure the safety of workers on the ground.

(2) Sequencing of work shall minimize equipment movement when personnel are in the work area.

(3) Workers in the area of operating machinery or vehicular traffic shall wear high visibility apparel, in accordance with Section 5.F. These workers include, but are not limited to flag persons, signalpersons, spotters, survey crews and inspectors.

e. Loaders, trackhoes, and other construction equipment in debris reduction areas shall have functional lights in the front and back in order to work at night or during periods of reduced visibility.

f. Aerial Lifts/Platforms/Bucket trucks shall conform to requirements identified in Section 22.M.

g. Unless provided by the manufacturer, seat belts are not required at the operator's station on articulating grapple trucks (knuckle boom trucks). If provided by the manufacturer, seat belts are required to be worn. Access ladders shall be a minimum of 12 in (30.5 cm) width with 16 in (40.6 cm) recommended.

10. Traffic Control.

a. Traffic control is extremely important on highways, in residential areas, and at construction sites. When traffic may pose a hazard to operations, public roads will be closed. Road closings shall be coordinated in writing with appropriate local agencies. Traffic controls and signage should comply with the DOT Federal Highway Administration's *"Manual on Uniform Traffic Control Devices* (MUTCD)".

b. When a road cannot be closed, the following precautions shall be taken:

(1) "FLAGGER" (MUTCD W-20-7) or "WORKERS AHEAD" (W21-1) or similar appropriate signs shall be placed along the roadway, 1,000 ft (304.8m) and 500 ft (30.5 m) before the work zone, on both sides of the work zone;

(2) Sufficient number of flag persons shall be used to control traffic within the work area;

(3) Flag persons shall be used and shall receive instruction in flagging operations before being placed in traffic. Flagger training shall be consistent with the requirements of the MUTCD and State DOT unless the State requirements have been waived for the emergency at which point training and certification, such as provided by the National Safety Council, is recommended;

(4) All flag persons shall wear high-visibility apparel in accordance with Section 05.F, safety-toed footwear and hard hats;

(5) "STOP/SLOW" paddles, preferably mounted on a 6 ft (1.8 m) staff, will be used for traffic control;

(6) Flag persons shall be able to communicate with each other and with the foreman, and effectively signal/direct the affected public;

(7) Two-way radios shall be used whenever visual contact between flaggers is not maintained.

c. When construction vehicles and all vehicles exceeding 1-1/2 tons (1360.8kg) are required to back up, an AHA shall be developed per Section 01.A.14 that considers all potential hazards and controls to include consideration for use of a spotter.

d. Fugitive dust emissions shall be kept to a minimum within the work boundaries especially when adjacent to debris towers.

11. Debris Reduction.

a. General information.

(1) The Contractor shall notify the local fire department and arrange for fire suppression support in case of fire beyond the Contractor's firefighting capability.

(2) Adequate supplies of water or fire extinguishers shall be readily available and fire watches shall be used. A fire watch shall be present continuously at debris collection/reduction sites anytime there is reduction taking place or visible flame and when the site is not being actively worked and the potential exists for spontaneous combustion or other fire hazard. The fire watch shall have at least one 20 lb ABC fire extinguisher available and the means to expediently communicate with the site supervisor and designated fire response agencies.

(3) No hazardous or containerized ignitable material shall be co-mingled with debris.

(4) Pits may not extend within 1 ft (30.5 cm) of the ground water table. Pits shall have a compacted clay layer (or similar) on the bottom to minimize migration of ash to the aquifer.

(5) Particulate emissions must meet State and EPA standards for burning operations. The site manager must be continuously aware of wind conditions and adjust accordingly to control smoke encroachment into residential areas. Wind meters must be available on site to track wind conditions. Personnel shall work out of direct smoke streams.

(6) Eye wash facilities shall be provided at all burning and grinding operations. > See Section 06.

(7) For night operations, adequate lighting of 55 lx (5 fc) shall be provided in all outdoor work areas.

(8) Signs shall be posted at entrances to debris collection/reduction areas indicating "NOTICE: AUTHORIZED PERSONNEL ONLY" (USACE SNO-07 or ANSI equivalent).

(9) A "Danger/Keep Back" sign shall be posted at the edge of the 100 ft (31 m) setback from air curtain incinerators and open burn areas as a warning to personnel (USACE UNS01 or ANSI-equivalent).

(10) All personnel working in debris collection/reduction areas shall wear safety shoes, hard hat, safety glasses, Class II (minimum) high-visibility vest, and have hearing protection available.

(11) A minimum 30 ft (9 m) wide fire lane shall be cleared around the full perimeter of the site with a silt fence along the perimeter. The fire lane shall be kept clear of all combustible materials.

(12) All burning operations, including air-curtain incinerators, shall be conducted at a distance of no less than 1000 ft (305 m) from an occupied dwelling or business or a dwelling or business in such condition that it can be occupied.

(13) For outbuildings such as barns, sheds, structures destroyed by the storms, tree lines and similar, the minimum separation distance is 300 ft (92 m) subject to local authority approval.

(14) Burning may not occur within 100 ft (31 m) of overhead utility lines.

b. Debris/mulch piles.

B

(1) At least 100 ft (31 m) is required between the debris/mulch piles and the burn area or incinerator.

(2) At least 1000 ft (305 m) is required between the debris/mulch piles and the nearest occupied dwelling or business or a dwelling or business in such condition that it can be occupied.

(3) Debris/mulch piles shall not be placed directly under transmission lines nor located within 100 ft (31 m) of transmission towers.

(4) A minimum 30 ft (9 m) wide fire lane shall be cleared around each debris/mulch pile. The fire lane shall be kept clear of all combustible materials.

(5) Mulch piles shall not be stacked greater than 20 ft (6 m) high for more than 7 days due to the increased risk of spontaneous combustion.

c. Air-curtain incinerator operations.

(1) Prior to operating an air-curtain incinerator, the contractor shall develop a written AHA and SOP. Employees will be briefed on the AHA/SOP, which will be readily available for their review. In addition, the contractor shall have all incinerator placements inspected by a USACE SOH professional prior to the start of burning and ensure that the design is maintained throughout the life of the activity.

(2) The design of air-curtain operations shall provide for efficient burning of materials.

(3) Equipment, such as trackhoes, that feed burn pits/debris piles shall have a fully enclosed cab equipped with an air filtration and pressurization system. Workers requiring respirators shall be enrolled in the respiratory protection program and all applicable requirements met in accordance with Section 5.

(4) There shall be a 1 ft (0.3 m) high warning barrier the length of the charging side of the pit to warn equipment operators. It shall be constructed of non-combustible material.

(5) Pits must be constructed out of highly compactable material that will hold its shape.

- If a manufactured fire box is not provided, the incineration pits shall be made of Type B soil (cohesive soil), and be reinforced with earth anchors, wire mesh, or other items in order to support the weight of loaders.

- The edges of the pit shall be checked for

integrity on a regular basis to prevent unexpected cave-ins or collapse.

- There shall be an impervious layer of clay on the bottom of the pit to attempt to seal the ash from the aquifer. This shall be replaced if scraped by dozers.

- The length of the air-curtain pit shall not be more than 6 in (15.2 cm) longer than the blower system at each end.

- The ends of the pit shall be near vertical and extend to the top of the pit.

(6) If a pick-and-drop debris pile is located within the 100 ft (30.5 m) minimum separation zone of the air curtain incinerator, the total volume of the pick-and-drop debris pile(s) supporting an incinerator shall not be more than four times the volume of the incinerator pit.

(7) A 12 in (30.5 cm) soil seal shall be placed on the lip of the air curtain incineration pit to seal the blower nozzle. The nozzle should be 3 in (7.6 cm) to 6 in (15.2 cm) from the edge of the pit.

d. Open burning operations.

(1) Open burning may involve one of the following:

- Ignition of brush piles in rows on top of the ground;

- Digging a fire pit in the ground or constructing the pit above ground using berms;

- Constructing a 3-sided bermed pit open at one end to allow equipment tending the fire to push the brush pile to one end and continue feeding, with all brush contained below the top of the bermed area.

(2) When open burning:

- AND sustained wind speeds reach 15 mph, additional material may not be added to the burn pile;

- Full burning may resume when sustained wind speeds drop below 15 mph;

- When sustained wind speeds reach 20 mph, fires shall be wetted or knocked down to control spread of fires.

(3) Each open burning area may not exceed 200 ft

by 200 ft (61 m x 61 m) in the horizontal plane.

- If space permits the use of multiple open burning areas, there will be a 30 ft (91.4 m) fire lane between the open burning areas.

- The load approach area of the pits shall be sufficiently compacted to provide a surface capable of supporting the loading equipment without damaging the integrity of the pit walls.

- A stop of non-combustible material shall be constructed no closer than 10 ft (3 m) of the edge of the pit to prevent equipment from falling into the pit.

(4) When burning in pits:

- AND the top of the brush pile remains below the top of the pit AND sustained winds reach 25 mph, additional material may not be added to the pile:

- AND sustained wind speeds reach 30 mph, fires shall be wetted or knocked down to control spread of fires.

- AND the brush pile extends above the top of the pit AND sustained wind speeds reach 15 mph, additional material may not be added to the burn pile.

- AND the brush pile extends above the top of the pit AND sustained wind speeds reach 20 mph, all fires must be wetted or knocked down.

- Debris may not be stacked in the burning area higher than 10 ft (3 m) above the original ground level.

e. Ash management.

(1) The burn shall be extinguished approximately 2 hours before anticipated removal of the ash mound. The ash mound shall be removed before it reaches 2 ft (0.6 m) below the lip of the incineration pit.

(2) The contractor shall exercise dust control measures while handling ash especially during transport. Ash shall not be transported until it is proven fully extinguished (soaked with water, producing no steam, and having no visible evidence of residual hot embers).

12. Temporary Roofing.

a. During emergency operations that involve residential temporary roofing, RFO Commanders may permit:

(1) The use of athletic footwear by workers performing temporary roofing operations only;

(2) The removal of hard hats by workers on roof tops;

b. Fall Protection shall be per Section 21 and fall protection during temporary roofing activities shall be in accordance with Figure B-1.

c. While workers are on the roof, weather shall be monitored as required in Section 01.E.01.

13. Tower Safety Requirements.

a. All towers shall be designed by a registered professional engineer (RPE) and clearly marked with weight capacities. The weight capacities shall not be exceeded under any circumstance.

b. All towers shall be GFCI (Ground Fault Circuit Interruption) protected, receptacles shall have gasket weather-proof coverings, and both electrical boxes and conduit shall be rated for outdoor use.

c. No modifications shall be made to the tower that will affect the structural stability of the structure without obtaining a sign-off by the design engineer.

d. Personnel shall not lean out of tower windows nor use stools or other steps to decrease fall protection provided by the window height. If visibility of load is obstructed, use of a mirror or other tool shall be utilized.

e. All portable generators shall be tagged green for having been inspected and deemed in compliance with the manufacturer's recommendations especially in regards to proper grounding.

f. Scissor lifts may be approved by the GDA during the initial 72 hours of the emergency operation during tower construction.

(1) Scissor lifts may not be occupied by more than two individuals at any given time unless the manufacturer allows additional occupancy.

(2) All personnel shall be provided with and required to wear proper fall protection with restraint lines while in the scissor lift, as required in Section 21.

(3) Scissor lifts shall be protected from impact by suitable impact protection equal to that required by

a tower in the same location.

g. All towers shall be provided sufficient traffic barrier protection such as would be provided by concrete jersey barriers.

14. Tree Maintenance. >*See Section 31.*

15. Defensive Driving Training. Personnel involved in emergency operations are at increased risk of motor vehicle accidents due to damaged roadways, debris/hazards in roadways, road closings, malfunctioning or missing traffic control devices, extended duty hours, and driving under challenging environmental conditions.

a. Safe driving programs shall be instituted and those deploying will have current Defensive Driver Training.

b. In addition, Government-owned vehicles operated by Contractor personnel (GOCO) shall also have current Defensive driver training. > *See Section 18.*

c. Personnel operating off-road vehicles shall be trained, prior to operation, in the use of such equipment. > *See Sections 18.C.02 and 18.D.*

16. Public Safety. Requirements for work area delineation, traffic control devices, and the use of flag persons shall be considered and as per ANSI A10.34. Public service announcements shall be used as needed to promote safety of the public exposed to USACE activities. Barriers and fencing shall be considered in restricting the public from operation sites. It is also necessary for all contact with the public to be handled in a courteous manner. > *See ANSI A10.34.*

17. Health Hazard Recognition.

a. Health hazards (e.g., asbestos, lead paint, radiation, hazardous chemicals, etc.) shall be identified and controlled through the recommendations of a qualified industrial hygienist(s). Instrumentation, as required, shall be provided for the detection and measurement of health hazards. After hazards have been identified, and measured, this information shall be posted at the work site and copies of this posting shall be kept by both the contractor and the relevant local USACE field office's Quality Assurance Team. Controls shall be instituted where required and a description of the controls shall be written as part of the APP.

b. Asbestos Recognition and Control. Before work begins where the *potential* exists for an exposure to asbestos containing material, an asbestos control plan shall be developed using age of the buildings, type of typical building supplies for the period and location, and any observations of debris or demolition areas.

(1) The plan shall be written by an industrial hygienist with asbestos training or an AHERA trained supervisor or manager.

(2) If possible, the potential work areas should be inspected by asbestos trained inspectors or an industrial hygienist to identify and quantify asbestos hazards.

(3) The plan shall address control mechanisms, such as wetting with water or surfactant, posting, worker and community protection, air sampling, and safe transport and disposal.

(4) As the asbestos volume and type may change, the pre-inspections of the debris and demolition areas shall continue for each new sector. > *See also Section 06.B.05.*

18. Mishap Reporting.

a. All mishaps (near-miss, incident or accident) shall be reported in accordance with AR 385-10 and applicable supplements.

b. Contractor motor vehicle mishaps occurring on public highways shall be reported for trend analysis only and shall not be considered recordable.

c. The RFO SOH Manager will report mishap experience during emergency operations by maintaining an onsite accident log and by creation of a Preliminary Accident Notification (PAN) in ENGLink under the event name for all recordable accidents. This information, as well as information regarding unsatisfactory SOH performance and/or unresolved SOH problems, will be periodically reported to the USACE National Program Manager for SOH Emergency Planning and Response.

19. Variances to Safety and Health Requirements. The on-site RFO SOH Manager may recommend variances to the requirements contained within this manual to the Geographic District SOHO.

a. The Geographic District SOHO must review the request, concur or non-concur. Geographic District SOHOs will exercise prudent judgment in their recommendations for granting variances with due consideration of existing disaster conditions.

b. The recommended variance is then coordinated with the KO/COR for concurrence and then given to the RFO Commander for approval.

c. The RFO Commander shall have the authority to approve or disapprove requests for variances.

d. All variances granted must be copied to Division and HQ SOHO <u>immediately</u> for information only. The variances approved by the RFO Commander will expire at the end of the emergency operation mission.

Figure B-1
Blue-Roof Mission
Fall Protection Chart

[1] Personal Fall Arrest System

[2] Warning Line System

[3] Other hazards, e.g. downed power lines or trees or obstructions from other sources, snow or ice, heavy rain or wind, roof load bearing risks, and insect/vermin hazards

Regulatory Requirements. Contractor shall submit a Fall Protection Plan specific to the mission which complies with the requirements in EM 385-1-1 Sections 21 and 24, and 29 CFR 1926.500. In addition, an Activity Hazard Analysis shall be developed for each roof prior to start of work.

APPENDIX C Process for Requesting Interpretations

The following process will be used for requesting an official interpretation of a requirement contained in this manual. Other DOD Components must submit their requests for interpretations through their chain of command.

1. Official requests for interpretation and all responses shall be in writing.

2. The requester must:

a. specifically identify the requirement for which he/she seeks an interpretation;

b. provide the exact citation and quote the requirement in question. A separate request must be made for each requirement;

c. state his/her source of confusion regarding the requirement;

d. provide all the information necessary to understand the context in which the requirement is being applied;

e. provide his/her interpretation of the requirement and his/her rationale;

3. Every effort shall be made to clarify the requirement at the lowest possible level.

a. The requester shall work the request for interpretation with the local USACE Safety and Occupational Health Office (SOHO). A Contractor must request interpretation of a requirement from the field office under which they work who will then coordinate with the local SOHO to provide a response. The local SOHO must then render a written interpretation of the requirement within 5 working days of receipt.

b. If either the field office or the requester is not satisfied with this response, either may appeal their position in writing to the Division SOHO. The entire package containing the requester's, and the local SOHO's interpretation, rationale, and supporting information shall be sent to the Division SOHO who shall render a written response to the local SOHO within 5 working days of receipt.

c. If the requester, the field office, or local SOHO is not satisfied with the Division SOHOs response, they may appeal it to the USACE-SO for final resolution. All of the information sent to the Division, the interpretation, rationale, and supporting information shall be provided. Within 5 working days of receipt, USACE-SO will provide a written interpretation to the Division SOHO for dissemination and it shall be final.

4. Interpretations apply ONLY to the specific time and the context in which the requirement is being applied. They may not be used as precedents to determine future applications of the requirement. USACE-SO will make the proper notifications if an interpretation may be applied globally.

5. Unofficial requests for interpretations/clarifications of requirements from local SOHOs may be made via email or telephone. However, the answers provided via this mode will be considered general guidance, not official interpretations.

6. USACE-SO will NOT accept requests for official interpretations from parties outside the USACE structure.

C

THIS PAGE INTENTIONALLY LEFT BLANK

APPENDIX D Process for Requesting Waivers/Variances

The following process shall be used when requesting a waiver or a variance from a requirement contained in this manual. Other DOD Components must submit their requests through their chain of command.

1. <u>Official requests for waivers or variances and all responses shall be in writing.</u>

2. Waiver/variance request package shall be complete and shall include the following:

a. Specific identity of the requirement for which relief is being sought, providing exact citation and quoting the requirement;

b. Statement as to whether a waiver (total elimination of the requirement) or a variance (retaining the basic requirement, but doing it differently) is being sought;

c. Details as to why it is not possible or practical to comply with the requirement;

d. All the information (maps, drawings, references, calculations, change analysis or impact, etc.) necessary to make an informed decision. The burden of proof rests with the requester. Failure to provide the necessary information may be justification for denial of the request. It is up to the requester to make the case as to why the requirement should be waived or varied;

e. Identification of specific time period and operation for which the request is being made. A waiver/variance will be granted for specific time periods and operations and may not be used as a defense for failure to comply with a requirement at another time or on another project;

f. Explanation of method they plan to use in lieu of the requirement and how it provides protection equal to or greater than the requirement being challenged;

g. A detailed AHA addressing the alternate procedure. Risk assessment should be a part of the AHA process;

h. Provision of any other requirements or standards addressing the requirement in question. It is incumbent upon the requester to research the literature to determine if any other requirement or standard exists addressing the requirement from which relief is being sought. If there is another standard(s), the requester must identify it and provide a copy. Requests for waivers/variances will

not be processed until this requirement has been met; and

i. A cover letter.

3. Requester shall work the action with the local USACE Safety and Occupational Health Office (SOHO) who will cover package with their official signed memorandum requesting consideration and including their concurrence or non-concurrence with the request. Package is then sent via mail in hard copy or via e-mail with attached PDF file to HQ USACE-SO with a copy furnished to Division SOH Manager <u>for concurrence or non-concurrence.</u>

4. HQ USACE-SO will then coordinate with Division SOH Manager to evaluate the request. USACE-SO shall have at least 10 working days from date of receipt to consider the request and to render a written decision.

5. A waiver or variance will not be carried over to other operations unless the evaluator extends the scope to include other times and operations. If warranted, HQ USACE-SO may issue a global variance based on an individual request, <u>however a global variance/waiver normally indicates a flawed requirement and hence, the actual requirement may be in need of correction/change.</u>

D

THIS PAGE INTENTIONALLY LEFT BLANK

APPENDIX E Assured Equipment Grounding Conductor Program

1. Program Overview. If an Assured Equipment Grounding Conductor Program (AEGCP) is used in place of ground-fault circuit interrupters (GFCIs) for ground-fault protection, the AEGCP shall consist of: written procedures for equipment inspections, tests, test schedule and results to assure equipment grounding conductors for all cord sets, receptacles that are not a part of the permanent wiring of the building or structure, and equipment connected by cord and plug are installed and maintained to protect employees on construction sites. AEGCP must be in compliance with OSHA, NESC and NEC requirements.

a. These procedures shall be made available when requested to GDA and affected persons. An AEGCP shall be continuously implemented and enforced at the site by one or more designated persons.

b. One or more competent persons shall be designated to implement and enforce the AEGCP.

2. Visual Inspections. Visually inspect all cord sets, attachment caps, plugs and receptacles, and any equipment connected by cord and plug **before each day's use** for external damage (i.e., deformed or missing pins, damaged insulation) and for indication of possible internal damage. Ensure flexible cords are being inspected and those arriving onsite between tests are identified and tested.

3. Removing Equipment. Equipment found to be damaged or defective or which fails any of the prescribed inspections or tests shall not be used until repaired or replaced.

4. Testing. Perform two required tests on all electrical equipment: a continuity test and a terminal connection test. Tests are required:

a. Before first use;

b. Before placing back in service following any repairs;

c. Before equipment is used after any incident that can be reasonably suspected to have caused damage (e.g., when a cord set is run over); AND

d. At intervals not to exceed 3 months, except that cord sets and receptacles that are fixed and not exposed to damage shall be tested at intervals not to exceed 6 months.

5. Recordkeeping. All inspections and tests shall be documented to identify all equipment that passed the inspection or test, the date of inspection or test, and the individual responsible for the inspection or test.

THIS PAGE INTENTIONALLY LEFT BLANK

APPENDIX F

Floating Plant and Marine Activities Diagrams

FIGURE F-1
Type A Railing

MARINE RAILING TYPE A, TWO TIER RIGID FALL PROTECTION RAILING

Type B Railings

FIGURE F-2
Type B Railings

MARINE TYPE B THREE TIER RIGID RAILING

FIGURE F-2 (Continued)
Type B Railings

MARINE TYPE B THREE TIER TENSIONED RAILING

FIGURE F-3
Type C Railings

MARINE TYPE C NON-TENSIONED RAILING (3" SAG SHOWN)

FIGURE F-3 (Continued)
Type C Railings

MARINE TYPE C FLEXIBLE/ SWING-AWAY RAILING WITH FLEXIBLE TIERS (3" SAG SHOWN)

MARINE TYPE C FLEXIBLE/ SWING-AWAY RAILING WITH RIGID TIERS

F

THIS PAGE INTENTIONALLY LEFT BLANK

APPENDIX G

Manning Levels for Dive Teams

1. General. Manning level tables shown are a minimum. Actual manning levels may increase, as determined by the DDC, after considering the diving support systems, the task at hand, weather conditions, dive platform and location, and other factors. Team members may rotate through the dive team positions as long as the minimum manning levels are maintained and team members are qualified and accepted for the position.

2. SCUBA: Untethered, 0 to 100 ft (0 to 30.5 m).

    <u>a.</u> Untethered SCUBA divers shall always be accompanied by another diver in continuous visual contact.

    <u>b.</u> When depth of dive is 0-100 ft (0-30.5 m), the minimum dive team will be composed as shown in Table G-1:

TABLE G-1 Dive Team Composition SCUBA - Untethered, 0 to 100 ft (0 to 30.5 m)	
Personnel	**Number**
Diving Supervisor	1
Divers (in visual contact)	2
Standby Diver*	1
TOTAL TEAM	4

    <u>3.</u> **SCUBA: Tethered with communications, 0 to 100 ft (0 to 30.5 m).** When depth of the dive is 0-100 ft (0-30.5 m), the minimum dive team will be composed as shown in Table G-2:

TABLE G-2 Dive Team Composition SCUBA – Tethered with communications, 0 to 100 ft (0 to 30.5 m)	
Personnel	**Number**
Diving Supervisor ***	1
Diver in water	1
Standby Diver* (tethered with communications)	1
Tender	1
TOTAL TEAM	4

    <u>4.</u> **Surface Supplied Air: 0 to 100 ft (0 to 30.5 m).**

    a. When surface supplied air is being used as the diving mode, the minimum dive team will be composed as shown in Table G-3:

TABLE G-3 Dive Team Composition Surface Supplied Air, 0 to 100 ft (0 to 30.5 m) Within No Decompression Limits			
Personnel	Number	Penetration Dive	
Diving Supervisor ***	1	1	
Diver	1	2	
Standby Diver*	1	1	
Tender	1	2	
TOTAL TEAM	4	6	

b. Deploying the Standby Diver as a Worker Diver. The Standby diver may be deployed as a working diver provided all of the following conditions are met:

(1) Surface-supplied no-decompression dive of 60 fsw or less;
(2) Divers are in close proximity, (based on site specific requirements), with unimpeded access to each other;
(3) Divers have communications with each other at all times;
(4) No entanglement hazards exist;
(5) Prior to deploying the standby diver, the work area shall be determined to be free of hazards (i.e., suctions, discharges) by the first diver on the job site;
(6) The dive is NOT a penetration or confined space dive;
(7) Each diver has a full-time tender (which brings the minimum number of team members to 5).

5. **Surface Supplied Air: 101 to 190 ft (30.8 to 57.9 m).**

When surface supplied air is being used as the diving mode, the minimum dive team will be composed as shown in Table G-4:

TABLE G-4 Dive Team Composition Surface Supplied Air, 0 to 100 ft Requiring Decompression and All Surface Supplied Air, 101 to 190 ft (30.8 to 57.9 m)			
Personnel	Dives within no decompression	Dives requiring decompression	Penetration Dive
Diving Supervisor	1	1	1
Chamber Operator**	**/1	****/1	1
Diver	1	1	2
Standby Diver*	1	1	1
Tender	1	1	2
Standby Diver Tender	1	1	1
TOTAL TEAM	5/6	5/6	8

6. **Surface Supplied Mixed Gas Diving.** For surface supplied mixed gas diving, to include OEA (Nitrox, etc.), the minimum dive team will be composed as shown in Table G-5:

TABLE G-5 Dive Team Composition Surface Supplied Mixed Gas Diving			
Personnel	Dives within no decompression limits	Dives requiring decompression	Penetration Dives
Diving Supervisor	1	1	1
Chamber Operator**	**/1	****/1	1
Diver	1	1	2
Standby Diver*	1	1	1
Tender	1	1	2
Standby Diver Tender	1	1	1
TOTAL TEAM	5/6	5/6	8

Notes:

* The standby diver will be rested and capable of performing emergency rescue assistance. When work is limited to no decompression limits, the standby diver shall be sufficiently free of residual nitrogen to allow for 25 minutes of bottom time at the working depth without exceeding "No Decompression Limits."

** The Competent Person/chamber operator may be any non-diving member of the dive team when the chamber is only for emergency use when diving within the no- decompression limits. Saturation diving requires that a life support technician will serve as the chamber operator.

*** The supervisor may be the standby tender for dives under 100 ft (30.5 m).

**** The Competent Person/chamber operator may be any non-diving member of the dive team if all diving ceases during chamber decompression.

G

THIS PAGE INTENTIONALLY LEFT BLANK

APPENDIX Q Definitions
This appendix defines the following terms for the purposes of this manual.

Abrasive blasting: the forcible application of an abrasive to a surface by pneumatic pressure, hydraulic pressure, or centrifugal force.

Absorbed dose: energy imparted to matter by ionizing radiation per unit mass of irradiated material at the place of interest in that material. The units of absorbed dose are the rad or the Gray (1 Gray equals 1 Joule/Kilogram equals 100 rad).

Accepted/Acceptable: a term denoting when a written procedure, practice, method, program, engineering design, or employee qualification criteria submittal, which, after a cursory review by a GDA, is determined to generally conform to safety and health or contractual requirements. Acceptance or acceptability of such submittals in no way relieves the submitting entity from ensuring employees a safe and healthful work environment or complying with all contractual requirements and good engineering practices.

Accident, recordable: One of 3 types of mishaps; meets the definition of an Army accident that involves a Government employee, Contractor, or member of the public that rises to the severity level that they are used to calculate accident experience modification rates.

Accident Prevention Plan (APP): a document that outlines occupational safety and health policy, responsibilities, and program requirements.

Accredited testing laboratory: a laboratory that an accrediting organization has determined has demonstrated the ability to conduct air quality testing according to their standard.

Activity Hazard Analysis (AHA): a documented risk management process by which the steps (procedures) required to accomplish a work activity/task are outlined and the actual/potential hazards of each step are identified. This is identification of "inherent risk". Safety measures, precautions and controls are then identified and put into place to reduce the level of hazard for each step. The risk level then identified, is called the residual risk for that step/activity. A risk acceptance code (RAC) is then assigned to the entire activity. The AHA is an analysis tool that the USACE uses, however, other similar analysis tools are acceptable (e.g., Job Hazard Analysis, JHAs; Job Safety Analysis, JSA;, etc) provided the information required on the AHA is included, steps are identified, hazards associated with each step are listed. > See also "Inherent Risk", "Risk Assessment Code" and "Residual Risk".

Aerial lift/device: any vehicle mounted device, telescoping or articulating, or both, which is used to position/elevate personnel to job sites/activities above the ground. May be made of metal, wood, fiberglass reinforced plastic (FRP) or other; may be powered or manually operated; Includes:
• Aerial ladder: an aerial device consisting of a single- or multiple-section extensible ladder;
• Articulating boom platform: an aerial device with two or more hinged boom sections;
• Insulated aerial device: an aerial device designed for work on energized lines and apparatus.
Related definitions:
• Mobile unit: a combination of an aerial device, its vehicle and related equipment;
• Platform: any personnel-carrying device, basket or bucket, which is a component of an aerial device.

Affected employee: a person whose position requires him/her to operate or use a system that is under lockout or tagout or whose position requires him/her to work in an area where a system that is under lockout or tagout is being serviced or maintained.

Air curtain incinerator: Means an incinerator that operates by forcefully projecting a curtain of air across an open chamber or pit in which burning occurs. If operating optimally, there should be minimal to no visible smoke plume above the pit.

Air-purifying respirator: a respirator with an air-purifying filter, cartridge, or canister that removes specific air contaminants by passing ambient air through the air-purifying element.

Air receiver: a tank used for the storage of air discharged from the compressor; used to help eliminate pressure pulsations in the discharge line.

All-Terrain Vehicles (ATVs): ATVs are motorized vehicles intended for off-road use that travel on four low-pressure tires with a seat designed to be straddled by the operator and handlebar for steering control.
Altered: any change to the original manufacturer's design configuration. These are:
• Replacement of weight-handling equipment parts and components with parts or components not identical with the original (i.e., change in material, dimensions, or design configuration);
• The addition of parts or components not previously

a part of the equipment;
- The removal of components that were previously a part of the load handling equipment; and
- Rearrangement of original parts or components.

Anchor handling barge: a floating work platform consisting of a pontoon or barge, hoisting equipment, and a fixed A-frame that cannot slew or change radius. An anchor barge is used to extract anchors or buoy weights only. The load is often unknown and is often not under the tip of the A-frame.

Anchorage (fall protection): a secured point of attachment that can safely withstand the forces exerted by activation of fall protection and rescue equipment. The anchorage is the rigid part of the structure that can be in the form of a beam, girder, column or floor.

Anchorage connector: a component or subsystem by which fall protection or rescue equipment is secured to the anchorage.

Anchorage system: a combination of anchorage and anchorage connector.

Anchored bridging: the steel joist bridging is connected to a bridging terminus point.

Anti-runaway: a safety device to stop a declining conveyor in case of mechanical or electrical failure.

Anti-two blocking (A2B) device: a device that is activated by two-blocking and disengages the particular function whose movement is caused by the two-blocking.

Approach-departure clearance surface: an extension of the primary surface and the clear zone at each end of the runway, first along an inclined plane (glide angle) and then along a horizontal plane, both flaring symmetrically about the runway centerline extended.

Arborist: Is a professional in the practice of arboriculture, which is the cultivation, management, and study of individual trees, shrubs, vines, and other perennial plants. Arborists generally focus on the health and safety of individual plants and trees. Arborists typically climb trees through rope ascending and have special training in this type of climbing.

Arc: A controlled electrical discharge between the electrode and the work piece that is formed and sustained by a gas that has been heated to such a temperature that it can conduct electric current.

Arc flash: An explosive release of energy caused by an electrical arc. An arc flash results from either a phase to ground or a phase to phase fault caused by such occurrences as accidental contact with electrical systems, build-up of conductive dust, corrosion, dropped tools, and improper work procedures.

Arc Rating: A value of the energy necessary to pass through any given fabric to cause with 50% probability a second or third degree burn. This value is measured in calories/cm². The necessary Arc Rating for an article of clothing is determined by a Hazard/Risk Assessment and the resulting HRC. Usually measured in terms of ATPV or EBT

Arc welding: a welding process that joins work pieces by heating them with an arc.

Articulating boom crane: a crane with a boom that has sections that are articulated by hydraulic cylinders. The boom may have a telescoping section. The crane can be stationary or mounted on a vehicle, track, locomotive, etc., and is used to lift, swing, and lower loads.

Associate Safety Professional (ASP): an individual who has achieved an interim designation denoting progress towards the Certified Safety Professional Certification offered by BCSP.

Atmosphere-supplying respirator: a respirator that supplies the respirator user with breathing air from a source independent of the ambient atmosphere, and includes SARs and SCBA units.

Attendant (confined space): an individual stationed outside one or more permit spaces who monitors the authorized entrants and who performs all attendant's duties assigned in the employer's permit space program.

Authorized Entrant: anyone entering the site that is assigned to the site but is not a site worker (e.g., security forces, other military forces, etc.).

Authorized Entrant (confined space): an employee who is authorized by the employer to enter a permit space.

Authorized Individual (Hazardous Energy Control): a qualified person who is designated, in writing by the designated authority, to request, receive, implement, and remove hazardous energy control procedures

Authorized Person, Fall Protection: a worker working at heights, exposed to fall hazards and using FP equipment; shall have a working understanding of and follow the employer's policy and procedures and the instructions of the Competent Person for FP regarding the use of fall protection and rescue systems.

Authorized Rescuer: A person assigned to perform rescue from fall protection.

Back cut: the final cut in a felling operation, made horizontally on the opposite side from the undercut. > See definition of notch.

Barricade: a physical obstruction, such as tape, screens, or cones, intended to warn of and limit access to a hazardous area.

Barrier: a physical obstruction that is intended to prevent contact with energized lines or equipment.
Beam platform: a work platform made up of wood beams (oriented vertically).

Bearer: a horizontal member of a scaffold upon which the platform rests and that may be supported by runners.

Benching: a method of protecting employees from cave-ins by cutting the sides of the excavation in the arrangement of one or more horizontal levels, usually with vertical or near-vertical walls between steps.

Blast area: the area in which explosive loading and blasting activities are being conducted and the area immediately adjacent that is within the influence of fly-rock and concussion.

Blast site: the area in which explosive materials are being loaded, or have been loaded, including all holes to be loaded for the same blast for a distance of 50 ft (15.2 m) on all sides.

Blaster: the person(s) authorized to use explosives for blasting purposes.

Blasting agent: any material or mixture, consisting of a fuel and oxidizer, intended for blasting, not otherwise classified as an explosive, and in which none of the ingredients is classified as an explosive, provided that the finished product, as mixed and packaged for use or shipment, cannot be detonated by means of a No. 8 blasting cap when unconfined.

Boatswain's chair: a suspended seat designed to accommodate one worker.

Body belt: a body support comprised of a strap with means for securing about the waist and attaching it to a lanyard, lifeline, or deceleration device (prohibited).

Body harness, full: straps connected together and secured about a body in a manner that distributes the arresting forces over at least the thighs, waist, chest, shoulders, and pelvis, with provision for attaching a lanyard, lifeline, or deceleration device.

Bolted diagonal bridging: diagonal bridging that is bolted to a steel joist or joists.

Bond: an electrical connection from one conductive element to another to minimize potential differences or providing suitable conductivity for fault current or for mitigation of leakage current and electrolytic action.

Bonding: the permanent joining of metallic parts to form an electrically conductive path that will ensure electrical continuity and capacity to conduct safely any current likely to be imposed.

Bonding jumper: a reliable conductor to ensure the required electrical conductivity between metal parts required to be electrically connected.

Boom: a member hinged to the superstructure or a crane/derrick and used for supporting hoisting tackle.

Boom angle: the angle above or below the horizontal of the longitudinal axis of the base of the boom section.

Boom angle indicator: a device that measures the angle of the boom to the horizontal.

Boom hoist mechanism: means for supporting the boom and controlling boom angle.

Boom, live: a boom in which lowering (free-fall) is controlled by a brake without aid from other lowering retarding devices.

Boom stop (crane):   a device used to limit the angle of the boom at the highest position.

Bottom time: the total elapsed time, measured in minutes, from the time when the diver leaves the surface in descent to the time that the diver begins ascent.

Braided sling: a sling made from braided rope.

Branch circuit: the circuit conductors between the final over current device protecting the circuit and the outlet(s).

Brazing: a welding process that joins materials by heating them to a temperature that will   not melt them but will melt a filler material which adheres to them and forms a joint.

Q

Bricklayers' square scaffold: a scaffold made up of a work platform (planking) supported on bricklayers' squares.

Bridge: that part of a gantry or overhead crane that carries the trolley(s).

Bridging clip: a device that is attached to the steel joist to allow the bolting of the bridging to the steel joist.

Bridging terminus point: a wall, a beam, tandem joists (with all bridging installed and a horizontal truss in the plane of the top chord) or other element at an end or intermediate point(s) of a line of bridging that provides an anchor point for the steel joist bridging. Bridle sling: multiple-leg-sling; the legs of the sling are spread to distribute the load.

Bucket conveyor: any type of conveyor in which the material is carried in a series of buckets.

Bucking: the act of sawing a felled tree or limbs into smaller sections.

Bus wire: an expendable wire used in parallel or series-in-parallel circuits to which are connected the leg wires of electric blasting caps.

Cable: a conductor with insulation, or a stranded conductor with or without insulation and other coverings (single-conductor cable), or a combination of conductors insulated from one another (multiple-conductor cable).

Cable laid endless sling: a wire rope sling made from one continuous length of cable laid rope with the ends joined by one or more metallic fittings.

Cable laid grommet, hand tucked: an endless wire rope sling made from one continuous length of rope formed to make a body composed of six ropes around a rope core. The rope ends are tucked into the body, forming the core. No sleeves are used.

Cable laid rope: a rope composed of several wire ropes laid as strands around a wire rope core.

Cable laid rope sling, mechanical joint: a wire rope sling made from a cable laid wire rope with eyes fabricated by pressing or swaging metal sleeves over the rope junction.

Caisson: a watertight chamber (of wood or steel sheeting or a concrete or steel cylinder) used in construction work underwater or as a foundation. When the bottom of the structure extends below the surface of free water, excavation is performed by workers in a working chamber at an air pressure greater than atmospheric pressure.

Canister or cartridge: a container with a filter, sorbent, or catalyst, or combination of these items, which removes specific contaminants from the air passed through the container.

Capable of being locked: an energy isolating device is considered "capable of being locked out" if it meets the following:
• Is designed with a hasp or other part to which a lock can be attached (i.e., a lockable electric disconnect switch);
• Has a locking mechanism built into it; or
• Can be locked without dismantling, rebuilding, or replacing the energy isolating device or permanently altering its energy control capability (i.e.,using a lock/chain assembly on a pipeline valve, a lockable valve cover, circuit breaker lockout or fuse block-out devices). Equipment that accepts bolted blank flanges and bolted slip blinds are considered to be capable of being locked out.

Carabiner: a connector component generally consisting of an oval or trapezoidal shaped body with a closed gate or similar arrangement

Carpenter's bracket scaffold: a scaffold made up of a work platform supported on wood or metal brackets.

Catch platform: a temporary structure erected around, attached to and abutting the building being demolished for the purpose of safeguarding and protecting the employees and the public by catching and retaining falling objects or debris.

Cathead: a spool shaped attachment on a winch around which rope is wound for hoisting and pulling.

Certificate Of Compliance (COC): A certificate provided by the contractor for each piece of Load Handling Equipment prior to the LHE being brought on site. The COC states that the LHE and rigging gear meet applicable regulations and requirements, is submitted to the GDA for acceptance and shall be posted on the LHE. See Certificate Of Compliance, Form 16-1.

Certified Anchorage: An anchorage for fall arrest, positioning, restraint, or rescue systems that a qualified person certifies to be capable of supporting the potential fall forces that could be encountered during a fall or that meet the criteria for a certified anchorage.

Certified Construction Heath and Safety Technician (CHST): an individual who is currently certified by the Council on Certification of Health, Environmental and Safety Technologists (CCHST).

Certified Health Physicist (CHP): an individual who is currently certified by the American Board of Health Physics.

Certified Industrial Hygienist (CIH): an individual who is currently certified by the American Board of Industrial Hygiene.

Certified Safety Professional (CSP): an individual who is currently certified by the BCSP.

Certified Safety Trained Supervisor (CSTS): an individual who is currently certified by the Council on Certification of Health, Environmental and Safety Technologists (CCHST).

Chain conveyor: any type of conveyor in which one or more chains act as the conveying medium.

Chemical Agent (CA). A chemical compound (to include experimental compounds) that, through its chemical properties, produces lethal or other damaging effects on human beings, and is intended for use in military operations to kill, seriously injure, or incapacitate persons through its physiological effects. Excluded are research, development, test and evaluation solutions; riot control agents; chemical defoliants and herbicides; smoke and other obscuration materials; flame and incendiary materials; and industrial chemicals.

Chicken Ladder: See "Crawling Board"

Choker: a sling used to form a slip noose around an object.

Christmas tree lifting – See Multiple Lift Rigging

Class A fire: a fire involving ordinary combustible materials such as wood, paper, clothing, and some rubber and plastic materials.

Class B fire: a fire involving flammable or combustible liquids, flammable gases, greases and similar materials, and some rubber and plastic materials.

Class C fire: a fire involving energized electrical equipment where safety to the employee requires the use of electrically nonconductive extinguishing media.

Class D fire: a fire involving combustible metals such as

magnesium, zirconium, sodium, and potassium.

Cleat: a mooring fitting having two horizontal arms to which mooring lines are secured.

Coarse laid rope: 6 x 7 wire rope (6 strands, 7 wires per strand).

Cofferdam: a temporary structure used to keep water (and earth) out of an excavation during construction of the permanent structure.

Collateral Duty Safety Officer (CDSO): An employee who is trained to assist with the SOH program as a minor duty (20% or less of the time) and upon appointment as CDSO, is designated in writing and provided SOH training commensurate with the scope of their assigned responsibilities, per 29 CFR 1960.58.

Column: a load-carrying vertical member that is part of the primary skeletal framing system. Columns do not include posts.

Command: the USACE Major Subordinate Command, District, Laboratory, or Field Operating Activity with responsibility for a particular activity.

Committed dose equivalent: The dose equivalent to organs or tissues of reference that will be received from an intake of radioactive material by a person during the 50-year period following the intake.

Committed effective dose equivalent: the sum of the products of the weighting factors applicable to each of the body organs or tissues irradiated and the committed dose equivalent to these organs or tissues.

Competent Person: one who can identify existing and predictable hazards in the working environment or working conditions that are dangerous to personnel and who has authorization to take prompt corrective measures to eliminate them.

Competent Person, Confined Space: A person with thorough knowledge of OSHA's Confined Space Standard, 29 CFR 1910.146, designated in writing by the employer to be responsible for the immediate supervision, implementation and monitoring of the confined space program, who through training, knowledge and experience in confined space entry is capable of identifying, evaluating and addressing existing and potential confined space hazards and, who has the authority to take prompt corrective measures with regard to such hazards.

Competent Person, Confined Spaces in ships and vessels (CPCSSV): a person who has the knowledge of the designation of spaces where the work is done;

Q

ability to understand and follow through on the air sampling, personal protective equipment and instructions of a Marine Chemist, Coast Guard authorized person, or Certified Industrial Hygienist.

Competent Person, Cranes and Rigging: A person meeting the competent person requirements as defined in the definitions of and 29 CFR Part 1926 who has been designated in writing by the employer to be responsible for the immediate supervision, implementation and monitoring of the Crane and Rigging Program, who through training, knowledge and experience in crane and rigging is capable of identifying, evaluating and addressing existing and potential hazards and, who has the authority to take prompt corrective measures with regard to such hazards.

Competent Person, Excavation/Trenching: A person meeting the competent person requirements as defined in the definitions of and 29 CFR Part 1926 who has been designated in writing by the employer to be responsible for the immediate supervision, implementation and monitoring of the excavation/trenching program, who through training, knowledge and experience in excavation/trenching is capable of identifying, evaluating and addressing existing and potential hazards and, who has the authority to take prompt corrective measures with regard to such hazards

Competent Person, Fall Protection: a person designated in writing by the employer to be responsible for immediate supervising, implementing and monitoring of the fall protection program, who through training, knowledge and experience in fall protection and rescue systems and equipment, is capable of identifying, evaluating and addressing existing and potential fall hazards and, who has the authority to take prompt corrective measures with regard to such hazards.

Competent Person, Scaffolding: a person, designated in writing by the employer to be responsible for immediate supervising, implementing and monitoring of the scaffolding program. The CP for Scaffolding has enough training, knowledge AND experience in scaffolding to correctly identify, evaluate and address existing and potential hazards and also has the authority to take prompt corrective measures with regard to these hazards. CP qualifications must be documented and shall include training - a minimum of 8-hours of scaffold training, to include training on the specific type of scaffold being used (e.g., mastclimbing, adjustable, tubular frame, etc.) and experience on specific scaffolding systems/types, assessment of the base material the scaffold will be erected upon, load calculations for materials and personnel, erection and dismantling.

Competent Person Trainer: An individual who by training, knowledge and experience is capable of conducting competent person training.

Competent Rescuer: An individual designated by the employer who by training, knowledge, and experience is capable of the implementation, supervision, and monitoring of the employer's fall protection rescue program.

Competent Rescuer Trainer: An individual who by training, knowledge and experience specific to fall protection rescue is capable of conducting rescue training.

Confined space: a space that
• Is large enough and so configured that a person can bodily enter and perform assigned work; and
• Has limited or restricted means for entry or exit [such that the entrant's ability to escape in an emergency would be hindered (e.g., tanks, vessels, silos, storage bins, hoppers, vaults, and pits are spaces that may have limited means of entry; doorways are not considered a limited means of entry or egress)]; and
• Is not designed for continuous worker occupancy.

Confined space on a ship or vessel: a compartment of small size and limited access such as a double bottom tank, cofferdam, or other space which by its small size and confined nature can readily create or aggravate a hazardous exposure.

Connector: an employee who, working with hoisting equipment, is placing and connecting structural members and/or components.

Constructability: the ability to erect structural steel members in accordance with 29 CFR 1926, Subpart R, without having to alter the over-all structural design.

Construction load: (for joist erection) means any load other than the weight of the employee(s), the joists and the bridging bundle.

Container: any vessel of 60 gal (0.23 m3) or less capacity used for transporting or storing liquids.

Contaminant: any material, that, by nature of its composition or reaction with other materials, is potentially capable of causing injury, death, illness, damage, loss, or pain.

Contaminated water: related to underwater diving; water

which contains any chemical, biological, or radioactive substance which poses a chronic or acute health risk to exposed personnel. Supervisory personnel are encouraged to contact local agencies to obtain information on local water contaminants and hazards.

Contractor: any individual or firm under contractual agreement with the government or its subunits for the performance of services and products, such as construction, maintenance, and hazardous waste activities, including subcontractors of a prime contractor.

Controlled Access Zone: a zone to restrict access to unprotected side or edge of a roof or floor.

Controlled decking zone (CDZ): an area in which certain work (e.g., initial installation and placement of metal decking) may take place without the use of guardrail systems, personal fall arrest systems, fall restraint systems, or safety net systems and where access to the zone is controlled.

Controlled load-lowering: lowering a load by means of a mechanical hoist drum device that allows a hoisted load to be lowered with maximum control using the gear train or hydraulic components of the hoist mechanism. Controlled load lowering requires the use of the hoist drive motor, rather than the load hoist brake, to lower the load.

Controlling Contractor: a prime contractor, general contractor, construction manager or any other legal entity which has the overall responsibility for the construction of the project – its planning, quality and completion.

Conveyor: a horizontal, inclined, or vertical device for transporting material in a path predetermined by the design of the device and having points of loading and discharge.

Conveyor, portable: a transportable conveyor that is not self-propelled, usually having supports that provide mobility.

Corrosive: is a substance that can cause destruction of living tissue or damage by chemical action, including acids with a pH of 2.5 or below or caustics with a pH of 11.0 or above.

Crane: a machine for lifting or lowering a load and moving it horizontally, with the hoisting mechanism being an integral part of the machine.

Crane, truck-mounted: a crane consisting of a rotating superstructure (center post or turn table), boom, operating machinery, and one or more operator's stations mounted on a frame attached to a commercial truck chassis, usually retaining a payload hauling capability whose power source usually powers the crane.

Crane, crawler: a crane consisting of rotating superstructure with a power plant, operating machinery, and a boom, mounted on a base and equipped with crawler treads for travel.

Crane, floating: a rotating superstructure, power plant, operating machinery, and boom, mounted on a barge or pontoon. The power plant may be installed below decks. The crane's function is to handle loads at various radii.

Crane, floor-operated: a crane that is pendant or nonconductive rope controlled by an operator on the floor or an independent platform.

Crane, gantry: a crane similar to an overhead crane except that the bridge is rigidly supported on two or more legs running on fixed rails or other runway.

Crane, hammerhead: a lifting machine arranged with a tower (mast), an upper structure that rotates, a horizontally-extended load jib (boom) with trolley, and a counterweight jib extending in the direction opposite of the load jib: neither jib are arranged for luffing. The trolley on the load jib traverses the length of the jib and contains the sheaves and accessory parts which make up the upper load block; the lower load block is suspended from the trolley.

Crane, locomotive: a crane mounted on a base or car equipped for travel on a railroad track.

Crane, luffing jib: a type of jib on a tower crane that is pivoted at the jib foot and supported by luffing cables. The hoist rope usually passes over a sheave at the jib point and the hook radius is changed by luffing, or changing the angle of inclination, of the jib. Rear pivoted luffing jibs are similar but the pivot is towards the rear of the top of the tower rather than at the jib foot.

Crane, mobile: a crane mounted on a truck or crawler.

Crane, overhead: a crane with a single- or multiple-girder movable bridge or fixed hoisting mechanism and traveling on an overhead fixed runway structure.

Crane, pillar: a fixed crane consisting of a vertical member, held in position at its base to resist overturning moment, and normally with a constant-radius revolving boom supported at the outer end by a tension member.

Crane, portal: a crane consisting of a rotating superstructure with operating machinery and boom, all

Q

of which is mounted on gantry structure, usually with a portal opening between the gantry columns or legs for traffic to pass through; may be fixed or traveling.

Crane, standby: a crane that is not in regular service but which is used occasionally or intermittently as required.

Crane, tower: similar to a portal crane but with a tower intervening between the upper structure and the gantry or other base structure; typically without a portal. To resist overturning moments, the assembly may be ballasted, fixed to a foundation, or a combination of both. The crane may be either fixed or on a traveling base.

Crane (hoist), under-hung: a crane that is suspended from the bottom flange of a runway track or a single-track monorail system.

Crane, wall: a crane having a jib with or without trolley and supported from a side wall or line of columns of a building. It is a traveling type and operates on a runway attached to the sidewall or columns.

Crane, wheel-mounted (multi-control stations): a crane consisting of a rotating superstructure, operating machinery, and operator's station and boom, mounted on a crane carrier equipped with axles and rubber-tired wheels for travel, a power source(s), and having separate stations for driving and operating.

Crane, wheel-mounted (single control station): a crane consisting of a rotating superstructure, operating machinery, and boom, mounted on a crane carrier equipped with axles and rubber-tired wheels for travel, a power source, and having a single control station.

Crane operator aids: devices that are used to assist a crane operator in the safe operation of the crane, including: two-block warning devices, two-block prevention devices, load and load moment indicator devices, boom angle and radius indicators, boom and jib stops, boom hoist disengaging devices, limit switches, drum rotation indicators, etc.

Crawling board (chicken ladder): a supported scaffold consisting of a plank with cleats spaced and secured to provide footing, for use on sloped surfaces such as roofs.

Cribbing: a system of timbers, arranged in a rectangular pattern, used to support and distribute the weight of equipment.

Critical Item Weld: A structural feature or structural

piece which requires welding and is in place to provide life saving support for people, e.g., personal fall arrest anchorages, scaffolding, shoring, forms, ladders, or piling. A critical item weld may also be on piping or ventilation systems containing hazardous materials, pressurized piping, bulkheads, tainter gates, catwalks, lifting or pad eyes for rigging, and cranes. This definition is not written to be complete in nature, but to provide guidance in determining critical item welds. This determination shall be made by a Qualified Person.

Critical lift: a non-routine crane lift requiring detailed planning and additional or unusual safety precautions.

Crossbraces: two diagonal scaffold members joined at their center to form an "X", used between frames or uprights or both.

Crotch: to pass a rope through the crotch of a limb, or false crotch, in such a way that the load will be supported by the main leader.

Cumulative trauma disorders: disorders of muscles, tendons, peripheral nerves, or vascular system. These can be caused, precipitated, or aggravated by intense, repeated, or sustained exertions, motions of the body, insufficient recovery, vibration, or cold.

Cylinder manifold: a multiple header for interconnection of gas sources with distribution points.

DANGEROUS Placard: A freight container, unit load device, transport vehicle, or railcar that contains non-bulk packages with two or more categories of hazardous materials that require different placards, may be placarded with a DANGEROUS placard instead of the separate placards specified for each of the materials.

Deadman control: a constant-pressure, hand or foot-operated control designed so that when released, it automatically returns to a neutral or deactivated position.

Debris net: a net designed to catch only debris. It must be used in conjunction with a personnel net if there is any possibility for personnel to fall.

Decelerating device: any mechanism that serves to dissipate energy during a fall.

Decibel (dB): a measure of sound pressure.

dB(A): A-weighted measure of sound pressure used with sound level meters; the weighting causes the sensitivity of the sound level meter to vary with the frequency and intensity of sound and in doing so duplicates the response of the human ear.

Decompression sickness: a condition with a variety of symptoms which may result from gas or bubbles in the tissues of divers after pressure reduction.

Decompression table: a profile or set of profiles of depth-time relationships for ascent rate and breathing mixtures to be followed after a specific depth-time exposure or exposures.

Derrick: an apparatus consisting of a mast or equivalent member held at the end by guys or braces, with or without a boom, for use with a hoisting mechanism and operating ropes.

Derrick, A-frame: a derrick in which the boom is hinged from a cross member or pedestal between the bottom ends of two upright members spread apart at the lower ends and joined at the top, the boom point secured to the junction of the side members, and the side members are braced or guyed from this junction point.

Derrick, floating: a mast or equivalent member held at the head by guys or braces, with or without a boom, for use with a hoisting mechanism and operating ropes, mounted on a barge or a pontoon. The power plant may be installed below decks.

Derrick, floor: an elevated floor of a building or structure that has been designated to receive hoisted pieces of steel prior to final placement.

Derrick, guy: a fixed derrick consisting of a vertical mast capable of being rotated 360° (but not continuous rotation) supported by guys, and a boom that is pivoted at the bottom and capable of moving in a vertical plane; a reeved rope between the head (top) of the mast and the boom harness (at the boom point) allows lifting and lowering of the boom and a reeved rope from the boom point allows lifting and lowering of the load.

Derrick, stiff leg: a derrick similar to a guy derrick except that the mast is supported or held in place by 2 or more stiff members (stiff legs) which are capable of resisting either tensile or compressive forces. Sills are generally provided to connect the lower ends of the stiff legs to the foot of the mast.

Design load: the maximum intended load: that is, the total of all loads including the worker(s), material, and the equipment placed on the unit.

Designated Dive Coordinator (DDC): a USACE employee assigned the responsibility for organizing, integrating, and monitoring the total dive program within a USACE Command. This individual and an alternate are appointed, in writing, by the USACE Commander/Director; shall successfully complete Diving Safety/Diving Supervisor Training Course; shall maintain certification (attending the diving refresher course every 4 years); are not required to perform 12 working/training dives unless they are also a USACE diver or USACE Diving Supervisor.

Designated person: An employee who has been trained or is qualified and assigned the responsibility to perform a specific task.

Designated Representative (DR): an individual that can substitute for an SSHO under certain conditions; See Section 01.A.17.
- DR supports and supplements the SSHO efforts in managing, implementing and enforcing the Contractor's safety and health program. DRs shall be individuals(s) with work oversight responsibilities, such as crew leader, masters, mates, seniors and/or foreman. DRs should not be in positions requiring continuous mechanical or equipment operations, such as equipment operators.

Dive location: a surface or vessel from which a diving operation is conducted.

Dive operation: the complete scope of work addressed in a single diving plan.

Dive team: divers and support employees involved in a diving operation, including the diving supervisor.

Dive tender: that individual on the dive team assigned to assist the diver with dressing in and out, entering and exiting the water, and continuously tend the tether or umbilical of the diver while in the water. The dive tender shall have experience and training that encompasses all aspects of tending in order to provide safe and efficient support to the diver.

Diving, Direct Source Compressor: Air compressor system used on-site as a direct source to supply air to SSA divers via the receiver tank, manifold, and air line – not compressors used onsite solely to fill SCUBA or other air cylinders.

Diving, Heavy Gear: Surface-supplied deep-sea diving gear including helmet (with or without breastplate), dry suit, and weighted shoes, with the helmet directly connected to the dry suit, forming a self-contained pressure envelope for the diver.

Diving Inspector: a USACE employee or other designated qualified person who inspects a Contractor

Q

diving operation while work is in progress (not an employee of the dive contractor); USACE Diving inspectors are designated in writing by local Commander; must successfully complete a USACE diving safety/ diving supervisor, Diving Inspector, or Dive Safety Administrator course and shall maintain certification via refresher every 4 years. Non-USACE Diving monitors/inspectors with other credentials will be considered on a case-by-case basis and may be approved in writing by the DDC with Command notification and concurrence.

Diving Safety Representative (DSR): the Safety and Occupational Health Office representative assigned the responsibility of dive safety; provides dive safety advice; actively participates in the review and comment process for diving plans and hazard analyses; on-site monitoring of diving operations; has successfully completed USACE diving safety/ diving supervisor, diving inspector, or Dive Safety Administrator course and maintain certification every 4 years.

Diving supervisor: the employer, or an employee designated by the employer, at the dive location in charge of all aspects of the diving operation that affect the safety and health of dive team members. The diving supervisor shall have experience and training in the conduct of the assigned diving operation.

Dose equivalent: the product of the absorbed dose in tissue, quality factor, and all other necessary modifying factors at the location of interest. The units of dose equivalent are the rem or Sievert (Sv) (1 Sievert equals 100 rem).

Dosimetry: the measure of radiological exposure.

Double-cleated ladder: a ladder, similar to a single cleat ladder but with a center rail, which allows simultaneous two-way traffic for employees ascending or descending.

Dragline: a bucket attachment for a crane that excavates by the crane drawing, with a cable, the bucket towards itself.

Dredge: any vessel fitted with machinery for the purpose of removing or relocating material from or in a body of water.

Drilled Shaft: a shaft constructed by excavating a cylindrical hole, placing reinforcing steel (if required) and filling the hole with concrete (also called drilled piers or caissons).

Drilling fluid (mud): fluid that is pumped into a drilled hole and used to wash cuttings from the hole: drilling mud is a type of drilling fluid made of a slurry of clay and water and that is used to coat and support the sides of the drill hole and seal off permeable strata.

Dry chemical: an extinguishing agent composed of very small particles of chemicals such as sodium bicarbonate, potassium bicarbonate, or potassium chloride supplemented by special treatment to provide resistance to packing and moisture absorption and to provide proper flow capabilities. Does not include dry powders.

Dry location: a location not normally subject to dampness or wetness; a location classified as dry may be temporarily subject to dampness or wetness, as in the case of a building under construction

Dry powder: a compound used to extinguish or control Class D fires.

Duck Pond: Openings between stationary vessels or vessels and other structures that create fully enclosed water areas (duck ponds) into which personnel could fall.

Dust: solid particles generated by handling, crushing, grinding, or detonation of organic or inorganic materials.

Duty cycle: operations involving repetitive pick and swing, such as with a dragline, grapple, or clamshell: such operations are conducted primarily for production as opposed to placement.

Duty time: time during which an individual is being compensated for his/her services.

Effective dose equivalent: the sum of the products of the dose equivalent to the organ or tissue and the weighting factors applicable to each of the body organs or tissues irradiated.

Effectively grounded: intentionally connected to earth through a ground connection or connections of sufficiently low impedance and having sufficient current-carrying capacity to prevent the buildup of voltages which may result in undue hazard to connected equipment or to persons.

Elevating aerial work platform: a vertically-adjustable, integral chassis, power operated work platforms, which may be horizontally extended or rotated relative to the elevating mechanism; an integral frame boom supported power operated elevating work platforms which either telescope, articulate, rotate, or extend beyond their base dimensions.

Emergency (marine): an unforeseen development that imposes an immediate hazard to the safety of the vessel, the passengers, the crew, the cargo, property, or the marine environment, requiring urgent action to remove or mitigate the hazard.

Employee: a Government or Contractor person engaged in work on a USACE project.

Employer: a Government or Contractor organization that has control over employees engaged in work on a USACE project.

Enclosed space: any space, other than a confined space, that is enclosed by bulkheads and overhead. This includes cargo holds, tanks, and quarters, as well as machinery and boiler spaces.

Endless rope: a rope with the ends spliced together.

End-of-service-life indicator (ESLI): a system that warns the respirator user of the approach of the end of adequate respiratory protection (e.g., that the sorbent is approaching saturation or is no longer effective).

End user: a person who has been trained and authorized by the employer on the use of assigned fall protection equipment in a typical fall hazard situation.

Energy (shock) absorber: a component whose primary function is to dissipate energy and limit the deceleration forces imposed on the body during fall arrest.

Energy control procedure: a written procedure (including responsibilities, procedural steps for lockout and tagout, and requirements for testing the effectiveness of energy control measures) to be used for the control of hazardous energy.

Energy isolation device: a physical device that prevents the transmission or release of energy. Includes, but is not limited to, manually operated circuit breakers, disconnect switches, slide gates, slip blinds, line valves, blocks, or similar devices, capable of blocking or isolating energy, with a position indicator. The term does not include push buttons, selector switches, and other control circuit type devices.

Energy ratio: a measure of the seismic energy impact of an explosive blast.

Energy source: includes electrical, mechanical, hydraulic, pneumatic, chemical, thermal, nuclear, stored, or other energy.

Engulfment: the surrounding and effective capture by a liquid or finely divided (flow able) solid substance that can be aspirated to cause death by filling or plugging the respiratory system or that can exert enough force on the body to cause death by strangulation, constriction, or crushing.

Enter with restrictions: refers to entry into a confined space when engineering controls, personal protective equipment, and time limitations are imposed by the competent person.

Entry permit (permit): the written/printed document provided to allow and control entry into a permit space and that contains the information specified in ENG Form 5044-R.

Entry supervisor (confined space): the person responsible for determining if acceptable entry conditions are present at a permit space where entry is planned, for authorizing entry and overseeing entry operations, and for terminating entry as required by this manual.

Erection bridging: the bolted diagonal bridging that is required to be installed prior to releasing the hoisting cables from the steel joists.

Escape-only respirator: a respirator intended to be used only for emergency exit.

Exceptional-exposure dive: dives in which the risk of decompression sickness, oxygen toxicity, and or exposure to the elements is substantially greater than normal working dives.

Explosion Proof: this term is usually seen when describing Class I Division 1 equipment. The device must be able to withstand an internal explosion if it should occur and it must work to prevent the spread of the internal explosion to the surrounding saturated atmosphere. Equipment is designed so as not to allow the explosion or other possible sources of ignition to reach the hazardous atmosphere.

Explosive: A substance or a mixture of substances that is capable by chemical reaction of producing gas at such temperature, pressure, and speed as to cause damage to the surroundings; includes all substances known as high explosives and propellants, together with igniters, primers, initiators, and pyrotechnics (e.g., illuminant, smoke, delay, decoy, flare, and incendiary compositions).

Explosive-actuated tool: a tool that uses the expanding gases from a power load to drive a fastener.

Exposure: a measure of the ionizing radiation produced in air by X or gamma radiation, equal to the sum of the electrical charges on all ions of one sign produced per unit mass of air. The special unit of exposure is the Roentgen equal to 2.58 x 10-4 Coulombs per Kilogram of air at standard temperature and pressure.

Exposure hours: the number of paid duty hours. Unpaid hours count as exposure when employees are quartered on-site. Exposures hours are used to calculate accident experience rates.

Exposure (respiratory hazard): exposure to a concentration of an airborne contaminant that would occur if the employee were not using respiratory protection.

Extension trestle ladder: A self-supporting portable ladder, adjustable in length, consisting of a trestle ladder base and a vertically adjustable extension section, with a suitable means for locking the ladders together.

Extinguisher classification: the letter classification given an extinguisher to designate the classes of fire on which it will be effective.

Extinguisher rating: the numerical rating given to an extinguisher that indicates the extinguishing potential of the unit.

Facility: may be classified as permanent or temporary and may include any of the following: building, structure, shed, tower, utility support system or utility conveyance system, swimming pool or other open concrete structure, whether above or below grade or any other item that is designated a facility by Government Designated Authority (GDA).

Fall arrest system: assembly of equipment, components and subsystems used to arrest a fall.

Fall arrestor (rope grab): a device that travels on a lifeline and will automatically engage or lock onto the lifeline in the event of a fall.

Fall Protection Program Administrator: a person responsible for the development, implementation, monitoring and evaluation of the managed FP Program; shall have a working knowledge of current FP regulations, standards, FP equipment and systems; May also function as a QP for FP or CP for FP, CP Trainer, QP Trainer or Competent rescue Trainer.

Fall Protection Program Manager: A person responsible for managing the fall protection program.

Fall Restraint System: A fall protection system that prevents the user from falling any distance. The system is comprised of body harness, along with an anchorage, connectors and other necessary equipment. The other components typically include a lanyard, and may also include a lifeline and other devices.

False crotch: a pulley, block, sling, lashing, or metal ring, affixed to a tree's leader of limb, through which a load line is passed, to raise or lower limbs or equipment.

Feeder: all circuit conductors between the service equipment, the source of a separately derived system, or other power supply source and the final branch-circuit over-current device.

Figure-four form scaffold: a scaffold consisting of a work platform supported by brackets designed in the shape of a "4."

Filter or air purifying element: a component used in respirators to remove solid or liquid aerosols from the inspired air.

Filtering facepiece (dust mask): a negative-pressure particulate respirator with a filter as an integral part of the facepiece or with the entire facepiece composed of the filtering medium.

Fire cut-offs: Building features (fire walls, automatic fire doors, etc.) designed to retard or restrict the spread of a fire within the building.

Fit factor: a quantitative estimate of the fit of a particular respirator to a specific individual, and typically estimates the ratio of the concentration of a substance in ambient air to its concentration inside the respirator when worn.

Fit test: the use of a protocol to qualitatively or quantitatively evaluate the fit of a respirator on an individual. > *See Qualitative fit test (QLFT) and Quantitative fit test (QNFT).*

Fixed extinguishing system: a permanently installed system that either extinguishes or controls a fire.

Fixed ladder: a ladder that cannot be readily moved or carried because it is an integral part of a building or structure.

Fixed lead: pile driving leads which are rigidly attached to a boom by horizontal struts extending from the leads to extended boom foot pins, thus providing a fixed triangular frame of boom, struts, and leads.

Flammable liquid: any liquid having a flashpoint at or below 199.4°F (93°C). Flammable liquids are divided into four categories as follows:
• Category 1 shall include liquids having flashpoints below 73.4°F (23°C) and having a boiling point at or below 95°F (35°C).
• Category 2 shall include liquids having flashpoints below 73.4°F (23°C) and having a boiling point above 95°F (35°C).
• Category 3 shall include liquids having flashpoints at or above 73.4°F (23°C) and at or below 140°F (60°C).
• Category 4 shall include liquids having flashpoints above 140°F (60°C) and at or below 199.4°F (93°C).

Flashback: a recession of the flame into or back of the mixing chamber of the oxy-fuel gas torch.

Floating plant/vessel: used to transport personnel, work boats, floating cranes and derricks, barges, patrol boats, etc.

Float/ship scaffold: a scaffold hung from overhead supports by means of ropes and consisting of a unit having diagonal bracing underneath: the scaffold rests upon and is securely fastened to two parallel planks bearers at right angles to the span.

Floor arch: the masonry arch shaped filling between steel floor beams or girders, whatever the type of flooring system.

Floor (roof) hole/opening: floor or roof holes/openings are any that measure over 2 in (51 mm) in any direction of a walking/working surface which persons may trip or fall into or where objects may fall to the level below.

Floor-operated crane: a crane which is pendant or nonconductive rope controlled by an operator on the floor or an independent platform.

Foam: a stable aggregation of small bubbles that flow freely over a burning liquid surface and form a coherent blanket that seals combustible vapors, thereby extinguishing the fire.

Foot-candle: the English and American traditional measurement unit of light (illuminance) as perceived by the human eye, and is roughly equal to 10.7 Lux.

Forklift: See Powered industrial truck (PIT).

Form scaffold: a scaffolding system integrated to formwork.

Free Fall Distance: The vertical distance traveled during a fall, measured from the onset of a fall from a walking working surface to the point at which the fall protection system begins to arrest the fall; excludes deceleration distance and the elongation of a lifeline or lanyard; includes any distance that a deceleration device slides before engaging or the distance that a self retracting lifeline or lanyard extends before fall arrest forces are applied; distance is measured using a common reference point, typically the fall arrest attachment.

Freestanding scaffold: a scaffold that is independent of and not rigidly attached to a structure.

Fuel gas: a gas (e.g., acetylene, hydrogen, natural gas, propane) used with oxygen in the oxy-fuel process and for heating.

Full body harness: See "Body Harness, Full".

Full personnel protection: when tagout is used in place of lockout, full personnel protection is provided when:
• The tagout device is attached at the same location as the lockout device would have been attached;
• All tagout-related requirements of this manual have been complied with; and
• Additional means have been taken to provide a level of safety commensurate with that of a lockout device. Such additional means include the removal of an isolating circuit element, blocking of a control switch, opening and tagging an extra (separated by distance) disconnecting device, or the removal of a valve handle to reduce the likelihood of being energized.

Fume: very small suspended solid particles created by condensation from the gaseous state.

Fusible plug: a device designed to relieve pressure and to indicate certain conditions that contribute to low water.

Gaffs: Spurs used to assist in climbing utility poles or trees.

Gangway: any ramp, stairway, or ladder provided for personnel to board/leave a vessel.

Gaseous agent: a fire-extinguishing agent that is in the gaseous state at normal room temperature and pressure and diffuses readily to diffuse itself uniformly throughout an enclosure.

Gas metal arc welding: an arc welding process that uses an arc between a continuous filler metal electrode and the weld pool. Shielding (from the atmosphere) is

Q

provided by an externally supplied gas.

Gate: a device or structure by means of which the flow of material may be stopped or regulated.

Generator, mobile: mobile describes equipment, such as vehicle-mounted generators, that is capable of being moved on wheels or rollers.

Generator, portable: portable describes equipment that is easily carried by personnel from one location to another.

Government Designated Authority (GDA): the senior person in charge or his/her appointed representative for the operation or activity being conducted/considered.

Grommet: an endless 7-strand wire rope.

Ground: (reference) - that conductive body, usually earth, to which an electric potential is referenced; (as a noun) - a conductive connection whether incidental or accidental, by which an electric circuit or equipment is connected to reference ground; (as a verb) - the connecting or establishing of a connection, whether by intention or accident, of an electric circuit or equipment to reference ground.

Grounded: connected to earth or to some conducting body that serves in place of the earth.

Grounded conductor: a system or circuit conductor that is intentionally grounded.

Grounded system: a system of conductors in which at least one conductor or point (usually the middle wire or neutral point of a transformer or generator windings) is intentionally grounded, either solidly or through a current limiting device (not a current-interrupting device).

Ground fault circuit interrupter: a device used to interrupt the electric circuit to the load when a fault current to ground exceeds some predetermined value that is less than that required to operate the over current protection device of the supply circuit.

Grounding conductor: a conductor used to connect equipment or the grounded circuit of a wiring system to a grounding electrode or electrodes.

Grounding electrode (ground electrode): a conductor embedded in the earth, used for maintaining ground potential on conductors connected to it, and for dissipating into the earth current connected to it.

Guarded by location: describes moving parts so protected by their remoteness from the floor, platform, walkway, or other working level, or by their location with reference to frame, foundation, or structure as to reduce the foreseeable risk of accidental contact by persons or objects. Remoteness from foreseeable, regular, or frequent presence of public or employed personnel may in reasonable circumstances constitute guarding by location.

Guardrail system: A rail system erected along open-sided floors, openings, and ends of platforms. The rail system consists of a toprail, midrail and their supports.

Halon: a colorless, electrically nonconductive gas that extinguishes fire by inhibiting the chemical chain reaction of fuel and oxygen. Halon 1211 is a liquefied gas, also known as bromochlorodifluromethane. Halon 1301 is also known as bromotrifluoromethane.

Hardware: rigid components or elements such as buckles, D-rings, snap-hooks, and associated devices used to attach the components of a personal fall protection system together.

Hazard: a dangerous condition, potential or inherent, that can bring about an interruption or interfere with the expected orderly progress of an activity. A source of potential injury to person or to property.

Hazardous (physical) agent: noise, non-ionizing and ionizing radiation, and temperature exposure of durations and quantities capable of causing adverse health effects.

Hazardous atmosphere: an atmosphere that may expose persons to the risk of death, incapacitation, impairment of ability to self rescue (i.e., escape unaided from a permit space), injury, or acute illness from one or more of the following causes:
  • Flammable gas, vapor, or mist in excess of 10% of its lower flammable limit (LFL);
  • Airborne combustible dust at a concentration that meets or exceeds its LFL;
  • Atmospheric oxygen concentration below 19.5% or above 23.5%;
  • Atmospheric concentration of any substance for which a dose or PEL is published and which could result in team member exposure in excess of its dose or PEL;
  • Any other atmospheric condition that is IDLH.

Hazardous energy control plan (HECP): the written plan that clearly and specifically identifies the hazardous energy sources and outlines the scope, purpose, responsibilities, and procedural steps for lockout and tagout and the requirements for testing the effectiveness of energy control measures to be used for the control of hazardous energy from stated sources.

Hazardous environment: an environment with an atmosphere that poses a risk of death, incapacitation, injury, or illness due to flammable or explosive hazards; hazardous substances or agents; oxygen concentrations below 19.5% or above 22%; or any other atmospheric condition recognized as IDLH.

Hazardous substance: any substance defined as a hazardous substance under 29 CFR 1910.120, 29 CFR 1926.65, or 40 CFR 302; any chemical determined to be a hazard as specified in 29 CFR 1910.1200 or 29 CFR 1926.59 to include a chemical (as a gas, liquid, vapor, mist, dust, or fume) which has been identified as causing adverse health effects in exposed employees.

Hazardous, toxic, radioactive waste (HTRW) activity: refers to overall project or worksite involving the investigation, assessment, or clean-up of HTRW or the emergency response to releases of hazardous substances, hazardous waste, or hazardous material at an HTRW site. Includes: activities undertaken for the EPA's Superfund Program, the Defense Environmental Restoration Program (which also includes FUDS and Installation Restoration Program activities), HTRW actions associated with Civil Works projects, and HTRW projects of other Government agencies. Includes, but are not limited to: preliminary assessments/site inspections; remedial investigations; feasibility studies; engineering evaluations/cost analyses; RCRA facility investigations/corrective measures studies/corrective measures implementations/closure plans/Part B permits; or any other pre-design investigations, remedial design, or remedial construction, operation or maintenance at known, suspected, or potential HTRW sites, activities conducted at containerized HTRW sites (leaking PCB transformers and leaking or suspected leaking USTs that contain hazardous substances).

Hazardous, toxic, radioactive waste (HTRW) operation: a specific function on an HTRW site, such as sampling, monitoring, excavation, drum removal, etc.

Hazardous, toxic, radioactive waste (HTRW) site: any facility or location that:
• Requires the planned or emergency clean-up of hazardous, toxic, radioactive waste; and
• Is designated as an uncontrolled hazardous waste site or covered by the RCRA.

Headache Ball: A weighted hook that is used to attach loads to the hoist load line of the crane.

Heating torch: a device for directing the heating flame produced by the controlled combustion of fuel gases.

Heavy gear: diver-worn deep-sea dress, including helmet, in-water stage: a suspended underwater platform that supports a diver in the water. Breastplate, dry suit, and weighted shoes, (e.g., U.S. Navy Mark V gear).

High efficiency particulate air (HEPA) filter: a filter that is at least 99.97% efficient in removing mono-disperse particles of 0.3 μm in diameter. The equivalent NIOSH 42 CFR 84 particulate filters are the N100, R100, and P100 filters.

High radiation area: any area, accessible to personnel, in which there exists radiation at such levels that a major portion of the body could receive in any 1 hour a dose in excess of 100 mrem.

High voltage: is a voltage of 600 volts or greater.

Hoist: a machinery unit that is used for lifting or lowering a freely suspended (unguided) load.

Hoisting Equipment: equipment, including excavators or forklifts, used WITH RIGGING to hoist and move a load, which causes this to become "load handling equipment" (see Section 16).

Hole: a gap or void more than 2 in (5.1 cm) in its least dimension and less than 12 in (30.5 cm) in its greatest dimension in a floor, roof, or other walking/working surface. Pre-engineered holes in cellular decking (for wires, cables, etc.) are not included in this definition.

Horizontal lifeline system: A fall arrest sub-system consisting of an assembly of components (flexible wire, rope or synthetic cable) spanned horizontally between two end anchorages.

Horse scaffold: a scaffold composed of work platforms supported by construction horses.

Hotline tools and ropes: those tools and ropes that are especially designed for work on energized high voltage lines and equipment. Insulated aerial equipment especially designed for work on energized high voltage lines and equipment shall be considered hot line.

Hot tapping: a procedure of attaching connections to equipment in service by welding and drilling.

Hot work: hot riveting, welding, burning, abrasive blasting, or other fire- or spark-producing operations.

Hot work, confined space: hot work in confined space: any activity involving riveting, welding, burning, powder-actuated tools, or similar fire-producing operations. Grinding, drilling, abrasive blasting, or similar spark-producing operations are also considered hot work except when such operations are isolated physically from any atmosphere containing more than 10% of the lower explosive limit of a flammable or combustible substance.

Hot work permit: written authorization to perform operations (for example, riveting, welding, cutting, burning, and heating) capable of providing a source of ignition.

Humboldt Notch: A notch cut used to fell a tree. A directional felling cut into the side of a tree, facing the intended direction of fall and consisting of a horizontal face cut and an angled cut below it, creating a notch of approximately 45 degrees. A Humboldt notch is usually reserved for larger trees on steep slopes.

Hydrostatic Testing: Test of strength and leak-resistance of a vessel, pipe, or other hollow equipment by internal pressurization with a test liquid, usually water.

Immediately dangerous to life or health (IDLH–respiratory hazard): an atmosphere that poses an immediate threat to life, would cause irreversible adverse health effects, or would impair an individual's ability to escape from a dangerous atmosphere.

Impulse noise: noise is considered impulse when the variations in sound-pressure level involve peaks at intervals greater than 1 second.

Incident: a mishap that adversely affects a mission and results in property damage and personal injury below the recordable threshold identified in Section 01.D.03 (e.g., a worker falls off a scaffold and incurs minor cut to his hand (no lost time, no property damage); a crane swings around to move a load and the load scrapes a parked vehicle, incurring minor damage to the vehicle, <$5K). > See also "Mishap".

Incidental employee: an employee who, under normal circumstances, would not be in an area where a system is under lockout and tagout but is required to enter or pass through such an area.

Incipient stage fire: a fire that is in the initial or beginning stage and that can be controlled or extinguished by portable fire extinguisher, Class II standpipe, or small hose systems without the need for protective clothing or breathing apparatus.

Independent wire rope core: a small 6 x 7 wire rope with a wire strand core; used to provide greater resistance to crushing and distortion of the wire rope.

Induced current: the generation of a current in a conductor caused by its proximity to a second alternating current source, a moving direct current source (such as a motor), or an extraneous voltage source (such as lightning).

Inherent Risk: the initial level of risk or danger associated with a work activity or task in the absence of any action to control or modify the circumstances. The inherent risk is identified by identifying the anticipated frequency of loss versus the severity of loss PRIOR to identifying and applying any safety measures, precautions and controls to reduce the level of hazard for each step; Identified by using an Activity Hazard Analysis AHA). > See also "Activity Hazard Analysis", "Risk Assessment Code" and "Residual Risk".

Inside post: the post nearest to the structure against which the scaffold is erected.

Intrinsically safe equipment: Equipment and associated wiring incapable of releasing sufficient electrical energy under normal or abnormal conditions to cause ignition of a specific hazardous atmospheric mixture; equipment incapable of igniting the atmosphere surrounding it.

In-water stage: a suspended underwater platform that supports a diver in the water.

Ionizing radiation: electromagnetic and particulate radiation that causes molecular ionization; includes alpha particles, beta particles, gamma rays, x-rays, neutrons, high speed electrons and protons, and other atomic matter.

Isolation: an activity that physically prevents the transmission or release of energy.

Jib: on hammerhead cranes, the horizontal structural member attached to the rotating superstructure of a crane and upon which the load trolley travels; on mobile cranes, an extension attached to the boom to provide added boom length for lifting specified loads.

Job-made ladder: a ladder fabricated by employees, typically at the construction site, and is not commercially manufactured.

Labeled: equipment or materials that has an attached label, symbol, or other identifying mark of an organization that is acceptable to the authority having jurisdiction and concerned with the product evaluation that maintains periodic inspection of production of labeled equipment or materials and by whose labeling the manufacturer indicates compliance with appropriate standards or performance in a specified manner.

Laboratory waste pack: a drum containing individual containers of laboratory materials normally surrounded by cushioning absorbent material.

Ladder: a device incorporating or employing steps, rungs, or cleats on which a person may step to ascend or descend.

Ladder climbing safety device: device that is connected to a harness or belt to prevent falls from ladders.

Ladder, combination: a portable ladder capable of being used either as a stepladder or as a single or extension ladder. It may also be capable of being used as a trestle ladder or a stairwell ladder. Its components may be used as single ladders.

Ladder, extension: a non-self-supporting portable ladder adjustable in length. It consists of two or more sections, traveling guides, or brackets or the equivalent and so arranged as to permit length adjustment.

Ladder, individual-rung/step: a ladder without a side rail or center rail support, made by mounting individual steps or rungs directly to the side or wall of the structure.

Ladder jack scaffold: a supported scaffold consisting of a platform resting on brackets attached to ladders. (prohibited)

Ladder, portable: a ladder that can readily be moved or carried, usually consisting of side rails joined at intervals by steps, rungs, cleats, or rear braces.

Ladder, sectional: a non-self-supporting portable ladder, nonadjustable in length, consisting of two or more sections, and so constructed that the sections may be combined to function as a single ladder.

Ladder, side-step, fixed: a fixed ladder that requires a person getting off at the top to step to the side of the ladder side rails to reach the landing.

Ladder, single cleat: a ladder consisting of a pair of side rails connected together by cleats, rungs, or steps.

Ladder, single rail: a portable ladder with rungs, cleats, or steps mounted on a single rail instead of the typical two rails.

Ladder, through-step, fixed: a fixed ladder that requires a person getting off at the top to step between the side rails of the ladder to reach the landing.

Ladder, trestle: a self-supporting ladder consisting of two single ladders hinged or joined at the top to form equal angles with the base.

Ladder type: the designation that identifies the working load.

Ladder-type platform: a platform that resembles a ladder covered by planking.

Lagging: timber planks, steel plates, or other structural members used for transferring loads and supporting soil or rock.

Lanyard: a component consisting of flexible rope, wire rope or strap, which typically has a connector at each end for connecting body support to a fall arrestor, energy absorber, anchorage connector, or anchorage.

Large area scaffold: a scaffold erected over substantially the entire work area. For example: a scaffold erected over the entire floor area of a room.

Laser: a device that produces an intense, coherent, directional beam of light.

Lead: the device on a pile driver that maintains the hammer in position during the driving. A lead typically is made up of two vertical rails or guides, held together by a frame, in which the hammer moves vertically.

Lead (leading) wire: an insulated expendable wire used between the electric power source and the electric blasting cap circuit.

Leader: the upper portion of the primary axis of a tree.

Leading edge: the unprotected side or edge of a floor, roof, or formwork for a floor or other walking/working surface (such as deck) that changes location as additional floor, roof, decking, or formwork sections are placed, formed, or constructed.

Ledger: is a horizontal scaffold member upon which bearers rest; the longitudinal member that joins scaffold uprights, posts, poles, and similar members.

Lifeline: a line (horizontal or vertical) for direct attachment between a worker's personal fall protection equipment and a point of anchorage.

Lift supervisor: the person designated to direct the load

handling activity; who must have a thorough knowledge of safety procedures as they relate to the crane, rigging and employee conduct and who has satisfactory level of experience of working with LHE, especially the type being used. The lift supervisor may be the crane operator or another individual.

Limbing: to cut limbs from a tree.

Limited Approach Boundary: An approach limit at a distance from an exposed energized electrical conductor or circuit part within which a shock hazard exists.

Liquefied petroleum gas (LP-Gas): any material that is composed predominantly of any of the following hydrocarbons (or mixtures of them): propane, propylene, butanes, and butylenes.

List: the angle of inclination about the longitudinal axis of a vessel.

Listed: equipment, materials, or services included in a list published by an organization acceptable to the authority having jurisdiction (AHJ) and concerned with the evaluation of products or services that maintains periodic inspection of production of listed equipment or materials or periodic evaluation of services and whose listing states either that the equipment, material, or service meets identified standards or has been tested and found suitable for a specified purpose.

Live-boating: The practice of supporting a SSA or mixed gas diver from a vessel that is underway.

Live-line bare-hand technique: a highly specialized technique (usually used on medium- and high-voltage transmission lines) where a qualified employee working from an insulated aerial platform is electrically bonded to an energized line, effectively canceling any electrical potential difference across the worker's body and protecting the employee from electric shock.

Live-line bare-hand work: work that is performed barehanded from an insulated aerial platform, with the linemen in the basket at the same potential as the live conductor on which they are working.

Live-line tools: tools used by qualified employees to handle energized conductors. The tool insulates the employee from the energized line, allowing the employee to perform the task safely. Also known as "hot sticks."

Load block: an assembly of hook or shackle, swivel,

pins, and frame.

Load Handling Equipment (LHE): a term used to describe cranes, hoists and all other hoisting equipment (hoisting equipment means equipment, including excavators or forklifts, used WITH RIGGING to hoist and move a load).

Load indicator: a device that measures the weight of the load.

Load moment indicator (rated capacity indicator): a device that indicates the bending moment on a crane by measuring both the load on a boom and the horizontal distance from the load (boom point) to the crane's axis of rotation. Load moment indicators are often equipped with warning devices or disengaging devices that are actuated before a crane is overloaded.

Load performance test: a test of a crane's performance, structural competence, and stability while lifting at a percentage of its rated load capacity.

Load-rated: the maximum allowable working load.

Load-working: the external load applied to the crane or derrick, including the weight of load-attaching equipment such as load blocks, shackles, and slings.

Local application system: a fixed fire suppression system that has a supply of extinguishing agent with nozzles arranged to automatically discharge extinguishing agent directly on the burning material to extinguish or control the fire.

Lockout: a form of hazardous energy control using the placement of a lockout device, in accordance with established procedures, on an energy-isolating device to ensure that the energy-isolating device and the system being controlled cannot be operated until the lockout device is removed.

Lockout device: a device that uses a positive means, such as a key or combination lock, to hold an energy-isolating device in the safe position and prevent the energizing of a system.

Long-bed end-dump trailer: a trailer with a length of 30 ft (9.1 m) or more, a length-to-width ratio of or exceeding 4:1, and which is used to transport and dump material.

Loose-fitting facepiece: a respiratory inlet covering that is designed to form a partial seal with the face.

Low-slope roof: a roof having a slope less than or equal

to 4:12 (vertical to horizontal).

Low voltage: voltage less than 600 volts.

Lux: the International System of Units measurement of light (illuminance) as perceived by the human eye.

Machinery and Mechanized equipment: equipment intended for use on construction sites or industrial sites and not intended for operations on public highways.

Manned vessels: vessels that operate with crews, or quartered personnel, or that have work areas that are occupied by assigned personnel during normal work activities.

Marine activities: operations and work involving proximity to or on water.
Mast (derrick): the upright member of the derrick used for support of the boom.

Mast climbing work platform: a hoist having a working platform used for temporary purposes to raise personnel and materials to the working position by means of a drive system mounted on an extendable mast which may be tied to a building.

Material Safety Data Sheet (MSDS): a sheet that provides information on substance identification; ingredients and hazards; physical data; fire and explosion data; reactivity data; health hazard information; spill, leak, and disposal procedures; and special precautions and comments.
Maximum arresting force: the peak force exerted on the boy when a fall protection system arrests or stops a fall.

Mechanical Demolition: removal of a structure involving the use of one or more pieces of heavy machinery to include: hydraulic excavators with various attachments; front end loaders (tracked or rubber-tired); cranes; bulldozers; etc.

Metal-clad cable (MC): a factory assembly of one or more conductors, each individually insulated and enclosed in a metallic sheath of interlocking tape or a smooth or corrugated tube.

Metal decking: a commercially manufactured, structural grade, cold-rolled metal panel formed into a series of parallel ribs; this includes metal floor and roof decks, standing seam metal roofs, other metal roof systems, bar gratings, checker plate, expanded metal panels, and similar products.

Miscellaneous-Type Hooks: Hooks that do not support a load in a direct-pull configuration, such as grab hooks,

foundry hooks, sorting hooks and choker hooks.

Misfire: an explosive charge that failed to detonate.

Mishap: an unplanned, undesired event that occurs during the course of activity being performed. The term "mishap" includes accidents, incidents and near-misses.

Mixed-gas diving: a diving mode in which the diver breathes mixture other than air, e.g., helium-oxygen, (OEA).

Mobile conveyor: a conveyor supported on a structure that is movable under its own power.

Monorail: a single run of overhead track.

Motor vehicle: a sedan, van, SUV, truck, motorcycle, or other mode of conveyance intended for use on public roadways, and includes construction equipment that is driven on public highways. It is not intended to apply to equipment designed exclusively for use off the highway.

Mud capping (bulldozing, adobe blasting, or dobying): blasting by placing a quantity of explosives against a rock or other object without confining the explosives in a drill hole.

Mudsill: a 2-in x 10-in x 8-in (5.1-cm x 25.4-cm x 20.3-cm) (minimum) wood plate that is used to distribute the scaffolding load over a suitable ground area. The size of the mudsill is determined by the load carried over a particular ground area and by the nature of the soil supporting the sills.

Multi-employer work site: a work site where more than one employer occupies the same work site. The Government considers the Prime Contractor to be the "controlling authority" for all subcontractors.

Multiple-Lift Rigging (Christmas Tree Lifting"): procedure allowed ONLY during steel erection activities and ONLY if specific criteria are met – found in 29 CFR 1926.753(e) and, Sections 15 and 16.

Multiple-lift Rigging Assembly (Christmas tree lifting): a rigging assembly manufactured by wire rope rigging suppliers that facilitates the attachment of up to five independent loads to the hoist rigging of a crane.

Multipurpose dry chemical: a dry chemical that is approved for use on Class A, Class B, and Class C fires.

Near miss: a mishap resulting in no personal injury and zero property damage, but given a shift in time or position, damage or injury may have occurred (e.g., a

Q

worker falls off a scaffold and is not injured; a crane swings around to move his load and narrowly misses a parked vehicle). > See also "Mishap".

Negative pressure respirator (tight fitting): a respirator in which the air pressure inside the facepiece is negative during inhalation with respect to the ambient air pressure outside the respirator.

No-decompression limits: the depth-time limits of the "no-decompression limits and repetitive dive group designation table for no-decompression air dives" as specified in the U.S. Navy Diving Manual or equivalent.

Nominal dimension: the dimension of material before it is surfaced and finished.

Non-Certified Fall Arrest Anchorage: An anchorage that a competent person can judge to be capable of supporting the predetermined anchorage forces.

Non-guided personnel hoist system: a hoist system used to transport personnel in a device that is not attached to fixed tracks or guide ropes (a boatswain's chair is an example of a non-guided personnel hoist).

Non-ionizing radiation: those electromagnetic radiations that do not cause ionization (but may be absorbed) in biological systems; includes low frequency ultraviolet light, infrared light, heat, laser, microwaves, and radio waves.

Nonmetallic-sheathed cable: a factory assembly of two or more insulated conductors having an outer sheath of moisture-resistant, flame-retardant, nonmetallic material.

Non-Permit Required Confined Space: a confined space that does not contain, or have the potential to contain an atmospheric hazard capable of causing death or physical harm. The atmosphere should be proven by air monitoring to be free of hazard.

Normally unoccupied remote facility: a facility operated, maintained, or serviced by employees who visit the facility only periodically to check its operation and to perform necessary operating or maintenance tasks. No employees are permanently stationed at the facility. Facilities meeting this definition are not contiguous with, and must be geographically remote from, all other buildings, processes, or persons.

Nosing: that portion of a tread projecting beyond the top of the tread immediately below.

Notch: when cutting a tree to be felled, a notch is cut into the tree on the same side to which the tree is to fall; the notch consists of a horizontal cut (of depth approximately onethird the tree's diameter); the top of the notch is cut at a 45° angle from a height of 2.5 in (6.4 cm) per 1 ft (0.3 m) of diameter above the base of the notch.

OEA: > See Nitrox Gas

OE Safety Specialist: A USACE employee who is qualified through experience and completion of the U.S. Army Bomb Disposal School, Aberdeen Proving Ground, Maryland, or U.S. Naval EOD School, Indian Head, Maryland ,or Eglin AFB, Florida, and is classified in the GS-0018 job series (CP-12 career series). Performs safety and occupational health support and oversight of projects involving MEC/RCWM.

Open conductors: wires that are run as separate conductors, in contrast to wires run through conduit, cables, or raceways.

Opening: a gap or void 12 in (30.5 cm) or more in its least dimension in a floor, roof, or other walking/working surface. Skylights and smoke domes that do not meet the strength requirements of 29 CFR 1926.754(e)(3) shall be regarded as openings.

Operational performance test: a test, conducted without a test load, to determine the proper operation of a crane or other load handling equipment (LHE).

Outrigger: extendable or fixed structural members with one end attached to the base of a piece of equipment and the other end resting on floats on the ground: used to distribute loads in supporting equipment.

Outrigger float: the pedestal (or bearing pad) on which an outrigger beam is supported.

Outside post: the post away from the structure against which the scaffold is erected.

Overexposure: an exposure to a safety or health hazard above the PEL or, if there is no PEL, above the published exposure levels for the hazard.

Overriding operational necessity: circumstances in which essential work cannot be delayed for safety or environmental reasons, or could not reasonably have been anticipated.

Oxyfuel gas cutting: an oxygen cutting process that uses heat from an oxyfuel gas flame.

Oxyfuel gas welding: a welding process that joins work pieces by heating them with an oxyfuel gas flame
Oxygen deficient atmosphere: an atmosphere with oxygen content below 19.5% by volume.

Oxygen enriched atmosphere: an atmosphere containing more than 23.5% oxygen by volume.

Peak particle velocity: a measure of how fast the ground moves during an explosive blast.

Pendant: a rope or strand of specified length with fixed end connections.
Performance test: a test to determine the proper operation of a crane and the ability of the crane to safely lift loads within its performance rating. A performance test includes operational performance tests and load performance tests.

Perimeter protection: measures taken to prevent personnel, vehicles, and materials from falling into an excavation:
 • Class I perimeter protection guarding against personnel falling into an excavation it shall meet the following:
 • Have the strength, height, and maximum deflection requirements for guardrails; o Provide fall protection equivalent to that provided by a toprail, midrail, and toeboard; and
 • Have post spacing equivalent to a standard guardrail.
 • Class I perimeter protection guarding against traffic (vehicles and/or equipment) falling into an excavation ishall be designed, by a qualified person, to withstand the potential forces and bending moments due to impact by traffic.
 • Class II perimeter protection: consists of warning barricades or flagging placed at a distance not closer than 6 ft (1.8 m) from the edge of the excavation: warning barricades or flagging do not have to meet the requirements for Class I perimeter protection but do need to display an adequate warning at an elevation of 3 ft (0.9 m) to 4 ft (1.2 m) above ground level.
 • Class III perimeter protection: warning barricades or flagging placed a distance not closer than 6 in (15.2 cm) nor more than 6 ft (1.8 m) from the edge of the excavation: warning barricades or flagging do not have to meet the requirements for Class I perimeter protection but do need to display an adequate warning at an elevation of 3 ft (0.9 m) to 4 ft (1.2 m) above ground level.
Permanent floor: a structurally completed floor at any level or elevation (including slab on grade).

Permit-required confined space (permit space): a confined space that has one or more of the following characteristics:
 • Contains or has the potential to contain a hazardous atmosphere,
 • Contains a material that has the potential for engulfing an entrant,
 • Has an internal configuration such that an entrant could be trapped or asphyxiated by inwardly converging walls or by a floor that slopes downward and tapers to a smaller cross-section, or
 • Contains any other recognized serious safety or health hazard.

Personal Eyewash Units: Personal eyewash units are portable, supplementary units that support plumbed units or self-contained units, or both, by delivering immediate flushing for approximately 15 minutes. May not be used by itself as eyewash protection.

Personal fall arrest system: an engineered system used to arrest an employee in a fall; consists of an anchorage, connectors, body harness, and may include a lanyard, deceleration device, lifeline, or suitable combination of these.

Personal fall protection system: an engineered system that protects employees from falls.

Physician: A licensed Doctor of Medicine (M.D) or Osteopathy (D.O.) in good standing who, by virtue of education, specialized training, and experience, has acquired a minimum of five (5) years experience and is knowledgeable of regulations and resources relating to occupational medicine such as OSHA, and Occupational Medicine Practice Guidelines (ACOEM).
 • For the purposes of this manual, physicals can be accomplished through other licensed health care providers, such as a Physician's Assistant, but shall be reviewed and signed by a licensed Doctor of Medicine or Osteopathy.
 • This term is intended to mean a Medical Doctor (M.D.) or Doctor of Osteopathy (D.O.).

Plank platform: a work platform made up of wood boards (oriented horizontally).

Planking: a wood board or fabricated component that is used as a flooring member.

Platform Ladder: a self-supporting portable ladder of fixed size with a platform provided at the intended highest standing level.

Point of anchorage: a secure point of attachment for lifelines, lanyards, or deceleration devices.

Portable electric tools: electric equipment intended to be moved from one place to another. Portable ladder: a ladder that can be readily moved or carried.

Portable tank: any closed vessel having a liquid capacity over 60 gal (0.23 m 3) and not intended for fixed installation.

Portal: the entrance to a tunnel.

Position hazard analysis (PHA): a documented process by which the duties (or tasks) of an employee's job position are outlined, the actual or potential hazards of each duty are identified, and measures for the elimination or control of those hazards are developed.

Positioning Device System: a body harness system rigged to allow a worker to be supported on an elevated vertical surface, such as a wall, and work with both hands free while leaning (e.g., working on rebar assembly, towers, poles or ladders).

Positive-pressure respirator: a respirator in which the pressure inside the respiratory inlet covering exceeds the ambient air pressure outside the respirator.

Potable Water: water which meets the quality standards prescribed in the U.S. Public Health Service Drinking Water Standards, published in 42 CFR Part 72, or water which is approved for drinking purposes by the State or local authority having jurisdiction.

Powered Air-Purifying Respirator (PAPR): an air-purifying respirator that uses a blower to force the ambient air through air-purifying elements to the inlet covering.

Powered industrial truck (PIT): a mobile power propelled truck used to carry, push, pull, lift, stack, or tier materials; Includes forklifts, pallet trucks, rider trucks, forktrucks, lifttrucks, telehandlers. Excluded are vehicles used for earth moving and over-the-road hauling.

Pre-discharge employee alarm: an alarm that will sound at a set time before actual discharge of an extinguishing system so that employees may evacuate the discharge area before system discharge.

Pre-entry briefings: an information briefing given by the site safety and health supervisor to employees before their entry to an HTRW site and instructing employees in the contents of the site-SSHP.

Premises wiring: the interior and exterior wiring, including power, lighting, control, and signal circuit wiring with all of the associated hardware, fittings, and wiring devices, both permanently and temporarily installed, which extend from the load-end of the service lateral conductors to the outlets.

Prescribed fire: any fire ignited to meet specific management objectives.

Pressure systems: all pipe, tubing, valves, controls, and other devices that operate or are maintained above atmospheric pressure. > See definition of Vacuum systems.

Primer: a cartridge or container of explosives into which a detonator or detonating cord is inserted or attached.

Prohibited condition: any condition in a permit space that is not allowed by the permit during the period in which entry is authorized.

Project Structural Engineer of Record: The registered, licensed professional responsible for the design of structural steel framing and whose seal appears on the structural documents.

Protective system: a method of protecting employees from cave-ins, from material falling into an excavation, or from the collapse of adjacent structures; includes benching, sloping, shoring, trench shields, underpinning, rock bolting, etc.

Qualified Evaluator of Signal Persons (not a third party): a person employed by the signal person's employer who has demonstrated that he/she is competent in accurately assessing whether individuals meet the Qualification Requirements in Section 16.B.06 for a signal person.

Qualified Evaluator of Signal Persons (third party): an entity that, due to its independence and expertise, has demonstrated that it is competent in accurately assessing whether individuals meet the Qualification Requirements in Section 16.B.06 for a signal person.

Qualified line-clearance tree trimmer: a tree worker who, through related training and on- the-job experience, is familiar with the hazards in line clearance and has demonstrated his/her ability in the performance of the special techniques involved.

Qualified line-clearance tree trimmer trainee: any worker undergoing line-clearance tree trimming training who, in the course of such training, is familiar with the hazards in line clearance and has demonstrated his/her ability in the performance of the special techniques involved.

<u>Qualified Mast-Climber Work Platform (MCWP) Operator: an employee designated in writing by the employer that has been trained by a CP for Scaffolding; shall be able to recognize hazards associated with mast-climbing scaffolds; have specific equipment familiarization prior to operation to include distributed loading and point loading characteristics; demonstrate a comprehensive working understanding of the controls and safety systems; read and understand all cautions and danger warnings on the machine and in the operator's manual, including the maximum uniformly distributed load allowable for the specific configuration, the maximum point load allowed for the configuration, information relating to the placement of these loads on the platform, and any load reductions or restrictions (e.g., planking and cantilevers); and successfully demonstrate a comprehensive knowledge of pre-use inspection criteria, specific for the make and model.</u>

Qualified person: one who, by possession of a recognized degree, certificate, or professional standing, or extensive knowledge, training, and experience, has successfully demonstrated his/her ability to solve or resolve problems related to the subject matter, the work, or the project.

Qualified Person, Electrical: One who, due to their knowledge, ability, experience, specialized training, and/or licensing can competently and safely perform required/assigned electrical duties or functions (construction, operations and/or maintenance); includes skills and techniques necessary to distinguish exposed live parts from other parts of electric equipment, to determine the nominal voltage of exposed live parts, the clearance distances and corresponding voltages to which the qualified person will be exposed.

➤Note 1: Whether an employee is considered to be a "qualified person" will depend upon various circumstances in the workplace, e.g., an individual may be considered "qualified" with regard to certain equipment in the workplace, but "unqualified" as to other equipment.

➤Note 2: An employee who is undergoing on-the-job training and who, in the course of such training, has demonstrated an ability to perform duties safely at his level of training and who is under the direct supervision of a qualified person is considered to be a qualified person for the performance of those duties.

Qualified Person, Fall Protection (QP for FP): a person

with a recognized degree or professional certificate and with extensive knowledge, training and experience in the fall protection and rescue field who is capable of designing, analyzing, evaluating and specifying fall protection and rescue systems; <u>shall have an advanced understanding of the regulatory requirements, physical sciences and engineering principles that affect equipment and systems for FP and rescue; be able to calculate forces generated by an arrested fall, the total loading and the deflection of the fall arrest anchorage, the impact on the structural members to which the fall arrest system is attached and shall be able to determine safe locations of anchorages; shall supervise the design, selection, installation and inspection of certified anchorages and horizontal lifelines.</u>

<u>Qualified Person Trainer: A qualified person who meets the requirements of these standards and who is also qualified to provide fall protection training.</u>

Qualified Rigger (Qualified Rigging Supervisor, Qualified Lift Supervisor): an employee that will rig loads or oversee the rigging of loads for hoisting. Employee must be at least 18 years of age; Be able to communicate effectively with the crane operator, the lift supervisor, flagman and affected employees on site; Have basic knowledge and understanding of equipment-operating characteristics, capabilities, and limitations; AND shall be able to demonstrate adequate knowledge and proficiency in the following: Personnel roles and responsibilities; Site preparation (terrain, environment); Rigging equipment and materials; Safe Operating procedures as related to rigging; Principles of safe rigging; Environmental hazards (overhead interferences); Rigging the load, handling the load, common causes of crane-related accidents.

Qualified tree worker: an individual who, through related training and on-the-job experience, is familiar with equipment, techniques, and hazards of tree maintenance and removal and with the equipment used in such operations and has demonstrated his/her ability in the performance of the special techniques involved.

Qualitative fit test (QLFT): a pass/fail fit test to assess the adequacy of respirator fit that relies on the individual's response to the test agent.

Quantitative fit test (QNFT): an assessment of the adequacy of respirator fit by numerically measuring the amount of leakage into the respirator.

Rad: a measure of the dose of ionizing radiation to the body tissue in terms of the energy absorbed per unit of mass of the tissue.

Q

Radiant energy: the energy of electromagnetic waves produced by movement of molecules excited by the heat of an electric arc, gas flame, or the passage of electric current. Includes ultraviolet, visible light, and infrared energy.

Radiation area: any area, accessible to personnel, in which there exists radiation at such levels that a major portion of the body could receive in any 1 hour a dose in excess of 5 mrem, or in any 5 consecutive 8-hour days a dose in excess of 100 mrem.

Radioactive material: any material that emits, by spontaneous nuclear disintegration, electromagnetic or particulate emanations.

Radiological device: machinery or equipment that produces or contains ionizing radiation, such as nuclear density meters and radiographic testing machines.

Rails: the side structural members of a ladder to which rungs, cleats, or steps are attached.

Rated Load (rated capacity): the maximum allowable working load established by the rigging hardware manufacturer. The terms "rated capacity" and "working load limit" are commonly used to describe rated load.

Recompression chamber: a pressure vessel for human occupancy such as a surface decompression chamber, closed bell, or deep diving system used to decompress divers to treat decompression sickness.

Reconfiguration: the addition or subtraction of boom, jib, counterweight or, for a fixed crane, a change in foundation.

Red Flag Barge/vessel: a barge/vessel carrying in bulk, hazardous cargoes regulated by SubChapter D (petroleum) and O (chemical) of Chapter I, Title 46 CFR of Certain Dangerous Cargoes (flammable or other hazardous materials) OR Vessels whose primary purpose is the transporting of flammable or other hazardous cargos e.g. oil tankers, chemical parcel tankers, liquid chemical barges, liquefied gas tankers, etc.).

Reeving: a rope system in which the rope travels around drums and sheaves.

REM (roentgen equivalent in man): a measure of the dose of ionizing radiation to body tissue in terms of its biological effect; the dose required to produce the same biological effect as one roentgen of high-penetration of x-rays.

Renovation: the process of remodeling or upgrading an existing structure. This process includes the selective interior demolition and possibly some exterior demolition of a structure as the first step before renovation begins.

Rescue system: an assembly of components and subsystems used for self-rescue or assisted-rescue Residential Type Construction. Regardless of structure size, projects where the materials, methods and procedures are essentially the same as those used in building a typical single-family home or townhouse. Wood framing (not steel or concrete), wooden floor joists and roof structures are characteristic of the materials used, and traditional wood frame construction techniques are used in construction. Structures that use metal studs are considered residential construction if they meet the other criteria for residential construction.

Residual Risk: the level of risk or danger of an activity or event that exists after an activity has been analyzed and safety measures have been applied. > See Activity Hazard Analysis.

Rest: a period of time during which the person concerned is off duty; is not performing work, including administrative tasks; and is afforded the opportunity for uninterrupted sleep. This does not include time for breaks, meals, or travel time to/from work.

Restraint system: a combination of anchorage, anchorage connector, lanyard (or other mean of connection), and body support that limits travel in such as manner that the user is not exposed to a fall hazard.

Restricted area: when used in conjunction with ionizing radiation, any area to which access is controlled by the employer for purposes of protecting individuals from exposure to ionizing radiation.

Rigging Hardware: Detachable rigging hardware used for load-handling activities; includes shackles, links, rings, swivels, turn-buckles, eyebolts, hoist rings, wire rope clips, wedge sockets, rigging blocks and load-indicating devices.

Risk Assessment: the systematic identification of potential hazards in the work place as a first step to controlling the possible risk involved; a fundamental process that is required by legislation.

Risk Assessment Code (RAC): quantitative estimate of risk associated with an activity/task; a product of the estimated probability (frequency) of loss from an activity/task and the severity of that loss. The RAC is

then used as a level of residual risk for that activity. This level must be approved by the appropriate level of authority prior to that work activity proceeding.
> See also "Activity Hazard Analysis", "Inherent Risk" and "Residual Risk".

Roll out: A process by which a snaphook or carabiner unintentionally disengages from another connector or object to which it is coupled.

Rope Access: a variety of advanced access techniques where roped and specialized equipment are used as the primary method for providing access and support to workers in their jobs at high or hard-to-reach places.

Rope Access Supervisor: A person with the training, skills, experience and qualifications necessary to assume responsibility for the entire rope access work site, including management and guidance of other Rope Access Technicians on the worksite; is capable of designing, analyzing, evaluating and specifying rope access systems and has the knowledge and experience to direct rescue operations from rope access systems, as well as the skills necessary to perform advanced rescue from rope access systems.

Rope Access Worker: A person with the appropriate training, skills, and qualifications for performing, under the direct supervision of a Rope Access Leader, Technician or Supervisor, standard rope access operations and, at a minimum, has the skills necessary to perform limited rescue from rope access systems.
Rope grab: see fall arrestor.

Rope-guided personnel hoist system: a hoist system, used to transport personnel in a cage, which is guided by wire ropes as differentiated from a hoist system using anchored rail arrangements.

Rotation resistant rope: a wire rope consisting of an inner layer of strand laid in one direction covered by a layer of strand laid in the opposite direction: this has the effect of counteracting torque by reducing the tendency of the finished rope to rotate.

Runner: a horizontal scaffold member that forms a tie between posts and may also support a bearer.

Runway: a personnel passageway elevated above the surrounding floor or ground level, such as a foot walk along shafting or a walkway between scaffolds.

Safe Clearance Procedure: Written procedure that identifies the steps to be taken for the implementation of proper controls of the known and potential hazards associated with a particular operation, piece of equipment, tool or system.

Safe for Workers: denotes a confined space on floating plant that meets the following criteria:
• The oxygen content of the atmosphere is at least 19.5 percent and below 22 percent by volume;
• The concentration of flammable vapors is below 10 percent of the lower explosive limit (LEL);
• Any toxic materials in the atmosphere associated with cargo, fuel, tank coatings, or inerting media are within permissible concentrations at the time of the inspection.
Safety belt: See "Body Belt".

Safety can: an approved container, of not more than 5 gal (18.9 L) capacity, having a spring-closing lid and spout cover and designed to safety relieve internal pressures under fire exposure.

Safety deck attachment: an initial attachment that is used to secure an initially placed sheet of decking to keep proper alignment and bearing with structural support members.

Safety factor: the ratio of the ultimate braking strength of a member or piece of material or equipment to the actual working stress or safe working load when in use.

Safety harness: See "Full Body Harness".

Safety Lashing: A rope, cord, chain, or other suitable material flexible lacing that is used to fasten two objects together securely and thus rendering the objects safe.

Safety Monitoring System: Safety System where Competent Person for Fall Protection is responsible for recognizing and warning employees of fall hazards.

Safety Point of Contact (POC): a worker that has knowledge of the work being performed and the associated hazards and controls associated with it.

Safety precaution area: those portions of approach-departure clearance zones and transitional zones where placement of objects incident to contract performance might result in vertical projections at or above the approach-departure clearance or the transitional surface.

Safety Professional: Because of the wide variety of safety, health and environmental responsibilities safety professionals undertake, a simple definition has not been widely accepted within the profession. Instead, industry looks to ANSI Z590.2, Criteria for Establishing the "Scope and Functions of the Professional Safety Position".

Q

Safety relief valves: valves that relieve excess pressure or vacuum (depending on their design) that would otherwise damage equipment or cause injury to personnel.

Safety sign: a visual alerting device in the form of a sign, label, decal, placard, or other marking that advises the observer of the nature and degree of the potential hazard(s) that can cause an accident. It may also provide other directions to eliminate or reduce the hazard and may advise of the probable consequences of not avoiding the hazard.

Safety sign alert symbol: a symbol that indicates a potential personal injury hazard. It is composed of an equilateral triangle surrounding an exclamation mark.

Safety sign message panel: area of the safety sign that contains those words related to: identification of the hazard, how to avoid the hazard, and probable consequences of not avoiding the hazard.

Safety sign panel: area of a safety sign having a distinctive background color different from adjacent areas of the sign or which is clearly delineated by a line or margin.

Safety sign signal word panel: area of the safety panel that contains the signal word.

Safety tag: a device usually made of card stock, paper, paperboard, plastic, or other material on which letters, markings, symbols, or combinations thereof, appear for the purpose of alerting persons to the presence of a temporary hazard or hazardous condition created by situations such as shipment, setup, service, or repair. The tag is removed when the hazard or hazardous condition no longer exists.

Scaffold: temporary elevated platform and its supporting structure used for supporting worker(s), materials, or both.

Scaffold, double pole: a scaffold supported from the base by a double row of posts. This scaffold is independent of support from walls and is constructed of posts, runners, horizontal platform bearers, and diagonal bracing (also known as independent pole scaffold).

Scaffold, float: a scaffold hung from overhead supports by means of ropes and consisting of a unit having diagonal bracing underneath. The scaffold rests upon and is securely fastened to two parallel plank bearers at right angles to the span (also known as ship scaffold).

Scaffold, Hanging: A scaffold consisting of a work platform supported by hooks or brackets that are part of the scaffold structure and are directly attached to or hanging on a wall, lock gate, or similar vertical structure, providing an elevated work area for those engaged in repairing or modifying the vertical structure.

Scaffold, horse: a scaffold for light or medium duty that is composed of horses supporting a platform.

Scaffold, interior-hung: a suspended scaffold consisting of a work platform suspended from the ceiling or roof structure by fixed length supports.

Scaffold, ladder jack (PROHIBITED): a light-duty supported scaffold consisting of a platform supported by brackets attached to ladders.

Scaffold, Large area: a scaffold erected over substantially the entire work area. For example: a scaffold erected over the entire floor area of a room.

Scaffold, Lean-to (prohibited): a supported scaffold which is kept erect by tilting it toward and resting it against a building or structure.

Scaffold, load ratings: maximum loadings for the following categories:
• Heavy duty: a scaffold designed and constructed to carry a working load of 75 lbs per square foot (366.2 kg/m2), that is intended for stone masonry work, with storage material on the platform.
• Medium duty: a scaffold designed and constructed to carry a working load of 50 lbs per square foot (244.1 kg/m2), that is intended for bricklayers or plasterers, with weight of material in addition to workers.
• Light duty: a scaffold designed and constructed to carry specific working load of 25 lbs per square foot (122.1 kg/m2), that is intended for workers only, with no material storage other than weight for tools.
• Special duty: a scaffold designed and constructed to carry specific types of objects, such as palletized materials. The design of planks and other types of scaffold units, the scaffold, and accessories shall be based on categories of load ratings.

Scaffold, manually propelled: a scaffold assembly supported by casters and moved only manually.

Scaffold, mason's multiple-point adjustable suspension: a scaffold having a continuous platform supported by bearers suspended by wire rope hoists from overhead supports.

Scaffold, metal frame: a scaffold consisting of a work

platform supported by prefabricated metal frames.

Scaffold, needle-beam: a platform resting on two bearers that is suspended by a line.

Scaffold, outrigger: a scaffold consisting of a work unit supported by outriggers projecting beyond the wall or face of the building or structure, the inboard ends of which are secured inside of such building or structure.

Scaffold, pump jack: a scaffold consisting of a work platform supported by movable support brackets mounted on vertical poles.

Scaffold, single-point suspension: a scaffold supported by a single wire rope from an overhead support so arranged and operated as to permit the raising or lowering of the platform to desired working position.

Scaffold, single pole: a unit resting on bearers or cross beams. The outside ends of this unit are supported on runners secured to a single row of posts or uprights, and the inner ends of this unit are supported on or in the wall.

Scaffold, stonesetters' multiple-point adjustable suspension: a swinging type scaffold having a unit supported by members that is suspended at four points.

Scaffold, system: a scaffold consisting of posts with fixed connection points that accept runners, bearers, and diagonals that can be interconnected at predetermined levels.

Scaffold, tube and coupler: a scaffold consisting of a work platform supported by individual pieces of tubing (uprights, bearers, runners, bracing) connected with couplers.

Scaffold, two-point suspension (swinging scaffold/swinging stage): a suspension scaffold consisting of a platform supported by hangers (stirrups) suspended by two ropes from overhead supports and equipped with means to raise and lower the platform.

Scaffold, window jack: a supported scaffold consisting of a platform supported by a bracket or jack that projects through a window opening.

Scaled distance: a scaled factor (ft/lb units) of the potential damage to a structure, based on the distance from the nearest structure to the blast site and the weight of explosives per delay.

Scaling: the removal of loose, overhanging, protruding, or otherwise precariously positioned material from above or along the sides of an excavation.

Scheduled work: Work that is regular and recurring, in that it forms a similar pattern for more than 50% of a working tour.

Scientific Diving: Diving performed solely as a necessary part of a scientific, research, or educational activity by employees whose sole purpose for diving is to perform scientific research tasks; Tasks are light to medium duty, such as environmental or ecological surveys, filming/ recording flora and fauna, biological sample collection, and placement of scientific monitoring equipment; does not include placing or removing heavy objects underwater, regardless of its purpose, or performing any tasks usually associated with commercial diving such as, but not limited to: inspection/ assessment of underwater pipelines, structures and similar objects for structural reasons; construction; demolition; cutting or welding; or the use of explosives.

Scissor lift: a raising/lowering device that is supported or stabilized by one or more pantograph leg sections.

SCUBA: an acronym for self-contained underwater breathing apparatus, in which the supply of breathing mixture carried by the diver is independent of any other source.

Sea-keeping: the aspects of a vessel's design and construction that determine its ability to operate efficiently in the body of water where it will operate (e.g., stability, strength, and speed).

Sea-worthy: a vessel that is fit in all aspects for the anticipated perils of the voyage and will carry the crew and cargo in a safe condition.

Self-contained breathing apparatus (SCBA): an atmosphere-supplying respirator for which the breathing air source is designed to be carried by the user.

Self-retracting lanyard: a deceleration device containing a drum wound line that automatically locks at the onset of a fall to arrest the user, but that automatically pays out from and retracts onto the drum during normal movement of the person to whom the line is attached, after onset of a fall, automatically locks the drum and arrests the fall.

Separately derived system: a premises wiring system whose power is derived from generator, transformer, or converter winding and has no direct electrical connection, including a solidly connected grounded circuit conductor, to supply conductors originating in another system.

Q

Service: the conductors and equipment for delivering electric energy from the serving utility to the wiring system of the premises served.

Service conductors: the conductors from the service point to the service disconnecting means.

Service drop: the overhead service conductors from the last pole or other aerial support to and including the splices, if any, connecting to the service-entrance conductors at the building or other structure.

Service life: the period of time that a respirator, filter or sorbent, or other respiratory equipment provides adequate protection to the wearer.

Service station (automotive): that portion of property where liquids used as motor fuels are stored and dispensed from fixed equipment into the fuel tanks of motor vehicles or approved containers and shall include any facilities for the sale and service of tires, batteries, and accessories.

Service station (marine): that portion of a property where liquids used as fuels are stored and dispensed from equipment on shore, piers, wharves, or floating docks into the fuel tanks of self-propelled craft.

Shackle: a U-shaped metal fitting with a pin through the ends.

Shaft: a passage made from the surface of the ground to a point underground; shafts cut through the ground at an angle greater than 20° to the horizontal. > See "Tunnel".

Shallow dose equivalent: applies to the external exposure of the skin or an extremity. It is taken as the dose equivalent at a tissue depth of 0.007 cm averaged over an area of 1.6 in2 (10 cm2).

Shear connector: headed steel studs, steel bars, steel lugs, and similar devices that are attached to a structural member for the purpose of achieving composite action with concrete.

Sheave: the grooved wheel of a pulley or block over which rope or cable is passed.

Sheeting: > See "Upright".

Shield: a structure that is designed to withstand the forces imposed on it by the walls of an excavation and prevents cave-ins.

Ship repair: includes any repair of a vessel including,

but not restricted to, alterations, conversion, installation, cleaning, painting, and maintenance work. This includes work in confined and enclosed spaces and other dangerous atmospheres in vessels, vessel sections, and on land-side operations regardless of geographic location.

Shoring: a support member that resists compressive forces imposed by a load.

Site control procedures: procedures delineated in the site control program that will be used to minimize any potential contamination of workers, protect members of the public from the site's hazards, and prevent vandalism.

Site Safety and Health Officer (SSHO): the superintendent or other qualified or competent person who is responsible for on-site safety and health.

Site Safety and Health Officer (HTRW): the person on-site with the responsibility for implementation of the APP and SSHP appendix at HTRW activities.

Site Safety and Health Manager (SHM): the CIH, CSP, or CHP responsible for development and enforcement of the APP and SSHP appendix for HTRW activities.

Site safety and health plan (SSHP): an appendix to the APP that describes the site-specific practices.

Site work zones: zones of differing work activities and hazards established to reduce the accidental spread of hazardous substances from a contaminated to an uncontaminated area and to control exposure of personnel to HTRW hazards. There are generally three categories of site work zones:
• Exclusion zones, where contamination does or could occur,
• Contamination-reduction zones, which are transition areas between contaminated areas and clean areas and where decontamination takes place, and
• Support zones, which are uncontaminated areas where administrative and support functions are located.

Sling: an assembly used for lifting when connected to a lifting mechanism at the sling's upper end and when supporting a load at the sling's lower end. > See Figure 15-4.

Sling - basket: loading with the sling passed under the load with both ends, end attachments, eyes, or handles on the hook or a single master link.

Sling - choker: loading with the sling passed through one end attachment, eye, or handle and suspended by the other.

Sloping: a method of protecting employees from cave-ins by cutting the sides of the excavation in the arrangement of slopes; The angle of the slope needed to prevent cave-in is a function of the soil type, environmental factors such as moisture and freezing weather, and the magnitude and location of any loads and vibration surcharged upon the slopes.

Sling - vertical: a load suspended on a single, vertical, part or leg.

Small hose system: a system of hose, ranging in diameter from 5/8 in (1.6 cm), that is for use by employees and provides a means for the control and extinguishment of incipient stage fire.

Snap hook: a connector comprised of a hook-shaped body with a normally closed gate, or similar arrangement that may be opened to permit the hook to receive an object and, when released, automatically closes to retain the object. The locking type has a self-closing, self- locking keeper that remains locked until unlocked and pressed open for connection or disconnection.

Snap-ties: a concrete wall-form tie, the end of which can be twisted or snapped off after the forms have been removed.

Snow Machine: any vehicle designed to travel over ice and snow using mechanical propulsion in conjunction with skis, belts, cleats or low-pressure tires.

Soft Demolition: removal of parts/systems of a structure which may include the following: removal of doors, windows, lay-in tile ceilings, fixtures, interior equipment, lighting, HVAC system components, floor covering, support systems, and other items deemed appropriate by the State in which the demolition permit is granted. Soft demolition does not include the facility enclosure, curtain walls, roof, slab, or the structural frame. Sound-pressure: steady state: sound that does not significantly change in intensity or frequency with time.

Specialty Vehicles: all other vehicles not meeting definition of motor vehicle, ATVs, ORVs, Utility Vehicles, machinery or mechanized equipment, dump truck, etc. Examples are golfcarts, Segway HT, snow machines/mobiles, etc.

Splice - eye: a splice formed by bending a rope's end back onto itself and splicing it into the rope so that a loop

is formed.

Splice - hand tucked: a loop formed in the end of a rope by tucking the end of the strands back into the main body of the rope.

Splice - long: a splice without an appreciable increase of circumference that is used when the rope must run over a sheave or through a hole.

Splice - mechanical: a loop formed in the end of a rope and connected by pressing (swaging) one or more metal sleeves over the junction of the rope.

Splice - short: a splice using less material than a long splice but increasing the circumference.

Sprinkler system: a system of piping designed in accordance with fire protection engineering standards and installed to control or extinguish fires. The system includes an adequate and reliable water supply, a network of specialty sized piping and sprinklers that are interconnected, and a control valve and device for actuating an alarm when the system is in operation.

SSHO: The SSHO for contract work shall meet the administrative, educational, experience and training requirements details in Section 01.A.17.a-d.

SSHO, Alternate: An employee that meets the definition of SSHO but is not the Primary SSHO.

Stable rock: natural solid mineral material that can be excavated with vertical sides and remain intact while exposed.

Standard Lift Plan: Written information and/or instruction used in support of planning a standard load handling activity; See also Form 16-2, Standard Lift Plan Checklist.

Standby diver: a diver at the dive location available to assist a diver in the water; standby divers will be dressed for immediate entry into the water.

Standpipe system:
• Class I standpipe system: a 2-1/2 in (6.4 cm) hose connection for use by fire departments and those trained in handling heavy fire streams.
• Class II standpipe system: a 1-1/2 in (3.8 cm) hose system that provides a means for the control or extinguishment of incipient stage fires.
• Class III standpipe system: a combined system of hose that is for use by employees trained in the use of hose operations and that is capable of furnishing effective water discharge during the more advanced

stages of fire (beyond the incipient stage) in the interior of workplaces.

Station bill: a placard that designates vessel personnel duties and procedures to be followed in the event of an emergency or emergency drill. Placards are permanently placed in personnel quarters and work areas, and are strategically located throughout the vessel.

Steel erection: the construction, alteration, or repair of steel buildings, bridges, and other structures, including the installation of metal decking and all planking used during the process of erection.

Steel joist: an open web, secondary load-carrying member of 144 ft (43.9 m) or less, designed by the manufacturer, used for the support of floors and roofs. This does not include structural steel trusses or cold-formed joists.

Steel joist girder: an open web, primary load-carrying member, designed by the manufacturer, used for the support of floors and roofs. This does not include structural steel trusses.

Steel truss: an open web member designed of structural steel components by the project structural engineer of record. A steel truss is considered equivalent to a solid web structural member.

Steep-sloped roof: a roof having a slope greater than 4:1 (vertical to horizontal).

Step stool: a self-supporting, foldable, portable ladder, non-adjustable in length, 32 in (81.3 cm) or less in height, with flat steps and without a pail shelf, designed to be climbed on the ladder top cap as well as all steps.

Stilts: a pair of poles or similar supports with raised footrests, used for walking above the ground or working surface.

Storage tank: any vessel having a liquid capacity that exceeds 60 gal (227.1 L) is intended for fixed installation and is not used for processing.

Stored energy: energy (electrical, mechanical, or chemical) that might be found in a charge capacitor, a loaded spring, chemical solutions, or other similar hazardous form.

Structural Demolition: the complete removal of a structure that is not occupied. Structures may include: buildings, chimneys, towers, foundations, utilities, bridges or similar.

Structural steel: a steel member, or a member made of a substitute material (such as, but not limited to, fiberglass, aluminum or composite members). These members include, but are not limited to, steel joists, joist girders, purlins, columns, beams, trusses, splices, seats, metal decking, girts, and all bridging, and cold-formed metal framing which is integrated with the structural steel framing of a building.

Supplied-air respirator (SAR) or airline respirator: an atmosphere-supplying respirator for which the source of breathing air is not designed to be carried by the user.

Support system: a structural means of supporting the walls of an excavation to prevent cave-ins; includes shields, shoring, underpinning, rock bolts, etc.

Surface-supplied air (SSA): a diving mode in which the diver in the water is supplied from the dive location with compressed air for breathing.

Swage fittings: fittings in which wire rope is inserted and attached by cold flowing method.

Swinger mechanism: the device that rotates a derrick mast.

Swinging (hanging) lead: pile-driving leads that are suspended from an extended boom point sheave pin at the top of the boom. The bottom points of the leads are positioned astride the pile location, the hammer is vertically above the top of the pile. Often the bottoms of the leads are pointed and the weight of the pile leads and hammer force the bottom points into the ground, holding them in position.

Switch: a device for connecting two or more continuous package conveyor lines; an electrical control device; or a mechanism that transfers a trolley, carrier, or truck from one track to another at a converging or diverging section.

System: includes machinery, equipment, and electrical, hydraulic, and pneumatic lines and their subsystems.

Systems-engineered metal building: a metal, field-assembled building system consisting of framing, roof, and wall coverings. Typically, many of these components are cold-formed shapes. These individual parts are fabricated in one or more manufacturing facilities and shipped to the job site for assembly into the final structure. The engineering design of the system is normally the responsibility of the systems-engineered metal building manufacturer.

Tackle: an assembly of ropes and sheaves arranged for lifting, lowering and pulling.

Tagout: a form of hazardous energy control procedure using the placement of a tagout device, in accordance with established procedures, on an energy-isolating device to indicate that the energy-isolating device and the system being controlled may not be operated until the tagout device is removed.

Tagout device: a prominent warning device, such as a tag with a means of attachment, which can be securely attached to an energy-isolating device in accordance with established procedures to indicate that the energy-isolating device and system being controlled may not be operated until the tagout device is removed.

Tailing crane lift: a procedure sometimes used in erecting large pressure vessels or structural elements in which one crane (lead crane) lifts the top of the load and a second crane (tail crane), rigged to the bottom of the load, either secures the bottom of the load from movement or assists in the horizontal positioning of the load.

Take-up: the assembly of the necessary structural and mechanical parts that provides the means to adjust the length of belts, cables, chains, and similar transmission mechanisms to compensate for stretch, shrinkage, or wear, and to maintain proper tension.

Tandem crane lift: the use of two or more cranes to lift a load.

Taut-line hitch: a knot used for securing all workers aloft to their climbing rope, and consisting of either one or two wraps over two wraps.

Thermite Welding: a welding process that produces coalescence of metals by heating them with superheated liquid metal resulting from a chemical reaction between a metal oxide and aluminum, with or without the application of pressure.

Three-point-contact: usually required when ascending/descending ladders; means that either both hands and one foot, or both feet and one hand are in contact with the climbing device at all times.

Threshold limit values (TLV): airborne concentrations of substances and represent conditions under which it is believed that nearly all workers may be repeatedly exposed day after day without adverse health effects.

Third (3rd) party, Nationally Accredited (ANSI, NCCA) SOH-related certification: safety and health related certifications that can be obtained by a safety and occupational health professional. They are Nationally Accredited, meaning the awarding organization must follow recognized, established national criteria for administration of the certification process AND provided by a 3rd Party.

CFPS - Certified Fire Protection Specialist
CIH - Certified Industrial Hygienist
CHP - Certified Health Physicist
CHMM - Certified Hazardous Materials Manager
CHMP - Certified Hazardous Materials Practitioner
CHST - Construction Health and Safety Technologist
CMSP - Certified Mine Safety Professional
COHN - Certified Occupational Health Nurse
COHN-S - Certified Occupational Health Nurse - Specialist
CSP - Certified Safety Professional
OHST - Occupational Health and Safety Technologist
STS - Safety Trained Supervisor

Tied in: the term that describes a tree climber whose climbing line has been properly crotched and attached to the saddle and whose taut-line hitch is tied.

Tight-fitting facepiece: a respiratory inlet covering that forms a complete seal with the face.

Toeboard: a vertical barrier at floor level erected along exposed edges of a floor opening, wall opening, platform, runway, or ramp to prevent materials from falling.

Tool rest (work rest): a device that prevents the tool or work piece from jamming between the abrasive wheel and the wheel guard.

Top running bridge: a bridge that travels over top of a runway track.

Toprail: the uppermost horizontal rail of a guardrail system.

Total effective dose equivalent: the sum of the deep-dose equivalent (for external exposures) and the committed effective dose equivalent (for internal exposures).

Total Fall Distance. The total vertical distance a person falls, measured from the onset of a fall to the point where the person comes to rest after the fall is stopped. Total fall distance includes free fall distance and deceleration distance, but excludes dynamic elongation.

Total flooding systems: a fixed suppression system that is arranged to automatically discharge a predetermined concentration of agent into an enclosed space for fire extinguishment or control.

Q

Toxic: pertaining to, or caused by, poison; poisonous; harmful.

Toxic chemical: is a chemical that produces serious injury or illness by absorption through any body surface.

Track-guided personnel hoist system: a hoist system used to transport personnel in a car that is attached to fixed tracks or guide members.

Travel restraint system: See "Restraint System".

Travel time (marine): time spent transiting to and from the rest location when not immediately adjacent to or aboard the work site.

Trench: an excavation that is narrow in relation to its length; in general, the depth is greater than the width, and the width is not greater than 15 ft (4.6 m).

Trestle Ladder Scaffold: A work platform supported by a trestle ladder. A trestle ladder is a self-supporting portable ladder that can be adjustable in length, consisting of two sections, hinged at the top to form equal angles with the base.

Trim (floating crane barge): the angle of inclination about the transverse axis of the barge or pontoon.

Trolley: the unit that travels on bridge rails and supports the load block.

Trolley conveyor: a series of trolleys supported from or within an overhead truck and connected by endless propelling means, such as chain, cable, or other linkage, with loads usually suspended from the trolleys.

Trolley line: a horizontal line for direct attachment to a worker's body belt, lanyard, or deceleration device.

Truck (crane): the unit consisting of a frame, wheels, bearings, and axles that supports the bridge girders or trolleys.

Tunnel: an excavation beneath the surface of the ground, the longer axis of which makes an angle not greater than 20° to the horizontal. > See "Shaft".

Turbine Maintenance Platform: a temporary work platform designed to fit into a hydropower turbine to facilitate maintenance of the turbine -usually erected with the turbine remaining in place.

Two-block damage prevention device: a system that will

stall when two-blocking occurs without causing damage to the hoist rope or crane machinery components.

Two-block warning device: a warning device to alert the operator of an impending twoblocking condition.

Two-blocking: the condition when the lower load block or hook assembly comes in contact with the upper load block, or when the load block comes in contact with the boom tip.

Unfired pressure vessels: vessels that can withstand internal pressure or vacuum but do not have the direct fire of burning fuel or electric heaters (heat may be generated in the vessel due to chemical reactions or the application of heat to vessel contents).

Unmanned vessels: vessels that carry cargo such as materials, supplies, equipment, or liquids, and do not have personnel on board during normal operations.

Unprotected sides and edges: any side or edge (except at entrances to points of access) of a walking/working surface (e.g., floor, roof, ramp or runway) where there is no wall or guardrail system.

Unsafe Condition: any physical state that is not acceptable, that presents risks to personal safety, or that has the potential to cause personal injury, illness, and/or damage to property, or that contributes to a reduction in the degree of safety normally present.

Upright: a vertical structural support member. In excavation support systems, uprights are placed in contact with the earth and are usually spaced so that individual uprights do not contact one another. Uprights that are spaced such that they are in contact with or interconnected to one another are referred to as sheeting.

USACE Diving Coordinator (UDC): a USACE employee assigned the responsibility for organizing, integrating, and monitoring the total dive program within a USACE Command; UDC and alternate are appointed, in writing, by the USACE Commander/Director; assures adherence to all applicable rules and regulations.

USACE motor vehicle: any vehicle (government-owned; POV or Rental Car if being used while on-duty in lieu of government-owned vehicle) provided for transportation of government and/or contractor personnel.

Utility Vehicles: Motorized off-highway vehicle capable of maneuvering over uneven terrain, having four or more low pressure tires, designed with side by side seats, seatbelts, steering wheel and optional cab/brush cage (not ROPS). Some offer ROPS as option. (e.g., Rangers, Rhino, M-Gators, Gators, and Mules).

Vehicle-mounted elevating and rotating work platforms: an elevating and rotating work platform mounted on the chassis of a commercial vehicle.

Vertical lifeline system: a vertically suspended flexible line with a connector at the upper end for tying it to a 5000 lbs (22.2 kN) single overhead anchorage along which a fall arrester (rope grab) travels.

Vessel: every type of watercraft or artificial contrivance used, or capable of being used, as a means of transportation on water, including special-purpose floating structures not primarily designed for or used as a means of transportation on water.

Visitor: anyone coming to the site for short-term action (e.g., inspection, meetings, deliveries, etc.).
Warning Line System (WLS): a barrier erected on a floor, roof, or edge of excavation area to warn workers that they are approaching an unprotected side or edge.

Weathervaning: wind induced rotation of a crane superstructure, when out-of-service, to expose minimal surface area to the wind.

Weighting factor: factor that represents the proportion of the total stochastic (cancer plus genetic) risk resulting from irradiation to tissue to the total risk when the whole body is irradiated uniformly.

Wet-bulb globe temperature (WBGT) index: a measurement of environmental factors that correlate with human deep body temperature and other physiological responses to heat.

Wet location: installations underground or in concrete slabs or masonry in direct contact with the earth and locations subject to saturation with water or other liquids, such as vehicle washing basins, and locations exposed to weather and unprotected.

Whaler: a horizontal structural member; in excavation support systems, whalers are placed parallel to the face of the excavation and bear against uprights or the excavation wall.

Whip Check: A cable-like device used on pressurized hoses that prevents serious injury due to hose or coupling failure and may also minimize damage to equipment, may also be referred to as "safety lashing.

Whipline (runner or auxiliary line): a separate hoist rope

system on a crane, usually of a lighter load capacity than the main hoist.

Wild land fire: a planned or an unplanned fire in wild land fuels.

Work positioning system: See "Positioning System".

Work stand (Portable Work Platform): a portable work stand commonly used by sheetrockers. They are designed to meet ANSI ladder standards rather than scaffold standards.

THIS PAGE INTENTIONALLY LEFT BLANK

ACRONYMS

A2B	Anti-two Blocking
A2LA	American Association of Laboratory Accreditation
AAUS	American Academy of Underwater Scientists
ABS	American Bureau of Shipping
ACDE	Association of Commercial Diving Educators
ACGIH	American Conference of Governmental Industrial Hygienists
ACI	American Concrete Institute
ACM	Asbestos-Containing Material
ADC	Association of Diving Contractors
ADCI	Association of Diving Contractors International
AED	Automatic External Defibrillator
AEGCP	Assured Equipment Grounding Conductor Program
AFFF	Aqueous Film Foaming Foam
AHA	Activity Hazard Analysis/Analyses
AHA	American Heart Association
AIHA	American Industrial Hygiene Association
ALARA	As Low As Is Reasonably Achievable
ALI	American Ladder Association
ALI	Annual Limits On Intake
ANSI	American National Standards Institute
API	American Petroleum Institute
APP	Accident Prevention Plan
AR	Army Regulation
ARA	Army Radiation Authorization
ARC	American Red Cross
ASCE	American Society of Civil Engineers
ASHRAE	American Society of Heating, Refrigeration& Air-Conditioning Engineers
ASME	American Society of Mechanical Engineers
ASP	Associate Safety Professional
ASSE	American Society of Safety Engineers
ASTM	American Society for Testing and Materials
ATV	All Terrain Vehicles
AWG	American Wire Gauge
AWPs	Aerial Work Platforms
AWS	American Welding Society
BBP	Blood Borne Pathogen
BCD	Buoyancy Compensation Device
BCSP	Board of Certified Safety Professionals
BRAC	Base Realignment and Closure
Btu	British thermal units

CA	Chemical Agent
C&D	Construction and Debris
Cd	Conductive Footwear
CDC	Centers for Disease Control
CDSO	Collateral Duty Safety Officer
CDZ	Controlled Decking Zone
CERCLA	Comprehensive Environmental Response, Compensation, and Liability Act
cfm	Cubic Feet per Minute
CFR	Code of Federal Regulations
CFS	Chemical Fire Suppression
CG	Center of Gravity
CGA	Compressed Gas Association
CHP	Certified Health Physicist
CHST	Certified Construction Health and Safety Technician
CIH	Certified Industrial Hygienist
cm	Centimeter
cm2	Centimeter Square
CMAA	Crane Manufacturer's Association of America
CO	Carbon Monoxide
CO2	Carbon Dioxide
COC	Certification of Compliance
CONUS	Continental United States
COR	Contracting Officer's Representative
COTS	Commercial, Off the shelf
CP	Competent Person
CPCSSV	Competent Person for Confined Spaces on Ships and Vessels
CPR	Cardiopulmonary Resuscitation
CRZ	Contamination Reduction Zone
CS	Confined Space
CSCP	Confined Space Competent Person
CSE	Confined Space Entry
CSMP	Cold Stress Management Plan
CSP	Certified Safety Professional
CSPP	Construction Safety and Phasing Plan
CSTS	Certified Safety Trained Supervisor
CSWI	Certified Senior Welding Inspector
CTSP	Certified Tree Care Safety Proffesional
CUSP	Certified Utility Safety Professional
CWM	Chemical Warfare Materiel
DA	Department of the Army
DA Pam	Department of the Army Pamphlet

DAC	Derived Air Concentration
DAN	Divers Alert Network
dB	Decibel
DDC	District Diving Coordinator
DDESB	DoD Explosives Safety Board
DEMA	Dive Equipment Manufacturer's Association
DFARS	Defense Federal Acquisition Regulation Supplement
DFOW	Defined Feature of Work
DMM	Discarded Military Munitions
DO	Doctor of Osteopathy
DOD	Department of Defense
DODI	Department of Defense Instruction
DOE	Department of Energy
DOT	Department of Transportation
DSR	Dive Safety Representative
EANx	Nitrox gas
ECC	Emergency Cardiovascular Care
ECP	Entry Control Point
ELSA	Emergency Life Support Apparatus
EM	Engineering Manual
EMR	Electromagnetic Radiation
EMR	Experience Modification Rate
EMS	Emergency Medical Services
EMT	Emergency Medical Technician
EO	Executive Order
EOD	Explosive Ordnance Disposal
EP	Engineering Pamphlet
EPA	Environmental Protection Agency
ER	Engineering Regulation
ERP	Emergency Response Plan
ERT	Emergency Response Team
ESLI	End-of-Service Life Indicator
ESSP	Explosives Safety Site Plan
ETS	Environmental Tobacco Smoke
EZ	Exclusion Zone
FAA	Federal Aviation Administration
FAR	Federal Acquisition Regulation
fc	Footcandle
FCAW	Flux Cored Arc Welding
FDA	Food and Drug Administration
FF	FreeFall

FGS	Final Governing Standards
FM	Field Manual
FMP	Fatigue Management Plan
FOA	field operating activities
FOB	Foreign Object Debris
FOPS	Falling Object Protective Structures
FP	Fall Protection
FRP	Fiberglass-Reinforced Plastic
ft	Foot
ft/min	Feet per Minute
ft2	Square foot
ft3	Cubic foot
FUDS	Formerly Used Defense Sites
FUSRAP	Formerly Used Sites Remedial Action Program
gal	Gallon
GDA	Government Designated Authority
GFCI	Ground Fault Circuit Interrupter
GMAW	Gas Metal Arc Welding
GPTC	Gas Piping Technology Committee
Gy	Gray
HAV	Hepatitis A virus
HAZCOM	Hazardous Communication
HAZWOPER	Hazardous Waste Operations and Emergency Response
HBV	Hepatitis B virus
HCP	Hearing Conversation Program
HCV	Hepatitis C virus
HE	High explosives
HEC	Hazardous Energy Control
HECP	Hazardous Energy Control Program
HEPA	High Efficiency Particulate Air
HIV	Human Immuno-Deficiency Virus
HLL	Horizontal Life Line
hp	Horsepower
HQUSACE	Headquarters, U.S. Army Corps of Engineers
HSMP	Heat Stress Monitoring Plan
HTRW	Hazardous, toxic, and radioactive waste
HVAC	Heating, ventilation, and air conditioning
Hz	Hertz
IAQ	Indoor Air Quality
IDLH	Immediately dangerous to life and health
IEEE	Institute of Electrical and Electronics Engineers

IESNA	Illuminating Engineering Society of North America
IME	Institute of Makers of Explosives
in	Inch
in2	Square inch
IRP	Installation Restoration Program
IRSC	Ionizing Radiation Safety Committee
ISEA	International Safety Equipment Association
ISO	International Organization of Standardization
JHAs	Job Hazard Analyses
JSAs	Job Safety Analyses
kA	Kiloamp
kg	Kilogram
kHz	Kilohertz
km	Kilometers
kN	KiloNewton
KO	Contracting Officer
kPa	Kilopascal
kV	Kilovolt
L	Liter
L/s	Liters per second
lb	Pound
LBP	Lead-based paint
LCDS	Ladder Climbing Devices
LEL	Lower Explosive Limit
LFL	Lower Flammable Limit
LHE	Load Handling Equipment
LID	Load Indicating Device
LLD	Load Limiting Device
LMI	Load Moment Indicating
LNP	Licensed Nurse Practioner
LOTO	Lockout Tagout
LP	Licensed Physician
LPA	Licensed Physician's Assistant
LP-Gas	Liquefied Petroleum Gas
LPN	Licensed Practical Nurse
lx	Luminance
m	Meter
m/s	Meters per second
m2	Square meter
M²S²	Military Munitions Support Services
m3	Cubic meter

MC	Metal-clad cable
MC	Munitions constituents
MD	Medical Doctor
MCRP	Marine Corps Reference Publication
MEC	Munitions and Explosives of Concern
mg	Milligram
mi	Miles
MILCON	Military Construction
MIL-STD	Military Standard
MLR	Multiple Lift Rigging
MM	Military Munitions
mm	Millimeters
MMAD	Mass Median Aerodynamic Diameters
MOA	Memorandum of Agreement
MOOTW	Military Operations Other Than War
MOU	Memorandum of Understanding
mph	Miles per hour
mrem	Millirems
MRS	Munitions Response Site
MSC	Major Subordinate Command
MSDS	Material Safety Data Sheet
MSHA	Mine Safety and Health Administration
MSS	Motion Stopping Safety System
mSv	Millisieverts
MT	Metric ton
MUTCD	Manual on Uniform Traffic Control Devices for Streets and Highways
MVA	Megavolt-amperes
NAA	Naval Architect Analysis
NAMS	National Association of Marine Surveyors
NASBLA	National Association of Safe Boating Law Administrators
NAUI	National Association of Underwater Instructors
NAVFAC	Naval Facilities NAVMED Navy Medical
NAVMED	Navy Medical
NAVSEA	Naval Sea Systems Command
NBBI	National Board of Boiler and Pressure Vessel Inspectors
NEC	National Electrical Code
NEMA	National Electrical Manufacturers Association
NESC	National Electrical Safety Code
NESHAP	National Emissions Standards for Hazardous Air Pollutants
NFPA	National Fire Protection Association
NIOSH	National Institute for Occupational Safety and Health

NIST	National Institute of Standards and Technology
NMFC	National Motor Freight Classification
NOAA	National Oceanic and Atmospheric Administrationn
NOTAM	Notice to Airmen
NPDWR	National Primary Drinking Water Regulatio
NPRCS	Non-permit Required Confined Space
NRC	Nuclear Regulatory Commission
NREMT	Nationally Registered Emergency Medical Technician
NRR	Noise reduction rating
NSC	National Safety Council
NVLAP	National Voluntary Laboratory Accreditation Program
OCONUS	Outside Continental United States/Overseas
OE	Ordnance and Explosives
OEA	Oxygen Enriched Air
OEBGD	Overseas Environmental Baseline Guidance Document
OEL	Occupational Exposure Limit
OEM	Original Equipment Manufacturer
OJT	On-the-job training
ORM	Other Regulated Devices
OSHA	Occupational Safety and Health Administration
Pa	Pascal
PA	Physician's Assistant (licensed and/or registered)
PADI	Professional Association of Diving Instructors
PAN	Preliminary Accident Notification
PAPR	Powered-Air Purifying Respirator
PCB	Polychlorinated biphenyls
pCi/L	Picocuries per liter
PDT	Project Delivery Team
PEL	Permissible Exposure Limit
PFAS	Personal Fall Arrest System
PFD	Personal Floatation Device
PHA	Position Hazard Analysis
PIT	Powered Industrial Truck
PLHCP	Physician-Licensed Healthcare Professional
PM	Project Manager
PMP	Project Management Plan
POC	Point of Contact
POL	Petroleum, oil, and lubricants
PPE	Personal Protective Equipment
ppm	Parts per million
PRCS	Permit-Required Confined Spaces

PrgMP	Program Management Plan
PRT	Planning and Response Teams
psf	Pounds per square foot
psi	Per square inch
psia	Per square inch absolute
QA	Quality Assurance
QASP	Quality Assurance Surveillance Plan
QC	Quality Control
QCP	Quality Control Plan
QCS	Quality Control Supervisor
QLFT	Qualitative Fit Test
QNFT	Quantitative Fit Test
QP	Qualified Person
QR	Qualified Rigger
RAC	Risk Assessment Code
RCRA	Resource Conservation and Recovery Act
RDS	Respirable Dust Standard
REL	Recommended Exposure Limit
REM	Roentgen equivalent in man
RF	Radio frequency
RFO	Recovery Field Office
RFP	Request for Proposal
RN	Registered Nurse
ROPS	Rollover Protective Structure
ROVs	Remotely Operated Vehicles
RPA	Respirator Program Administrator
RPE	Registered Professional Engineer
RSA	Runway Safety Area
RSC	Radiation Safety Committee
RSO	Radiation safety officer
RSSO	USACE Radiation Safety Staff Officer
RT	Rough Terrain
SAE	Society of Automotive Engineers
SAMS	Society of Accredited Marine Surveyors
SAR	Supplied-Air Respirator
SCBA	Self-Contained Breathing Apparatus
SCUBA	Self-Contained Underwater Breathing Apparatus
SDS	Safety Data Sheet
SHM	Safety and Health Manager
SIA	Scaffold Industry Association
SLP	Standard Lift Plan

SMS	Safety Monitoring System
SOH	Safety and Occupational Health
SOHO	Safety and Occupational Health Office
SOP	Standard Operating Procedure
SPCD	Safety Plan Compliance Document
SPF	Sun protection factor
SRL	Self Retracting Lanyard
SRL-LE	Self Retracting Lanyard Leading Edge
SSA	Surface-supplied air
SSHO	Site Safety and Health Officer
SSHP	Site Safety and Health Plan
SUR-D- O2	Surface Decompression with Oxygen
Sv	Sieverts
SZ	Support zone
T&M	Time and materials
TB	MED Technical Bulletin, Medical
TDP	Test Designated Position
TEDE	Total Equivalent Dose Exposure
TIP	Tie-in point
TLV	Threshold Limit Value
TMPs	Turbine Maintanance Platforms
TSD	Treatment Storage and Disposal
TWA	Time-Weighted Average
UDC	USACE Command Diving Coordinator
UFC	Uniform Freight Classification
UFGS	Unified Facilities Guide Specification
UL	Underwriters Laboratory
USACE	U.S. Army Corps of Engineers
USCG	U.S. Coast Guard
USEPA	U.S. Environmental Protection Agency
USPHS	U.S. Public Health Service
UST	Underground storage tank
UV	Utility Vehicles
UV	Ultraviolet
UVA	Ultraviolet A-region
UVB	Ultraviolet B-region
UXO	Unexploded ordnance
VLL	Vertical Life Line
WBGT	Wet Bulb Globe Temperature
WLL	Working Load Limit
WLS	Warning Line System

WP	White Phosphorous
μSv	Microsieverts
μCi/g	Microcuries per gram

INDEX

-A-

-C-

-D-

-J-

-K-

-L-

-M-

-S-

-T-